Praise for *The Moral Vision of the New Testament*

"Hays has pulled off, with a success for which I can think of no contemporary parallel, one of the most difficult tasks in theological and biblical writing today. . . . [He] has produced one of the boldest and most successful attempts to demonstrate how the New Testament can effectively provide norm and guidance for contemporary ethics. This book will provide a stimulus and model for scholarly and church discussion (and decision making!) about the New Testament and ethical issues as no other has."

James D. G. Dunn, Lightfoot Professor of Divinity, University of Durham

"This book combines scholarly excellence with contemporary impact. . . . [Hays's] description of the variegated ethical vision of the early church is state-of-the-art, and the application of that vision to contemporary issues is hermeneutically skillful and morally challenging. Few on either right or left will agree entirely with this book, but none should ignore it."

George Lindbeck, Pitkin Professor Emeritus of Historical Theology,
Yale University Divinity School

"This is a significant book. Written with clarity and subtlety, it leads its reader through the ethical insights of various New Testament writings, provides summaries of how such insights have been used by theologians and ethicists, gives careful consideration to the interpretative task, and concludes with specific examples of how the New Testament can function as the authoritative source for Christian ethical reflection and action. . . . The book will be valuable to pastor and teacher alike, and it ought to be high on anyone's list of books to be read and seriously pondered."

Paul J. Achtemeier, editor of *The HarperCollins Bible Dictionary*

"Hays makes a creative contribution to the conversation concerning the use of the New Testament within the church. . . . He challenges readers to move beyond easy affirmations and accommodations about either experience or texts, and invites them to the discipline of careful reading and clear thinking."

Luke Timothy Johnson, Robert W. Woodruff Professor of New Testament
and Christian Origins, Emory University; author of *The Real Jesus*

"A gem that sparkles on every page. . . . This profoundly theological book grapples with some of the major ethical issues of our time. A rare delight."

Graham Stanton, professor of New Testament studies,
King's College, University of London

"This study is important, above all, for its thoughtful and thought-provoking proposals about how the New Testament's moral vision should be determinative for Christians today. It is unquestionably a book to be taken seriously—and perhaps especially by those who are inclined to other views."

Victor Paul Furnish, University Distinguished Professor of New Testament,
Southern Methodist University

"Many people interested in the relation of Scripture and Christian ethics have been waiting and watching for Hays's new book. They will not be disappointed when they read it. Hays carefully describes the moral teachings of New Testament texts, attentive to and appreciative of the diversity of those texts. He brings these teachings together in a compelling vision of their coherence and of their embeddedness in the gospel. He takes up and helps his readers through the questions about how these texts should be used in contemporary moral arguments. And he displays how these texts might form and inform Christian lives and communities. It is an extraordinary accomplishment."

Allen Verhey, Blekkink Professor of Religion, Hope College

"Since this book eschews the safe course taken by many scholars of remaining silent or vague about controversial issues, it is certain to inspire criticism as well as praise. But both for its audacity and for its lucid and comprehensive address to a question central to the life of all Christian communities—How can we be morally formed by the New Testament?—it is also sure to be widely read and greatly welcomed. I am pleased to have an opportunity to express my admiration for the care, vigor, and passion of this work."

Sondra Ely Wheeler, assistant professor of Christian ethics,
Wesley Theological Seminary

"Combining rigorous scholarship and theological insight, Hays offers a powerful account of the moral vision of the New Testament. . . . Hays's method and proposals will undoubtedly stir debates, but they will also prove a benchmark for future scholarship. His book should receive a wide audience in both the church and the academy."

L. Gregory Jones, co-editor of *Modern Theology* and author of *Embodying Forgiveness*

"If the New Testament is to be treated as authoritative at all for Christians, the key area in which that authority is exhibited is in ethics. Can Christians live by the New Testament? This book is clearly a major contribution to this question. . . . Hays offers this book to open, not to terminate, conversation about the New Testament and ethics. Whether one is inclined sympathetically or critically in response to Hays's positions, this book certainly deserves to be read, for it can stimulate the conversation Hays seeks to promote."

Larry Hurtado, professor of New Testament language,
literature, and theology, University of Edinburgh

" Hays has written a rare and fine book: one which succeeds in synthesizing a mass of detailed scholarship, of which he is a master, and presenting it in lively style for a wide readership; one which is not afraid to engage with contemporary issues, while addressing clearly the difficult questions of interpretation that make such an undertaking hazardous. An intelligent, sharp-minded, controversial book; a major contribution to contemporary debate about our vision of the good life."

John K. Riches, professor of divinity and biblical criticism, University of Glasgow

The Moral Vision of the New Testament

The Moral Vision of the New Testament

Community, Cross, New Creation

A Contemporary Introduction
to New Testament Ethics

Richard B. Hays

continuum
T&T CLARK

T&T Clark
an imprint of
Continuum
The Tower Building
11 York Road
London SE1 7NX

15 East 26th Street
New York
NY 10010

www.continuumbooks.com

Permission acknowledgements appear on page 485, which constitutes
a constitution of this copyright page.
Originally published in the United States of America by
HarperCollins Publishers, 10 East 53rd Street, New York 10022

This edition published under licence from HarperCollins Publishers
by T&T Clark Ltd, The Tower Building, 11 York Road, Waterloo, London SE1 7NX

First published 1997
Latest impression 2001, 2003
Reprinted 2004

ISBN 0 567 08569 4

British Library Cataloguing-in-Publication Data
A catalogue record for this book is available from the British Library

Printed and bound in Great Britain by Biddles Ltd., King's Lynn

To my students at Yale Divinity School, 1981–1991

οὕτως ὁμειρόμενοι ὑμῶν εὐδοκοῦμεν μεταδοῦναι ὑμῖν
οὐ μόνον τὸ εὐαγγέλιον τοῦ Θεοῦ ἀλλὰ καὶ τὰς ἑαυτῶν ψυχάς,
διότι ἀγαπητοὶ ἡμῖν ἐγενήθητε.
(1 Thess. 2:8)

Contents

Preface

This book has grown out of years of wrestling, together with many students and colleagues in ministry, with the question of how the New Testament might inform our perennially inadequate efforts to respond faithfully to God's calling of the church to a common life of discipleship. The readings and arguments set forth in these pages are offered not as definitive pronouncements on the moral issues that vex our time but as provisional discernments about how the witnesses of the New Testament speak to our situation.

No one can publish such a book without being acutely aware of the dangers attending the enterprise: the possibilities for misreading, abuse, serving one's own interests, and premature closure are ever present. I would invite the reader, therefore, to the same task to which I try to invite students in the classroom: the task of *critical, reflective conversation in which we stand together under the judgment and guidance of Scripture.* My hope is not that this book will settle all disputes but that it will facilitate a clearer discussion about how to read the New Testament and how to live in imaginative obedience to its moral vision. I invite those who may disagree with me on particular issues to join me in the discipline of listening closely to the New Testament witnesses and to offer their own readings for the edification of the church. I have no doubt that I, as well as others, will learn much from the ensuing conversation.

It has not been easy for me to let this book go. Scholars are disposed, by inclination and training, to close every possible loophole, cite every relevant book and article, consider every alternative line of argument, and—most important—defer judgment indefinitely. Given the broad scope of this book and the endless sea of secondary literature on the problems discussed here, I am painfully aware of how incomplete this study remains. The works cited in the notes and bibliography represent only a fraction of the literature from which I have learned materially, and that fraction in turn represents an even tinier fraction of what has been published on these topics. My discussions of particular New Testament texts and of specific moral issues remain all too sketchy. Nonetheless, I am convinced that one must at some point make some interpretive decisions and render some response to the New Testament's urgent ethical summons. The church cannot suspend judgment forever; action is necessary. Surely the vocation of biblical scholarship within the church is to inform such judgment and action. Unless scholarship is merely self-enclosed and self-serving, it is necessary for those of us who have studied the New Testament texts for years to take the risk of making some calls, venturing to speak within the church about the meaning of these texts for us and about their claim upon us. Thus, this book risks—after years of scholarly agonizing—what every preacher must risk every Sunday: articulating the concrete implications of the Word of God for the community of faith. It is my greatest hope that this book will be of some help to those serving or preparing to serve in the parish, equipping all God's people for the work of ministry.

Because this book has been germinating for almost twelve years, since I first started teaching a course on New Testament ethics at Yale Divinity School in 1984, I have a long list of debts to acknowledge. Thanks are due first of all to the Pew Charitable Trusts, whose substantial grant provided for research support, for leave time to work on the manuscript during the spring semester of 1993, and for the organization of a major conference at Duke University ("The New Testament and Ethics: Problems and Prospects") in the spring of 1995. That conference and the conversations surrounding it contributed in important ways to the refinement of the arguments set forth here.

Next, I want to express my gratitude to Austin Presbyterian Theological Seminary for the invitation to deliver the Thomas W. Currie Lectures (January 30 through February 1, 1995). Significant portions of this manuscript were drafted for that occasion, and I profited greatly from the stimulating exchanges that followed the lectures. Thanks are due also to President Jack L. Stotts and to members of the faculty for their generous hospitality on that occasion.

Other parts of this book have also been presented in lecture form, in settings both academic and ecclesial, over the past several years, including the Yale Divinity School Convocation (1989), the Duke Divinity School Ministers' Week (1991), the AMBS Theological Lectureship at the Associated Mennonite Biblical Seminaries in Goshen, Indiana (1993), the Simeon Lectures at Trinity Episcopal School for Ministry in Ambridge, Pennsylvania (1993), the North Park Symposium on the Theological Interpretation of Scripture (1994), the Lund Lectures at North Park Theological Seminary in Chicago (1994), and a plenary address at the Society of Christian Ethics meeting in Alexandria, Virginia (1995). I would also like to thank the following groups and institutions for providing opportunities to lecture on aspects of New Testament ethics: the Pastors' School of the Oklahoma Annual Conference of the United Methodist Church (1988), the Catholic Biblical Association in New York City (1989), the Ottawa Summer School of Biblical and Theological Studies (1989), the Graduate Institute on Contemporary Christian Thought at St. Joseph College in Hartford, Connecticut (1992), and the School of Ministry of the Florida Annual Conference of the United Methodist Church (1992). On all these occasions, I learned much from the thoughtful responses of those who heard and sometimes challenged what I had to say. The ideas in this book are richer and more nuanced because of the conversations that attended these public occasions.

Thanks are due also to the editors of several journals that have given permission for the republication, in revised form, of material that first appeared in various articles. This book contains material adapted from the following previously published essays: "Relations Natural and Unnatural: A Response to John Boswell's Exegesis of Romans 1," *Journal of Religious Ethics* 14/1 (1986): 184–215; "Scripture-Shaped Community: The Problem of Method in New Testament Ethics," *Interpretation* 44 (1990): 42–55; "Awaiting the Redemption of Our Bodies," *Sojourners* (July 1991): 17–21 (subsequently revised and expanded in Jeffrey S. Siker, ed., *Homosexuality in the Church: Both Sides of the Debate* [Louisville: Westminster/John Knox, 1994]: 3–17); "Ecclesiology and Ethics in 1 Corinthians," *Ex Auditu* 10 (1994): 31–43; and "New Testament Ethics: The Theological Task," *Annual of the Society of Christian Ethics* (1995): 97–120.

Bible quotations, unless otherwise noted, are from the New Revised Standard Version of the Bible. Biblical quotations marked "(RH)" are my own translations, and adaptations of the NRSV are marked "(AA)."

If it is true, as I contend in this book, that we must discern the will of God in and for the community of faith, it follows that a book such as this could have been written only with the support and stimulation of others who have sought alongside me to listen responsively to the Word. It is impossible to mention all the individuals who have played a formative role in shaping my reading of the New Testament's moral vision, but I want at least to offer special thanks to those who have read and critiqued various portions of this manuscript at different stages of its development—not least to those who have posed serious challenges to my project. I have profited enormously from their wisdom, even if I have not always heeded their advice.

A few colleagues have worked through a penultimate draft of the book in its entirety and made numerous suggestions, small and large, for its improvement. For this service, I offer my deepest gratitude to Daniel Boyarin of the University of California at Berkeley, Nancy Duff of Princeton Theological Seminary, Kathryn Greene-McCreight of Yale University, A. Katherine Grieb of Virginia Theological Seminary, Luke Timothy Johnson of Emory University, L. Gregory Jones of Loyola College, George Lindbeck of Yale University, and, among my present doctoral students at Duke, Bruce Fisk and Audrey West. The usual disclaimer is in this instance perhaps more than usually pertinent: none of these friends and colleagues should be held responsible for the judgments I have made in this book. Indeed, several of them stand in serious disagreement with me on issues of method and on one or more of the normative positions that I take in the book's final section. Nonetheless, I am privileged to count them as colleagues and to learn from their insights.

A much longer roster of friends, colleagues, and students has also helped me by reading some portions of the work in progress or by providing assistance on particular points. While I am in every case mindful of their particular contributions, it will have to suffice merely to list them here with gratitude: Carole Alderman, Jim Buckley, Ellen Charry, Regina Plunkett Dowling, Gina Giannini, Marvin Hage, Judy Hays, Craig Hill, Timothy Jackson, Joan Walczak Kloc, Steve Kraftchick, Dale Martin, Ben Ollenburger, Sally Purvis, Scott Saye, Christopher Seitz, Barry Seltser, Jeff Siker, George Steffey, Diana Swancutt, Willard Swartley, Allen Verhey, and Sondra Wheeler.

Special mention should be made of Stanley Hauerwas and John Howard Yoder, who graciously read and critiqued my analyses of their own work; even where my differences with them remain, my reading has been sharpened and clarified by their responses. I also want to give special acknowledgment to a group of colleagues at Yale who met occasionally during the late 1980s to discuss issues concerning the relationship between Scripture and ethics: Margaret Farley, Leander Keck, David Kelsey, Abraham Malherbe, Wayne Meeks, Gene Outka, and Robert Wilson. I profited not only from their comments on an early programmatic draft of the design for the present book but also from our discussions of their own work in this field.

The manuscript of this book could never have been completed without the tireless work of Audrey West, my research assistant for the past three years under the auspices of the Pew grant. With unfailing competence and good humor, she has tracked down bibliographical references, photocopied articles, provided background analyses of various problems, filled in gaps, and smoothed the way for my writing. No doubt she will be relieved to see this book finished so that she can devote her energies to her own work. My thanks also to J. Ross Wagner, who prepared the Index of Scripture and Other Ancient Writings and Author Index with meticulous care.

The only person more glad than Audrey to see this project brought to completion will be my wife, Judy, who has awaited this consummation with increasing holy impatience. Her support and service over the years have been indispensable to my work. When I say, as I do in Chapter 15, "Marriage is hard," she might with justification add, "Yes, especially for those married to New Testament professors!" The richly fulfilling pilgrimage that she and I have shared for the past twenty-five years, seeking to follow Jesus and to discover authentic Christian community, has brought me to the place where it is possible to write this book; consequently, her long-suffering love undergirds every page.

Finally, a word must be said about those to whom this book is dedicated, my students at Yale Divinity School from 1981 to 1991. During those years, I came to see the necessity of attempting to write such a book as this, and the basic design of this study was hashed out in countless hours of vigorous conversation, both inside and outside the classroom, with my students. They were a contrary and unpredictable lot, eclectically drawn from across the spectrum of Christian confessions around the world. Their probing questions and spirited responses provided both a tremendous challenge and bracing encouragement to a young professor trying to think his way through the intractable problems of New Testament ethics. Thus, the outlines of this study took shape, hammered out in debate with an ever-changing collection of superb and stimulating students. To them this book is dedicated, in the hope that it will be of value in the ministries to which they have been called.

Richard B. Hays
Durham, North Carolina
August 10, 1995

The Moral Vision of the New Testament

Introduction

The Task of New Testament Ethics

1. New Testament Ethics As a Problem

"The Devil can cite Scripture to his purpose," so my grandmother used to say. Or, as we prefer to say now in the academy, "The text has inexhaustible hermeneutical potential."[1] No matter how we choose to phrase it, the problem is the same. Despite the time-honored Christian claim that Scripture is the foundation of the church's faith and practice, appeals to Scripture are suspect for at least two reasons: the Bible itself contains diverse points of view, and diverse interpretive methods can yield diverse readings of any given text.

This hermeneutical crisis is nowhere more acutely embarrassing for the church than with regard to ethical questions. The 1988 presidential election in the United States offered a vivid illustration of the problem, as two Christian ministers ran unsuccessfully for the presidency: Jesse Jackson and Pat Robertson, each appealing to the Bible as the ground of his convictions, championed widely divergent visions of Christian morality. Although appeals to Scripture featured less prominently in the 1992 campaign, the competing parties still struggled to claim biblical support for their particular ethical concerns. Many Republicans claimed some sort of biblical sanction for the "family values" that they advocated, and Bill Clinton, in his acceptance speech at the Democratic convention, quoted the Bible (loosely) several times and described his political program—with perhaps a trace of audacity—as a "new covenant."

After Clinton's victory in the election, some conservative Christians were scandalized by Billy Graham's decision to participate in the inaugural festivities. They drafted a letter of protest asking Graham not to pray for Clinton.[2] "Bill Clinton ran for office as an outspoken advocate of abortion on demand and legitimized homosexuality," they wrote. "Of course, we realize that other presidents have been endorsed by church leaders who might not have held biblical positions on all issues,[3] but never in recent history has a presidential candidate with such an explicitly unbiblical platform been elected to our nation's highest office."[4] Graham, undeterred by this protest, did participate in the inauguration, where he heard Clinton bring his inaugural address to its climax by quoting Galatians 6:9, KJV: "Let us not be weary in well doing, for in due season we shall reap, if we faint not."

Such uses of biblical language in political rhetoric exemplify a perennial difficulty: everybody wants to claim the Bible.[5] Christians of all sorts, even those who might not subscribe formally to a "high" doctrine of biblical inspiration, have always deemed it essential that their ethical teachings and practices stand in continuity with Scripture.[6] Thus, we see Christians distributed across the various ethical spectrums—from Oliver North to Daniel Berrigan, from Phyllis Schlafly to Elisabeth Schüssler Fiorenza, from Jerry Falwell to Bishop John Shelby Spong—all insisting that the Bible somehow informs their understanding of God's purposes. Of course, the problem is not merely a matter of the right and left wings in politics; these examples are cited only to illustrate the range of disagreements prevalent among serious Christians. The ethical issues that confront Christians who try to discern the will of God in Scripture are, as I shall try to show in this book, far more nuanced than a simple conservative/liberal polarity would suggest. One reason that the church has become so bitterly divided over moral issues is that the community of faith has uncritically accepted the categories of popular U.S. discourse about these topics, without subjecting them to sustained critical scrutiny in light of a close reading of the Bible.

One more story, again involving Billy Graham, illustrates the dilemma. At the beginning of the Gulf War in January of 1991, Graham went to the White House to pray with President George Bush as he launched the Desert Storm attack on Iraq. Only hours earlier, however, Edmond Browning, the presiding bishop of the Episcopal Church—Bush's own denomination—had joined an ecumenical group of Christians in a candlelight vigil outside the White House fence, praying for peace rather than success in war. Which group of Christians, those inside the White House or those outside the fence, had rightly discerned the Word of God?

In light of such profound disagreements about the message—or application—of Scripture, an outsider's skepticism might be understandable: Is it not nonsense for Christians to pretend that the Bible can regulate moral understanding? The dilemma is most poignant, however, when seen from within the community of faith: How can the church become a Scripture-shaped community, even where it earnestly longs to do so? Those who can naively affirm the bumper-sticker slogan, "God said it, I believe it, that settles it," are oblivious to the question-begging inherent in the formulation: there is no escape from the imperative of interpreting the Word. Bumper-sticker hermeneutics will not do.

Nor, sad to say, can more and better exegesis bring us all the way to a solution. Indeed, careful exegesis heightens our awareness of the ideological diversity within Scripture and of our historical distance from the original communities (in ancient Israel and the earliest churches) to whom these texts were addressed. In other words, critical exegesis exacerbates the hermeneutical problem rather than solving it. That is why seminary students sometimes come away from Bible courses puzzled and alienated. As Oliver O'Donovan once remarked, interpreters who think that they can determine the proper ethical application of the Bible solely through more sophisticated exegesis are like people who believe that they can fly if only they flap their arms hard enough.[7]

Unless we can give a coherent account of our methods for moving between text and normative ethical judgments, appeals to the authority of Scripture will be hollow and unconvincing. It is my aim in this book, therefore, to articulate as clearly as possible a framework within which we might pursue New Testament ethics[8] as a normative theological discipline: the goal of the inquiry will be to clarify how the church can read Scripture in a faithful and disciplined manner so that Scripture might come to shape the life of the church.

2. The Fourfold Task of New Testament Ethics

The project of studying New Testament ethics is multiplex; it requires us to engage in four overlapping critical operations that we may designate as the *descriptive*, the *synthetic*, the *hermeneutical*, and the *pragmatic* tasks. The four tasks interpenetrate one another, of course, but it is useful to distinguish them for heuristic purposes. Indeed, much confusion can arise from the failure to distinguish these operations appropriately.[9]

(a) The Descriptive Task: Reading the Text Carefully

The *descriptive* task is fundamentally exegetical in character. The first thing we must do in order to understand the ethics of the New Testament is to explicate in detail the messages of the individual writings in the canon,[10] without prematurely harmonizing them. When we read the texts in this way, we note distinctive themes and patterns of reasoning in the individual witnesses: Luke has a special concern for the poor, the pastoral Epistles emphasize order and stability in the community, and so forth. Likewise, whenever we ask a specific question such as, "What is the meaning of *porneia* in the exception clause that Matthew appends to Jesus' prohibition of divorce?"[11] we are operating at the descriptive level.

This last example contains a hidden complication that exemplifies the difficulty of doing New Testament ethics even at the descriptive level: my formulation assumes that the exception clause originates with Matthew (or his community tradition) rather than with the historical Jesus. As this observation implies, the descriptive task requires attention to the developmental history of moral teaching traditions within the canon.[12]

Our descriptive work cannot be confined, however, to the explicit moral teachings of the New Testament texts; the church's moral world is manifest not only in *didachē* but also in the stories, symbols, social structures, and practices that shape the community's *ethos*. A text such as the Gospel of John, for example, may have relatively little explicit ethical teaching, but its story of a "man from heaven" who comes to reveal God's truth to an unbelieving world is fraught with ethical implications for the community that accepts the message and finds itself rejected by the world.[13] Thus, the work of the historical critic entails reconstructing a "thick description" of the symbolic world of the communities that produced and received the New Testament writings.[14]

Part I of this book ("The Descriptive Task: Visions of the Moral Life in the New Testament") will undertake a descriptive survey of the major New Testament writings, asking how each one portrays the ethical stance and responsibility of the community of faith. The survey will not aim at exhaustive exposition of the ethical content of the New Testament; rather, my intent is to sketch the distinctive moral vision embodied in each of these texts.

(b) The Synthetic Task: Placing the Text in Canonical Context

If we are pursuing New Testament ethics with theological concerns in view, however, we must move on to ask about the possibility of coherence among the various witnesses. When we ask this question, we move from the descriptive to the *synthetic* task. Is it possible to describe a unity of ethical perspective within the diversity of the canon?[15]

This is the phase of the operation that Wayne Meeks deems impossible; he takes the canon's ideological diversity to be irreducible.[16] If that is so, then he is right that we should give up talking about "New Testament ethics" and concentrate instead on the ethos and practices of the individual communities represented by the New Testament documents. I shall contend, on the contrary, that the task of discerning some coherence in the canon is both necessary and possible. The difficult problem, however, is to know what methods might allow us to give an appropriate account of this canonical coherence.

Often the problem is addressed through attempts to reconcile apparent contradictions. Does Matthew's demand for a higher righteousness (Matt. 5:20) contradict

Paul's gospel of the justification of the ungodly (Rom. 4:5)? Does Luke's concern for an ongoing church in history betray the early church's radical eschatological ethic? How does the command for the people of God to "come out . . . and be separate" (2 Cor. 6:14–7:1) relate to Jesus' notorious preference for eating with tax collectors and sinners? How does the principle that in Christ "there is no longer male and female" (Gal. 3:28) relate to specific pastoral admonitions that women should keep silent in churches (1 Cor. 14:34–35) and submit to their husbands (Eph. 5:22–24)? Is the state God's servant for good (Rom. 13:1–7) or the Beast from the abyss that makes war on the saints (Rev. 13)?

Such particular intracanonical tensions can be handled (with something more substantial than ad hoc harmonizing rationalizations) only if they can be located within a comprehensive characterization of the New Testament's moral concerns or themes.[17] This problem is not always clearly confronted in the literature on New Testament ethics. What—if anything—makes these diverse writings hang together as a guide to the moral life?[18]

Some interpreters who have addressed this problem have sought to isolate a single great principle that anchors the New Testament's moral teaching. Love is sometimes singled out as the great imperative at the center of the New Testament's witness. This proposal can, of course, claim the precedent of Mark 12:28–34 and 1 Corinthians 13. Nevertheless, for reasons that will emerge in the course of this investigation, I want to argue that the concept of love is insufficient as a ground of coherence for the New Testament's moral vision.[19]

Instead, I shall propose in Part II ("The Synthetic Task: Finding Coherence in the Moral Vision of the New Testament") that no single principle can account for the unity of the New Testament writings; instead, we need a cluster of focal images to govern our construal of New Testament ethics. The unifying images must be derived from the texts themselves rather than superimposed artificially, and they must be capable of providing an interpretive framework that links and illumines the individual writings. Such a framework is supplied, I shall propose, by the focal images of *community*, *cross*, and *new creation*. The significance of these images—and their application to the task of canonical reading—will be explored in Part II.

(c) The Hermeneutical Task: Relating the Text to Our Situation

Even if we should succeed, however, in giving some satisfactory synthetic account of the New Testament's ethical content, we will still find ourselves perched on the edge of a daunting abyss: the temporal and cultural distance between ourselves and the text. How can we bridge this chasm? This is the hermeneutical task. How do we appropriate the New Testament's message as a word addressed to us?

The problem was put to me in a striking way by a Methodist pastor in Kansas. While conducting a three-day class on Romans for a pastors' school, I had insisted that Paul's letter to the Romans should not be read as a tract about personal salvation; rather, Paul's central concern in the letter is to explicate the relation of Jews and Gentiles in God's redemptive purpose while insisting that the gospel does not abrogate God's faithfulness to Israel. On the last day, one of the pastors said, "Professor Hays, you've convinced me that you're right about Romans, but now I don't see how I can preach from it anymore. Where I serve out in western Kansas, Israel's fate isn't a burning issue for my people, and there's not a Jew within a hundred miles of my church." The objection deserves a thoughtful answer.

What this pastor came to see about Romans is true of the New Testament in its entirety. These texts were not written in the first instance for residents of the United States at the end of the twentieth century. When we read Paul's letters to his churches, we are reading the mail of people who have been dead for nineteen hundred years; when we read the Gospels, we are reading stories told for the benefit of ancient communities whose customs and problems differed vastly from ours.[20] Only historical ignorance or cultural chauvinism could lead us to suppose that no hermeneutical "translation" is necessary for us to understand these texts. The more we understand, the more we will find ourselves appreciating the force of the Kansas pastor's question: How can we preach from these texts anymore? How can we take our moral bearings from a world so different from ours? If the New Testament's teachings are so integrally embedded in the social and symbolic world of first-century communities, can they speak at all to us or for us? Worse still, is the very effort to derive guidance from these texts doomed as an exercise in inauthenticity—either playacting or repressive heteronomy?

The task of hermeneutical appropriation requires an *integrative act of the imagination.* This is always so, even for those who would like to deny it: with fear and trembling we must work out a life of faithfulness to God through responsive and creative reappropriation of the New Testament in a world far removed from the world of the original writers and readers. *Thus, whenever we appeal to the authority of the New Testament, we are necessarily engaged in metaphor-making, placing our community's life imaginatively within the world articulated by the texts.*[21] It is an easy thing to say that such analogical appropriation is necessary; to show how it can be done is a harder task. The form of this imaginative integration of text and situation can never be exactly specified a priori, but certain guidelines can be set forth. This book seeks to offer some such guidelines. A musical analogy might suggest what I hope to do. When a blues-rock band jams, the lead instrumentalist plays improvisationally, but the improvisation occurs within a framework: the key, the time signature, and perhaps even the chord structure are stable configurations within which the soloist plays freely. What this book seeks to do is to describe a framework for New Testament ethics within which the constructive improvisation of moral judgment can take place.

The third major section of this book ("The Hermeneutical Task: The Use of the New Testament in Christian Ethics") will examine ways in which selected theological ethicists have in fact dealt with the hermeneutical task. After comparing their various strategies for employing Scripture, I shall propose a set of hermeneutical guidelines for critical evaluation of normative appeals to the New Testament.

(d) The Pragmatic Task: Living the Text

The final task of New Testament ethics is the pragmatic task: embodying Scripture's imperatives in the life of the Christian community. Without this living embodiment of the Word, none of the above deliberation matters. After all the careful exegetical work, after reflective consideration of the unity of the New Testament's message, after the imaginative work of correlating our world with the New Testament's world, the test that finally proves the value of our theological labors is the "fruits test": "A good tree cannot bear bad fruit, nor can a bad tree bear good fruit. . . . Thus you will know them by their fruits" (Matt. 7:18, 20). The value of our exegesis and hermeneutics will be tested by their capacity to produce persons and communities whose character is commensurate with Jesus Christ and thereby pleasing to God.[22]

Distinguishing the pragmatic task from the hermeneutical is easier in theory than in practice; as we shall see, the New Testament texts themselves frequently insist that there can be no true understanding apart from lived obedience, and vice versa. It would be possible to group the two tasks together under the heading of *application:* the hermeneutical task is the cognitive or conceptual application of the New Testament's message to our situation, and the pragmatic task is the enacted application of the New Testament's message in our situation.

The living out of the New Testament cannot occur in a book; it can happen only in the life of the Christian community. It is possible, however, to indicate how the interpretations and proposals put forward in this book might issue forth into action. Thus, the final section of the book ("The Pragmatic Task: Living Under the Word—Test Cases") will offer some particular judgments on how the New Testament might address moral issues of concern to the church at the end of the twentieth century: violence, divorce, homosexuality, racism, and abortion. In this way, readers will be able to see how the positions I take on these controversial questions grow out of my interpretation of the New Testament texts and out of the methodological decisions I have made along the way.

3. Possible Objections

Any decision to structure a discussion of New Testament ethics in this way rather than that will entail gains and losses. The approach that I am undertaking will undoubtedly raise significant objections from various quarters. Before plunging into the substance of the investigation, it would be well to note several major possible objections to the working method of this book and to provide a preliminary response to these objections.

First of all, some readers will find the fourfold division of the task to be artificial. Does my design encourage an illusion that exegesis is an objective science and that hermeneutical concerns can be deferred until a late stage in the interpretive process? To be sure, the four tasks described here always overlap in practice. The work of description and synthesis can never be wholly divorced from the interpreter's hermeneutical concerns, and—if the above remarks about embodiment of the Word are correct—our own experience of the pragmatic enactment of Scripture will condition our reading from start to finish. No one should suppose, then, that the four tasks are simple sequential steps; when Scripture is actually employed in the church, as in the work of preaching, the interpreter integrates the four tasks. Nonetheless, it is useful to break the tasks of interpretation down for analytical purposes. This heuristic division of the tasks gives us a way of systematically reviewing our integrative judgments and uses of the New Testament.

A more radical version of this objection might be put forward by interpreters influenced by the postmodernist turn in hermeneutics, who would insist that there is no "text" external to the interpretive traditions and practices of particular reading communities.[23] In my analysis of the work of Stanley Hauerwas (see Chapter 12.4), I offer a more extensive account of the difficulties with this position. For the present, it may be sufficient to say that this position—if rigorously and consistently articulated—is true neither to the actual function of Scripture in the theological discourse of classic Christianity nor to the general human conviction that texts have determinate ranges of meaning.[24] It is, of course, true that all interpreters are embedded in cultural contexts and traditions, but to acknowledge that is very different from saying that there is no text or that the text itself has no power to generate or constrain interpretations. Historically, the church has looked to Scripture as a word *extra nos*, a voice that can correct or even challenge tradition; such a view of Scripture was foundational for the Reformation. One may, of course, repudiate this construal of Scripture's role in the church, but not without far-reaching theological consequences. At the same time, those who have immersed themselves deeply in Scripture repeatedly bear witness to the experience of hearing the text say things that they did not know or expect, things not borne to them by the ecclesial traditions in which they were raised, things that they perhaps did not want to hear. How are such experiences to be explained? Self-deception? The revelatory power of the Word of God? Or—more modestly—the commonsense acknowledgment that texts do have determinate ranges of semantic possibility and that a text's world of signification can be meaningfully distinguished from the tradition's construal of it? This last option represents the working assumption of the present study. Tradition shapes and orders our reading in deeply significant ways, but there remains a persistent creative tension between the text and the tradition; Scripture has its own voice, and the responsibility of the faithful interpreter is to listen for that voice both through and apart from the community's interpretive traditions.

Another possible objection to my approach is that it pays too little attention to the historical context and development of the New Testament's ethical teachings. By concentrating on the witness of the canonical documents, do we produce a distorted picture of the realities of life in the early Christian communities? Actually, there are three issues here. First, should New Testament ethics concern itself with *what lies behind the texts?* Much traditional historical-critical scholarship has understood its primary role as offering quasi-causal explanations of where the ideas in the texts "came from." A study of New Testament ethics so conceived would focus on the sources, known and hypothetical, behind the New Testament writings, perhaps with particular attention to reconstructing the ethical teachings of the historical Jesus, in distinction from the canonical portrayals of his teaching.[25] Second, should New Testament ethics concern itself with charting the *developmental trajectories* of early Christian ethical teaching? Such an undertaking could not be confined to the canonical texts; the historian would have to weigh equally the evidence of extracanonical material.[26] Third, should New Testament ethics concern itself with *the social ethos and practices* of the earliest Christian communities? A study with such interests would treat the New Testament writings as windows through which we can look—even if through a glass darkly—upon the social world and daily experiences of the first-century Christians.[27] All of these questions are interesting in their own right, even though they may be less susceptible of definitive answers than earlier generations of New Testament scholars sometimes supposed.

It will be evident to the reader of the following pages that I stand on the shoulders of others; my readings of the individual canonical documents are informed by the results of previous scholarly studies of the sources, development, and social settings of these writings. All of these matters belong to what I have called the descriptive task. Any serious close reading of the texts must take such factors into account; this book could not have been written without the contributing insights of historical criticism. The primary goal of this book, however, is something else: *to engage the theological problem of how the New Testament ought to shape the ethical norms and practices of the church in our time.* With regard to this aim, questions about the historical context of the New Testament are subsidiary. I would therefore respond to the objection by saying that my approach, rather than ignoring historical issues, takes them up into a larger interpretive project. Given the scope of the present book, it is impossible to pursue historical issues in detail. Readers desiring fuller treatments of particular historical problems may consult the literature cited in the endnotes.

Still another potential objection is that I have left the Old Testament out of the account. Given the historic decision of the church to recognize Israel's sacred writings as Scripture, is it not necessary to consider the entire canon in any discussion of biblical norms for ethics? In other words, does my concentration on New Testament ethics imply a Marcionite bias against the Old Testament? On the contrary, the reader of the pages that follow will see that my approach to the New Testament is fundamentally shaped by the conviction that the New Testament is intelligible only as a hermeneutical appropriation of Israel's Scriptures.[28] Thus, although it is impossible here to treat the Old Testament writings independently—another, and much larger, volume would be required for that—my exegetical work on the New Testament texts will seek to show how deeply the convictional structure of the New Testament writers is shaped by the witness of the Old Testament. (For a more extensive discussion of this issue, see Chapter 13.4.)

A final possible objection to the methodology of this book is that it accords preeminent authority to the New Testament without ever giving a reasoned defense for ascribing such normative weight to this particular collection of documents. Indeed, this study proceeds on the working assumption that the canonical Scriptures constitute the *norma normans* for the church's life, whereas every other source of moral guidance (whether church tradition, philosophical reasoning, scientific investigation, or claims about contemporary religious experience) must be understood as *norma normata*. Thus, normative Christian ethics is fundamentally a *hermeneutical* enterprise: it must begin and end in the interpretation and application of Scripture for the life of the community of faith. Such a pronouncement will prove controversial in some circles,[29] but it represents the classic confessional position of catholic Christianity, particularly as sharpened in its Reformation traditions. In this book, therefore, I do not attempt to offer a formal apologetic argument in defense of the authority of Scripture. Readers who wonder why the Bible should be accorded some normative status will have to look elsewhere. Such a limitation of scope is necessitated by the size and complexity of the topic, but there is also a theological intuition underlying my decision to bypass the apologetic enterprise: the most powerful argument for the truth of Scripture is a community of people who exemplify the love and power of the God that they have come to know through the New Testament. Apart from the witness of such communities, formal arguments for the authority of Scripture carry little weight. Consequently, this book is written primarily for readers who stand within a community whose identity is constituted by its confession that the New Testament is normative. In such a community, the truly interesting and urgent questions bear upon the way in which the New Testament may be claimed to authorize and shape the church's life. For such readers, this study will offer an account of how the church might understand its vocation to be a Scripture-shaped community.

NOTES

1. Indeed, the plasticity of textual "meaning" is so great that it has become a fashionable truism in postmodernist circles that the "meaning" of any text is constituted not by any determinate features of the text itself but rather by the conventions of particular communities of readers. Stanley Fish (1980) has whimsically carried this claim to its logical end by denying the existence of a "text": there are no texts, only readers.

2. This political demand seems curious coming from Christian leaders concerned to uphold the authority of the Bible: Did they not consider 1 Tim. 2:1–2 as pertinent? ("First of all, then, I urge that supplications, prayers, intercessions, and thanksgivings be made for everyone, for kings and all who are in high positions, so that we may lead a quiet and peaceable life in all godliness and dignity.")

3. One assumes that the writers meant to say, ". . . church leaders have endorsed other presidents who might not have held biblical positions on all issues."

4. Patrick Mahoney and Bill Devlin, as quoted in *Christian Century* 110/2 (Jan. 20, 1993): 49.

5. In fact, Bishop Spong (1991) has volunteered to rescue it.

6. For a case-study approach that shows how the Bible has been used to support conflicting positions on controversial issues, see Swartley 1983.

7. I heard O'Donovan use this simile in a lecture at Yale Divinity School in the fall of 1987.

8. Wayne Meeks (1986c) suggests that the term "New Testament ethics" confuses historical and normative categories and should therefore not be used. More recently, he has conceded that Christians who seek to derive their ethical standards from the NT might appropriately speak of "'New Testament ethics'—but that would be a normative category, not a historical or descriptive one." Even in this case, he would prefer to speak of "bib-

lical ethics" in order to indicate that the NT is read as part of a larger canon (1993, 3–4). Several notable studies in recent years have addressed the methodological issues: in addition to Swartley 1983, see also Schnackenburg 1965; Childs 1970; Gustafson 1970; Hauerwas 1981, 53–71; Ogletree 1983; Wall 1983; Verhey 1984; Longenecker 1984; Schulz 1987; Countryman 1988; Goldsmith 1988; Birch and Rasmussen 1989; Lohse 1991; Fowl and Jones 1991; Sleeper 1992; Scroggs 1993; Marxsen 1993; McDonald 1993; Spohn 1995.

9. For extended discussion of one instance of such confusion, see Hays 1986.

10. As is done, e.g., by Schrage 1988.

11. Matt. 5:32, 19:9; cf. Mark 10:11–12.

12. For a presentation of NT ethics that attends closely to tradition history, see Schulz 1987.

13. Meeks 1972.

14. See, e.g., Meeks 1986b; N. Petersen 1985. The term "thick description" is a phrase borrowed by Meeks from the work of anthropologist Clifford Geertz (1973). Of course, the thicker the description, the more challenging will be the subsequent synthetic phase of the project.

15. The problem of unity and diversity has long been a central issue of NT theology. For helpful discussions, see Dunn 1977; Boers 1979; Räisänen 1990.

16. Meeks 1986c.

17. Important attempts to address this synthetic problem have recently been offered by Collange 1980 and Lohse 1991. Of these two, Collange is more careful methodologically, though his treatment is restricted to an examination of the coherence between Jesus and Paul. Marxsen (1993), on the other hand, insists that even on so basic a matter as the conception of God, the different NT witnesses "resist harmonization" and contradict one another. Thus, he argues that an exercise of critical discernment is necessary to distinguish the authentically Christian theology and ethics within the NT from the merely nominal Christian thought that already finds expression there.

18. One scholar who has addressed the problem is Allen Verhey. He proposes that the "key" to understanding the message of Scripture is "the resurrection of the crucified Jesus of Nazareth." This is not merely "one doctrine among many to be brought into systematic coherence with the others." Rather, the resurrection "stands as the basis and at the center of the New Testament"; it is the "prism" through which all sources of moral wisdom must pass (1984, 181–183). Cf. Oliver O'Donovan 1994.

19. See Chapter 10.

20. For an approach to the ethics of the NT that emphasizes its cultural distance from the modern world, see Countryman 1988.

21. For elaboration of this point, see Chapter 13.2.

22. Fowl and Jones (1991) offer an approach to ethics that stresses the pragmatic aspect of biblical ethics.

23. Hauerwas 1993; cf. Cartwright 1988.

24. Apart from the assumption that texts have limited ranges of meaning, ordered social discourse would be impossible. For example, the signifier STOP on a traffic sign is not susceptible of infinitely various construals.

25. For further discussion of this problem, see Chapter 7—"Excursus: The Role of 'the Historical Jesus' in New Testament Ethics."

26. This approach would be analogous to the program for NT theology described by William Wrede in his seminal 1897 essay, "The Task and Methods of 'New Testament Theology,'" (English translation in Morgan 1973, 68–116). Tellingly, in order to defend this conception of the project, Wrede was forced to contend that the designation "New Testament theology" was "wrong in both its terms."

27. This approach is exemplified by Meeks 1986b, 1993.

28. For an extended demonstration of this point with regard to one NT writer, see Hays 1989.

29. Indeed, there are many—including some who would identify themselves as Christian theologians—for whom the Bible is seen as a source of oppression and moral blindness, particularly with regard to issues of sexual ethics; for such interpreters, the most crucial question about the moral teaching of the NT is how we can get critical leverage against it. (For a survey of several recent expressions of such a view, see S. C. Barton 1994.) Such forthright repudiation of biblical authority by self-identified Christian thinkers is a historical phenomenon that is both relatively recent and unlikely to exercise any lasting influence within the church.

PART ONE

The Descriptive Task

Visions of the Moral Life in the New Testament

The first task of New Testament ethics is to describe the content of the individual writings in the New Testament canon. But how is such a description to be attempted? A systematic exegetical treatment of the ethical teachings of the New Testament could fill several volumes.[1] Because this book seeks to move beyond description to the synthetic, hermeneutical, and pragmatic tasks, we must limit ourselves to summary accounts of the moral visions of the major New Testament witnesses. Taking in turn each writing or body of writings (e.g., Paul's letters, the Johannine literature), we shall ask what sort of moral logic informs the writer's vision of a life lived faithfully before God. What are the major symbols, themes, and concerns that come to expression in the text, and what are the underlying assumptions and convictions about the shape of the Christian life? How does each author reason in discerning God's will for the community of faith? We shall, in other words, offer a sketch of the moral perspective embodied in each of these texts.

The selection of sketches will be representative rather than comprehensive, concentrating attention on the witnesses that are most important by virtue of their substance and historic influence: Paul, the four Gospels, Acts, and Revelation.[2] As a consequence of this approach, the Pauline letters will receive selective coverage, with the letters usually classed as deutero-Pauline (i.e., Colossians, Ephesians, and the pastoral Epistles) receiving only cursory attention; the Johannine Epistles will be considered along with the Gospel of John; and Hebrews and the general Epistles (James, 1 and 2 Peter, and Jude) will not be discussed at all. If the texts not fully treated in this survey did in fact contain ethical emphases or teachings that stood in tension with the other New Testament texts, they would have to be reckoned with in Part II ("The Synthetic Task"); however, in my judgment, that is not the case. The goal of this first part of the book is not to present an exhaustive account of the ethical content of the New Testament but to illustrate the descriptive enterprise and to display a representative sample of the material with which we must work in doing New Testament ethics.

The order in which the texts are to be explored here is a matter demanding some explanation. Most surveys of New Testament ethics begin with a historical reconstruction of the ethics of Jesus and then trace the development of traditions through the early church and into the Gospels.[3] I have chosen, however, to begin with Paul. Why? There are three compelling reasons not to follow the customary pattern.

First, beginning with the Gospels tends to create a perspectival distortion. The letters of Paul are actually the earliest extant Christian writings, the oldest texts in the New Testament. When we begin with Jesus and the Gospel traditions, we foster, consciously or unconsciously, the impression that Paul is interpreting or reacting to the Gospels. In fact, however, the Gospels that we know were written well after Paul's death, and Paul makes only a few passing references to the teachings of Jesus (e.g., 1 Cor. 7:10, 11:23–25). The virtual absence of references in Paul to synoptic Jesus-tradition is a classic problem for New Testament research; for the purposes of the present study, we cannot pursue the arguments about possible allusions to Jesus' teaching in Paul's letters.[4] In any case, we stand a better chance of appreciating Paul's distinctive patterns of moral reasoning if we consider his letters in their own right before turning to the Gospel materials.

Second, of all the New Testament writers, Paul offers the most extensive and explicit wrestling with ethical issues. In his correspondence we can see how he encounters specific problems and reasons his way through to a solution. The processes of moral logic are, as it were, exposed and on the surface, so that we can see how his reasoning unfolds. Thus, for heuristic reasons, it is useful to begin with Paul: reading his work will allow us to develop analytical categories that will prove useful in examining other New Testament texts in which the logic of moral argument is less explicit.

Finally, the purpose of this book is not to present a developmental history of early Christian ethics; it is, rather, to reflect critically on the ethical import of the canonical New Testament. Our primary interpretive interest lies not in the hypothetical prehistory of the texts but in their final form and subsequent interpretation.[5] The reconstructive historical task is valid and interesting—perhaps even necessary—but it is subsidiary to the concerns of New Testament ethics as a theological discipline. Does it matter for the church's normative ethical reflection whether Jesus of Nazareth really told the parable of the unforgiving servant (Matt. 18:23–35) or whether it is an imaginative creation of Matthew's community? In either case, the parable stands in the canonical texts and exerts a normative claim on the Christian tradition. Without minimizing the complexity and importance of our efforts to understand the original historical setting of the New Testament texts, the present study focuses on the witness of the canonical documents.

Why, then, it might be asked, is the Gospel of Mark discussed in this book before the Gospel of Matthew? Why not simply follow the canonical order? Again, this order of presentation seeks to avoid perspectival distortion. For many reasons, a majority of New Testament scholars agree that Mark is the earliest of the canonical Gospels.[6] The particular emphases of Matthew and Luke stand out more sharply when their portrayals of Jesus are seen as adaptations and supplementations of the portrait painted by Mark. On the other hand, the order in which the texts are read here is merely a question of heuristic clarity. Our basic concern is to hear the voice of each witness individually; consequently, nothing crucial would be lost if the order of presentation were different.

NOTES

1. The point is illustrated by the existence of several book-length studies of the ethics of individual NT writers: e.g., Via (1985) on Mark; Furnish (1968) and Sampley (1991) on Paul. This is not to mention the extensive body of commentaries and monographs on even smaller units, such as the Sermon on the Mount.

2. To focus an extended discussion on "the ethics of Jude," for example, would be an exercise in excessive critical scrupulosity.

3. For example, Schnackenburg 1965; J. T. Sanders 1975; Verhey 1984; Schrage 1988; Schulz 1987.

4. See Furnish 1964; Dungan 1971; Allison 1982; Furnish 1993; Wenham 1995.

5. For a spirited defense of the legitimacy of such interpretive interests, see Levenson 1993.

6. For presentation of the argument, see Streeter 1924; Kümmel 1975 [1973], 52–64, 84–85; Sanders and Davies 1989.

Chapter 1

Paul

The Koinōnia *of His Sufferings*

1. Is Paul's Ethic Theologically Grounded?

Paul was first of all a missionary, an organizer of far-flung little communities around the Mediterranean that united clusters of disparate people in the startling confession that God had raised a crucified man, Jesus, from the dead and thus initiated a new age in which the whole world was to be transformed. The letters of Paul that survive in the New Testament are his pastoral communications with these mission outposts. Though separated from them, he continued to offer them exhortation and counsel about how to conduct their common life "in a manner worthy of the gospel of Christ" (Phil. 1:27).

All of the letters except Romans were written to communities that Paul himself had founded, communities that were well acquainted with his preaching and teaching; consequently, much is left unsaid, taken for granted. As belated readers of the letters, we are left to imagine how the gaps should be filled in. How had Paul preached the gospel to them originally? What norms of behavior had he already sought to inculcate? What shared assumptions were so fundamental that they remained implicit rather than explicit in Paul's correspondence? The letters give us some clues, but when we read them we repeatedly encounter the tantalizing challenge of the unspoken, just as though we were listening to one end of a telephone conversation.

Paul nowhere sets forth a systematic presentation of "Christian ethics." Nor does he offer his communities a "manual of discipline," a comprehensive summary of community organization and duties. Such summaries were not uncommon in the ancient world: in various ways, the genre is represented by the Community Rule (1QS) found among the Dead Sea Scrolls, the presentation of Jesus' teaching in the Gospel of Matthew, the Didache, and the codification of Jewish Halakah in the Mishnah. Paul, however, does not formulate such a code. As we shall see, he has theological reasons for preferring not to do so. Instead, he responds ad hoc to the contingent pastoral problems that arise in his churches. Should Gentile believers be circumcised? Should converts to Paul's movement divorce their unbelieving spouses? Are Christians obligated to obey the Roman authorities? In every case, Paul offers answers.

But are his answers based on some coherent set of theological convictions?[1] Has he unreflectively taken his moral norms from traditional sources, or are they derived from a logic internal to his gospel?

New Testament scholars have sometimes suggested that there is no direct connection between Paul's ethical prescriptions and his theological proclamation. Martin Dibelius, one of the founders of form criticism, proposed that the blocks of moral advice that characteristically occur at the end of Paul's letters should be understood as *parenesis*, general collections of maxims adopted from popular Hellenistic philosophy.[2] According to Dibelius, the early Christians expected the end of history to occur almost immediately; consequently, they did not concern themselves with formulating an ethic. When the parousia did not occur as expected, they filled the ethical vacuum by appropriating philosophical *parenesis*. Thus, in Dibelius's view, the ethical teachings in, for example, Galatians 5–6 and Romans 12–15 are not integrally related to Paul's gospel or derived from "revelation" (see Gal. 1:12); rather, they recycle a general moral wisdom widely shared in Hellenistic culture.[3]

Although Dibelius's description of the Pauline ethical material has been strongly challenged,[4] his sharp disjunction between the theological and ethical aspects of the letters has continued to find significant support. For example, Hans Dieter Betz, in his major commentary on Galatians, writes this with regard to Galatians 5:1–6:10:

> Paul does not provide the Galatians with a specifically Christian ethic. The Christian is addressed as an educated and responsible person. He is expected to do no more than what would be expected of any other educated person in the Hellenistic culture of the time. In a rather conspicuous way Paul conforms to the ethical thought of his contemporaries.[5]

According to Betz's account, Paul's gospel may provide motivation to do what is right, but it does not generate a singularly Christian account of "what is right"; Paul adopts his moral *norms* from the surrounding educated culture.

The implications of such an analysis are great: if there is no integral relation between Paul's ethics and his theology, the normative status of his particular ethical teachings is tenuous. When the Christian gospel moves in time or space to a different culture, one could presumably substitute a different set of cultural norms without difficulty. (One frequently hears this sort of argument made with regard to Paul's pronouncements on sexual ethics.) If, on the other hand, Paul's ethic does have a material relation to his theology, then the normative status of his moral teaching is inextricably bound up with the authority of his gospel. Such hermeneutical concerns cannot, of course, predetermine the result of our analysis, but it is well to recognize what is at stake in the question.

Thus, we confront a cluster of critical questions for our study of Pauline ethics: Are Paul's ethical norms grounded in the gospel? On what is his pastoral counsel based? Is Paul a sort of early Christian advice columnist or editorial writer who addresses the issues of the day by appealing to commonsense standards of morality and decency? Or is his advice distinctively shaped by the gospel? Does the truth of the gospel require the particular counsel that he gives?

In the pages that follow, I will offer a reading of Paul that seeks to demonstrate how his ethical teachings are rooted in his theological thought. Only if we back off some distance from the actual content of the Pauline letters can we posit a dichotomy between Paul's *theology* and his *ethics*—or between *kerygma* (the proclamation of the gospel) and *didachē* (the teaching of standards of conduct), or between *indicative* (what God has done in Christ) and *imperative* (what human beings are called upon to do). The more closely we read Paul's letters, the more fragile these familiar dichotomies appear. In these texts, it is difficult to draw a clear distinction between theology and ethics.[6] They are packed together, under pressure: specific pastoral problems in Paul's churches elicit his theological reflection. Thus, we see theology in progress, unfolding. Paul is not simply repeating already formulated doctrines; rather, he is theologizing as he writes,[7] and the constant aim of his theological reflection is to shape the behavior of his churches. Theology is for Paul never merely a speculative exercise; it is always a tool for constructing community.

Paul is driven by a theological vision of extraordinary breadth: everything is brought under scrutiny of the gospel, and the attempt is made to speak to all pastoral problems in light of the gospel. Meat offered to idols, proper behavior at church potluck dinners, speaking in tongues, or sex counseling for married couples: Paul has something to say on every topic that comes up. Yet behind his various responses to the *contingencies* of the community's struggle to live faithfully stands, according to Paul, a singular *coherent* gospel.[8] "When I came to you, brothers and sisters" he writes to the Corinthians, "I did not come proclaiming the mystery of God to you in lofty words or wisdom. For I decided to know nothing among you except Jesus Christ, and him crucified" (1 Cor. 2:1–2). This singular message of Christ crucified is made to address all the particular problems of conduct faced by his infant communities. But how, exactly, does the gospel of Christ crucified apply to the various ethical issues that Paul faces? That is the question we must investigate in the following pages.

Because Paul's letters are situationally specific, the best approach to Pauline ethics would be to take them one at a time, exploring the particular problems and Paul's response to them.[9] Regrettably, the scope of this book precludes an inductive exegetical treatment of the individual letters. Instead, the goal of our exposition must be a summary sketch of Paul's moral vision, taking into account evidence from all the letters.[10] Our discussion will be structured in the following way:

First, we will explore three recurrent, interlocking theological motifs that provide the framework for Paul's ethical teaching: eschatology, the cross, and the new community in Christ. This general account of Paul's thought is necessary because, as Victor Furnish observed in his landmark study *Theology and Ethics in Paul*, the study of Pauline ethics must begin with "the theological convictions which underlie Paul's concrete exhortations and instructions."[11]

Second, having surveyed these theological bases for Paul's ethic, we will ask a set of analytic questions about its internal logic: *Why* be obedient to God, *what* does the gospel call us to do, and *how* can we do the will of God after we have identified it? These three questions can be rephrased in the conventional language of ethical analysis: What are the *warrants* for obedience to God, what are the *norms* of conduct, and what is the source of *empowerment* for the moral life?

Finally, we will give particular attention to Paul's teaching on sex within marriage and the roles of men and women in ministry. Although these matters are not central in Paul's moral vision, they are of great concern to readers at the end of the twentieth century, and the passages where he deals with them provide a helpful illustration of his theological thought at work, shaping the life of the communities that received his witness.

2. The Theological Framework for Pauline Ethics

(A) NEW CREATION: ESCHATOLOGY AND ETHICS According to Paul, the death and resurrection of Jesus was an apocalyptic event that signaled the end of the old age and portended the beginning of the new. Paul's moral vision is intelligible only when his apocalyptic perspective is kept clearly in mind:[12] the church is to find its identity and vocation by recognizing its role within the cosmic drama of God's reconciliation of the world to himself.

> *[W]e are convinced that one has died for all; therefore all have died. And he died for all, so that those who live might live no longer for themselves, but for him who died and was raised for them. From now on, therefore, we regard no one according to the flesh. . . . So if anyone is in Christ, there is a new creation: everything old has passed away; see, everything has become new! All this is from God, who reconciled us to himself through Christ, and has given us the ministry of reconciliation.* (2 Cor. 5:14b–18, AA)

The image of "new creation" belongs to the thought-world of Jewish apocalypticism. One of the fundamental beliefs of apocalyptic thought was its doctrine of the "two ages": the present age of evil and suffering was to be superseded by a glorious messianic age in which God would prevail over injustice and establish righteousness in a restored Israel.[13] Paul's use of the phrase "new creation" echoes Isaiah's prophecy of hope:

> *For I am about to create new heavens*
> *and a new earth;*
> *the former things shall not be remembered*
> *or come into mind.*
> *But be glad and rejoice forever*
> *in what I am creating;*
> *for I am about to create Jerusalem as a joy,*
> *and its people as a delight.*
> *I will rejoice in Jerusalem,*
> *and delight in my people;*
> *no more shall the sound of weeping be heard in it,*
> *or the cry of distress.* (ISA. 65:17–19)

When we hear 2 Corinthians 5 in the context of Isaiah's fervent prophetic hope for the renewal of the world, we understand that Paul is proclaiming that the church has already entered the sphere of the eschatological age.

The apocalyptic scope of 2 Corinthians 5 was obscured by older translations that rendered the crucial phrase in verse 17 as "*he is* a new creation" (RSV) or—worse yet—"*he is* a new *creature*" (KJV). Such translations seriously distort Paul's meaning by making it appear that he is describing only the personal transformation of the individual through conversion experience. The sentence in Greek, however, lacks both subject and verb; a very literal translation might treat the words "new creation" as an exclamatory interjection: "If anyone is in Christ—new creation!" The NRSV has rectified matters by rendering the passage, "If anyone is in Christ *there is* a new creation." Paul is not merely talking about an individual's subjective experience of renewal through conversion; rather, for Paul, *ktisis* ("creation") refers to the whole created order (cf. Rom. 8:18–25). He is proclaiming the apocalyptic message that through the cross God has nullified the *kosmos* of sin and death and brought a new *kosmos* into being. That is why Paul can describe himself and his readers as those "on whom the ends of the ages have met" (1 Cor. 10:11).[14] The old age is passing away (cf. 1 Cor. 7:31b), the new age has appeared in Christ, and the church stands at the juncture between them.

But for Paul there is also a critical caveat that must be spoken: while the church stands at this juncture, it must also *wait* for the consummation of its hope. Salvation will be fully accomplished only at the parousia, the coming of the Lord Jesus Christ in glory; his appearing will be accompanied by the general resurrection of the dead and the final judgment (1 Thess. 4:13–18; 1 Cor. 15:20–23). Thus, Paul thinks of the present time as an anomalous interval in which the "already" and the "not yet" of redemption exist simultaneously in dialectical tension.[15] The ends of the ages have overlapped.

On the one hand, the power of the old age persists: mundane obligations (e.g., marriage, obedience to ruling authorities) remain in force, and sin and suffering continue to beset the church. Paul drives this point home again and again. In Romans 8, acknowledging "the sufferings of the present time," he speaks of redemption as a future hope: "For in hope we were saved. Now hope that is seen is not hope, for who hopes for what is seen?" (Rom. 8:24–25).

On the other hand, the new creation is not just a future hope, as in most forms of Jewish apocalyptic thought; rather, the redemptive power of God has already broken into the present time, and the form of this world is already passing away. The presence of the Holy Spirit in the church is an eschatological sign, a foretaste and assurance of God's promised redemption. In 2 Corinthians 1:22 and 5:5, Paul speaks metaphorically of the Spirit as an *arrabōn*, a kind of "earnest money" or "first installment" that guarantees the final payoff. Thus, the Spirit-endowed church stands within the present age as a sign of what is to come, already prefiguring the redemption for which it waits.

How does this radical eschatological perspective inform Pauline ethics? Modern critics for whom apocalyptic eschatology seems a wild and foreign thought-world have often found the connection of eschatology and ethics problematical, supposing that the imminent expectation of the end must render ethical judgments pointless. J. L. Houlden, for example, sees Paul's eschatological convictions as the source of "inconsistent moral judgments," because belief in the imminence of the end "deals a crippling blow to the ordinary processes of ethical argument."[16] Alternatively, the imminent expectation of the end is sometimes thought to have produced an "enthusiastic" interim ethic that proved far too radical for the long haul as the church continued to live in history. For example, Paul's endorsement of celibacy (1 Cor. 7:8, 25–35) is predicated partly on the assumption that time is running out (1 Cor. 7:29–31). A common supposition, then, is that radical eschatology must lead either to moral quietism (saving one's own soul and letting the world go to hell) or to moral fanaticism.

There may be some truth to the view that in the modern era imminent eschatological expectation has sometimes led to an abandonment of social responsibility. That does not mean, however, that the same thing was true in the first century. It is important not to impose anachronistic preconceptions on Paul's eschatology. Let us consider a sampling of passages to see how eschatological language and images actually function in Paul's effort to shape the behavior of his churches.

1 Thessalonians. In 1 Thessalonians, the earliest of Paul's extant letters, the future eschatological expectation plays a prominent role. In the letter's opening section (1:2–10), Paul gives thanks for the way in which the Thessalonians' reception of the gospel has become a powerful witness to others who have heard "how you turned to God from idols, to serve a living and true God, and to wait for his Son from heaven, whom he raised from the dead—Jesus, who rescues us from the wrath that is coming" (1:9b–10). No doubt we see here a rough sketch of the content of Paul's original missionary preaching. Paul's summary highlights apocalyptic motifs: the resurrection of Jesus from the dead and the expectation that he will come again from heaven to rescue his people from the wrath of God's last judgment.

The role of the Thessalonian community in the eschatological interval between resurrection and parousia is not only "to wait" (v. 10) but also "to *serve* [*douleuein*] . . . God" while they wait. This point is underscored by Paul's recollection of their "work of faith and labor of love and endurance of hope in our Lord Jesus Christ" (v. 3). The future-directed hope is directly connected with a transformation of the Thessalonians' lives in such a way that they are, according to Paul, engaged in active works of love as a means of serving God. We cannot tell from Paul's concise formulation exactly what they have been doing (except for welcoming Paul himself graciously [v. 9]), but we do know that their reception of the apocalyptic gospel has led to loving action rather than passivity.

In 1 Thessalonians 3:12–13, Paul offers a prayer of intercession for his Thessalonian readers:

> *And may the Lord make you increase and abound in love for one another and for all, just as we abound in love for you. And may he so strengthen your hearts in holiness that you may be blameless before our God and Father at the coming [**parousia**] of our Lord Jesus with all his saints.*

This is, let it be observed, not an exhortation but a prayer. The Thessalonians are not being told to do something; rather, Paul is asking that *God* act in their lives to increase their love for one another and to sanctify them in preparation for the parousia. Paul conceives the church as a people being prepared by God for the fullness of God's kingdom; the holiness that will make them ready for the final judgment finds expression in the love that abounds within the community. The importance of these themes is reiterated in the letter's concluding prayer (5:23–24):

> *May the God of peace **himself** sanctify you entirely; and may your spirit and soul and body be kept sound and blameless at the coming [**parousia**] of our Lord Jesus Christ. The one who calls you [i.e., God] is faithful, **and he will do this.*** (*emphasis mine*)

Eschatological motifs surface also in 1 Thessalonians 4:13–18, where Paul addresses a particular concern of the Thessalonians.[17] What about believers who die before the parousia? Are they to be deprived of life in the messianic kingdom? Paul's answer demonstrates in the clearest possible way that his hope was fixed on the resurrection of the dead rather than immortality of the soul. He could have said, "Don't you know that when your loved ones die, their souls are with Jesus in heaven?" But he offers no such response. Instead, he answers the question by narrating a story about the resurrection of the body: those who have died will rise first; then "we who are alive, who are left," will be caught up *together with them* to meet the Lord. The crucial point of the story is to affirm the hope of reunion with "those who have fallen asleep." The story functions not to warn the readers of judgment at the last day but rather to reassure them: "Therefore encourage one another with these words" (4:18).

The following paragraph, however, modulates the reassurance into admonition (5:1–11). Paul exhorts the community to stay awake and sober in preparation for the day of the Lord, putting on the triad of faith, love, and hope as defensive armor for the struggle at hand (5:8). The battle imagery, lightly touched upon here, is characteristic of apocalyptic portrayals of the community of the faithful in the last days: they will come under assault from the powers of evil, and they must be prepared (cf. Eph. 6:10–20 and the "War Scroll" of the Qumran community). To be sure, the armor is not literal battle equipment[18] but the very same virtues that were said in 1:3 to characterize the Thessalonians. The unit concludes with a reprise of themes sounded earlier:

> God has destined us not for wrath but for obtaining salvation through our Lord Jesus Christ [cf. 1:9–10], who died for us, so that whether we are awake or asleep we may live with him [cf. 4:13–17]. Therefore encourage one another [cf. 4:18] and build up each other, as indeed you are doing [cf. 3:12].

Thus, throughout this short letter, Paul's use of eschatological language serves to comfort the community and to call community members into relationships of loving mutual edification. The eschatological hope should leave them, according to Paul, neither in a state of passivity nor in a state of fevered striving; instead, they should gladly acknowledge that God is at work among them preparing them for the day of the Lord precisely through the works of love that characterize their common life.

2 Corinthians. If 1 Thessalonians emphasizes the future horizon of apocalyptic expectation, other passages in Paul's correspondence lay equal stress on the inbreaking of the new creation in the present. In 2 Corinthians, as we have already seen, Paul describes the community as living on the "already" side of the turn of the ages: "[E]verything old has passed away; see, everything has become new" (2 Cor. 5:17). Because the death and resurrection of Christ have already occurred, the church is said to be living in the "day of salvation" (6:2). It would be a serious misreading of Paul, however, to take these statements out of context as indicators that Paul had shifted his thought wholly in the direction of realized eschatology.

Paul highlights eschatological fulfillment in 2 Corinthians 5 in order to undergird the authority of his apostolic ministry, which has been challenged by rival preachers at Corinth.[19] These rivals, whom Paul caustically characterizes as "super-apostles" (11:5), have emphasized their Jewish ancestry (11:22), compared the authority of their ministry to that of Moses, and produced letters of recommendation, perhaps from the church in Jerusalem, attesting the validity of their ministry. They have also raised questions about Paul. Where are his letters of recommendation (3:1)? Is he a legitimate apostle?

In responding to this challenge, Paul makes bold claims grounded in his apocalyptic worldview. He needs no letters of recommendation, no proofs of continuity with Moses or Jerusalem, because the Spirit is the source of his authority (3:4–6).

The distinctions in which the super-apostles pride themselves belong to the old age, but Paul is an "ambassador for Christ" (5:20), announcing a new order, announcing the apocalyptic message of the reconciliation of the world to God. Those who continue to demand traditional credentials simply do not know what time it is: When a new world is bursting upon the scene, why look back?

In light of this situation, Paul warns the Corinthians against getting caught up in the standards of the old age and being drawn away from the gospel:

> *But we also speak to you as your fellow-workers, adding our exhortation that you should not let God's proffered grace go for nothing. For he says, "At an acceptable time I have heard you, and in a day of salvation I have helped you." Behold, now is the well-favored time; behold, now is the day of salvation.* (6:1–2, QUOTING ISA. 49:8 LXX; RH)[20]

The apocalyptic turn of the ages has created a new Spirit-inspired ministry. Those who are still trapped in the script of the old age do not understand it. "A veil lies over their minds" (3:15b). Indeed, "the god of this age has blinded the minds of the unbelievers" (4:4, AA), those who are perishing. (This sort of soteriological dualism is another prominent characteristic of apocalyptic thought.) But Paul and his converts are among those who have turned to the Lord and had the veil lifted. Thus, "all of us, with unveiled faces, seeing the glory of the Lord as though reflected in a mirror, are being transformed into the same image from one degree of glory to another; for this comes from the Lord, the Spirit" (2 Cor. 3:18).[21]

This eschatological transformation of the community explains Paul's extraordinary affirmation that the purpose of God's reconciling work in Christ is "that we might become the righteousness of God" (5:21). He does not say "that we might *know about* the righteousness of God," nor "that we might *believe in* the righteousness of God," nor even "that we might *receive* the righteousness of God." Instead, the church is to *become* the righteousness of God: where the church embodies in its life together the world-reconciling love of Jesus Christ, the new creation is manifest. The church incarnates the righteousness of God.

Thus, Paul's defense of his own apostolic ministry turns out to be inextricably fused with the proclamation that the church community is a sneak preview of God's ultimate redemption of the world. This is a grandiose-sounding claim, but its potential triumphalism is tempered by the other side of Paul's eschatological dialectic, the "not yet." After his astounding claims about the Spirit-empowered transforming effects of the gospel, Paul adds a crucial qualifier about the specific form his ministry takes:

> *But we have this treasure in clay jars, so that it may be made clear that this extraordinary power belongs to God and does not come from us. We are afflicted in every way, but not crushed; perplexed, but not driven to despair; persecuted, but not forsaken; struck down, but not destroyed. . . . For while we live, we are always being given up to death for Jesus' sake, so that the life of Jesus may be made visible in our mortal flesh.* (4:7–9, 11)

If the church manifests the righteousness of God, it does so in just the way Jesus did: through suffering and death for the sake of others. The vocation of God's people entails suffering. Lest we miss the point, Paul repeats—just after his ringing declaration that "now is the day of salvation"—an extended catalog of the hardships he has suffered as God's servant (6:3–10). The apparent tension between Paul's suffering and his claim that the new creation has already arrived is not a sign of contradiction in Paul's thought. It is, rather, a consequence of his conviction that the church lives in the time between the times. Those who stand at the collision point of the two ages live under the sign of the cross. "We walk by faith, not by sight" (5:7).

Romans 8. Paul's apocalyptic vision of Christian existence between the times, in which glory and suffering paradoxically intermingle, is most vividly expressed in Romans 8. This section of the letter begins with Paul's triumphant declaration that "there is therefore *now* [i.e., since the death of Christ; cf. Rom. 5:8] no condemnation for those who are in Christ Jesus" (8:1). God has dealt with sin through Christ's death, with the result that "the just requirement of the Law might be fulfilled in us, who walk not according to the flesh but according to the Spirit" (8:4, AA). The presence of the eschatological Spirit of God in the community is the basis for confidence and rejoicing: "You are not in the flesh; you are in the Spirit, since the Spirit of God dwells in you" (8:9). The Spirit also attests that believers now belong to the family of God: "When we cry, 'Abba! Father!' it is that very Spirit bearing witness with our spirit that we are children of God, and if children, then heirs, heirs of God and joint heirs with Christ" (8:15c–17a).

So far the picture painted here is one of glorious fulfillment: the community in Christ experiences freedom from the power of the flesh and, through the presence of the Holy Spirit, participates already with Christ in the promised inheritance. Suddenly, however, Paul's account of life in Christ takes a sharp turn: ". . . joint heirs with Christ—if, in fact, we suffer with him so that we may also be glorified with him" (8:17b). The conditional clause introduces the "eschatological reservation" that constantly qualifies Paul's understanding of Christian existence on this side of the parousia. The wrenching time at the turn of the ages is a time of suffering: to speak more precisely, it is a time in which the community participates in the suffering of Christ. Those who enjoy the blessings detailed in 8:1–17a are, paradoxically, those who suffer with Christ in the present time.

Having sounded this crucial reservation, Paul moves into a meditation on the ambiguity of life between the times:

> *I consider that the sufferings of the present time are not worth comparing with the glory about to be revealed to us. For the creation [***hē ktisis***] waits with eager longing for the revealing of the children of God . . . in hope that the creation itself will be set free from its bondage to decay and will obtain the freedom of the glory of the children of God. We know that the whole creation has been groaning in labor pains*[22] *until now; and not only the creation, but we ourselves, who have the first fruits of the Spirit, groan inwardly while we wait for adoption, the redemption of our bodies. For in hope we were saved. Now hope that is*

*seen is not hope. For who hopes for what is seen? But if we hope for what we do not see, we wait for it with patient endurance [**hypomonē**].* (8:18–25, AA)

Remarkably, those who have received "the first fruits of the Spirit" are not thereby exempted from suffering; on the contrary, they groan along with the unredeemed creation,[23] awaiting a redemption that is to be complete only at the resurrection, "the redemption of our bodies." For Paul, redemption is finally to be understood in bodily terms; there is no thought here of "redemption *from* our bodies," as though the body itself were evil. On the contrary, Paul passionately awaits the Creator's final act of liberating the whole creation from "bondage to decay." In the meantime, believers stand in a relation of solidarity with the pain of an unredeemed creation. If anything, the shared pain is sharpened by the tension between hope and reality. Those who have experienced the freedom and power of God's Spirit continue to hope for a reality that they do not yet see; thus, they wait and groan and rejoice.

Summary. We began by asking how Paul's eschatology actually functions in shaping the counsel he gives to his churches. On the basis of our survey of passages in 1 Thessalonians, 2 Corinthians, and Romans, we offer the following observations:

- The eschatological perspective allows Paul to counsel a high tolerance for ambiguity. Suffering and joy are present together, and the church should expect this paradoxical condition to persist until the parousia. Nonetheless, the promise of God's ultimate making right of all things allows the community to live faithfully and confidently no matter how bad things may look in the present.
- The community is engaged in a cosmic conflict. As the advance representatives of God's new creation in an unwilling and hostile world, the church should expect to experience the same sort of opposition that Jesus did, the same sort of opposition that Paul himself encounters. The battle is to be fought, however, not "according to the flesh"—not with weapons of violence—but with proclamation of the truth (cf. 2 Cor. 10:3–6).
- The sense of imminence of the coming of the Lord heightens rather than negates the imperatives of ethical action. The community is called to pursue with urgency the tasks of love and mutual service.
- At the same time, however, *God* is at work preparing the community for the day of the Lord. It is striking how seldom Paul uses eschatological judgment as a threat to motivate obedience. More characteristically, he points to the sanctifying work of God's Spirit, already underway in the community, as a ground of reassurance and hope.
- Paul's gospel proclaims the redemption of all creation; it is not an otherworldly hope of escape from material reality. Consequently, the dualism characteristic of apocalyptic schemes is tempered by Paul's insistence that even those who have received the Spirit still groan along with the unredeemed world.

In sum, Paul's eschatology locates the Christian community within a cosmic, apocalyptic frame of reference. The church community is God's eschatological beachhead, the place where the power of God has invaded the world.[24] All Paul's ethical judgments are worked out in this context. The dialectical character of Paul's eschatological vision (already/not yet) provides a critical framework for moral discernment: he is sharply critical not only of the old age that is passing away but also of those who claim unqualified participation already in the new age. To live faithfully in the time between the times is to walk a tightrope of moral discernment, claiming neither too much nor too little for God's transforming power within the community of faith.

(B) THE CROSS: PARADIGM OF FAITHFULNESS Paul's letters offer very little information about the man Jesus. But when Paul does refer to what Jesus did, the references point, over and over again, to the cross. This concentration on the death of Jesus is the outworking of Paul's determination "to know nothing . . . except Jesus Christ, and him crucified" (1 Cor. 2:2).

The cross is a complex symbol in Paul's thought-world, encoding a rich variety of meanings.[25] The cross signifies the pivot-point of the ages, the place where Christ took "the curse of the law" upon himself (Gal. 3:13) so that blessing might accrue to the Gentiles, the ultimate demonstration of God's righteousness (Rom. 3:24–26) and God's love (Rom. 5:8), the event in which God acted for the redemption of the world. It is the mystery that confutes human wisdom and shames human power (1 Cor. 1:21–31).

For the purpose of our study of New Testament ethics, we must focus attention on one aspect of Paul's interpretation of the cross that is determinative for his understanding of the church's ethical responsibility. For Paul, Jesus' death on the cross is an act of loving, self-sacrificial obedience that becomes paradigmatic for the obedience of all who are in Christ.

Jesus' death on the cross is not an accident or an injustice that befell him; it is, rather, an act of sacrifice freely offered for the sake of God's people. In the salutation of his letter to the Galatians, Paul wishes them peace from "the Lord Jesus Christ, who gave himself for our sins to set us free from the present evil age, according to the will of our God and Father" (Gal. 1:3–4). The aorist participle *dontos* ("gave") refers specifically to Jesus' giving up his life, as is clear also in Galatians 2:20, where the affirmation that "the Son of God . . . loved me and gave himself for me" is explicated by surrounding references to crucifixion (2:19) and Christ's death (2:21).

To be sure, the death of the Son of God on a cross is a unique event, unrepeatable, reconciling humanity to God. It is an event fraught with singular metaphysical significance, not merely a good example of how people ought to live and die. Nonetheless, it does become for Paul also an example, a paradigm for the life of faith. When Paul writes in Galatians 6:2, "Bear one another's burdens, and in this way you will fulfill the law of Christ," he has taken the pattern of Christ's self-giving (1:4, 2:20) and projected it into an imperative for the community to serve one another in love.[26] Paul reads the cross as a metaphor for other actions (burden-bearing) that correspond analogically to the self-giving exemplified by Jesus' death. This metaphorical interpretation of the cross in Galatians 6:2 is exactly consonant with Paul's use of the same image elsewhere in his letters.

In Romans 15, Paul takes Christ's death as an example that should constrain the behavior of "the powerful," who might otherwise be inclined to despise those who are "weak in faith" (Rom. 14:1).

> *We who are powerful ought to bear [**bastazein**, the same verb used in Gal. 6:2] the weaknesses of the powerless, and not to please ourselves. Each of us must please our neighbor for the good, to the end of building up [the community].*[27] *For the Christ*[28] *did not please himself, but, as it is written, "The insults of those who insult you have fallen upon me." . . . Welcome one another, therefore, as the Christ has welcomed you, for the glory of God.*
> (ROM. 15:1–3, 7, RH)

This passage is a little obscure, because Paul assumes without explanation that his readers will understand his citation of Psalm 69:9b ("The insults of those who insult you have fallen on me") as an allusion to the passion of Jesus.[29] Once we recognize that allusion, Paul's point comes into focus: just as the crucified Messiah took upon himself suffering for the sake of others, so the "powerful" in the Roman church should welcome the others even if it means putting up with their "weaknesses." In this case the "weakness" in question is a matter of dietary scruples: "Some believe in eating anything, while the weak eat only vegetables" (14:2). It may seem almost ludicrous to draw an analogy between Jesus' giving up his life in crucifixion and the duty of the strong to give up eating certain foods for the sake of the weak, but the point of comparison is the voluntary surrender of prerogatives for the sake of the other. Indeed, the rhetorical force of Paul's appeal is rooted precisely in the incongruity of the metaphor. "Do not let what you eat cause the ruin of one for whom Christ died" (14:15b). Jesus was willing to die for these people, says Paul, and you aren't even willing to modify your diet?

The paradigmatic significance of Jesus' death is most fully developed in Philippians, where the "Christ hymn" of Philippians 2:6–11 becomes the centerpiece of the letter.[30] Writing from prison (1:12–14), Paul exhorts the Philippians to conduct themselves "in a manner worthy of the gospel of Christ" in the face of opposition and suffering (1:27–30). Their suffering is "for Christ," and it is therefore a "privilege" (1:29). It is also described as "the same struggle" that Paul himself has experienced as an apostle. Thus, the opening of the letter establishes a solidarity in suffering between Paul and his readers.

At the beginning of the second chapter of the letter, Paul exhorts his readers to a life of *koinōnia* (fellowship, sharing) and mutual support. This exhortation is grounded in the story of Christ, as sketched in a poetic passage that may have been an early Christian hymn already familiar to the Philippians.

If, therefore, there is any encouragement in Christ, if there is any consolation of love, if there is any koinōnia *of the Spirit, if there are any compassion and mercy, fulfill my joy: be of the same mind, having the same love, being common-souled and of one mind. Do nothing in accordance with envy or conceit, but in humility let each member of the community count all the others as having higher rank.*[31] *Let each of you look not to your own interests, but to the interests of others. Let this mind be in you that was also in Christ Jesus,*

Who, though in the form of God
Did not count equality with God
As something to be exploited,[32]
But he emptied himself,
Taking the form of a slave
And being found in human form.
He humbled himself
And became obedient all the way to death,
Death on a cross.
Therefore God also highly exalted him
And granted to him the name
That is above every name
So that in the name of Jesus
Every knee should bend
Of beings in heavenly places and on earth and under the earth
And every tongue should confess that
Jesus Christ is Lord
To the glory of God the Father.

Therefore, my beloved, just as you have always obeyed,[33] *not only in my presence but now much more in my absence, work out your own salvation with fear and trembling, for God is the one who is working in you both to will and to work for his good pleasure.*
(PHIL. 2:1–13, RH)

Christ's obedience to the point of death (2:8) is offered to the Philippians as a pattern for their own obedience (2:12). Just as he obediently suffered, so the Philippians should stand firm in the gospel, even when it requires them to suffer (1:27–30). Just as he humbled himself (*etapeinōsen*, 2:8) and took the form of a slave, so the Philippians should in humility (*tapeinophrosynē*, 2:3) become servants of the interests of others. Thus, Paul takes a hymn whose original purpose is doxological and employs it in service of moral exhortation.[34] Christ becomes an "exemplar"[35] who illuminates the way of obedience.

This interpretation of the Christ hymn as ethical paradigm has been out of favor with many New Testament exegetes in the latter half of the twentieth century, as a result of influential studies of the passage by Ernst Käsemann and Ralph Martin.[36] Käsemann emphasized the impossibility of imitating the cosmic action of a divine being's descent from heaven and ultimate exaltation above all creation; in his view, only a naive and sentimental "ethical idealism" could see a moral example here. A key to Käsemann's interpretation is his reading of verse 6. The Greek says literally, "Let this mind be among you which also in Christ Jesus." Käsemann proposed that the ellipsis should be understood to mean "Let this mind be among you which [you have] also in Christ Jesus." In other words, the sentence would point not to Jesus' action as an example but to the sphere of being "in Christ" that defines the context for the church's action. This interpretation of the passage, which was adopted in the RSV, finds felicitous phrasing in the NEB: "Let your bearing towards one another arise out of your life in Christ Jesus."

More recent interpretations of the passage, however, have observed that Käsemann's exegesis fails to account for the function of the hymn in its context and for the extensive correspondences developed in the letter between Christ, Paul, and the Philippians. Furthermore, Käsemann's rejection of a literal imitation of Christ's cosmic act depends on a rigid notion of one-to-one correspondence between example and imitator. If we adopt a more supple notion of metaphorical correspondence, the dissimilarities between Christ and his people are to be expected, because metaphor always posits a startling likeness between unlike entities. In Philippians, Paul offers a metaphorical reading of Christ's self-emptying and death; the power of the metaphor is precisely a function of its daring improbability, inviting the readers to see their own lives and vocations as corresponding to the gracious action of the Lord whom they acclaim in their worship.[37] Consequently, the decision of the NRSV translation committee to return to the "exemplar" interpretation is to be welcomed: "Let the same mind be in you that was in Christ Jesus."

This correspondence to the pattern of Jesus is exemplified for the Philippians by Paul's account of his own story in Philippians 3. Once upon a time, he explains, he had it made as a successful and respected religious person who knew all the answers. Unlike Martin Luther, Paul the Pharisee did not struggle with a terrified conscience; with respect to righteousness under the Law, he was "blameless" (Phil. 3:4–7).[38] But his encounter with Christ led him to empty himself of these claims and privileges. He has left his former status behind: "I have suffered the loss of all things, and I consider them crap,[39] in order that I might gain Christ and be found in him." Having surrendered his credibility within the social world of Jewish culture, Paul has become a disreputable traveling preacher; he writes this letter from a prison cell. It takes no great leap of imagination to discern the correspondence that Paul sees between his own career and the trajectory of Christ's obedience in the hymn of Philippians 2.

Furthermore, just as Christ was highly exalted by God, Paul hopes also to share ultimately in Christ's vindication:

> *. . . to know Christ and the power of his resurrection and the* **koinōnia** *of his sufferings, by becoming like him in his death, if somehow I may attain the resurrection from the dead.* (3:10–11)

The *koinōnia* of his sufferings: that is Paul's picture of the life in Christ. In community with others, believers find themselves conformed to the death of Christ. Thus, the cross becomes the ruling metaphor for Christian obedience, while the resurrection stands as the sign of hope that those who now suffer will finally be vindicated by God. As the wider context makes apparent, the suffering of which Paul speaks is not merely suffering for the sake of suffering; rather, it is suffering incurred for "the faith of the gospel" (1:27) and through service to others (2:1–4).

For all these reasons, Paul presumes to invite his readers to "become fellow-imitators of/with me[40] and observe those who walk according to the pattern [*typos*] you have in us" (Phil. 3:17, RH). Paul poses himself as an example because his own life is conformed (however imperfectly: cf. Phil. 3:12) to Christ: through imitating him, his churches will be joining him in imitating Christ. The point, implicit in the whole structure of the argument in Philippians, is made concisely explicit in 1 Thessalonians 1:6: "You became imitators of us and of the Lord."

The twin themes of conformity to Christ's death and the imitation of Christ are foundational elements of Paul's vision of the moral life. (For other passages in which these themes emerge with particular clarity, see Rom. 6:1–14; 8:17, 29–30; 15:1–7; 1 Cor. 10:23–11:1; 2 Cor. 4:7–15; 12:9–10; Gal. 2:19–20; 5:24; 6:14.) Obedience to God is defined paradigmatically—in the metaphorical way we have discussed above—by Jesus' death on the cross.

The paradigmatic role of the cross is suggested also by the contrast in Romans 5:12–21 between Christ's obedience and the disobedience of Adam. Adam is the initiator and prime symbol of humanity's rebellion against the will of God; Jesus, through his radical obedience, reverses the consequences of Adam's sin and becomes the initiator of a new, obedient humanity:

> *Therefore just as one man's trespass led to condemnation for all, so one man's act of righteousness leads to justification and life for all. For just as by the one man's disobedience the many were made sinners, so by the one man's obedience the many will be made righteous.* (5:18–19)

The obedience of Jesus, enacted in his death on the cross, is the prototype for "the obedience of faith" that Paul's preaching aims to inculcate (1:5).[41] Indeed, "the one man's obedience" (5:19) should be understood as a virtual synonym for "the faith of Jesus Christ" (3:22), through which the righteousness of God is revealed.

This last point has been somewhat obscured by translations that render the expression *pistis Iēsou Christou* as "faith *in* Jesus Christ" rather than "faith *of* Jesus Christ." I have presented at length elsewhere the exegetical arguments for the latter interpretation.[42] The meaning of "the faith of Jesus Christ" comes into focus when we perceive that Paul understands the cross as a pattern for the life of Christians.

When Paul declares in Romans 3:21–22 that the righteousness of God has been shown forth apart from the Law "through the faith of Jesus Christ," he is providing the answer to seemingly insuperable difficulties raised in 3:1–20. Does the unfaithfulness (*apistia*) of Israel nullify the faithfulness (*pistis*) of God toward his covenant people (3:3)? Is God unjust (*adikos*) to inflict wrath (3:5)? If all human beings are deeply implicated in sin, Jews and Gentiles alike, all in a state of *apistia*, despite Israel's advantage of having been given the Law, does that mean that God's redemptive intentions have been thwarted? In Romans 3:21–26 Paul offers a resounding no! to all of these troubling questions: God has vindicated his own righteousness (*dikaiosynē*) by putting forward Jesus, whose faithfulness in death atones for human sin/unfaithfulness and demonstrates God's continuing faithfulness to his covenant promises. When these verses are read together with Romans 5:15–19, a consistent picture emerges. Jesus' death is an act of faithfulness[43] that simultaneously reconciles humanity to God and establishes a new reality in which we are set free from the power of sin, able to be conformed to the pattern of his life. That is what Paul means when he says

> *I have been crucified with Christ; and it is no longer I who live, but it is Christ who lives in me. And the life I now live in the flesh I live by the faith of the Son of God, who loved me and gave himself for me.*
>
> (GAL. 2:19–20, *the translation given here follows the translation given in the NRSV footnote*)

The faith(fulness) of Jesus Christ becomes the animating force in our lives. However mysterious such claims appear, they show that there is a deep connection in Paul's thought between Christology and ethics:[44] to be in Christ is to have one's life conformed to the self-giving love enacted in the cross, "always carrying in the body the death of Jesus, so that the life of Jesus may also be made visible in our bodies" (2 Cor. 4:10).

(C) REDEEMED COMMUNITY: THE BODY OF CHRIST Paul did not write general theological tractates; instead, he wrote letters to churches.[45] Paul's strong thematic emphasis on community is partly to be explained by the original occasion and purpose of these letters: they were written to strengthen and support group identity in fledgling mission churches. The weight placed on community formation is not, however, merely a matter of practical necessity; Paul develops his account of the new community in Christ as a fundamental *theological* theme in his proclamation of the gospel.[46]

What is God doing in the world in the interval between resurrection and parousia? According to Paul, God is at work through the Spirit to create communities that prefigure and embody the reconciliation and healing of the world. The fruit of God's love is the formation of communities that confess, worship, and pray together in a way that glorifies God (see, e.g., Rom. 15:7–13).

Those who are baptized, Paul insists, have become "one in Christ Jesus," no longer divided by former distinctions of ethnicity, social status, or gender (Gal. 3:28). Because in Christ they are all "sons of God,"[47] they all belong together in a single family, in which all are joint heirs.[48] His passionate opposition to Cephas at Antioch (Gal. 2:11–21) sprang from his urgent conviction that Jews and Gentiles must be one in Christ, not separated by social barriers. The basic problem with the desire of Jewish Christians to maintain Torah observance was, according to Paul, not that it engendered "works righteousness" but rather that it fractured the unity of the community in Christ.[49] John Barclay has well summarized the ethical issue at stake: "The problem here is not legalism (in the sense of earning merit before God) but cultural imperialism—regarding Jewish identity and Jewish customs as the essential tokens of membership in the people of God."[50]

It is important to realize, however, that Paul could equally be accused of promulgating a reverse "cultural imperialism." He has relativized and disqualified the distinctively Jewish signs of membership in God's covenant community ("works of Law" = circumcision, food laws, Sabbath observance), but he has at the same time inevitably set up new marks of participation in that community (confession of faith, baptism, experience of the Holy Spirit). Daniel Boyarin, in an important and provocative study of Paul, describes Paul's vision of community as "particularist universalism."[51] It should not be forgotten that the community whose unity Paul passionately seeks is not the human community as a whole, nor is it a pluralistic community within the *polis*. It is, rather, always the particular community of the church. To be sure, Paul hopes for the ultimate triumph of God's grace over all human unbelief and disobedience (Rom. 11:32, Phil. 2:9–11). Until that eschatological consummation, however, Paul speaks only to the community of faith. He articulates no basis for a general ethic applicable to those outside the church.

Paul's concern for communal unity surfaces clearly in the concluding hortatory portion of the letter to the Galatians.[52] Not only is his list of "works of the flesh" (5:19–21) heavily weighted toward offenses against the unity of the community ("enmities, strife, jealousy, anger, quarrels, dissensions, factions, envy"), but the vice and virtue lists of 5:16–24 are also bracketed by clear directives against conflict in the church (5:13–15; 5:25–6:5). The conformity of the Galatians to Christ is to be expressed in their communal practice of loving, mutual service: "Through love become slaves to one another. . . . Bear one another's burdens, and in this way you will fulfill the law of Christ" (5:13c; 6:2).

Concern for unity of the community is also a fundamental theme of 1 Corinthians.[53] The letter's introductory thanksgiving concludes with this affirmation: "God is faithful; by him you were called into the *koinōnia* of his Son, Jesus Christ our Lord" (1 Cor. 1:9). This call to the fellowship of Jesus in turn becomes the immediate ground of a plea for unity:

> *Now I appeal to you, brothers and sisters, through the name of our Lord Jesus Christ, that all of you be in agreement and that there be no divisions [**schismata**] among you, but that you be united in the same mind and the same purpose.* (1:10)

This exhortation is necessary because Paul has received word that there are indeed quarrels within the Corinthian community. (Some of the particular causes of these divisions are discussed during the course of the letter.) Paul regards such disunity in the church as contrary to the word of the cross (1:18–2:5) and as a sign of the Corinthians' immaturity in the faith.

And so, brothers and sisters, I could not speak to you as spiritual people, but rather as people of the flesh, as infants in Christ. I fed you with milk, not solid food, for you were not ready for solid food. Even now you are still not ready, for you are still of the flesh. ***For as long as there is jealousy and quarreling among you, are you not of the flesh, and behaving according to human inclinations?*** (3:1–4, *emphasis mine*)

Dissension in the church is deeply worrisome to Paul, for the aim of his apostolic labors has been to build community, not just to save souls. He has "laid a foundation" (3:10), and he is concerned that other contractors are botching the subsequent construction job. The quality of construction matters urgently, because the community is "God's building" (3:9). Indeed, Paul dares to assert more: the community is the place where God dwells. "Do you not know," he asks, "that you [plural] are God's temple and that God's Spirit dwells in you [plural]?" (3:16). To read this last sentence as though it spoke of the Spirit dwelling in the body of the individual Christian would be to miss the force of Paul's audacious metaphor: the apostolically founded community takes the place of the Jerusalem Temple as the place where the glory of God resides.[54] When the community suffers division, the temple of God is dishonored. But the presence of the Spirit in the community should produce unity rather than conflict.

These broad themes are brought into close focus by Paul's long discussion of speaking in tongues and other spiritual gifts in the community's worship in 1 Corinthians 12–14. This passage forcefully holds up the norm of communal edification as the standard by which spirituality is to be measured and guided.

Apparently some of the Corinthians were priding themselves on their rich endowments of spiritually inspired "speech and knowledge" (cf. 1:5). In the opening of the letter, Paul gives thanks, perhaps with a trace of irony, that the Corinthians "are not lacking in any spiritual gift" (1:7). He does not give a direct description of the problems surrounding spiritual manifestations in the Corinthian assembly, but his counsel suggests that some members of the community must have been claiming spiritual superiority and dominating the community's worship with virtuoso displays of glossolalia.

In responding to this situation, Paul develops an account of the church's interdependent common life:

Now there are varieties of gifts, but the same Spirit; and there are varieties of services, but the same Lord; and there are varieties of activities, but it is the same God who activates all of them in everyone. To each is given the manifestation of the Spirit for the common good. (12:4–7)

The diversity of God's gifts is necessary "for the common good" of the community. Paul underscores his point by employing the analogy of the human body in which all the parts are necessary to healthy functioning of the organism: "If one member suffers, all suffer together with it; if one member is honored, all rejoice together with it" (12:26). Then Paul introduces his foundational metaphor for the church's corporate life: "Now you are the body of Christ and individually members of it" (12:27).

Common participation in the body of Christ becomes the basis for Paul's particular directions concerning the regulation of the community's worship. Speaking in tongues is a spiritual experience, a fine thing in itself, says Paul (14:2, 5a), but it does not edify the community. All actions, however ostensibly spiritual, must meet the criterion of constructive impact on the church community. Consequently, intelligible prophecy, which offers "upbuilding and encouragement and consolation" for the community (14:3), is to be more highly valued and sought: "Those who speak in a tongue build up themselves, but those who prophesy build up the church" (14:4). The noun *oikodomē* ("building up, edification") and the cognate verb *oikodomein* occur repeatedly in this chapter. The task of community-building, which was originally Paul's apostolic work, is transferred to the community itself; thus, the purpose of corporate worship becomes community formation. It is crucial, however, that the work of community-building be a shared, participatory enterprise; the worship assembly is not to be monopolized by any one member. Instead,

> *When you come together,* ***each one*** *has a hymn, a lesson, a revelation, a tongue, or an interpretation. Let all things be done for building up [****oikodomē****].* (14:26, *emphasis mine*)

Thus, the gathered community's worship reflects and symbolizes the interdependence of the body of Christ.

Sandwiched between chapters 12 and 14 is Paul's great panegyric on love. Whether this is an independent piece of tradition inserted here by Paul or whether it was composed for the occasion at hand, the placement of this discourse shows that Paul interprets love in terms of the ecclesial context elaborated in the surrounding chapters. Love, rightly understood, should constrain those superspiritual Corinthians whose behavior threatens the good of the community. Love binds the body of Christ together in mutual suffering and rejoicing; love seeks the upbuilding of the whole community rather than private advantage. It is striking that Paul places this discourse on love in the midst of his response to the tongue-speaking controversy rather than, say, in his discussion of marriage in 1 Corinthians 7. Why so? For Paul, love has its primary locus in the common life of the church.

One final passage will serve to illustrate the fundamental emphasis on community in Paul's thought. Having completed the long theological exposition of Romans 1:16–11:36, in which he defends the integrity of God's promises to Israel and articulates the mystery of God's grace, Paul turns to explicit exhortation in Romans 12.

> *I appeal to you, therefore, brothers and sisters, by the mercies of God, to present your bodies [****sōmata**** (plural)] as a living sacrifice [****thysian**** (singular)], holy and acceptable to God, which is your spiritual worship. Do not be conformed to this age, but be transformed by the renewing of your minds, so that you may discern what is the will of God—what is good and acceptable and perfect.* (Rom. 12:1–2, AA)

The metaphor of "living sacrifice" describes the vocation of the community: the addressees of the letter are called to present their bodies together as a single collective sacrifice of obedience to God. This act of rightful worship must be performed by the community as a whole. Modern readers accustomed to interpreting biblical texts as discourse addressing the private individual will find this image of a corporate sacrifice a strange picture, but it is fundamental to Paul's understanding of his mission. For instance, in Romans 15:14–19, he invokes the metaphor of himself as a priest presenting "the offering of the Gentiles" to God; this "offering" (*prosphora*) is then explicated as "the obedience of the Gentiles" (v. 18). In this passage, Paul is the metaphorical "priest" presenting the offering, whereas in Romans 12:1–2 the community performs the act of self-presentation. In both cases, however, the content of the sacrifice is the community's corporate obedience. That Paul has the community explicitly in mind in Romans 12 is confirmed by the fact that he immediately reintroduces the "one body in Christ" metaphor in verses 4–8, again emphasizing, as in 1 Corinthians 12, the complementarity of different gifts for the common good.

Paul's thought moves in Romans 12:2 from the community's sacrificial self-surrender to the community's transformation. Having offered themselves to God, community members are to find themselves transformed, set free from the confining power of this age. Their mind (*nous*, again singular) is to be made new by God so that they can rightly discern God's will. The meaning of this vision is substantially the same as the picture of the church in 2 Corinthians 5:14–21, already discussed above, in which the church, as new creation in Christ, is said to "become the righteousness of God." In 2 Corinthians 5, the new creation is expressed as a present reality, whereas in Romans 12, the readers are exhorted to present themselves and be transformed. This is one more instance of the coincidence of indicative and imperative in Paul's thought; present reality and future hope overlap at the turn of the ages. The constant factor is that he imagines God's eschatological salvation in corporate terms: God transforms and saves a *people*, not atomized individuals. Consequently, the faithful find their identity and vocation in the world as the body of Christ.

These three closely linked themes, then, frame Paul's ethical thought: new creation in collision with the present age, the cross as paradigm for action, and the community as the locus of God's saving power. Within this framework, let us turn to examine the processes of Paul's moral reasoning.

3. Paul's Moral Logic: Warrants, Norms, and Power

(A) WHY OBEY GOD? WARRANTS FOR THE MORAL LIFE Does grace undo ethics? Paul himself was forced to worry about this problem, because his detractors were already asserting that his gospel did away with Law and order, removing the necessary restraints on human sinfulness. Many of his Jewish compatriots, including fellow Jewish Christians, were scandalized by the freedom with which Paul dismissed the particular commandments of the Torah, fearing that his preaching provided carte blanche for the flesh.[55] (It is a peculiar irony that in the modern—and "postmodern"—world, Christianity has come to be regarded as narrow and moralistic. Originally, it was quite the reverse: figures such as Jesus and Paul were widely regarded as rebels, antinomians, disturbers of decency.)[56]

Paul saw the danger that his gospel could be heard as license for antinomianism; that is why, after his passionate defense of Christian freedom from the Law in Galatians, he introduces the final section of his argument with a major caveat: "For you were called to freedom, brothers and sisters; only do not use your freedom as an opportunity for the flesh" (Gal. 5:13, AA). He then distinguishes schematically between "the works of the flesh" and "the fruit of the Spirit," contending that "those who belong to Christ Jesus have crucified the flesh with its passions and desires" (5:16–26). The crucifixion of Jesus is a watershed event; the Galatian believers are said to have undergone with Christ a death and resurrection, with the result that they have (or *should* have) left behind the divisive and self-indulgent practices of the past. Those who "live by the Spirit" are called to "be guided by the Spirit"—that is, to let their conduct correspond appropriately to the life-giving power of God that they have experienced. The metaphor of "fruit" suggests that the sanctified conduct Paul expects of the Galatians is not so much the product of moral striving as that of allowing the mysterious power of God's Spirit to work in and through them. Where God's Spirit is at work, Paul contends, the result will be peace and holiness, not moral anarchy.

Similar issues receive further elaboration in Paul's letter to the Romans. In Romans 3, Paul is building a case that "all, both Jews and Greeks, are under the power of sin." Consequently, human beings are radically dependent on God's act of grace: the gospel is "the power *of God* for salvation" (Rom. 1:16). The argument is shocking not only because it seems to deny the privileged status of Israel as God's elect people but also because it threatens to undercut all motivation for seeking to live in obedience to God. Paul has already heard this objection to his message, and he raises it himself rhetorically in Romans 3:7–8.

> *But if through my falsehood God's truthfulness abounds to his glory, why am I still being condemned as a sinner? And why not say (as some people slander us by saying that we say), "Let us do evil so that good may come"? Their condemnation is deserved!*

At this stage of the letter, Paul does not really answer the objection except by rejecting it as a "slander," a reprehensible misconstrual of his gospel. By raising this issue, however, he has run ahead of the structure of his argument; consequently, he brackets the question momentarily in order to develop more fully his account of grace in Romans 3:21–5:21.

Paul's depiction of grace builds to its climax in Romans 5: "For while we were still weak, at the right time Christ died for the ungodly. . . . God proves his love for us in that while we were sinners Christ died for us" (Rom. 5:6, 8). Christ's death was an act of cosmic significance, the typological antithesis and overcoming of Adam's fall: "Just as one man's trespass led to condemnation for all, so one man's act of righteousness leads to justification and life for all" (Rom. 5:18). When the claim is formulated in these cosmic terms, however, the submerged question of Romans 3:7–8 starts to resurface: Does Jesus' obedience (see Rom. 5:19) render ours irrelevant? Indeed, Paul provocatively restates his message of grace in terms perilously close to the "slander" he had rejected earlier:

> *But where sin increased, grace abounded all the more, so that, just as sin exercised dominion in death, so grace might also exercise dominion through [Christ's] righteousness leading to eternal life through Jesus Christ our Lord.* (ROM. 5:20b–21)

The more sin, the more grace? It is not hard to see how Paul's opponents might have accused him of suggesting such a thing.

Thus, in Romans 6, he at last addresses the problem he had adumbrated in 3:7–8: "What then shall we say? Should we continue in sin in order that grace may abound?" This time he is ready to confront the issue directly, and he opens with an emphatic rejoinder: "No way!" (The conventional translation, "By no means," does not sufficiently render the force of Paul's *Mē genoito.)*

The reasons for this forceful denial follow. First of all, Paul argues, we have been united with Christ in baptism: thus, in a mysterious way, we participate in the effects of his death and resurrection. We have died to sin and we are enabled, in union with the risen Christ, to "walk in newness of life" (Rom. 6:2–5). The gospel that Paul preaches deals not merely with forgiveness but with *transformation.* To be baptized is to pass from the realm of sin and death into the realm of righteousness and life. Because Christ died, "our old self was crucified with him so that . . . we might no longer be enslaved to sin" (Rom. 6:6); because Christ was raised from the dead, "death no longer has dominion over him" (Rom. 6:9b). Consequently, Paul concludes, "you also must consider yourselves dead to sin and alive to God in Christ Jesus" (Rom. 6:11). This notion of effective transformation through union with Christ is fundamental to Paul's theological ethics.

Closely related to participation in Christ's death is the theme of *transfer of lordship.* Paul portrays sin as a slavemaster from whom we have been rescued. Through baptism, believers are transferred from one sphere of power to another, like prisoners of war liberated to serve their rightful authority. Thus, "sin will have no dominion over you, since you are not under law but under grace" (Rom. 6:14).

But this formulation causes Paul, in order to avert any possible misunderstanding, to raise the rhetorical question yet one more time: "What then? Should we sin because we are not under law but under grace? No way!" (Rom. 6:15). Still using the slavery metaphor, Paul frames a final response in terms of *transfer of allegiance,* this time stressing the human response to God's gracious act: "For just as you once presented your members as slaves to impurity and to greater and greater iniquity, so now present your members as slaves to righteousness for sanctification" (Rom. 6:19bc). The result of God's liberating grace is not to make us into free moral agents; rather, "you have been freed from sin and enslaved to God" (Rom. 6:22a). The appropriate response to God's grace, Paul insists, is a response of self-presentation in obedience to the one who rescued us from slavery to sin and death.

Thus, Paul mounts a vigorous rejoinder to the charge that his gospel undercuts the imperative of obedience to God's will. On the contrary, he asserts that it is only through God's gracious act in Christ that believers are transformed and set free for obedience. The gospel does not destroy the ethical imperative; those who suppose that it does, Paul contends, have simply failed to understand that his gospel proclaims an act of God that grasps us and remakes us.

We have noted so far three fundamental warrants for obedience that are intrinsic to Paul's gospel:

- Through union with Christ, we undergo transformation that should cause us to "walk in newness of life."
- Because God has liberated us from the power of sin, we should transfer our allegiance to the one who has set us free.
- Because the Holy Spirit is at work in the community of faith, the fruit of the Spirit should be manifest in the community's life.

It is striking that these are all positive warrants that ground the moral imperative in what God has already done or is doing in the midst of the community. There is, interestingly, no emphasis in Paul on gratitude as a motive for obedience. (He never says, in effect, "God has done something nice for us, so we should return the favor by doing something nice for God.") Instead, Paul seems to see moral action as a logical entailment of God's redemptive action. For Paul, God's transforming act in Christ conditions all of reality. Insofar as we perceive the truth about God's redemptive work in the world, we will participate gladly in the outworking of God's purpose; conversely, if we fail to act in a way consonant with God's will, we are living in a state of contradiction: we are failing to understand what is going on about us. Consequently, much of Paul's moral exhortation takes the form of reminding his readers to view their obligations and actions in the cosmic context of what God has done in Christ.

Any full account of moral warrants in Paul, however, must also acknowledge the presence of negative warrants, sanctions against sinful behavior. One of Paul's fundamental convictions is the belief that God will ultimately pronounce judgment on the whole world, including the community of faith; in accordance with this conviction, Paul sometimes seeks to influence the behavior of his communities through threats of punishment for disobedience. The expectation of future judgment becomes an explicit warrant for moral action: ". . . [W]e make it our aim to please [God]. For all of us must appear before the judgment seat of Christ, so that each may receive recompense for what has been done in the body, whether good or evil" (2 Cor. 5:9b–10; see also Rom. 2:1–16; 14:10–12; 1 Cor. 3:10–17; 11:27–32; 1 Thess. 4:23–25).

Furthermore, as a correlate of this belief in God's eschatological judgment, Paul issues stern apostolic warnings to his young churches. The Corinthians, for example, receive several such admonitions:

> *I warned those who sinned previously and all the others, and I warn them now while absent, as I did when present on my second visit, that if I come again, I will not be lenient.* (2 Cor. 13:2)

> *But some of you, thinking that I am not coming to you, have become arrogant. But I will come to you soon, if the Lord wills, and I will find out not the talk of these arrogant people, but their power. For the kingdom of God depends not on talk but on power. What would you prefer? Am I to come to you with a stick, or with love in a spirit of gentleness?* (1 Cor. 4:18–21)

The apostle's own promised return to the community for judgment prefigures Christ's parousia.[57] It is not completely clear what Paul is threatening to do if the Corinthians fail to fall into line. Probably we find some clues in the enigmatic passage 1 Corinthians 5:1–13, where he counsels the expulsion of an offender from the community. This act of excommunication is starkly described as "handing this man over to Satan for the destruction of the flesh, so that [the/his] spirit may be saved in the day of the Lord."[58] We shall return to this passage below; for now, we simply note that in some contexts, Paul wields strong negative warrants to discourage certain behaviors in his churches.

Such threats, however, appear to be measures of last resort. Paul generally prefers suasion to sanctions; he characteristically produces painstaking arguments setting forth the positive warrants for the actions he commends to his churches. For example, in Paul's brief and rhetorically tactful letter to Philemon—actually sent to the church that meets in Philemon's house—he refrains from ordering Philemon directly to release the slave Onesimus, preferring instead to appeal to Philemon's good graces.[59]

> *Though I am bold enough in Christ to command you to do your duty, yet I would rather appeal to you on the basis of love. . . . Confident of your obedience, I am writing to you, knowing that you will do even more than I say.* (Philem. 8–9a, 21)

Only when the theological arguments seem to be failing (as in the case of the notoriously difficult Corinthian community) does he begin appealing to negative warrants.

On the surface of the matter, it might appear that the negative warrants stand in some tension with the fundamental message of Paul's gospel. If "Christ has redeemed us from the curse of the law by becoming a curse for us" (Gal. 3:13), does that not mean that the conditional curses and blessings of Deuteronomy 27 and 28 have been suspended, so that God's blessing of the covenant people no longer depends upon their obedience? Indeed, it is precisely this theme of God's preemptive grace that explains Paul's strong preference for the carrot over the stick as a strategy of moral exhortation. Nonetheless, the deepest logic of Paul's message reveals a dialectic of judgment and grace. Any account of his gospel that occludes the inescapable truth of God's eschatological judgment is a misleading account: "Do not be deceived; God is not mocked" (Gal. 6:7). The message of God's judgment is actually an integral part of Paul's gospel, not an antithesis to it.

Still, Paul's usual manner of address to his communities emphasizes the transforming grace of God as an assurance that they are not simply stuck in a pattern of life that would make them subject to God's condemnation.

> *Do you not know that the unrighteous will not inherit the kingdom of God? Do not be deceived. Fornicators, idolaters, adulterers, male prostitutes, sodomites, thieves, the greedy, drunkards, revilers, robbers—none of these will inherit the kingdom of God. And this is what some of you used to be. But you were washed, you were sanctified, you were justified in the name of the Lord Jesus Christ and in the Spirit of our God.* (1 COR. 6:9–11)

The rhetoric of this passage treats the readers as participants already in a new life. The statement that evildoers will not inherit God's kingdom is set forward not as a threat to the Corinthian community but rather as an invitation to them to claim their own baptismal identity as a sanctified people under the lordship of Christ, no longer living under the power of sin.

(B) WHAT IS THE SHAPE OF OBEDIENCE? NORMS FOR THE MORAL LIFE

Even after it becomes clear that Paul employs a theologically sophisticated range of warrants for obedience to God, it is another matter to ask how that obedience is to be defined. It would be possible for Paul to have a richly developed theological grounding for his ethics without necessarily having a distinctively Christian ethic. Paul's norms could be derived from Hellenistic philosophy or from what was "in the air" in Hellenistic popular culture. For example, near the end of a labored argument about head coverings, he asks the Corinthians, "Does not nature itself teach you that if a man wears long hair, it is a disgrace for him?" (1 Cor. 11:14, AA). Alternatively, some of his norms could be retained from his pharisaic Jewish heritage, despite his formal rejection of the Torah as a directly binding set of regulations for his churches.[60] Many of his standards for sexual morality, for example, are carried forward directly from Jewish tradition. The formulation of 1 Thessalonians 4:3–5 is telling: "For this is the will of God, your sanctification: . . . that each one of you know how to control your own body in holiness and honor, not with lustful passion, like the Gentiles who do not know God."[61]

Both of these suggestions obviously contain elements of truth. Paul's thought-world reflects the fusion of cultures; there are many clear instances where his ethical categories and vocabulary are drawn from his Jewish and Hellenistic cultural backgrounds. Nonetheless, when we examine Paul's actual ethical arguments, we find that such cultural traditions play a relatively slight role in comparison to two fundamental norms to which he points repeatedly: the unity of the community and the imitation of Christ. We have already examined some of the passages in which these norms are expressed, but a careful examination of 1 Corinthians 8:1–11:1 will demonstrate how they work together in Paul's response to a particular issue.

The Corinthians have written to Paul about several matters (1 Cor. 7:1), including the problem of food sacrificed to idols (8:1, 4). In Greco-Roman culture, a person who offered a sacrifice to the god in a pagan temple would often invite family members and friends to share in a feast at which the meat of the sacrificial animal was consumed; the feast was held in the temple of the god (cf. 8:10). In some respects, such social occasions were more like dinner parties than religious ceremonies, but their association with the pagan gods would surely have made many Jews and Christians uneasy about participating. The temptation to participate would have been strong, however, not only because of social pressure to conform to normal cultural practices but also because such occasions were among the relatively few opportunities many people would have had to eat meat.[62] Some of the Corinthians, confident in their knowledge (*gnōsis*) that "there is no idol in the world" and that "there is no God but one" (8:4) have decided that there is no harm in participating in such meals celebrated in pagan temples. Others, however, whom Paul calls "the weak" (8:7), are either scandalized by this behavior or—what Paul considers worse—drawn by the example of the "strong"[63] to join in such temple meals despite their own scruples (8:7, 10; cf. Rom. 14:23: "Those who have doubts are condemned if they eat, because they do not act from faith; for whatever does not proceed from faith is sin").

Remarkably, Paul does not seek to settle the disagreement among the Corinthians by issuing a simple ruling on the disputed point. Instead, he appeals to those who do possess "knowledge" to act in loving acknowledgment of their familial interdependence with their brothers and sisters in the community who do not share their convictions. His counsel is already implied in the pithy comment with which he leads off the discussion of the problem: "Knowledge puffs up, but love builds up [*oikodomei*]" (8:1b; cf. 10:23–24). Those who insist on their own spiritual prerogatives and refuse to place concern for the community first are pursuing a disastrous course: "So by your knowledge the weak one is destroyed, the brother for whom Christ died" (8:11, RH). The alternative is a way of life that surrenders freedom and prerogatives for the spiritual welfare of others. Paul declares his own intention to choose this way: "Therefore, if food causes my brother to fall, I will never eat meat, so that I may not cause my brother to fall" (8:13, RH).[64]

This formulation provides the transition into an extended discussion of Paul's own apostolic conduct as an example of the self-surrendering behavior that he is recommending (9:1–27). As an apostle, Paul asserts, he has the right to receive financial support for his ministry; indeed, "the Lord [Jesus] commanded that those who proclaim the gospel should get their living by the gospel" (9:14; cf. Matt. 10:10, Luke 10:7). Nonetheless—contrary to the direct authority of the tradition of Jesus' teaching!—he refuses to accept support, in order to "make the gospel free of charge" (9:18). The operative norm here is relinquishment of self-interest for the benefit of others.

Paul restates and generalizes this norm in 9:19–23, a passage that bears a striking structural similarity to the Christ hymn of Philippians. "For though I am free with respect to all," he declares, "I made myself a slave to all,[65] so that I might win more of them"(9:19). This passage is often read as a statement of Paul's cultural flexibility for the sake of his mission; rightly so, but its deeper point is Paul's willingness to relinquish his own freedom for the sake of the gospel. With a telling self-description, he signals that he has not forgotten the idol-meat issue: "To the weak I became weak, so that I might win the weak" (9:22). That is, of course, precisely what he wants the "strong" Corinthians to do: to become weak. He is offering himself as a model for imitation. Because he presents himself as one "not seeking my own advantage, but that of many" (10:33), he can at last articulate the exhortation that undergirds the entire idol-meat discussion: "Be imitators of me, as I am of Christ."

Thus, we see that Paul addresses this pastoral problem at Corinth not by seeking to determine the appropriate halakah in the Torah,[66] not by pointing to the authoritative teaching of Jesus or the pronouncement of an Apostolic Council (Acts 15) but by urging the strong members of the Corinthian church to follow the example of Christ and the example of the apostle by surrendering their place of privilege. The *telos* of such action is not just to enhance personal virtue and humility but also to secure the unity of the community in Christ. The ethical norm, then, is not given in the form of a predetermined rule or set of rules for conduct; rather, the right action must be *discerned* on the basis of a christological paradigm, with a view to the need of the community.

Paul's reluctance to specify narrow behavioral norms was perhaps one of the factors that led to trouble in the Corinthian community. Acting in light of their own spiritual discernment, some of the Corinthians were conducting themselves in ways that Paul found deeply objectionable. In 1 Corinthians 5:1–5, for example, he condemns an incestuous relationship between a man and his mother-in-law as "sexual immorality of a kind that is not found even among the Gentiles."[67] Here he gives no reason for his rejection of this behavior; he merely pronounces condemnation. He formulates his moral indignation in a manner ("not found even among the *Gentiles*") suggesting that this particular normative judgment is rooted in Jewish cultural sensibilities, based ultimately on Leviticus 18:8: "You shall not uncover the nakedness of your father's wife." This background, however, remains implicit.

Even in this disturbing passage, however, the specific directive that Paul gives to the Corinthian church ("Drive out the wicked person from among you" [5:13]) is motivated by a concern for the unitary holiness of the community: "Do you not know that a little yeast leavens the whole batch of dough? Clean out the old yeast so that you [plural] may be a new batch, as you really are unleavened" (5:6b–7a). Thus, concern for the health and purity of the community remains the constant factor in which more specific norms must be grounded.

(C) HOW IS OBEDIENCE POSSIBLE? POWER FOR THE MORAL LIFE It is one thing to understand our ethical obligations, but it is quite another thing to live in accordance with what we understand. Romans 7, a generative passage for theological anthropology in the Christian tradition, offers a classic expression of the rift between intention and action.

> *For what I am doing, I do not know. For I do not do what I will to do; but that which I hate, this I do. . . . Thus I find it to be a law that the bad lies close at hand to the "me" that wills to do the good. For I delight in the Law of God according to my inner self, but I see another law in my members fighting against the law of my mind and taking me captive to the law of sin that is in my members. Wretched person that I am! Who will rescue me from this body of death?* (ROM. 7:15, 21–24, RH)

The great difficulty with the Law of Moses, according to Paul, was that it could only *point* to righteousness, never actually produce it. There is a powerful and inexplicable "law of sin" at work in human hearts that constantly defeats our solemn intention to do the good and to obey the will of God. Consequently, even where the hearer of the Law applauds the vision of the moral life conveyed by the Torah—as indeed we should, since the commandment of the Law is "holy and just and good" (Rom. 7:12)—the Law can produce only condemnation and frustration. This gap between intention and performance prefigures the human predicament evoked by T. S. Eliot's "The Hollow Men":

> Between the idea
> And the reality
> Between the motion
> And the act
> Falls the Shadow.

One influential interpretive tradition rooted in the Lutheran Reformation holds that Paul's answer to this human dilemma is found in "justification by faith alone," understood as equivalent to God's forgiveness of sinners. Those who put their faith in Jesus Christ will find mercy despite their inability to do what God's Law requires. Consequently, the Christian who believes in Jesus remains *simul iustus et peccator*: "at the same time righteous and a sinner." According to this reading, Paul's gospel provides a solution to the problem of the "terrified conscience," but it does not fundamentally alter the ethical predicament of Romans 7 (except by setting the individual free from paralyzing feelings of guilt).[68]

The great strengths of this interpretive tradition lie in its realism about human fallibility and its reverence for the radical grace of God. The "Lutheran" reading honors Paul's dictum that "all have sinned and fall short of the glory of God" (Rom. 3:23) as a hermeneutical key. The danger, however, is that the slogan *simul iustus et peccator* may underestimate the transformative power of God's grace and obscure major emphases of Paul's moral vision. Romans does not end after chapter 3 or chapter 7. The agonized struggle of Romans 7 is hardly offered by Paul as a normative account of Christian experience.[69] Rather, it is an account of existence "in Adam" or under the Law or both. When Paul breaks into praise in Romans 7:25a ("Thanks be to God through Jesus Christ our Lord"), he is not merely offering thanks for forgiveness; he is celebrating liberation from the bondage and paralysis that formerly blocked obedience to God's will.

> *There is therefore now no condemnation for those who are in Christ Jesus. For the law of the spirit of life in Christ Jesus has set you free from the law of sin and of death. For God has done what the Law—weak on account of the flesh—could not do: by sending his own Son in the likeness of sinful flesh, and as a sin offering,*[70] *he condemned sin in the flesh, so* ***that the just requirement [dikaiōma] of the Law might be fulfilled in us, who walk not according to the flesh but according to the Spirit.*** (ROM. 8:1–4, AA, *emphasis mine*)

A decisive transition occurs in verse 4: after declaring that Christ's death is a "sin offering" that terminates God's "condemnation," Paul moves to the affirmation that the Holy Spirit is a source of power enabling Christ's people to "walk" in a way that fulfills the real meaning of the Law. To be sure, this Spirit-empowered obedience remains subject to the eschatological proviso of Romans 8:17–30: the present is a time of suffering and waiting, not a time of unambiguous triumph. Still, the fundamental force of Paul's claim must not be missed: God is present in power in the church, changing lives and enabling an obedience that would otherwise be unattainable. This motif of transformation by the Spirit appears repeatedly in Paul (e.g., Rom. 12:1–2, 1 Cor. 6:9–11, 2 Cor. 3:12–18, Gal. 5:16–26). "God . . . is at work in you, *enabling* you both to will and to work for his good pleasure" (Phil. 2:12–13, emphasis mine).[71] We can overlook this major theological theme in Paul only if we assume a priori that his doctrine of justification somehow makes obedience religiously irrelevant.[72] By Paul's own account, the purpose of his gospel preaching is to inculcate "the obedience of faith" among the Gentiles (Rom. 1:5).

In such passages, however, human moral action is given a distinct place in the syntax of the divine-human relationship; obedience is a consequence of salvation, not its condition. The Holy Spirit is not a theological abstraction but the manifestation of God's presence in the community, making everything new. Those who respond to the gospel have entered the sphere of the Spirit's power, where they find themselves changed and empowered for obedience.

Of course, there are instruments and mediating structures through which the Spirit works: Scripture, Paul's own teaching, the emissaries that Paul sends back to his churches (see, for example, Phil. 2:19–30), the community's worship. But fundamental to all of these is the power of the Spirit. For Paul, the moral life can never be a matter of reason controlling the passions (as in Platonist philosophical traditions) or of any exercise of unaided human will or capacity: "[T]hose who are in the flesh cannot please God" (Rom. 8:8). Obedience is possible at all only because God has broken the power of sin and begun the work of conforming believers to the image of Jesus Christ. "And all of us, with unveiled faces, seeing the glory of the Lord as though reflected in a mirror, *are being transformed into the same image* from one degree of glory to another; *for this comes from the Lord, the Spirit*" (2 Cor. 3:18, emphasis mine).

(D) CONCLUSION: OUR STORY IN CHRIST'S In sum, Paul sees the community of faith being caught up into the story of God's remaking of the world through Jesus Christ. Thus, to make ethical discernments is, for Paul, simply to recognize our place within the epic story of redemption. There is no meaningful distinction between theology and ethics in Paul's thought, because Paul's theology is fundamentally an account of God's work of transforming his people into the image of Christ.

Within the story, everything points to the death and resurrection of Jesus as the pivot-point of the ages; the old cosmos has met its end, and God's eschatological righteousness/justice has broken in upon the present, making everything new. This appearance of God's justice confirms the integrity of his promises to Israel: God calls a covenant community and models love and truth through that community. When Israel's Torah is read through the hermeneutical lens of the new community in Christ, Paul asserts, its real meaning comes clear for the first time, and its fulfillment appears in the community of faith, whose vocation is to proclaim and embody that fulfillment.

The distinctive shape of obedience to God is disclosed in Jesus Christ's faithful death on the cross for the sake of God's people. That death becomes metaphorically paradigmatic for the obedience of the community: to obey God means to offer our lives unqualifiedly for the sake of others. Thus, the fundamental norm of Pauline ethics is the christomorphic life. To imitate Christ is also to follow the apostolic example of surrendering one's own prerogatives and interests.

Within this world shaped by the story of Jesus Christ, the community wrestles with the constant need for spiritual discernment to understand and enact the obedience of faith. Ethics cannot be sufficiently guided by law or by institutionalized rules; instead, Spirit-empowered, Spirit-discerned conformity to Christ is required. The community is called to act in creative freedom in order to become "a living sacrifice, holy and acceptable to God" (Rom. 12:1). In so doing, the community discovers *koinōnia* with one another in the sufferings of Christ and in the hope of sharing his glory.

4. Appendix: Paul on the Relation between Men and Women

Many readers will be surprised at how little has been said here about sexual morality and about Paul's teaching concerning the relation of men and women. The omission has been deliberate: our aim has been to explicate the foundational logic of Paul's moral vision. With regard to that foundational logic, sex is a minor concern. One sees this clearly in Romans: apart from the rhetorically charged depiction of sexual immorality as an outward and visible sign of humanity's alienation from God in Romans 1:24–27, Paul has very little to say about sexual conduct in this most extensive exposition of his teaching.

Nonetheless, Paul was compelled by circumstances to deal with issues of sexual behavior in his churches, particularly at Corinth; his responses in 1 Corinthians have been of fateful import historically for Christian teaching about sex. Furthermore, as issues of sexual conduct are hotly debated at the end of the twentieth century, Paul is alternately invoked or inveighed against by various disputants. Consequently, we cannot responsibly leave our consideration of Paul without asking how his understanding of sex fits into his larger moral vision.[73]

(A) SEX AT THE TURN OF THE AGES: 1 CORINTHIANS 7 People who know nothing else about the apostle Paul may know that he wrote, "It is well for a man not to touch a woman" (1 Cor. 7:1b). This statement, however, is surely one of the most widely misinterpreted texts in the New Testament. Precisely for that reason, it offers an excellent illustration of the importance of careful descriptive exegesis as the first step in the construction of New Testament ethics. On the basis of 1 Corinthians 7:1, lifted out of its context, Paul is often castigated as a misogynistic character with pathological attitudes about sex. While the apostle's ideas certainly do not correspond to conventional late-twentieth-century notions of "healthy sexuality," it would be a serious mistake to treat this text as a polemic against sex. Let us examine the passage carefully.

First of all, we must remember that we are reading one side of a conversational exchange. Paul is not setting out to write a general treatise on sex and marriage; rather, he is responding to a Corinthian concern. This is made explicit at the beginning of the sentence: "Now concerning the matters about which you wrote . . ." (1 Cor. 7:1a). This is a major structural transition in the letter. Through the first six chapters, Paul has been responding to reports about the Corinthian community (1:11, 5:1); now he turns to questions they have raised directly in correspondence. Therefore, in order to understand Paul's response, we need to reconstruct the question they have asked and the situation it presupposes.

Several times in 1 Corinthians Paul quotes a slogan popular among some of his readers in order to correct or qualify it, or to challenge the conclusions that the Corinthians were drawing from it. For example, in 1 Corinthians 6:12–14, just a few lines before the passage we are considering, Paul scripts the following exchange:

Corinthians: "All things are lawful for me."

Paul: But not all things are beneficial.

Corinthians: "All things are lawful for me."

Paul: But I will not be dominated by anything.

Corinthians: "Food is meant for the stomach and the stomach for food," and God will destroy both one and the other.

Paul: The body is meant not for fornication but for the Lord, and the Lord for the body. And God raised the Lord and will also raise us by his power.[74]

In ancient Greek manuscripts there were no quotation marks to set off the Corinthians' lines from Paul's responses, but readers at Corinth who were familiar with the slogans would have had no trouble in following the dialogical character of this passage. The NRSV translators have provided quotation marks to help us read the dialogue rightly.

In 1 Corinthians 8:1, which is structurally analogous to 7:1, we encounter a similar pattern:

> *Now concerning food sacrificed to idols: we know that "all of us possess knowledge." Knowledge puffs up, but love builds up.* (CF. ALSO VV. 4–6, 8–9)

Paul does not attack the Corinthian slogan; he first accepts it, then deflates it. He is quoting (or perhaps characterizing) their position in order to set up a foil for his response.

Once we recognize this rhetorical pattern in the letter, it becomes clear that 1 Corinthians 7:1 is another instance of the same technique:

Corinthians: "It is well for a man not to touch a woman."

Paul: But because of cases of sexual immorality, each man should have his own wife and each woman her own husband.

Thus, we see that the antisex slogan almost certainly comes from the Corinthians rather than from Paul himself.[75] This is one of "the matters about which you wrote" (7:1a). As the punctuation in the NRSV indicates, Paul is quoting a statement from their letter back to them to identify the topic of discussion.

Paul does not directly challenge the slogan; indeed, he is sympathetic with it (cf. v. 8). Nonetheless, he poses a corrective to it. What exactly is he trying to correct? The key lies in the proper interpretation of verse 2: ". . . each man should *have* his own wife and each woman her own husband." The sentence is often read as an encouragement for unmarried people to pair up and get married. Careful reflection will show, however, that this interpretation is impossible: Paul's advice to the unmarried in this same chapter is that they should remain unmarried if at all possible (vv. 8–9, 20, 24, 25–27, 39–40). What, then, does verse 2 mean? The passage makes perfect sense when we recognize that the verb *echein* ("to have") is a common euphemism for sexual intercourse. For instance, it occurs in this sense in 1 Corinthians 5:1: "It is actually reported that there is sexual immorality among you, and of a kind that is not found even among Gentiles: for a man to *have* his father's wife" (RH). If this is the sense of the verb "have" in 1 Corinthians 7:2, then Paul must be speaking to those who are already married and urging them to continue to have sexual intercourse. This same exhortation is explicitly repeated in verse 3.

But why would such advice be necessary? To readers at the end of the twentieth century, this counsel to married couples may appear foolishly superfluous, as though Paul had written to remind his churches to breathe and eat. But in the first-century context, such teaching about sex was not at all unnecessary. In the first place, the correlation between piety and celibacy was a common feature of Hellenistic culture. The physical body, belonging to the material world, was deprecated and regarded as inferior to the rational soul; the goal of the wise philosopher was to discipline the body by bringing its animal urges under the control of reason. We find a reaction against such teachings in the letter to the Colossians:

> *Why do you submit to regulations, "Do not handle, Do not taste, Do not touch"? All these regulations refer to things that perish with use; they are simply human commands and teachings. These have indeed an appearance of wisdom in promoting self-imposed piety, humility, and severe treatment of the body, but they are of no value in checking self-indulgence.* (COL. 2:20b–23)

In many circles, ascetic wisdom was understood to entail sexual abstinence. Celibacy was seen as a sign of spiritual power, because it symbolized freedom from attachment to the crude realm of the material. In short, we might say aphoristically that in the ancient world celibacy had "sex appeal."

Second, it is not implausible that there were factors within the earliest Christian traditions that made sexual abstinence appear attractive or even mandatory for participants in this new faith. The baptismal formula that Paul cites in Galatians 3:28 declares that in Christ "there is no longer male and female." In other words, Genesis 1:27 ("So God created humankind in his image; . . . male and female he created them") has been superseded by the new creation, in which sexual differences are abolished.[76] How then can Christian couples continue to indulge their sexual desires? Is sex not incompatible with life in the new creation? (It is probably not coincidental that when Paul cites the baptismal formula to the Corinthians in 1 Corinthians 12:13, he omits the "no longer male and female" phrase.) Particularly if—as some scholars have argued—some of the Corinthians believed that they were already living in the state of resurrection life (cf. 4:8), they might well have concluded that married couples should cease having sex. Consider the saying of Jesus reported in Luke 20:34–36:

> *Those who belong to this age marry and are given in marriage; but those who are considered worthy of a place in that age and in the resurrection of the dead neither marry nor are given in marriage. Indeed they cannot die anymore, because they are like angels and are children of God, being children of the resurrection.*

It is not at all improbable that some of the Corinthians, who understood themselves to be capable of speaking in "the tongues of angels" (1 Cor. 13:1), might have regarded themselves as having been translated into such an angelic state.[77]

Thus, we propose the hypothesis that *Paul is seeking to counteract radical Corinthian asceticism.* Against an idealistic hyperspirituality that forswears sexual union even within existing marriages, Paul urges that married couples may and *must* continue to have sexual relations:

> *Let the husband give to his wife what is owed her, and likewise the wife to the husband. For the wife does not have authority over her own body, but the husband does. Likewise also the husband does not have authority over his own body, but the wife does.*
> (7:3–4, RH)

The emphasis here on mutuality is striking. In contrast to a patriarchal culture that would assume a one-way hierarchical ordering of the husband's authority over the wife, Paul carefully prescribes *mutual submission.*[78] Neither marriage partner controls his or her own body: in the marriage covenant, one surrenders authority over one's own body to the spouse. (In passing, we should note how sharply this picture of mutual submission contrasts to the twentieth-century notion of the sexual autonomy of each individual.) Those who have already entered marriage relationships, Paul directs, should continue to honor their commitments; to do otherwise is to deprive the spouse of what he or she might legitimately expect from a marriage partner.

Indeed, withdrawal into celibacy is not only a breach of faith with the spouse, it is also dangerous. Why? Because Satan may tempt the superspiritual ascetic to find sexual fulfillment elsewhere (7:5), perhaps through fornication with a prostitute. (Paul has just spoken sternly against such practices in 1 Cor. 6:12–20.) In order to understand Paul's concern, we must picture the sadly comic scenario in which a Christian married couple plays a charade of sexual abstinence with one another while indulging in clandestine extramarital affairs. Though the prospect seems ridiculous, Paul is a realistic observer of the deceitfulness of the human heart,[79] and he knows—as we have seen in recent sex scandals involving television evangelists—that hyperspiritual people are hardly immune to sexual temptations. Thus, he thinks it safer to counsel the continuance of normal sexual relations within marriage.

He does make one concession, however, to the Corinthians' desire to pursue ambitious spiritual disciplines:

> *Do not deprive one another except perhaps by agreement [**ek symphōnou**] for a set time, to devote yourselves to prayer, and then come together again, so that Satan may not tempt you because of your lack of self-control.* (7:5)

Marriage partners may agree "with a common voice" (*ek symphōnou*) to temporary abstinence—analogous to fasting—for a special season of prayer, as long as the time is strictly bounded, with the understanding that they will resume sexual relations. This permission for a temporary moratorium on sex is the "concession" mentioned in verse 6: "This I say by way of concession, not of command." Traditionally, the text has been interpreted to mean that Paul grudgingly concedes the legitimacy of sex within marriage. In view of the foregoing exegesis, however, the passage makes better sense if the pronoun *touto* ("this") in verse 6 is understood to refer to the immediately preceding verse 5: Paul's concession to the Corinthian ascetics is his cautious approval of a temporary suspension of sexual relations.

In light of these exegetical observations, we can construct a paraphrase of 1 Corinthians 7:1–9, filling in some of the silences and gaps in the conversation. The words in italics are supplied as explanatory expansions to show how Paul's advice seeks to address the particular issues raised by the Corinthians.

> (1) Now I will respond to the matters about which you wrote. *You propose that, for the sake of holiness and purity, married couples should abstain from sexual intercourse. As you say,* "It is a fine thing for a man not to touch a woman." (2) But—*since that is unrealistic*—let each husband have sexual intercourse with his own wife, and let each wife have sexual intercourse with her own husband. (3) *Marriage creates a mutual obligation for a couple to satisfy one another's needs; therefore,* let the husband give the wife what he

> owes her, and likewise let the wife give what she owes to her husband. (4) For the wife does not rule her own body; the husband does. Likewise, the husband does not rule his own body; the wife does. (5) Do not deprive one another, unless you decide—in harmony with one another—to abstain from intercourse for a time so that *both of* you can devote yourselves to prayer. But *(when the time is up)* come together again, so that Satan will not be able to tempt you. (6) I am not commanding this *practice of temporary abstinence*; rather, I am saying this as a concession *to your proposal* (see v. 1, above). (7) I wish that everyone could be *in control of sexual desire* like me. *Obviously, however, that is not the case.* But each person has his/her own gift from God: *if not celibacy, then something else,* one in one way and another in some other way.
>
> (8) To the unmarried and to the widows, on the other hand, I say that it is a fine thing for them to remain *unmarried* as I am. (9) But if they are not in control of themselves, let them marry, for it is better to marry than to burn *with passion.*

It is important to note what is *not* said in this passage about sex within marriage. Perhaps most striking is the absence of any reference to sexual union as an expression of love. As we have already noted, Paul appeals to love as a motive for behavior when he addresses the problems of idol-meat and speaking in tongues, but he does not do so when he speaks of sex. Perhaps love is implied in Paul's call for mutual submission of marriage partners, but he does not make the point explicit. Second, nothing is said here about the procreative purpose of sex. Husband and wife are to continue having intercourse because sexual union is a part of the obligation of marriage and because it protects them against temptation, but nothing is said here about conceiving children. Presumably, Paul's belief in the imminent eschaton made him relatively indifferent to the raising of families; in this respect his teaching stands in stark contrast to Jewish tradition and to later Christian teaching about procreation as the fundamental purpose of marital sex. Finally, there is no suggestion whatever of differing standards for clergy and laity; indeed, the distinction is anachronistic. Paul knew nothing of a special class of "ordained" persons who were subject to special standards of sexual behavior.

In sum, we see that the passage has been subject to drastic misinterpretation. Rather than deprecating women or sex, Paul is actually arguing *against* those who regard sexual intercourse as inappropriate for Christians. He stoutly and realistically affirms the necessity of mutual sexual satisfaction within marriage.[80]

Why, then, does Paul advise the unmarried to remain unmarried (7:8)? At this point, we see the effects of his apocalyptic eschatology:

> *I mean, brothers and sisters, the appointed time has grown short; from now on, let even those who have wives be as though they had none, and those who mourn as though they were not mourning, and those who rejoice as though they were not rejoicing, and those who buy as though they had no possessions, and those who deal with the world as though they had no dealings with it. For the present form of this world is passing away.* (7:29–31)

If the present order of things is about to be swept away, why enter into marriage? Paul's rule of thumb is stated clearly and insistently in 7:17–24: "Let each of you remain in the condition in which you were called." The only thing that matters in the present time between the times is "unhindered devotion to the Lord." Marriage inevitably brings with it a concern for "the affairs of the world" and thereby hinders total devotion to the mission of the church at the turn of the ages (7:32–35). That mission is "the present necessity"[81] that leads Paul to opine that singleness is preferable to marriage. Of considerable importance is the fact that Paul clearly marks this preference as his own opinion on a matter where he has no command of the Lord (7:25).

At the same time, Paul knows that the power of the present age still exercises influence over the lives of believers. They are subject to temptation and to burning physical desire. Unlike the hyperspiritual enthusiasts that he seeks to correct, he knows that the resurrection remains a future hope rather than a present reality. Consequently, the "not yet" pole of his eschatology leads him to give sober realistic counsel to the Corinthians, permitting marriage and encouraging sexual relations within marriage. The important thing is that the members of the community, whether married or unmarried, remain in a state of watchful readiness and obedience.

(B) WOMEN AND MEN IN THE MINISTRY OF THE PAULINE CHURCHES

Apart from questions of sex and marriage, what role did women play in the social organization and worship life of the Pauline churches? The letters seem to send mixed signals. On the one hand, we find the radical egalitarian declaration of Galatians 3:26–28:

> *For in Christ Jesus you are all children of God through faith. As many of you as were baptized into Christ have clothed yourselves with Christ. There is no longer Jew or Greek, there is no longer slave or free, there is no longer male and female; for all of you are one in Christ Jesus.*

On the other hand, we find in 1 Corinthians 14:34–35 a stringent suppression of the public role of women in the worshiping community:

> *Let women be silent in the churches.*[82] *For it is not permitted to them to speak, but let them be subordinate, just as the Law also says. And if they want to learn something, let them ask their own husbands at home. For it is a shameful thing for a woman to speak in church.* (RH)

How is the tension between these texts to be understood? Are women equal partners with men within the community of faith, or does Paul assign them a subordinate role?

The best way to approach this question is to examine the evidence concerning the roles *actually* played by women in the Pauline communities. Since this matter has been studied extensively in recent New Testament scholarship, we can summarize the pertinent findings briefly here.[83]

First, we know from 1 Corinthians 11:3–16 that Paul expected women to pray and prophesy in the community's worship. His major concern in this passage is that they should arrange their hair (or cover their heads)[84] in a seemly manner while praying or prophesying. Wayne Meeks summarizes the thrust of the passage aptly: "In brief, he leaves unquestioned the right of women, led by the Spirit, to exercise the same leadership roles in the assembly as men, but insists only that the conventional symbols of sexual difference, in clothing and hair styles, be retained."[85] Thus, this passage seems to stand in contradiction to the directive of 1 Corinthians 14:34–35, which mandates silence for women in the assembly.

Second, numerous incidental references in Paul's letters show that women were included among Paul's co-workers. Some of these women exercised leadership roles in the communities. For example, Paul describes Phoebe as "a deacon [*diakonos*] of the church at Cenchreae" (Rom. 16:1). It is not clear whether the term *diakonos* should be understood as designating a formal office in the church (as in Phil. 1:1), or whether it is simply a generic term for "servant/minister," as in 1 Corinthians 3:5 and 2 Corinthians 3:6, where Paul uses exactly the same word to describe his own role. In either case, Paul thinks of Phoebe as having some important work to do at Rome, and he instructs the Romans to help her "in whatever she may require of you," adding that "she has been a benefactor [*prostatis*] of many and of myself as well" (Rom. 16:2). The term *prostatis* (literally "one who stands before") can be used to describe one who leads or presides over a group; here it probably has the more general sense of "patron" or "benefactor."

Prisca and Aquila, a wife and husband team, are among Paul's "co-workers in Christ Jesus." Paul mentions that "all the churches of the Gentiles" give thanks for their ministry, and he mentions that they host a house-church in their home (Rom. 16:3–4, AA; cf. Acts 18:18–28). None of Paul's comments about them suggests any subordination of the wife to the husband; she appears to be a full participant in ministry. Several other women appear as "workers in the Lord" in Paul's long list of salutations in Romans 16:1–16, including Mary, Tryphaena, Tryphosa, Persis, and Junia, who along with Andronicus (perhaps her husband) is described as "prominent among the apostles" (16:7). In Philippians 4:2–3 Paul urges the women Euodia and Syntyche—who have "struggled beside me in the work of the gospel"—to mend their differences and "be of the same mind in the Lord." They are not explicitly described as leaders of the Philippian church, but the prominence that Paul accords them in this letter addressed to the whole church suggests that they are persons with an important role in the community.

The cumulative weight of this evidence suggests that women did play a significant role in the ministry of the Pauline churches, including serving as members of the apostolic mission teams. Certainly, women participated in the activity of prophecy, which had as its purpose the upbuilding of the church (1 Cor. 14:1–25). In many respects, women in these communities enjoyed a greater measure of freedom and dignity than they could have experienced in Greco-Roman society outside the Christian fellowship. Indeed, the relatively egalitarian social structure of the Pauline communities made them particularly attractive to "upwardly mobile" urban women whose education or economic position ("achieved status") exceeded their hereditary social position ("attributed status").[86]

How, then, are we to understand the injunction to silence in 1 Corinthians 14:34–35? At least four different explanations have been proposed by scholars.

- The passage does not forbid women from exercising leadership or speaking in edifying ways to the community; rather, it forbids disruptive speech during the community's worship. Perhaps the women at Corinth, moving into a new position of freedom in the church, were interrupting worship with questions (v. 35) and creating disorder. Thus, the injunction is not a general rule but a pastoral directive aimed at a specific situation. This explanation makes sense of verse 35 ("If they want to learn something, let them ask their own husbands at home"), but it overlooks the generalizing force of verse 34b ("Let them be subordinate, just as the Law also says") and requires a special narrow sense for the common verb *lalein* ("speak") in verses 34 and 35; it would have to mean something like "chatter." If verse 33b ("as in all the churches of the saints") is read with verse 34, this argument becomes impossible, because Paul would be asserting female silence and subordination as a rule for all communities, not just for some particular problematical situation at Corinth.
- The passage refers only to married women, whereas the women who are permitted to pray and prophesy (1 Cor. 11:3–16) must be unmarried.[87] Women who marry become subordinate to their husbands and should keep quiet. This interpretation resolves the apparent contradiction, but it requires us to supply a condition not stipulated in 1 Corinthians 11:3–16 (that female prophets must be unmarried), and it overlooks the evidence that married women such as Prisca and Junia did play leadership roles in the Pauline communities.
- The passage is an interpolation,[88] not written by Paul but added to his letter by a later scribe or editor, such as the author of the pastoral Epistles (cf. 1 Tim. 2:8–15). This hypothesis finds some support in the existence of a number of ancient manuscripts that place verses 34–35 at the end of the chapter rather than between verses 33 and 36. The verses do appear intrusive in Paul's discussion of order in the exercise of prophetic gifts; when they are removed, the passage reads smoothly. Furthermore, on material grounds it is difficult to imagine these words coming from Paul's hand: the Paul who wrote 1 Corinthians 11:3–16 certainly did not think that it was "shameful for a woman to speak in church." There are, however, no extant manuscripts that omit verses 34–35; if these verses were added to the text secondarily, they were added at a very early stage.[89]
- Antoinette Wire, rejecting the interpolation theory, has recently argued that 1 Corinthians 14:34–35 is the rhetorical goal and climax of the entire letter, which is constructed to lead up to Paul's silencing of female prophets at Corinth.[90] (She leaves open the question whether Paul intentionally structures the whole argument to lead to this conclusion or whether he arrives at it through wrestling with the community's problems.) On this reading, 1 Corinthians 11:3–16 is interpreted not as an endorsement of prophecy by women but

as a preliminary restriction on the dress and behavior of the female prophets; having gained an inch rhetorically in chapter 11, Paul takes a mile in chapter 14, promulgating a far more comprehensive restriction on the Corinthian women. Of the four options considered here, this is the least plausible: it depends on an elaborate speculative reconstruction of the role of women prophets at Corinth, it construes the whole letter as an instance of manipulative and repressive rhetoric, and—most tellingly—it clashes flagrantly with the evidence enumerated above concerning the actual roles of women in Paul's churches.

All things considered, the third of these explanations—the interpolation theory—is the likeliest, the one most consistent with the picture that Paul's letters otherwise convey of the role of women in worship and ministry. Whether Paul wrote these words or not, however, they give expression to a theological judgment that appears again in the pastoral Epistles; consequently, a New Testament ethic that seeks to be responsive to the full witness of the canonical New Testament must take 1 Corinthians 14:34–35 into account in the synthetic and hermeneutical stages of normative reflection. In other words, we cannot end our consideration of this text by saying, "Paul did not write it." In a later stage of our work, we will have to deal with the New Testament's differing attitudes concerning the role of women in the church.

Regardless of our judgment concerning the interpretation of 1 Corinthians 14:34–35, we must recognize a certain built-in tension concerning the role of women in Paul's symbolic world. The deepest logic of his gospel declares that men and women are one in Christ and ought to live in relations of loving mutuality. His instructions on marriage are remarkable for their time in their careful, egalitarian balancing of the obligations of husband and wife. In his missionary work he joyfully acknowledges the contributions of female colleagues, fellow "workers in the Lord." Yet in some passages, such as 1 Corinthians 11:3–16, he insists—with labored and unpersuasive theological arguments—on the maintenance of traditional markers of sexual distinction; despite the ingenious efforts of exegetes at the end of the twentieth century, it is impossible to deny the hierarchical implications of such symbolic markers. Indeed, Paul seems to have found the Corinthian church's experiments in gender equality somewhat unsettling; consequently, he sought to constrain what he saw as excesses.

In this matter as in so many others, Paul's ethical stance is comprehensible only in light of his dialectical eschatology: already men and women enjoy equality in Christ; however, not yet can that equality sweep away all the constraints and distinctions of the fallen order. Sexual distinctions do persist, and sexual relations are fraught with danger. The transformation of gender roles was not a programmatic emphasis of Paul's mission; rather, it was an unintended consequence, as the Spirit worked in the churches. The calling of Christians at the turn of the ages, according to Paul, is to live sacrificially within the structures of marriage and community, recognizing the freedom of the Spirit to transform institutions and roles but waiting on the coming of the Lord to set all things right. In the meantime, apostle and community find themselves poised on a tightrope, seeking to discern the will of God in circumstances where old norms no longer hold. "Do not be conformed to this age, but be transformed by the renewing of your minds, so that you may discern what is the will of God—what is good and acceptable and perfect" (Rom. 12:2, AA).

How does this exhortation work itself out in the community's understanding of the right relation of women and men? Perhaps on no other issue do we see Paul struggling so visibly to get it right. In that respect, the church at the end of the twentieth century stands to learn something from Paul, since—as he wrote to the Philippians in another context—"you are having the same struggle that you saw I had" (Phil. 1:30).[91] Any sexual ethic that takes its bearings from Paul will shape the community's discernment with respect to the three fundamental theological motifs that we have identified in Paul's thought: How do our actions manifest the presence of the new creation in a sin-dominated world, how do our actions correspond to the self-sacrificial love of the cross, and how do our actions serve the good of the community? We rightly understand Paul's particular teachings about sex only when we see them as attempts to answer these questions for the communities that he was forming.

NOTES

1. Some critics have portrayed Paul's ethical teaching as an amalgam of relatively undigested ideas without a clear governing rationale. See, e.g., Houlden 1973; Räisänen 1983; Sampley 1991.

2. Dibelius 1936 [1926], 143–144, 217–220. See also Dibelius 1930; Dibelius and Greeven 1976 [1964], 1–5.

3. "Christian writings have become the transmitters of popular ethics of antiquity" (Dibelius and Greeven 1976 [1964], 5).

4. For example, by Furnish 1968. For a detailed survey of interpretations of Pauline ethics in nineteenth- and twentieth-century scholarship, see pp. 242–279.

5. Betz 1979, 292. For challenges to Betz, see Hays 1987; Barclay 1988.

6. Rightly argued by Furnish 1968.

7. The term *theologizing* is clumsy, but it reminds us that for Paul theology is an activity. For a helpful discussion, see Jouette Bassler, "Paul's Theology: Whence and Whither?" and Steven J. Kraftchick, "Seeking a More Fluid Model: A Response to Jouette Bassler," in Hay 1993, 3–17, 18–34.

8. The dialectic of "contingency" and "coherence" in Paul's thought has been a major theme of J. Christiaan Beker's work (1980, 1991).

9. This is the method adopted by the Society of Biblical Literature Pauline Theology Group. See Bassler 1991; Hay 1993.

10. For purposes of methodological clarity, I shall deal here only with the seven uncontested Pauline Epistles, although I am inclined to regard 2 Thessalonians and Colossians as authentic Pauline letters also.

11. Furnish 1968, 212.

12. As Furnish (1968, 214) observes, "The Pauline eschatology is not just one motif among numerous others, but helps to provide the fundamental perspective within which everything else is viewed."

13. See, for example, 2 Esdras 7:50, 112–115, 8:1; 2 Enoch 66:6; 2 Baruch 15:7–8, 44:8–15.

14. Here again, Paul's apocalyptic perspective is blurred by translations that treat Paul's plural *ta telē tōn aiōnōn* ("the ends of the ages") as a singular "the end of the ages," as in the RSV. Likewise, the verb *katēntēken* means "met," not "come." For seminal discussions of the importance of the two-age schema in Paul's thinking, see W. D. Davies 1980, 285–320; Martyn 1967.

15. Hence the title of J. Paul Sampley's helpful book highlighting the eschatological context of Pauline ethics: *Walking Between the Times* (1991).

16. Houlden 1973, 28, 12.

17. It is usually assumed that Paul is here addressing a question or concern of his readers. It is possible, however, that he is anticipating rather than responding to a question.

18. The point is crucial for Christian ethics. There is a long and tragic history of zealous but misguided readers reading the NT's military metaphors at a literal rather than figurative level. For more on this point, see Chapter 14.

19. For the most extensive reconstruction of Paul's Corinthian opponents, see Georgi 1986.

20. For further comment on this text and my translation of it, see Hays 1989, 171, 225–226 nn. 46–48.

21. On this passage, see Wright 1987.

22. This is a common apocalyptic image. For a helpful account of this metaphor in apocalyptic tradition, see Gaventa 1990.

23. Ernst Käsemann's important essay on this passage, "The Cry for Liberty in the Worship of the Church" (1971 [1969], 122–137), argues that Paul's statements about the spirit here are polemical: against enthusiasts who claim their ecstatic utterances as signs of an already realized redemption, Paul interprets the early church's Spirit-inspired worship as inarticulate groaning along with creation.

24. The "invasion" metaphor may be traced back to Oscar Cullmann 1964 [1946], 84.

25. See Cousar 1990.

26. This interpretation of Gal. 6:2 is defended at length in Hays 1987.

27. The Greek text simply says *pros oikodomēn*: "to the end of building up." The NRSV interprets this elliptical formulation in an individualistic fashion: "building up the neighbor." Paul's characteristic usage of this language, however, suggests that he surely has in mind the edification of the community as a whole. See 1 Cor. 14:3–5, 12, 26; 2 Cor. 12:19, 13:10; Eph. 4:12, 16; cf. 1 Cor. 12:7.

28. The presence of the definite article here and in v. 7 suggests that *Christos* is being used as a title rather than, as often elsewhere in Paul, a proper name. See Dunn 1988 (vol. 2), 840.

29. Note the way in which Ps. 69:21 is echoed in the synoptic passion narratives. Also, Ps. 69:9a is cited with reference to Jesus in John 2:17 in a context that foreshadows his death. It is probable that the psalm was generally understood in the early church as a messianic lament psalm. On this whole question, see Hays 1993.

30. On the role of the hymn in the argument of the letter, see Fowl 1990, 78–101, and the literature cited there.

31. This last phrase is very difficult to translate. The Greek says, literally, "count one another as surpassing yourselves." The verb *hyperechein* ("surpassing") often refers to the possession of higher rank or authority, as in Rom. 13:1, where *exousiai hyperechousai* are "the ruling authorities." Paul's exhortation is paradoxical: each member of the community is to submit to the authority of all the others. I have given a periphrastic rendering.

32. This translation of *harpagmos* is taken from the NRSV.

33. The NRSV supplies the pronoun *me* as the direct object of the verb *obeyed*, but there is no object in the Greek.

34. For extended discussion of Paul's hortatory use of hymnic material, see Fowl 1990. On Philippians, see especially pp. 49–101.

35. On this term, see Fowl 1990, 92–95.

36. Käsemann 1950; Martin 1983.

37. See the important essay of Kraftchick 1993.

38. This passage is a key for Krister Stendahl's important reassessment of Paul: "The Apostle Paul and the Introspective Conscience of the West" (1976, 78–96).

39. Greek *skybala*, literally "dung." Apart from this change in wording, my citation follows Phil. 3:8b–9a, NRSV.

40. The Greek *symmimētai mou* is ambiguous: Does "become my fellow imitators" mean "join together in imitating me" or "join me in imitating Christ"? Both interpretations are possible, but in the end they come to the same thing.

41. Many commentators have interpreted *pisteōs* in Rom. 1:5 as an epexegetical genitive: "the obedience which is faith." Insofar as such an interpretation renders a portrayal of a Pauline gospel concerned only about cognitive believing and unconcerned about obedience in conduct, it is certainly to be rejected. On this interpretation, many other parts of the letter become contradictory or unintelligible (e.g., 6:12–23, 8:1–11, 12:1–15:13). A far more coherent view of Paul's message results if Rom. 1:5 is interpreted to mean "the obedience that springs from faith" or simply "faithful obedience." For discussion and survey of the literature, see G. N. Davies 1990, 25–30.

42. See Hays 1983; Hays 1991b. For a defense of the "objective genitive" interpretation, see Dunn 1991a.

43. It is important to bear in mind that the semantic range of the noun *pistis* is focused on meanings such as "trust, loyalty, fidelity" rather than "believing."

44. See Hays 1987.

45. Even the letter to Philemon, confronting an issue that might have been considered a private pastoral matter, is addressed not just to Philemon but also to Apphia and Archippus and to "the church in your house" (Philem. 2). Paul insists on laying the decision-making process open to the community's scrutiny. On the

rhetorical effects of Paul's addressing the letter to the whole church, see Petersen 1985. The pastoral Epistles (1 and 2 Timothy and Titus) are addressed to individuals, but their authorship is debatable.

46. See Banks 1994.

47. Paul uses the term *huioi* ("sons") to include both men and women, as the continuing explanation in 3:28 makes clear. The decision of the NRSV translators to render the term as "children" in 3:26 and 4:5–7 is hermeneutically justifiable, though it diminishes the rhetorical effect of some of Paul's turns of phrase—e.g., 4:6: ". . . and because you are sons, God has sent the Spirit of his Son into our hearts, crying 'Abba! Father!'"

48. Nowhere does Paul speak of all humanity as "children of God." All are God's creatures, but the language of *family* relationship is reserved for the elect community.

49. Hays 1987, 289–290. On the problem of why Cephas and others shunned table fellowship with Gentile converts, see E. P. Sanders 1990.

50. Barclay 1988, 239. Barclay is building here on the insights of E. P. Sanders 1977; Dunn 1983a; Dunn 1983b; and Watson 1986.

51. Boyarin 1994.

52. Barclay (1988) has demonstrated that this ethical concern pervades the letter to the Galatians and that the hortatory material in chapters 5 and 6 is thematically integral to the letter. See also Gaventa 1986.

53. Mitchell (1992) has demonstrated conclusively by means of rhetorical analysis that "1 Corinthians is a unified letter which throughout urges the course of unity on the divided Corinthian church" (17).

54. A similar hermeneutical shift occurred in the Qumran writings: the community of Qumran covenanters was seen as replacing the corrupt Temple in Jerusalem. See Gärtner 1965.

55. Of course, a similar critique was later directed at one of Paul's most passionate interpreters, Martin Luther, by his Catholic and Anabaptist opponents, and subsequently by John Wesley.

56. See Keck 1976.

57. Funk 1967, 263–266.

58. The possessive pronoun *his* does not appear in the Greek text. Worthy of serious consideration is the argument of A. Y. Collins (1980) that the "spirit" to be saved is the Spirit present in the community.

59. On the rhetorical strategy of this letter, see the analysis of N. Petersen 1985.

60. For a sustained attempt to demonstrate the presence of Jewish legal traditions in Paul's moral instruction, see Tomson 1990.

61. NRSV. The point I am making here, that Paul's sexual ethic derives from Jewish tradition, does not require an exegetical decision about the exact meaning of the difficult v. 4, which may mean either "that each one of you know how to keep his own sexual organ in holiness and honor" or "that each one of you know how to take a wife in holiness and honor." See discussions in Best 1979, 161–163; R. F. Collins 1984, 328–333; Yarbrough 1985, 7–29, 68–73.

62. Theissen 1982, 125–129.

63. Paul does not actually use the term *strong* in 1 Corinthians 8; however, the term does appear in his discussion of a very similar problem in Rom. 14:1–15:6. See also the rhetorically freighted remark of 1 Cor. 1:27: "God has chosen the foolish things of the world to shame the wise, and the weak things of the world to shame the strong."

64. The NRSV employs various circumlocutions in vv. 11–13 to avoid using the masculine word "brother." Paul's repeated use of this word, as reflected in my translation here, aims to emphasize that "the strong" at Corinth are harming fellow members of God's *family*, as the NRSV's rendering of v. 12 rightly emphasizes.

65. On the topos of the "enslaved leader," see D. Martin 1990, 86–116.

66. Contrary to the opinion of Tomson 1990, 187–220.

67. The word translated "pagans" in the NRSV is *ethnē*, Paul's ordinary word for non-Jews.

68. This account of a "Lutheran" understanding of justification is a caricature of Luther's own position, whose nuances need not concern us here. For an account of Luther's thought on justification, see Althaus 1966, 224–250; Althaus 1972, 3–24. For an analysis of how subsequent Lutheran theology appropriated Luther's justification doctrine, see Gritsch and Jenson 1976, 36–68; Braaten 1983. Luther's reading of Paul is eloquently defended by Westerholm 1988.

69. This position is convincingly argued by Kümmel 1929 and Stendahl 1976. For a recent review of the issues, see Dunn 1988 (vol. 1), 374–412.

70. On the translation of *peri hamartian*, see Wright 1991, 220–225.

71. The Catholic tradition (including the Wesleyan movement) has always emphasized this aspect of Paul's thought in a way that has made Lutheran and Reformed thinkers distinctly uneasy.

72. See Hays 1992 and the literature cited there.

73. The topics of divorce and homosexuality will be more thoroughly treated in Part IV of this book; consequently, they will not be the focus of our attention here.

74. For analysis of the structure of vv. 13–14, see Fee 1987, 253–257, who argues persuasively that the phrase "God will destroy both one and the other" expresses not Paul's view but "the Corinthian view of spirituality,

which looked for a 'spiritual' salvation that would finally be divested of the body" (257).

75. For a thorough exegetical defense of this interpretation, see Fee 1987, 266–286. See also Furnish 1985, 29–38.

76. For an account of the diverse ways in which this symbolism was interpreted in early Christianity, see Meeks 1974.

77. There is no indication in the letter that the Corinthians knew this specific tradition of Jesus' teaching or that their self-imposed sexual abstinence was based on appeal to dominical tradition. The point is simply that the Lukan saying gives independent expression to the wider cultural assumption that sexuality is alien to eschatological existence.

78. Tomson (1990, 107), while noting that Paul's teaching is parallel to rabbinic traditions that stress the wife's marital rights on the basis of Exod. 21:10, also observes that the "remarkable reciprocity" of Paul's statements transcends "the accepted Rabbinic conception."

79. See Via 1990.

80. This reading differs in emphasis from Daniel Boyarin's incisive and nuanced interpretation of the same passage (Boyarin 1994, 180–200). Boyarin stresses more heavily Paul's preference for a genderless, spiritualized ideal of Christian existence (as articulated in Gal. 3:28); thus, Paul's statements in 1 Cor. 7 must be read as a reluctant compromise: "Paul settled for something else, something less than his vision called for, and thus the continuation of the domestic slavery of marriage for those not called to the celibate life" (p. 193). My difference from Boyarin on the reading of this text is part of a larger debate between us about the extent to which Paul's anthropology parallels the systematic dualism expressed more clearly in Philo of Alexandria. Nonetheless, the differences are primarily matters of where to place the accents in Paul's discourse. I can agree entirely with Boyarin when he writes, "Paul maintains a two-tiered system of thought regarding sexuality: celibacy as the higher state but marriage as a fully honorable condition for the believing Christian" (p. 192).

81. The translation "impending crisis" (7:26), despite its appearance in the RSV and the NRSV, is indefensible. The participle *enestōsan* clearly means "present," as in 1 Cor. 3:22, where it is juxtaposed to *mellonta*, "things to come."

82. Many modern translations, following the lead of Nestle-Aland, punctuate the text so that the sentence begins in v. 33b: "As in all the churches of the saints, let the women be silent in the churches." For several reasons, this analysis of the text's structure is to be rejected. First, it creates a redundancy: "As in all the churches . . . in the churches." Second, several ancient manuscripts move vv. 34–35 to the conclusion of chapter 14. This suggests that these verses may be an interpolation (see below); at the very least, it demonstrates that the scribes responsible for the textual displacement understood v. 33b to belong with the foregoing sentence rather than with v. 34. Finally, Paul characteristically places the appeal to common practice of the church at the end of arguments (as in 1 Cor. 11:16) rather than at the beginning. If v. 33b does belong with the foregoing sentence, it must be connected to v. 32, with v. 33a being read as parenthetical: "And the spirits of prophets are subject to prophets—for God is not a God of disorder but of peace—as in all the churches of the saints."

83. For more detailed discussion, see Schüssler Fiorenza 1983, 205–241; Furnish 1985, 83–114; Witherington 1980.

84. For discussions of this disputed passage, see Schüssler Fiorenza 1983, 226–230; Furnish 1985, 94–101; D. Martin 1995a.

85. Meeks 1983, 220 n. 107.

86. Meeks 1983, 70–73.

87. Schüssler Fiorenza 1983, 230–233.

88. For an extended defense of this argument, see Fee 1987, 699–708. For a counterargument defending the authenticity of the verses, see Wire 1990, 149–152.

89. Significantly, however, a recent article by Philip Payne (1995) identifies previously unnoticed evidence from the sixth-century Codex Fuldensis suggesting that vv. 34–35 were regarded as an interpolation by Bishop Victor of Capua, under whose authority the manuscript was produced. My thanks to Dr. Payne for allowing me to consult a prepublication copy of his essay.

90. Wire 1990, 135–158.

91. As Boyarin remarks, "People in late antiquity had not thought their way out of a dilemma which catches us on its horns even now—in *very* late antiquity" (1994, 200).

Chapter 2

Developments of the Pauline Tradition

1. Witnesses to the Legacy of Paul

What was the fate of Paul's vision for community? In the continuing history of the communities that he founded, how was his moral vision received and appropriated? As time goes on, can a community tolerate the tension of living at the turn of the ages? Is it possible to sustain a community in which the only law is "the law of Christ"? Can a people who walk by the guidance of the Spirit form a coherent human social order? In short, did Paul's vision provide a theologically stable basis for ethics? The presence in the New Testament canon of the deutero-Pauline letters invites us to consider these problems.

Our sketch of Pauline ethics has been based on the seven letters whose authorship is generally uncontested (Romans, 1 and 2 Corinthians, Galatians, Philippians, 1 Thessalonians, and Philemon). The other six letters in the Pauline corpus (2 Thessalonians, Colossians, Ephesians, 1 and 2 Timothy, and Titus) are considered by the majority of New Testament scholars to be pseudepigraphical compositions written under Paul's name by followers after his death. This judgment is, however, by no means unanimous. The question of authorship must be considered for each letter independently.[1] My own view is that the arguments against Pauline authorship of 2 Thessalonians and Colossians are not compelling; I am inclined to regard these as authentic Pauline letters. Ephesians and the pastoral Epistles (1 and 2 Timothy and Titus), on the other hand, differ so markedly from the other letters in the corpus, both theologically and stylistically, that they should probably be understood as later compositions written by someone else in Paul's name. Even within this latter group of letters, different degrees of certainty obtain: 2 Timothy bears fewer marks of non-Pauline authorship than do the other pastorals.[2]

For the purposes of this book, I will adopt the working hypothesis that Ephesians and the pastorals are products of second-generation Pauline Christianity. My reading of these letters, therefore, will try to show how they interpret and develop the legacy of Paul. I will concentrate on Ephesians and 1 Timothy as illustrative samples. As in the discussion of Paul's own letters, the governing heuristic question will be, "What vision of the moral life is presented in these texts?"

From one point of view, the question of authorship is irrelevant for New Testament ethics. Even if Paul is the author of these letters, their portrayal of the church and of the faithful Christian life diverges so significantly from the picture drawn by the other letters that they would in any case demand separate consideration, perhaps as the vision of the "late Paul" as opposed to the "early Paul" of Galatians, the Corinthian correspondence, and Romans.[3] In order to write a biographical account of Paul's development as a thinker, one would have to make a firm decision about the authorship and relative chronology of these letters. Since the aim of my study, however, is to listen to the different voices in the canon, this critical decision is less crucial. Whether the pastorals represent a second-generation adaptation of the Pauline tradition or the voice of a "sadder but wiser" Paul who has come to believe in the necessity of firmly structured institutional order in the church, their witness stands apart from the earlier Pauline letters. (New Testament scholars are sometimes oddly resistant to the idea that Paul could have developed or even declined as a theological thinker. When the topic of pseudonymous composition arises, I like to ask my students whether all those albums issued under the name of Bob Dylan for the last fifteen years can possibly be the work of the same person who performed "Highway 61 Revisited.")

While the nature of the evidence may not permit a finally decisive resolution of the authorship question, the deutero-Pauline Epistles are more hermeneutically suggestive if they are interpreted as second-generation texts. Why so? If so read, they show us the church's effort to allow the voice of Paul to continue to speak in a historical situation different from that of the first generation. "Timothy" and "Titus"—the addressees of the pastorals—become symbols for those who carry on the mission after Paul's time, preserving and interpreting the gospel that has been entrusted to them. In other words, these letters provide instances of the transmission and reinterpretation of the apostolic heritage within the New Testament itself.[4] That is the perspective from which we will now examine the moral witness of these texts.

2. Ephesians: Cosmic Ecclesiology

The letter to the Ephesians opens with a long mystical meditation on the themes of election and cosmic reconciliation. This meditation, which takes up half the length of the letter (chapters 1–3), is composed in a florid Greek style with very long sentences padded by extended participial phrases and relative clauses; for example, Ephesians 1:3–14 is a single Greek sentence. English translations usually break the long periods of Ephesians down for the sake of readability, but one may gain a more accurate impression of the letter's style by reading Ephesians 1:3–14 in the King James Version:[5]

> *Blessed be the God and Father of our Lord Jesus Christ, who hath blessed us with all spiritual blessings in heavenly places in Christ, according as he hath chosen us in him before the foundation of the world, that we should be holy and without blame before him in love, having predestinated us unto the adoption of children by Jesus Christ to himself, according to the good pleasure of his will, to the praise of the glory of his grace, wherein he hath made us accepted in the beloved, in whom we have redemption through his blood, the forgiveness of sins, according to the riches of his grace, wherein he hath abounded toward us in all wisdom and prudence, having made known unto us the mystery of his will, according to his good pleasure which he hath purposed in himself, that in the dispensation of the fulness of times he might gather together in one all things in Christ, both which are in heaven, and which are on earth, even in him in whom also we have obtained an inheritance, being predestinated according to the purpose of him who worketh all things after the counsel of his own will, that we should be to the praise of his glory, who first trusted in Christ, in whom ye also trusted, after that ye heard the word of truth, the gospel of your salvation, in whom also after that ye believed, ye were sealed with that holy Spirit of promise, which is the earnest of our inheritance until the redemption of the purchased possession, unto the praise of his glory.*

Despite the un-Pauline ornate style, the theological motifs of this passage are characteristically Pauline: election, redemption, adoption as God's children through Christ, the Holy Spirit as sign and seal of the promised inheritance. In striking distinction from other Pauline letters, however, these motifs are offered as general doctrinal reflections with no discernible link to any particular problem or situation in a specific congregation. Indeed, the fact that some important manuscripts lack the words "in Ephesus" in the greeting (1:1) has suggested to some scholars that the letter might originally have been composed as a circular letter to be sent to a number of churches, perhaps as a cover letter for a collection of Paul's Epistles.

Also distinctive here is the great emphasis placed on the cosmic significance of the church, which is described as the fulfillment of God's design to gather all things together in Christ. God has "put all things under his feet and has made him the head over all things *for the church*, which is his body, the fullness of him who fills all in all" (Eph. 1:22–23). The long-hidden "plan [*oikonomia*] of the mystery" of God's wisdom is said to be at last revealed "*through the church* . . . to the rulers and authorities in the heavenly places" (3:9–10). This exalted cosmic ecclesiology represents a theologically noteworthy development of Paul's view that the church, being transformed into the image of Christ, reflects the glory of God (2 Cor. 3:18). In Ephesians, the church is not only the recipient of revelation (1:9) but also the singular medium of revelation to the whole creation, including the cosmic powers that still oppose God's purposes (3:10, 6:10–20).

For that reason, the visible unity of the church is crucial. In the church, God has "broken down the dividing wall" between Jews and Gentiles. Indeed, the primary effect of the death of Christ is to bring this division to an end:

> *For he is our peace; in his flesh he has made both groups into one and has broken down the dividing wall, that is, the hostility between us. He has abolished the law with its commandments and ordinances, that he might create in himself one new humanity in place of the two, thus making peace, and might reconcile both groups to God in one body through the cross, thus putting to death that hostility through it.* (2:14–16)

As a result of Christ's death, Jews and Gentiles alike now have "access in one Spirit to the Father" (2:18). This is God's secret wisdom that the church now proclaims by its very existence. The long meditative introduction of Ephesians is, then, a prayer for the church's imagination: the apostle prays that his readers will find "the eyes of [their] heart" illuminated (1:18) to grasp the overwhelmingly glorious significance of God's plan to bring about the reconciliation of the whole universe in and through Christ's cosmic body, the church (cf. 3:14–19). Chapter 3 concludes with a doxological acknowledgment, however, that no matter how empowered the church's imagination may be, it will never grasp fully the scope of God's power and grace:

> *Now to him who by the power at work among*[6] *us is able to accomplish abundantly far more than all we can ask or imagine, to him be glory* **in the church** *and in Christ Jesus to all generations, forever and ever. Amen.* (3:20–21, *emphasis mine*)

All of this serves as an elaborate preamble to the moral exhortation and instruction that appears in the last half of the letter (chapters 4–6). Because the church is the manifestation in the world of God's reconciling power, the readers are exhorted

> *to lead a life worthy of the calling to which you have been called, with all humility and gentleness, with patience, bearing with one another in love, making every effort to maintain the unity of the Spirit in the bond of peace.* (4:1b–3)

The unity of the one body of Christ, which shares "one faith, one baptism" is the correlate of the oneness of God, who undergirds and sustains the community's life.

Ephesians 4:1–5:20 presents a visionary description of the character of the reconciled community. The diverse gifts in the church have as their common purpose "to equip the saints for the work of ministry, for building up the body of Christ until all of us come to the unity of the faith and . . . to maturity, to the measure of the full stature of Christ" (4:12–13). Thus, as in 1 Corinthians 12, ministry is conceived as the work of the entire community, not of a specially designated class of spiritually gifted persons. The interplay of gifts in the church is designed to bring the community as a whole to full maturity, so that the church might ultimately stand unambiguously as "the body of Christ," the complete embodiment of Christ in the world. The imagery of growth suggests that this visionary goal is not to be understood as a future instantaneous transformation (i.e., at the resurrection of the dead) but as the end result of a process already underway in the community.

In its growth toward maturity, the body of Christ must withstand "every wind of doctrine" and every scheme that seeks to lead the community astray (4:14). The community must "no longer live as the Gentiles live, in the futility of their minds"; rather, they are to clothe themselves in the character qualities that they have learned "in Jesus" (4:17–24). In 4:25–5:2, there is a brief sketch of the positive behaviors that characterize the new life in Christ: speaking the truth in love, doing honest labor, sharing with the needy, using disciplined edifying speech, avoiding bitterness and anger, "forgiving one another, as God in Christ has forgiven you." All of this is summed up by a commandment that expands the familiar Pauline exhortation to imitate Christ: "Therefore be imitators of God, as beloved children, and live in love, as Christ loved us and gave himself up for us, a fragrant offering and sacrifice to God" (5:1–2).

The section concludes with a series of warnings against the "unfruitful works of darkness" (5:11) and a call for those in the church to "walk as children of light," redeeming the time in the midst of evil days (5:8, 15–16). The language of this passage is reminiscent of the apocalyptic exhortations in other Pauline letters (cf. Rom. 13:11–14), but there is no explicit reference to the parousia or a future judgment. The resurrection appears to be interpreted, curiously, as an awakening to moral consciousness (5:14) rather than as a future hope. Indeed, one of the most striking theological developments in this letter is the relative suppression of Paul's future-oriented apocalyptic hope, which seems to have been supplanted by a belief in the progressive redemption of the world through the growth of the church.

In 5:21–6:9, the moral exhortation shifts from general counsel for the whole church to a series of admonitions addressed to persons in particular roles within the household: wives/husbands, children/parents, slaves/masters. The passage belongs to the genre of *Haustafeln* (tables of household duties), other examples of which occur in Colossians 3:18–4:1, Titus 2:1–10, and 1 Peter 2:18–3:7.

Four distinctive features of the household code in Ephesians are noteworthy. First, the particular admonitions are subsumed under a general exhortation to the whole church to "be subject to one another out of reverence for Christ" (5:21); thus, the hierarchical structure of the relations described is tempered by a comprehensive vision of the church as a people living in humility and mutual submission. The conventional authority structures of the ancient household are thereby subverted even while they are left in place. Second, the formal structure of the code is unusual in its pattern of addressing the subordinate persons in the social order (wives, children, and slaves) as moral agents who must *choose* to "be subject."[7] More typically, ancient *Haustafeln* address the holders of power and instruct them on their duties toward those who are subject to them. Third, the household code in Ephesians is notable for its reciprocity. It does not merely call upon the less powerful to submit (as does, e.g., Titus 2:9–10); it equally charges the more powerful (husbands, fathers, and masters) to act with gentleness toward and concern for those over whom they exercise authority. Finally, and most important, the commandments laid down in this code are given an explicitly theological elaboration that seeks to show how these norms are warranted by the gospel. This is most evident in the author's reading of marriage as a symbol of the relationship between Christ and the church. This symbolic correlation becomes a powerful warrant for husbands to love their wives with self-sacrificial care, "just as Christ loved the church and gave himself up for her" (5:25). (Because this text calls for wives to be subject to their husbands [vv. 22–24], it has sometimes been alleged to justify grave mistreatment and even physical abuse of women. Such a use of the text can only be judged a bizarre and tragic misreading: the author of Ephesians, by charging husbands to "love their wives as they do their own bodies" [vv. 28–29], clearly aims to preclude precisely such abuses within Christian marriages.)[8]

In all these respects, then, the household code of Ephesians articulates a vision for a community whose social relations are impacted by the gospel of Jesus Christ. The vision is not egalitarian, if measured anachronistically by twentieth-century ideals of social equality; Elisabeth Schüssler Fiorenza aptly describes this social order as "love patriarchalism."[9] The love patriarchalism of Ephesians is not, however, closed and static in character. When masters are told to stop threatening their slaves because "you have the same Master in heaven, and with him there is no partiality" (6:9), a theological image is invoked that unsettles the conventional patterns of master-slave relations. Similarly, if marriage is a metaphor for the relationship between Christ and the church, the exalted ecclesiology of Ephesians must deconstruct static patriarchal notions of marriage. The church, in Ephesians, is not dominated by Christ; rather, in unity with Christ, it is nurtured into full maturity, into "the measure of the full stature of Christ" (4:13). What, then, must the *telos* of marriage be?

The climactic passage of Ephesians (6:10–20) depicts the church as engaged in spiritual warfare against "the schemes[10] of the devil":

> *For our struggle is not against enemies of blood and flesh, but against the rulers, against the authorities, against the cosmic powers of this present darkness, against the spiritual forces of evil in the heavenly places.* (6:12)

The weapons that are to be employed against these cosmic powers are not to be forged of steel by any human technology; instead, the war is to be fought with prayer (6:18) and with the renewed character of the holy community. The armor is mostly defensive, enabling the church to ward off the assaults of "the evil one":

Belt: truth
Breastplate: justice
Shoes: the gospel of peace(!)

Shield: faith

Helmet: salvation

The one offensive weapon to be carried by the church is "the sword of the Spirit, which is the word of God." Thus, the passage offers no sanction for conventional holy war ideology. Rather, it depicts the church standing firm in the battle against cosmic powers armed only with the gospel that promises God's triumph. By its peaceful existence in the world, the church community stands (6:13) as a challenge to the power of evil. By speaking truth and living in forgiveness, the church shatters the dominion of the principalities and powers and reveals "the plan of the mystery hidden for ages in God who created all things" (3:9).

In sum, how does Ephesians adapt the Pauline heritage? As we have seen, the explicit eschatological framework has been deemphasized, though not abandoned, and the cosmic significance of the church has been greatly highlighted. The church's common life is a sign of God's grace, for the church is "God's work of art,[11] created in Christ Jesus for good works, which God prepared beforehand, in order that we might walk in them" (2:10, JB). The unity of Jews and Gentiles in Christ, an important theme in Romans, is interpreted here as a sign of God's plan to unify the cosmos and to reconcile it to himself. If Ephesians 5:21–6:9 is an elaboration of the simpler *Haustafel* of Colossians 3:18–4:1, we see that the author's attempt to develop theological warrants for the wife's submission has generated a richly suggestive symbolism that offers a more positive account of love within marriage than anything elsewhere in the Pauline literature.

The most striking difference between Ephesians and the other letters in the Pauline corpus lies in its lack of situational specificity; it takes Paul's various interpretations of the significance of local church communities and develops them into a speculative portrayal of the mystical role of the church within God's plan to gather the whole world into a redeemed unity. Within that plan, the church's moral action has two fundamental aims: to manifest the truth of God's cosmic design and to extend God's reconciling power into the world through the growth of the body of Christ toward full maturity.

3. 1 Timothy: How to Behave in the Household of God

In 1 Timothy, we encounter a blueprint for a community characterized by institutional order and stability. The figure of the apostle Paul is represented as writing to his younger co-worker, Timothy, and setting forth a series of instructions for organizing and guiding the church in Ephesus (1 Tim. 1:3).[12]

> *I hope to come to you soon, but I am writing these instructions to you so that, if I am delayed, you may know how one ought to behave in the household of God, which is the church of the living God, the pillar and bulwark of the truth.*[13] (3:14–15)

The institution of the *household* provides the controlling metaphor for the church in this letter—"controlling" in more senses than one, for the prevailing concern here is that the leadership of the church should prudently constrain the members of the church, who otherwise are likely to be led astray. One of the primary qualifications for an *episkopos* ("overseer": the common translation "bishop" suggests a more developed ecclesiastical structure than is appropriate to the late first century) is that "he must manage his own household well, keeping his children submissive and respectful in every way—for if someone does not know how to manage his own household, how can he take care of God's church?" (3:4–5; cf. 3:12). The church becomes the Greco-Roman household writ large, and the authority of the household head becomes the model for the exercise of authority in the church.[14]

1 Timothy places a high value on forming "a quiet and peaceable life" for the community (2:2) and on presenting a respectable appearance to outsiders (e.g., 3:7, 5:14, 6:1), so that the church might be undisturbed:

> *First of all, then, I urge that supplications, prayers, intercessions, and thanksgivings be made for everyone, for kings and all who are in high positions, so that we may lead a quiet and peaceable life in all godliness [**eusebeia**] and dignity.* (2:1–2)

This admonition does not imply that the church has become part of the social and political establishment; rather, a peaceful environment is judged to be conducive to the spreading of the gospel (2:3–4). Thus, the church should pray for political tranquility. Despite the reference to Jesus' "good confession" before Pontius Pilate (6:13), there is no hint in this letter that the gospel might present a challenge to the political order of the time.

Within the community of the church, the directions for orderliness are emphatic. Women are especially enjoined to a subordinate role:

> *Let a woman learn in silence with full submission. I permit no woman to teach or to dominate*[15] *a man; she is to remain silent. For Adam was formed first, then Eve; and Adam was not deceived, but the woman was deceived and became a transgressor. Yet she will be saved through childbearing, provided they continue in faith and love and holiness, with modesty.* (2:11–15)

This is one of the passages in the letter that could hardly have come from the pen of Paul. The assertion that women will be saved through bearing children clashes flagrantly with Paul's profound conviction that all human beings are saved only by virtue of the death of Christ. The lame exoneration of Adam (2:13–14) also sits oddly in conjunction with Paul's portrayal in Romans 5:12–21 of Adam as the source of sin and typological representative of sinful humanity. The peculiarity of the passage has given rise to various imaginative exegetical attempts at damage control, but the overall sense of the text is finally inescapable: women (or perhaps wives) are to be silent and submissive and to bear children.[16] According to 1 Timothy, that is what good order in the church requires.

The one permissible exception to this norm is the group of widows (5:3–16).[17] These were older women, financially supported by the church, who devoted themselves to prayer (5:5) and service (5:10). 1 Timothy sanctions this arrangement but insists on certain tests for acknowledging "real widows": they must be at least sixty years of age, they must have been married only once, and they must have devoted themselves to good works. Only those who meet these standards should be enrolled as official widows, eligible to receive support from the community. Younger widowed women should remarry; otherwise, says the writer, they will fall prey to lust, idleness, and gossip (5:11–14; note the contrast to Paul's advice to widows in 1 Cor. 7:8, 39–40). Slaves, too, are to remain submissive for the sake of the church's good reputation.

> *Let all who are under the yoke of slavery regard their masters as worthy of all honor, so that the name of God and the teaching [**didaskalia**] may not be blasphemed. Those who have believing masters must not be disrespectful to them on the ground that they are members of the church; rather, they must serve them all the more, since those who benefit by their service are believers and beloved.* (6:1–2)

If Christian slaves become too uppity with their Christian masters, it will bring "the teaching" (of the church) into disrepute.

In contrast to Colossians 3:18–4:1 and Ephesians 5:21–33, 1 Timothy speaks no counterbalancing word to husbands and masters. The univocal message is that the household of the church must be kept in order. The women and slaves are not addressed directly; rather, Timothy, the emissary of Paul, is instructed to keep them in line (6:2c: "Teach and urge these duties").

In order to maintain the desired order, the church community must clearly designate positions of leadership and authority. In contrast to the relatively chaotic situation of charismatic freedom implied in letters such as Galatians and 1 Corinthians, where we find no reference to positions of authority in the local assembly, 1 Timothy makes explicit provision for the appointment of "overseers" and "deacons" and spells out criteria for their selection (3:1–13). These criteria point primarily not to endowment with spiritual gifts and graces but rather to mundane civic virtues:

> *Now an overseer must be above reproach, married only once, temperate, sensible, respectable, hospitable, an apt teacher, not a drunkard, not violent but gentle, not quarrelsome, and not a lover of money.* (3:2–3)

As noted above, these church leaders are to keep their own households in order, just as they are to keep the church in order. Those who do well are to receive financial compensation for their service (5:17–18); however, those who "persist in sin" are to be publicly castigated by Timothy "so that the rest also may stand in fear" (5:20). As this last instruction suggests, a major function of the leaders is to serve as role models of Christian character for others in the community.

The one ministerial function implied in the lists of qualifications for leaders is the teaching role. Indeed, teaching is of great importance in 1 Timothy, for "sound teaching" (4:6) is the essential antidote to "deceitful spirits and teachings of demons" (4:1) and to all manner of immoral conduct (1:8–11). The authoritative transmission of "the sound words of our Lord Jesus Christ and the teaching [*didaskalia*] that is in accordance with godliness [*eusebeia*]" (6:3) is the special task of Timothy (4:11–16); presumably, the local church leadership is also to participate in this teaching ministry, under Timothy's direction (cf. 2 Tim. 2:2, Tit. 1:9). Timothy has received this sound teaching from Paul, and he is to "guard" it faithfully, as a *parathēkē*: a "deposit" or "thing entrusted" to him (6:20). This conception of Christian doctrine as a fixed body of tradition that must be protected has precedent in other Pauline letters (see, e.g., Rom. 6:17; 1 Cor. 11:2, 15:1–3), but nowhere else is it given the singular emphasis that it receives in 1 Timothy and the other pastorals (cf. 2 Tim. 1:13–14, 2:2; Tit. 2:1).

The content of this authoritative deposit of tradition is not described in detail; presumably, Timothy knows it well already. On the basis of the hints provided in the letter, we can surmise that it includes at least two sorts of material: confessional traditions and moral instruction. The relation between these elements—if indeed there is one—remains unclear. The confessional traditions appear in pithy formulations such as the following:

> *The saying is sure and worthy of full acceptance, that Christ Jesus came into the world to save sinners.* (1:15)

> *There is one God; there is also one mediator between God and humanity, the man Christ Jesus, who gave himself as a ransom for all.* (2:5–6)

> *He was revealed in flesh,*
> *justified in spirit,*
> *seen by angels,*
> *proclaimed among Gentiles,*
> *believed in throughout the world,*
> *taken up in glory.* (3:16)

The moral instruction, on the other hand, some of which we have already noted above, seems to focus on the development of *eusebeia* (2:2, 4:7–8, 6:3–6, 6:11). Most modern English translations render this word as "godliness," but a better translation is "piety," in the root sense of the Latin *pietas*, connoting dutiful reverence. This word appears nowhere in the Pauline corpus outside the pastoral Epistles, where it appears ten times (eight times in 1 Timothy alone). Whatever significance one assigns to these statistics,[18] it is hard to avoid the impression that the vision of the Christian life in 1 Timothy is characterized by conformity to fixed conventions of respectable, law-abiding behavior. The characteristic Pauline themes of freedom, suffering with Christ, costly love for the sake of the community, and living in the creative tension between the ages have been drastically deemphasized, if not entirely abandoned.[19] In their place we find the modest, mundane virtues of the orderly household.

One other special ethical emphasis of 1 Timothy deserves note: its strong disparagement of financial ambition and greed. The opponents criticized by the author, in addition to all their other manifold faults, make the fatal error of "imagining that godliness [*eusebeia*] is a means of gain" (6:5). The accusation is a stock charge in ancient polemics against sophists or other philosophical adversaries. The author of 1 Timothy warns his readers against the seductive dangers of the desire for wealth:

> *But those who want to be rich fall into temptation and are trapped by many senseless and harmful desires that plunge people into ruin and destruction. For the love of money is a root of all kinds of evil, and in their eagerness to be rich some have wandered away from the faith and pierced themselves with many pains.* (6:9–10)

That is why an overseer must be "not a lover of money" (3:3). The church should learn to be satisfied with modest circumstances: "If we have food and clothing, we will be content with these" (6:8).

On the other hand, the letter presupposes that there will be rich Christians in the community; no radical demands are made for them to surrender their goods. Instead, Timothy is instructed to encourage them to monitor their attitudes about wealth and to share their resources generously.

> *As for those who in the present age are rich, command them not to be haughty, or to set their hopes on the uncertainty of riches, but rather on God who richly provides us with everything for our enjoyment. They are to do good, to be rich in good works, generous, and ready to share, thus storing up for themselves the treasure of a good foundation for the future, so that they may take hold of the life that really is life.* (6:17–19)

This moderate counsel is in keeping with the general tendency of the letter to accept the status quo of social reality in the world in which the church finds itself. (Cf. also 1 Cor. 7:17–24.)

How then shall we sum up the development of the Pauline ethical tradition in 1 Timothy? As in the case of Ephesians, we witness here some diminishment of the earlier Pauline eschatological tension. There are passing allusions to eschatological judgment and hope, but these allusions play little direct role in the articulation of the ethical stance. The death of Jesus is promulgated as a confessional mystery, but again it plays no visible role in the formulation of ethical norms. The strongest thread of continuity with the other Pauline letters is the emphasis on the moral formation of the community as a matter of central concern. Even on this point, however, a shift of emphasis is discernible: while 1 Timothy vigorously promotes *norms* for the community, the well-being of the community does not figure prominently as a *warrant* in ethical argumentation (as it does in, e.g., 1 Cor.).

Indeed, there is scant ethical argumentation of any kind in 1 Timothy. The moral norms are assumed to be known already in the tradition, and little attempt is made to offer theological justification for these norms. Here lies the greatest difference between 1 Timothy and the authentic Pauline letters. Paul wrestles constantly with the hermeneutical task of relating the gospel freshly to the situation in his "target" churches; 1 Timothy assumes that the norms must be merely guarded and passed along. Indeed, there is a positive impatience with theological argumentation: those who disagree with the officially sanctioned "sound teaching" are said to manifest "a morbid craving for controversy and for disputes about words" (1 Tim. 6:4). It is difficult to imagine Paul dismissively avoiding theological controversy in this manner. Do we see here the evidence of a bad case of apostolic burnout?

The likelier explanation is that 1 Timothy represents a second-generation reception of the Pauline heritage; the writer takes the fundamental theological and ethical questions as already settled by the great apostolic exemplar. Thus, ironically, the dynamic union of theology and ethics that we saw in Paul disintegrates in 1 Timothy *precisely because it is taken for granted.* 1 Timothy articulates the moral vision of a Christian community that has achieved a measure of institutional and symbolic stability; the writer is no longer thinking through ethical issues from their theological foundations. All that needs to be done is to guard the tradition entrusted by the apostle. The result? A gain in stability, but a loss in profundity and freedom. In the authentic Pauline letters, the churches are repeatedly exhorted to discern the will of God anew under the guidance of the Holy Spirit; in 1 Timothy, there is no call for discernment because the will of God has already been sufficiently made known in the "sound teaching" of the tradition.

Perhaps the moral vision of the pastorals was inevitable (and even necessary) for the church at the end of the first century to achieve social cohesion and to survive external pressures. Some have suggested that a similar vision might be necessary for the church at the end of the twentieth century to maintain orderly households in an increasingly chaotic pagan culture.[20] Whether that be so or not, the presence of the pastorals in the New Testament canon requires the church to ponder the importance, as well as the dangers, of order in the household of God.

NOTES

1. On authorship, see Kümmel 1975 [1973], 264–269, 340–346, 357–363, 370–374; L. Johnson 1986, 255–257, 266–267, 357–359, 367–372, 381–388.
2. Noted with particular clarity by L. Johnson 1986, 381–389.
3. Romans is usually regarded as the last of the authentic Pauline letters. On the question of the dating of the various letters, see Jewett 1979; Lüdemann 1984; Soards 1987.
4. For a discussion of the later NT writings from this point of view, see R. E. Brown 1984.
5. I have modified the KJV punctuation here slightly in order to reflect the unbroken syntax of the Greek text.

6. In view of the context, *en hēmin* here should almost certainly be translated "among us" (i.e., "in the corporate life of the church"), rather than "within us," as in the NRSV.

7. Yoder 1994, 162–192 [1972, 163–192].

8. For further discussion of this point, see Chapter 15.2.

9. Schüssler Fiorenza 1983, 218.

10. Greek, *tas methodeias.* The NRSV's "wiles" is slightly archaic.

11. This is the Jerusalem Bible's happy translation of *poiēma,* "a thing made."

12. The differences in tone and content between this letter and the letter to the Ephesians are made all the more striking by this geographical link.

13. It is hard to imagine the Paul of the uncontested seven letters describing the church as "the pillar and bulwark of the truth." This formulation is, however, cognate with the ecclesiology of Ephesians. Cf. especially Eph. 2:20.

14. Verner 1983.

15. Greek *authentein.* This word, which appears only here in the NT, is not the ordinary term meaning "to have authority" (though that is the translation given it by the NRSV); rather, it probably connotes willful or abusive exercise of authority. See Scholer 1986.

16. For recent literature on the passage, see Donelson 1988; S. Porter 1993.

17. See Bassler 1984.

18. Towner (1989) thinks that the opponents attacked in the pastorals were using this terminology to describe their own teaching and that the author of these letters simply appropriates their terminology.

19. To be sure, "suffering with Christ" is a major theme of 2 Timothy. This is one of the ways in which this letter differs strikingly from 1 Timothy and Titus. I am indebted to Luke Johnson for calling my attention to this point in "The Use of the New Testament in Christian Ethics: A Response to Richard Hays," a paper delivered at the symposium "The New Testament and Ethics: Problems and Prospects," Duke University, April 1, 1995.

20. E.g., Oden 1979, 130–147.

Chapter 3

The Gospel of Mark

Taking Up the Cross

1. Finding "Ethics" in the Story of Jesus: Reflections on Method

When we turn from the corpus of Pauline letters to the Gospels, we find ourselves dealing with a different kind of literature. The letters present explicit moral teaching and advice to particular communities, but the Gospels simply tell stories about Jesus. Although these stories are written and crafted by the evangelists to bear witness in their own time, forty to sixty years after the death of Jesus, they are not explicitly addressed to any particular community or situation. Rather, by adopting a narrative mode of presentation, the Gospels clothe their message in the form of a story about the past and thus allow their message to address the whole church, wherever and whenever the church understands its destiny to be shaped by the events of Jesus' life and death.

To be sure, the Gospels—especially Matthew—do contain stories that represent Jesus as a moral teacher, but the moral meaning of the Gospels cannot be limited to these explicitly didactic passages. Stories form our values and moral sensibilities in more indirect and complex ways, teaching us how to see the world, what to fear, and what to hope for; stories offer us nuanced models of behavior both wise and foolish, courageous and cowardly, faithful and faithless. That is why, as Amos Wilder remarked, "the road to a moral judgment is by way of the imagination."[1]

Consequently, the ethical significance of each Gospel must be discerned from the shape of the story as a whole. In order to grasp the moral vision of the evangelist, we must ask how Jesus' life and ministry are portrayed in the story and how his call to discipleship reshapes the lives of the other characters. We must also ask what conceptions of time and history and human possibility are woven into the texture of the narrative. In particular, we must ask how Jesus' violent and unjust death is interpreted as meaningful. All of these questions are pertinent to New Testament ethics.

The Gospel of Mark provides a clear illustration of the importance of this approach, for it contains very little explicit ethical teaching.[2] Even passages that appear to offer ethical instruction (e.g., the "tribute to Caesar" text in Mark 12:13–17) often turn out, on closer inspection, to be elusive riddles whose purpose is to establish claims about the identity and authority of Jesus, rather than to set clear guidelines for the community's conduct. Thus, to investigate the ethical import of Mark's story of Jesus, we must look beyond such brief didactic units and attend to the broader contours of Mark's narrative world.

This approach differs significantly from two prevalent methods for interpreting Markan theology. It differs first of all from a redaction-critical method that would seek to identify Mark's theology and ethics by isolating distinctive Markan material or Markan transformations of a critically reconstructed pre-Markan tradition.[3] The redactional approach to the Gospel materials is exemplified by Wolfgang Schrage's *The Ethics of the New Testament.* After a long account of the ethics of (the historically reconstructed) Jesus and a chapter on "Ethical Beginnings in the Earliest Congregations" (i.e., a reconstruction of presynoptic traditions), Schrage offers a very brief sketch of "Ethical Accents in the Synoptic Gospels." The title of this chapter is revealing: the evangelists are treated as "spin doctors" who add minor accents or emphases to the Jesus tradition. In the case of Mark, the earliest Gospel,[4] this method yields slim results, because we have no text of a pre-Markan Gospel; consequently, the attempt to distinguish between Mark's sources and his distinctive editorial contribution involves a great deal of guesswork. Schrage himself acknowledges the limitations of his method: "It would be possible to suggest many additional theories about details of Mark's ethics, but his redactional hand is always highly hypothetical."[5] By contrast, the more literary method adopted in this book allows us to say a good deal about Markan ethics by analyzing the total shape of the narrative that Mark produced. It does not matter how much of this narrative is original with Mark; what matters is how the story as a whole depicts the shape of Christian discipleship.

Second, for similar reasons, my reading of Mark lays little stress on the attempt to identify the precise historical circumstances of the composition of the Gospel. Several recent studies of Mark have proposed detailed hypothetical reconstructions of the Markan community and interpreted the Gospel predominantly in relation to these conjectural historical contexts.[6] All such reconstructions, however, are highly speculative; we simply do not have enough evidence to determine the exact date and setting of this Gospel's composition. Whatever value such speculations may have as history, they do not fundamentally affect our account of the shape of the narrative. My portrayal of Markan ethics would be compatible with several of the competing reconstructions, but it does not require any of them for its intelligibility.

Let us turn, then, to a reading of Mark's Gospel, asking how its narrative renders an account of a life lived faithfully before God.

2. Mark's Christology: A Story of the Crucified Messiah

The central question of Mark's Gospel is asked by Jesus himself in the conversation at Caesarea Philippi that stands at the hinge-point of the story: "But who do you say that I am?" (Mark 8:29). In order to appreciate the force of this question, we must consider its place within the plot of Mark's story.

The Gospel of Mark begins with a succinct superscription: "The beginning of the gospel of Jesus Christ, the Son of God" (Mark 1:1).[7] This opening revelation sets up a dramatic irony that serves as the mainspring of the story: we as readers know the identity of Jesus from the first line, but none of the characters in the story knows it—except, as we shall see, the demons. Consequently, Mark is not at all like a detective story, where the reader must assemble clues to figure out Jesus' true identity; rather, the story's suspense arises, as in *Oedipus Rex*, from the awful tension between the reader's knowledge and the ignorance of the actors. The reader knows from the beginning of the narrative that Jesus is "the Son of God," a designation confirmed by a voice from heaven at Jesus' baptism (1:11) and again at the transfiguration (9:7). To read the story rightly, then, is to join the evangelist in this confession.

But what does it mean to make such a claim about the particular person Jesus? Mark's narrative is carefully constructed to lead us to grasp the strangeness of such a confession about a man who was crucified. The honorific title "Son of God" is given its distinctive and surprising meaning by the story that Mark tells. Only at the end of that story does a human character rightly utter the confession; the outsider Gentile centurion, witnessing Jesus' ignominious death on a cross, speaks the truth: "Truly this man was God's Son!" (15:39). Here at the climax of the story we find the goal toward which Mark's narrative presses: Jesus can be known as "Son of God" only when he is known as the crucified one.

Throughout the first half of the Gospel (1:1–8:26), we might have expected a rather different ending to the tale. Jesus bursts on the scene proclaiming the arrival of the kingdom of God and doing mighty works: he casts out demons, heals the sick, raises the dead, calms the sea and the wind, walks on water, and twice multiplies bread to feed large crowds.[8] In short, in the first half of the story, the Jesus of Mark's Gospel looks very much like a Hellenistic wonder-worker or magician.[9] He acts as a superhero who exercises the power of God to subdue the forces of evil.

At the same time, however, running parallel with Mark's account of Jesus' deeds of power is a sustained portrayal of the disciples' incomprehension of Jesus' identity. Although the disciples have witnessed all the marvels recounted in the first half of the Gospel, they remain stupidly uncomprehending. Although Jesus declares that it has been given to them to know the secret of the kingdom of God (4:11), they do not understand Jesus' parables (4:13, 7:17–18), they are afraid and have "no faith" (4:40), and they fail to understand the meaning of the multiplication of the loaves (6:52). Their incomprehension is made painfully apparent when they seem to have forgotten by 8:4 all about the earlier miraculous feeding: "How can one feed these people with bread here in the desert?"

Why are the disciples portrayed in this negative light? Some New Testament scholars have argued that Mark has a polemical purpose: he is trying to discredit the original followers of Jesus, the founders of the church in Jerusalem, in order to justify his own version of the gospel.[10] According to various versions of this hypothesis, the Jerusalem apostles are said to represent a gospel characterized by rigid Law observance, or by excessive emphasis on the miraculous, or by "orality" in contrast to Mark's preference for the written word. This sort of speculative historical explanation is implausible for many reasons, not least the fact that Mark's Gospel foretells the reunion of the disciples with the risen Lord (14:28; 16:7) and prophesies their destiny as faithful witnesses and martyrs for the gospel (13:9–13). Furthermore, as Robert Tannehill has argued persuasively, the narrative is constructed to elicit the reader's identification with the disciples; through vicariously experiencing their failure (e.g., Peter's denial of Jesus), Christian readers find themselves exhorted to receive forgiveness and to live more faithfully.[11]

Most important, the negative portrayal of the disciples leads the reader to a fundamental reevaluation of power. The juxtaposition of Jesus' mighty works with the disciples' incomprehension invites us to recognize that power is not self-attesting. Those who know Jesus only as a worker of wonders do not understand him at all, for the secret of the kingdom of God is that Jesus must die as the crucified Messiah. The tension between Jesus' miraculous acts of self-disclosure and the disciples' obtuseness provokes a crisis of understanding—a crisis that starts to come to a head in the latter part of Mark 8.

After the second feeding miracle (8:1–10), Jesus and the disciples get into a boat to cross the Sea of Galilee. Jesus, who has just brushed off a group of Pharisees asking for a sign from heaven (8:11–13), warns the disciples to "beware of the yeast of the Pharisees and the yeast of Herod" (8:15). The disciples, however, who have "only one loaf with them in the boat" (8:14), suppose that Jesus is scolding them for forgetting to bring along sufficient provisions. Their anxiety is absurd: Jesus has just fed four thousand people with only seven loaves! Jesus' incredulous response shows that he is fast losing patience with them:

> *Why are you talking about having no bread? Do you still not perceive or understand? Are your hearts hardened? Do you have eyes, and fail to see? Do you have ears, and fail to hear?* (8:17–18)

His questions echo the words in which he had earlier explained to the disciples the mysterious purpose of his teaching in parables:

> *To you has been given the mystery of the kingdom of God, but for the outsiders, everything comes in parables, in order that they may indeed see, but not perceive, and may indeed hear, but not understand, so that they may not turn again and be forgiven.*[12] (4:11–12, RH)

Through their failure of perception, the disciples have become "outsiders." Jesus' mighty deeds have been for them like enigmatic parables whose interpretation remains obscure. Although they have witnessed the feeding miracles, they still fret about not having enough bread, even with Jesus in their presence. They fail to recognize who it is in the boat with them.

Jesus walks them through the details of the two feeding incidents, and then asks plaintively, "Do you not yet understand?" (8:21). No answer is given; the question dangles provocatively at the end of the scene, inviting the reader to supply the response.

The next scene is a brief healing story (8:22–26) with a noteworthy peculiarity. Jesus heals a blind man, but the healing—unlike any other healing in the Gospels—proceeds in two stages.

> *He took the blind man by the hand and led him out of the village; and when he had put saliva on his eyes and laid his hands on him, he asked him, "Can you see anything?" And the man looked up and said, "I can see people, but they look like trees, walking." Then Jesus laid his hands on his eyes again; and he looked intently and his sight was restored, and he saw everything clearly.*

In light of the heavy emphasis placed on "not seeing" in the immediately preceding dialogue in the boat (8:14–21), we would be singularly myopic readers if we failed to see the symbolic implications of this story. Mark has placed this odd episode immediately before the pivotal conversation at Caesarea Philippi in order to signal that the disciples are about to undergo the process of having their vision healed—but gradually, rather than all at once.

The first stage of the healing will take place as Jesus interrogates the disciples concerning his identity (8:27–30). Jesus first asks the disciples, "Who do people say that I am?" After they report the popular scuttlebutt, Jesus asks them to offer their own answer to the question: "But you—who do you say that I am?"[13] Peter blurts out an answer: "You are the Messiah."

At this point, we must read carefully to see how Mark tells the story. The distinctive character of Mark's account of Peter's confession is often overlooked, because the Matthean version of the story (Matt. 16:13–20)—in which Peter is extolled as the rock on which the church will be built—has exercised such a powerful influence on the development of Christian tradition. Mark, however, recounts the event differently. Rather than praising Peter for his divinely gifted insight (cf. Matt. 16:17), Jesus abruptly rebukes the disciples: "And he rebuked [*epetimēsen*] them so that they might speak to no one about him" (8:30, RH). Many translations soften the force of Mark's strong word: e.g., "And he sternly ordered them not to tell anyone about him" (NRSV). The verb "rebuked" is, however, the same word used in Mark

3:12, where Jesus rebukes and silences the demons, who have shouted out, "You are the Son of God." In both cases, Jesus sharply censures speakers who declare the truth about his identity.[14] Why?

First, we should consider what Peter's confession means: "You are the *Christos*." Despite the impression created by the Matthean form of the story, the terms "Messiah" and "Son of God" are not synonymous. Nowhere in pre-Christian sources is there any suggestion that the Messiah was expected to be a supernatural or divine figure. Nor, indeed, was there necessarily a single clearly defined set of expectations about "the Messiah" (literally "anointed one") in Judaism.[15] Nevertheless, in the first-century context, the term "Messiah" might well have evoked in the popular imagination the image of an anointed ruler who would overthrow Israel's enemies (particularly the Romans) and restore the royal throne of David. The expectation of such a messianic figure is vividly expressed in the Psalms of Solomon, a collection of Jewish prayers composed in the first century B.C.E.

> *See, Lord, and raise up for them their King,*
> *The son of David, to rule over your servant Israel*
> *in the time known to you, O God.*
> *Undergird him with the strength to destroy the unrighteous rulers,*
> *to purge Jerusalem from gentiles*
> *who trample her to destruction;*
> *in wisdom and in righteousness to drive out*
> *the sinners from the inheritance;*
> *to smash the arrogance of sinners like a potter's jar;*
> *To shatter all their substance with an iron rod;*
> *to destroy the unlawful nations with the word of his mouth. . . .*
> *He will gather a holy people*
> *whom he will lead in righteousness;*
> *and he will judge the tribes of the people*
> *that have been made holy by the Lord their God. . . .*
> *And he will be a righteous king over them, taught by God.*
> *There will be no unrighteousness among them in his days,*
> *for all shall be holy,*
> *and their king shall be the Lord Messiah.*[16]

With such fervent hopes in the background, Peter's designation of Jesus as "Messiah" carries with it a range of connotations that are strongly nationalistic and oriented to the exercise of power. Peter has begun to "see" Jesus, but imperfectly, like the man who saw "trees walking." Consequently, Jesus' rebuke of the disciples, while not rejecting the title "Messiah," signals the beginning of a teaching project of massive proportions:

> *Then he began to teach them that the Son of Man must undergo great suffering, and be rejected by the elders, the chief priests, and the scribes, and be killed, and after three days rise again.* (8:31)

The meaning of the term "Messiah" must be redefined in terms of the suffering Son of Man.[17]

Peter, not surprisingly, finds this hard teaching decidedly uncongenial. It triggers a mutual rebuking contest between Peter and Jesus:

> *And Peter took him aside and began to rebuke [**epitiman**] him. But turning and looking at his disciples, he rebuked [**epetimēsen**] Peter and said, "Get behind me Satan! For you are setting your mind not on divine things but on human things."* (8:32b–33)

The characterization of Peter as Satan here is purposeful. In this scene, Peter is functioning as tempter and adversary. Jesus has defined his identity and his vocation as Messiah in a way that contradicts all expectations and all normal canons of political efficacy. Peter's apparently reasonable objection is in fact nothing less than a suggestion that Jesus deny himself and his mission, thus capitulating to Satan. By uncompromisingly rejecting Peter's position, Jesus affirms that he is to be a suffering Messiah. That is what obedience to God requires of him.

But that is not all. He goes on to say that his vocation of suffering is not unique; all who follow him are summoned to a similar vocation.

> *He called the crowd with his disciples, and said to them, "If anyone wants to follow after me, let him deny himself and take up his cross and follow me. For whoever wants to save his life will lose it, and whoever loses his life for my sake and for the sake of the gospel will save it."* (8:34–35, RH)

Those who are the Messiah's disciples are called to follow him in the way of suffering, rejection, and death. And yet Mark designates this message as a "gospel": good news. What sort of good news can this be?

In any case, it is clear that though the disciples may have recognized that Jesus is the Messiah, they have yet much to learn about what that means. As with the blind man, their vision is only partially restored. They will not see all things clearly until much later, after the crucifixion. Indeed, Mark never explicitly narrates their unambiguous recognition of the true shape of the messianic vocation; the narrative strategy of Mark challenges the reader to draw the conclusion, to answer the question, "Who do you say that I am?" by acknowledging Jesus as the crucified Messiah. That acknowledgment, however, carries with it a corollary of somber significance for Markan ethics: to be Jesus' disciple means to allow one's own identity to be stamped by the identity of the one who died forsaken on the cross. When we embrace Mark's answer to the question, "Who do you say that I am?" we are not just making a theological affirmation about Jesus' identity; we are choosing our own identity as well.

After Jesus' pivotal conversation with his disciples at Caesarea Philippi (8:27–9:1), the mighty works very nearly cease: we find only one exorcism (9:14–29), one healing (10:46–52), and the withering of one fig tree (11:12–13, 20–21). Even the single exorcism is marked by Jesus' impatient reluctance: "You faithless generation, how much longer must I be among you? How much longer must I put up with you? Bring him to me" (9:19). The working of miracles seems to have become a distraction to his mission rather than an expression of it. The action of the story moves inexorably toward Golgotha.

From the vantage point of Caesarea Philippi, we see that Mark has crafted the story to gain hermeneutical control over the traditions of Jesus as a miracle-worker. Those who perceive Jesus as a purveyor of power—whether supernatural or political—have failed to understand him. He can be rightly understood only as the Son of Man who will surrender power in order to suffer and die. The cross becomes the controlling symbol for interpreting Jesus' identity. Thus, the question, "Who do you say that I am?" finds its final answer in the confession, "Truly this man was the Son of God," a confession that can be rightly uttered only at the foot of the cross.

As the story unfolds, we learn that the cross is not only integral to Jesus' identity but is also mysteriously necessary for the sake of others. Although Mark does not attempt to explain in detail how Jesus' death is effective for the salvation of his followers, the bare fact of its vicarious effect is asserted in two passages placed at prominent points in the narrative. In 10:45, Jesus declares that "the Son of Man came not to be served but to serve, and to give his life as a ransom for many." Later, at his final meal with the disciples, anticipating his impending death, Jesus performs an act of prophetic symbolism by distributing bread and wine to the disciples, with the interpretive words, "Take; this is my body," and "This is my blood of the covenant, which is poured out for many" (14:22–24). Here Jesus' death is construed as a sacrifice that seals a covenant with God for the sake of "many." The tightly compressed saying of 10:45 also echoes the depiction of Isaiah's suffering-servant figure (Isa. 52:13–53:12), who was made "an offering for sin" and bore the iniquities of many.[18] With these theologically fraught narrative clues before us, we cannot fail to read Mark's extended passion narrative as the story of a sacrificial action on Jesus' part, a giving-up of his own life for the people of God.

3. Discipleship: Following the Crucified Messiah

While Mark depicts Jesus' death as a vicarious sacrifice, he stresses even more emphatically its exemplary character: Jesus' death on the cross establishes a pattern for his disciples to follow. We have already noted the way in which Jesus' response to Peter at Caesarea Philippi discloses—for the first time in the story—the daunting information that the call to discipleship is also necessarily a call to take up the cross. Indeed, this theme is so crucial to Mark that he hammers it home repeatedly in a carefully composed central unit of the Gospel, extending from 8:27 to 10:45, structured around three passion predictions (8:31, 9:31, 10:32–34) and framed by two bookend stories of healing blind men (8:22–26, 10:46–52). Within this central unit,

Jesus presses forward his pedagogical project of reshaping the disciples' understanding of his mission and of theirs.

Each of the three passion predictions triggers a similar sequence: the disciples respond in a way that demonstrates their resistance or failure to understand, and Jesus in turn provides corrective teaching that focuses attention on the call to suffering discipleship. These sequences, which constitute the structural backbone of Mark 8:27–10:45, may be represented diagrammatically as follows:

PASSION PREDICTION	MISUNDERSTANDING	CORRECTIVE TEACHING
8:31	8:32–33	8:34–9:1
9:31	9:33–34	9:35–37 (–50?)
10:32–34	10:35–41	10:42–45

The first of these sequences has been discussed above, with emphasis on its christological significance. The third sequence (to which we now turn), offering the most detailed prediction of Jesus' suffering, provides also the most explicit commentary on the correspondence between his fate and the vocation of the disciples.

Apparently trying to shock the disciples into hearing the warning, Jesus gruesomely details his coming suffering: "... [T]hey will mock him, and spit upon him, and flog him, and kill him" (10:34). Immediately thereafter, however, the brothers James and John approach Jesus with a request that suggests they have hardly been listening: "Grant us to sit, one at your right hand and one at your left, in your glory" (10:37). Jesus, startled at their temerity, replies, "You do not know what you are asking. Are you able to drink the cup that I drink [cf. 14:36], or be baptized with the baptism that I am baptized with?" With naive bravado, they answer flatly, "We are able." Jesus, who knows that they will "be scandalized" and flee when his hour of crisis arrives (14:27, 50), informs them, still employing the metaphors of cup and baptism, that they will indeed undergo suffering with him but that there are no guarantees of special honor to be had; that is a matter for God to decide. (The sentimental hymn "Are Ye Able?" often sung in Protestant churches, retells this story with stunning tone deafness to its irony, encouraging the congregation to join James and John in a chorus of oblivious self-congratulation: "Lord, we are able!")

Not surprisingly, the other ten disciples resent the attempt of James and John to hustle their way into the places of honor. Jesus seizes the moment to make one final attempt at teaching them explicitly what discipleship entails.

> *You know that among the Gentiles those whom they recognize as their rulers lord it over them, and their great ones are tyrants over them. But it is not so among you; but whoever wishes to become great among you must be your servant, and whoever wishes to be first among you must be slave of all. For the Son of Man came not to be served but to serve, and to give his life as a ransom for many.* (10:42–45)

The continuing attempts of the disciples to scramble for position in a pecking order (9:33–34, 10:35–37) show that they have not yet grasped the nature of God's kingdom or of their calling. Those who are called into the community of Jesus' disciples are to be servants, and the pattern for this servanthood is definitively shown by Jesus, who came to give up his own life for the sake of others. The full impact of this pattern will become apparent only in the detailed account of his passion and death, but his teaching about discipleship has now been set forth with all possible clarity: to be Jesus' follower is to share his vocation of suffering servanthood, renouncing the world's lust for power. Among "Gentiles," domination and self-assertion are the rule, but in the new community of Jesus' followers, another logic is at work.

With the character of discipleship now firmly established, Jesus' fundamental teaching project has reached its conclusion. To be sure, the disciples will still fail and fall away, but no more will they challenge or misunderstand Jesus' conception of their mission. (When Jesus speaks again of his impending demise on his last evening with the disciples, Peter and all the rest declare their determination not to fall away [14:27–31]. The determination proves empty, but their failure is a failure of nerve rather than understanding: "The spirit indeed is willing, but the flesh is weak" [14:38b].) Chapter 10 concludes with the story of the healing of the blind man Bartimaeus, who pointedly addresses Jesus as "Son of David," a messianic title. This time, in contrast to the earlier two-stage healing, the healing is immediate and complete: "Immediately he regained his sight and followed him on the way" (10:52). Just as the first healing symbolized the beginning of a process of the disciples' reorientation, so the second healing symbolizes the sealing of that process. The phrase "followed him on the way" suggests faithful discipleship, echoing the same verb (*akolouthein*) that Jesus had used in his call to take up the cross at the beginning of this narrative unit (8:34).[19] Those who are willing to follow Jesus on his way can rightly call him Son of David, Messiah. Now the narrative can move forward to the climactic confrontation in Jerusalem.

Because that climactic confrontation involves the disciples' desertion of Jesus at the time of his arrest, most vividly enacted in Peter's threefold denial, we cannot avoid considering the significance of discipleship failure in Mark's vision of the moral life. Mark's portrayal of the disciples discloses a sober view of human impotence. In Mark's Gospel, even Jesus' closest followers, who have been given the secret of the kingdom of God, fall away in time of trial. At the moment of Jesus' final struggle in prayer to accept his vocation of suffering, the disciples comically nap rather than keep watch while Jesus prays (14:32–42). Peter's declaration of uncompromising allegiance to Jesus ("Even though I must die with you, I will not deny you," 14:31) proves empty bluster, and Peter must finally break down and weep at his own faithlessness (14:72). In short, Mark is hardly a cheerful optimist about the human capacity to fulfill the will of God. He knows well the weakness of the flesh, the deceitfulness of the heart, and the darkness of the mind.

Nonetheless, the call to discipleship is given and repeated again and again. There is not the slightest hint in this Gospel that the requirements of God must be prudentially tailored or "realistically" limited because of human weakness. Rather, the demand for self-sacrificial discipleship is uncompromising. Just as the sower in Mark's programmatic parable of the sower (4:3–9) sows seed indiscriminately on good soil and bad, so Mark's call to discipleship is for anyone who has "ears to hear." The seed may be wasted on many, but those who "hear the word and accept it" will in the end yield a rich harvest, "thirty and sixty and a hundredfold."

Mark focuses (in contrast, as we shall see, to Matthew) on simple external obedience rather than on motivation or the intention of the heart. There is no visible concern with the problem of *how* it is possible to obey. Unlike Paul, Mark places no emphasis at all on the empowerment of the Holy Spirit as a necessary condition for obedience. His single reference to the Spirit's empowerment appears in Jesus' teaching to the disciples about the apocalyptic birthpangs of the coming kingdom:

> *As for yourselves, beware; for they will hand you over to councils; and you will be beaten in synagogues; and you will stand before governors and kings because of me, as a testimony to them. . . . When they bring you to trial and hand you over, do not worry beforehand about what you are to say; but say whatever is given you at that time, for it is not you who speak, but the Holy Spirit.* (13:9, 11)

The Spirit will inspire the testimony of Jesus' followers under persecution, but nowhere else in Mark is there any reference to a "gift" of the Holy Spirit or to the Holy Spirit as a continuing presence that will comfort and guide the community or facilitate its obedience. Instead, we encounter the stark call to suffering discipleship and the simple expectation that those who hear will follow. How? It remains a mystery.

For example, in Mark 10:17–31, Jesus promulgates an astounding teaching about wealth.[20] He tells a rich seeker after "eternal life" to sell all his possessions, give the money to the poor, and join the ranks of Jesus' itinerant disciples. The man goes away "grieving, for he had many possessions." This predictable response elicits from Jesus the entirely unpredictable remark that "it is easier for a camel to go through the eye of a needle than for someone who is rich to enter the kingdom of God." In response to the disciples' astonished query, "Who then can be saved?" Jesus offers an enigmatic response: "For mortals it is impossible, but not for God; for God all things are possible." The capacity to respond in obedience is a mysterious possibility granted by God, as this seed parable suggests:

> *The kingdom of God is as if someone would scatter seed on the ground, and would sleep and rise night and day, and the seed would sprout and grow, he does not know how. The earth produces of itself, first the stalk, then the head, then the full grain in the head. But when the grain is ripe, at once he goes in with his sickle, because the harvest has come.* (4:26–29)

Indeed, this connection between Jesus' teaching on possessions and the seed parables is strengthened by his further promise that those who have abandoned goods and families for the sake of radical discipleship will "receive a *hundredfold* now in this age—houses, brothers and sisters, mothers and children, and fields with persecutions[!]—and in the age to come eternal life" (10:30, emphasis mine). The hundredfold reward recalls the hundredfold yield proclaimed in 4:8 and 4:20 for seed that falls on good soil. In both cases, the initiative is God's and the gift of fruitfulness is God's mysterious doing.[21]

Thus, Mark presents a rigorously challenging account of the life of discipleship. One may be called upon to give up possessions, honor, and security. There are, to be sure, compensations: participation in the community of the faithful is itself a blessing. This is how Mark 10:30 should probably be understood: the community of disciples becomes one's new family; those who do the will of God are Jesus' "brother and sister and mother" (3:35). Furthermore, an eschatological reward is promised to those who endure faithfully; those who follow Jesus are assured that they will find life by losing their lives for the sake of the gospel (8:35). In the meantime, however, there are no easy roads, for the life of faithfulness leads to the cross. The story insists repeatedly that discipleship should never be understood as instrumental to the end of gaining glory or blessing. Each time the disciples lapse into calculating their future rewards, they appear foolish and heedless, and they are given firm correction by Jesus (e.g., 9:33–35, 10:35–45). One follows Jesus not because of some promised good result but simply because he brings "a new teaching—with authority" (1:27). Even if the way that he teaches—the way of the cross—is one that appears to make no sense in prudential terms, it is nonetheless to be followed undeviatingly. The promised eschatological vindication is to be left in the hands of God.

The *norm* for discipleship is defined by the cross. Jesus' own obedience, interpreted as servanthood (10:45), is the singular pattern for faithfulness. Strikingly, the concept of love, a common theme of early Christian teaching, receives very little attention in Mark. Only one passage focuses on it (12:28–34), and this is in a controversy discourse rather than in Jesus' teachings to his disciples. In response to a question from a scribe about which commandment of the Torah is "first of all," Jesus answers by linking the Shema (Deut. 6:4–5) with Leviticus 19:18 to form the double love commandment, exhorting love of God and neighbor. When the scribe endorses Jesus' answer, adding that love is "much more important than all whole burnt offerings and sacrifices," Jesus responds, with tempered approbation, "You are not far from the kingdom of God." The passage is certainly an important indicator of Mark's evaluation of the Law; it summons God's people to radical love of God and of one another.[22] Mark 12:28–34 demonstrates that many of the zealous observers of the Law, such as the Pharisees who condemn healing on the Sabbath (3:1–6) and the scribes who "devour widows' houses" (12:38–40), stand condemned by the substance of their own acknowledged norms. Nowhere, however, does the Markan Jesus promulgate love as a distinctive mark of discipleship. The disciples are summoned to follow, and the single fundamental norm is laid down in the narrative of Jesus' own death on the cross. Unlike Paul and John, Mark nowhere explicitly interprets Jesus' death as an act of "love." The way of the cross is simply the way of obedience to the will of God, and discipleship requires following that way regardless of cost or consequences.

4. Eschatological Expectation in Mark: "Keep Awake"

From the opening lines of Mark's Gospel, we are plunged into an atmosphere of intense eschatological expectation. The Gospel begins with a rapid-fire series of prophecies and fulfillments:

Prophecy: Isaiah prophesied a messenger to prepare the way of Lord.

Fulfillment: John the Baptizer appears in the wilderness (1:2–4).

Prophecy: John prophesies the coming of one more powerful (1:7–8).

Fulfillment: Jesus comes to be baptized, and a heavenly voice proclaims him "my Son, the Beloved" (9–11).

Prophecy: Jesus proclaims the arrival of the kingdom of God (1:14–15).

Fulfillment? When does the kingdom arrive?

The movement of this opening sequence leads us to expect the immediate fulfillment of Jesus' message: "The time is fulfilled, and the kingdom of God has come near" (1:15). Thus, we read through the rest of the Gospel waiting for the other shoe to drop.

We are given numerous tantalizing signs of the imminence of God's kingdom: Jesus' power over demons and his healing miracles are signs of the inbreaking of God's new order. Nonetheless, we are reminded constantly that the fulfillment is not yet. Jesus' silencing of the demons is, among other things, an indicator that the time is not yet right for the final disclosure. He speaks in parables (4:1–34), a mode of discourse that offers a veiled revelation appropriate to the time between the times. Although Jesus declares to his disciples that "there are some standing here who will not taste death until they see that the kingdom of God has come with power" (9:1), they are called in the interim to take up the cross and follow Jesus' example of suffering. His transfiguration (9:2–8) is a proleptic disclosure of his eschatological glory, but the disciples are warned not to speak of it yet (9:9–10). His protest action in the Temple (11:15–17) evokes Isaiah's prophecy of the eschatological inclusion of Gentiles along with Israel as God's people so that the Temple might be "a house of prayer for all nations," yet Mark (unlike Luke-Acts) never programmatically narrates the conversion of Gentiles; instead, we have hints and signs in the exorcism of the Gerasene demoniac (5:1–20), the faith of the Syrophoenician woman (7:24–30), and the confession of the centurion at the foot of the cross (15:39).

Mark's most extensive treatment of the impending end appears in Jesus' discussion with his disciples on the Mount of Olives concerning his prophecy of the destruction of the Temple (13:1–37). On the one hand, this discourse contains numerous warnings not to anticipate the eschatological consummation prematurely:

Beware that no one leads you astray. Many will come in my name and say, "I am he!" and they will lead many astray. When you hear of wars and rumors of wars, do not be alarmed; this must take place, but the end is still to come. For nation will rise against nation, and kingdom against kingdom; there will be earthquakes in various places; there will be famines. This is but the beginning of the birthpangs. . . . And if anyone says to you at that time, "Look! Here is the Messiah!" or "Look! There he is!"—do not believe it. False messiahs and false prophets will appear and produce signs and omens, to lead astray, if possible, the elect. But be alert; I have already told you everything." (13:5–8, 21–24)

Speculation about the exact time of the coming of the Son of Man in power is fruitless: ". . . [A]bout that day or hour no one knows, neither the angels in heaven, nor the Son, but only the Father" (13:32).

On the other hand, the discourse pulses with the fervent expectation that the destruction of the Temple, the coming of the Son of Man, and the gathering of the elect will occur in the very near future: the "birthpangs" have begun. The disciples will be persecuted and put to death for their testimony to the gospel, and "the one who endures to the end will be saved" (13:9–13). They are to watch out for the setting up of "the desolating sacrilege" in the Temple and to flee to the mountains when this sign occurs; luckily, for the sake of the elect, the Lord has "cut short" the days of suffering (13:14–20). The promise of 9:1 is reiterated in 13:30: "Truly I tell you, this generation will not pass away until all these things have taken place." Consequently, the community is called to a posture of intense watchfulness:

Beware, keep alert; for you do not know when the time will come. It is like a man going on a journey, when he leaves home and puts his slaves in charge, each with his work, and commands the doorkeeper to be on the watch. Therefore, keep awake—for you do not know when the master of the house will come, in the evening, or at midnight, or at cockcrow, or at dawn, or else he may find you asleep when he comes suddenly. And what I say to you I say to all: Keep awake. (13:33–37)

The drowsy disciples at Gethsemane (14:32–42) serve as a foil for this exhortation to the readers of the Gospel, who are suddenly addressed directly in 13:37; Jesus turns, as it were, to face the camera with an urgent summons to "Watch!"

The passion and death of Jesus are presented by Mark as climactic eschatological events. All that happens to Jesus fulfills what has been written in Scripture (14:27, 49), and Jesus, when interrogated by the high priest, tears away the veil of secrecy by explicitly identifying himself with the Son of Man prophesied in Daniel 7:13–14. The tearing of the Temple curtain at Jesus' death (15:38) is also to be understood as a sign of the end of the present age.

The final disclosure of God's eschatological power in this Gospel is the resurrection of Jesus. But here Mark supplies a surprising twist: an empty tomb, but no resurrection appearances. The original ending of the Gospel is Mark 16:8: "And they said nothing to anyone, for they were afraid."[23] The last words spoken in this story are those of the enigmatic young man in a white robe sitting in the tomb where Jesus had been laid:

> *Do not be alarmed; Jesus you seek, the Nazarene, the Crucified One.*[24] *He has been raised; he is not here. But go, tell his disciples and Peter that he is going ahead of you to Galilee; there you will see him, just as he told you.* (16:6–7, RH)

The women who have come to the tomb to anoint Jesus' dead body—Mary Magdalene, Mary the mother of James, and Salome—flee in terror. And there, astoundingly, the Gospel ends. No resurrection appearances of the risen Lord, no reconciliation with Peter, no commissioning of the apostles, no gift of the Holy Spirit, no ascension of Jesus into heaven, no book of Acts to narrate the glorious expansion of the church into the world—only the word of promise that the disciples *will* see Jesus again in Galilee, and the terrified silence of the women at the tomb.

How are we to read this enigmatic ending? The problem has elicited a prodigious body of commentary,[25] but a few basic observations will suffice for our purposes here. The abrupt ending without a resurrection appearance points emphatically to the still *future* character of the kingdom of God. Jesus' disciples at the end of the story find themselves suspended between the news of the resurrection and the experience of the risen Lord. "Galilee" becomes a symbol of the future encounter with Jesus at the parousia.[26] For now, the identity and presence of Jesus remain elusive: "He has been raised; he is not here" (16:6). Even in resurrection, Mark's Jesus eludes us. He remains just around the corner, "at the very gates" (13:29b).

How does Mark's eschatological expectation shape his vision of the moral life? At least three implications are immediately apparent.

First, the intensity of imminent expectation excludes all possibility of compromising the radical demands of discipleship. Those who follow Jesus must "endure to the end" regardless of what consequences may come. The community is to live in a state of watchful readiness.

Second, the imminence of the inbreaking kingdom dramatically relativizes the norms of the old order, which for Mark certainly includes the Torah. Jesus in Mark's Gospel declares—in dramatic contradiction to pharisaic traditions—that nothing external can defile a person, thus "declar[ing] all foods clean" (7:1–23). Throughout the narrative, Jesus disregards the Law's purity codes, heals on the Sabbath, and challenges the authority of Israel's religious leaders. The explanation for this behavior is simple and consistent: in Jesus the new order of God's kingdom is present, and new wine cannot be put into old wineskins (2:21–22). With regard to matters such as Sabbath observance, "the Son of Man is lord even of the sabbath" (2:28). Thus, the new eschatological reality eclipses the old rule-based norms, which are portrayed as rigid and sterile. For example, the climactic episode of the Gospel's first cycle of controversy stories (2:1–3:6) depicts Jesus preparing to heal a man's withered hand on the Sabbath. Addressing the Pharisees, he asks:

> *"Is it lawful to do good or to do harm on the sabbath, to save life or to kill?" But they were silent. He looked around at them with anger; he was grieved at their hardness of heart and said to the man, "Stretch out your hand." He stretched it out, and his hand was restored.*

The Pharisees went out and immediately conspired with the Herodians against him, how to destroy him. (3:4–6)

This is the first indication in Mark's Gospel that Jesus will meet a violent end. That end is portrayed as the result of an apocalyptic collision between God's compassionate new order and the violent hardness of heart of those who are locked into the old order.[27]

Finally, in the time between the times, the community of Jesus' followers is called to live out their vocation of suffering discipleship without the immediate presence of the Lord. Jesus provides a pattern for discipleship and leaves the community to carry it out while awaiting the eschatological consummation. In striking contrast to Matthew and John, however, Mark offers no comforting promises of Jesus' presence with the community. "He has been raised; he is not here." There will be consolation when the Son of Man comes in glory, but for the present there is only the sober call to take up the cross and follow.

5. Mark's Narrative World As Context for Action

If an account of Markan ethics must reckon with the "world" rendered by the narrative as a whole, what conclusions may be drawn about the way in which this Gospel defines the context of moral action? I would offer six observations about the contours of Mark's narrative world.

First, the world according to Mark is *a world torn open by God.* From the moment when the heavens are torn apart (*schizomenous*) at Jesus' baptism (1:10) to the moment when the curtain of the Temple is torn (*eschisthē*) in two at his death (15:38), this is a story of God's powerful incursion into the created order. The Gospel of Mark offers an answer to the impassioned cry of Isaiah:

Look down from heaven and see,
from your holy and glorious habitation.
Where are your zeal and your might?
The yearning of your heart and your compassion?
They are withheld from me.
For you are our father,
though Abraham does not know us
and Israel does not acknowledge us;
you, O Lord, are our father;
our Redeemer from of old is your name.
Why, O Lord, do you make us stray from your ways
and harden our heart, so that we do not fear you?
Turn back for the sake of your servants,
for the sake of the tribes that are your heritage.
Your holy people took possession for a little while;
but now our adversaries have trampled down your sanctuary.

We have long been like those whom you do not rule,
like those not called by your name.
O that you would tear open the heavens and come down,
so that the mountains would quake at your presence—
as when fire kindles brushwood
and the fire causes water to boil—
to make your name known to your adversaries,
so that the nations might tremble at your presence!
When you did awesome deeds that we did not expect,
you came down, the mountains quaked at your presence.
From ages past no one has heard,
no ear has perceived,
no eye has seen any God besides you,
who works for those who wait for him. (Isa. 63:15–64:4, *emphasis mine*)

The appearing of the kingdom of God in Jesus ruptures the status quo, just as new wine bursts old wineskins. Illusions of stability and authority—both the authority of Roman rule (12:13–17) and the authority of the Jewish religious establishment (11:27–12:12)—are stripped away. History cannot be seen as a closed system of immanent causes and effects; God's abrupt intervention fractures apparent historical continuities, and human life is laid bare before God. The cries of the demons are the sure sign of a cataclysmic disturbance in the cosmic order: "What have you to do with us, Jesus of Nazareth? Have you come to destroy us?" (1:24). The answer is yes: in the coming of Jesus, God has mounted a decisive campaign against the powers of evil that oppress humanity.[28] But the campaign is waged in a mysterious way that no one could have expected, culminating in the cross.

Second, because the cosmic conflict is underway, *time becomes compressed.* "The time is fulfilled" (*peplērōtai ho kairos,* 1:15); all the prophecies point to the present time, and all of human history hinges on this moment. Consequently, everything is happening fast, and there is a tremendous sense of urgency about action in the present. The urgent forward thrust of Mark's narrative is powerfully conveyed in the opening scenes of the Gospel. In chapter 1 alone, Mark uses the word *euthys* ("immediately") no less than eleven times. This is not just a clumsy device to link separate pericopes; rather, it describes the breathless pace with which God's apocalyptic campaign is unfolding. The effect is like watching a multimedia presentation in which slides flash across the screen so rapidly that there is no time to absorb the details; we perceive the forward thrust of events and find ourselves caught up in them. Mark's Jesus has no time for leisurely discourses about the lilies of the field. This Gospel plunges us into the midst of a cosmic conflict careening forward; if we want to follow the story, we need to pick up the pace.

Third, God's apocalyptic invasion of the world has also wrought an inversion: *God has reversed the positions of insiders and outsiders.* Those who are in positions of authority and privilege reject Jesus and his message; even Jesus' own disciples are slow to understand his teaching. Outsiders, however—people of low or despised position in the social world of first-century Jewish culture—receive the gospel gladly, for their need is great. The lepers, the demon-possessed, the woman with the hemorrhage (5:25–34), the Syrophoenician woman (7:24–30), the little children (10:13–16), blind Bartimaeus (10:46–52), the nameless woman who anoints Jesus at Bethany "for burial" (14:3–9), the Gentile centurion at the cross (15:39)—these are the examples put forward by Mark of faithful response to Jesus. "Many who are first will be last, and the last will be first" (10:31). Those of us who are lulled by familiarity with the story should not underestimate the shock of this inversion.

Fourth, Mark's Gospel *redefines the nature of power and the value of suffering.* Because Jesus uses power to serve rather than to be served, authentic power is shown forth paradoxically in the cross. Those who exercise power to dominate others, to kill and oppress, are shown not only as villains but also, surprisingly, as pawns of forces beyond their control. This is particularly evident in the cases of Herod (6:14–29) and Pilate (15:1–15). On the other hand, Jesus' apparently powerless passion becomes the true expression of the power of God. Suffering is portrayed as meaningful and necessary in the mysterious working of God's will. This counterintuitive account of power and suffering can function in two very different ways in the formation of the community of believers. On the one hand, a suffering community will find in Mark's story encouragement and validation of their struggle. The writer of 1 Peter formulates a word of consolation that aptly reflects the hortatory function of a text such as the Gospel of Mark:

> *Beloved, do not be surprised at the fiery ordeal that is taking place among you to test you, as though something strange were happening to you. But rejoice insofar as you are sharing Christ's sufferings, so that you may also be glad and shout for joy when his glory is revealed.* (1 PET. 4:12–13)

On the other hand, readers who occupy positions of power and privilege will find in Mark's Gospel a stern challenge to their life of ease. Like the rich man in 10:17–22, they are called to surrender their privileges and follow Jesus on the way of the cross.[29]

Fifth, Mark's vision of the moral life is profoundly *ironic.* Because God's manner of revelation is characterized by hiddenness, reversal, and surprise, those who follow Jesus find themselves repeatedly failing to understand the will of God. If God's self-disclosure takes the form of riddle and enigma, there can be no place for smugness or dogmatism in ethical matters. Those who think they have the rules firmly in hand are those who suffer from hardness of heart (3:1–6, 7:1–23). The story's notorious lack of closure should engender openness in the readers. If our sensibilities are formed by this narrative, we will learn not to take ourselves too seriously; we will be self-critical and receptive to unexpected manifestations of God's love and power.

Finally, this Gospel's lack of closure calls for *active response* from the reader. We have noted that Mark is fond of concluding narrative units with questions or exhortations that aim beyond the characters in the story and address the reader directly (e.g., "Do you not yet understand?"; "Keep awake!") The strange ending of the Gospel works in the same way. What kind of a story is this whose message of joyous hope ends with the abrupt and enigmatic words, "And they said nothing to anyone, for they were afraid" (16:8)? It is a Gospel of uninterpreted gestures and suggestive silences. Precisely for that reason, it summons readers to supply the ending by taking up the cross and completing the interpretation in their own lives of discipleship. The Gospel of Mark cannot be "understood" from outside; it can be read rightly only through following Jesus in self-involving, self-sacrificial service.

NOTES

1. Wilder 1971, 60. Wilder's dictum is cited and developed insightfully by Via 1978, 1985. See also Beardslee 1970.

2. See the comments of Houlden (1973, 41–46) on the "paucity of ethical material" in this Gospel. Houlden maintains that "even the ethical material which Mark includes is for the most part not present as a result of purely ethical interest."

3. For a telling critique of redaction-critical methods, see Black 1989.

4. Despite various recent challenges, the great majority of NT scholars continue to believe that the hypothesis of Markan priority offers the most satisfactory solution to the complex problem of the literary relationships among the synoptic Gospels. I concur firmly with this consensus, and I shall assume it throughout my discussion of the Gospel materials. It will be evident, however, that my method of expositing the moral vision of each Gospel individually places relatively little emphasis on any particular theory of Gospel origins and relationships.

5. Schrage 1988, 143.

6. For important examples, see Kelber 1974; Kee 1977; Myers 1988; Marcus 1992. For a critique of the methodology of these studies, see D. N. Peterson 1995.

7. Some ancient manuscripts lack the words "Son of God," but these words are almost certainly an original part of the text. Their omission can be accounted for by transcriptional factors. See Metzger 1975, 73.

8. It is often proposed that Mark has employed a traditional collection of miracle stories, or perhaps two cycles of miracle stories (hence the duplication of the feeding miracle). One of the most careful efforts to delineate the structure of the pre-Markan tradition is that of Achtemeier 1970, 1972. See also Fowler 1981. It is important to recognize, however, that the miracle-working motif appears not only in the blocks of tradition but also in Mark's redactional summaries (1:32–34, 3:7–12, 6:53–56, 7:37).

9. This does not mean, however, that Mark or his sources had a fixed concept of the "divine man." See Holladay 1977.

10. Weeden 1971; Kelber 1974; Kelber 1983.

11. Tannehill 1977.

12. For a brilliant interpretation of this passage, see Kermode 1979.

13. The position of the pronoun *hymeis* ("you") is emphatic; Jesus turns the question pointedly to the disciples. Hence, my modification of the NRSV.

14. Here we encounter the distinctive Markan motif of the "messianic secret." For important studies, see Wrede 1971 [1901]; Tuckett 1983; Marcus 1986. Wrede was right to identify this theme as a central element of Markan theology but wrong to see it as an apologetic justification for the transmutation of a nonmessianic historical Jesus into a messianic figure. As our ensuing discussion will show, the secrecy motif serves Mark's purpose of focusing the interpretation of Jesus' identity on the cross.

15. Evidence from the period suggests that there were diverse expectations about a coming Messiah. Furthermore, messianic expectations may have been more peripheral to Jewish piety than subsequent Christian interpreters have tended to suppose. On the whole question, see de Jonge 1966; Neusner 1987; E. P. Sanders 1992, 295–298; Wright 1992, 307–320; Horsley 1992.

16. Psalms of Solomon 17:21–24, 26, 32; translation by R. B. Wright in Charlesworth 1983 (vol. 2), 667. For the OT background of this idea, see, e.g., 2 Sam. 7:12–13; Isa. 9:7, 11:1–10; Jer. 23:5–6; Mic. 5:1–5a. For other expressions of the messianic hope in first-century Judaism, see also 2 Esdras 7:28–29, 12:32–34; 1 Enoch 52:4.

17. The background of the term "Son of Man" is too complex an issue to discuss here. It is evident from Mark 14:62 that the title is derived from Daniel. In Mark, however, the term, used exclusively as a self-designation by Jesus, refers distinctively to his future destiny as a suffering and glorified figure: cf. Mark 9:31, 10:33–34. Nickelsburg (1992) discusses the "double uses" of "Son of Man" as referring both to the human Jesus and to his future

exalted status. The human Jesus already possesses an authority that belongs to the "future" Son of Man (e.g., 2:1–12, 23–28); he also will have authority (8:38), but all this is tied to the necessity of suffering. Thus, in Mark, the term has "purposeful ambiguity" (144).

18. The connection of Mark 10:45 to Isaiah's prophecy is a controversial issue in NT scholarship. Hooker (1959) vigorously denies any direct connection. The position taken here reflects the work of Stuhlmacher 1986 [1981], 16–29, and Marcus 1992, 186–196.

19. Kingsbury 1978.

20. On this passage, see Wheeler 1995, 39–56.

21. Via (1985, 164–165) emphasizes this point: "[F]or Mark discipleship would be impossible without a divine miracle. Apart from the latter there is no opening of the eyes (10:52); following Jesus is not a human possibility but must be enabled by God (10:21–22, 26–27)." Tolbert (1989, 310) notices the same feature of Mark's account but finds it objectionable:

> The difficulty Mark furnishes for modern appropriation is not its negative assessment of the human situation but its solution to the problem. Mark argues that only direct divine intervention can save the elect from the mess this generation is making of the cosmos. While some even now may wish to continue affirming Mark's view, such acquiescence has unfortunately permitted this generation to keep increasing the mess for almost two thousand years. Mark's analysis should be valued, but Christians today must work, not individually, but in solidarity with others to bring to fruition this abundant and lovingly created vineyard that is God's intended kingdom.

While appreciating Tolbert's candor in offering her frank corrective to Mark, one must wonder whether a gospel that places its fundamental trust in human effort rather than divine intervention can any longer be called a gospel. Such questions, however, anticipate the concerns of Part III of the present study.

22. The story also demonstrates that Mark offers no blanket condemnation of the Jewish people; authentic individual response to the Law is recognized and affirmed.

23. Despite the strangeness of this ending, the manuscript evidence is decisive: all manuscripts that supply "endings" beyond 16:8 are late and secondary (Metzger 1975, 122–126; Lane 1974, 601–605). Thus, unless the original ending was lost at a very early stage, we must reckon with a text that ends enigmatically. As I shall seek to demonstrate, such an ending is consonant with Mark's overall vision.

24. My translation here reflects the Greek word order, which has the effect of laying emphasis on the perfect participle *estaurōmenon* and turning it virtually into a title: "the Crucified One." Even after the resurrection, Jesus is rightly identified as the one who was and remains (hence the perfect tense) crucified.

25. For references, see Farmer 1974; Lane 1974; N. Petersen 1980.

26. Even if Mark's formulation comes from an early stage of the tradition that literally expected the immediate return of Jesus to occur in Galilee (Marxsen 1969 [1956], 57–95), the language has taken on a richer symbolic significance within the world of Mark's narrative (Tolbert 1989, 298).

27. It is important to recognize that Mark has shaped the story to highlight the elements of apocalyptic conflict and that this highlighting may produce a skewed view of first-century Judaism. In a significant communication, Daniel Boyarin notes that "in cases of threat to life and limb, rabbinic Judaism sanctions, even demands, healing on the Sabbath. . . . Keeping the Sabbath is not irreconcilable with compassion, and Mark's Jesus here is engaged in a rhetorical, eschatological attack on the Sabbath more than an act of compassion for its own sake" (private communication, Jan. 18, 1995).

28. Myers 1988; Marcus 1992.

29. The fact that Mark's Gospel can be read as a two-edged sword, comforting the afflicted and afflicting the comfortable, should warn us against framing hypotheses that too narrowly circumscribe the original purpose or social setting of the text.

Chapter 4

The Gospel of Matthew

Training for the Kingdom of Heaven

If Mark's Gospel ends without closure, requiring readers to supply the imaginative completion of the message in their own lives, Matthew adopts a very different narrative strategy. The ending of Matthew's Gospel explicitly draws together the threads of the story and commissions the disciples—and Matthew's readers—with a clear task.

> *Now the eleven disciples went to Galilee, to the mountain to which Jesus had directed them. When they saw him, they worshiped him; but some doubted. And Jesus came and said to them, "All authority in heaven and on earth has been given to me. Go therefore and make disciples of all nations, baptizing them in the name of the Father and of the Son and of the Holy Spirit, and teaching them to obey everything that I have commanded you. And remember, I am with you always, to the end of the age.* (MATT. 28:16–20)

Mark ends with a promise that Jesus "is going ahead" to Galilee, but the risen Lord does not appear. "He has been raised; he is not here." Matthew ends with the immediate presence of the risen Lord, who promises to remain present always, until the end of the age. This reassuring word grounds the life and mission of the church on solid rock (cf. Matt. 7:24–25).

The contrast between Matthew and Mark is not limited to their endings; it is characteristic of their stories from start to finish. Matthew, who incorporates almost all of Mark's material, consistently seeks to resolve ambiguities, explain mysteries, and bring closure.

A typology of narrative modes suggested by John Dominic Crossan provides a helpful way of categorizing the differences between the narrative sensibilities of these two Gospels. Crossan proposes that narratives may be classified according to their point of view toward "world." (The term "world" here signifies the conventional understanding of reality prevalent in the culture to which the narrative is addressed.) The narrative text renders its own fictive world; Crossan's heuristic question, then, is how the world of the narrative is related to the "world" of its cultural environment. He suggests that narratives may be ranged along a spectrum that encompasses five categories: myth, apologue, action, satire, and parable. The differences among these narrative types are encapsulated as follows: "Myth establishes world. Apologue defends world. Action describes world. Satire attacks world. Parable subverts world."[1]

Crossan develops this typology in order to demonstrate that Jesus' parables are world-disrupting. We may borrow the typology, however, to elucidate the striking differences between Matthew and Mark. (To use these categories does not imply any particular judgment about the historical factuality of the traditions employed by the evangelists; both history and fiction create narrative worlds. The historical writings of Josephus, for example, clearly belong to the category of apologue.) In terms of Crossan's categories, Mark is a parable, whereas Matthew falls somewhere at the myth/apologue end of the spectrum.

Matthew is both creating an ordered, symbolic world, in which Jesus possesses all authority in heaven and on earth, and defending it against rival worldviews. The way in which Matthew constructs that world may be seen in his representation of Jesus as teacher, his account of discipleship as community formation, and his adaptation of eschatology as a warrant for ethics. After considering each of these themes in turn, I shall offer some brief remarks about the historical background against which Matthew's creative use of the Jesus-tradition must be read, along with some conclusions about Matthew's narrative world as a context for moral discernment and action.

1. Matthew's Christology: Jesus As Teacher

Matthew has marshaled the traditions at his disposal in a way that highlights Jesus' role as the authoritative teacher of the people of God. Taking Mark's narrative outline as a framework, he fills out the story in two important ways.

First, he gives the story a beginning (genealogy and birth narratives, 1:1–2:23) and an end (resurrection appearance and commissioning of the disciples, 28:8–20). The effect of these narrative bookends is to establish the basis for Jesus' authority. He is by birth "the Messiah, the son of David, the son of Abraham" (1:1), who was conceived by the Holy Spirit; furthermore, the strong Moses typology of the birth narrative material establishes the interpretive expectation that Jesus will assume and fulfill Moses' role as deliverer and law-giver for God's people.[2] The ending of the Gospel establishes his divine authority by virtue of the resurrection; that is why all nations—not just Israel—should be taught to obey his commandments.

The content of those commandments is spelled out through Matthew's second major supplementation of the Markan narrative: he makes incisions in Mark's outline in five places and inserts extensive blocks of teaching material (5:1–7:27, 10:5–42, 13:1–52, 18:1–35, and 23:1–25:46).[3] At the end of each of these five sections, Matthew calls attention to the discourse unit by using the formula, "When Jesus had finished [*etelesen*] these words . . . ,"[4] which once again underscores the Moses typology (cf. Deut. 31:1, 32:45). Thus, the narrative line becomes the cargo vehicle for large shipments of didactic material, and Jesus' role as teacher of the church is accentuated.

The programmatic placement of the Sermon on the Mount at the beginning of Jesus' ministry also ensures that the image of Jesus as authoritative teacher will dominate this Gospel's Christology. (Indeed, as a consequence of Matthew's placement as the first Gospel in the New Testament canon, this image of Jesus as pedagogue came to exercise a disproportionately weighty influence in the early church's piety.) At the conclusion of the Sermon on the Mount, Matthew remarks that "the crowds were astonished at his teaching, for he taught them as one having authority, and not as their scribes" (7:28–29).[5] To know the Matthean Jesus rightly, then, is to acknowledge his authority by obeying his word.

> *Not everyone who says to me, "Lord, Lord," will enter the kingdom of heaven, but only the one who does the will of my Father in heaven. On that day many will say to me, "Lord, Lord, did we not prophesy in your name, and cast out demons in your name, and do many deeds of power in your name?" Then I will declare to them, "I never knew you; go away from me, you evildoers."* (7:21–23)

Those who obey Jesus' teachings are like the wise man who built his house on rock, and those who disobey are like the foolish man who built his house on sand (7:24–27). Thus, while Matthew retains the Markan material that speaks of following Jesus' example by taking up the cross, Jesus' distinctive role in Matthew is more didactic: he becomes the "one teacher" who supplants all other rabbis (23:8). The Messiah expounds Torah in a new and authoritative way.

Jesus' continuity with the Torah is an important thematic emphasis for Matthew. A programmatic statement in Matthew 5:17–20 asserts that Jesus has come not to abolish the Law and the prophets but to fulfill them. The rest of the Sermon on the Mount then elaborates the meaning of this statement. The six antitheses of 5:21–48 ("You have heard that it was said . . . , but I say to you. . . .") explicitly counterpose the authority of Jesus to the authority of traditional understandings of the Law: rather than reading the Law's requirements as rules that fix the normative standards of righteousness, Matthew's Jesus sees them as pointers to a more radical righteousness of the heart, intensifying the demand of God far beyond the letter of the Law. Where the Law forbids murder and adultery, Jesus calls for the renunciation of anger and lust; where the Law poses regulative limitations on divorce and revenge, Jesus calls his followers to renounce these options altogether. Where the Law limits the obligation of love to the neighbor (i.e., the fellow Israelite), Jesus calls for love of enemies. In short, he tells his disciples to "be perfect [*teleios*] . . . as your heavenly Father is perfect" (5:48). This is one of the senses in which Jesus is said to "fulfill" the Law: he elucidates its inner intent, demanding of his followers a righteousness that "exceeds that of the scribes and Pharisees" (5:20). Probably Matthew's insistence on this point reflects an urgent debate in his own time concerning the authentic interpretation of Torah; perhaps responding to charges from the "Pharisees" (i.e., those representing nascent rabbinic Judaism) that Christians are antinomians, Matthew insists that it is Jesus—not the punctilious Pharisees—who truly instructs his followers to do what the Law requires.[6]

At the same time, however, Jesus also "fulfills" the Torah, in the sense that his life is the typological completion of numerous Old Testament prophecies and stories. Matthew, distinctively among the evangelists, repeatedly offers authorial asides to the reader, declaring that various events in Jesus' career happened in order to fulfill what the prophets had spoken. There are more than a dozen such "formula quotations" in Matthew.[7] One effect of this Matthean narrative technique is to highlight the "scripted" character of salvation history; nothing is random or uncertain, for all events are under the authority of God's providence. Reality has an orderly pattern: no loose ends are left dangling, because Jesus the Messiah has tied them all up. Matthew sees it as his business to demonstrate the continuity of Jesus—both in his teaching and in his person—with the Torah; thus, he argues for a harmonious correspondence between Law and gospel.

By Matthew's time, about fifty years after the death of Jesus, the teaching authority of Jesus had to be mediated somehow to the church; the formula quotations stand as evidence that within Matthew's community there were scribes and teachers who undertook the task of collecting the traditions about Jesus, arranging them for pedagogical purposes, and seeking out correlations with the Torah.[8] Matthew himself is best understood as a scribe of this sort, whose signature may be traced in the saying of Jesus—found only in this Gospel—that concludes the collection of parables in Matthew 13: "Therefore every scribe who has been trained for the kingdom of heaven is like the master of a household who brings out of his treasure what is new and what is old" (13:52). The new and the old together are collected, treasured up, and "brought out" by this "scribe trained for the kingdom of heaven." Nothing is lost, not a jot or a tittle; everything finds its place within the fullness of Jesus' messianic kingdom.

2. Training for the Kingdom

It follows naturally that when Jesus is conceived as a teacher, the church is seen primarily as a community of those who are taught—which is, of course, the meaning of the word "disciples." The formation and discipling of the church occurs through the instruction offered by this Gospel. The "great commission" at the conclusion of Matthew's Gospel is pointedly a mandate to teach: "Make *disciples* of all nations . . . *teaching* them to *obey* everything that I have commanded you." Matthew is not interested merely in soliciting converts; the gospel, according to Matthew, summons people to join a disciplined community of Jesus' followers who put his teachings into practice.

There can be no question here of a purely individualized spiritual formation. Matthew is strongly ecclesially oriented. Indeed, only in Matthew's Gospel does Jesus speak of the *ekklēsia* ("church"). Though the term appears just twice, the contexts of its occurrence are highly significant. The first is Jesus' declaration to Peter at Caesarea Philippi (Matt. 16:18: "On this rock I will build my church"; note the absence of this theme from the parallels in Mark 8:27–30 and Luke 9:18–21); the second is Jesus' instruction that unrepentant offenders should be disciplined by the church (18:17). Unmistakably, Matthew depicts Jesus as the founder of the church. To join his movement is to join the community of disciples that he has expressly called, taught, and authorized. Matthew pointedly omits Mark's story of Jesus' tolerant response to "the strange exorcist," with its concluding aphorism, "Whoever is not against us is for us" (Mark 9:38–40). Indeed, in the context of one of his polemics against the Pharisees, Matthew's Jesus provocatively reverses the aphorism: "Whoever is not with me is against me, and whoever does not gather with me scatters" (Matt. 12:30). One cannot follow Jesus, according to Matthew, except by becoming part of the community that he trained to carry out his mission in the world.

(A) A COMMUNAL ETHIC OF PERFECTION But what is the character of that community, and what specific teachings shape its life? The Sermon on the Mount calls for a life of uncompromising rigor in discipleship. The community of Jesus' followers is to be a model community living in obedience to God: the salt of the earth, the light of the world, a city set on a hill (5:13–16). This task of modeling obedience is an integral part of the community's mission: "[L]et your light shine before others, so that they may see your good works and give glory to your Father in heaven" (5:16). The church is a demonstration plot in which God's will can be exhibited. For that reason, the righteousness of Jesus' disciples must exceed that of the scribes and Pharisees; otherwise, the church will not be a compelling paradigm of the kingdom that Jesus proclaimed.

The character of the community is sketched, though not legislated in detail, in the Sermon. First of all, the Beatitudes pronounce Jesus' blessing upon those who are meek, merciful, and pure, those who make peace, and particularly those who suffer for righteousness' sake (5:3–12). The counterintuitive paradoxes of the Beatitudes alert us to the fact that Jesus' new community is a contrast society, out of synch with the "normal" order of the world. What sense does it make to say, "Blessed are those who mourn"? Such a judgment can be made only in view of the eschatological promise that accompanies it: ". . . for they will be comforted." The community of Jesus' followers lives now in anticipation of ultimate restoration by God. They do not seek to enforce God's way through violence; rather, they await God's act of putting things right. To be trained for the kingdom is to be trained to see the world from the perspective of God's future—and therefore askew from what the world counts as common sense.

The teachings of the rest of the Sermon, then, specify the character of a community that seeks to embody this eschatological vision of God's righteousness. Community members are to put away anger, lust, violence, hypocrisy, pride, and materialism. In place of these self-asserting and self-preserving behaviors, they are to love their enemies, keep their promises (including promises to their marriage partners), forgive freely as they have been forgiven by God, give alms in secret, and trust God to provide for their material needs.

When we compare these teachings to the halakic rulings of the Mishnah or the detailed regulations for community life codified in the Community Rule of the Qumran covenanters (1QS), we can hardly help noticing the rather broad and incomplete character of Matthew's programmatic presentation. As Wayne Meeks observes,

> . . . [W]e have here no system of commandments. The rules are exemplary not comprehensive, pointers to the kind of life expected in the community, but not a map of acceptable behavior. Still less does Matthew's Jesus state philosophical principles from which guidelines for behavior could be rationally derived. We are left with the puzzle that while Jesus plays the role of a conventional sage in Matthew, his teachings recorded here do not add up to an ethical system. It is not in such a program of teaching, apparently, that Matthew understands the will of God to be discovered.[9]

Matthew's rigorous summons to moral perfection cannot be rightly understood as a call to obey a comprehensive system of rules. Despite his emphasis on the church's commission to teach obedience to Jesus' commandments, Matthew sees such teaching as instrumental to a deeper goal: the transformation of character and of the heart. As Thomas W. Ogletree remarks, "Matthew is expressing in the language of law and commandment what might more appropriately be stated in the language of virtues."[10] Of course, "the language of law and commandment" is given as a part of Israel's heritage, which Matthew eagerly claims, while subjecting it to a hermeneutical transformation in light of Jesus' teaching. Whether, as Ogletree suggests, it would be more appropriate to use "the language of virtues" is a debatable point: the power of Matthew's vision is generated precisely by the paradoxical tension between his stable deontological moral categories and his message that the coming of the kingdom transforms everything, including the people who live under accountability to those categories.

While rules and commandments provide an orderly structure for the moral life, Matthew also thinks of actions as growing organically out of character. False prophets, for instance, may be recognized "by their fruits," for "a good tree cannot bear bad fruit, nor can a bad tree bear good fruit" (7:15–20). The fruit-bearing metaphor appears again in Jesus' denunciation of the Pharisees who have accused him of casting out demons "by Beelzebul, the ruler of the demons" (12:24):

> *Either make the tree good, and its fruit good; or make the tree bad, and its fruit bad; for the tree is known by its fruit. You brood of vipers! How can you speak good things, when you are evil? For out of the abundance of the heart the mouth speaks.* (12:33–34)

Speech and action are the outward manifestations of what is in the heart. Presumably that explains why, in Jesus' great parable of the final judgment, the "sheep" who inherit the kingdom prepared for them from the foundation of the world did not even know that their actions were serving Jesus: they were simply, to mix the metaphor, bearing fruit, giving expression to the goodness of their character. How is this "expressivist" view of ethics related to Matthew's emphasis on obedience to Jesus' words? Matthew gives no systematic account of the matter, but the solution to the puzzle is probably to be sought along the following lines. Action flows from character, but character is not so much a matter of innate disposition as of training in the ways of righteousness. Those who respond to Jesus' preaching and submit to his instruction will find themselves formed in a new way so that their actions will, as it were, "naturally" be wise and righteous. They will learn the skills and discernments requisite to living faithfully. In this respect, Matthew's moral vision has much in common with Israel's wisdom tradition, though Matthew is more concerned with community formation than with the cultivation of wisdom and virtue in the individual.

(B) THE HERMENEUTIC OF MERCY One of the most important character qualities that Jesus seeks to inculcate in those who heed his words is the quality of *mercy*. On two different occasions—again in dispute with the Pharisees—he cites Hosea 6:6: "I desire mercy and not sacrifice" (Matt. 9:13, 12:7). It has often been noted that this passage was cited by the great rabbi Yohanan ben Zakkai, the founder of the rabbinic academy at Jamnia, as a word of reassurance for Israel after the destruction of the Temple, when the prescribed sacrifices were no longer possible.[11] Thus, Matthew is citing a passage that had been given great hermeneutical prominence in pharisaic Judaism precisely contemporary with his composition of the Gospel, but he applies it in a different way, as we shall see. The repetition of the citation marks it as a matter of special importance for understanding Matthew's ethic.[12]

On the first occasion (9:10–13), the Pharisees are grumbling about Jesus' practice of eating with tax collectors and sinners; he replies with the proverb, "Those who are well have no need of a physician, but those who are sick." Thus far Matthew's account follows Mark 9:15–17 closely. Next, however, he inserts the Hosea quotation: "Go and learn what this means, 'I desire mercy, not sacrifice.'" The conclusion of the pericope returns to the Markan source: "For I have come to call not the righteous but sinners." What Hosea 6:6 means, according to Matthew's use of it here, is that God's mercy is extended to sinners. Nothing is said here about the destruction of the Temple, or about acts of loving-kindness as *atoning* for sin, as in Yohanan ben Zakkai's teaching, but the discussion of these issues was surely in the background for Matthew's original readers. His citation of this key scriptural text has a polemical point, as John Meier notes: "Mercy, not sacrifice, is God's will.

And, if mercy replaces the chief act of cult, how much more does it take precedence over Pharisaic rules of purity!"[13] Jesus shows God's mercy on sinners and suggests that this is precisely what the Law requires of others as well.

The second citation of Hosea 6:6 appears in the controversy over plucking grain on the Sabbath (12:1–8). Here again Matthew is following a Markan story about conflict with Pharisees, but he introduces two arguments in defense of the disciples' action that are not found in his source.

> *Or have you not read in the law that on the sabbath the priests in the temple break the sabbath and yet are guiltless? I tell you, something greater than the temple is here. But if you had known what this means, "I desire mercy and not sacrifice," you would not have condemned the guiltless.* (12:5–7)

The christological claim that Jesus is greater than the Temple and that therefore those who serve him are, like priests in the Temple, not subject to the ordinary restrictions on Sabbath activity is an extraordinarily bold—some would say nearly blasphemous—assertion; in the aftermath of the Temple's destruction, it takes on a specially freighted import. To this christological argument is coupled once again an appeal to the Hosea text: the "hermeneutic of mercy" supplants or relativizes the Law's specific commandments (cf. Exod. 34:21).[14]

In these passages we see the outworking of Matthew's earlier claim in the Sermon on the Mount that Jesus fulfills rather than negates the Law. When that formula is applied to test cases, such as eating with sinners and harvesting grain on the Sabbath, we see that the Law is understood to bear witness to what Matthew elsewhere calls "the weightier matters of the law: justice and mercy and faith" (23:23). Jesus' teaching provides a dramatic new hermeneutical filter that necessitates a rereading of everything in the Law in light of the dominant imperative of mercy. In contrast to the scribes and Pharisees, who are said to "tie up heavy burdens, hard to bear, and lay them on the shoulders of others" (23:4), the wisdom taught by Jesus yields a very different reading of Torah:

> *Come to me, all you that are weary and are carrying heavy burdens, and I will give you rest. Take my yoke upon you, and learn from me; for I am gentle and humble in heart, and you will find rest for your souls. For my yoke is easy, and my burden is light.* (11:28–30)

The language of this invitation echoes the call of the traditionally personified figure of Wisdom, often virtually equated with the Torah (see, for example, Prov. 8; Sirach 24, especially vv. 19–23; Sirach 53:23–28; Baruch 3:9–4:4). Those who take upon themselves Jesus' yoke are in effect taking up the yoke of Torah as interpreted by Jesus, but his yoke—in light of his hermeneutic of mercy—is not burdensome, in contrast to the systematic interpretations of the Torah being promulgated by Matthew's pharisaic rivals. (The invidious characterization of the Pharisees reflects a bitter conflict located in Matthew's specific historical setting, a point to which we must return below, but the reading of mercy as the real aim of the Law is a positive component of Matthew's moral vision.)

The pronouncement story about the greatest of the commandments (22:34–40) again highlights Matthew's hermeneutical transformation of the Law. In response to the Pharisee's test question, Jesus first quotes the Shema (Deut. 6:5) as the greatest of the commandments (an obvious answer for any Jew), then links to it the commandment of Leviticus 19:18: "You shall love your neighbor as yourself." So far, Matthew agrees with Mark. Once again, however, he appends his own tag line to sum up the significance of what Jesus has said: "On these two commandments hang all the law and the prophets" (22:40). This introduces a subtle but important claim. It is not merely that the two love commands are the greatest of the Torah's commandments, as Mark had affirmed (Mark 12:28–34). Rather, everything else in the Torah "hangs" upon them; everything else must be derivable from them. In consequence, the double love command becomes a hermeneutical filter—virtually synonymous with Hosea 6:6—that governs the community's entire construal of the Law. This has wide-ranging consequences for the specific content of Matthew's moral vision. Those who are trained for the kingdom of heaven are trained to evaluate all norms, even the norms of the Law itself, in terms of the criteria of love and mercy. In the community that lives this vision, then, acts of love and mercy should abound.

(C) COMMUNITY DISCIPLINE AND FORGIVENESS In light of the foregoing observations, we see that Matthew's narrative sets up a serious tension between rigor and mercy. On the one hand, the community is called to perfection: as a city set on a hill, the community is to exemplify a rigorous standard of righteousness exceeding even that of the scribes and Pharisees. On the other hand, the community is called to interpret the Torah in light of a hermeneutic of mercy that leads them to subordinate the Law's specific commandments to its deeper intent; consequently, following the example of Jesus, the community must receive tax collectors and sinners and deal mercifully with human weakness and failure. Thus, rigor and mercy are set side by side in Matthew's story. How are these apparently contradictory demands to be held together in the life of the community?

It is characteristic of Matthew that he never provides a systematic theological solution to this problem. But the fourth major discourse unit in this Gospel (18:1–35), dealing with community discipline and forgiveness, offers some guidelines for the community's practice.

> *If your brother sins against you,*[15] *go and tell him his fault, between you and him alone. If he listens to you, you have gained your brother. But if he does not listen, take one or two others along with you, that every word may be confirmed by the evidence of two or three witnesses. If he refuses to listen to them, tell it to the church; and if he refuses to listen even to the church, let him be to you as a Gentile and a tax collector. Truly, I say to you, whatever you bind on earth shall be bound in heaven, and whatever you loose on earth shall be loosed in heaven. Again I say to you, if two of you agree on earth about anything they ask, it will be done for them by my Father in heaven. For where two or three are gathered in my name, there am I in the midst of them.*[16] (18:15–20, RSV)

In this passage Jesus makes it clear that sin is not to be tolerated or ignored within the community. Someone—in the first instance, the offended party—must go to the sinner and confront him.[17] The stipulation that this initial conversation is to be "between you and him alone" is an important one: this rule, if followed, would eliminate much gossip and backbiting in the church. It also provides the opportunity for the offender to receive the word of admonition and repent without public scandal. This directive is by no means an innovation on the part of Jesus: it is a restatement of Leviticus 19:17, where the admonition to reprove the erring neighbor is an integral part of the obligation to "love your neighbor as yourself" (see Lev. 19:17–18). Not surprisingly, the Qumran community, with its urgent concern for the holiness of the community, also stressed the importance of mutual rebuke and correction, explicitly citing Leviticus 19 as the scriptural basis for this practice.[18] The requirement of additional witnesses is also based on Old Testament precedent (Deut. 19:15), although Matthew 18:16 changes the setting from a legal proceeding to the context of pastoral admonition within the community. The final step of expulsion of the unrepentant sinner from the community (18:17) indicates how seriously the imperatives of righteousness are to be taken. One cannot be an unrepentant sinner and remain within the community of Jesus' disciples.

The entire procedure prescribed in Matthew 18:15–17, however, aims at regaining the brother; the familial language of the passage is not insignificant. In the wider narrative context of the Gospel of Matthew, to say that the expelled sinner must be "as a Gentile and a tax collector" cannot mean that the person becomes a pariah to be shunned by the church; it means, rather, that the person becomes an object of the community's missionary efforts. As we have already seen, Jesus notoriously sought out fellowship with tax collectors and sinners, and he commissioned his disciples to preach the gospel to all nations (*ethnē* = "Gentiles"). Thus, the community's necessary action of expelling the offender must be read together with the immediately preceding parable of the shepherd who leaves ninety-nine sheep to search for the one that went "astray" (18:12–14). Because "it is not the will of your Father in heaven that one of these little ones should be lost," the goal of the community's disciplinary action must always be the restoration of the sinner to fellowship. Thus, the three-step disciplinary procedure of Matthew 18:15–17 both upholds the community's rigorous moral norms and provides for forgiveness and reintegration of the wrongdoer into the community's life.

At the same time, enormous authority is given to the community. In exercising its disciplinary power of "binding" and "loosing," the church effectually acts as God's agent in the world. This authority—in contrast to Matthew 16:19, where the authority to bind and loose is granted specifically to Peter—is said to be exercised by the community as a whole in its corporate decisions.[19] How can so much spiritual power be entrusted to the *ekklēsia?* The answer lies in the remarkable promise of Jesus' continuing presence in and with the gathered praying community: "For where two or three are gathered in my name, I am there among them." The community can exercise Jesus' authority because Jesus is present with them (cf. also 28:20). Thus, they are not acting merely on their own authority; they are acting under Jesus' instructions and under his continuing guidance.

Might a church entrusted with such disciplinary power be tempted to develop a proud and censorious spirit? This danger is immediately recognized and dealt with by Matthew in verses 21–35. Peter, upon hearing Jesus' instruction concerning the three-step process for calling sinful members back to the fellowship, recognizes the potential here for a never-ending cycle of sin and repentance; quite reasonably, he asks how many second chances the offender should receive. Showing a graciousness far more liberal than the widespread enthusiasm in late-twentieth-century America for a "three-strikes-and-you're-out" policy toward lawbreakers, Peter asks whether he should forgive his brother as many as seven times. Jesus' stunning answer proclaims the superabundance of divine mercy that the church is called to display to the world: "I do not say to you seven times, but seventy times seven" (18:21–22, RSV). Here again rigor and mercy are strangely combined. Jesus' disciples are faced with a demand that seems humanly incredible: to be as infinitely forgiving as is God.

The climax of this discourse on discipline and forgiveness is the parable of the unforgiving slave (18:23–35). The king in the parable forgives the slave a debt of ten thousand talents, a staggering sum that is something on the order of the national debt. ("Herod's total annual income amounted to only nine hundred talents, and the taxes imposed on Galilee and Perea together only two hundred.")[20] The slave then turns around and bullies and threatens another slave, who owes him the comparative pittance of a hundred denarii. When this comes to the attention of the king, he is furious at the unforgiving slave:

> *You wicked slave! I forgave you all that debt because you pleaded with me. Should you not have had mercy on your fellow slave, as I had mercy on you? And in anger his lord handed him over to be tortured until he would pay his entire debt. So my heavenly Father will also do to every one of you, if you do not forgive your brother or sister from your heart.* (18:32b–35)

The parable hints at the theological underpinnings of this whole chapter on church discipline and forgiveness—indeed, at the underpinnings of Matthew's understanding of the relation between God's mercy and God's demand. Mercy precedes everything: that, and only that, is why the announcement of the kingdom of heaven[21] is good news.

Shakespeare dramatizes a similar message in *Measure for Measure.* The hypocritical and judgmental Angelo declares to the pleading Isabella, the sister of a man condemned to die, "Your brother is a forfeit of the law,/ and you but waste your words." She replies,

> Why, all the souls that were were forfeit once;
> And He that might the vantage best have took
> Found out the remedy. How would you be
> If He, which is the top of judgment, should

But judge you as you are? O, think on that;
And mercy then will breathe within your lips,
Like man new made.[22]

Similarly, Matthew's summons to the disciples to forgive, to obey Jesus' words, is nothing other than a logical extension of God's mercy. And yet the threat of God's future judgment hangs over those who despise God's grace.

3. Matthew's Eschatology: "I am with you always, to the end of the age"

Matthew retains intact the early tradition's apocalyptic eschatology: his story confidently affirms the future coming of the Son of Man in glory, the resurrection of the dead, and God's final judgment (e.g., 16:27; 22:23–33; 24:3–44; 13:24–27, 36–43). Nonetheless, in contrast to the earlier role of apocalyptic traditions as the ground of hope in Paul and Mark, a subtle shift has occurred in the ethical use to which Matthew puts these eschatological motifs and in the way they relate to other elements in his theology. The nature of that shift has significant implications for understanding Matthew's moral vision.

(A) RELAXATION OF ESCHATOLOGICAL URGENCY First of all, the imminence of the eschatological expectation seems to have receded slightly in Matthew. The shift of emphasis here is subtle, for Matthew continues to affirm that "the Son of Man is coming at an unexpected hour" (24:44) and that the church should therefore remain in a state of readiness. Nonetheless, the passage of time has inevitably caused certain adjustments of perspective. Jesus has been raised from the dead, but the world goes on as before—for fifty years or more by the time Matthew writes this Gospel. The passing of years is marked by Matthew's comment on the story spread among the Jews that Jesus' disciples had stolen his body: "And this story is still told among the Jews to this day" (28:15). The Temple has been destroyed (see 24:1–2), but still history goes on as before. Various indications in the story show that Matthew has settled into the expectation of a protracted historical period prior to the eschatological consummation. Jesus established a church, an institution built on the confession of Peter (16:18), and that church has a mission to proclaim the gospel to the whole world (24:14), a project that will take time. Even within the church, some have begun to say, "My master is delayed," and to behave irresponsibly (24:48–49). Matthew warns against this attitude, but the very fact that he has to warn against it is significant (cf. 2 Pet. 3:3–4). Thus, when the Gospel concludes with Jesus' promise to be present with his community "always until the end of the age," some temporal duration for the present age is indicated. The reality of the final judgment is crucial for Matthew, but not its timing.

(B) THE PRESENCE OF JESUS One factor that allows Matthew to settle more patiently into the present age is his conviction that the risen Lord is present in and with his church. Unlike Mark, whose Gospel depicts the present as a time of absence and grim waiting for the parousia, Matthew assures his readers in numerous ways of the powerful and abiding presence of Jesus with his people. The theme first appears in the narrative as a prophecy before Jesus' birth, when the angel in Joseph's dream declares that Mary's pregnancy has occurred in accordance with God's will:

> *All this took place to fulfill what had been spoken by the Lord through the prophet:*
>
> > *"Look, the virgin shall conceive and bear a son*
> > *and they shall name him Emmanuel,"*
>
> *which means, "God with us."* (1:22–23)

This final lexical gloss is a characteristically Matthean gesture, making sure that no one can possibly miss the point. Jesus is to be the one in whom God is present to his people.

As we have already seen, the same point is made again in Jesus' instructions on church discipline. Wherever two or three gather in his name, he is there. This promise suggestively echoes a rabbinic tradition about the study of Torah: "If two sit together and words of the Law [are spoken] between them, the Divine Presence rests between them."[23] If such a tradition was already current in Matthew's time, then Matthew 18:20 serves as one more provocative claim that Jesus himself has now supplanted the Torah. How are we to understand the mode of his presence? Is he, like the *Shekinah* ("Divine Presence") in rabbinic lore, mediated textually, so that to gather in Jesus' name is virtually equated with gathering to study his words as collected in Matthew's Gospel? More likely, Matthew thinks of him as present—in a way closer to Paul's vision—as a powerful spiritual presence in the worshiping community. The *magisterium* is neither confined to an authoritative text nor transmitted through an institutional authority. It remains grounded in the personal presence of Jesus in the *ekklēsia.* In any case, his presence gives the church an experience in the present of sufficiency, clarity, and authority. The urgency of his coming again is somewhat mitigated by the consolation of his presence already.

Finally, it is no accident that the conclusion of Matthew's Gospel sounds this same note of Jesus' presence: he is present as the one who authorizes the disciples' mission (28:16–20). Beginning, middle, and end, Matthew explicitly structures this theme as the backbone of his narrative. Similarly, Matthew has also handled much of his other material in a way that reinforces the proclamation of "God with us" in Jesus, so that it underlies the whole Gospel as a ground figure. The narrative is to be read not merely as an account of historically past events but as a figurative portrayal of Jesus' ongoing presence and activity in the church. One illustration will have to suffice.

Matthew's adaptation of the Markan story of Jesus walking on the sea (Mark 6:45–52, Matt. 14:22–33) exemplifies his reading of the miracle traditions as allegories of Jesus' presence. Matthew introduces two major changes in his retelling of the story. First, he adds the tale of Peter's getting out of the boat to walk on the water along with Jesus (14:28–31). The story cries out to be read allegorically. The boat (read: church) is battered by waves and wind (read: persecution and adversity); Jesus comes mysteriously to rescue them. Peter, the leader and symbol of the disciples, ventures to emulate Jesus' miraculous actions but starts to sink and has to be saved by Jesus. Peter, still the symbolic figure, is rebuked by Jesus for his little faith. When they get into the boat and the wind ceases, the disciples worship Jesus, saying, "Truly you are the Son of God."

This last event is Matthew's second major modification of the story. In Mark, when Jesus gets into the boat and the wind ceases, the author remarks acerbically, "And they were utterly astounded, for they did not understand about the loaves, but their hearts were hardened" (6:52). No understanding, no worship, no confession, just bewilderment. Matthew finds this eminently unsatisfactory and gives this epiphany story a proper doxological ending, even though his doing so renders Peter's subsequent confession at Caesarea Philippi anticlimactic. The disciples in the boat worshiping Jesus as Son of God are manifestly a figure for the church in Matthew's own time—or any future time—which may also pray for and expect Jesus to rescue them from trials and tribulations. The meaning of the story for Matthew can be grasped only when it is interpreted as an allegorical promise of Jesus' continuing presence with the church—and therefore also as an exhortation to eschew doubt. Such promises of Jesus' presence do not supersede the hope of the parousia, but they prefigure it so palpably in the church's experience that they diminish its urgency.

(C) ESCHATOLOGY AS ETHICAL WARRANT The final shift in Matthew's use of apocalyptic eschatology is the most obvious one: in Matthew, eschatology becomes a powerful *warrant* for moral behavior. The motivation for obedience to God is repeatedly grounded in the rewards and punishments that await everyone at the final judgment. To be sure, we have seen this idea in Paul and Mark also, but Matthew greatly increases the emphasis that it receives. This is nowhere more evident than in Matthew 24:37–25:46, where he appends to the Markan apocalyptic discourse five units of additional material stressing in various ways the necessity of being prepared for the coming of the Son of Man. The first of these units (24:37–44) is a composite group of sayings highlighting the suddenness and uncertainty of the hour of judgment, comparing the coming of the Son of Man to the flood in the days of Noah or to a thief breaking into a house in the middle of the night. The other four units are all parables of judgment: the parable of the faithful and unfaithful slaves (24:45–51), the parable of the wise and foolish virgins (25:1–13), the parable of the talents (25:14–20), and the parable of the sheep and the goats (25:31–46). The primary point of the wise and foolish virgins is the same as that of 24:37–44: "Keep awake therefore, for you know neither the day nor the hour" (25:13). The other three parables, however, all underline the direct connection between faithful stewardship and one's fate in the final judgment. Those who beat the other slaves, waste the master's resources, and fail to respond to the needs of the hungry, the sick, and the prisoners will be cast into "the outer darkness, where there will be weeping and gnashing of teeth" (25:30); however, those who do their duty, make imaginative use of the resources given them, and minister to the needs of the poor will go "into eternal life" (25:46). The aim of such stories is to instill godly fear in the hearers and to motivate them to do the will of God while they still have opportunity, before the judgment comes upon them.

It would not be correct to say that these stories provide only *warrants* for obedience to God; they also define significant ethical *norms* having to do primarily with just and merciful treatment of others and with responsible use of property. (In view of the earlier teaching on possessions in Matthew [6:19–34; 19:16–30], however, the parable of the talents must be interpreted allegorically; it is not just a literal teaching about the wise investment of money.) The parable of the sheep and the goats, with its powerful portrayal of care for the needy as the basic criterion for God's eschatological judgment of human deeds, has had a powerful impact on the church's imagination; the story reinforces Matthew's earlier emphasis on mercy as the hallmark of the kingdom of God.

4. Historical Setting: Matthew As Ecclesiastical Diplomat

We can speak only hypothetically about Matthew's historical setting; we do not know with any certainty even where this Gospel was written, though recent scholarship has gravitated toward a consensus that Antioch is the likeliest location. Matthew's distinctive shaping of the story does, however, lead us to certain plausible hypotheses that make sense of many of the features of this challenging text.

The likeliest historical hypothesis is that Matthew was written sometime during the last twenty years of the first century, after the destruction of the Jerusalem Temple by the Romans. The definitive separation between church and synagogue had occurred only recently, leaving rancorous feelings on both sides, as both groups found themselves in a critical period of identity formation.[24] Matthew's Christian community was engaged in a struggle with the representatives of emergent rabbinic Judaism, each side claiming to represent the authentic interpretation of the Torah and of Israel's traditions. The strategy of the rabbis, whose roots were in pharisaic Judaism, was to circle the wagons, establishing strong group boundaries defined in terms of orthopraxy. Matthew, on the other hand, represents an originally Jewish-Christian community that chose to spiritualize the meaning of the Torah by means of a love hermeneutic and to create an inclusive community that reached out to Gentiles. Subsequent history shows that Matthew was spectacularly successful in formulating a foundational narrative for Gentile mission and almost completely unsuccessful in keeping that mission grounded in Judaism.

The crucial question that separated Matthew from "formative Judaism" was christological, for his distinctive claims about the proper reading of the Law are all grounded in his more fundamental claim that Jesus is the fulfillment and definitive interpreter of the Law. It is noteworthy that Matthew shows no trace of the earlier

Christian debates over the requirements of circumcision and dietary laws in the church. Is that because these debates were all over and Matthew's church was well on its way to becoming the Gentile "early catholic" church? Or is it because Matthew remained, on such questions, within the orbit of Judaism?[25] The general line of development of early Christianity would suggest the former as the likelier situation, but the evidence does not permit a certain decision on this point. In any case, Matthew saw the destruction of the Temple as God's definitive judgment on a corrupt and faithless generation of Jews who had rejected God's Messiah. (See extended discussion of this point in Chapter 17.) This is the situation that underlies Matthew's sharp polemic against the Pharisees.

At the same time, Matthew probably faced divisive tendencies within his own community. The warning against judging one another (7:1–5) and the procedures for resolving grievances against other members of the community (18:15–17) are of universal applicability, but we may assume that they were pertinent to actual issues in Matthew's church. The parable of the wheat and the weeds (13:24–30) and its interpretation (13:36–43) suggest that there was an active debate in Matthew's community concerning whether the church should seek to be a community of the pure or whether it should accept a more ambiguous status as *corpus mixtum* awaiting the final judgment. Matthew clearly opts for the latter view but tries to do so in a way that takes the demand for righteousness seriously. Some studies have suggested that Matthew, in writing this Gospel, was seeking (among other things) to bridge differences in the church, including social-ethical differences between wandering charismatic prophets and a more stable urban Christian community.[26] At the literary level, Matthew brings together diverse sources, including Mark's Gospel and some collection or collections of sayings of Jesus. Whether these different literary sources should be linked with specific social groups in Matthew's church is purely speculative.

In any case, the composition of this Gospel was a grand act of synthesis, pulling together disparate traditions into a master narrative that could unify the community in its confession of Jesus.[27] If this reconstruction of the situation is correct, then Matthew should be seen as "an astute church diplomat,"[28] creating a conciliatory platform for a pluralistic church. This hypothesis would explain some of the unresolved systematic tensions in Matthew, such as the tension between rigor and mercy that we have explored above. The theological tensions within the text are the conceptual deposit left by the specific challenges that Matthew confronted in his own time.

The unavoidable question is whether Matthew's synthesis *works*. Is there a coherent theological and moral vision in this text, or has Matthew simply produced an unstable compromise? To the extent that the synthesis works, it works not through systematic coherence but through the power of narrative to bind together disparate elements and hold them in solution. Matthew narrates a Jesus who proclaims the kingdom of God but at the same time demands radical ethical obedience and teaches mercy toward sinners, a Jesus who commissions the church strictly to teach and obey his commandments and yet at the same time remains present with the community to enable more flexible discernments. Leander Keck's assessment of the result is judicious: "It is precisely the logical instability of the text which prevents an ideological position from forming permanently, on the one hand, and which, on the other, makes it possible for different parts of the text to emerge with special power from one situation to the next."[29]

Thus, Matthew presents in microcosm the same possibilities—and problems—for ethics that we see on a larger scale in the New Testament canon as a whole.

5. Matthew's Narrative World As Context for Action

How does Matthew's moral vision impart a particular shape to the tasks of discipleship? In light of the foregoing observations, I offer some summary conclusions about the way in which this Gospel defines the context of moral action.

First, the world according to Matthew is *a world stabilized and given meaning by the authoritative presence of Jesus Christ.* Doubt and ambiguity have no legitimate place in the community of those who follow Jesus. Right and wrong are defined with clarity, and full-hearted obedience is to be expected as the norm within the church. The Father of Jesus Christ is the same God who gave the Torah through Moses; even though Jesus has brought a new interpretative perspective on the Torah, it remains abidingly valid. Thus, the moral order of God's dealing with the world remains stable and continuous.

Second, although the future judgment of God is sure, the present age has significance in its own right. *The present is the time of the church's mission to make disciples of all nations,* a mission that may extend into the foreseeable future. During the present age, the church stands as a model of the will of God for human community. The gates of hell cannot prevail against this community founded upon the word of Jesus.

Third, God's ultimate judgment of all will be based upon *concrete works of love and mercy,* in accordance with the teaching of Jesus. Confessional orthodoxy counts for nothing unless it is accompanied by obedience to the will of God. The kingdom of God is characterized by compassionate outreach to the weak and needy.

Fourth, the *bitter conflict with the synagogue* is a salient aspect of Matthew's world. According to Matthew, the leaders of the Jewish people have imposed upon them intolerable burdens and have led them astray from true obedience to God. The battle between Matthew's community and emergent rabbinic Judaism has left indelible scars upon Matthew's Gospel, in the form of scathing prophetic denunciations of the scribes and Pharisees. Matthew's text provides no clues about how this implacable hostility toward the traditional representatives of Israel is to be integrated with Jesus' teaching concerning the love of enemies.

Fifth, within the church, however, Matthew envisions a *community characterized by humility, patience, and concern for the "little ones"* who may stumble or be weak in faith. Love is prized above theological consistency, and forgiveness is the hallmark of the community's life. No one should be quick to judge others, for all are radically dependent upon the mercy of God.

Sixth, even though individuals will continue to sin, so that correction and forgiveness are necessary aspects of the community's life, Matthew offers no hint that the propensity to sin is related to some deep flaw in the self or, as in Paul, to a state of bondage to powers beyond the control of the will. *Obedience is represented as a simple possibility* for those who hear the word of Jesus.[30]

Seventh, the cumulative effect of these teachings is that the church is represented as a community in which people can find *security* and can act with *moral confidence*. The distinction between insiders and outsiders is clear, and those who are inside are granted to know the secrets of the kingdom of heaven. The will of God is clearly revealed in the teaching and example of Jesus, and the church is expected to obey all that he has commanded, to the end of the age.

NOTES

1. Crossan 1975, 59.
2. For a thorough summary of the evidence, see Allison 1993, 140–165. Cf. France 1989, 186–189.
3. Some of the material in these units is taken from the Markan source; however, in each case, Matthew has supplemented it significantly.
4. The precise formula appears in 7:28 and 19:1, with minor variations in 11:1 and 13:53 (the parallelism is clearer in the Greek text than in most English translations). The last time the formula occurs (26:1), Matthew emphasizes the finality of the foregoing discourse with an emphatic cadence: "When Jesus had finished *all* these words. . . ." Kingsbury's argument (1975) that Matthew should be read as having a tripartite structure downplays this clear evidence of authorial structuring and points instead to the phrase "From that time Jesus began . . ." (4:17, 16:21) as a major structural marker. Kingsbury's reading is to be rejected, not least because it splits the Caesarea Philippi pericope (16:13–28; cf. Mark 8:27–9:1) in half.
5. The sentence is taken from Mark 1:22, where it refers to Jesus' teaching in the synagogue at Capernaum; Mark, however, neglects to tell us the actual content of Jesus' teaching. For him, the authority of Jesus is manifested more decisively in his power over demons (Mark 1:27) than in his Moses-like instruction in the way of righteousness.
6. One of the most thoroughgoing demonstrations that the Sermon on the Mount must be read in the context of debates with emergent rabbinic Judaism is W. D. Davies's magisterial work *The Setting of the Sermon on the Mount* (1964). Despite criticism of various particulars of Davies's work, its central thesis remains persuasive and has commanded virtually universal scholarly assent.
7. Scholars count as few as eleven or as many as fourteen, depending on how strictly the formula is defined. See 1:22–23, 2:5–6, 2:15, 2:17–18, 2:23, 3:3, 4:14–16, 8:17, 12:17–21, 13:14–15 (referring to the people who do not understand), 13:35, 21:4–5, 26:56 (no text explicitly cited), and 27:9–10 (referring to Judas). The foundational study of these passages is Stendahl 1968 [1954].
8. Stendahl (1968 [1954]) suggests that this sort of organized scribal activity might have occurred within a "school" of Christian scribes.
9. Meeks 1986b, 140.
10. Ogletree 1983, 111.
11. Noted by Ernst von Dobschütz, "Matthew as Rabbi and Catechist," in Stanton 1983, 20; W. D. Davies 1964, 306–307.
12. The following passages are best read with the aid of a synopsis of the Gospels, such as Throckmorton 1992, or, for those who can use the Greek text, Aland 1985.
13. Meier 1980, 94–95.
14. The apt phrase "hermeneutic of mercy" is taken from Meier 1980, 130.
15. Although the words "against you" appear in the majority of later Greek texts, they are absent from some of the oldest and best manuscripts. A good case can be made that they do not belong to the original form of the text. For an argument in favor their inclusion, however, see Davies and Allison 1991 (vol. 2), 782 n. 3.
16. In this case I have cited the RSV in preference to the NRSV, whose laudable effort to employ inclusive language in the passage renders it cumbersome and loses the crucial familial metaphor in v. 15: the offender is not

just "another member of the church" (NRSV) but "your brother" (RSV, translating the Greek text literally). Of course, the provisions of the passage apply to male and female members of the community alike.

17. Since I have quoted the RSV, I will continue here to use masculine pronouns to refer to the offender. The reader is trusted to supply the tacit understanding that women, as well as men, can be sinners in need of admonition and discipline.

18. 1QS 5.25–6.1; CD 9.2–4.

19. The verbs in 18:18 are second-person plural, in contrast to the second-person singular verbs in the parallel formulation of 16:19.

20. E. Schweizer 1975, 377.

21. Matthew prefers the phrase "kingdom of heaven" to "kingdom of God," the characteristic phrase in Mark and Luke. Matthew's usage does not reflect a conception of the kingdom as otherworldly; rather, it is a pious circumlocution—in accord with Jewish practice—to avoid using the name of God.

22. *Measure for Measure*, act II, scene iii.

23. m.Aboth 3.2.

24. For a balanced and helpful discussion of the historical evidence, see Stanton 1992, 113–281.

25. Luz 1989, 79–95, takes the latter view. "Matthew obviously does not know Paul and his theology; but it is basically the case that he would belong to the side of the opponents of Paul" (87).

26. Keck 1984, 42–43, following the work of Theissen 1978.

27. For a carefully nuanced discussion of Matthew's achievement in this regard, see R. E. Brown 1984, 124–145.

28. Keck 1984, 43.

29. Keck 1984, 55.

30. Keck 1984, 41–42.

Chapter 5

Luke-Acts

Liberation through the Power of the Spirit

The Gospel of Luke and the Acts of the Apostles are two parts of a single grand literary work in which Luke tells the story of salvation history in a stately and gracious manner. God's mighty act of deliverance through Jesus Christ is narrated as an epic, in such a way that the church might discover its location in human history, particularly within the history of God's dealings with his people Israel.[1] The two-part structure of the work allows the author[2] to present the emergence of the church as a clear and necessary sequel to the activity of Jesus. The opening of the second volume makes this relation between the parts abundantly clear:

> *I made the first book, Theophilus, about everything that Jesus began to do and to teach until the day when—after giving instructions through the Holy Spirit to the apostles whom he chose—he was taken up.* (Acts 1:1–2, RH)

This literal rendering of the Greek calls attention to Luke's significant turn of phrase suggesting that the Gospel narrates only the beginning of what Jesus set out to accomplish; the apostles whom he chose and instructed are to carry the action forward in the second book, under the guidance of the Holy Spirit.

Although Luke used Mark as a source for his Gospel, his style and sensibility differ dramatically from Mark's. To move from reading Mark to reading Luke is like moving from Beowulf to Milton. In both cases, the former presents a shadowy world whose bleak passion we can comprehend only in part, through a glass darkly; the latter portrays a well-lit civilized world informed by the social and literary conventions of classical antiquity. Part of Luke's literary achievement is to make the foreboding story of Jesus seem reasonable and inviting to a more cultured readership in the Hellenistic world.

Luke announces in the prologue of the Gospel that he intends to narrate everything *kathexēs:* "in good order."

> *Since many have undertaken to set down an orderly account of the events that have been fulfilled among us, just as they were handed on to us by those who from the beginning were eyewitnesses and servants of the word, I too decided, after investigating everything carefully from the very first, to write an orderly account for you, most excellent Theophilus, so that you may know the truth concerning the things about which you have been instructed.*
> (LUKE 1:1–4)

Luke's designation of the account as "orderly" does not mean just that he aims for historical accuracy. Rather, it means that he intends to narrate a well-wrought tale, telling the story in such a way that the reader will come to perceive and trust the orderliness of God's plan in history.[3] The Greek word translated "truth" in the NRSV ("so that you may know the truth") is *asphaleia,* which means "firmness," "certainty," or "security"; the English word "asphalt" is derived from this root. We might paraphrase Luke's claim by saying that he aims to assure his readers of the *solidity* of the instruction that they have received. Thus, "Theophilus"[4] should be reassured by Luke's two-part story of the reliability of the Christian tradition, and moved—as are so many characters in Luke's story—to glorify God.

The constancy of God's purpose is to be discerned above all in the deep correspondences between the Old Testament and Luke's Gospel story. Unlike Matthew, who focuses on the fulfillment of prophetic *predictions*, Luke has a subtler perception of the continuity between Scripture and his own narrative. That continuity is manifest first of all in Luke's language, which consciously adopts septuagintal diction, especially in the birth narratives of Luke 1–2. As Nils Dahl observes, Luke's imitation of biblical style hints that he is consciously composing "a continuation of Biblical history."[5] Furthermore, not only the language but also the plot structure of Luke's narrative reflects patterns derived from the Old Testament. The birth and infancy narratives, for instance, resound with echoes of the stories of Sarah and Abraham (Gen. 17–18) and Hannah (1 Sam. 1–2).[6] Luke neither quotes these passages nor calls attention to the typology by means of any citation formula; nonetheless, the reader who knows the Old Testament background will discern how Luke has woven these motifs seamlessly into his story.[7]

Most significantly, Luke presents the events surrounding Jesus' life as the fulfillment of God's *promises* to Israel. Scripture is read not as a book of oracular predictions about future events but as a book of promises to God's chosen people, promises that have been made good in the dramatic events of Jesus' ministry, death, and resurrection as well as in the subsequent experience of the church. God's word to Israel is a binding, self-involving commitment that can find fulfillment only in God's action of saving the people. The climax of Mary's song of praise (the Magnificat) in Luke 1:47–55 declares that this saving action has become—or soon will become—a reality through the child that she bears in her womb.

He has helped his servant Israel,
in remembrance of his mercy,
according to the promise he made to our ancestors,
to Abraham and to his descendants forever. (LUKE 1:54–55)

The repeated stress on promise and fulfillment is a distinctive and foundational motif of Luke-Acts; consequently, Lukan ethics becomes comprehensible only as an aspect of his larger vision for the people of God as the bearers of the fulfilled promise.

In order to see how Luke relates the narrative of Jesus' career to his normative vision for the church, we must look first at Luke's representation of Jesus, then at his portrayal of the Spirit-empowered community, and finally at the way in which Luke's eschatology frames his ethics. After considering these themes in turn, we shall attempt to summarize how Luke's narrative world provides a context for moral discernment and action.

1. Luke's Christology: "The Spirit of the Lord is upon me"

As we have already observed, there is a strong correlation between each evangelist's portrayal of Jesus and his consequent ethical vision for the community. Thus, it is important to bring Luke's Christology clearly into focus in order to understand Lukan ethics. No single christological conception, however, systematically governs Luke's presentation of Jesus. In an eclectic fashion, he has combined a number of christological traditions.

In contrast to later Christian theology, Luke is not particularly concerned to make ontological claims about Jesus' person; indeed, the notion that one could distinguish between the *work* of Jesus and his *person* and then talk about the latter in substantialist categories is foreign to Luke's thought-world. Unlike John, Luke has no doctrine of Christ's preexistence, nor does he share the conviction of Matthew and John that the risen Jesus remains present in the church; that role is taken in Luke's narrative by the Holy Spirit poured out on the church. Luke's Christology is functional: Jesus is understood in terms of what he has done, in terms of the role he has played in bringing God's salvation to the world. That is why Luke's use of Scripture is generally allusive rather than overt: he is not trying to prove that Jesus is, for instance, the servant of God prophesied by Isaiah; rather, Jesus fulfills God's promise to Israel by accomplishing the deliverance that the servant prefigured.

Out of the numerous christological images employed by Luke, we shall consider here three of the most consequential: the Spirit-empowered servant, the prophet like Moses, and the righteous martyr. Each of these will have a bearing on Luke's subsequent portrayal of the church's vocation.

(A) THE SPIRIT-EMPOWERED SERVANT In Luke's narrative, immediately following the temptation in the wilderness, Jesus returns "with the power of the Spirit" to Galilee and appears in the synagogue at Nazareth on the Sabbath. Here Luke has rearranged the Markan narrative sequence. Whereas Mark places Jesus' appearance in his hometown synagogue much later in the story (Mark 6:1–6a), after a large number of healings, controversies, and teachings, Luke has moved the story to the very beginning of Jesus' public ministry and turned it into a programmatic statement.[8] Whereas Mark says merely that Jesus "began to teach in the synagogue," Luke offers a full account of what Jesus said on that occasion. His teaching is nothing less than a public announcement of his messianic vocation.

> *When he came to Nazareth, where he had been brought up, he went to the synagogue on the sabbath day, as was his custom. He stood up to read, and the scroll of the prophet Isaiah was given to him. He unrolled the scroll and found the place where it was written:*
>
> > *"The Spirit of the Lord is upon me,*
> > *because he has anointed me to bring good news to the poor.*
> > *He has sent me to proclaim release to the captives*
> > *and recovery of sight to the blind,*
> > *to let the oppressed go free,*
> > *to proclaim the year of the Lord's favor."*[9]
>
> *And he rolled up the scroll, gave it back to the attendant, and sat down. The eyes of all in the synagogue were fixed on him. Then he began to say to them, "Today this scripture has been fulfilled in your hearing."* (LUKE 4:16–21)

At first the crowd responds favorably to Jesus' "gracious words" (4:22), but things quickly turn ugly when he suggests, using stories about the prophets Elijah and Elisha, that God's "favor" is not restricted to Israelites (4:25–27): the people are "filled with rage" and try to throw him off a cliff, but he makes his escape (4:28–30).

If Luke's story of Jesus' proclamation in the synagogue at Nazareth should be read as a messianic manifesto, what does it tell us about Jesus' identity and mission? Several major Lukan themes appear here.

- ➢ The appeal to Isaiah 61:1–2 (and 58:6) places Jesus squarely in line with Israel's prophetic tradition. Jesus both claims the authority of that tradition as authorization of his own proclamation and claims that the tradition is to be fulfilled in his own activity. In effect, he takes the mantle of the *pais theou*, the "servant of God" depicted in Isaiah's prophecy.

- Jesus is implicitly identified here as God's anointed one, the Messiah. Because the Spirit has anointed (*echrisen*) him, he is the *Christos*. Luke has already told us that the Spirit descended upon Jesus at his baptism (3:21–22) and that Jesus is empowered by the Spirit (4:1, 14). The close linkage of servant, Messiah, and Spirit is distinctively Lukan.
- The servant's vocation is to proclaim good news to the poor, the blind, the captives, and the oppressed. Thus, for Luke, Jesus' messianic activity is the work of *liberation*, and the direct link of the gospel to the message of the prophets is to be found in the prophetic call for *justice*. (The contrast here to Matthew's primary interest in prophecy as predictive of discrete events in the Messiah's career is striking.) The particular Isaiah texts that are conflated in Luke's account are significant: Isaiah 61 promises the deliverance and restoration of Israel, and Isaiah 58 is a powerful statement of God's demand for service to the poor:

  Is not this the fast that I choose:
  to loose the bonds of injustice,
  to undo the thongs of the yoke,
  to let the oppressed go free,
  and to break every yoke?
  Is it not to share your bread with the hungry,
  and bring the homeless poor into your house;
  when you see the naked, to cover them,
  and not to hide yourself from your own kin? . . .
  Then you shall call, and the Lord will answer;
  you shall cry for help, and he will say, Here I am. (ISA. 58:6–7, 9)

  By evoking these texts at the beginning of his ministry, Luke's Jesus declares himself as the Messiah who by the power of the Spirit will create a restored Israel in which justice and compassion for the poor will prevail. All of Jesus' miracles and healings throughout Luke's Gospel are therefore to be read as signs of God's coming kingdom, in which the oppressed will be set free. A similar understanding of Jesus' activity is articulated in Acts 10:38: "God anointed Jesus of Nazareth with the Holy Spirit and with power; . . . he went about doing good and healing all who were oppressed by the devil, for God was with him" (cf. Luke 7:18–23).
- The dramatic development of the story prefigures the message that God's salvation is for everyone whom God may call, including Gentiles. Already the opening scene of Jesus' public ministry foreshadows both the extension of God's grace beyond the boundaries of Israel and the hostility of many in Israel to this inclusive message of grace. The issues and tensions set in motion here will continue right through to the last page of Acts.

In sum, the announcement in the synagogue at Nazareth is a declaration that Jesus has been empowered by the Spirit to inaugurate the liberation of God's people. The book of Acts will subsequently show how this liberation unfolds in the life of the church.

(B) THE PROPHET LIKE MOSES As in Matthew, so also in Luke there are intimations that the ministry of Jesus corresponds typologically to that of Moses, although Luke's thematic emphasis falls less on Moses as teacher and law-giver than on Moses as prophetic liberator of his people.[10] In the Lukan transfiguration story, for instance, Moses and Elijah speak with Jesus concerning "his *exodus*, which he was going to *fulfill* in Jerusalem" (Luke 9:31, RH, emphasis mine). The passage of Jesus through death into resurrection life is interpreted here as the antitype of Israel's journey out of bondage in Egypt into the promised land. Indeed, some interpreters have suggested that Jesus' journey to Jerusalem in Luke 9:51–19:44 corresponds structurally to Deuteronomy 1–26. As David Moessner has concluded,

> The career of Moses has indeed converged with the career of Jesus, who fulfills "all the prophets" "beginning with Moses" (Luke 24:27). As he is sent on a New Exodus, Jesus brings the promises of the covenant life to fulfillment precisely as he is rejected by an unrepenting people. . . . [This] leitmotiv of Deuteronomy is thus the driving force of Luke's plotting of the anointed prophet sent to Israel in the Central Section [of Luke's Gospel]. . . . Luke then presents the journeying Jesus of the Central Section as *the prophet like Moses of Deut 18:15–19.*[11]

Whether or not one accepts the hypothesis that Deuteronomy provides a detailed foundation for Luke's structuring of material in his Gospel, it cannot be denied that Luke understands Jesus to be Deuteronomy's "prophet like Moses," for two passages in Acts make this identification explicit.

Following the healing of a lame man in the Temple, Peter calls the assembled crowd of hearers to repentance, claiming directly that Jesus, whom God had "raised up," was the prophet whom Moses had foretold:

> *Moses said, "The Lord your God will raise up for you from your own people a prophet like me. You must listen to whatever he tells you. And it will be that everyone who does not listen to that prophet will be utterly rooted out of the people" [Deut 18:15, 19].*[12] *And all the prophets, as many as have spoken, from Samuel and those after him, also predicted these days. . . . When God raised up his servant, he sent him first to you, to bless you by turning each of you from your wicked ways.* (ACTS 3:22–23, 25)

The mighty work of healing the lame man in Jesus' name is analogous to the "signs and wonders" done by Moses (cf. Deut. 34:10–12). The miracles done first by Jesus and now by his apostles are warnings to the people: they must accept Jesus as the prophet like Moses and repent and obey his words if they are to find life. Those who remain stubborn and refuse to follow him will be cut off from the covenant people.

Luke Johnson has demonstrated that this typological correspondence between Jesus and Moses governs the retelling of the Moses story in Stephen's speech just before his martyrdom (Acts 7), which once again refers explicitly to Moses' word that God would raise up a prophet "as he raised me up" (7:37). Johnson comments:

> Moses is . . . sent twice, the first time in weakness, the second time in power. There are two offers of salvation to the people. The first is rejected out of ignorance, and leads to a

> second chance. When this is refused despite the overwhelming evidence of signs and wonders, God rejects the people. These elements strikingly parallel Luke's account of Jesus. . . . Luke in his portrayal of Moses has given us the essential clue for understanding his overall story.[13]

The "necessity" of Jesus' suffering is determined by the necessity of conformity to the Mosaic typology.

All of this has major implications for understanding the ethical imperatives that confront the church. As the new people of God summoned by the prophet like Moses, they are to journey with him, to heed his teachings, to know themselves as the new covenant people who are to fulfill the Deuteronomic vision of Israel's destiny.

(C) THE RIGHTEOUS MARTYR Luke's passion narrative, more than any of the other Gospels, stresses the innocence of Jesus. Pilate three times declares that "he has done nothing to deserve death" (Luke 23:4, 13–15, 22). One of the criminals crucified alongside Jesus mocks him, but the other rebukes the mocker:

> *Do you not fear God, since you are under the same sentence of condemnation? And we indeed have been condemned justly, for we are getting what we deserve for our deeds, but this man has done nothing wrong.* (23:40–41)

At the moment of Jesus' death, the Roman centurion "praised God and said, 'Certainly this man was innocent [*dikaios*]'" (23:47). This last instance is particularly noteworthy, for Luke has placed this declaration of innocence in the centurion's mouth in place of Mark's "Truly this man was God's Son" (Mark 15:39).

How are we to interpret this emphasis on Jesus' innocence? The standard explanation, classically articulated by Hans Conzelmann, has been that it is a piece of political apologetic, designed to present the church in the best light before Roman authority, as a politically harmless group.[14] Several substantial arguments have been mounted against this interpretation; perhaps the most telling of these is the objection that it overlooks the scriptural background of the Lukan declarations of Jesus' innocence.[15] The description of Jesus as *dikaios* may recall Isaiah 53:11 LXX, which speaks of a "Righteous One" who will take away the sins of many. But a more apposite parallel still is to be found in Wisdom of Solomon 2:12–20. In the following translation, I have underlined the expressions that might have been read by Luke as prefiguring Jesus:

> *Let us lie in wait for the Righteous One [**ton dikaion**],*
> *because he is inconvenient to us and opposes our actions;*
> *he reproaches us for sins against the law,*
> *and accuses us for sins against our training.*
> *He professes to have knowledge of God,*
> *and calls himself a child of the Lord [**paida kyriou**]. . . .*
> *Let us see if his words are true,*

and let us test what will happen at the end of his life;
*for if the Righteous One is God's Son [**ho dikaios huios theou**], he will help him,*
and will deliver him from the hand of his adversaries.
Let us test him with insult and torture,
so that we may find out how gentle he is,
and make trial of his forbearance.
Let us condemn him to a shameful death,
for, according to what he says, he will be protected.
(WISDOM OF SOLOMON 2:12–13, 17–20, AA)

When Luke's account of Jesus' innocence is read against the background of Wisdom of Solomon, it fits smoothly into the larger pattern of the suffering and vindication of the righteous man, as seen repeatedly in the lament Psalms. The centurion's declaration that this man was *dikaios* is then seen to be an instance of Lukan dramatic irony. The centurion intends no more than to say, "He was innocent," but the reader who hears the echoes of Wisdom of Solomon hears, "He was the Righteous One."[16]

This reading of the Lukan passion narrative is strongly reinforced by two retrospective references to the death of Jesus in Acts. In Peter's speech in Acts 3, he reproaches his Jerusalem hearers with their culpability for Jesus' crucifixion:

> *[T]he God of our ancestors has glorified his servant [**pais**] Jesus, whom you handed over and rejected in the presence of Pilate, though he had decided to release him. But you rejected the Holy and Righteous One [**ton hagion kai dikaion**] and asked to have a murderer given to you, and you killed the Author of life, whom God raised from the dead. To this we are witnesses.* (ACTS 3:13–15)

Similarly, in Acts 7 the climax of Stephen's speech again accuses the people of killing the Righteous One:

> *You stiff-necked people, uncircumcised in heart and ears, you are forever opposing the Holy Spirit, just as your ancestors used to do. Which of the prophets did your ancestors not persecute? They killed those who foretold the coming of the Righteous One [**tou dikaiou**], and now you have become his betrayers and murderers.* (ACTS 7:51–52)

The cumulative effect of these passages is to demonstrate that Jesus died in accordance with the Scriptures, as the Righteous One prefigured in Isaiah, the lament psalms, and Wisdom of Solomon.[17] His death once again confirms that the true prophet must be rejected, and it also establishes a pattern for his followers—as the martyrdom of Stephen shows.

Jesus in the Lukan passion narrative remains serene and steadfast, forgiving his enemies (23:34), speaking compassionately to one of the criminals crucified with him (23:43), and commending his spirit into God's hands (23:46). The latter passage once again exemplifies Luke's artful transformation of his Markan source. In Mark's narrative, the dying Jesus cries, "My God, my God, why have you forsaken me?"

seizing in his anguish upon the words of Psalm 22:1. Luke, finding this portrayal inconsistent with his interpretation of Jesus, substitutes the words of a different royal lament psalm, Psalm 31:5:

> *Into your hand I commit my spirit;*
> *you have redeemed me, O Lord, faithful God.*

Thus, while maintaining the claim that Jesus' death was in all its particulars in accordance with Scripture, Luke depicts Jesus as a model martyr[18] like the Maccabean martyrs whose deaths are narrated in 2 Maccabees 6–7 and 4 Maccabees 5–18. A single example, the death of Eleazar as told in 4 Maccabees, will illustrate the similarity:

> *When he was now burned to his very bones and about to expire, he lifted up his eyes to God and said, "You know, O God, that though I might have saved myself, I am dying in burning torments for the sake of the law. Be merciful to your people, and let our punishment suffice for them. Make my blood their purification, and take my life in exchange for theirs."* (4 Macc. 6:26–29)

Commenting on this same martyr's death, the author of 2 Maccabees remarks, "So in this way he died, leaving in his death an example of nobility and a memorial of courage, not only to the young but to the great body of his nation" (2 Macc. 6:31). The martyr's manner of death is seen to be not a disconfirmation of his righteousness or relation to God; rather, by heroically surmounting suffering and death, the martyr demonstrates the depth of his faith and the truth of his convictions. Jesus, by the manner of his death, proves himself truly to be the Righteous One and at the same time supplies a paradigm of faith.

None of these images adequately sums up Jesus' significance for Luke. They are like strands woven together with others into a rope that is larger and more substantial than any of the individual strands. Jesus is more than a Spirit-anointed servant who proclaims justice, more than a prophet like Moses, more than a righteous martyr who gives a noble example of faithfulness: he is the one who fulfills the promises implicit in all these scripturally foreshadowed figures. He is the pivot-point of God's plan to bring salvation to the world. Still, each of these significant strands in Luke's Christology has a role to play in his constructive vision for the life of the community that is liberated by Jesus.

2. The Church in the Power of the Spirit

(A) JESUS AS PARADIGM FOR THE CHURCH'S MINISTRY In the Acts of the Apostles, the ministry inaugurated by Jesus is transferred over to the church. "Everything that Jesus began to do and to teach" (Acts 1:1, RH) is now to be carried forward by those who act in his name.

Just as Jesus was anointed by the Spirit to bring good news to the poor, so in Acts the church is anointed by the Spirit to proclaim the gospel to all nations. The outpouring of the Spirit at Pentecost is the event that empowers the church to continue Jesus' work. At the conclusion of Luke's Gospel, after the resurrection, Jesus instructs the disciples to remain in Jerusalem to await this anointing with power:

> *Thus it is written, that the Messiah is to suffer and to rise from the dead on the third day, and that repentance and forgiveness of sins is to be proclaimed in his name to all nations, beginning from Jerusalem. . . . And see, I am sending upon you what my Father promised; so stay here in the city until you have been clothed with power from on high.*
> (LUKE 24:46–49)

The promise is repeated at the beginning of Acts, before Jesus' ascension to heaven: "You will receive power when the Holy Spirit has come upon you; and you will be my witnesses in Jerusalem, in all Judea and Samaria, and to the ends of the earth" (Acts 1:8). Although Luke's primary interest here is in the Spirit's conferral of power for witnessing about Jesus, we must remember that Jesus had defined his own mission in terms of good news for the poor, release to the captives, and letting the oppressed go free. Thus, the apostles' Spirit-empowered preaching about Jesus will necessarily include the same message of liberation.

Despite Luke's special interest in telling the story of the apostles as successors to Jesus, his vision of the power of the Spirit in the church extends in a more comprehensive and egalitarian way to the whole people of God. In his Pentecost sermon, Peter explains the outpouring of the Spirit on the whole community by citing a prophecy from Joel:

> *In the last days it will be, God declares,*
> *That I will pour out my Spirit upon all flesh,*
> *and your sons and your daughters shall prophesy,*
> *and your young men shall see visions,*
> *and your old men shall dream dreams.*
> *Even upon my slaves, both men and women,*
> *in those days I will pour out my Spirit;*
> *and they shall prophesy.* (ACTS 2:17–18, quoting JOEL 2:28–29)

The Spirit does not fall just upon the apostles; rather, "the promise is for you, for your children, and for all who are far away, everyone whom the Lord our God calls to him" (Acts 2:39). Implied in this gift of the Spirit for all is the empowering of all to take up Jesus' vocation of proclaiming liberty to the captives. Indeed, the call to repentance (Luke 24:47, Acts 2:38), which lies at the heart of the gospel proclamation for Luke, includes precisely the call to reform individual lives and community practices in accordance with the prophetic vision of justice, as set forth in the Isaiah texts that stand as the keynote for Jesus' proclamation of the kingdom of God.

Just as Jesus was revealed to be the prophet like Moses, so now the apostles are revealed to be prophets like Jesus: they carry forward his vocation "to heal and to reveal."[19] Like him, they are to proclaim repentance and forgiveness, liberation from bondage. Like him, they are to do "signs and wonders" which are both acts of divine mercy and warnings to Israel to acknowledge the divine authority of Jesus' name. Many of the miracle stories in Acts deliberately mirror the Gospel's account of Jesus' deeds. To cite one particularly dramatic example, Peter's raising of Dorcas from death (Acts 9:36–43) closely recapitulates Jesus' raising of the daughter of Jairus (Luke 8:40–42, 49–56).[20] Like Moses and Jesus, the apostles teach and shape the community of God's people (Acts 2:42–47, 4:32–37).

The homology between Jesus and the church extends also to his role as righteous martyr. As we have already noted, the death of Stephen (Acts 7:54–60) is modeled on the account of Jesus' death. James the brother of John also suffers a martyr's death (Acts 12:1–2), and the proclaimers of the gospel throughout the narrative suffer mob opposition and arrest in a manner reminiscent of the passion narrative. Paul's resolution to go to Jerusalem, where he will be arrested (Acts 19:21; 21:10–14), recapitulates Jesus' setting his face to go to Jerusalem (Luke 9:51); both of them face the prospect of death with the confidence that their suffering is part of the divine plan. In short, the apostolic hardships of the Acts narrative can be read as the fulfillment of Jesus' call to surrender everything and take up the cross in order to follow him (Luke 9:23–27; 14:25–33). Despite the power unleashed in the church by the Holy Spirit and the joy attending the spread of the gospel, Luke does not minimize suffering; to join "the Way" is to volunteer for risky duty.

(B) THE NEW COMMUNITY: "GREAT GRACE WAS UPON THEM ALL" From the beginning of Luke's Gospel, it is evident that God's saving action intends the formation of a *people,* not merely the salvation of individuals. The angel Gabriel, appearing to Zechariah, declares that the son to be born to him and his wife Elizabeth—that is, John the Baptist—will have as his mission "to make ready a people prepared for the Lord" (Luke 1:17). The canticles of the birth narrative repeatedly interpret Jesus' birth as a sign of God's deliverance of Israel (Luke 1:54–55; 1:68–79; 2:29–32), and the interpretation of John's preaching in terms of Isaiah 40:3–5 sets the scene for understanding Jesus' activity as a restoration of Israel, in accordance with the prophetic vision (Luke 3:1–6). Broadly speaking, the plot line of the Gospel—particularly the "journey narrative" of 9:51–19:44—shows Jesus calling and instructing the nucleus of the new covenant people that God is calling into existence, as Luke Johnson notes:

> On the way to Jerusalem to face his rejection and death at the hands of the leaders, the prophet Jesus is forming the true people of God around himself. The crowds are being called to repentance, and those who respond are being instructed in the nature of discipleship. But those who reject the prophet are being warned of their own rejection by God.[21]

Thus, by the time Jesus reaches Jerusalem, Luke can speak of "the whole multitude of the disciples" welcoming Jesus as king (Luke 19:37).

The formation of the new community, however, becomes most visible after Pentecost. With the outpouring of the Spirit, thousands of new believers are added to the original nucleus, and the community in Jerusalem takes on a distinctive form of life:

> *They devoted themselves to the apostles' teaching and fellowship, to the breaking of bread and the prayers. Awe came upon everyone, because many wonders and signs were being done by the apostles. All who believed were together and had all things in common; they would sell their possessions and goods and distribute the proceeds to all, as any had need. Day by day, as they spent much time together in the temple, they broke bread at home and ate their food with glad and generous hearts, praising God and having the goodwill of all the people. And day by day the Lord added to their number those who were being saved.* (ACTS 2:42–47)

In Acts 4 Luke offers another description of this newly formed fellowship:

> *Now the whole group of those who believed were of one heart and soul, and no one claimed private ownership of any possessions, but everything they owned was held in common. With great power the apostles gave their testimony to the resurrection of the Lord Jesus, and great grace was upon them all, for there was not a needy person among them; for as many as owned lands or houses sold them and brought the proceeds of what was sold. They laid it at the apostles' feet, and it was distributed to each as any had need.* (ACTS 4:32–35)

Here I have altered the NRSV slightly. That version places a full stop between verses 33 and 34 and leaves the word *gar* ("for") at the beginning of verse 34 untranslated. The Greek syntax (". . . great grace was upon them all, *for* there was not a needy person among them"), however, indicates a causal relationship between the clauses: the absence of needy persons in the community is itself the warrant for the preceding theological claim that "great grace was upon them all."

Whether these descriptions are historically factual or not,[22] Luke here portrays the church after Pentecost as the fulfillment of two ancient ideals: the Greek ideal of true friendship and the Deuteronomic ideal of the covenant community. Already in Aristotle's *Nicomachean Ethics*, it is assumed that the ideals of sharing and unity of soul between friends are truisms: "All the proverbs agree with this: 'Friends have one soul between them' and 'Friends' goods are common property.'"[23] Thus, the Jerusalem community embodies in its life together the Greek vision of authentic friendship, not just between two people or within a small intimate circle but now exponentially expanded into the life of a community of thousands. Hostility, mistrust, and selfishness are replaced by a communal ethic of sharing that treats all members of the community as friends in accordance with the philosophical ideal. At the same time, this community in which it can be said that "there is no needy person among them" shows itself to be the authentic Israel, living in accordance with the covenant provisions of Deuteronomy 15:

> *There will, however, be no one in need among you, because the Lord is sure to bless you in the land that the Lord your God is giving you as a possession to occupy, if only you will obey the Lord your God by diligently observing this entire commandment that I command you today. . . . If there is among you anyone in need, a member of your community in any of your towns within the land that the Lord your God is giving you, do not be hard-hearted*

or tight-fisted toward your needy neighbor. You should rather open your hand, willingly lending enough to meet the need, whatever it may be. (DEUT. 15:4–5, 7–8)

Accordingly, in the church's common life of economic sharing, we see the fruition—or at least the first fruits—of the mission that Jesus announced in Luke 4:16–21: to bring into being a restored Israel in which good news is proclaimed and enacted for the poor and oppressed.

The community's practice of distributing goods to meet the needs of the poor is also a response of obedience to Jesus' teaching throughout Luke's Gospel, which shows a distinctive concern about this problem. It is possible here to note only a few of the most important Lukan texts that manifest this urgent concern for the sharing of resources with the needy. The Lukan Beatitudes pronounce blessing simply upon the poor and the hungry, not (as in Matthew) upon the "poor in spirit" and those who "hunger and thirst for righteousness" (Luke 6:20–21; cf. Matt. 5:3, 6). That Luke rejects the spiritualizing interpretation of these Beatitudes is shown unmistakably by the accompanying pronouncement of prophetic woes:

But woe to you who are rich,
for you have received your consolation.
Woe to you who are full now,
for you will be hungry.
Woe to you who are laughing now,
for you will mourn and weep. (LUKE 6:24–25)

This condemnation of the rich receives dramatic expression in two powerful Lukan parables: the rich fool (12:13–21) and the rich man and Lazarus (16:19–31). In both cases, the heaping up of wealth is exposed as a terrible miscalculation, even as a cause for eternal torment. The latter parable paints a graphic contrast between the rich man, who "feasted sumptuously every day," and the poor man Lazarus, covered with sores, who lay at the rich man's gate and "longed to satisfy his hunger with what fell from the rich man's table." When their fortunes are reversed in the afterlife, the rich man begs Abraham(!) to send Lazarus back from the dead to warn his five brothers. Abraham replies, "They have Moses and the prophets; they should listen to them." For example, they should read Deuteronomy 15 and Isaiah 58. The rich man—apparently knowing that his brothers are not avid Bible readers—persists: "No, father Abraham; but if someone goes to them from the dead, they will repent." Abraham's chilling answer reveals much about Lukan theology and ethics: "If they do not listen to Moses and the prophets, neither will they be convinced even if someone rises from the dead." Even the resurrection—even Jesus' own resurrection—remains futile, a mute apparition, for those who harden their hearts against Moses and the prophets. On the other hand, those who heed Jesus will understand that the message of Scripture calls the community to precisely the sort of generous sharing that is exemplified by the Jerusalem church in the early chapters of Acts.

Luke also offers two contrasting pronouncement stories illustrating righteous and unrighteous responses to wealth in light of Jesus' summons to discipleship. The rich ruler (Luke 18:18–30) sadly declines Jesus' invitation to sell his goods and distribute the money to the poor, whereas Zacchaeus (Luke 19:1–10), upon encountering Jesus, spontaneously repents and promises to give half of his possessions to the poor and to restore fourfold any ill-gotten gains.[24] To him, Jesus responds by saying, "Today salvation has come to this house, because he too is a son of Abraham." This story illustrates that Luke has no mechanical standard or requirement for total renunciation of possessions as a universal requirement of discipleship, despite some passages that would seem to demand this (e.g., 14:33). In the case of Zacchaeus, giving up half his possessions seems to be sufficient. Would the rich ruler have accepted that arrangement if Jesus had offered it? As Luke Johnson has convincingly demonstrated, possessions in Luke-Acts function as symbols of response to God.[25] Zacchaeus's uncoerced generosity is a sign of repentance and faith, whereas the hesitant stinginess of the rich ruler—or, worse, the dishonesty of Ananias and Sapphira (Acts 5:1–11)—betrays an unrepentant heart, closed toward the grace of God.

Thus, the "glad and generous hearts" (Acts 2:46) of the Jerusalem community are the sure signs of the presence of God's Spirit in their midst, and their sharing of their goods so that there is no needy person among them is the outward and visible sign of God's effectual grace. Indeed, the *power* of the apostles' "testimony to the resurrection of the Lord Jesus" is linked directly by Luke to the community's economic sharing (Acts 4:32–35). The testimony is credible because the evidence of God's power is palpable in the community's life.

(C) THE CHURCH AND THE EMPIRE: TURNING THE WORLD UPSIDE DOWN

How is the new community in which the kingdom of God is manifest related to the kingdoms of this world? An episode that focuses this question sharply occurs when Paul and Silas begin preaching in Thessalonica (Acts 17:1–9). Soon they find themselves opposed by a mob organized by Jews who are "jealous" of their initial missionary success. Failing to find Paul and Silas, the mob drags some other believers before the city authorities, shouting,

> *These people who have been turning the world upside down have come here also. . . . They are all acting contrary to the decrees of the emperor, saying that there is another king named Jesus.* (ACTS 17:6–7)

A crucial question for the interpretation of Luke-Acts is whether this accusation against the believers is to be understood as a false charge—thus serving Luke's political apologetic by showing that innocent believers are falsely accused of stirring up trouble—or whether the angry crowd rightly discerns something true about the impact of the gospel in the Roman world. Jesus is, after all, a "king" who claims an ultimate allegiance that transcends Caesar's jurisdiction. Is there a sense in which the Christian movement described in Acts does "turn the world upside down" and threaten the existing political order?

The question has been extensively debated by scholars. For nearly a generation, Hans Conzelmann's thesis held the field: Luke seeks to formulate an apology that will show Christianity to be politically harmless within the Roman world.[26] According to Conzelmann's reading of Luke-Acts, Christians are docile subjects, and trouble arises only when Jews rouse the populace with false accusations against the church. This reading of the texts, however, has been strongly challenged, first by Richard J. Cassidy and subsequently by other Lukan scholars.[27] Cassidy interprets Luke's Jesus as a nonviolent social dissident who was actually a potential danger to the Roman empire "in approximately the same way that Gandhi was dangerous to British rule in India."[28] Cassidy takes note of Jesus' concern for outcasts, his condemnation of the wealthy, his critique of unjust and oppressive structures, his call for social relations to be based on service and humility, and his opposition to violence. In view of these factors, he draws the following conclusion about the Lukan Jesus:

> Although Jesus did not constitute the same type of threat to Roman rule as the Zealots and the Parthians, the threat that he posed was, ultimately, not less dangerous. . . . [B]y espousing radically new social patterns and by refusing to defer to the existing political authorities, Jesus pointed the way to a social order in which neither the Romans nor any other oppressing group would be able to hold sway.[29]

Both Conzelmann and Cassidy do us the service of reminding us that these texts must be read in a concrete historical and political context. More than any other New Testament author, Luke is concerned to situate the events that he narrates within wider world history: he dates the birth of Jesus in relation to the reign of Caesar Augustus and the governorship of Quirinius in Syria (Luke 2:1–2),[30] explicitly dates the beginning of Jesus' ministry "in the fifteenth year of the reign of Emperor Tiberius" (3:1), and introduces into his narrative—especially in Acts—many specific rulers and public officials. As Paul says in a speech before the Roman governor Festus and King Herod Agrippa II, after recounting his own career, "Indeed the king knows about these things, . . . for this was not done in a corner" (Acts 26:26). The events of Jesus' life and the subsequent emergence of the church are played out on the stage of public affairs. It is therefore entirely reasonable to ask how Luke sees the church in relation to these political authorities. Even if both Conzelmann and Cassidy force the limited evidence to bear too much weight and underplay the counterevidence, their debate raises significant issues that demand investigation.

Although much discussion has surrounded Jesus' response to the trick question about paying taxes to the emperor (Luke 20:20–26), the passage actually sheds very little light on this range of issues. Christendom's traditional interpretation takes Jesus' response as one of acquiescence to the taxing authority of the ruler, thus establishing a "two kingdoms" theory of separation between the secular and the religious realms. But this is clearly an inadequate reading, for it leaves unexplained why Jesus' adversaries are "amazed" and silenced by his answer. If his answer simply means, "Yes, pay the tax to Caesar," then his adversaries have successfully trapped him into advocating an accommodationist stance that would be unpopular with the people and in apparent conflict with his own proclamation of the coming of the kingdom of God. (It should never be forgotten that talk about the "kingdom of God" was potent political language in Jesus' time: it would have been heard as declaring the restoration of an Israel free from outside domination.)[31] A careful reading of the passage will show that Jesus' answer confounds his interlocutors because it poses a parabolic demand for discernment: What really belongs to God?

A more adequate way to assess Luke's understanding of the political vocation of the church is to examine the narratives in Acts that actually describe the interaction of the church with political authorities. This would require a lengthier study than is possible to carry out here, but several summary observations can be offered. First of all, there is significant evidence that appears to support Conzelmann's thesis: Roman officials are generally portrayed as fair and respectful in their treatment of Christians, and the apostles are certainly not seeking to foment rebellion against the empire. On the other hand, Cassidy's reading also finds some support in the text of Acts: the fledgling Christian community repeatedly upsets conventions and stands in tension with the established social order.

In Acts 4, Peter and John come into conflict with the Jewish authorities in Jerusalem. A council including the rulers, elders, and scribes, along with the high priest and the high-priestly family, arrests them and charges them not to speak or teach in the name of Jesus. The apostles, however, explicitly reject this demand: "Whether it is right in God's sight to listen to you rather than to God, you must judge; for we cannot keep from speaking about what we have seen and heard" (Acts 4:19–20). Of particular interest is the response of the assembled community when Peter and John are released. Luke reports a long prayer that is spoken, apparently in unison, by the whole community:

> *Sovereign Lord, who made the heaven and the earth, the sea, and everything in them, it is you who said by the Holy Spirit through our ancestor David, your servant:*
>
> *"Why did the Gentiles rage,*
> *and the peoples imagine vain things?*
> *The kings of the earth took their stand,*
> *and the rulers have gathered together*
> *against the Lord and against his Messiah."*
>
> *For in this city, in fact, both Herod and Pontius Pilate, with the Gentiles and the peoples*[32] *of Israel, gathered together against your holy servant Jesus, whom you anointed, to do whatever your hand and your plan had predestined to take place. And now, Lord, look at their threats, and grant to your servants to speak your word with all boldness, while you stretch out your hand to heal, and signs and wonders are performed through the name of your holy servant Jesus.* (Acts 4:24b–30, quoting Ps. 2:1–2)

It is striking that, although the immediate brush of Peter and John with authority has been with the Jewish Jerusalem Council, the prayer, reflecting the content of Psalm 2, interprets the event as part of a wider conflict with Gentile and Jewish authorities together. The defiance of Peter and John is emblematic of the church's larger conflict with "the kings of the earth," who oppose the Lord and his Messiah. Such opposition is of course futile, from Luke's point of view, for God is not just a local deity but the creator of heaven and earth. Even Jesus' death at the hands of these rulers was merely part of what God had predestined. Thus, however improbable the church's power may appear for the present, those who oppose the proclaimers of Christ are imagining "a vain thing." The power of God will prevail in the end, for it is precisely through the church that God is now stretching out his hand to do signs and wonders.

A similar sequence of events is repeated in Acts 5:17–42. This time, when the apostles are again brought before the council, Peter articulates the great foundation of Christian civil disobedience: "We must obey God rather than any human authority" (5:29; the NRSV's paraphrastic translation captures the sense well). No tame acquiescence to authority here: the church has its own agenda, which, as we have seen, includes not only preaching about Jesus but also reshaping the community's life in response to Jesus' teachings. If any authority tries to hinder this mission, the church can only stand and testify against that authority. As the stories surveyed so far indicate, God will often intervene miraculously to vindicate the church's resistance—for instance, by sending angels to let the apostles out of prison (5:19–21).

One final illustration will indicate that the preaching of the gospel is—in Luke's estimation—a threat not just to Jewish authorities but also to the status quo in the Gentile social world. The silversmiths of Ephesus become distraught over the prospect that Paul's preaching against idolatry will undermine their lucrative business of selling silver shrines of Artemis. Consequently, they orchestrate an exuberant public demonstration against the Christians, chanting for hours on end, "Great is Artemis of the Ephesians" (Acts 19:23–41).

(Americans at the end of the twentieth century may find the idea of such a public display of religious sentiment to be peculiar. To transfer this story hermeneutically into our situation, we might think of the silversmiths as defense contractors worried that the Christians will put them out of business by turning everybody into pacifists. The mob's chant, then—instead of "Great is Artemis of the Ephesians"—would simply be "U-S-A! U-S-A!")

There is no indication that Paul has taken any direct initiative against the silversmiths or their trade. He has simply been about the business of preaching repentance and integrating people into the fellowship of the church. Yet in case after case, this sort of community-building seems to introduce an explosive new catalyst into the sociopolitical order. The book of Acts portrays a movement that is turning people in large numbers "from the power of Satan to God" (Acts 26:18) and resocializing them into a community that lives by very different norms—the norms defined by Jesus' life and teachings. Such a movement—when lived with integrity—inevitably has an explosive effect in the surrounding culture. That is Luke's vision for the transformative power of the church: it turns the world upside down not through armed revolution but through the formation of the church as a counterculture, an alternative witness-bearing community.[33]

3. Luke's Eschatology: "Why do you stand looking up toward heaven?"

Our treatment of Lukan eschatology can be somewhat abbreviated, since Luke, writing in the same general time period as Matthew, confronts some of the same issues and makes some similar adaptations of the early church's apocalyptic eschatology.[34] Like Matthew, Luke reckons with a deferred parousia and a consequent relaxation of eschatological tension. Also like Matthew, Luke places increased emphasis on the theme of eschatological judgment as a warrant for moral behavior in the present time. Luke does, however, contribute some distinctive accents to the eschatological picture by opening up a longer constructive prospect for the church's continuing existence in history and by highlighting the role of the eschatological Spirit in the church's present existence.

(A) THE CHURCH IN HISTORY In various subtle ways, Luke mutes the apocalyptic trumpet that sounds from every page in Mark's Gospel. Luke's tempering of the tradition may best be seen by observing his redactional handling of the material that he inherited. The following Lukan editorial touches may best be scrutinized with the aid of a synopsis.

- The final unit of teaching material in the journey narrative before Jesus' entry to Jerusalem is the parable of the pounds (Luke 19:11–27), the Lukan parallel to the Matthean parable of the talents. Luke's introduction to the parable explains that Jesus told it to his disciples "because he was near Jerusalem, and because they supposed that the kingdom of God was to appear immediately" (Luke 19:11). Having reached the climactic point of the journey, the disciples expect Jesus to march into the city and inaugurate the kingdom of God at once. Thus, the ensuing parable functions in Luke's narrative to cool the eschatological fervor of the disciples. Jesus spins an allegory of a nobleman who goes away "to a distant country to get royal power for himself and then return," leaving each of his slaves in charge of ten pounds (19:12). Almost surely the nobleman represents Jesus himself, who is to "go away" to the right hand of God (Acts 2:33) and return ultimately in power. The parable stresses the importance of trustworthy stewardship in the interim, the duration of which remains uncertain.
- When Jesus returns to Galilee (Luke adds "in the power of the Spirit") after his temptation in the wilderness, Luke omits Mark's account of the content of his proclamation. In Mark, Jesus announces, "The time is fulfilled, and the kingdom of God has come near" (Mark 1:15). Luke merely tells us that "he began to teach in their synagogues and was praised by everyone" (Luke 4:15).
- At the conclusion of the interpretation of the parable of the sower, Luke adds that the good seed represents those who *hold it fast in an honest and good heart* and bear fruit *with patient endurance* (*hypomonē*). Luke's interpretation pays less attention to the superabundant harvest and more to the staying power of those who hear the word in good faith.

- Even the call to take up the cross and follow Jesus is given a distinctive redactional twist by Luke: "If anyone wants to come after me, let him deny himself and take up his cross *daily* and follow me" (Luke 9:23, RH; cf. Mark 8:34). By the simple addition of *kath hēmeran,* Luke transforms the summons from a dramatic once-for-all decision to a matter of dailiness, living the life of discipleship day by day.
- In the climactic dialogue of the trial scene in the passion narrative, Luke downplays the allusion to Daniel 7:13–14, omitting any reference to the Son of Man's "coming with the clouds of heaven" (or indeed to any future coming at all). Luke's Jesus says, "[F]rom now on the Son of Man will be seated at the right hand of the power of God" (Luke 22:69).
- In the apocalyptic discourse, when warning against deceivers who will seek to lead the faithful astray, Jesus cautions that they will say not only "I am he" but also "The time is near! [*ho kairos ēggiken*]"—very close to what Mark's Jesus says in Mark 1:15! (Luke 21:8). In the sentence following that verse, Luke changes Mark's "But the end is not yet" (Mark 13:7, RH) to "The end will not follow immediately" (21:9). Finally, in 21:19, Luke changes Mark's "But the one who endures to the end will be saved" (Mark 13:13) to "Possess your souls in patient endurance [*hypomonē*]" (my translation).[35]
- By adding the references to "Jerusalem surrounded by armies" and "trampled on by the Gentiles" (21:20, 24), Luke effectually shifts the emphasis of this discourse away from apocalyptic future tribulations and toward events that are for him and his readers lodged in the immediate historical past: the Roman conquest of Jerusalem in 70 C.E.

Any one of these modifications of the tradition taken by itself might weigh rather lightly, but cumulatively they suggest that Luke has systematically sought to defuse any immediate apocalyptic expectation. To be sure, he continues to affirm the future judgment, as his ending to the apocalyptic discourse (21:34–36) makes clear, but he has taken pains to tell the story in such a way that Jesus never encourages the notion of an immediate end. The conversation between Jesus and the apostles just before his ascension to heaven at the beginning of Acts is emblematic of Luke's handling of eschatology. The apostles ask—quite reasonably—whether the time has at last come, following Jesus' resurrection, for the restoration of the kingdom to Israel. But Jesus replies:

> *It is not for you to know the times or periods that the Father has set by his own authority. But you will receive power when the Holy Spirit has come upon you; and you will be my witnesses in Jerusalem, in all Judea and Samaria, and to the ends of the earth.*
> (ACTS 1:7–8)

These are Jesus' final words to the community in Luke-Acts: forget the eschatological timetable; your job is to be my witnesses. Despite the subsequent angelic affirmation that Jesus will return in the same way that the apostles have seen him go, the emphasis is shifted away from future expectation ("Why do you stand looking up toward heaven?") and toward the immediate mission (Acts 1:10–11).

John Carroll's study of Lukan eschatology argues that it is important to distinguish between the narrated world of Luke's story and the historical situation of Luke's community; in Carroll's view, Luke has deliberately distanced Jesus from predictions of an immediate eschatological consummation precisely in order to defer such expectations into his own time, thus keeping imminent expectation alive in the church: "Delay [in the narrative] does not oppose but undergirds expectation of an imminent end in Luke's own situation."[36] While Carroll's analysis of Luke's original motivation is persuasive, the end result of Luke's adaptation is somewhat different when the text of Luke-Acts continues to be read in the church over a long period of time. By reducing the urgency of Jesus' expectation of the end and by pushing the day of judgment into an indefinite future, Luke in effect creates an infinitely expanding historical "middle" in which the role of the church is paramount. As Joseph Fitzmyer puts it, Luke has sought "to shift Christian attention from an exclusive focus on imminence to a realization that the present Period of the Church also has place in God's salvation history."[37] This making room for the church in history is one of Luke's most important contributions to New Testament theology and ethics.

(B) THE ESCHATOLOGICAL SPIRIT IN THE CHURCH The life of the community within its ongoing history is by no means—again in sharp contrast to Mark—a time of grimly determined waiting for the promised deliverance. The community has already received "the promise of the Father": the Holy Spirit, which is the source of great power, joy, and confidence. Luke's description of the Jerusalem community is not only a fulfillment of the Old Testament's covenant vision but also an anticipation of the "time of universal restoration [*apokatastasis*]" (Acts 3:21). The fact that Luke understands the Spirit as an eschatological sign is shown by the fact that he alters the opening of the Joel quotation in Acts 2:17 from "afterwards" to "in the last days." The outpouring of the Spirit prefigures the end, and thus the community that lives and acts in the power of the Spirit is an eschatological community, bringing God's future into being in communal life and thus witnessing to the world about the power of the resurrection. This conviction imparts to the book of Acts its tremendous energy and forward thrust.

The Spirit supplies both power for the mission and very specific guidance. To take one example, chosen virtually at random, Philip is guided by the Spirit to initiate a conversation with the Ethiopian eunuch: "The Spirit said to Philip, 'Go over to this chariot and join it'" (Acts 8:29; see also 11:12; 13:2; 16:6–7; 20:23; 20:28; 21:11). Likewise, the momentous decision of the Jerusalem Council not to impose the requirements of circumcision and Torah observance on Gentile converts is said to be guided by the Spirit: "It has seemed good to the Holy Spirit and to us . . ." (15:28). Not without reason has it often been said that the book should really be called, rather than the Acts of the Apostles, the Acts of the Holy Spirit. Where the Spirit is at work in the church, nothing is static: old barriers and conventions fall as the Spirit gathers and shapes a new people.

(C) ESCHATOLOGICAL REVERSAL The eschatological outpouring of the Spirit brings with it a pervasive reversal of fortunes for the powerful and the oppressed, as Mary foresees in her song at the beginning of Luke's Gospel:

He has brought down the powerful from their thrones,
and lifted up the lowly;
he has filled the hungry with good things,
and sent the rich away empty. (LUKE 1:52–53)

We have already noted several illustrations of this reversal motif: the Lukan Beatitudes, the story of the rich man and Lazarus, and the acceptance of tax collectors and sinners into the kingdom of God. The Lukan parable of the prodigal son (15:11–32) makes a similar point: the wastrel son is welcomed with a lavish party while the dutiful son stands outside and grumbles. This parable should be read—among its several possible levels of interpretation—as prefiguring the analogous reversal in Acts, where many Gentiles receive the preaching of the gospel with joy while many Law-observant Jews balk and raise qualms about this missionary development.[38]

It is under this heading that we could—were there world enough and time—investigate Luke's striking portrayal of women as fully rounded characters essential to the unfolding of salvation history, characters whose personal response to God counts for everything. They are given voice in Luke's story, reversing their conventional lowliness of status. As Mary sings, God "has looked with favor on the lowliness of his servant" and done "great things" for and through her. The roster of significant female characters in Luke-Acts is far longer than that of any other New Testament writing. This is not because Luke was consciously a feminist; the term is an anachronism when applied to a first-century writer. Rather, it is because the Spirit's eschatological power of reversal was at work in the tradition that Luke knew, raising women to a status they had not formerly enjoyed:

In the last days it will be, God declares,
that I will pour out my Spirit upon all flesh,
and your sons ***and your daughters*** *shall prophesy . . .*
Even upon my slaves, ***both men and women****,*
in those days I will pour out my Spirit
and they shall prophesy. (ACTS 2:17–18, *emphasis mine*)

Thus, the significant role given by Luke to women is not based on some a priori conviction about the inherent equality of the sexes; rather, it is another sign of eschatological reversal, of God's setting the world right by deposing the powerful and lifting up the lowly.

To make a full list of similar reversals narrated in Luke's long story would be a lengthy but illuminating project, for the overturning of the expected is a motion that lies in the deep structure of Luke's construal of the good news.[39] In this respect, Luke's moral vision is theologically consonant with Paul's insight that the gospel of the cross overturns the world's notions of wisdom and power. The unexpected keeps happening in Luke's story. This is not merely a sign of the author's literary inventiveness; rather, it is the outworking of his conviction that the eschatological "year of the Lord's favor" has arrived. The Spirit is at work releasing captives and setting the oppressed free. Where such signs and wonders are breaking loose, the community of believers can live in the present with joy, without undue anxiety about when the final hour of judgment will arrive.

As we have seen, Luke's handling of eschatological traditions enables him to deal in patient, imaginative ways with the theological and pastoral problems created by the delay of the parousia. How is the church to cope with reality when the dream of Christ's triumphant return, so fervently awaited by the first Christian generation, becomes indefinitely deferred? This problem was, in Luke's time, analogous to the problem of disappointment addressed nineteen centuries later by Langston Hughes in his poem "Dream Deferred."[40]

What happens to a dream deferred?
    Does it dry up
    like a raisin in the sun?
    Or fester like a sore—
    And then run?
    Does it stink like rotten meat?
    Or crust and sugar over—
    like a syrupy sweet?
    Maybe it just sags
    like a heavy load,
    Or does it explode?

Some unsympathetic interpreters of Luke-Acts, seeing it as a nostalgic and triumphalist piece of propaganda for emergent "early catholicism," have in effect argued that in these texts early Christian eschatology has been allowed to "crust and sugar over—like a syrupy sweet."[41] But the foregoing discussion has sought to show, instead, that Luke has rendered an "orderly account" that gives the community of faith a firm foothold in time and history. What happens to a dream deferred? It becomes, in Luke, the sustaining vision for a community setting out on a long and joyful pilgrimage.

4. Luke's Narrative World As Context for Action

The extended narrative of Luke-Acts erects a capacious framework within which the church's moral discernment and action can be situated. The following points constitute a summary of my observations about the narrative world of this two-part work.

First, Luke offers his readers a sense of *orientation within time and history.* For Luke, Christian existence cannot be understood as a matter of the individual's isolated momentary encounter with God. It is, in Eliot's phrase, "Not the intense moment / Isolated, with no before and after."[42] Rather, for Luke, the community of those who confess the name of Jesus Christ stands within the great unfolding story of God's redemptive faithfulness. God's people have come from a past superintended by providence; they are going toward the end securely promised within God's plan. This temporal locatedness provides the security (*asphaleia*) that Luke promises his readers in the Gospel's prologue. Thus, Luke-Acts is to the church as the Aeneid is to Rome.

Second, an important aspect of the church's orientation in time is its direct *continuity with Israel.* The community's identity is rooted in a specific salvation history, and the God who is at work in the church is the same God who elected and delivered the people Israel in the past. The church's present experience, therefore, must be prefigured in and consistent with the promises of God in Scripture.

Third, precisely because the community is identified as Israel, standing in typological correspondence to the Old Testament narratives, it must understand itself as *participating in a journey,* an exodus to a promised destination not yet reached. Such a journey entails suffering, risk, and sacrifice; there will be unanticipated turns of fortune, and the community must remain open to follow God's leading along the way. This vision of the church's life is far more conducive than Matthew's to flexibility and innovation. But the journey is of course neither aimless nor unmapped. Jesus, the great prophetic leader "like Moses," has led the way, and the community must follow the way he has marked out—hence, Luke's characteristic description of the Christian movement as "the Way" (Acts 9:2; 18:25; 19:9, 23; 22:4; 24:14, 22).

Fourth, Luke's deep confidence in God's providence imparts to the story a positive, robust, *world-affirming* character.[43] Unlike the Johannine community (see Chapter 6), the church in Luke-Acts is not a defensive community withdrawing from an evil world; instead, it acts boldly on the stage of public affairs, commending the gospel in reasoned terms to all persons of goodwill and expecting an open-minded response. Closely correlated with this optimistic assessment of the church's political situation is Luke's rather elegant aesthetic sense, his obvious delight in beauty and order. His very telling of the tale breathes a subtle appreciation of human literary skill, of art and culture.

Fifth, the affective tone of the narrative is characterized by *joy and praise.* The canticles in the birth stories virtually invite the reader to join the heavenly host—as generations of readers have done—in singing:

> *Glory to God in the highest heaven,*
> *and on earth peace among those whom he favors.* (Luke 2:14)

As the church's mission unfolds in Acts, the community manifests "glad and generous hearts," and even in the face of imprisonments and hardships, rejoicing is the order of the day; for instance, when the apostles are interrogated and flogged, Luke tells us that "they rejoiced that they were considered worthy to suffer dishonor for the sake of the name [of Jesus]" (Acts 5:41). Acts 13:52 can stand as a thumbnail sketch of the church that Luke portrays: "And the disciples were filled with joy and with the Holy Spirit."

Sixth, *the Holy Spirit empowers the work and witness of the church.* Luke, like Matthew (but for a different reason), entertains no dark doubts concerning the capacity of believers to do the will of God, nor does he wrestle with any complex issues of religious psychology. Repentance is required, to be sure, in order to receive God's forgiveness and blessing (Acts 2:38). But where the Spirit is poured out on the church, it sweeps the believers along as though in a great river of obedience, praise, and mighty works. Empowered by the Spirit, the community can dare and hope great things, seeing visions, dreaming dreams, turning the world upside down. (The idea that Acts sanctions a pallid and stultifying "early catholicism" can only have been promulgated by academics utterly oblivious to the lure of the Spirit's power. This text is, if anything, an expression of "early pentecostalism," not "early catholicism.")[44] Preeminently, the Spirit energizes the community to bear witness in word and deed to the power of the resurrection.

Seventh, where the Spirit is at work, *liberation is underway:* good news to the poor, release to the captives, recovery of sight to the blind, deliverance to the oppressed. The purpose of God's outpouring of the Spirit is to establish a covenant community in which justice is both proclaimed and practiced. Because the language of liberation has been so widely appropriated in the interest of various political causes, it is important to specify what Luke does and does not have in mind. The book of Acts gives no evidence of the apostles seeking to reform political structures outside the church, either through protest or by seizing power. Instead, Luke tells the story of the formation of a new human community—the church—in which goods are shared and wrongs are put right. In this way the apostolic testimony to the resurrection is made effectual. The question that Luke-Acts puts to the church—then and now—is not "Are you reforming society?" but rather "Is the power of the resurrection at work among you?" The community's sharing of its material resources so that there is no needy person among them is the most powerful sign of the Spirit's liberating work.

NOTES

1. The theme of God's fulfillment of promises to Israel is surprisingly omitted in Schrage's treatment of Luke-Acts (Schrage 1988, 152–161).

2. I follow convention in referring to the author as Luke, though the identity of the author cannot be known with certainty. For extended discussion, see Fitzmyer 1981, 35–53. As Fitzmyer rightly concludes, "In fact it makes little difference to the interpretation of the Lucan Gospel whether or not one can establish that its author was the traditional Luke, a sometime companion of Paul, even a physician" (p. 53).

3. Schneider 1977. On "the plan of God" in Luke-Acts, see Squires 1993.

4. The name means "Godlover." In its present context, it may well be a fictional form of address to any interested reader.

5. Dahl 1976, 88.

6. For detailed analysis of the patterns of correspondence, see R. E. Brown 1979a, 233–499; for a more recent consideration of the issues, see Green 1995.

7. On Luke's technique of using the OT, see Holtz 1968; Rese 1969; Craddock 1985; Bock 1987; Barrett 1988; Evans and Sanders 1993; Kimball 1994.

8. The artificiality of Luke's placement of the scene is indicated by the unexplained reference in Luke 4:23 to "the things that we have heard you did at Capernaum." This is simply an editing glitch on Luke's part; according to Luke's story, Jesus has not yet done anything in Capernaum.

9. The quotation conflates Isa. 61:1–2 with Isa. 58:6. There is no reason to suppose that a text containing this conflation was actually in use in Galilean synagogues; Luke has created the composite to express his interpretation of Jesus' identity and vocation.

10. Susan Garrett (1990) has made the intriguing proposal that Jesus' deliverance of God's people from bondage to Satan in Luke-Acts is structured by a Moses-Exodus typology. I find her argument, which cannot be adequately summarized here, richly suggestive. If she is right, Jesus is "like Moses" in a more comprehensive way than commentators on Luke-Acts have traditionally realized.

11. Moessner 1989, 262–263, emphasis in the original. See also C. F. Evans 1955; Evans and Sanders 1993, 121–139.

12. On Luke's significant alteration of Deut. 18:19 in this citation, see my discussion of the passage in Chapter 17.

13. L. T. Johnson 1991, 19–20. See also L. T. Johnson 1986, 208–210.

14. Conzelmann 1961 [1953], 137–141. For further discussion of this thesis, see section 2.c of this chapter.

15. See Daryl Schmidt, "Luke's 'Innocent' Jesus: A Scriptural Apologetic," in Cassidy and Scharper 1983, 111–121.

16. One explanation for Luke 23:47 is rarely given the weight it deserves: Luke, who is retelling the story *kathexēs*, simply does not regard Mark's account of the centurion's confession as historically plausible. By substituting *dikaios* for *huios theou*, he avoids the anachronism and at the same time suggests theologically provocative scriptural echoes.

17. For discussion of the history of this motif, see Hays 1988 and the literature cited there.

18. Luke does not actually use the word "martyr" of Jesus. The Greek word *martys* simply means "witness," as in Acts 3:15. Only later did the term come to be applied predominantly to those who suffer and die for the faith. When I speak of Jesus as a paradigmatic martyr in Luke, I am applying the term in its later connotation to describe the pattern present in Luke-Acts.

19. Minear 1976.

20. For other examples of such parallelism, see Acts 3:1–10 in conjunction with Luke 5:17–26; Acts 5:15, 19:11–12 and Luke 8:44; Acts 7:59–60 and Luke 23:34, 46.

21. L. T. Johnson 1986, 219.

22. Although commentators frequently dismiss these accounts as idealized fictions (e.g., Conzelmann 1987, 24), there are reasons to be suspicious of this dismissal as an a priori judgment in reaction against egalitarian or communistic normative claims based upon such texts. For a recent argument in support of the historical credibility of these traditions, see Bartchy 1991.

23. Aristotle, *Nicomachean Ethics* 9.8.1168b, 6ff.

24. Some interpreters have read Zacchaeus's declaration in 19:8 not as an expression of repentance but as a self-justification, describing his habitual practice of giving half his goods to the poor. There are serious arguments to be made in defense of this reading (see Fitzmyer 1985, 1220–1222), but they founder on the emphatic *sēmeron* ("today") in Jesus' pronouncement in v. 9. Unless Zacchaeus had undergone a change of heart, what sense would it make for Jesus to proclaim that "*today* salvation has come to this house"? Thus, somewhat against the tide of recent interpretation, I continue to read the story as a story of repentance, fitting Luke's characteristic schema: repentance is the gateway to salvation.

25. L. T. Johnson 1977; L. T. Johnson 1981.

26. Conzelmann 1961 [1953].

27. Cassidy 1978; Cassidy and Scharper 1983.

28. Cassidy 1978, 80.

29. Cassidy 1978, 79.

30. Whether Luke's chronology is correct or internally consistent is not material to this point; I am simply noting that Luke places his characters on the stage of recognizable political events and actors.

31. Batstone 1992; Wright 1992, 302–307.

32. Here I have amended the NRSV, which reads "people." By using the plural *laois Israēl*, Luke signals that he is expositing Ps. 2:1: the psalm foreshadows that Gentiles and Israel would join together against Jesus. I am indebted to Bruce Fisk for calling this point to my attention.

33. Thus, rightly, Charles Talbert, "Martyrdom in Luke-Acts and the Lukan Social Ethic," in Cassidy and Scharper 1983, 99–110.

34. For a helpful summary of the extensive body of research on Lukan eschatology, see Carroll 1988, 1–30.

35. My translation here, in accordance with Nestle-Aland, follows the reading *ktēsasthe* (aorist imperative) rather than *ktēsesthe* (future indicative).

36. Carroll 1988, 166.

37. Fitzmyer 1981, 235.

38. This is of course not the original sense of the parable in the life setting of Jesus; instead, it is an acquired sense of the parable within the present literary context of the two-volume work.

39. Allen Verhey's *The Great Reversal* is in important respects a Lukan reading of NT ethics, not only because Verhey takes the resurrection as the key to the NT's message (Verhey 1984, 181–183) but also because of the emphasis suggested in the title.

40. Cited here from Hughes 1992, 14. The poem was published in some earlier anthologies under the title "Harlem."

41. E.g., Käsemann (1964 [1960], 63–94) contends that in Acts "a *theologia gloriae* is now in process of replacing the *theologia crucis*" (92). See also Käsemann 1969 [1965], 236–251.

42. "East Coker," in Eliot 1952 [1930], 129.

43. L. T. Johnson 1991, 21–22; cf. Pervo 1987.

44. Regarding "early catholicism," see the Käsemann essays cited in n. 41, above, and Conzelmann 1987. For a reading more attuned to the narrative forces that I have identified here, see Willimon 1988.

Chapter 6

The Gospel and Epistles of John

Loving One Another

For readers seeking ethical themes, the Gospel of John is a puzzling text. It contains almost none of the specific moral teaching found in the synoptics: no instruction here about violence or possessions or divorce. Jesus is represented in John not as a teacher but as a relentless revealer of a single metaphysical secret: that Jesus himself is the one who has come from God to bring life.[1] He offers minimal moral instruction for the community of his disciples. There are repeated injunctions to the community to keep Jesus' commandments (14:15, 21; 15:10; cf. 1 John 2:3–6), but, remarkably, the actual content of these commandments is never spelled out in the text. If we had only the Fourth Gospel in the New Testament canon, it would be difficult indeed to base any specific Christian ethic on the teaching of Jesus.

Similarly, the Law of Moses plays no explicit role in John's moral vision; it is read as prefiguring Jesus, and its meaning is seemingly absorbed into his person.

> *You search the scriptures because you think that in them you have eternal life; and it is they that testify on my behalf. Yet you refuse to come to me to have life. . . . If you believed Moses, you would believe me, for he wrote about me. But if you do not believe what he wrote, how will you believe what I say?* (John 5:39–40, 46–47)

Nowhere in John do we find any appeal to the Law as prescriptive of moral conduct; it cannot be assumed that the Torah implicitly remains normative for John's community.[2] Nor are there any traces in the Johannine literature of the early Christian debate over the binding character of the commandments of circumcision and food laws. The entire conflict with Judaism is focused on christological issues, not on ethics or praxis.

The Gospel and Epistles of John—which surely represent a common stream of tradition, even if they are not produced by the same author[3]—portray the community of believers as deeply alienated from the world, perhaps even ontologically distinct from the world. In his lengthy prayer for the disciples at the conclusion of the farewell discourse, John's Jesus prays to the Father: "I have given them your word, and the world has hated them because they do not belong to the world, just as I do not belong to the world" (John 17:14). The strongly sectarian character of the Johannine vision stands at the opposite pole within the New Testament from Luke's optimistic affirmation of the world and its culture. It is not without reason that H. Richard Niebuhr, in his classic study *Christ and Culture*, selected 1 John as his parade example of the "Christ against Culture" mentality within the Christian tradition.[4]

One of the most striking manifestations of the apparently isolationist tendency of the Johannine tradition is the fact that the love commandment, which plays a central role in this literature, is applied only *within* the community of believers: "I give you a new commandment: that you should love one another" (John 13:34a). As Ernst Käsemann correctly observed,

> . . . [T]he concept of love in the Fourth Gospel is not without its problems. . . . John demands love for one's brethren, but not for one's enemies. . . . There is no indication in John that love for one's brother would also include love toward one's neighbour, as demanded in the other books of the New Testament.[5]

This intracommunal focus causes some interpreters to find the Johannine literature ethically deficient. J. L. Houlden asserts disapprovingly that "for John the believer has no duties towards 'the world,' but only towards those who like himself are saved from it."[6] A particularly strong statement of protest is articulated by Jack T. Sanders, who speaks of the "weakness and moral bankruptcy of the Johannine ethics":

> Here is not a Christianity that considers that loving is the same as fulfilling the Law (Paul) or that the good Samaritan parable represents a demand (Luke) to stop and render even first aid to the man who has been robbed, beaten, and left there for dead. Johannine Christianity is interested only in whether he believes. "Are you saved, brother?" the Johannine Christian asks the man bleeding to death on the side of the road. "Are you concerned about your soul?" "Do you believe that Jesus is the one who came down from God?" "If you believe, you will have eternal life," promises the Johannine Christian, while the dying man's blood stains the ground.[7]

Is Sanders's indictment a fair one? It does look as though ethics has been crowded out by Christology, especially in John's Gospel. (As we shall see, 1 John supplies some corrective balance to the Gospel on this point.) As I have repeatedly argued, however, the ethical significance of the New Testament narratives cannot be restricted to their didactic content. John, even more pointedly than the other Gospels, shows that a fuller reading of the story is necessary in order to grasp its implications for shaping the life of the Christian community. The sectarian character of this material is undeniable, but Sanders's harsh verdict on its ethical quality is overhasty, neglecting both the specific historical circumstances of its origin and the more complex way in which this story frames the world within which its readers live and move.

As with the other Gospels, we shall begin with an account of the text's Christology, turn next to its picture of the church, move then to the ethical implications of its eschatology, and finally turn to some summary remarks about the way in which John's story creates a symbolic context for moral discernment. Although we shall focus primarily on the Gospel of John, evidence from the Epistles will be drawn into the discussion at pertinent points. Since our concern is to trace the major moral visions represented within the New Testament canon, we need not discriminate too finely between the Epistles and the Gospel, or indeed between the various possible redactional layers within the Gospel. The governing assumption of the following discussion is that the Johannine tradition represents a distinctive and theologically coherent trajectory. The writer of 1 John articulates that trajectory in a way that seeks to preclude certain possible misunderstandings, but his additions to the tradition are friendly amendments, seeking to clarify what he and his community had "from the beginning" taken to be the meaning of "the message we have heard from him and proclaim to you" (1 John 1:1–5).

1. John's Christology: The Man from Heaven

The Jesus portrayed in the Fourth Gospel is, from the first lines of the Gospel onward, revealed as a divine figure who has come into the world to bring light and salvation. He is fully conscious of his divine origin and destiny, and he proclaims his divinity openly to all who will listen—and to many who will not. Despite the failure of many to believe, there is no secretiveness about Jesus' identity in this Gospel; after his arrest, he can truthfully declare to the high priest, "I have spoken openly to the world. . . . I have said nothing in secret" (John 18:20).

He is the preexistent Logos who was with God before creation, through whom the world was made. Although the title Logos ("Word") is not applied to Jesus again in the rest of the Gospel, many other features of the narrative reinforce this claim for his unity with God. He asserts his own preexistence in prayer to the Father ("So now, Father, glorify me in your own presence with the glory that I had in your presence before the world existed"; John 17:5) and in his stunning public declaration:

"Very truly, I tell you, before Abraham was, I am" (8:58). We are told repeatedly that he has come down from heaven (3:31, 6:51–58), and he pointedly contrasts his heavenly origin to that of "the Jews," saying, "You are from below, I am from above; you are of this world, I am not of this world" (8:23).[8]

Other details of the Johannine portrait bear witness to Jesus' exalted supernatural status. He has supernatural knowledge of what is in the hearts of people (2:23–25), he apparently does not hunger for ordinary material food (4:31–34, a narrative element that surely gave aid and comfort to the docetic heresy that the author of 1 John later battled against), and he mysteriously disappears from hostile crowds (7:30, 8:59). He greets the news of the death of his friend Lazarus with gladness because it will provide him with a useful teaching aid for his disciples (11:14–15). His miracles are interpreted as "signs" that elicit from Jesus himself long meditative interpretations, as in the "bread of life" discourse in John 6. Unlike the synoptic Jesus, the Jesus of John's Gospel breaks repeatedly into lengthy christological discourses in which he proclaims his identity and his oneness with God. In short, we find here a Jesus in whom the divine glory is manifest from start to finish, "God going about on the earth."[9] The "glory" witnessed by the believing community (1:14) threatens—by its very brightness—to obliterate the confession that the Word (really) became flesh. That is why, in Käsemann's well-known formulation, the Christology of John is in danger of slipping into "naive docetism," an unintentional denial of the humanity of Jesus.[10]

It is likely that the docetic schismatics against whom 1 John rails—those who denied that "Jesus Christ has come in the flesh" (1 John 4:2–3)—were in fact taking their cues from these elements in the Fourth Gospel.[11] Against such a reading, 1 John—with the author's remarkable claim not only to have seen the Word of life but also to have "touched [it] with our hands" (1 John 1:1)—seeks to interpret the heritage of the Fourth Gospel in a way that underscores the genuine humanity of Jesus. Such an interpretation is not without foundation, for John's narrative also contains numerous features that convey the physical concreteness and human reality of the incarnation. John gives us a Jesus who gets thirsty and asks a Samaritan woman for a drink (4:7; cf. 19:28), a Jesus who weeps at Lazarus's grave (11:35), a Jesus who strips off his clothes, takes a towel, and washes the grimy feet of his followers (13:3–5). Jesus is the Word become flesh (1:14), and his flesh is not merely a vestment donned for a revelation-play; he is a man who knows pain and the joys and sorrows of embodied existence.

In the sustained paradoxical tension between these two emphases in John's portrait of Jesus—the divine and the human—lies the genius of Johannine Christology. John has made extraordinary claims about the figure of Jesus, describing him in language and imagery appropriate to the universal Logos of Stoicism, the preexistent Sophia of Jewish wisdom tradition (who is "a pure emanation of the glory of the Almighty"; Wis. 7:25), and the Word of God as described in Israel's prophetic tradition (see Ps. 33:6, Isa. 55:10–11). He is all these things and more, rolled into one. And yet he is also a particular historical person who lived in the flesh, who could be handled and wounded. This is the claim that transcends and threatens to shatter the symbolic worlds that provide the background for John's representation of Jesus. Saint Augustine—trained in Platonist thought prior to his conversion—places the world-transforming character of John's Christology into perspective:

> [In] certain books of the Platonists . . . I read, not indeed in the very words, but to the very same purpose, enforced by many and divers reasons, that In the beginning was the Word, and the Word was with God, and the Word was God. . . . But, that He came unto His own, and His own received Him not; but as many as received Him, to them gave He power to become the sons of God, as many as believed in His name; this I read not there. Again I read there, that God the Word was born not of flesh nor of blood, nor of the will of man, nor of the will of the flesh, but of God. But that the Word was made flesh, and dwelt among us, I read not there.[12]

Language threatens to crack and strain under the pressure of this mind-boggling confession. W. H. Auden's lines capture the paradox:

> How could the Eternal do a temporal act,
> The Infinite become a finite fact?
> Nothing can save us that is possible.[13]

Yet the gospel according to John is precisely this: that God has done the impossible in order to save us. Jesus, the man from heaven, has become a "finite fact" for the sake of the finite world. "No one has ever seen God," says John at the conclusion of his prologue, but by becoming flesh Jesus, "the only Son, who is close to the Father's heart, . . . has exegeted (*exēgēsato*) him" (1:18, RH). Jesus is the definitive interpretation, in human form, of God—and therefore of the will of God.

Among the many consequences of John's incarnational Christology, one of the most important is that the figure of Jesus, who is at once heavenly and earthly, deconstructs the story's otherwise powerful dualism. In contrast to later Gnostic redeemer myths, the redeemer from heaven in the Fourth Gospel is also the creator of the world, and he validates the creation by entering it fully. Thus, creation and redemption are held together. The importance of this for ethics is considerable, as we shall see.

2. Loving One Another: The Friends of Jesus

(A) ABIDING IN JESUS By coming into the world, Jesus gathers to himself a community of believers who adhere to him closely—indeed, they enter into union with him. John spins a kaleidoscope of metaphors for this relation of the church to Jesus. He is the bread of life, and in order to have life believers must ingest his flesh and blood (6:35–59). Or again, he is the good shepherd, and they are the sheep given him by the Father; they recognize his voice, and no one can snatch them out of his hand (10:1–30). Or again, he is the vine and they are the branches who must abide in him in order to have life and bear fruit (15:1–8). Their identification with Jesus is very strong; indeed, they are given the task of carrying on his mission and contending with the same rejection that he experienced at the hands of the world. In his farewell discourse, he offers them affectionate words of simultaneous warning and encouragement:

> *If the world hates you, be aware that it hated me before it hated you. If you belonged to the world, the world would love you as its own. Because you do not belong to the world, but I have chosen you out of the world—therefore the world hates you. Remember the word that I said to you, "Servants are not greater than their master." If they persecuted me, they will persecute you; if they kept my word, they will keep yours also. But they will do all these things to you on account of my name, because they do not know him who sent me.* (15:18–21)

In a similar vein, he prays for their mission just before his departure from the world:

> *I am not asking you to take them out of the world, but I ask you to protect them from the evil one. They do not belong to the world, just as I do not belong to the world. Sanctify them in the truth; your word is truth. As you have sent me into the world, so I have sent them into the world.* (17:15–18)

Their commission is formally initiated on the day of the resurrection: Jesus appears to the disciples huddled together in a locked house "for fear of the Jews" and declares, "Peace be with you. As the Father has sent me, so I send you" (20:21).

Thus John—like Paul, Mark, and Luke—affirms that the community of believers is to carry on Jesus' mission, patterning their lives after his and sharing his destiny: "Whoever serves me must follow me, and where I am, there will my servant be also" (12:26). 1 John drives home the same message in terms that highlight the ethical entailment of the disciples' union with Jesus: "By this we may be sure that we are in him: whoever says, 'I abide in him,' ought to walk just as he walked" (1 John 2:5b–6). The bond between Jesus and believers is determinative for the community's ethical norms.

The difficulty, however, is how this formal assertion of Jesus as ethical pattern is to be unpacked in terms of specific behaviors. Jesus in the Fourth Gospel does not actually do much of anything except make grandiloquent revelatory speeches. The actions that he does perform are primarily of a miraculous character: changing water into wine, healing the blind and lame, and raising Lazarus from the dead. Can these serve as patterns for the community's action?

We must reckon with the possibility that John does indeed envision the church as continuing to perform miraculous healings. The promise of Jesus to his disciples would seem to suggest such a course of action:

> *Very truly, I tell you, the one who believes in me will also do the works that I do and, in fact, will do greater works than these, because I am going to the Father. I will do whatever you ask in my name, so that the Father may be glorified in the Son. If in my name you ask me for anything, I will do it.* (14:12–14)

The purpose clause—"so that the Father may be glorified in the Son"—indicates the underlying logic of all the miracles in the Fourth Gospel: they are not, as in Luke-Acts, mighty works that portend the coming of God's kingdom and exemplify God's passionate concern for the poor and needy. Rather, they serve primarily as signs of Jesus' divine authority. Each miracle provides a new occasion for Jesus to launch into a self-referential revelatory discourse; for example, the feeding of the five thousand (6:1–14) provides the narrative occasion for the "bread of life" discourse. Furthermore, John has evidently interpreted some of the miracle stories symbolically. The restored sight of the blind man in John 9 becomes a symbol for faith in Jesus, whereas the Pharisees who do not believe are shown, in an ironic reversal, to be blind. Thus, even if the Johannine community continues to do miraculous "works" of healing like those of Jesus, these are instrumental to the larger purpose of evangelism. The community's preeminent responsibility is to glorify God by proclaiming the truth about Jesus so that all, through believing, may have life in his name (see 20:31).

(B) LOVE WITHIN THE COMMUNITY The one clear directive that Jesus issues for his followers is that they should love one another in the same way that he has loved them (13:34). This too has the purpose of giving testimony to the world: "By this everyone will know that you are my disciples, if you have love for one another" (13:35). The character of love is specified in the Fourth Gospel not by an extended body of teaching, as in Matthew's Sermon on the Mount, but by a single enacted parable: Jesus' washing of the disciples' feet.

> *Jesus, knowing that the Father had given all things into his hands, and that he had come from God and was going to God, got up from the table, took off his outer robe, and tied a towel around himself. Then he poured water into a basin and began to wash the disciples' feet and to wipe them with the towel that was tied around him. . . . After he had washed their feet, had put on his robe, and had returned to the table, he said to them, "Do you know what I have done to you? You call me Teacher and Lord—and you are right, for that is what I am. So if I, your Lord and Teacher, have washed your feet, you also ought to wash one another's feet. For I have set you an example, that you also should do as I have done to you."* (13:3–5, 12–15)

This narrative sets the scene for the "new commandment" of 13:34–35. Jesus instructs the disciples to love one another as he has loved them only after demonstrating in action what "love" means: humble service of others. One does not have to be an exceptionally perceptive reader to see that the foot-washing scene, placed in John's story immediately preceding the passion narrative, serves to prefigure the death of Jesus and to interpret Jesus' laying down of his life for his followers as an act of love and servanthood. Indeed, as we continue to read the farewell discourse material, the link between the love commandment and laying down one's life is made explicit.

> *This is my commandment, that you love one another as I have loved you. No one has greater love than this, to lay down one's life for one's friends. You are my friends if you do what I command you. . . . I am giving you these commands so that you may love one another.* (15:12–14, 17)

Thus, Jesus' death is depicted by John, in a manner closely analogous to Pauline thought, as an act of self-sacrificial love that establishes the cruciform life as the norm for discipleship. Those within the community may be called upon literally to lay down their lives for one another.

The point is important, because John's emphasis on intracommunal love is sometimes construed as a license for sentimental complacency within the church. Such a reading fails to take into account the dramatically countercultural position of the Johannine community (see section c, below), and it also underestimates the seriousness of John's call to costly service within the community. We should also note that John unmistakably understands the death of Jesus as being for the sake of the whole world (1:29; 3:16): God loved the world so much that he gave his only Son up to death. Consequently, even though their primary mandate is to manifest love and service within the community, the disciples who share in Jesus' mission in the world can hardly remain indifferent to those outside the community of faith. The call to lay down one's life may have broader implications than those explicitly articulated in the "new commandment."

The writer of 1 John reiterates the imperative for members of the community to love one another and gives the commandment a pragmatic spin by applying it to the question of economic justice:

> *For this is the message you have heard from the beginning, that we should love one another. . . . We know love by this, that he laid down his life for us—and we ought to lay down our lives for one another. How does God's love abide in anyone who has the world's goods and sees a brother or sister in need and yet refuses help? Little children, let us love, not in word or speech, but in truth and action.* (1 JOHN 3:11, 16–18)[14]

Although this admonition is not developed at length, it shows that the Johannine talk of love does have practical implications. Love within the community is not merely a matter of warm feelings; rather, it is a matter of action. The sharing of "the world's goods" is only one example of what it might mean in practice to "love one another." One suspects, then, that a general formulation such as 1 John 3:23 is intended to cover a considerable range of behaviors that are not actually specified: "And this is his commandment, that we should believe in the name of his Son Jesus Christ and love one another, just as he has commanded us."

It is fashionable to derogate the Johannine exhortations to love within the community as sectarian retreats from the more universal call to love the neighbor, broadly defined as in Luke, or even the enemy, as in Matthew. Given the actual level of conflict and struggle within the church historically, however, John's vision of a community living in loving fellowship is hardly to be disparaged as trivial. The indissoluble link between love of God and love within the community of faith needs to be affirmed again and again:

> *Those who say, "I love God," and hate their brothers or sisters, are liars; for those who do not love a brother or sister whom they have seen, cannot love God whom they have not seen. The commandment we have from him is this: those who love God must love their brothers and sisters also.* (1 JOHN 4:20–21)

This may not be the last word to be said about Christian ethics, but it is not a bad place to begin.

(C) THE HISTORICAL SETTING In order to grasp the Johannine conception of the church rightly, we must take account of the specific pastoral issues being addressed by this literature. Critical study of the Johannine literature in the past generation has revolutionized our understanding of the historical context out of which the Fourth Gospel and the Johannine Epistles emerged.[15] The distinctive Johannine traditions took shape within a closely knit community of Jews who had come to confess Jesus as Messiah. The precise location of the community is unknown, but we should think in terms of a community localized within a particular urban setting such as Ephesus, with satellite communities (as suggested by the evidence of 2 and 3 John) in other towns.[16] During the early years of the community's life, these followers continued to live and move within the world of Judaism, maintaining membership in the synagogue and participating in Jewish festivals, all the while seeking to convince their fellow Jews that Jesus was the Messiah. Not surprisingly, their involvement in the Jewish community increasingly produced tensions, as the majority of Jews rejected their claims about Jesus. At a crucial point in the community's history—sometime after the destruction of the Temple in 70 C.E.—they were expelled from participation in the synagogue.[17] This explusion, referred to three times in the course of the Gospel (9:22, 12:42, 16:2), caused painful wounds and left scars on the community's tradition. "The Jews" became a term of opprobrium (see my extended discussion of this problem in Chapter 17), and the Johannine community withdrew into a defensive posture. David Rensberger aptly describes the plight of the small cluster of Johannine Christians after the traumatic experience of being declared *aposynagōgos* ("put out of the synagogue"):

> The Christians who were expelled would have been cut off from much that had given identity and structure to their lives. Expulsion would have meant social ostracism and thus the loss of relationship with family and friends, and perhaps economic dislocation as well. It would certainly have meant religious dislocation. The synagogue meetings, the public liturgy, the festivals and observances were all now denied them, and the authoritative interpretation of sacred scripture itself was in the hands of their opponents. What was threatened was thus the entire universe of shared perceptions, assumptions, beliefs, ideals, and hopes that had given meaning to their world within Judaism.[18]

Under these circumstances, the community necessarily defined itself sharply against the synagogue and against "the world," which came to be seen as a hostile and untrustworthy place. The Johannine Christians circled the wagons, defined their confessional boundaries still more rigidly, and raised the stakes of the argument by claiming that Jesus in his own person supplanted—and more than compensated for—everything in Judaism from which the community was now cut off. With the world inexplicably refusing to receive Jesus as the bearer of God's truth (1:10–11), the community of faith came to be seen as the only sphere within which life and love could be found. This perception is powerfully articulated in 1 John:

> *Do not be astonished, brothers and sisters, that the world hates you. We know that we have passed from death to life because we love one another. Whoever does not love abides in death. . . . We know that we are God's children, and that the whole world lies under the power of the evil one.* (1 JOHN 3:13–14; 5:19)

Because the world is under the power of evil, the readers of 1 John are warned, "Do not love the world or the things in the world" (1 John 2:15). Loving the world merely leads the community astray, "for all that is in the world—the desire of the flesh, the desire of the eyes, the pride in riches—comes not from the Father but from the world" (2:16). Love for the brothers and sisters within the community of faith, under these siege conditions, becomes not only an act of communal self-preservation but also of prophetic resistance: in a world governed by hate, pride in riches, and the power of the Evil One, the love of the believing community for one another stands as a sign of the light that shines in the darkness and has not been extinguished.

When the Fourth Gospel is read against the background of this historical situation, as a response to a communal crisis of identity, its exhortations for love within the community sound less exclusionary and more like an urgent appeal for unity within an oppressed minority community. The urgency of that appeal had increased by the time of the composition of the Epistles, as the minority community itself had begun to undergo schism (see 1 John 2:18–27; 4:1–6; 2 John 7–11; 3 John 9–10). In this context, the distinctive Johannine appeal for love within the church is a poignant cry for solidarity in a church beset by external and internal stress.

(D) SOCIAL RELOCATION: "MY KINGDOM IS NOT OF THIS WORLD" In his important book *Johannine Faith and Liberating Community*, David Rensberger argues persuasively that the Johannine vision cannot be understood as a call merely for individual religious conversion or the acceptance of a set of doctrines. Rather, hearers of the Fourth Gospel's message were being called upon to step across a fateful line into a new community. This step entailed "a dangerous social relocation."[19] His analysis of the Nicodemus story (John 3) shows that the Fourth Gospel is calling upon Jewish secret sympathizers to make "a public transfer of allegiance" to Jesus:

> [T]he Fourth Evangelist seems to appeal to the secret Christians in high places to make an open confession and take their stand with the oppressed community. We should not underestimate the risk he is asking them to take. . . . They are being asked, in fact, to switch sides from persecutor to persecuted. The group they are being asked to join has no status, no power, no place in the world. They are being asked to dislocate and displace

> themselves socially, to undertake an act of deliberate downward mobility. Quite possibly they are being asked to risk their lives.[20]

Consequently, the alienation of John's community from its Jewish cultural context is fundamentally determinative for the ethics of the Fourth Gospel: one cannot become a follower of Jesus in this Gospel's narrative world without surrendering a position of privilege. Jesus' own fate of death by crucifixion is a powerful precedent and symbol for the social experience of those who follow him.

Furthermore, the community of believers in Jesus adopts a countercultural stance not only in its relation to Judaism but also in relation to Roman power and culture. This is most vividly dramatized in the scene of Jesus' trial before Pontius Pilate, where Jesus' kingship is ironically juxtaposed against the authority of Rome. Jesus declares, in response to Pilate's interrogation, that his kingdom is "not of this world"; the clearest sign of that fact is that his followers do not fight to resist Jesus' being handed over (18:36). In response to Pilate's claim to have power to crucify him, Jesus pointedly asserts that Pilate actually has no power over him; God has merely granted Pilate a temporary and limited authority in order that God's own purpose (the "lifting up" of Jesus by crucifixion) might be fulfilled (19:10–11). The whole dialogue subverts Roman claims of sovereignty and subordinates Roman power to the power of God. Readers within the community that finds its identity in Jesus are thereby encouraged to see their own relation to the world in an entirely new way. Again Rensberger:

> The sovereignty that Jesus asserts against Caesar is that of Israel's God, but precisely as *God's* sovereignty and not as the world's it is not won by violence. . . . What is involved is first of all a revolution of consciousness, the alienation of their allegiance away from the idolatrous and oppressive orders of the world toward the truth of God, the truth that makes free. . . . Allegiance to God's sovereignty through Jesus the King subverts the orders of the world and only this subverts them truly.[21]

Because the choice is drawn so clearly between the kingdom of this world and the kingdom of Jesus, the response of the chief priests is intensely ironic. When Pilate asks, "Shall I crucify your King?" they reply—in a de facto denial of Israel's God—"We have no king but the emperor" (19:15). In making that cynical declaration, they cast their lot with the powers of the world. Readers of John's Gospel, however, are exhorted to make the opposite choice, to declare, in effect, "We have no king but Jesus," and to live out the social consequences of that uncompromised allegiance.

3. Johannine Eschatology: "We know that we have passed from death to life"

Of all the texts in the New Testament, the Gospel of John undertakes the most radical reformulation of early Christian eschatological expectation. This Gospel bears telltale traces of a time when the death of the first generation of apostolic witnesses was posing a crisis for the community's faith.[22] For example, the author of the Gospel—or at least of its epilogue in John 21—has to squelch the rumor that Jesus had predicted that the Beloved Disciple, the source of the special tradition behind this Gospel, would not die before the parousia (21:20–23). This issue would likely arise as a problem for the community only if the Beloved Disciple had in fact died. Another important indication of the community's situation is found in Jesus' "high-priestly prayer" in John 17. Jesus prays in succession for himself (17:1–5), for his original disciples ("those whom you gave me from the world"; 17:6–19), and for the second generation of believers ("those who will believe in me through their word"; 17:20–26). The great burden of the prayer is "that they all may be one," united in Jesus despite their separation in time, "so that the world may know that you have sent me and have loved them even as you have loved me" (17:23). Such a prayer appears to address the concerns of a second generation of believers, reassuring them of their continuing relation to Jesus despite the loss of the link provided by the Beloved Disciple and other first-generation believers. For such readers, the words of the risen Jesus to Thomas would come as a comforting benediction: "Have you believed because you have seen me? Blessed are those who have not seen and yet have come to believe" (20:29).

In such a situation, the delay of Jesus' coming might have posed doubts and difficulties for the church. The Johannine tradition, however, had shaped its faith in such a way that the community was equipped to deal theologically with the delay of the parousia. Two distinctive elements in Johannine theology enabled the Fourth Gospel to cope with this situation: the conviction that judgment has already occurred in Jesus' encounter with the world, and the conviction that the Paraclete, the Holy Spirit, remains actively present in the community of faith. We shall examine each of these themes briefly before noting a handful of Johannine texts that continue also to speak of a future eschatological expectation.

(A) ***KRISIS*** The Fourth Gospel makes the extraordinary claim that God's eschatological judgment, rather than awaiting a future consummation associated with the resurrection of the dead and the return of Jesus in glory, has *already* occurred as a result of Jesus' coming into the world.

> *Indeed, God did not send the Son into the world to condemn the world, but in order that the world might be saved through him. Those who believe in him are not condemned; but those who do not believe are condemned already, because they have not believed in the name of the only Son of God. And this is the judgment [**krisis**], that the light has come into the world, and people loved darkness rather than light because their deeds were evil.*
> (3:17–19)

As Rudolf Bultmann observes, "The judgment takes place in just the fact that upon the encounter with Jesus the sunderance between faith and unfaith, between the sighted and the blind, is accomplished."[23] It is as though Jesus' coming had introduced a giant magnetic field into the world, and all human beings perforce lined up around either the positive or the negative pole. On the negative side, those who reject Jesus as God's messenger of salvation are beyond hope; they are "condemned already." On the positive side, those who believe have already passed through the critical moment and entered into eternal life: "Very truly, I tell you, anyone who hears my word and believes him who sent me has eternal life, and does not come under judgment, but has passed from death to life" (5:24).

Thus, for those in the believing community, eternal life is now. The eschatological event has already occurred. Believers need no longer await some future manifestation of God's kingdom in glory, for the glory of the kingdom was and is fully manifest in Jesus. Therefore, judgment is not a future event "out there" at the end of time; rather, it is happening now wherever the Word of God is preached. By our response to the Word we come under judgment or enter into life. That is John's eschatological vision.

That is why Jesus can respond to Martha's expression of faith that her dead brother Lazarus will rise again in the resurrection on the last day by offering an even more extravagant, though profoundly paradoxical, promise: "I am the resurrection and the life. Those who believe in me, even though they die, will live, and everyone who lives and believes in me will never die" (11:25–26). The person who knows Jesus as the one sent from the Father already possesses eschatological life in all its fullness. Therefore, mere physical death becomes a trivial matter. Jesus' subsequent action of raising Lazarus (11:38–44) becomes, then, an outward and visible sign of the spiritual truth that Jesus is more powerful than death, that death cannot snatch out of his hand those whom he loves.

Such a theological view, if carried out fully and consistently, transforms "death" and "life" into symbols for the quality and mode of existence in the present. Insofar as this has happened in the Fourth Gospel, the early Christian apocalyptic eschatology has been transformed into realized eschatology. Future judgment no longer hangs over the community, as in Matthew, as a warrant to motivate obedience in the present. Nor is the continuing history of the church to be understood, as in Luke, as a time in which the church carries out its patient mission of preparing a people for God, whose final judgment will establish cosmic justice. Least of all is the present time, as for Mark, a bleak time of keeping the faith and urgently longing for the return of the Son of Man. Rather, the community already lives in the fullness of eschatological life given by God to those who are in union with Jesus. In this assurance, the writer of 1 John can say, "We know that we have passed from death to life because we love one another" (1 John 3:14). The love within the community is the sign and guarantee that those who belong to Jesus are free from the grip of death. It hardly needs to be emphasized, therefore, that actual failures of love and schisms within the community—of the sort vividly reflected in the Johannine Epistles—pose a serious threat to the coherence of this sort of realized eschatology.

(B) THE PARACLETE John's distinctive doctrine of the Paraclete also answers the need created by the delay of the parousia and the death of the first-generation witnesses. The farewell discourse in the Fourth Gospel offers repeated reassurance that Jesus' departure will not leave the community "orphaned" (14:18).

> *If you love me, you will keep my commandments. And I will ask the Father, and he will give you another Advocate [**paraklētos**], to be with you forever. This is the Spirit of truth, whom the world cannot receive, because it neither sees him nor knows him. You know him, because he abides with you, and he will be among you.*[24] *. . . I have said these things to you while I am still with you. But the Advocate, the Holy Spirit, whom the Father will send in my name, will teach you everything, and remind you of all that I have said to you.* (14:15–17, 25–26)

Though Jesus must go away, returning to heaven to be with the Father, he will send the Paraclete to "abide" in the midst of the community. (The notion that the Spirit is to dwell individually within each believer—though fondly held by sentimental forms of Christian pietism—is a doubtful interpretation of these texts: John thinks of the Spirit present and speaking within the community of the faithful.) The function of the Paraclete is to teach the community, to remind followers of what Jesus had taught, and to testify about Jesus before the world (15:26, 16:7–11).[25] Most important, the Paraclete will provide continuing guidance, even about matters concerning which Jesus left no instructions.

> *I still have many things to say to you, but you cannot bear them now. When the Spirit of truth comes, he will guide you into all the truth; for he will not speak on his own, but will speak whatever he hears, and he will declare to you the things that are to come. He will glorify me, because he will take what is mine and declare it to you.* (16:12–14)

In short, the Paraclete is to provide not only God's continuing presence within the community but also a source of continuing revelation.

How does the Fourth Gospel envision this continuing guidance as taking place? The usual modern inclination is to think of some sort of intuitive knowledge in the hearts of individual believers, but in the setting of first-century Christianity it is far more likely, as D. Moody Smith and others have suggested, that we should think of the Paraclete as guiding the community through Spirit-inspired prophecy uttered in the worshiping assembly.[26] Indeed, the distinctive form of the words of Jesus found in the Fourth Gospel's *egō eimi* ("I am") discourses is best explained as the result of just this sort of charismatic prophetic activity.

Thus, any reflection about Johannine ethics must take seriously the community's expectation of being led by the Spirit. Indeed, that expectation may provide a partial explanation for the near absence of specific moral instruction in these texts. As 1 John says, "I write to you, not because you do not know the truth, but because you know it. . . . [T]he anointing that you received from him abides in you ['in your midst' (*en hymin*)], and so you do not need anyone to teach you" (1 John 2:21, 27a). Of course, the actual situation that elicits the letter suggests that the author's confidence on this point may be either a rhetorical gesture or wishful thinking, for "many false prophets have gone out into the world," and indeed "the world listens to them" (1 John 4:1, 5). The community has apparently experienced a split based on the claims of rival Spirit-inspired leaders speaking in the name of Jesus. The author of 1 John has a simple test for distinguishing truth from error in this situation: "We are from God. Whoever knows God listens to us, and whoever is not from God does not listen to us. From this we know the spirit of truth and the spirit of error" (1 John 4:6).

In any case, the active presence of the Paraclete in the community of believers is both a source of comfort and an aspect of the eternal life that the community already knows by abiding in Jesus. Thus, the urgency of any hope for future salvation is drastically diminished in the Johannine vision, especially in the Fourth Gospel.

(C) RESURRECTION ON THE LAST DAY Nonetheless, future hope has not disappeared altogether in these writings, nor can it, for reasons both theological and practical. As long as death, conflict, and schism remain in the world, no Christian community that seeks to hold creation and redemption together can collapse salvation entirely into the present. Thus, even in the Fourth Gospel we find alongside the spiritual realized eschatology several texts reaffirming the traditional early Christian future-oriented eschatology. The latter are, to be sure, a secondary theme in this Gospel, but their presence is crucial in keeping this Gospel from sliding over the brink into Gnosticism.

> *Do not be astonished at this; for the hour is coming when all who are in their graves will hear his voice and will come out—those who have done good, to the resurrection of life, and those who have done evil, to the resurrection of condemnation.* (JOHN 5:28–29)

This affirmation is the more significant because it follows hard upon the more characteristic Johannine assertion that "the hour is coming, *and is now here*, when the dead will hear the voice of the Son of God, and those who hear will live" (5:25, emphasis mine). In that assertion, "the dead" must be understood figuratively; however, the addition of verses 28–29, which reaffirm the future apocalyptic horizon of the gospel, shows that the Fourth Gospel is unwilling to dissolve the resurrection into a purely figurative sense.

Bultmann proposed that passages such as 5:28–29 were the handiwork of an "ecclesiastical redactor" who sought to accommodate John's radical theological vision to a more conventional early Christian framework of thought.[27] Other scholars have proposed more complicated hypotheses: Raymond Brown, for instance, regards 5:28–29 as older Johannine community tradition that was not originally included in the Fourth Gospel but was added at a later stage by a redactor—perhaps the author of 1 John?—who sought to preclude misinterpretations (such as Bultmann's!) of the Fourth Gospel's figurative language about realized eschatology.[28] It is, however, only a matter of conjecture that such passages (see also 6:39–40, 44, 54; 12:48) were added by anyone at a stage later than the original composition of the Gospel. The hypothesis is not impossible, but all we have before us is the text as it stands, with present and future eschatology side by side in a seemingly paradoxical relation to one another. (For a very compact formulation of the tension, see 6:54: "Those who eat my flesh and drink my blood have eternal life, and I will raise them up on the last day.") If, as Brown rightly observes, "within Jesus' own message there was a tension between realized and final eschatology,"[29] it is hard to see why we should deny that a similar tension might have been inherent in the message of the Fourth Evangelist. The best explanation for the tension, in other words, might be theological rather than source-critical.

John stresses, more than any of the other Gospels, the importance of the judging and life-giving power of God's Word in the present. But this message would be gravely truncated without the simultaneous future hope of the resurrection of which the present experience of "eternal life" is an anticipation. John seeks not to *supplant* future hope with present glory but rather to emphasize the fullness of life that Jesus offers in the present to those who believe. The ethical implications of this theological vision are not very fully worked out in the Fourth Gospel, but we may offer a few suggestions about the direction that such an outworking might take. Both the warrants and the norms for ethics are to be located almost exclusively in conformity to the person of Jesus. Future rewards and punishments play a minimal role in motivating ethical conduct; the thing that matters is living in the present in a way that authentically manifests the love of God in Christ. The specific behavior that issues from union with Jesus need not be spelled out in detail, for those who abide in Jesus will intuitively know what is right and do it. Indeed, 1 John can even make the extraordinary claim that "those who have been born of God do not sin . . . ; they cannot sin, because they have been born of God" (1 John 3:9). And yet the same author earlier insisted that "if we say that we have no sin, we deceive ourselves, and the truth is not in us" (1 John 1:8). How is the powerful tension between these assertions to be resolved? For the Johannine literature, as for the rest of the New Testament, the only possible resolution of the paradoxical conflict between the indicative and the imperative is to be found in the future eschatological hope:

> *Beloved, we are God's children now; what we will be has not yet been revealed. What we do know is this: when he is revealed, we will be like him, for we will see him as he is. And all who have this hope in him purify themselves, just as he is pure.* (1 JOHN 3:2–3)

4. John's Narrative World As Context for Action

Having traced the contours of John's symbolic world, we may now draw together some conclusions about the way in which that world establishes a framework for moral discernment and action.

First, in the Johannine narrative world, *time blurs and recedes into the background.* Because Jesus is the eternal Logos, he is not bound to past historical events and traditions; he can speak to the community at any time within history. The community's spiritual union with Jesus is so profound that the experiences of the community need not be sharply distinguished from the events of Jesus' life; the past and the present can be superimposed upon one another as a "two-level drama," so that the story of Jesus becomes the story of the community and vice versa.[30] The temporal distance between Jesus and the writer's time is dissolved. Thus, John's representation of temporality is closest to Matthew's and at the opposite pole from Luke's concern for chronological sequence and orderliness. The future dimension of eschatological hope is partially, but not entirely, eclipsed by John's celebration of oneness with Jesus in the present.

Second, the world according to John is characterized by *binary polarities*: light and darkness, above and below, good and evil, truth and lies, life and death. These antitheses admit of no ambiguity and no mediation. One must choose to declare for one or the other, and in that critical choice judgment already is accomplished. Despite the strongly dualistic character of these formulations, it is not quite correct to describe John's worldview as a cosmic dualism, for the powers of light and darkness are not equally counterposed. There is never any doubt of God's ultimate sovereignty and triumph over evil. The power of darkness is only illusory and temporary; thus, Jesus can say to his followers just before his passion, "In the world you face persecution. But take courage; I have conquered the world" (John 16:33).

Third, the social implications of this polarized worldview are a pervasive factor in shaping the Johannine tradition. The Fourth Gospel reflects on almost every page a history of acrimonious controversy with the Jewish community from which the Johannine community emerged. Compromise and accommodation were seen as impossible; the result was thoroughgoing *alienation of the Johannine church from its cultural roots and immediate social environment*. Thus, John depicts the community of faith as necessarily countercultural and wary of the world.

Fourth, within the community of the faithful, however, the Johannine tradition offers a glowing vision of *solidarity and fellowship*. Jesus' followers are marked by their powerful love for one another. (The popular—indeed, overworked—Christian song "They'll Know We Are Christians by Our Love" expresses vintage Johannine theology.) The love in question is not merely personal affection; it is expressed in servanthood for other members of the group, as definitively modeled in Jesus' act of foot-washing.

There is scant indication in the Johannine literature of hierarchical structure in the community. While figures such as the Beloved Disciple and the elder who wrote 2 and 3 John were revered leaders, the Johannine vision is notably egalitarian. All members of the group are said to be anointed by the Spirit and to know the truth (1 John 2:18–27). Most strikingly, Jesus addresses his followers no longer as servants but as his friends (John 15:13–15). (The remarkable character of this text may be most clearly seen if we try, by contrast, to imagine Matthew's Jesus addressing his disciples in similar terms!) Indeed, friendship is explicitly given an important role in John's picture of the Christian life. Jesus exemplifies a special love for selected characters in the story: Martha and Mary (11:5), Lazarus (11:36), and of course the Beloved Disciple. Thus, within the comprehensive love of the Christian fellowship, John allows for and even encourages special relations of love and friendship in a way that no other Gospel writer does.

The egalitarian character of the Johannine community may also have important implications for the role of women. The Johannine literature offers no hint that women are to play a subordinate role in the life of the church. Women appear in the Fourth Gospel as fully formed characters who interact with Jesus and embody authentic faith. Martha utters the same breakthrough revelatory confession about Jesus that Matthew ascribes to Peter ("You are the Messiah, the Son of God," 11:27); Jesus reveals himself as Messiah to the Samaritan woman, who then effectively proclaims the news about him to others (4:28–30, 39); Mary Magdalene becomes the first witness to the resurrection and the first bearer of the good news to the disciples (20:1–18).[31] Thus, women fully share and embody the mission of the community to confess and proclaim Jesus to the world.

Fifth, although the Johannine tradition gives little evidence of wrestling with the problem of how to distinguish between right and wrong conduct, there is *a clear formal rejection of sin and a mandate to live righteously.* This comes out most clearly in 1 John 3:4–10, which insists that "no one who abides in him sins" (v. 6). As we have noted, this assertion cannot be taken simply at face value, for the opening section of the letter clearly assumes that members of the community do in fact sin. The distinguishing mark of the community is not so much sinlessness as the willingness to bring their sins into the light, to confess them, and to receive forgiveness and cleansing by the blood of Jesus (1 John 1:5–9). If Jesus is "the Lamb of God who takes away the sin of the world" (John 1:29), then the church must be the community of those who know themselves to be forgiven sinners. Indeed, those who claim to be sinless are liars (1 John 1:10). Thus, the puzzling passage in 3:4–10 is best read as polemic against the secessionist opponents, who may be claiming to be "born of God" while committing flagrant sin.[32] This reading is confirmed by the conclusion of the unit:

> *The children of God and the children of the devil are revealed in this way: all who do not do what is right are not from God, nor are those who do not love their brothers and sisters.* (1 John 3:10)

The overall Johannine stance on the problem of sin is best summed up in 1 John 2:1: "My little children, I am writing these things to you so that you may not sin. But if anyone does sin, we have an advocate with the Father, Jesus Christ the righteous."

Sixth, *the presence of the Paraclete to guide the community of believers* provides comfort and moral confidence for the community. In the face of persecution and rejection by the world, the Holy Spirit—manifested through prophetic utterances in the community—sustains and directs the church in difficult times. Because the Spirit continues to reaffirm the life-giving power of Jesus, John's vision of the Christian life is deeply joyful despite all adversity.

Seventh, *the Word of God subverts the world's conception of power.* The Jewish leaders and Roman officials alike are shown to be mere pretenders who try to exert control over events that elude their grasp. Gail O'Day aptly describes Jesus' trial before Pilate: "What the narrative shows the reader is a ruler with all the accoutrements of power, with the authority to take away life, who stands powerless in the face of true power, authority, and life."[33] Because the cross is the event whereby Jesus is lifted up and glorified, the character of power is permanently and paradoxically redefined. In this, John stands unified with all the other New Testament witnesses. The point is of fundamental importance for all ethical reflection about the exercise of power.

Eighth, the subversion of power is only one manifestation of a distinctively *ironic vision of the world.* John delights in dramatic irony, in dialogues that have a double sense hidden from Jesus' interlocutors but evident to the informed Christian reader.[34] Such irony produces group solidarity within a community of interpreters who can respond appropriately to the evangelist's nods and winks. For example, when the high priest Caiaphas declares, "You know nothing at all! You do not understand that it is better for you to have one man die for the people than to have the whole nation destroyed" (John 11:49b–50), he means something like "To make an omelet, a few eggs must be broken." His words, however, are perceived by John and his readers as true in a sense far different from the one he intended. Irony is not, however, merely a clever literary device; it is also the necessary expression of the theological conviction that the world has failed to know the one through whom it came into being (cf. John 1:10–11). One comes to know who Jesus really is only through the ironic mode in which God has revealed him.

Finally, in the Fourth Gospel *incarnation deconstructs dualism.* Despite John's wariness about the world, his theological vision is ultimately not docetic or hostile to creation. Rather, at the level of deepest theological conviction, the Word made flesh affirms the goodness and significance of creation. All creation breathes with the life of the Logos, apart from whom there is no life (1:1–4). This conviction finds subliminal expression in John's masterful use of elemental, earthy symbols to articulate the Word: water, wine, bread, light, door, sheep, seed, vine, blood, fish. The truth of the Logos is manifest only in and through the medium of these symbols. No other New Testament writing so vividly visualizes the eternal in, with, and under the ordinary. The effect of such archetypal imagining is that the ordinary is transfigured. Despite the simplicity of this Gospel's language, it paints an aesthetically rich and powerful portrait of Jesus. The reader who responds to this portrait with imaginative sympathy can hardly lapse into the ethical blindness—as caricatured by J. T. Sanders[35]—of ignoring the dying man's blood and thinking only of his soul. Those who follow the Jesus of the Fourth Gospel—the Jesus who washes filthy feet and weeps at the tomb of Lazarus—will learn an ethic that loves "not in word or speech, but in truth and action," 1 John 3:18), for they follow a Lord who gives his own flesh fot the life of the world (John 6:51).

NOTES

1. "He does not *communicate anything,* but *calls men to himself.* . . . Thus it turns out in the end that Jesus as the Revealer of God *reveals nothing but that he is the Revealer*" (Bultmann 1955 [vol. 2], 41, 66).
2. For an opposing view, *see* Verhey 1984, 142–143.

3. For detailed discussion of the problems of authorship, see Brown 1982, 14–35. Schrage rightly decides to treat these writings as a unit with regard to their ethical content and implications (1988, 297). I follow the same procedure here.
4. H. R. Niebuhr 1951, 46–49.
5. Käsemann 1968, 59.
6. Houlden 1973, 36.
7. J. T. Sanders 1975, 100.
8. On the crucial question of John's attitude toward "the Jews," see Chapter 17.
9. Käsemann 1968, 8–9.
10. Käsemann 1968, 26.
11. In this observation and in the following analysis of the situation presupposed in 1 John, I depend heavily on R. E. Brown 1979b.
12. Augustine 398, 130–131.
13. "For the Time Being," in Mack, Dean, and Frost 1961, 215.
14. The NRSV's paragraph division, setting v. 18 apart as the beginning of the following section, is peculiar. I follow Nestle-Aland in taking v. 18 as the conclusion of the foregoing material.
15. The following sketch is built upon the work of Martyn 1979; Meeks 1972; R. E. Brown 1979b; R. E. Brown 1982; Wengst 1983; Smith 1984; and Rensberger 1988.
16. R. E. Brown 1982, 101–102.
17. J. Louis Martyn's pathbreaking study of the historical setting of the Fourth Gospel proposed that the formal exclusion of Jewish Christians from the synagogue should be traced to the reformulation, in the rabbinic academy at Jamnia, of the *Birkat-ha-Minim* ("benediction against heretics"), somewhere around 85 C.E. (Martyn 1979). For challenges to this view, see Kimelman 1981; Katz 1984.
18. Rensberger 1988, 26–27.
19. Rensberger 1988, 113.
20. Rensberger 1988, 114.
21. Rensberger 1988, 116–117.
22. Minear 1984; R. E. Brown 1984, 84–123.
23. Bultmann 1955 (vol. 2), 38.
24. Translating *en hymin*, with the NRSV footnote, as "among you," rather than "in you."
25. Again I must demur from the NRSV's rendering: *peri mou* in 15:26 means "about me" rather than "on my behalf."
26. Smith 1984, 15–17, 30–31; Boring 1979; cf. Johnston 1970, 119–148.
27. Bultmann 1955 (vol. 2), 39.
28. R. E. Brown 1966, cxxi.
29. R. E. Brown 1966, cxix.
30. Martyn 1979.
31. These points are noted by Käsemann 1968, 29–31; for fuller development of these observations, see R. E. Brown 1979a, 183–198; R. E. Brown 1984, 94–95; Schneiders 1982; and Schüssler Fiorenza 1983, 323–334.
32. Smith 1991, 82–88.
33. O'Day 1986, 112.
34. For accounts of Johannine irony, see Meeks 1972; Culpepper 1983; Duke 1985; and especially O'Day 1986.
35. See the Sanders quote in the first section of this chapter.

Chapter 7

Excursus

The Role of "the Historical Jesus" in New Testament Ethics

1. Why Not Begin with Jesus?

Books on New Testament ethics often begin with an extensive treatment of the ethical teachings of Jesus. Wolfgang Schrage's *The Ethics of the New Testament*, for example, devotes more than one hundred pages to a discussion of "Jesus' Eschatological Ethics," before turning to a brief sketch (twenty-five pages) of "Ethical Accents in the Synoptic Gospels."[1] In such a presentation, the focus of interest lies on Schrage's historical reconstruction of the figure of Jesus, while the Gospel writers are treated as editors who make slight adjustments to a received body of historical tradition. In the present book, I have placed much less emphasis on the historical Jesus and much more on the ethical perspectives of the individual evangelists. A word of explanation for this methodological decision is perhaps in order. Why not begin with a reconstruction of the ethics of the historical figure Jesus of Nazareth?

First of all, I reiterate that the purpose of this book is not to trace the history of early Christian ethics. A study intending to present the historical background and development of Christian ethics would, to be sure, have to begin with some account—however sketchy—of the ethics of Jesus. But that is a different matter from the aim of this book: to reflect on how the church's life should be shaped by the New Testament witnesses.

Second, despite the apparent objectivity of beginning with an appeal to the "historical," the history of New Testament research demonstrates that efforts to reconstruct the historical Jesus have been beset by subjectivity and cultural bias. Albert Schweitzer's classic study *The Quest of the Historical Jesus* amply documented this difficulty in nineteenth-century "life of Jesus" research,[2] and the problem continues unabated in the present renewed outpouring of studies of the historical Jesus.[3] The temptation to project upon the figure of Jesus our own notions of the ideal religious personality is nearly irresistible.[4] As Martin Kähler sagely observed almost one hundred years ago, the critic who reconstructs a "historical Jesus" inevitably becomes a "fifth evangelist," cutting and pasting the tradition so as to articulate a new vision of Jesus for his or her own time.[5] Sometimes this outcome of historical inquiry is explicitly embraced, as in the programmatic comments of Robert Funk, the founder of the "Jesus Seminar":

> We are having increasing difficulty these days in accepting the biblical account of the creation and of the apocalyptic conclusion in anything like a literal sense. . . . But our crisis goes beyond these terminal points: it affects the middle as well. . . . To put the matter bluntly, we are having as much trouble with the middle—the messiah—as we are with the terminal points. What we need is a new fiction that takes as its starting point the central event in the Judeo-Christian drama. . . . In sum, we need a new narrative of Jesus, a new gospel, if you will, that places Jesus differently in the grand scheme, the epic story.[6]

Funk's remarks clearly acknowledge a point not always stated with such candor: the act of historical reconstruction is necessarily a hermeneutical endeavor. Insofar as the historian rejects the interpretive frameworks of the Gospel writers, some other framework must be provided. This is not necessarily a bad thing, but the recognition of this point does undercut one of the principal arguments for beginning the study of New Testament ethics with the historical Jesus: to do so is not to attain some greater degree of objectivity or factual security. It would be a curious act of intellectual hubris to suppose that our speculative reconstruction could give us a picture of Jesus immune to the vicissitudes of subjectivity.

In fact, we have a better chance of holding our own predispositions in abeyance—and thus allowing our communities to be shaped by Scripture—if we follow the procedure adopted in this book of treating each Gospel individually and attending to its narrative logic, its representation of the figure of Jesus, and its consequent moral world. Because each Gospel has a determinate structure and content, the interpretive imagination is given a set of constant constraints that guide and limit the range of viable readings. This range is narrower than the range of possible critical reconstructions of Jesus. Thus, we are more likely to reach consensus about literary and theological readings of the individual Gospel texts than about the historical figure who stands behind them all. The evidence for this claim may be found in the scholarly secondary literature; there is a far higher degree of agreement about, say, the theology of Matthew than about the content of the teaching of the Jesus of history. Of course, this is not to say that the Gospels are "foolproof" compositions[7] or that each Gospel has a univocal meaning. Debates still rage about various points, such as Luke's attitude toward Judaism. Mark is a more ambiguous text than the other three Gospels, offering less narrative closure and therefore inviting a greater diversity of interpretations. Nonetheless, it makes sense to claim modestly that New Testament ethics will find a more stable starting place if we begin with the moral visions of the individual texts than if we try to begin by reconstructing Jesus.

That is one of the reasons that Rudolf Bultmann opined that the preaching of Jesus belongs not to the theology of the New Testament but to its presuppositions.[8] Jesus is, after all, not one of the New Testament writers. His life and death constitute the subject matter for the New Testament's narration and reflection, but if the aim of our inquiry is the ethics of the New Testament, the ethical teaching of the historical Jesus will enter the picture only indirectly, as it is filtered through the compositional purposes of the evangelists. The theological function of the New Testament canon is to designate precisely these interpretations of Jesus as authoritative for the continuing life and practice of the community. Therefore, the historian's reimagining of Jesus, however informative and interesting, can never claim the same normative theological status as the four diverse canonical accounts. Consequently, in a work (such as the present one) that aims to read the New Testament as normative for the church's ethical reflection, it makes more sense to stay with the texts and to interpret the moral visions that confront us there, in the Jesus rendered by the individual evangelists.

Having said all that, however, it must be acknowledged that the question about the Jesus of history will not go away, because the question of truth looms. If the canonical accounts of Jesus were in fundamental conflict with what actually happened, if they were sheer fabrications of religious fanaticism or wishful thinking,[9] then Christians would be, in Paul's words, of all people most to be pitied. If the New Testament writers based their moral visions on a distorted or fundamentally mistaken view of what Jesus of Nazareth actually did and taught, then the church's subsequent reliance on these texts would be misplaced. Historical inquiry can never prove the truth of the kerygma, but historical inquiry might *disconfirm* it; consequently, intellectual integrity demands some investigation of what can be known historically about Jesus, even if our historical knowledge is subject to serious limitations. As Ernst Käsemann formulated the problem, the Jesus of history must ultimately serve as a criterion against which the New Testament's diverse formulations of the kerygma must be measured; otherwise, we are in danger of "falling into docetism and depriving ourselves of the possibility of drawing a line between the Easter faith of the community and myth."[10] By pressing the question about the Jesus of history, we seek to avoid falling into an enthusiastic religious subjectivity that ignores the question of what God has done *extra nos* in the world.

It is far beyond the scope of the present book to undertake a full treatment of the problem of the historical Jesus. Nonetheless, it is perhaps not a gratuitous gesture for me to give a brief account of the general outlines of my understanding of Jesus, especially since much attention has been given in the popular press to revisionist representations of Jesus as an itinerant Cynic philosopher specializing in aphoristic wisdom sayings. The Jesus portrayed in the findings of the Jesus Seminar is indeed far removed from the Jesus depicted by Matthew, Mark, Luke, and John.[11] The following sketch will display my own assessment of the evidence, pointing to a historical figure who might reasonably stand behind the canonical traditions.

2. Methods for the Quest

What methods should be followed in assessing the historical value of the traditions about Jesus that are available to us? The following list of methodological guidelines indicates the procedures that I think appropriate in seeking to reconstruct the Jesus of history. Although I cannot defend in detail here my reasons for adopting these guidelines, they offer the reader some basis for understanding and evaluating the conclusions that follow.[12]

- Jesus must be located organically within first-century Palestinian Judaism. He neither rejected nor sought to supersede the faith of his people.
- Jesus' life and teaching stand in some relation of continuity with the movement that he initiated—that is, the church.[13] (The effect of these first two guidelines is to counteract the "criterion of dissimilarity," which decrees that we can be most confident of the authenticity of the tradition when it represents Jesus as standing out of synch with first-century Judaism and with emergent Christianity.)
- A reconstructed narrative account of Jesus' life must yield some plausibly continuous picture of how Jesus' activity and fate led, within the social and religious world of ancient Judaism, to the formation of the church. How did events move from *a* to *b*? What is necessary to account for the development?[14]
- The reconstruction must pose some plausible explanation for the relation between Jesus' life and teaching, on the one hand, and his death, on the other.[15] Why did Jesus die on a cross? And how could his death have been interpreted at such an early date as having redemptive efficacy?
- The sayings traditions must not be weighed more heavily than the historical narrative materials. Both are essential to a coherent picture of Jesus.[16]
- The Gospel of John should not be dismissed in principle as a historical source, despite its heavily theological agenda. All four Gospels, after all, are theological. The Fourth Gospel claims to be based on eyewitness testimony. Even though John is more difficult to use with confidence as a historical source, its claims should not be dismissed out of hand.

- The Gospel of Thomas is a second-century Gnostic text. Though it may contain some independently transmitted traditions of Jesus' sayings, it is demonstrably dependent upon the synoptic tradition,[17] and it is therefore of secondary value as a historical source. Similarly, the Gospel of Peter, alleged by some to contain tradition older than the synoptic passion narratives,[18] is a second-century text derived loosely from the synoptic accounts; it has little or no independent historical value.[19]
- The burden of proof lies upon claims concerning the inauthenticity of material in the Gospel tradition, not upon claims for authenticity. The criteria of multiple attestation and coherence are far more important than the criterion of dissimilarity, which is useful primarily for targeting points of maximum historical probability.
- Wisdom lies in humility. Claims to historical knowledge should not transgress the constraints of modesty. We know less than we are fond of supposing.[20]

3. The Life and Teachings of Jesus: A Proposed Reconstruction

(A) THE CENTER Jesus was a Jew from Nazareth in Galilee who was put to death in approximately 30 C.E. by the Roman governor Pontius Pilate on a charge of insurrection.

That is the center, the fixed datum and reference point from which our reconstruction must proceed. Beyond this, all our other remarks will possess decreasing historical certainty. I do not believe that we can reconstruct the sequence of events in Jesus' public career. We know the beginning (his baptism by John) and the end (his crucifixion), and we have a drawerfull of snapshots that go somewhere in the middle, but we cannot confidently reconstruct a dramatic development. The one event that can be placed with some confidence is his demonstration in the Temple against the money-changers and sellers of animals. Presumably, this Temple incident was the precipitating factor in his arrest and execution.[21]

(B) JESUS' BACKGROUND Jesus came from Galilee. This is in itself a significant fact, for it indicates that his roots were in a region that was marginal in relation to the established religious and political centers of power in Judaism.[22] About his early life we know almost nothing. Tradition says that he was an artisan or the son of an artisan (Mark 6:3; Matt. 13:55). He seems to have studied the Scriptures deeply, but this does not necessarily imply formal training as a rabbi. We can trace his public career from his baptism by John the Baptist, an event that the Gospels retain in memory despite a certain embarrassment about it (e.g., Matt. 3:13–15). It is possible, but not certain, that Jesus may have been, prior to his baptism, a disciple of John. This would mean that he would have held an apocalyptic expectation of the coming of God's Messiah to establish the rule of God's righteousness (i.e., the kingdom of God).

(C) JESUS' MOVEMENT Jesus soon struck out on his own and became a controversial public figure, a man who was widely perceived as a prophet mighty in word and deed. He assembled a group of disciples around himself and taught them. He singled out twelve of them as symbolic heads of the new eschatological Israel, which he proclaimed and hoped to bring into being. This symbolic act is a clear sign that he understood his movement in terms of "restorationist eschatology"; in other words, he was anticipating that God would act to restore Israel to its lost glory.[23]

Jesus also attracted a large following among the fringe and outcast groups in Palestinian society.[24] Sinners and tax collectors, cripples, lepers, prostitutes—all the folks who were disdained by educated citizens with taste and theological education: this was the constituency of the Jesus movement. (One thinks of the characters in Flannery O'Connor's short stories.) Part of his appeal for these groups derived from his reputation as a healer and miracle-worker. I think that we should credit the historical truth of this picture.[25] Even where the Gospels show some discomfort with this portrayal of Jesus, it is never denied, only qualified so that he is seen as a reluctant miracle-worker who intends his healings to point to a truth that continues to elude the popular perception.

(D) JESUS' MESSAGE Jesus spoke characteristically in parables and stories that declared the imminent bursting in of God's kingdom, bringing grace and mercy in unexpected ways in unexpected places. (Interestingly, Jesus' mode of parabolic discourse was generally not emulated in the early Christian tradition.) The parables of the coming kingdom must be taken closely together with his warnings of apocalyptic judgment: he preached that the kingdom of God would bring the radical restoration of God's justice, setting things right but bringing judgment and destruction on those who resist God's will. The tendency in some recent New Testament scholarship to sever the message of grace from the message of judgment and to regard the latter as inauthentic is the natural—and misleading—consequence of isolating Jesus from the Jewish prophetic tradition within which all his words and actions must be understood.

Jesus' message was controversial and threatening to the established institutions of religious and political power in his society: the message carried with it a fundamental transvaluation of values, an exalting of the humble and a critique of the mighty. The theme of *reversal* seems to have been pervasive in his thought. To "the chief priests and the elders of the people," for example, he declared: "The tax collectors and the prostitutes are going into the kingdom before you" (that is, becoming adherents of the Jesus movement; Matt. 21:31). This reversal motif is built into the deep structure of Jesus' message, present in all layers of the tradition; thus, the criterion of multiple attestation validates this theme as a foundational element of Jesus' teaching. We find it in *sayings*—for example, "Whoever would save his life will lose it, and whoever loses his life for my sake and the gospel's will find it" (Mark 8:35, RSV)—and in the *Beatitudes*, especially in the Lukan version (Luke 6:20–26), which is likely to be more original than Matthew's spiritualized account. We find it in *parables*: the prodigal Son (Luke 15:11–32), the unjust steward (Luke

16:1–8). We find it in controversy pronouncements: for example, Matthew 21:31, cited above. And, perhaps most tellingly, we find it in Jesus' *actions*, his association with the unclean and outcasts.

It is unlikely that Jesus proclaimed an abrogation or even a critique of the Law. His critique seems to have been directed instead at those who *professed* allegiance to the Law while ignoring its weightier demands, its fundamental thrust toward justice and mercy. In this respect, he stood squarely in the prophetic tradition. This is first and foremost the way in which the historical Jesus should be understood: he was a prophet in the tradition of the prophets of Israel, warning of God's judgment on Israel, calling Israel to repentance and acknowledgment of God's justice in human affairs.

It is likely that Jesus explicitly interpreted his own mission in terms of paradigms provided by Israel's prophetic texts. If he understood himself to be gathering the eschatological Israel, surely he thought of this action in terms suggested by Isaiah (cf. Luke 7:18–23). If he pronounced a word of judgment on the Temple when Israel refused his summons, he did so in terms that evoked echoes of Jeremiah's Temple sermon (Mark 11:15–17; cf. Jer. 7:1–15).

Jesus spurned violence as the appropriate instrument of God's righteousness (see Mark 10:42–45). He taught love of enemies and rejected any suggestion of armed resistance to authority, even Roman authority. This combination of nonresistance with his inflammatory critique of those in power inevitably finds its consequence in the cross. Thus, it is not improbable that Jesus came to understand his own vocation in terms of necessary suffering and death.

(E) THE RESPONSE: VIOLENT REJECTION Jesus' activity and proclamation brought him squarely into conflict with the guardians of order in Jewish society. Whether it was Jesus' intention or not, his proclamation of the kingdom of God was inevitably heard as a revolutionary manifesto; the whole Gospel tradition is full of evidence of this. People wanted to make him king (John 6:15), and Peter's confession (Mark 8:29) means nothing other than this. It was this popular perception that finally proved his undoing: the inscription on the cross proves that he was executed as one who claimed to be "king of the Jews." And indeed, it would appear that he refused to get himself off the hook by denying the charge. Thus, we have a situation pregnant with ambiguity. The whole shape of the tradition indicates that Jesus—in contrast to other figures in Jewish history of the era, such as Bar Kochba—persistently refused to claim that he was the Messiah (cf. John 10:24). His whole message entailed a rejection of the violence and nationalism implied in the popular understanding of that title. Yet his words and deeds incited in the people a vivid expectation that he might, after all, be the one who would deliver Israel. There is a deep irony here. One might almost see Jesus as a victim crushed between the jaws of opposing historical forces. He rejected the way of violent revolution and so disappointed the hopes of many of his own followers; but because he excited—perhaps contrary to his own intention—messianic hopes, he was executed by the authorities as a potential danger to the stability of the social order. The reasons for his demise may have been similar to those adduced by Josephus for the execution of John the Baptist:

> When others too joined the crowds about him, because they were aroused to the highest degree by his sermons, Herod became alarmed. Eloquence that had so great an effect on mankind might lead to some form of sedition, for it looked as if they would be guided by John in everything that they did. Herod decided therefore that it would be much better to strike first and be rid of him before his work led to an uprising, than to wait for an upheaval, get involved in a difficult situation and see his mistake.[26]

So Jesus also was executed as a revolutionary, or at least as a potential security threat—as indeed he was, though not in quite the sense the authorities feared.

(E) GOD'S ANSWER: RESURRECTION Shortly after Jesus' death, the same followers who had fled in terror when he was arrested began proclaiming that he had been raised from the dead and had appeared to them. They understood this as a vindication of his whole life and message, particularly of his status as God's anointed one, the Messiah. They also saw his resurrection as the proleptic realization of the final triumph of God's kingdom in history, the foreshadowing of the general resurrection of the dead: as lightning is to thunder, so Jesus' resurrection is to the consummation of all things. There were no independent witnesses to the disciples' claim outside the community, however—no "independent sightings." Jesus did not appear in the Temple and chastise his opponents; he did not appear to Pilate or in Rome to Caesar.

Nonetheless, the resurrection, just as much as the other events of the story, must be assessed as a historical event. It is told as such in the narratives. Certainly, it is a mysterious event, but it is *not* presented as a vision, a dream, a theological inference, or an ineffable event in the hearts of those who loved him. It is told as another remarkable event within the narrative, as the bodily resurrection of the man Jesus, leaving the tomb empty, conversing with his disciples, showing them his hands and his feet, eating fish with them. This is the historical event that alone renders the development of the church historically explicable. This is the historical event in the light of which all our history must be interpreted anew.

With this conclusion, I part company with many New Testament scholars and theologians who think it inappropriate to describe the resurrection as a historical event.[27] One may readily concede that the historical factuality of the resurrection cannot be affirmed with the same level of confidence as the historical factuality of the crucifixion. All historical judgments can be made only with relative certainty, and the judgment that Jesus rose from the dead can be offered—from the historian's point of view—only with great caution. The character of the event itself hardly falls within ordinary categories of experience.[28] Still, something extraordinary happened shortly after Jesus' death that rallied the dispirited disciples and sent them out proclaiming to the world that Jesus had risen and had appeared to them. Reductive psychological explanations fail to do justice to the widespread testimony to this event within the original community and to the moral seriousness of the movement that resulted from it. The best explanation is to say that God did something beyond all power of human imagining by raising Jesus from the dead.

To make such a claim is to make an assertion that redefines reality.[29] If such an event has happened in history, then history is not a closed system of immanent causes and effects. God is powerfully at work in the world in ways that defy common sense, redeeming the creation from its bondage to necessity and decay. That, of course, is precisely what the early Christians believed and proclaimed:

> *I pray that the God of our Lord Jesus Christ, the Father of glory, may give you a spirit of wisdom and revelation as you come to know him, so that, with the eyes of your heart enlightened, you may know what is the hope to which he has called you, what are the riches of his glorious inheritance among the saints, and what is the immeasurable greatness of his power for us who believe, according to the working of his great power.* ***God put this power to work in Christ when he raised him from the dead*** *and seated him at his right hand in the heavenly places, far above all rule and authority and power and dominion, and above every name that is named, not only in this age but also in the age to come.*
> (EPH. 1:17–21, *emphasis mine*)

4. Implications for Christian Ethics

All of this has far-reaching implications for Christian ethics. If God really did raise Jesus from the dead, everything that Jesus taught and exemplified is vindicated by a God more powerful than death. He must therefore be seen as the bearer of the truth and the definitive paradigm for obedience to God. The New Testament writers seek in their own ways to develop the moral implications of this confession for the life of the community.

The foregoing historical sketch of the figure of Jesus of Nazareth is fundamentally congruent with the witness of the evangelists, though each of them highlights different aspects and introduces other themes not included in this minimal historical reconstruction. We may summarize some of the motifs within New Testament ethics that would be highlighted if my historical account were read in counterpoint with the canonical witnesses:

- The continuity of the gospel with Israel's heritage would be highlighted. Jesus' activity pointed toward the creation of a restored Israel, proleptically figured in the community of his disciples. Insofar as the church seeks to maintain continuity of its life and witness with the historical Jesus, it must consciously ground its identity in the tradition of Israel and wrestle with the issues posed both by Israel's election and by Israel's unfaithfulness. The struggle with this tension was central to Jesus' career.
- The apocalyptic character of Jesus' preaching would remain determinative for the symbolic world of the Christian community. The historical reality of the resurrection validates both apocalyptic hope and apocalyptic critique of the status quo in a world alienated from its Creator.

- The reversal of "normal" conceptions of status and power was central to the message of Jesus and would remain central for a community that carries on his legacy. The kingdom of God belongs to the poor, the outcasts, the weak, the children. Wherever the church becomes acclimated and deferential to conventional human authority that rests upon pride and coercion, it has lost continuity with the Jesus of history.
- Jesus' emphatic reaffirmation of the prophetic call for justice and mercy as the hallmarks of God's covenant people suggests that a community bearing his name ought to return again and again to the prophets to find its ethical bearings.
- Jesus' rejection of violence and his call to love the enemy would be given prominence in any ethic that looked to the historical Jesus for direction.
- Jesus of Nazareth died on a cross. Those who follow him can hardly expect better treatment from the world. Insofar as the community of faith follows the path of the Jesus of history, it should expect suffering as its lot.

As we have seen, each of these points is dramatized in one way or another by the canonical evangelists. Thus, in one sense, the reconstruction of the historical Jesus adds nothing new to New Testament ethics. If it adds anything at all, it is merely what Luke calls *asphaleia*, a confidence in the truth of the things about which we have been instructed by the storytellers who wrote the Gospels. They did not invent their portrayals of Jesus out of whole cloth; rather, they were assembling pieces already cut according to his pattern. For the church, it is perhaps important to know that the obedience of faith was lived out in history by the flesh-and-blood man Jesus, for his example teaches us that to trust in the power of God over history is not to trust in vain.

NOTES

1. Schrage 1988. See also Verhey 1984.
2. Schweitzer 1968 [1906].
3. See, for example, Luke T. Johnson's evaluation of John Dominic Crossan's exhaustive study, *The Historical Jesus: The Life of a Mediterranean Jewish Peasant* (Crossan 1991): "Perhaps after all these authors [Crossan and John P. Meier] have not escaped the tendencies so acutely described by Schweitzer. Does not Crossan's picture of a peasant cynic preaching inclusiveness and equality fit perfectly the idealized ethos of the late twentieth-century academic?" (L. T. Johnson 1992, 26).
4. For a broad account of different images of Jesus as mirrors of general cultural history from the first century to the present, see Pelikan 1985.
5. Kähler 1964 [1896].
6. Funk 1985, 5–6.
7. As Sternberg (1985, 48–56, 230–235) claims for the Hebrew Bible.
8. Bultmann 1951 (vol. 1), 3.
9. As claimed, for example, by Mack 1988.
10. Käsemann 1964 [1960], 15–47 (quotation from p. 34); cf. Käsemann 1969 [1965], 23–65. For an exposition of Käsemann's views on this topic, see Ehler 1986, 161–273.
11. For my critique of the Jesus Seminar, see Hays 1994. See also Witherington 1995, 42–57; L. T. Johnson 1996.
12. Readers conversant with the literature in the field will recognize that my approach to method has been significantly shaped by Dahl 1976; Dahl 1991; and E. P. Sanders 1985; E. P. Sanders 1993.
13. Dahl 1991, 81–111.
14. See Riches 1982; Harvey 1982.

15. Dahl 1991, 98–99; E. P. Sanders 1985, 22.

16. E. P. Sanders (1985) gives priority to narrative materials about events in Jesus' career. This is a helpful corrective to the prevailing tendencies of previous research. I would insist, however, that the significance of the events can hardly be understood apart from the sayings traditions.

17. Tuckett 1988; Wright 1992, 440–443.

18. See, e.g., Crossan 1988.

19. R. E. Brown 1987; R. E. Brown 1994, 1317–1349.

20. Thus, I am less confident than Ben Witherington (1990) that we can gain access, as historians, to Jesus' self-understanding. See L. T. Johnson 1996, 81–104.

21. E. P. Sanders 1985, 61–76.

22. Meier (1991), who emphasizes the marginality of Jesus, writes, "Jesus, the poor layman turned prophet and teacher, the religious figure from rural Galilee without credentials, met his death in Jerusalem at least in part because of his clash with the rich aristocratic urban priesthood. To the latter, a poor layman from the Galilean countryside with disturbing doctrines and claims was marginal both in the sense of being dangerously anti-establishment and in the sense of lacking a power base in the capital. He could be easily brushed aside into the dustbin of death" (9).

23. E. P. Sanders 1985.

24. Crossan 1991.

25. Here again I find myself in agreement with Crossan 1991, 303–353.

26. Josephus, *Antiquities* 18.118.

27. For example, Bornkamm 1960 [1956], 180: "The event of Christ's resurrection from the dead, his life and his eternal reign, are things removed from historical scholarship. History cannot ascertain and establish conclusively the facts about them as it can with other events of the past. The last historical fact available to them is the Easter faith of the first disciples." For different assessments, more open (in varying degrees) to considering the resurrection as a historical event, see Pannenberg 1977 [1964], 80–106; L. T. Johnson 1986, 98–113; E. P. Sanders 1985, 320; E. P. Sanders 1993, 276–281.

28. See the helpful discussion by L. T. Johnson 1986, 98–113.

29. The epistemological—and therefore ethical—consequences of faith in the resurrection are far-reaching. The topic is too massive to be examined here. One theologian who has seen the dimensions of the issue is Oliver O'Donovan, in his book *Resurrection and Moral Order* (1994). See also my discussion of Karl Barth in Chapter 12.2.

Chapter 8

Revelation

Resisting the Beast

Friedrich Nietzsche characterized the book of Revelation as "the most rabid outburst of vindictiveness in all recorded history."[1] In the book's spectacular depiction of God's eschatological destruction of the wicked, Nietzsche saw the ultimate fantasy of *ressentiment:* the repressed hatred of pious weaklings toward the powerful. For slightly different reasons, Jack T. Sanders registers moral revulsion toward the Apocalypse: because of its imminent eschatology, it exemplifies a "retreat from ethical responsibility." According to his interpretation, it encourages individuals to withdraw from attempting to solve social problems. To the extent that this is so, "its existence and its place in the canon are, in the fullest sense of the word, evil."[2] Krister Stendahl has described the scenario sketched by Revelation as a "script for a horror movie."[3] Are these negative construals justified? Such strong reactions are evoked by a strong text, one that symbolizes cosmic conflict in vivid imagery and calls the community of the faithful to an unambiguous witness against the regnant powers of the world. But is Revelation devoid of ethical value? Such questions can be answered only through a closer reading of the text's apocalyptic symbolism.

The entire content of the book is presented as a visionary revelation (*apokalypsis*, Rev. 1:1) granted to someone named John, who identifies himself only as "your brother who share[s] with you in Jesus the persecution and the kingdom and the patient endurance [*hypomonē*]" (1:9).[4] Exiled on the island of Patmos "because of the word of God and the testimony of Jesus," he received these visions while he was "in the spirit on the Lord's Day" (1:9–10). The book draws heavily on the symbolic lexicon of Jewish apocalyptic tradition, especially the book of Daniel, but—as we shall see—it subjects that tradition to some important hermeneutical modifications in light of the story of Jesus.

The epistolary framework of the book indicates that its prophetic message is addressed to "the seven churches that are in Asia" (1:4)—that is, the seven churches to whom the seven letters of 2:1–3:22 are addressed. The work's frequent references to persecution are usually taken to indicate that it was written during the reign of the Emperor Domitian (81–96 C.E.), under whom the cult of emperor worship flourished in the province of Asia. Presumably, the churches were suffering persecution because of their refusal to participate in veneration of the emperor. Whether the persecution was a matter of official imperial policy is a debated issue; it is perhaps more likely to have involved sporadic local harassment.[5] Indeed, some features of the text suggest that the churches were threatened less by organized oppression than by comfortable complacency.

Nonetheless, whatever the precise historical circumstances in which it originated, the book of Revelation is above all else a political resistance document. It refuses to acknowledge the legitimacy and authority of earthly rulers and looks defiantly to the future, when all things will be subjected to the authority of God. It seeks to rally the seven churches to a stance of courageous witness against a culture that dangles seductive defilements before the people of God, seeking if possible to lead even the saints astray. This situation must be kept in mind as we assess the moral vision of the Apocalypse.

1. Apocalyptic Symbolism: The Interpretive Choice

In every generation, interpreters have strained to make sense of the phantasmagoric imagery of the Apocalypse. Because the book's symbolism is elaborate and obscure, it remains open to many possible readings. In order to proceed with the interpretation of this work, we must make some preliminary decisions about the literary genre of the book and about the strategies appropriate to grasping it. How shall we read? How are we to construe this proliferation of bizarre visions and imagery? Broadly speaking, we may distinguish three basic interpretive approaches: the *predictive*, the *historical*, and the *theopoetic*.[6]

(A) PREDICTIVE The predictive interpretive strategy, which has persisted throughout the history of the church, reads the text as a literal transcript of future historical events. Certainly, the superscription of the work creates that expectation: "The revelation of Jesus Christ, which God gave him to show his servants what must soon take place" (1:1). Because the book's visions are revealed from the heavenly throneroom, they grant to the elect a privileged foreknowledge of what is to happen very soon (cf. 22:6, 10). Each generation that follows this reading strategy tends to consider itself the last before the final great cosmic battle and the establishment of the messianic kingdom on earth. The text is then read as a coded allegory of contemporary political events.

Hal Lindsey's popular book *The Late Great Planet Earth,* originally published in 1970, is an excellent example of this approach.[7] By identifying the Soviet Union with the Beast from the abyss, Lindsey promoted hard-line Cold War politics in the name of evangelical Christianity. The book sold more than seven million copies,[8] but its reading of Revelation was summarily disconfirmed by the demise of the Soviet Union and the collapse of the Iron Curtain at the end of the 1980s. There was nothing surprising about this outcome, of course; ever since the second century, interpreters who have adopted similar reading strategies have experienced similar disappointments. Whether the Beast was identified with the pope or Cromwell or Napoleon or Hitler or Gorbachev, the result has been the same: history goes on, and the ardent predictions of the interpreters are consigned to the junkyard of exegetical curiosities. Yet history's inexorable disconfirmation of all such attempts never seems to discourage new generations of readers from thinking that now at last the pattern of events concealed in Revelation's mysterious symbolism is coming to light in the present time.

Thus, during the early stages of the Gulf War in 1991, there was feverish speculation in some quarters that this war might lead to the great final battle of Armageddon (see Rev. 16:14–16). As a New Testament professor, I received telephone calls from newpaper reporters from Hartford to Houston asking whether I thought Saddam Hussein might be the Antichrist. I told them that if they really wanted to know what light the Bible might shed on this war, I would suggest some other places to start! (See Chapter 14.) Few of them, however, were interested in hearing that the fundamental witness of the New Testament was to forbid Christians to fight; that made less titillating copy for feature stories.

It will be evident from these remarks that I believe the predictive reading strategy to be fundamentally mistaken, not just in its particular identification of the symbols in the text but in its fundamental perception of the genre of the text. The book was not written to predict particular historical events two thousand years in the future of its original author and audience. To construe it in that way is to make a foolish category mistake and—most important—to misread its word to the church.

Perhaps an analogy will clarify the point. Let us suppose that a sect should arise promulgating the view that J. R. R. Tolkien's *The Lord of the Rings* was actually an inspired prophecy forecasting political events that must occur before the year 2000. The members of the sect would then busy themselves in attempting to work out the symbolic correlations between the story's characters and the dramatis personae of the world's political stage in the 1990s. Some of the proposals might be enormously detailed and ingenious, but surely we would have to say to such interpreters, "No, you've got it all wrong; *The Lord of the Rings* is not that sort of text at all." Something similar must be said to those who read Revelation as predictive in this way.

(B) HISTORICAL Should the book then be read not as a prediction of future events but as commentary on political events and figures of the author's own time? Clearly, this is a far more promising strategy. Texts of the apocalyptic genre demonstrably worked this way in Jewish tradition: Daniel, for instance—like Revelation, a resistance document—must be read as commentary and exhortation to the Jewish community during the oppressive reign of Antiochus IV Epiphanes in the second century B.C.E.[9] By appropriating the symbolic vocabulary of this tradition, Revelation virtually demands to be read in an analogous fashion. The original audience of the book would have read such symbolism "as fluently as any modern reader of the daily papers reads the conventional symbols of a political cartoon."[10] (For example, American readers of a political cartoon featuring an elephant and a donkey immediately know that the elephant symbolizes the Republican party and that the donkey symbolizes the Democrats.) As Adela Yarbro Collins maintains, "[T]he hardest won and most dearly held result of historical-critical scholarship on the Revelation to John" is that its imagery must be interpreted with reference to "contemporary [i.e., first-century] historical events and to eschatological images current at the time."[11] Thus, according to this interpretive strategy, in order to interpret the text we must decode its symbolism by finding referents in first-century persons and events known through other historical sources. This approach shares with the strategy of reading Revelation as a prophetic disclosure of things to come the assumption that the text must be interpreted through one-to-one decoding of its symbols. The difference is that the historical realities to which the text refers are taken to lie not in the future but in the past.

Such a reading of the book recognizes that the Beast of Revelation 13 symbolizes the Roman Empire (or one of its emperors) and that "Babylon the great, mother of whores and of earth's abominations" (17:5), symbolizes the city of Rome itself, "seated" on seven mountains (17:9, 18). The conflicts figured forth in the text are to be understood first of all in terms of the experience of the churches of Asia as they faced persecution and adversity during the reign of Domitian. The question then becomes how far the specific decoding of the images can be pursued: How many of the Apocalypse's images refer to historically identifiable first-century persons and events? Unfortunately, this reading strategy produces surprisingly slight results. On the one hand, we do not have enough information to crack the code in detail; on the other hand, many of the images in the narrative refer to heavenly events, not earthly. Furthermore, much of the symbolism, taken over from the conventions of Israel's prophetic and apocalyptic literature, expresses the author's vision of what should or might occur, not necessarily what actually did occur in history. Consequently, to read the book only as political allegory is to leave much of it out of account.

The value of this approach, however, is that it forces us to reckon concretely with the book as a message written for the church in a specific situation, just as the Gospels and Paul's letters were written to address particular circumstances. In particular, this reading strategy forces us to reckon seriously with Revelation's adamant resistance to the Roman Empire. As we seek to understand the causes and effects of this resistance, we will find ourselves immersed in the central ethical issues posed by this strange text.

(C) **THEOPOETIC** Another possibility exists. Rather than reading the text as a puzzle to be solved by identifying the dramatis personae and events, we could read it as a visionary theological and poetic representation of the spiritual environment within which the church perennially finds itself living and struggling.[12] Elisabeth Schüssler Fiorenza describes the book's presentation as "theo-ethical rhetoric": it performs "a symphony of images" that have the power to evoke "imaginative participation" within the community that the seer envisions.[13] The Apocalypse's visions are written for particular churches in their first-century situation, but they cannot necessarily be read off as one-to-one signifiers of particular persons and events—or at least their significance is not exhausted by such a reading. Rather, the visions unmask the illusory power of "realistic" politics and disclose God's truth about human historical experience. For those who have eyes to see, the present order of the earthly city, built upon exploitation and violence, is a foul demonic parody of the city of God. A great battle for sovereignty over the world is already being waged as God, through the death of Jesus and the power of the proclaimed Word, reclaims the world from the powers of evil. Paul Minear describes Revelation in this way:

> In this vision, then, John, as an apocalyptic prophet, was disclosing to the churches in Asia the range of cosmic powers which had been active in the story of Jesus, which had become present in a hidden form in the solidarity that bound these Christians to the sufferings of their Lord, and which were daily seeking to deceive them through apparent control over both the present and the future.[14]

Thus, in Revelation, we have an elaborate imaginative vision for the church as an alternative community pitted in conflict with the powers that be. The Apocalypse is a prophetic confrontation of all earthly pretensions to power, all symbolic orders other than that of the Lamb that was slaughtered. To read it in this way is the most adequate interpretive strategy, and the most productive for New Testament ethics.

2. The Lamb That Was Slaughtered

In the book of Revelation, Christ's lordship stands in flat antithesis to Caesar's. The fundamental political claim of this resistance document is articulated in the hymn sung by loud voices in heaven at the blowing of the seventh trumpet:

> *The kingdom of the world has become the kingdom of our Lord*
> *and of his Messiah,*
> *and he will reign forever and ever.* (11:15)

God's kingdom is not some otherworldly realm; rather, Christ has taken control over "the kingdom of the world." Thus, unlike Luke, who presents the conflict between Rome and the gospel as incidental, Revelation makes it inevitable and necessary, for the eschatological lordship of Christ necessarily excludes all other claims.[15] No compromise is possible. A. Y. Collins has rightly perceived the radical stance of opposition taken by this writing:

> Given a situation of persecution a variety of responses are possible. One might decide to write an apology for the Christian faith rather than an apocalypse. The fact that the author chose to write an apocalypse and one which involves such a thorough-going attack on the authority of Rome is an indication that he shared the fundamental theological principle of the Zealots: that the kingdom of God is incompatible with the kingdom of Caesar.[16]

No wonder, then, that John has been exiled and that his churches are facing persecution; they really do stand against the Roman Empire.

The crucial difference between the Zealot perspective and that of the Apocalypse, however, appears clearly when we consider the central christological metaphor of the book: Jesus is "the Lamb that was slaughtered." This image, used of Jesus twenty-eight times in Revelation, first appears in the heavenly throneroom scene, where someone is being sought to open the scroll with seven seals. John begins to weep because no one is deemed worthy to open the scroll, but he is comforted by one of the "elders" who sits in the presence of God's throne: "Do not weep. See, the Lion of the tribe of Judah, the Root of David, has conquered, so that he can open the scroll and its seven seals" (5:5). The description leads us to expect Jesus to appear as a glorious figure, as in 1:12–20: "[H]is eyes were like a flame of fire . . . his voice was like the sound of many waters. . . . [F]rom his mouth came a sharp, two-edged sword, and his face was like the sun shining with full force." But when "the lion of Judah" appears in the heavenly throneroom to open the scroll, he does not come in conquering kingly form; rather, we see his true aspect: "Then I saw between the throne and the four living creatures and among the elders a Lamb standing as if it had been slaughtered . . ." (5:6). The shock of this reversal discloses the central mystery of the Apocalypse: God overcomes the world not through a show of force but through the suffering and death of Jesus, "the faithful witness [*martys*]" (1:5). The comments of David L. Barr accurately assess the effect of this image reversal:

> A more complete reversal of value would be hard to imagine. . . . [T]he Lamb *is* the Lion. Jesus is the Messiah, but he has performed his messianic office in a most extraordinary way, by his death. Yet his death is not defeat, for it is just this that makes him worthy to open the scroll revealing the will of God. Jesus conquered through suffering and weakness rather than by might. John asks us to see both that Jesus rejects the role of Lion, refuses to conquer through supernatural power, and that we must now give a radical new valuation to lambs; the sufferer is the conqueror, the victim the victor.[17]

Rome rules by the power of violence, but the one who is the true King of kings and Lord of lords rules by virtue of his submission to death—precisely the opposite of armed violence against the empire. That is why he alone is worthy.

When, in the climactic battle scene in Revelation 19, Jesus appears as the conquering rider on a white horse, he is "clothed in a robe dipped in blood." Our first inclination is to see this as a mark of the divine warrior splattered with the blood of enemies whom he has killed, as in Isaiah's symbolic vision of a figure who comes "in garments stained crimson":

> *I trampled down peoples in my anger,*
> *I crushed them in my wrath,*
> *and I poured out their lifeblood on the earth.* (Isa. 63:6)

In Revelation 19:13, however, the rider's robe is dipped in blood *before* the battle, and he is leading "the armies of heaven, wearing fine linen, white and pure" (19:14). Thus, once again we are dealing with a dramatic symbolic reversal: the rider is the Lamb, and the blood with which he is stained is his own. He is called "the Word of God," and the sword with which he strikes down the nations comes from his mouth. We are to understand that the execution of God's judgment occurs through the proclamation of the Word. The message of the text is poignantly captured in the lines of Martin Luther's "A Mighty Fortress":

> Though hordes of devils fill the land, all threatening to devour us,
> We tremble not, unmoved we stand; they cannot overpower us.
> This world's prince may rage, in fierce war engage.
> He is doomed to fail; God's judgment must prevail!
> *One little word subdues him.*[18]

Those who read the battle imagery of Revelation with a literalist bent fail to grasp the way in which the symbolic logic of the work as a whole dismantles the symbolism of violence. Oliver O'Donovan perceptively describes the literary effect:

> There is, of course, as has often been observed, something highly paradoxical about the picture of the Prince of Martyrs constituting himself the head of an army of conquest. It is an image which negates itself, canceling, rather than confirming, the significance of the political categories on which it draws.[19]

A work that places the Lamb that was slaughtered at the center of its praise and worship can hardly be used to validate violence and coercion. God's ultimate judgment of the wicked is, to be sure, inexorable. Those who destroy the earth will be destroyed (11:18); those who have shed the blood of the saints and prophets will find their own blood poured out on the earth. But these events are in the hands of God; they do not constitute a program for human military action. As a paradigm for the action of the faithful community, Jesus stands as the faithful witness who conquers through suffering.

3. The Vocation of the Saints

The vocation of the church follows naturally from the above analysis of the Christology of Revelation. What is said of the 144,000 redeemed is true of all God's people, of whom they are the first fruits: "[T]hese follow the Lamb wherever he goes" (14:4). Just as Jesus suffered for his word of testimony, so those who follow him must testify and suffer. The repeated call to the community is to endure and to bear witness faithfully. Their role is celebrated by the voice from heaven:

> *Now have come the salvation and the power*
> *and the kingdom of our God*
> *and the authority of his Messiah,*
> *for the accuser of our brothers has been thrown down,*
> *who accuses them day and night before our God.*
> ***But they have conquered him by the blood of the Lamb***
> ***and by the word of their testimony,***
> *for they did not cling to life even in the face of death.* (12:10–11, AA, *emphasis mine*)

The church follows Jesus by bearing prophetic witness against the violence, immorality, and injustice of an earthly empire that claims the authority that belongs rightly to God. This means that Jesus' followers worship God, not the empire; they refuse to receive the mark of Beast, thereby excluding themselves from the normal activities of the economic system (13:16–17; 14:6–11). They imitate Jesus' example of powerless suffering and refuse to succumb to the illusion that power equals truth.

The most detailed inventory in Revelation of particular actions that are commended or proscribed is to be found in the letters to the seven churches (2:1–3:22). The structure of each letter is essentially the same, with minor variations: it begins with a description of Jesus, from whom the message comes; then follows an account of the praiseworthy characteristics of the individual community; then a listing of the community's failings, introduced by the phrase, "but I have this against you"; a summons to repent; a promise given "to everyone who conquers"; and finally the admonition to listen to what the Spirit is saying to the churches. Even in this material, however, we find surprisingly little specific content given to the behaviors approved and condemned. The prophetic indictments focus on two basic issues: involvement in idolatry through eating idol-food (2:14–15, 20) and complacency (2:4–5; 3:1–3; 3:15–17), perhaps related to excessive wealth. The commendations of the communities are equally general in character: love, faith, service, and patient endurance are singled out for praise (2:19; cf. 2:2–3, 13; 3:10), along with testing the claims of false apostles (2:2). In contrast to the self-satisfied church in Laodicea, the churches in Smyrna and Philadelphia are saluted simply for remaining steadfast in poverty and affliction; interestingly, these are the only two of the seven churches who receive no critique and no call to repent. To the Philadelphians, the prophecy says, "I know that you have but little power, and yet you have kept my word and have not denied my name" (3:8b). Faithful adherence to the confession of Jesus' name seems to be the fundamental issue. Those who do remain faithful constitute a powerless minority and suffer for their confession; those who make compromises with the surrounding culture may avoid suffering, but they incur God's judgment. Thus, the aim of the letters to the seven churches is simultaneously to comfort the afflicted (Smyrna, Philadelphia) and to afflict the comfortable (Sardis, Laodicea).

The withering judgment pronounced on the church at Laodicea ("[B]ecause you are lukewarm, and neither cold nor hot, I am about to spit you out of my mouth," 3:15–16) is of particular interest for our purposes.

> *For you say, "I am rich, I have prospered, and I need nothing." You do not realize that you are wretched, pitiable, poor, blind, and naked. . . . I reprove and discipline those whom I love. Be earnest, therefore, and repent.* (3:17, 19)

This church has been lulled to sleep by the hypnotic power of affluence and coopted by the economic system of the Roman Empire. John regards this as a back door into idolatry; the materially wealthy community is de facto compromised and therefore spiritually poor. Thus, although there are no specific commandments or teachings about possessions in Revelation, there is a clear symbolic correlation between wealth and idolatry.

The overall message of the seven letters is to call for sharper boundaries between the church and the world. Those who advocate eating idol-food apparently think that they can blend in as "normal" members of their society; perhaps some even argue that Christians can accommodate the emperor cult as a civic obligation without betraying their faith in Jesus. Against such thinking, John sounds an alarm. It is no accident that the letter to Laodicea comes as the climax of this section. There can be no compromise, John insists, and the church that thinks it can live comfortably within the empire's economic system is in spiritual danger.

A similar condemnation of wealth applies not only to prosperous Christians but also to outsiders. John's account of the fall of "Babylon" focuses to a great extent on economic issues. The kings, the merchants of the earth who trade in luxury items and slaves, and the shipmasters who "grew rich by her wealth" are the ones who especially lament her demise (18:11–20), and it is charged that they have been implicated in her "fornication." The latter term, following Old Testament symbolic conventions, applies less to literal sexual offenses than to idolatrous practices. John also disapproves, of course, of sexual immorality: fornicators are listed along with "the cowardly, the faithless, the polluted, the murderers, . . . the sorcerers, the idolaters, and all liars" among those who will be thrown into "the lake that burns with fire and sulfur, which is the second death" (21:8). But—as this list also indicates—sexual morality is not a major preoccupation of the Apocalypse.

The fall of Babylon remains for John a prophetic vision, not a political reality. Thus, in the present time the fundamental calling of the people of God is to bear witness and endure the onslaught of opposition that is to come from a world filled with hostile powers. This necessarily will entail following the way of Jesus by submitting even to death without recourse to violence.

One of the clearest indications that this is indeed the church's vocation appears in the midst of the central chapter (Revelation 13), in which the rising power of the Beast is described. The Beast is allowed to make war on the saints and to conquer them; meanwhile, "all the inhabitants of the earth" worship the Beast except for those whose names are written "in the book of life of the Lamb that was slaughtered" (13:7–8). It is a dire scenario, seemingly calling for desperate measures. Should the saints seek to oppose the power of the Beast with the sword? John breaks into his narration of the vision to address the community directly with a prophetic word, just as the seven churches had been addressed at the beginning of the book:

> *Let anyone who has an ear listen:*
> *If you are to be taken captive,*
> *into captivity you go;*
> *if you kill with the sword,*[20]
> *with the sword you must be killed.*
>
> *Here is a call for the endurance and faith of the saints.* (13:9–10)

This call for radical endurance (*hypomonē*) and trust (*pistis*) summons the church to resist the impulse to violence, even in these extreme circumstances. G. B. Caird's explanation of this puzzling summons is worth citing at length:

> If God allows the monster to wage war on his people and conquer them, what must God's people do? They must allow themselves to be conquered as their Lord had done, so that like their Lord they may win a victory not of this world. . . . [T]he church must submit without resistance to the conquering attack of the monster, since only in this way can the monster be halted in its track. Evil is self-propagating. Like the Hydra, the many-headed monster can grow another head when one has been cut off. When one man wrongs another, the other may retaliate, bear a grudge, or take his injury out on a third person. Whichever he does, there are now two evils where before there was one; and a chain reaction is started, like the spreading of a contagion. Only if the victim absorbs the wrong and so puts it out of currency, can it be prevented from going any further. And this is why the great ordeal is also the great victory.[21]

This explanation of the call to martyrdom—which of course goes well beyond John's explicit statements—deepens our understanding of the observation made by Collins that Revelation embodies "a synergistic understanding of righteous suffering" in which the unjust death of the martyrs actually makes a contribution toward the coming of the kingdom.[22] She suggests that, for the author of Revelation, the death of the martyr arouses God to vengeance against the enemy and that there is a divinely fixed number of martyrs who must die before the end can come (cf. 6:9–11, where both of these motifs are present). Without denying that these elements are part of the martyrological tradition that the Apocalypse inherits and passes on, we can affirm that Caird's explanation touches on the deeper mystery of the correspondence between the Lamb and his followers.[23] Those who follow him in persecution and death are not filling a randomly determined quota of martyrs; rather, they are enacting the will of God, who has chosen to overcome evil precisely in and through righteous suffering, not in spite of it. That is why those who bear the name of the Lamb on their foreheads must also share his fate.

4. A New Heaven and a New Earth

No New Testament book is more pervasively concerned with eschatological issues than Revelation. From beginning ("The time is near," 1:3) to end ("Come, Lord Jesus!" 22:20), the author looks fervently to the imminent future consummation of God's judgment and restoration of the world. The point is too obvious to require demonstration. But how does the book's apocalyptic eschatology shape its moral vision? Several observations may be offered.

First, the future hope is essential to the critique of the present order. Only the prophetic vision of eschatological salvation enables the believing community to recognize the lies and illusions of the Beast and the false prophet. Thus, apocalyptic eschatology sustains the possibility of resistance to the present unjust order of the world. Only the assurance of ultimate vindication gives the martyrs the confidence to resist the power of the Beast. The workings of this logic can be illustrated by observing the organization of material in Revelation 14. Verses 1–5 present a vision of the redeemed 144,000 standing on Mount Zion with the Lamb; verses 6–7 declare that the hour of judgment is at hand; verses 8–11 depict the fall of "Babylon the great" and the torment of those who have worshiped the Beast; finally, verse 12 summarizes the significance of these visions: "Here is a call for the endurance of the saints, those who keep the commandments of God and hold fast to the faith of Jesus." Readers are thus encouraged to remain constant in the way of those who are marked by the Lamb (14:1) rather than by the Beast (14:9).[24] The visions of the end serve as warrants for the seer's call to the church to "hold fast" and to live the alternative order for which the faithful witness, Jesus, is the model. The ultimate triumph of that alternative order is both assured and imminent, for Jesus promises, "*Surely I am coming soon*" (22:20).

In the meantime, while the community waits for Jesus' coming, the eschatological vision provides consolation. (This consolatory element is far more explicit in Revelation than in Mark, which shares many aspects of Revelation's apocalyptic eschatology.) In John's vision of the great multitude that have come through "the great ordeal," an angel speaks comforting words about their fate:

They will hunger no more, and thirst no more;
the sun will not strike them,
nor any scorching heat;

for the Lamb at the center of the throne will be their shepherd,
and he will guide them to springs of the water of life,
and God will wipe away every tear from their eyes. (7:16–17)

This promise anticipates the book's final vision of the new Jerusalem, in which

[God] will dwell with them as their God;
they will be his peoples,
and God himself will be with them;
he will wipe every tear from their eyes.
Death will be no more;
mourning and crying and pain will be no more,
for the first things have passed away. (21:3–4)

While these poetic descriptions of eschatological salvation point to the future, their powerful language already works as performative utterance in the present, offering consolation to those who mourn and suffer, assuring them that the love of God ultimately superintends their misfortunes.

Third, the threat of judgment as a warrant for obedience is implicitly present in Revelation (e.g., 20:11–15), but it plays a significantly smaller role than, for instance, in Matthew. Because the Apocalypse is addressed entirely to the elect community, it shows little interest in calling outsiders to repent before the judgment. Indeed, one passage seems to suggest that there is too little time left for repentance to do any good:

Do not seal up the words of the prophecy of this book, for the time is near. Let the evildoer still do evil, and the filthy still be filthy, and the righteous still do right, and the holy still be holy. See, I am coming soon; my reward is with me, to repay according to everyone's work. (22:10–12)

More prominent than calls to repentance based on eschatological warrants are positive eschatological rewards promised to the church, explicitly to those who "conquer": for example, "To everyone who conquers, I will give permission to eat from the tree of life that is in the paradise of God" (2:7b). To "conquer" is to remain faithful, overcoming obstacles from the world; as Schrage notes, the word "suggests the struggle inherent in Christian life between the ages."[25] Thus, the word of eschatological promise provides motivation for the church to bear up under suffering and to endure faithfully.

In view of the foregoing observations, it is not quite right to say that the eschatology of Revelation inculcates passivity in its readers. Instead, it calls them to an alert resistance to the seductive powers of the present age and an active obedience to a merciful God who wills to make all things new. Nor is the eschatology of Revelation otherworldly: it is not insignificant that the New Jerusalem comes down from heaven *to earth* and that the proclamation of final salvation declares that "the dwelling of God is with human beings," not vice versa (21:2-3, RH). These things occur, to be sure, in "a new heaven and a new earth" (21:1), but this means—in the Apocalypse just as in the prophetic visions upon which it draws (Isa. 65:17–25, 66:22)—that God will have redeemed and transformed the creation, not abolished it.

5. The Narrative World of the Apocalypse As Context for Action

Revelation, read as a visionary document of resistance to an idolatrous sociopolitical order, calls the church repeatedly to vigilance and discernment. Its vivid symbolic world creates the context for the community of God's elect to live out a distinctive witness to Jesus Christ as the Alpha and the Omega, in whom God's will is fully embodied. Let us summarize some of the salient aspects of John's prophetic vision.

First, the world according to Revelation is sundered by a series of *sharp dualisms.* The world is caught up in a cosmic conflict between God and "that ancient serpent, who is called the Devil and Satan, the deceiver of the whole world" (12:9). In this conflict there is no possibility of compromise: one must choose whom to worship, and neutrality is impossible. In this respect, Revelation stands close to the Johannine Gospel and Epistles, with which Christian tradition has associated it, although Revelation's mythic symbolizations of evil are far more lavishly imaginative. As in the Gospel and Epistles of John, there seems to be little need or allowance for ethical reflection and debate: good and evil, right and wrong, are so thoroughly assumed as givens that the author hardly bothers to define them. Also as in the other Johannine writings, the cosmic dualism is qualified by the confidence that God is ultimately in control and will triumph decisively over evil.

Second, the cosmic dualism finds expression also in *a sharp social polarization between the Christian community and the hostile world.* Because the Christian community is a tiny and powerless minority within its culture, the Apocalypse's sympathies lie entirely with the persecuted and marginal elements in society. This insight has been most fully developed by Elisabeth Schüssler Fiorenza in her various works on Revelation:

> . . . [T]he author of Revelation has adopted the "perspective from below" and has expressed the experiences of those who were poor, powerless, and in constant fear of denunciation. Revelation's world of vision responds to the experience and predicament of those Christians who are powerless in terms of the political powers of their times.[26]

The book's stinging critique of wealth and commercial activity is one expression of this social perspective.

Third, corresponding to this social division is a powerful sense of *solidarity within the community of the faithful.* Jesus' followers alone have refused the mark of the Beast, and they alone can grasp the full significance of the obscure apocalyptic symbolism of the work. Their voices join the heavenly chorus of praise, and they rejoice with the heavenly hosts over the destruction of the oppressors:

We give you thanks, Lord God Almighty,
who are and who were,
for you have taken your great power
and begun to reign.
The nations raged,
but your wrath has come,
and the time for judging the dead,
for rewarding your servants, the prophets
and saints and all who fear your name,
both small and great,
and for destroying those who destroy the earth. (11:17–18)

It is this celebration of the destruction of the wicked that gave rise to Nietzsche's reading of the book as an "outburst of vindictiveness." There is some truth in this characterization; whether we find this morally problematic will depend to some extent on whether we grant a sympathetic ear to the victims of oppression or whether, like Nietzsche, we regard them with contempt. In any case, we find no trace in Revelation of an imperative to love the enemy. The boundaries between the church and the world are sharply defined and absolute; the enemy, within this symbolic world, is portrayed simply as demonic.

Fourth, the sense of *eschatological urgency* in Revelation's world is very strong. The cataclysmic events prophesied are to occur very soon, and the existing order of things is therefore insubstantial. That is why the complacency of the church at Laodicea is not only reprehensible but also foolish. Jesus says, "See, I am coming soon; my reward is with me, to repay according to everyone's work" (22:12).

Fifth, in contrast to its perception of the insubstantial order of the status quo, Revelation manifests a deep underlying confidence in the *moral orderliness of the universe.* This is characteristic of the apocalyptic genre, which is deeply engaged with issues of theodicy, with the problem of who finally has dominion over the world.[27] The souls of those who have been "slaughtered for the word of God and for the testimony they had given" cry out to God, asking, "Sovereign Lord, holy and true, how long will it be before you judge and avenge our blood on the inhabitants of the earth?" (6:9–10). They are told to wait a little longer, but the narrative as a whole answers their question: in due time God will settle all scores and make all things right. The wicked who prosper now will be punished, and the righteous who suffer now will be rewarded; the logic is precisely the same as that of the Lukan Beatitudes and woes (Luke 6:20–26). God is not capricious or arbitrary; in the end his justice will prevail.

Sixth, since the world is presently under the sway of powers hostile to God and to the saints, God's justice will necessarily bring *radical reversal.* A major purpose of the revelatory prophecy is to disclose the truth about the world from God's perspective and thereby to *remake the community's understanding of reality.* Concerning this aspect of Revelation's impact, Wayne Meeks writes:

> The business of this writing is to stand things on their heads in the perceptions of its audience, to rob the established order of the most fundamental power of all: its sheer facticity. The moral strategy of the Apocalypse, therefore, is to destroy common sense as a guide for life.[28]

In order to break Satan's power of illusion, Revelation must reimagine the world; and so it does. The book's imaginative power annihilates the plausibility structure on which the status quo rests and replaces it with the vision of a new world. The authority of the Roman Empire is thereby delegitimated, and the way is prepared for the community to receive the truth about God's coming order. The implications of this are wide-ranging; it suggests, for instance, that J. T. Sanders's dismissal of Revelation as encouraging a withdrawal from social and political problems is far too hasty. By contrast, consider Oliver O'Donovan's analysis of the political witness of the Apocalypse:

> It conveys to us a hope that in the life which we are summoned to live with Christ we may experience, as a social reality, that authority of truth and righteousness which our experience of political society on earth has consistently denied us. We must not fail to observe the implications of this. If it is right to say that the basis for a new order of society is God's word of judgment pronounced in Christ, then it follows that *the witnesses who proclaimed that word to challenge the prevailing political order were not acting anti-politically at all, but were confronting a false political order with the foundation of a true one.* We must claim John for the point of view which sees criticism, when founded in truth, as genuine political engagement.[29]

In particular, as we have suggested, Revelation's critique of the prevailing false political order is a critique of the unjust and oppressive use of wealth and power. In Schüssler Fiorenza's words, "Revelation constructs a world of vision that challenges the symbolic discourse of Rome's hegemonic colonizing power."[30] No one can enter imaginatively into the world narrated by this book and remain complacent about things as they are in an unjust world.

This means that Revelation can be read rightly only by those who are actively struggling against injustice. If Revelation is a resistance document, its significance will become clear only to those who are engaged in resistance. It is no coincidence that the most powerful modern readings of Revelation have come from interpreters in socially marginalized positions who were seeking to call the church to countercultural resistance movements: for example, Martin Luther King, Jr., William Stringfellow, and Alan Boesak.[31] Something very strange happens when this text is appropriated by readers in a comfortable, powerful, majority community: it becomes a gold mine for paranoid fantasies and for those who want to preach revenge and destruction. Thus, as Schüssler Fiorenza insists, "Revelation will elicit a fitting theo-ethical response only in those sociopolitical situations that cry out for justice."[32] This sort of reading of the Apocalypse was nowhere more eloquently performed than in the simple anthem of the U.S. Civil Rights movement: "We Shall

Overcome." The word "overcome" was taken from the King James Version's rendering of the verb *nikan,* used pervasively in Revelation and translated in most modern versions as "conquer."[33] The word is used in the refrain of promise that concludes each of the letters to the seven churches. For example, "To him that overcometh will I grant to sit with me in my throne, even as I also overcame, and am set down with my Father in his throne" (3:21, KJV). As freedom marchers from the black churches joined hands and sang, "We shall overcome someday," they were expressing their faith that, despite their lack of conventional political power, their witness to the truth would prevail over violence and oppression. The movement's commitment to nonviolent resistance made the allusion to Revelation particularly apt: even if the marchers were to be beaten and killed, they would overcome the world by remaining peaceful, just as the Lamb had before them. This example is not exactly "exegesis" of Revelation in the strict sense, but it illustrates the social posture from which the text is appropriately to be read.

Finally, the ethical staying power of the Apocalypse is a product of its *imaginative richness.* The text throbs with theopoetic energy, expressed in its numerous songs of praise and worship. It is no accident that Milton drew inspiration from Revelation or that Handel found the lyrics for the climactic choruses of the *Messiah* ("Hallelujah" and "Worthy Is the Lamb") in the poetry of Revelation: "The kingdom of this world is become the kingdom of our Lord and of his Christ, and he shall reign for ever and ever" (based on Rev. 11:15). To sing such a song is a political act, and the political power of the act is the greater because it is sung, for others can join the chorus and fix it in aural memory. Interestingly, Revelation opens with a blessing on those who are to "perform" it: "Blessed is the one who *reads aloud* the words of the prophecy, and blessed are those who *hear* and who keep what is written in it" (1:3). For this work to have its full effect, it must be read aloud; that is the sort of text that it is, like the script for a play—a play in which the readers now find themselves the performers. Despite the strangeness and obscurity of Revelation at the level of linear reason, its imaginative vividness has made it a perennial source of art and liturgy in the church and has thereby supplied the power to sustain countercommunity in a world feverishly worshiping the Beast. Let anyone who has an ear listen.

NOTES

1. Nietzsche 1956 [1887], 185.
2. J. T. Sanders 1975, 115.
3. Stendahl 1976, 39.
4. There is nothing in the text to suggest that he should be identified with the John who was one of the original disciples of Jesus.
5. A. Y. Collins 1981; A. Y. Collins 1984, 97–99; Thompson 1990, 95–167.
6. For a similar discussion that delineates a more complex range of interpretive options, see Schüssler Fiorenza 1991, 5–20.
7. Lindsey 1970.
8. Schüssler Fiorenza 1991, 8.
9. J. J. Collins 1984, 68–92.
10. Caird 1966, 6.

11. A. Y. Collins 1977, 241.
12. The term "theopoetic" is borrowed from Wilder 1971. The view of Revelation indicated here is represented in various ways by Caird 1966; Minear 1968; Minear 1981; Stringfellow 1973; O'Donovan 1986; Meeks 1986b; Schüssler Fiorenza 1991.
13. Schüssler Fiorenza 1991, 31, 117–139.
14. Minear 1981, 101.
15. This reading stands in marked contrast to that of Cullmann (1956, 71–85), who thinks that the Apocalypse's view of the state is basically compatible with passages such as Rom. 13:1–7. Both texts, in Cullmann's view, allow Christians to oppose the state if and only if it assumes demonic idolatrous pretensions.
16. A. Y. Collins 1977, 252. See also Schüssler Fiorenza 1991, 84.
17. Barr 1984, 41.
18. Luther c. 1529; emphasis mine.
19. O'Donovan 1986, 90.
20. There is some slight manuscript support for the reading "if anyone is to be killed with the sword." This reading, which both conforms the text to Jer. 15:2 and 43:11 and creates a syntactical parallelism with the preceding line (Rev. 13:10a), is to be rejected as a secondary correction. Some scholars—including, apparently, the editors of Nestle-Aland, are suspicious of the better-attested reading "if you kill with the sword," because it makes John's prophetic word echo Matt. 26:52: "[A]ll who take the sword will perish by the sword." But that is the point: John has echoed Jeremiah's oracle of prophetic judgment, filtering it through the tradition of Jesus' saying in such a way that it becomes a divinely ordained vocation rather than a tragic necessity.
21. Caird 1966, 169–170.
22. A. Y. Collins 1977.
23. My only quarrel with Caird's exposition of the passage is that it is formulated too individualistically ("[W]hen one man wrongs another . . . "). John's vision is for the *community* of the Lamb's followers as a countersign to the world's violence.
24. The fact that the 144,000 "have not defiled themselves with women" does not mean that Revelation requires all Christians to be celibate; there is no indication of such a concern anywhere else in the text. As the commentators note, this narrative detail is a reflection of the requirements for soldiers to participate in Israel's holy wars (Caird 1966, 179). The 144,000 are in a state of symbolic ritual purity, ready to participate in the Lamb's war against the Beast. Schüssler Fiorenza (1991, 88) suggests that the sexual symbolism, here as elsewhere in Revelation, is metaphorical, signifying that these pure ones have not participated in the idolatry of the imperial cult.
25. Schrage 1988, 337.
26. Schüssler Fiorenza 1991, 128. See also Schüssler Fiorenza 1985.
27. Schrage 1988, 331.
28. Meeks 1986b, 145.
29. O'Donovan 1986, 90, emphasis mine.
30. Schüssler Fiorenza 1991, 124.
31. King, Jr. 1963; Stringfellow 1973; Boesak 1987.
32. Schüssler Fiorenza 1991, 139.
33. The statistics on incidence of this verb in the NT are as follows: it appears seventeen times in Revelation, six times in 1 John, and only five times in the rest of the NT (once in Luke, once in John, and 3 times in Romans).

PART TWO

The Synthetic Task

Finding Coherence in the Moral Vision of the New Testament

Chapter 9

Diverse Voices in the New Testament Canon

The New Testament is not a simple, homogeneous body of doctrine. It is, rather, a chorus of diverse voices. These voices differ not only in pacing and intonation but also in the material content of their messages. No matter how devoutly we might wish it otherwise, we cannot hear these texts as a chorus speaking in unison. Indeed, a rigid determination to make the texts speak univocally will at best limit our perception of the range of these witnesses and at worst produce distortion of their messages.

1. Cacophony or Polyphony?

The foregoing survey of the various New Testament writings has been governed by a rigorous intent to let the individual texts have their say, to allow the distinctive voice of each to be heard. Even if Mark's apocalyptic vision sounds bleak and foreboding, we must resist the temptation to soften it by supplying subtle—or not-so-subtle—correctives from Matthew or Luke. Even if John's dualistic invective against "the Jews" sounds hateful, we must resist the temptation to explain it away by reading into it Paul's eschatological hope for the unity of Jews and Gentiles in Christ. Even if Paul's teaching about subordination to "the authorities" in Romans 13 sounds like tepid acquiescence in an unjust order, we must not rationalize it away by overdubbing the stentorian voice of Revelation 13 upon it.

We must let the individual voices speak if we are to allow the New Testament to articulate a word that may contravene our own values and desires.[1] Otherwise, we are likely to succumb to the temptation of flipping to some comforting cross-reference to neutralize the force of any particularly challenging passage we may encounter. Does Jesus say in Luke's Gospel, "None of you can become my disciple if you do not give up all your possessions" (Luke 14:33)? This is a disturbing word; how are we to understand it? Flipping to 2 Corinthians 8–9, we find a less exacting norm: Paul exhorts the Corinthians merely to contribute generously to his collection for the Jerusalem church, "in order that there may be a fair balance" (*isotēs*, 2 Cor. 8:14). Paul advocates sharing, not renunciation of possessions. Thus, a homogenizing interpretation might filter Luke's stringent teaching through Paul's account of economic responsibility and conclude that Luke 14:33 cannot mean literally what it appears to say; its hyperbolic language is "really" to be understood as a way of urging sharing or inner detachment from wealth. When the text is interpreted in this way, however, the Gospel of Luke's radical call to discipleship is muffled.[2]

To be sure, our sinful ingenuity may find ways of evading the New Testament's moral demands even without the dodge of the neutralizing cross-reference. We are less likely to delude ourselves, however, if we establish a firm methodological ground rule that we must listen to the whole witness of each individual text with care. Luke 14:33 must be understood, in the first instance, in light of *Luke's* larger narrative depiction of the early church's economic practices (especially the pertinent passages in Acts that describe the Jerusalem church's sharing of possessions), not in light of *Paul's* pastoral instruction. Luke and Paul stand in some tension with one another on this issue, and we cannot interpret one in terms of the other. Only when we set their differing perspectives side by side will we rightly perceive the synthetic problem. Our first responsibility as interpreters is to listen to the individual witnesses.

Having listened, however, we find ourselves inescapably confronted by the question of coherence. Is the New Testament a complex polyphonic choral composition scored by God and performed by human voices under the direction of the Holy Spirit? Or is the New Testament a chaotic cacophony of many voices uncoordinated? The church has traditionally regarded the New Testament as a guide to faith and practice, but how can it serve as a guide if it is not internally consistent? "If the trumpet gives an unclear sound [*phōnē*], who will get ready for battle?" (1 Cor. 14:8, RH). How do these various ancient texts function as a canon? (The term "canon" comes from the Greek *kanōn*, "rule" or "measuring rod.") Is there some way of discerning a wholeness or unity among the canonical writings? Only if we can give an affirmative answer to this last question can we speak of New Testament ethics as a normative theological discipline.

When we seek to form some judgment about the unity of the various New Testament texts, we have moved from simple description to the synthetic task, in the root sense of the Greek word *synthesis:* "putting together." We turn now to the task of putting together the diverse voices within the New Testament canon. The adjective "synthetic" can carry the connotation of "artificial," signifying that an entity (e.g., a fabric) is the product of human artifice rather than a "naturally" occurring substance. Similarly, we cannot escape acknowledging that any synthetic account of the unity of the New Testament's moral vision will be a product of our artifice, an imaginative construct of the interpreter—or, perhaps better, since interpreters do not form their readings in isolation—of the interpretive community. Of course, this acknowledgment in no way denies the necessity or legitimacy of the synthetic judgment; it merely alerts us to exercise due modesty about our own synthetic proposals. Every proposed construal of the unity of the New Testament canon is a "performance," one analogous to a director's reading of a Shakespeare play—a reading that seeks to discern and articulate the shape and meaning of the whole.[3]

How, then, shall we proceed in seeking to discover moral coherence within the canon? There is no methodologically airtight way to derive proposals about the unity of the canonical witness; we can only read the texts carefully, asking what common ground they share, what themes and images appear repeatedly, what convictions undergird their various stories and exhortations. The approach, in other words, must be inductive, beginning with a close reading of the individual texts. Then, having first displayed our reading of the texts (Part I), we proceed by trial and error, testing various synthetic intuitions against the evidence. The task is dauntingly difficult, but it is inescapable if the church is to take its ethical bearings from the New Testament.[4] Thus, we plunge ahead to the task, while acknowledging that our synthetic reading of the texts will always be subject to critique or supplementation by other members of the community of faith who may teach us to see things more clearly. In the pages that follow, then, I shall first lay down some procedural ground rules and then propose a set of focal images that enable us to perceive significant unity among the New Testament's witnesses.

2. Three Procedural Guidelines

(A) CONFRONT THE FULL RANGE OF CANONICAL WITNESSES When we begin to seek the unity of New Testament witnesses—whether in general or on a particular issue—all of the relevant texts must be gathered and considered. Selective appeals to favorite prooftexts are illegitimate without full consideration of texts that stand on the opposite side of a particular issue. The more comprehensive the attention to the full range of New Testament witnesses, the more adequate a normative ethical proposal is likely to be. Beware of the interpreter who always quotes only the *Haustafeln* (e.g., Col. 3:22: "Slaves, obey your earthly masters in everything") and never wrestles with Galatians 5:1 ("For freedom Christ has set us free. Stand firm, therefore, and do not submit again to a yoke of slavery")—or vice versa.

(B) LET THE TENSIONS STAND However acute the tension between two different witnesses may appear, it must not be resolved through exegetical distortion of the texts. The individual witnesses must be allowed their own voices. A classic example of such distortion is the reading of Matthew's Sermon on the Mount through Pauline lenses (or, rather, Pauline lenses as interpreted by the Reformation): in such a reading, the rigorous demands of the Sermon on the Mount are treated as impossible commandments designed to drive sinners to recognize their absolute need of grace. In such a reading, Matthew's voice is suppressed, and the Sermon on the Mount becomes an instrument of a particular Reformation construal of Pauline theology.[5] Such flattening of the individual witnesses is to be rejected.

Likewise, we must not force harmony through abstraction away from the specific messages of the New Testament texts. Confronted with the diversity of New Testament witnesses, we are often tempted to dissolve the plurality of perspectives by appealing to universal principles (love, justice, and so on) or dialectical compromises. Such conceptual movements away from a text's specific imperatives are often escape routes from its uncomfortable demands. For example, Romans 13 and Revelation 13 are *not* two complementary expressions of a single principle or a single New Testament understanding of the state;[6] rather, they represent radically different assessments of the relation of the Christian community to the Roman Empire. Nor can we average them out and arrive at a position somewhere in the middle that will allow us to live comfortably as citizens of a modern democratic state. If these texts are allowed to have their say, they will force us either to choose between them or to reject the normative claims of both. Whatever synthetic account we give of the unity of New Testament witnesses, it must be sufficiently capacious to recognize and encompass tensions of this kind.[7] The synthesis that we seek will not require a forced harmonization of the New Testament's diverse perspectives.

(C) ATTEND TO THE LITERARY GENRE OF THE TEXTS In the effort to "use" the New Testament for doing ethics we may find ourselves seeking to extract universal maxims or principles from texts whose literary form is not readily amenable to such reductionistic analytic procedures. Parables, for example, resist paraphrase, as does visionary apocalyptic imagery. What moral principle shall we extract from the parable of the growing seed, which mysteriously sprouts and grows without our understanding how (Mark 4:26–29), or from the parable of the dishonest manager (Luke 16:1–8)? What moral maxim shall we deduce from the vision of the New Jerusalem, which "has no need of sun or moon to shine on it" (Rev. 21:9–22:5)? In our eagerness to discern ethical relevance, we must not force tone-deaf, literarily insensitive interpretations upon the texts. The New Testament is, after all, not a collection of general treatises on ethics. Its major texts are narratives (the Gospels and Acts), pastoral letters to specific congregations (the Pauline letters), and a richly symbolic apocalyptic vision (Revelation); only the catholic

Epistles take the form of general moral wisdom for the church at large. In our effort to discern the unity of New Testament ethics, we must take care to respect the character of these witnesses. The sort of unity that we discover here will have to be a unity appropriate to texts that are neither theoretical nor propositional in their mode of expression.

These three guidelines serve to keep us honest by ensuring that our synthetic proposals respect rather than erode the texts with which we work. They serve to ensure that we have all the pieces of the puzzle on the table and that we have not snipped off any of the corners of the funny-looking individual pieces. Taken by themselves, however, these guidelines might lead to disintegration rather than synthesis: we might find more tension than unity. We might find the New Testament texts to proffer a disparate collection of incommensurable moral perspectives. Ernst Käsemann posed the dilemma sharply in his famous dictum: "[T]he New Testament canon does not, as such, constitute the foundation of the unity of the Church. On the contrary, it provides the basis for the multiplicity of the confessions."[8] The problem, then, is whether we may legitimately speak of a unity that somehow underlies the multiplicity. Specifically with regard to ethical issues, is it possible, while respecting the above guidelines, to discern within the New Testament firm common ground on which a New Testament ethic can be constructed? The Christian church has historically affirmed that such a discernment of unity is possible. Our task now is to articulate wherein that unity lies.

NOTES

1. Anyone conversant with recent hermeneutical discussion will realize at once how problematical such a recommendation is: we have learned to suspect that all interpretation serves the power needs of the interpreter. Nonetheless, the claim that texts do have their own voices (i.e., that they do express meanings distinguishable from our own whims and predispositions, and that reasoned discussion can approximate consensus about these meanings) is a necessary assumption for any discourse that attributes authority to the Bible; it is also a necessary assumption for living daily life in a world where there are laws, street signs, and other "texts" that are presumed to constrain our behavior.

2. On the question of possessions in Luke-Acts, see L. T. Johnson 1977; Wheeler 1995, 57–72.

3. I am indebted to George Lindbeck (1995), whose critique of an earlier draft of this section caused me to place greater emphasis on the theme of "performance interpretation," a category that Lindbeck in turn derives from Wolterstorff 1995.

4. In a symposium on "The New Testament and Ethics" (Duke University, Apr. 1, 1995), Luke Johnson posed the interesting question of whether it is really necessary to articulate a synthesis before the NT texts can be used in ethical reflection. The alternative, presumably, would be to use the various texts in some sort of eclectic fashion, discerning ad hoc which text might speak to a given set of circumstances. Such a model has evident advantages, but it would seem to leave the church in one of two situations: either the church would lack a coherent moral vision, or the coherence would be provided by some set of norms or principles extrinsic to Scripture. In the latter case, the NT texts would become simply illustrative rather than constitutive of Christian ethics; in the former case, the risk of arbitrariness and moral anarchy is great. I would contend that the church's task of moral discernment—which is inevitable and necessary (on this point Johnson and I are in agreement)—can most fruitfully be pursued by the community within the framework of some synthetic account of the unity of the canonical witness.

5. See, however, my discussion of Paul in Chapter 1 for an argument that the understanding of Pauline theology presupposed by this harmonizing move is also fundamentally inaccurate.

6. But see Cullmann (1956, 86), who can speak of "a fundamental unity in the valuation of the State."

7. In Part IV, I shall argue that when we find ourselves caught between contradictory NT teachings, it is better to choose one resolutely, using clearly articulated theological criteria, than to waffle or seek artificial compromises. See especially the discussion of anti-Judaism in Chapter 17.

8. Käsemann 1964 [1960], 103. See also his provocative lecture on "Unity and Multiplicity in the New Testament Doctrine of the Church," delivered at the Fourth World Conference for Faith and Order in Montreal, July 16, 1963 (Käsemann 1969 [1965], 252–259). It should never be forgotten that Käsemann's relentless insistence on applying the gospel as a *critical* norm against false forms of Christianity—even if they be somehow based on an appeal to the NT canon—was inspired by his experience of seeing the church of his own land and time captured by Nazism's "German Christianity."

Chapter 10

Three Focal Images

Community, Cross, New Creation

The unity that we discover in the New Testament is not the unity of a dogmatic system. Rather, the unity that we find is the looser unity of a collection of documents that, in various ways, retell and comment upon a single fundamental story.[1] That story may be summarized roughly as follows:

The God of Israel, the creator of the world, has acted (astoundingly) to rescue a lost and broken world through the death and resurrection of Jesus; the full scope of that rescue is not yet apparent, but God has created a community of witnesses to this good news, the church. While awaiting the grand conclusion of the story, the church, empowered by the Holy Spirit, is called to reenact the loving obedience of Jesus Christ and thus to serve as a sign of God's redemptive purposes for the world.

Different New Testament writers emphasize different aspects of this story; for example, Luke places great emphasis on the role of the Holy Spirit in empowering the church's witness, whereas Mark mentions it only in passing (e.g., Mark 13:11). Various particular elements are elucidated using different conceptual categories, and a different "spin" is put on the story by each writer; for example, we find widely different evaluations of the degree of continuity between Israel and the church. Consequently, it would be impossible—or, at best, infelicitous—to put these different accounts into the blender so as to produce a single harmonized telling of the story, a late-twentieth-century Diatessaron.[2]

What we can do, however, is to identify certain key *images* that all the different canonical tellings share. Why look for images, rather than concepts or doctrines, as a ground of coherence? As David Kelsey has demonstrated, every theological reading of Scripture depends upon "a single synoptic, imaginative judgment" in which the interpreter "tries to catch up what Christianity is basically all about."[3]

> In short: at the root of a theological position there is an imaginative act in which a theologian tries to catch up in a single metaphorical judgment the full complexity of God's presence in, through, and over-against the activities comprising the church's common life and which, in turn, both provides the *discrimen* against which the theology criticizes the church's current forms of speech and life, and determines the peculiar "shape" of the "position."[4]

This single metaphorical judgment not only shapes "decisions about how to construe and use particular passages of scripture" but also governs "the sort of 'wholeness' each [theologian] concretely ascribes to Scripture."[5] In other words, the unity and sense of Scripture can be grasped only through an act of metaphorical imagination that focuses the diverse contents of the texts in terms of a particular "imaginative characterization." Kelsey does not use the word "image" to describe this imaginative characterization; indeed, his examples ("ideational mode," "concrete actuality," and "ideal possibility") suggest that he is thinking in terms of concepts (*Begriffe*) rather than images (*Vorstellungen*). Given his emphasis on the role of metaphor and imagination in the formation of such synoptic judgments, however, I propose that Kelsey's insight can best be developed by identifying a particular biblical image (or images) in which the synthetic metaphorical judgment is concretized. (For example, liberation theology takes the image of "liberation"—evoking the Exodus story—as the distillation of what Scripture is all about.) I propose, then, to identify images of this kind within the New Testament that concretely represent its narrative coherence.

This strategy seeks to respect the form in which the texts present themselves to us. (See the third procedural guideline outlined in Chapter 9.2). Though some of the New Testament texts, especially the letters of Paul, engage in second-order conceptual reflection,[6] many of the most important texts take the form of stories with minimal explicit second-order commentary. By looking for fundamental images, we stand a better chance of identifying common elements present in these different types of discourse without imposing conceptual abstractions on narrative texts and without forcing pastoral letters into a narrative mode. The images we seek, if they are to give adequate expression to the unity of the New Testament's moral vision, must arise from the texts themselves rather than being artificially superimposed upon them.

One might think of such images as root metaphors embedded in the New Testament texts: they encapsulate the crucial elements of the narrative and serve to focus our attention on the common ground shared by the various witnesses.[7] Thus they serve as *lenses* to focus our reading of the New Testament: when we reread the canonical documents through these images, our blurry multiple impressions of the texts come more sharply into focus. In this respect, such images would function in a way formally analogous to the Rule of Faith used by Irenaeus and other patristic interpreters: the images would simultaneously summarize the story told in (or presupposed by) Scripture and govern the interpretation of individual texts by placing them within a coherent narrative framework.[8] It is crucial to see that such synthetic images do not *replace* the New Testament texts; rather, they serve to focus and guide our readings and rereadings of the New Testament, which itself remains the primary source and authority for our theology and ethics.

It will be immediately evident that the focal images we choose will become pivotal for our subsequent normative use of the New Testament in ethical argument and formation of the community. For example, if it were decided that a major focal image in the New Testament were "the orderly household"—as one might conclude if the pastoral Epistles were seen as the center of gravity in the New Testament—the church would be led to adopt hierarchical structures and practices that emphasize authority and stability. On the other hand, if the key image were taken to be "freedom from Law and tradition"—as one might conclude if Galatians and Mark 7:1–23 were seen as the center of gravity—the church would be led to reject authority structures and to adopt practices that emphasize Spirit-inspired spontaneity. The divergent character of such hypothetical proposals[9] shows that we need to articulate criteria for critical evaluation of judgments about the unity of the New Testament. How can we tell a good synthetic proposal from a bad one?

I would offer three criteria for evaluating themes or images proposed as focal lenses for discerning the coherence of the New Testament's moral vision:

- Does the proposed focal image find a textual basis in all of the canonical witnesses? The more widely represented a particular theme or image is across the spectrum of the New Testament writings, the more claim it has to articulate a part of the New Testament's coherent moral vision.
- Does the proposed focal image stand in serious tension with the ethical teachings or major emphases of any of the New Testament witnesses? If so, this would count against the viability of the proposal.
- Does the proposed focal image highlight central and substantial ethical concerns of the texts in which it appears? One might find agreement across the canonical spectrum on some matter of minor significance (e.g., opposition to adultery) that would nonetheless fail to provide a sufficiently broad view of the New Testament's range of moral concern.

The two hypothetical proposals above ("the orderly household" and "freedom from Law") fall afoul of all three of these criteria. One might, however, make some differentiated judgments: with regard to the first criterion, "freedom from Law" is arguably a more widely represented theme in the New Testament than is "the orderly household"; thus, on the basis of this criterion alone, the former would appear to have a better claim as a synthetic image for New Testament ethics. On the other hand, with regard to the second criterion, "freedom from law" stands in deep tension with several important New Testament witnesses (Matthew, James, and the pastorals), whereas "the orderly household" is not exactly in opposition to the central teaching of any New Testament texts—though the demands of radical discipleship in the synoptic Gospels are potentially disruptive of family order (e.g., Mark 3:31–35, 10:28–31; Luke 14:26). Thus, on the basis of the second criterion alone, "freedom from Law" is more problematic as a ground of unity than is "the orderly household." With regard to the third criterion, both proposals fail: either proposal, taken alone, represents a severely truncated account of the New Testament's moral perspective.

No single image can adequately encapsulate the complex unity of the New Testament texts. Because these texts retell and interpret a narrative, their message reflects the complexity and temporal movement of emplotted experience; consequently, we need a cluster—or, better, a sequence—of images to represent the underlying story and bring the texts into focus. On the basis of the descriptive survey of the New Testament texts treated in Part I of this book, I would suggest three such focal images as guidelines for synthetic reflection about the New Testament canon: *community*, *cross*, and *new creation*. Reading the diverse New Testament texts through these focal images will enable us to see them all more clearly within Scripture's overarching story of God's grace. Let us consider each of the three in turn.

1. Community

The church is a countercultural community of discipleship, and this community is the primary addressee of God's imperatives. The biblical story focuses on God's design for forming a covenant *people*. Thus, the primary sphere of moral concern is not the character of the individual but the corporate obedience of the church. Paul's formulation in Romans 12:1–2 encapsulates the vision: "Present your bodies [*sōmata*, plural] as a living sacrifice [*thysian*, singular], holy and well-pleasing to God. . . . And do not be conformed to this age, but be transformed by the renewing of your mind" (RH). The community, in its corporate life, is called to embody an alternative order that stands as a sign of God's redemptive purposes in the world. Thus, "community" is not merely a concept; as the term is used here, it points to the concrete social manifestation of the people of God. We could equally well use the term "church," though it is subject to being misunderstood in terms of an institutional hierarchy. The term "community" more adequately connotes the corporate participatory character of the people of God in Christ. Many New Testament texts express different facets of this image: the church is the body of Christ, a temple built of living stones, a city set on a hill, Israel in the wilderness. The coherence of the New Testament's ethical mandate will come into focus only when we understand that mandate in *ecclesial* terms,[10] when we seek God's will not by asking first, "What should *I* do," but "What should *we* do?"[11]

2. Cross

Jesus' death on a cross is the paradigm for faithfulness to God in this world. The community expresses and experiences the presence of the kingdom of God by participating in "the *koinōnia* of his sufferings" (Phil. 3:10). Jesus' death is consistently interpreted in the New Testament as an act of self-giving love, and the community is consistently called to take up the cross and follow in the way that his death defines. (When "imitation of Christ" is understood in these terms, the often-proposed distinction between discipleship and imitation disappears.[12] To be Jesus' disciple is to obey his call to bear the cross, thus to be like him.) The death of Jesus carries with it the promise of the resurrection, but the power of the resurrection is in God's hands, not ours. Our actions are therefore to be judged not by their calculable efficacy in producing desirable results but by their correspondence to Jesus' example.[13] Consequently, the role of the community appears paradoxical: "While we live, we are always being given up to death for Jesus' sake, so that the life of Jesus may also be made visible in our mortal flesh" (2 Cor. 4:11). That is the vocation and job description of the church. Common sense protests this account of Christian faithfulness, just as Peter did when scandalized by Jesus' talk of cross-bearing (Mark 8:31–38), but the New Testament texts witness univocally to the *imitatio Christi* as the way of obedience: "Bear one another's burdens, and in this way you will fulfill the law of Christ"[14] (Gal. 6:2).

In view of the reservations expressed by some theologians about the use of the cross as a paradigm for Christian ethics, an additional word of clarification is necessary in order to avert misunderstanding.[15] The image of the cross should not be used by those who hold power in order to ensure the acquiescent suffering of the powerless. Instead, the New Testament insists that *the community as a whole* is called to follow in the way of Jesus' suffering. The New Testament writers consistently employ the pattern of the cross precisely to call those who possess power and privilege to *surrender* it for the sake of the weak (see, e.g., Mark 10:42–45, Rom. 15:1–3, 1 Cor. 8:1–11:1). In the New Testament's one clear application of this pattern to the patriarchal marriage relationship, it is *husbands* (not wives) who are called to emulate Christ's example of giving themselves up in obedience for the sake of the other (Eph. 5:25). To read such a text—which calls for husbands to love and tenderly care for their wives—as though it somehow warranted a husband's domination or physical abuse of his wife can only be regarded as a bizarre—indeed, blasphemous—misreading. It is precisely the focal image of the cross that ensures that the followers of Jesus—men and women alike—must read the New Testament as a call to renounce violence and coercion.[16]

3. New Creation

The church embodies the power of the resurrection in the midst of a not-yet-redeemed world. Paul's image of "new creation" stands here as a shorthand signifier for the dialectical eschatology that runs throughout the New Testament.[17] In the present time, the new creation already appears, but only proleptically; consequently, we hang in suspense between Jesus' resurrection and parousia. "The whole creation has been groaning in travail together until now; and not only the creation, but we ourselves, who have the first fruits of the Spirit, groan inwardly as we wait for adoption, the redemption of our bodies" (Rom. 8:22–23, adapted from RSV). The eschatological framework of life in Christ imparts to Christian existence its strange temporal sensibility, its odd capacity for simultaneous joy amidst suffering and impatience with things as they are. We can never say—as do the guys in a popular beer commercial—"It doesn't get any better than this," because we know it will; we are, like T. S. Eliot's Magi, "no longer at ease here, in the old dispensation." The church is, in Paul's remarkable phrase, the community of those "upon whom the ends of the ages have met" (1 Cor. 10:11, RH).[18] In Christ, we know that the powers of the old age are doomed, and the new creation is already appearing. Yet at the same time, all attempts to assert the unqualified presence of the kingdom of God stand under judgment of the eschatological reservation: not before the time, not yet. Thus, the New Testament's eschatology creates a critical framework that pronounces judgment upon our complacency as well as upon our presumptuous despair. As often as we eat the bread and drink the cup, we proclaim the Lord's *death . . . until he comes.* Within that anomalous hope-filled interval, all the New Testament writers work out their understandings of God's will for the community.[19]

These three images, I would propose, can focus and guide our reading of the New Testament texts with respect to ethical issues. Having introduced this proposal, I want to address several points about the derivation, use, and limits of these suggested criteria.

First, no one should suppose that these images have been derived in some strictly scientific or objective manner from exegesis of the individual New Testament texts. It is true that I have settled on these categories through a period of years of teaching on the various New Testament texts and reflecting inductively on the question of their coherence. (Some of the results of that inductive study are presented in Part I.) At the same time, however, it is equally true that my critical reading of the texts is shaped and informed by my participation in a living community of faith that has schooled me from an early age in the art of reading the Scriptures as coherent expressions of a story about God's grace. Thus, George Lindbeck, having read an earlier draft of my synthetic proposal, rightly remarks that it is "dependent on the mainstream Christian tradition of canonical reading that goes back to

Irenaeus" and that it articulates a theological framework "fully consistent with the christological, trinitarian and anti-Marcionite decisions of the church."[20] Thus, both my descriptive readings and my synthesis of these readings are influenced by community traditions of interpretation and practice. This is a clear illustration of a point made earlier: that the four tasks of New Testament ethics inevitably interpenetrate and overlap.

Second, my readings and my proposed synthesis are not *merely* repetitions of a traditional perspective. They offer a new interpretative "performance," the product of a fresh encounter with the texts that poses questions not necessarily asked by the tradition. I have sought to do what any serious interpreter must do: to *listen* to the texts with the aid of the best critical methods available and to discern their witness for the present time. (My reading of the Gospel of Mark is a good illustration of my point: though the interpretation set forth in Chapter 3 would enjoy general acceptance among contemporary New Testament scholars, no one in the church before the late twentieth century ever read this Gospel as embodying an ironic vision of the moral life and resisting epistemological closure.) But if my descriptive and synthetic accounts are a contingent interpretive performance, then they can hardly be claimed to be permanently definitive; the only interesting question is whether they are illuminating. Other equally serious readers might construe the texts in a different pattern. We are not compelled to read the New Testament texts as expressions of and reflections about the story encapsulated in the images of community, cross, and new creation; all that is claimed here is that a synthetic reading guided by these focal images will in fact fruitfully discover a coherent moral vision in the texts.

Third, reading the diverse New Testament witnesses in light of these focal images will not automatically resolve all tensions and difficulties, nor will it end debates about how to appropriate these texts for our time. All that is offered by these synthetic images is a framework within which the next step—hermeneutical reflection—can proceed. Indeed, the actual function of the images will become clear only as we employ them in Part IV of this book to shape our reading of the New Testament texts in relation to particular ethical issues.

Fourth, it might be asked whether the order of the three images is significant. I would suggest that the sequence *is* important. By placing *community* first, we are constantly reminded that God's design of forming a covenant people long precedes the New Testament writings themselves, that the church stands in fundamental continuity with Israel.[21] By placing *cross* in the middle, we are reminded that the death of Jesus is the climax and pivot-point of the eschatological drama. By placing *new creation* last, we are reminded that the church lives in expectation of God's future redemption of creation. In other words, the images are to be understood within a plot; they figure forth the story of God's saving action in the world.

Finally, it might be asked whether community, cross, and new creation become de facto a canon within the canon when they are employed in the way I have suggested.[22] The answer is yes, though in a way different from the common use of the term. The three images do serve as a canon within the canon in the sense that they provide a "rule" or guide for interpretation. They do not, however, replace or exclude any of the canonical writings. The function of these synthetic images must be kept clearly in mind. They should not be treated as principles that can be applied independently to the analysis of ethical issues without reference to the texts from which they are derived; rather, they are *lenses* that bring our reading of the canonical texts into sharper focus as we seek to discern what is central or fundamental in the ethical vision of the New Testament as a whole.

4. Why Love and Liberation Are Not Sufficient

Some readers will be surprised to find that I have not proposed love as a unifying theme for New Testament ethics. It is widely supposed that love is the basic message of the New Testament. Indeed, the letters of Paul, the Gospel of John, and the Johannine Epistles explicitly highlight love as a (or *the*) distinctive element of the Christian life: it is the "more excellent way" (1 Cor. 12:31–13:13), the fulfillment of the Law (Rom. 13:8), the new commandment of Jesus (John 13:34–35), and the revelation of the character of God that is to be reflected in relationships within the community of believers (1 John 4:7–8). Certainly, in these writings love is fundamental to the moral life.

Nonetheless, my omission of love from the above list of unifying images is not an oversight. For several reasons, love cannot serve as a focal image for the synthetic task of New Testament ethics.

First of all, love notably fails to meet my first criterion for evaluating focal images (discussed at the beginning of this chapter). For a number of the major New Testament writers, love is not a central thematic emphasis.

In the Gospel of Mark, Jesus' promulgation of the double love commandment (Mark 12:28–34) stands as an isolated element, not supported by other references to love in the story. In its narrative context, this pericope, part of a cycle of controversy discourses (11:27-12:44), serves to demonstrate that the Jewish religious authorities stood condemned by the norms that they themselves professed.[23] In this one passage, to be sure, love is assigned great importance: the greatest commandments in the Torah are love of God (Deut. 6:4–5) and love of neighbor (Lev. 19:18). For Mark, however, the Torah has been eclipsed by the coming of Jesus; consequently, the call of Christian discipleship cannot be understood simply in terms of continuity with the commandments of the Law, even the greatest ones. Nowhere in Mark's Gospel does Jesus teach or command his disciples to love; discipleship is defined not by love but by taking up the cross and following Jesus. If Mark were the only Gospel in the New Testament canon, it would be very difficult to make a case for love as a major motif in Christian ethics.[24]

In Hebrews and in Revelation, we encounter only scattered incidental references to love, mostly with regard to God's love of human beings, as in Hebrews

12:6, quoting Proverbs 3:12: "[T]he Lord disciplines those whom he loves." Only once in Hebrews is love held forth as an ideal or an imperative:

> *Let us hold fast to the confession of our hope without wavering, for he who has promised is faithful. And let us consider how to provoke one another to love and good deeds, not neglecting to meet together, as is the habit of some, but encouraging one another, and all the more as you see the Day approaching.* (HEB. 10:23–25)

The prevailing vision of the moral life in Hebrews—as one can see even in this exhortation—is characterized not so much by love as by patient endurance, holding fast the confession, following the example of Jesus' suffering obedience (5:7–10, 12:1–2). Similarly, as we have seen, the moral vision of Revelation focuses attention primarily on the testimony and the endurance of the saints, who "loved not their lives even unto death" (Rev. 12:11, RSV). The only references to love as an attribute or obligation of the community appear in two brief passages in the letters to the seven churches. The church at Thyatira is commended—somewhat perfunctorily in contrast to the stinging rebuke that is to follow (Rev. 2:20–23)—for its love, as one element in a list of virtues: "I know your works—your love, faith, service, and patient endurance" (Rev. 2:19). The church at Ephesus, on the other hand, is scolded for a lack of love:

> *But I have this against you, that you have abandoned the love you had at first. Remember then from what you have fallen; repent, and do the works you did at first.* (REV. 2:4–5)

One cannot say that the authors of Hebrews and Revelation are indifferent to love, but the paucity of references is striking. In each case where love is mentioned, it is closely identified with good works, and only in Revelation 2:4 is there a hint that love is anything more than a conventional description for good behavior. In sum, these two writings join the Gospel of Mark in bearing witness to a vision of the moral life in which love is not a major constitutive factor. Instead, all three of these major New Testament witnesses call the church to a rigorous, suffering obedience following the example of Jesus.

Perhaps the most striking evidence, however, comes from the Acts of the Apostles. Nowhere in this book does the word "love" appear, either as a noun or as a verb. Nowhere in any of the Lukan summaries of the apostolic preaching do we find any references to love; this foundational account of the early church neither commends love nor exhorts readers to experience or practice it. Even the programmatic accounts of the common life of the early Jerusalem community (2:42–47 and 4:32–37) emphasize unity and the power of God rather than the virtue of love. Christian readers are perhaps so accustomed to thinking of love as the preeminent characteristic of the Christian life that they subconsciously read it into Acts, but to do so is sloppy reading. The absence of the word "love" from Acts is not merely a lexical fluke; it is a true indicator of Luke's vision of the church. Acts is a book not about love but about power. Its fundamental theme is the triumphant march of the Spirit-empowered church throughout the Roman world. Certainly, Luke was not opposed to love; several passages in his Gospel (though fewer than one might suppose) commend love as a norm or as an appropriate response to Jesus (Luke 6:27–36, 7:36–50, 10:25–28 [with the parable of the good Samaritan in 10:29–37 as an exemplification of the meaning of loving the neighbor]). Nonetheless, his narrative account in Acts of the emergence and growth of the church does not lend itself to being synthesized with the rest of the New Testament under the rubric of "love."

This quick survey of the evidence demonstrates that at least four major New Testament witnesses—Mark, Acts, Hebrews, and Revelation—resist any attempt to synthesize their moral visions by employing love as a focal image. Or, to state the problem differently, a synthesis of the New Testament's message based on the theme of love drives these texts to the periphery of the canon. Surely this is an unacceptable result. The images of community, cross, and new creation more adequately bring these texts into focus along with the rest of the canonical witnesses. Despite the powerful theological uses to which the motif of love is put by Paul and John, that motif cannot serve as the common denominator for New Testament ethics.

The second reason that love is unsatisfactory as a focal image is that it is not really an image; rather, it is an interpretation of an image. What the New Testament means by "love" is embodied concretely in the *cross*. As 1 John 3:16 declares with powerful simplicity, "We know love by this, that he laid down his life for us—and we ought to lay down our lives for one another." The content of the word "love" is given fully and exclusively in the death of Jesus on the cross; apart from this specific narrative image, the term has no meaning. Thus, to add love as a fourth focal image would not only be superfluous, but it would also move in the direction of conceptual abstraction, away from the specific image of the cross.

The third reason for the inadequacy of love as a focal image is closely related to the second. Love covers a multitude of sins in more ways than one. The term has become debased in popular discourse; it has lost its power of discrimination, having become a cover for all manner of vapid self-indulgence. As Stanley Hauerwas has observed, "The ethics of love is often but a cover for what is fundamentally an assertion of ethical relativism."[25] One often hears voices in the church urging that the radical demands of Christian discipleship should not be pressed upon church members because the "loving" thing to do is to include everyone without imposing harsh demands—for example, disciplines of economic sharing or sexual fidelity. Indeed, love is sometimes invoked even to sanction sexual relations outside marriage or the use of violence. Surely in such cases the term has been emptied of its meaning. The biblical story teaches us that God's love cannot be reduced to "inclusiveness": authentic love calls us to repentance, discipline, sacrifice, and transformation (see, e.g., Luke 14:25–35; Heb. 12:5–13). We can recover the power of love only by insisting that love's meaning is to be discovered in the New Testament's story of Jesus—therefore, in the cross.[26]

This last reason shades over into concerns that are more properly hermeneutical than synthetic. Taken alone, it would not be a sufficient reason to resist using love as a synthetic lens. In combination with the above considerations, however, it suggests that love as a focal image might produce more distortion than clarity in our construal of the New Testament's ethical witness.

The arguments against using liberation as a focal image are somewhat similar. We find a powerful emphasis on this theme in Luke-Acts and in Paul. It is even possible, as David Rensberger has demonstrated, to read the Gospel of John as a witness for God's liberation of a community oppressed by the alienating powers of "the world."[27] It is difficult to see, however, how several of the other New Testament witnesses provide textual support for this image: Ephesians and the pastoral Epistles would be particularly resistant to a reading through the lens of liberation, though Matthew also presents a vision of the Christian life that is oriented more to orderly obedience than to deliverance from oppressing powers. Thus, although liberation finds a broader base of textual support than does love, it remains unable to bring the full spectrum of New Testament witnesses into focus. Indeed, the image of liberation actually stands in severe tension with the ethic of the pastoral Epistles. (See the second criterion discussed at the beginning of this chapter.) Thus, while liberation theology can rightly claim to be an authentic development of themes found in some of the New Testament witnesses, it does not represent a ground for synthesis; indeed, if the image of liberation were taken to be normative, it would have to serve as a critical principle to silence some of the voices within the canon.

The term "liberation" does have advantages; it offers a more specific image than the term "love." Indeed, the theme of liberation has proven theologically potent precisely because its allusive appeal to the Exodus story is so richly evocative: it touches the imagination, and it links the New Testament compellingly with the Old. Furthermore, unlike love, liberation is unlikely to fade into a conceptual abstraction, because it points resolutely to social and economic realities.

One potential danger in the use of liberation as a focal image, however, is that it can easily be understood in a purely immanent sense as a political term, thus losing touch with the New Testament's emphasis on the power of God as the sole ground of hope and freedom. When this happens, the New Testament's "eschatological reservation" (the "not yet" of salvation) may slip from view, so that the delicate balance of the eschatological dialectic is lost. For the New Testament writers who use the term, liberation is not a political program that human beings can implement; rather, it is the promised eschatological action of God.[28] Consequently, just as love is best understood through the focal image of the cross, so also liberation is best understood through the focal image of new creation: liberation is already given to us through Christ (Gal. 5:1), yet we still await liberation—the redemption of our bodies—while groaning along with the creation in bondage to decay (Rom. 8:18–25).

Thus, New Testament ethics will speak of love and liberation, and speak with urgent conviction, so long as these terms are understood as subheadings under the more fundamental categories of cross and new creation.[29] The latter categories serve as lenses that shape and focus our reading of the New Testament texts that speak of love and freedom. When love and liberation are removed from the focusing power of the cross and new creation, however, they can become distorted. And if we try to use love and liberation as focal images in their own right, we will produce reductive and truncated readings of the New Testament's canonical witness.

Taken together, the three images of *community, cross,* and *new creation* bring the moral vision of the New Testament canon into focus and provide a matrix within which we can speak meaningfully about the unity of New Testament ethics. But can this matrix of images be normative for us? That is the question to be pursued in the next part of this book.

NOTES

1. This claim is, of course, potentially controversial. For discussions that lend support in various ways to this assertion, see Dodd 1936; Frei 1975; Hays 1983; Wright 1992, 371–417. The earliest creeds characteristically articulate the content of Christian faith in narrative form. For recent discussion of the problem of the narrative character of Christian convictions, see the essays collected in Hauerwas and Jones 1989.

2. The Diatessaron was a late-second-century harmony of the four canonical Gospels, melding the four narratives into one. See W. L. Petersen 1992.

3. Kelsey 1975, 159.

4. Kelsey 1975, 163.

5. Kelsey 1975, 167, 197.

6. As I have argued elsewhere, however, this second-order reflection presupposes and comments upon a narratively structured gospel. See Hays 1983 and my essay "Crucified with Christ" in Bassler 1991, 227–246.

7. Images of this sort have much in common with Northrop Frye's conception of *dianoia,* adapted from Aristotle. Whereas the *mythos* of a literary work is its linear plot, the *dianoia* is its theme, the narrative pattern seen as a synoptic unity. "The word narrative or *mythos* conveys the sense of movement caught by the ear, and the word meaning or *dianoia* conveys, or at least preserves, the sense of simultaneity caught by the eye. . . . [A]s soon as the whole is clear in our minds, we 'see' what it means" (Frye 1957, 77). For further exposition and discussion, see Hays 1983, 20–28.

8. As Rowan A. Greer observes, "Irenaeus at every step of the way draws upon Scripture in articulating the framework by which he believes it must be interpreted" ("A Framework for Interpreting a Christian Bible," in Kugel and Greer 1986, 155–176; quotation from p. 174). I am indebted to Kathryn Greene-McCreight for calling my attention to the formal similarity between my proposal and the hermeneutical function of the Rule of Faith. For further reflections on the relation between "ruled reading" and "the literal sense" of the Bible, see Greene-McCreight 1994.

9. Of course, these proposals are not entirely hypothetical; one may in fact identify particular groups of Christians that do, de facto, read the NT through these particular focal lenses.

10. See Lohfink 1984 [1982]; Hütter 1994.

11. Allen Verhey, in private correspondence, suggests that the NT does not neglect individual responsibility but frames it with constant reference to communal discipline and discernment; thus, in some texts, the key question becomes, "What should I do as a member of this community?" Consequently, Christian discipleship involves the resocialization of the individual into the social patterns of a new community. The point is well taken: the NT does certainly offer moral exhortation and guidance for individuals. Nonetheless, I stand by the statement that the corporate obedience of the community is the primary concern of the NT writers. This concern differs so markedly from the usual individualistic assumptions of Western liberal culture that strongly worded guidelines are necessary in order to recall us to the NT's ecclesially oriented perspective.

12. Cf. Betz 1967.

13. The point has been argued compellingly by Yoder 1994.

14. On this text, see Hays 1987.

15. The following comments treat matters that pertain more properly to the hermeneutical and pragmatic tasks than to the problem of synthesis. I have nevertheless placed them here in the discussion, because my experience of lecturing on these texts has shown that the mere mention of the cross raises a red flag for many hearers—particularly for some feminist theologians. This is partly a consequence of the inescapable *skandalon* of the cross, but it is also, sadly, a consequence of the way in which patriarchal cultures have sometimes twisted the proclamation of the cross into a rhetorical instrument for subjugating women and the powerless. Such

abuse—both of the texts and of human beings—must be emphatically repudiated by NT ethics. For feminist critiques of the theology of the cross, see D. S. Williams 1993; Heyward 1984; Brock 1988.

16. Ellen Charry (1993) has argued eloquently that the cross and its attendant character-forming implications (humility, self-sacrifice, etc.) are precisely the most powerful theological instruments that can be brought to bear *against* male abuse of power. This seems to me to be exactly correct. I would add only that the NT's call for self-sacrificial service cannot be restricted only to men; to exempt women from the summons to be conformed to Christ's example of self-giving would be—paradoxically—to patronize them by excusing them from the call to radical discipleship.

17. The Gospel of John is the one NT text that may not fit easily into this synthetic account. John's emphasis on the realized element of eschatology is so strong that it threatens to dissolve the tension of unrealized promise found elsewhere in the NT. This Gospel continues, however, to look forward to a resurrection "at the last day," which cannot be identified with the fulfillment of coming to know Jesus in the present life. See the discussion of Johannine eschatology in Chapter 6. Also, when the Gospel is read in canonical context along with 1 John, the future eschatological emphasis is more clearly preserved: see, e.g., 1 John 2:28, 3:2, 4:17.

18. See the discussion of this passage in Chapter 1.2.a. Most English translations obscure Paul's conviction that the community stands at the point of the collision or overlapping of two ages.

19. My explication of this image owes much to the work of Ernst Käsemann, J. Christiaan Beker, and J. Louis Martyn. See also Finger 1989.

20. Lindbeck 1995, 19.

21. Indeed, if these same images were described by the terms "Israel, cross, and resurrection," I would not object so long as "Israel" were understood to include the Gentile Christians grafted into what Paul calls "the [eschatological] Israel of God" (Gal. 6:16) and so long as "resurrection" were understood to refer not only to the resurrection of Jesus (the already) but also to the general resurrection at the last day (the not yet).

22. This question was put to me by Ben Ollenburger in private correspondence (Feb. 24, 1993).

23. See my discussion of the passage in Chapter 3.

24. One possible strategy for making such a case would be to highlight the passages in which Mark portrays Jesus as having compassion on the crowds (6:34, 8:2) or as loving the rich man who asks what he must do to inherit eternal life (10:21). If these passages are taken as indicators of Jesus' general attitude toward people, then the call to follow Jesus might be interpreted to include sharing his disposition toward love. This strategy, however, is problematical. Mark (in contrast to John) does not encourage his readers to emulate Jesus' love; furthermore, if Jesus' compassion is taken to be exemplary, what are we to do with the passages in which Jesus manifests intolerance (7:27), impatience (8:17–21, 9:19), and anger (11:12–17, 1:41 [taking *orgistheis* ("being angry") as the original reading; see Lane 1974, 84 n. 141])? Mark's Jesus is not so much a loving figure as a powerful, somber, enigmatic one. The healings, exorcisms, and other miracles in Mark are not so much signs of love as signs of the power of God's inbreaking kingdom.

25. Hauerwas 1981b, 124.

26. Hauerwas's comment is again apt: "The ethic of the Gospel is not a love ethic, but it is an ethic of adherence to this man [Jesus] as he has bound our destiny to his, as he makes the story of our life his story. As an ethic of love the Gospels would be an ethic at our disposal, since we would fill in the context of love by our wishes . . ." (Hauerwas 1981b, 115).

27. Rensberger 1988; cf. Cassidy 1992.

28. One might compare the critique of liberation as a descriptive category for reading Exodus in Levenson 1993, 127–159.

29. Similarly, justice is rightly to be comprehended through the focal image of community. In other words, within NT ethics, justice (*dikaiosynē*) names the narratively rendered account of the covenant relation between God and God's people. For further discussion, see Hays 1992.

PART THREE

The Hermeneutical Task

The Use of the New Testament in Christian Ethics

Chapter 11

How Do Ethicists Use Scripture?

Diagnostic Questions

How can we read the New Testament texts as a message addressed to us? Once we have given a synthetic account of the basis for unity in New Testament ethics, we must move on to confront the hermeneutical task. What interpretive strategies shall we adopt to allow these ancient writings to continue speaking nineteen hundred years after their composition? When we confess these texts to be authoritative for the church, what precisely do we mean? Are certain parts or aspects of the New Testament authoritative in ways that other parts are not? What does it mean to say that a narrative text (such as Acts or one of the Gospels) is authoritative?

In order to approach these difficult questions, it will be useful to examine the ways in which a representative cross-section of theologians have in fact used the New Testament in setting forth normative accounts of Christian ethics. By examining their practices of interpreting and employing Scripture, we can gain a sense of the range of possible hermeneutical strategies and see what is at stake in their differing methodological decisions. In other words, before attempting to prescribe how we *should* use the New Testament in doing ethics, it is wise to consider how theologians *do* in fact use it.[1] I propose to investigate the role of Scripture in the ethics of five major twentieth-century interpreters: Reinhold Niebuhr, Karl Barth, John Howard Yoder, Stanley Hauerwas, and Elisabeth Schüssler Fiorenza. All five have been widely influential voices in the church. Although only Schüssler Fiorenza is a biblical scholar by trade, all five grant a major role to the New Testament in the formation of Christian ethics. I do not claim that their uses of the New Testament represent a comprehensive typology of hermeneutical strategies. All five, for example, are scholars who represent the academic culture of Europe and America. Four of the five are Protestants; only Schüssler Fiorenza is a Roman Catholic, and, as we shall see, her position is in no way representative of the dominant Thomist tradition in Catholic moral theology. Nonetheless, these five figures are sufficiently diverse to exemplify an instructive spectrum of hermeneutical options. One could expand the spectrum by adding representatives of other theological and cultural traditions (e.g., a Thomist, a Pentecostal, a Third World liberation theologian, and so forth); the range of possibilities is in principle infinite.[2] For the purposes of this book, however, the five thinkers selected for attention here will serve to raise the major hermeneutical issues for New Testament ethics. Readers are invited to extend this survey for themselves by posing the diagnostic questions developed in this part of the book to the work of other theologians.

Rather than attempting a complete survey of the use of the New Testament in the work of each of these writers, I will focus particularly on their treatments of war and violence. This specific test case will reveal much about their various methodological commitments, and it will provide a convenient point of comparison among the five.

After completing the comparative analysis of the hermeneutical strategies of these five theologians, I will offer some overall assessments and normative proposals about the role of the New Testament in Christian ethics. I do not expect that every reader will assent to my normative proposals; however, I hope that the categories employed in this chapter will at least clarify some of the differences in our interpretive practices within the church. At the same time, this discussion of hermeneutical methodology may encourage a more rigorous examination of the ways in which we appeal to Scripture as a basis for our ethical convictions.

Before we undertake the discussion of the use of the New Testament by Niebuhr, Barth, Yoder, Hauerwas, and Schüssler Fiorenza, it will be useful to set forth some diagnostic categories, a list of questions to pose to these five interpreters. This list of questions will focus the analysis and facilitate comparisons.

1. Modes of Appeal to Scripture

Hermeneutical appropriation of the New Testament requires us to make decisions about the *mode* of ethical discourse in which biblical warrants may function authoritatively. What sorts of work does Scripture do in ethical discourse? What sorts of affirmations does it authorize? We may distinguish four different modes of appeal to the text in ethical argument.[3] Theologians may appeal to Scripture as a source of the following:

- *Rules:* direct commandments or prohibitions of specific behaviors.
- *Principles:* general frameworks of moral consideration by which particular decisions about action are to be governed.
- *Paradigms:* stories or summary accounts of characters who model exemplary conduct (or negative paradigms: characters who model reprehensible conduct).
- A *symbolic world* that creates the perceptual categories through which we interpret reality.[4] (We may distinguish for analysis two different, but correlated, aspects of the New Testament's symbolic world: its representations of the human condition and its depictions of the character of God.)

Each of these modes of discourse may be found *within* Scripture as well as in secondary theological reflection about Scripture's ethical import. For example, the *rule* mode is illustrated by the New Testament's prohibition of divorce (Mark 10:2–12 and parallels). The *principle* mode is exemplified by Jesus' linking of Deuteronomy 6:4–5 with Leviticus 19:18 to form the double love commandment (Mark 12:28–31, parallels). The *paradigm* mode is illustrated by Jesus' use of the parable of the good Samaritan to answer the question "Who is my neighbor?" (Luke 10:29–37) and by Paul's offering himself as an example to be imitated (1 Cor. 10:31–11:1); an example of a negative paradigm is the story of Ananias and Sapphira (Acts 5:1–11). The *symbolic world* as context for moral discernment is by definition pervasive in New Testament texts. As examples, consider the following instances: Romans 1:19–32 offers a diagnosis of the fallen *human condition* without explicitly articulating any moral directives, and Matthew 5:43–48 proffers a *characterization of God* (who makes his sun rise on the evil and on the good, and sends rain on the just and on the unjust) in order to establish a framework for discipleship.

The presence of all these modes of discourse within the New Testament suggests that all of them are potentially legitimate modes for our own normative reflection.[5] Thus, the hermeneutical task is—in part—the task of rightly correlating our ethical norms with the modes of Scripture's speech. Our investigation will seek to determine the characteristic mode(s) of appeal to Scripture for each of the five theologians to be considered.

2. Other Sources of Authority

The other major hermeneutical issue that New Testament ethics must confront is the question of the authority of the New Testament's ethical vision in relation to other sources of authority for theology. No matter how seriously the church may take the authority of the Bible, the slogan of *sola Scriptura* is both conceptually and practically untenable, because the interpretation of Scripture can never occur in a vacuum. The New Testament is always read by interpreters under the formative influence of some particular tradition, using the light of reason and experience and attempting to relate the Bible to a particular historical situation. Thus, the hermeneutical task in New Testament ethics requires an attempt to specify as clearly as possible the relationship between Scripture and other sources of authority. These other sources are often characterized under the rubrics of *tradition, reason,* and *experience.*[6] This categorization is heuristically serviceable, but we must define carefully what is meant by each of these terms.

When we speak of *tradition* as an authority for theology, we refer not to general cultural customs but specifically to the church's time-honored practices of worship, service, and critical reflection. Included under this heading are first of all the ancient ecumenical creeds and dogmatic definitions; tradition also includes, however, the writings of individual theologians, particularly those who have been widely read and revered in the church over long periods of time (e.g., Augustine, Aquinas, Luther, Calvin, Wesley). As some of these examples suggest, tradition can also take more local forms: particular denominations or cultural groups within the church universal bear their own distinctive forms of belief and practice, which play a significant role in the way ethical issues are addressed. In Christian theology, tradition can never be treated as sacrosanct; we must bear in mind Jesus' warning against those who "abandon the commandment of God and hold to human tradition" (Mark 7:8 and parallels). The classic formula remains serviceable: Scripture is *norma normans* ("the norming norm"), while tradition is *norma normata* ("the normed norm"). Still, tradition gives us a place to start in our interpretation of Scripture; it teaches us how to read with imaginative sympathy and an obedient spirit. Only where there is an appropriate concern for the witness of tradition in the church will we find it possible to sustain what Hauerwas calls a "conversation with one another and God . . . across generations."[7]

When we speak of *reason* as an authority for theology, we refer to understandings of the world attained through systematic philosophical reflection and through scientific investigation. With regard to hermeneutical issues, reason is a necessary tool in weighing the intelligibility of the text, its correspondence to the world as perceived through other media of knowledge. Additionally, critical reason has played a major role in the historical study of the Bible, enabling us to understand more about the cultural context of scriptural writings and their processes of composition and development. The relationship of reason to the New Testament as an authority is sometimes problematical. That is so not because the New Testament is unreasonable but because reason itself is always culturally influenced. One important insight of philosophical reason in the late twentieth century has been the recognition that we have no access to a universal objective "reason."[8] Rationality is a contingent aspect of particular symbolic worlds. Consequently, when we ask about the relation between Scripture and "reason" as sources of authority, we are in effect seeking the best way to coordinate the cultural logic of the New Testament writings with the cultural logic of our own historical setting. The possibility of significant—perhaps irreconcilable—tensions between these sources can hardly be ruled out a priori.

When we speak of *experience* as an authority for theology, we refer not just to the religious experience of individuals but also to the experience of the community of faith collectively. Private revelatory experiences may prove edifying, but they can claim normative status in the interpretation of Scripture only insofar as they are received and validated in the wider experience of the community. (A classic example is Luther's experience of finding grace and forgiveness in Scripture; his personal experience became paradigmatically illuminating for many and thus became hermeneutically normative for an important theological tradition.) Experience serves not only to illuminate the meaning of the text but also to confirm the testimony of Scripture in the hearts and lives of the community. This is what the tradition calls *testimonium internum Spiritus Sancti,* what John Wesley meant when he spoke of "experimental religion": experience is the living appropriation of the text, which becomes self-attesting as it is experienced in faith.

> I love to tell the story, because I know 'tis true;
> it satisfies my longings as nothing else can do.[9]

The satisfaction of longings becomes evidence for the truth of Scripture's testimony. But what about experience that seems to contradict the witness of Scripture? That is a difficult problem that must be explored in our study of representative theological ethicists. In any case, just as tradition and cultural norms of rationality inescapably form our sensibilities, so also we are formed as interpreters by our personal experiences of God and the world. This formative role of experience must be acknowledged and reckoned with in our account of New Testament hermeneutics.

The right relation of Scripture to each of these other sources of authority has been a perennial problem for theology. The challenge has taken slightly different forms in different historical eras, but the church must always struggle to get the balance among these four factors right. The Reformation fought its hermeneutical battles over the relation of church *tradition* to Scripture; the Enlightenment wrestled with the relation of *reason* to Scripture, a battle that continued into the early years of the twentieth century. Now, however, we have passed into an era in which the urgent question is the relative authority of Scripture and *experience.* Many feminist and liberation theologians are willing to assert explicitly that the authority of Scripture is in principle subordinate to the authority of the critical insight conferred by the experience of the oppressed or of women. Here great caution is necessary to distinguish the appropriate—indeed, inevitable—role of experience in shaping our interpretation of the text from the bolder claim that personal experience can be treated as a source of theological authority independent of Scripture.

As we assess the hermeneutical strategies of Niebuhr, Barth, Yoder, Hauerwas, and Schüssler Fiorenza, we must ask how each one weighs the relative importance of these four sources for theology and how their interpretations of New Testament ethics are shaped by that methodological decision. But still one more factor remains to be considered.

3. The Enactment of the Word

As we survey the hermeneutical strategies of our five representative interpreters, we must ask finally in each case about the concrete embodiments of their moral visions. What sort of communities have resulted or might result from putting their readings of Scripture into practice? When we ask this question, we have moved imperceptibly across the indistinct theoretical line that distinguishes the hermeneutical task from the pragmatic.[10] If we want to assess the normative implications of differing readings of New Testament ethics, this movement to the pragmatic question is inescapable.

When we pose this question as an integral part of an inquiry into New Testament ethics, we are acknowledging the force of James's insistence that "faith without works is dead" (James 2:26b). Or, to put the point in a slightly different way, we are subjecting various accounts of New Testament ethics to the "fruits test" that Jesus proposed for distinguishing false prophets from true: "You will know them by their fruits" (Matt. 7:20). It is important to note, however, that we are not pursuing an ad hominem inquiry about the moral quality of the personal lives of these theologians. Rather, we are asking how their programmatic proposals for the use of the New Testament in ethics have been put into practice in living communities of faith. The operative assumption of this inquiry, then, is that a clearly articulated and faithful reading of the ethics of the New Testament ought to contribute to the formation of communities that palpably embody the love of God as shown forth in Jesus Christ.

4. A Diagnostic Checklist

In view of the above considerations, we may now formulate a diagnostic checklist to be employed in assessing the role of Scripture in the work of various theological ethicists. The overall structure of the checklist corresponds to the four-part structure of this book, distinguishing, for the sake of analysis, the *descriptive, synthetic, hermeneutical*, and *pragmatic* aspects of New Testament ethics. One could elaborate these diagnostic questions considerably; the questions posed in Parts I and IV of the list are broadly formulated, asking for summary judgments about complex matters. For our present purposes, however, this list will suffice as a structuring device for the discussion.

THE USE OF SCRIPTURE IN ETHICS

I. *Descriptive*

How accurate/adequate is the exegesis of texts used?

II. *Synthetic*

A. Range: How comprehensive is the scope of texts employed?

B. Selection: Which biblical texts are used and not used? Is there a canon within the canon? How is selection determined?

C. How does the interpreter handle texts that are in tension with his or her position?
D. What focal images are employed?

III. ***Hermeneutical***

A. What is the mode of appeal to the text? What sort of work does Scripture do? What sorts of proposals does it authorize?
   1. Rules
   2. Principles
   3. Paradigms
   4. Symbolic world
      a. The human condition
      b. The character of God

B. What other sources of authority do the interpreters rely on?
   1. Tradition
   2. Reason
   3. Experience

IV. ***Pragmatic***

The fruits test: How is the vision embodied in a living community? Does the community manifest the fruit of the Spirit (Gal. 5:22–23)?

NOTES

1. Kelsey (1975) gives an exemplary account of the various ways in which theologians appeal to Scripture to authorize theological claims. The present study, while drawing significantly on his insights, focuses more narrowly on a special case of the more general problem analyzed by Kelsey: the use of the NT in theological ethics.

2. For a comprehensive study of the use of Scripture by a somewhat wider range of theological ethicists, see Siker (forthcoming). My decision to treat Barth, Yoder, and Hauerwas entails a decision to give more intensive attention to a certain particular band within the spectrum, for there are definite family resemblances among these three in their use of Scripture. Because all three of them share my concern to grant Scripture a constitutive role in Christian ethics, I have found it instructive to clarify my own position by delineating more carefully the differences between them—differences that in my judgment turn out to be of considerable importance.

3. Here I follow Gustafson 1970, though I have modified his categories slightly.

4. Cf. the work of Berger and Luckmann 1966 and its application to the study of early Christian ethics by Meeks 1986b and 1993.

5. But see Verhey 1984, 176–177, who would exclude appeals to the NT at the "moral-rule" level.

6. The four sources of theological authority thus outlined correspond to the Wesleyan Quadrilateral described by Albert Outler, which has become widely influential as a framework for discussion in much recent Protestant thought. For Outler's own account of these categories, see Albert C. Outler, "The Wesleyan Quadrilateral—In John Wesley," in Langford 1991, 75–88. For a historical critique of Outler's attribution of these categories to Wesley himself, see Ted A. Campbell, "The 'Wesleyan Quadrilateral': The Story of a Modern Methodist Myth," in Langford 1991, 154–161. Anglican theology does not treat "experience" as a separate category, identifying instead a threefold authority for theology: Scripture, tradition, and reason. In effect, this classification treats contemporary religious experience as part of the data to be weighed by reason. While this is a workable schema, I believe it is more heuristically useful to consider experience as a separate category, thus distinguishing between scientific and philosophical investigations (i.e., reason) on the one hand and the evidence of intuitive and anecdotally reported spiritual *experience* on the other.

7. Hauerwas 1981a, 64.

8. For example, MacIntyre 1988 points out that "standards of rational justification" are embodied in and emerge from particular traditions (p. 7). Although the Enlightenment promised to provide standards of reason

"undeniable by any rational person and therefore independent of . . . social and cultural particularities," it failed (p. 6); there is no universal reason, because reason itself is tradition- and history-bound.

9. Katherine Hankey, "I Love to Tell the Story," *The United Methodist Hymnal* (Nashville: United Methodist Publishing House, 1989), 156. (Originally written in 1868.)

10. See my discussion of these terms in the Introduction.

Chapter 12

Five Representative Hermeneutical Strategies

1. Reinhold Niebuhr: Christian Realism

Reinhold Niebuhr (1902–1971) has been the most influential American Protestant theological ethicist of the twentieth century. As a young pastor and active advocate for organized labor in Detroit during the 1920s, he harbored strong socialist and pacifist sympathies. However, his 1932 book, *Moral Man and Immoral Society*—written after he had become a professor of Christian ethics at Union Theological Seminary in New York—marked an intellectual and political watershed. Niebuhr had come to regard his earlier political idealism as unrealistic; his subsequent career was devoted to championing his vision of "Christian realism," which he understood as a biblically informed prophetic critique of ideologies both on the right and on the left. Niebuhr's influence can hardly be overestimated; his essays and books came to define mainstream Protestant ethics during the middle part of this century. He became an adviser to presidents and Washington policy-makers during the Cold War era, and his picture appeared on the cover of *Time* magazine in 1948. What appears to be commonsense political ethics to the majority of Protestant churchgoers today is actually a popularized version of Niebuhr's Christian realism.

In recent years, Niebuhr's intellectual pilgrimage and public career have been amply documented in a steady stream of publications debating the implications of his legacy for Christian ethics at the end of the twentieth century.[1]

In the discussion that follows, I aim not at a comprehensive account of his wide-ranging thought but at a summary of his views on the "love ethic" of Jesus and its relevance for normative judgments about Christian participation in war and acts of violence. Our discussion will therefore focus particularly on two important essays: "The Ethic of Jesus" and "The Relevance of an Impossible Ethical Ideal," both published in 1935 in Niebuhr's *An Interpretation of Christian Ethics*.[2] An investigation of this theme will disclose important dimensions of the overall structure of Niebuhr's thought. Our particular concern here, however, is to analyze the way in which he employs the New Testament in the construction of his position.[3]

Niebuhr's Approach to Theological Ethics

Niebuhr understands the ethic of Jesus to be a radical ideal concerned only with the individual's attainment of complete moral perfection.[4] "Its ideal of love has the same relation to the facts and necessities of human experience as the God of prophetic faith has to the world."[5] That is to say, the ethic of Jesus transcends human historical possibility. His uncompromising demand of self-emptying love stands as a norm over all human action, but "it transcends the possibilities of human life in its final pinnacle as God transcends the world."[6] This ethic, according to Niebuhr, is marked particularly by its ideal of complete self-abnegation.

> The absolutism and perfectionism of Jesus' love ethic sets itself uncompromisingly not only against the natural self-regarding impulses, but against the necessary prudent defences of the self, required because of the egoism of others. . . . Every form of self–assertion is scrutinized and condemned in words which allow of no misinterpretation.[7]

Niebuhr has in mind here preeminently the teachings of the Sermon on the Mount. Jesus forbids concern for even one's own minimal needs: "Do not worry about your life, what you will eat or what you will drink, or about your body, what you will wear" (Matt. 6:25). Jesus' teachings against accumulation of possessions (Matt. 6:19–24) and against pride are also read by Niebuhr as indicators of his demand for self-abnegation.

The most compelling expression of the radical love ethic of Jesus, however, is to be found in his teachings on nonresistance and love of enemy:

> Jesus' attitude toward vindictiveness and his injunction to forgive the enemy reveals more clearly than any other element in his ethic his intransigence against forms of self-assertion which have social and moral approval in any natural morality.[8]

Throughout his presentation of Jesus' ethic, Niebuhr unremittingly polemicizes against all attempts to water down the force of these radical teachings or to assimilate them to any sort of prudential ethic. Jesus' ethic "demands an absolute obedience to the will of God without consideration of those consequences of moral action which must be the concern of any prudential ethic."[9] For example, Jesus' teaching of nonresistance to evil (Matt. 5:39) should neither be interpreted as a strategy for changing the enemy's behavior nor be translated into a mere prohibition against violent resistance. Indeed, according to Niebuhr, "[T]here is not the slightest support in Scripture for this doctrine of non-violence. Nothing could be plainer than that the ethic uncompromisingly enjoins non-resistance and not non-violent resistance."[10] Consequently,

> When . . . liberal Christianity defines the doctrine of non-resistance, so that it becomes merely an injunction against violence in conflict, it ceases to provide a perspective from which the sinful element in all resistance, conflict, and coercion may be discovered. Its application prompts moral complacency rather than contrition, and precisely in those groups in which the evils which flow from self-assertion are most covert. This is the pathos of the espousal of Christian pacifism by the liberal Church, ministering largely to those social groups who have the economic power to be able to dispense with the more violent forms of coercion and therefore condemn them as un-Christian.[11]

Looking at Jesus' teachings on turning the other cheek, going the second mile, loving the enemy, and forgiving seventy times seven (Matt. 5:38–48, 18:21–22), Niebuhr sees the clear expression of an absolute divine standard that will admit no compromise.

The difficulty, however, is that the moral demand of these texts exceeds the possibility of human fulfillment: "Jesus thus made demands upon the human spirit, which no finite man can fulfill, without explicitly admitting this situation."[12] Christian theology and preaching, then, ought to acknowledge the transcendent character of Jesus' demands: "The modern pulpit would be saved from much sentimentality if the thousands of sermons which are annually preached upon these texts would contain some suggestions of the impossibility of these ethical demands for natural man in his immediate situations."[13]

Furthermore, Niebuhr is equally insistent that these teachings envision only an individual religious ethic concerned with "disinterestedness" and "the integrity and beauty of the human spirit";[14] they cannot be applied in the sphere of human social or political life.

> The ethic of Jesus does not deal at all with the immediate moral problem of every human life—the problem of arranging some kind of armistice between various contending factions and forces. It has nothing to say about the relativities of politics and economics, nor of the necessary balances of power which exist and must exist in even the most intimate social relationships. . . . It does not establish a connection with the horizontal points of a political or social ethic or with the diagonals which a prudential individual ethic draws between the moral ideal and the facts of a given situation. It has only a vertical dimension between the loving will of God and the will of man.[15]

Thus, Niebuhr has framed the dilemma that he attempts to address in his essay "The Relevance of an Impossible Ethical Ideal." Jesus did not teach a social ethic; indeed, "Christianity really had no social ethic until it appropriated the Stoic ethic."[16] The ethic of love that Jesus did teach is of a transcendent character, presenting an ideal of personal purity and self-denial that can never be realized in any human historical community. How then does the ethic of Jesus pertain to normative Christian ethics?

It is difficult to see how Niebuhr's account of the ethic of Jesus avoids the pitfall of docetism. If Jesus' ethic "does not deal at all with the immediate moral problem of every human life," one may fairly ask whether Jesus' own life was a human life.[17] Does Niebuhr think of Jesus as a historical human being? He touches on this problem, without resolving it, in a cryptic remark in the midst of his "Impossible Ethical Ideal" essay.

> The relation of the Christ of Christian faith to the Jesus of history cannot be discussed within the confines of this treatise in terms adequate enough to escape misunderstanding. Perhaps it is sufficient to say that the Jesus of history actually created the Christ of faith in the life of the early church, and that his historic life is related to the transcendant Christ as a final and ultimate symbol of a relation which prophetic religion sees between all life and history and the transcendant.[18]

Here the influence of Niebuhr's colleague Paul Tillich, acknowledged in the preface of *An Interpretation of Christian Ethics,* is evident.[19] Niebuhr's formulation, however, not only posits a docetic Christology (by distinguishing ontologically between Jesus and the transcendent Christ) but also fails to solve the problem of the historical practicability of Jesus' ethic. If Jesus of Nazareth was a historical figure who lived—as all persons in history do—amidst "contending factions and forces," how could his ethic fail to address the moral problem of human life? On the other hand, if the life of the historical man Jesus symbolizes a transcendent reality, why is it "impossible" for other human beings also to act in ways that participate in that symbolization? It seems that Niebuhr has unintentionally created a theological problem for himself by placing Jesus' teachings on a superhuman pedestal; this distancing of Jesus from the human condition contradicts the portrayals of Jesus in the New Testament and in the christological definition of Chalcedon.

In any case, Niebuhr answers the question about the relevance of an impossible ideal by suggesting that Jesus' pure ideal of love can be approximated in history through the principle of equal justice, for equality is "a rational, political version of the law of love."[20] This idea, which appears repeatedly in Niebuhr's works, is stated succinctly in *An Interpretation of Christian Ethics:*

> It is impossible to construct a social ethic out of the ideal of love in its pure form, because the ideal presupposes the resolution of the conflict of life with life, which it is the concern of the law to mitigate and restrain. . . . As the ideal of love must relate itself to the problems of a world in which its perfect realization is not possible, the most logical modification and application of the ideal in a world in which life is in conflict with life is the principle of equality which strives for an equilibrium in the conflict.[21]

The major task of Christian social ethics, then, is to formulate realistic policies, working through existing political systems to achieve a social equilibrium that maximizes equal justice. The impossible ideal remains relevant because it provides both "the source of the norms of justice" and "an ultimate perspective by which their limitations are discovered."[22] Thus, "Christ and the Cross reveal not only the possibilities but the limits of human finitude in order that a more ultimate hope may arise from the contrite recognition of those limits."[23]

In light of the above considerations, it is evident that the formal structure of Niebuhr's ethic is emphatically *consequentialist,* determining the rightness of any course of action by assessing its consequences or anticipated consequences. Scripture does not give us fixed rules of conduct; rather, it serves as a source of general principles that must be applied to specific situations as we reckon the likely results of our actions. Of course, as creatures living within the amibiguities of history, we can never be sure in advance about the outcomes of our actions; all we can do is to make the best judgment possible, often being forced to choose the lesser of conflicting evils as we seek to promote justice.

For this reason, violence and war as instruments of Christian action cannot be rejected in principle. In *Moral Man and Immoral Society,* Niebuhr explicitly sets forth an argument for recourse to violence in a revolutionary cause.

> If a season of violence can establish a just social system and can create the possibilities of its preservation, there is no purely ethical ground upon which violence and revolution can be ruled out. . . . Once we have made the fateful concession of ethics to politics, and accepted coercion as a necessary instrument of social cohesion, we can make no absolute distinctions between non-violent and violent types of coercion or between coercion used by governments and that which is used by revolutionaries. If such distinctions are made they must be justified in terms of the *consequences* in which they result. The real question is: what are the political possibilities of establishing justice through violence?[24]

This appeal to *consequences* ("establishing justice") as the ultimate justification for revolutionary violence—without regard to the legal authorization of the agent employing violent coercion—distinguishes Niebuhr's position from traditional Christian just war theory, which stresses that armed violence can legitimately be ordered only by duly constituted state authority.

In most of his writings, however, Niebuhr is less concerned with legitimating revolutionary violence than with sanctioning the use of violence by existing government authority. Writing within the context of the U.S. democratic state, he assumes that the government is fundamentally the defender of justice against the forces of disorder, and he supposes that Christians will find themselves assuming responsibility for defending justice through the use of force.

> The very essence of politics is the achievement of justice through equilibria of power. A balance of power is not conflict; but a tension between opposing forces underlies it. Where there is tension there is potential conflict, and where there is conflict there is potential violence. *A responsible relationship to the political order, therefore, makes an unqualified disavowal of violence impossible.* There may always be crises in which the cause of justice will have to be defended against those who will attempt its violent destruction.[25]

Christian pacifism is valuable in the church as a "symbolic portrayal of love absolutism in a sinful world";[26] that is, it reminds us of the final norm of Jesus' love ethic, but it can never be justified as a pragmatic course of action.

Clearly, from Niebuhr's point of view, pacifism remains a peripheral option, one only for ascetics. Those Christians who want to be "responsible" participants in society will recognize that there is no possibility of living in history without sinning and that we must—however reluctantly—get our hands dirty in the rough-and-tumble of politics and violence. "With Augustine, we must realize that the peace of the world is gained by strife."[27]

For Niebuhr, this normative position on violence in no way constitutes a rejection of the authority of the New Testament. It is, rather, an attempt to respect the authority of the love ideal of Jesus by "realistically" approximating what it requires, using violence if necessary.

The necessity of some such adaptation is, in Niebuhr's view, underscored by the New Testament's portrayal of human nature. Again and again, Niebuhr quotes Romans 7 to characterize the anthropological perspective of the Bible:

> Prophetic Christianity . . . demands the impossible; and by that very demand emphasizes the impotence and corruption of human nature, wresting from man the cry of distress and corruption, "The good that I would do, I do not: but the evil that I would not, that I do. . . . Woe is me. . . . [W]ho will deliver me from the body of this death?"[28]

Pacifists, utopians, and liberal optimists fail to reckon seriously with "the insights of a religion which knows that the law of love is an impossible possibility and knows how to confess, 'There is a law in my members which wars against the law that is in my mind.'"[29] Human beings are caught in a dialectical dilemma between freedom and finitude; though they have the capacity for self-transcendence, they are also caught in the self-contradiction of sin. The fallenness of human nature ensures that egoism will continue to assert itself in historical circumstances, requiring countervailing coercion and violence in order to restore and maintain the equilibrium of forces demanded by the principle of equal justice. It is this ambiguous human condition, disclosed in its full depths only by the biblical portrayal of humanity, that mandates violence as an inescapable part of any realistic Christian ethic.

Posing the Diagnostic Questions

In light of the foregoing sketch of Niebuhr's position, let us now seek to characterize his hermeneutical strategy using the diagnostic questions developed in the previous chapter. (Readers may want to refer to the outline of those questions at the conclusion of Chapter 11 as a map for the following discussion.)

(A) DESCRIPTIVE How accurate and adequate is Niebuhr's exegesis of the texts that he cites? On the whole, Niebuhr cannot be considered a careful reader of the New Testament. His interest lies in big theological ideas and themes, not in close exposition of biblical texts.[30] He tends to treat the texts as illustrative material rather than as the generative source of his theological reflection.

Niebuhr rarely engages in any sort of exegetical discussion. He tends to cite brief passages, hardly ever more than a sentence at a time, as maxims or articulations of religious truth. In using Gospel materials, Niebuhr does not attend to the narrative context of the sayings he cites, nor does he make an attempt to distinguish between authentic sayings of the historical Jesus and the subsequent additions of the community. Since Niebuhr's own training and most of his writing antedated the development of redaction criticism, it is not surprising that he gives no consideration to the theologies of the individual evangelists. With regard to Paul, Niebuhr's reading is strongly shaped by Reformation traditions that center on the message of the sinner justified by faith; this one great theme eclipses the specific ethical teachings of the Pauline letters, and Niebuhr—again, not surprisingly for a critic of his generation—does not perceive the Pauline doctrine of justification in its historical context as Paul's response to the problems of Jewish-Gentile relations.

Occasionally, we catch glimpses of a demythologizing hermeneutic at work, as for instance when Niebuhr interprets Luke 10:20 ("Rejoice not that the devils are subject unto you, but rather rejoice because your names are written in heaven") to mean, "Find your satisfaction not in the triumph over evil in existence, but rather in the conformity of your life to its ultimate essence."[31] Niebuhr characteristically does not mount exegetical arguments for such interpretations; rather, he presents them as self-attesting distillations of the meaning of the texts.

(B) SYNTHETIC As we have seen, Niebuhr employs a relatively narrow range of New Testament texts in the construction of his ethical position. In the Gospels, he focuses on "the ethic of Jesus" as expressed particularly in the Sermon on the Mount; in other words, he concentrates on Jesus' sayings to the virtual exclusion of the narrative framework. His reading of Paul is highly selective, focusing on Romans 7 as a classic evocation of "the impotence and corruption of human nature"[32] but giving scant weight to Romans 8, with its depiction of transformed life in the Spirit. Niebuhr makes almost no use of the rest of the New Testament: the Gospel of John, the Acts of the Apostles, the pastoral Epistles, Hebrews, James, and Revelation do not seem to be part of his functional canon.[33] What about Old Testament texts? Niebuhr does point with some frequency to Israel's classical prophets as exemplars of "prophetic religion," but he rarely cites particular passages from the prophetic literature. All in all, this narrowly circumscribed use of biblical sources is a weakness of Niebuhr's method.

The texts that stand in tension with his synthetic construal of the message of the New Testament are treated, as we have seen, as expressions of an "impossible ideal." Rather than contradicting his program of Christian realism, they express idealized norms that must be approximated in practice. Similarly, New Testament passages that articulate apocalyptic visions or speak of the coming of the kingdom of God are read by Niebuhr as symbolic expressions of the truth that "only a final harmony of life with life in love can be the ultimate norm of [human] existence."[34] Such symbols, however, must be taken "seriously but not literally," for if they are taken literally, "the Biblical conception of a dialectical relation between history and superhistory is imperiled."[35] In other words, the force of the New Testament's eschatology is to affirm that "a continued element of contradiction in history is accepted as its perennial character."[36] An interpretive strategy of demythologizing (though Niebuhr did not use Bultmann's term) is necessary in order to bring the New Testament's writers into unison as witnesses for a perennially paradoxical human condition.[37] It is to Niebuhr's credit that he devotes so much attention to the hard cases, the passages that threaten to disconfirm his approach to Christian ethics. Attention to these texts is essential for Niebuhr's program, because the New Testament itself offers almost no direct support for a "realistic," consequentialist approach to ethics; nonetheless, Niebuhr finds biblical support for it precisely by pressing the radical character of the New Testament's demands and then applying an accommodationist hermeneutic.

Since Niebuhr does not really attempt to produce a comprehensive synthesis of the New Testament's ethical teaching, it is not easy to point to a focal image that governs his reading of the New Testament texts. The ideal of love is the fundamental unifying theme of the New Testament witness, in Niebuhr's view, but the images of "struggle" and "balance" (or "equilibrium") become the key images in his actual application of the New Testament to normative ethical issues.

(C) **HERMENEUTICAL** Niebuhr's manner of appealing to the New Testament texts is crucial for the development of his constructive ethic. He shows no interest in applying Scripture's specific *rules* to the moral issues of his day; rather, he sees Scripture as providing, above all else, *principles* that guide moral reflection—or, at an even higher level of abstraction, ideals (for example, love), from which principles (such as equal justice) may be derived. Moral decisions must be made by deciding in specific situations which actions best correspond to these principles. Niebuhr never treats the New Testament as a source of *paradigms* for action; this is a corollary of his lack of attention to the narrative dimension of the texts. Nowhere does Niebuhr hold forth the stories of Jesus or Paul or the early church as models of conduct.

The *symbolic world* of the New Testament, however—particularly its portrayal of human nature—is a critical element in Niebuhr's ethic; it is no accident that the title of Niebuhr's theological magnum opus is *The Nature and Destiny of Man.* The portrayal of the human being as caught in the dialectical tension between finitude and freedom, between the capacity for self-transcendence and the inevitable pull of sinful self-assertion, is at the root of Niebuhr's account of Christian ethics. He regards this ambiguous portrayal of human possibility and limits as a central insight of the Bible, one that challenges the pretensions of all human ideological systems. On the other hand, the biblical portrayal of God as the redeemer and transformer of human life plays a smaller role in Niebuhr's constructive ethic. For this reason, Martin Luther King, Jr., for whom Niebuhr had been a significant influence, finally came to believe that his account of the New Testament's symbolic world was unbalanced:

> I came to see that Niebuhr had overemphasized the corruption of human nature. His pessimism concerning human nature was not balanced by an optimism concerning di-

> vine nature. He was so involved in diagnosing man's sickness of sin that he overlooked the cure of grace.[38]

Whether that judgment is correct or not, it can hardly be denied that Niebuhr's appeals to biblical authority characteristically highlight biblical anthropology, especially the reality of sin and finitude as disclosed in texts such as Romans 7.

How does Scripture relate to other sources of authority in Niebuhr's ethic? While Niebuhr locates himself in the broad stream of tradition influenced by Augustine, and while his anthropology is profoundly shaped by Reformation perspectives, *tradition* is not explicitly assigned a major role in the formation of his normative judgments. "Orthodoxy" has a negative valence in Niebuhr's lexicon; the term designates for him a stagnant Christianity that values order over love. Niebuhr's account of "prophetic religion" is presented as an explicit critique of tradition (and, at the same time, of more recent Protestant liberalism). In this respect, Niebuhr's theological perspective is classically Protestant: he advocates a biblically informed faith as a critical norm against which tradition must be measured. Even when he argues for the necessity of violence, for example, he does not appeal to the just war tradition in Christian theology; instead, he develops an independent argument. In the formal structure of Niebuhr's hermeneutic, then, tradition weighs lightly.

Both *reason* and *experience*, on the other hand, are assigned major normative roles in Niebuhr's ethic. The consequentialist character of his thought necessarily places great importance on rational calculation and on assessment of living human experience. It is reason and experience that testify to the "impossible" character of Jesus' ethic of love. In a telling passage in the middle of "The Relevance of an Impossible Ethical Ideal," Niebuhr, after citing Pelagius's argument that God would not impose upon human beings commandments too hard to be obeyed, comments:

> There is a certain plausibility in the logic of these words, but unfortunately, *the facts of human history* and *the experience of every soul* contradict them. The faith which regards the love commandment as a simple possibility rather than an impossible possibility is rooted in a faulty analysis of human nature. . . .[39]

Pelagius argued his position on the basis of Scripture and an account of the character of God: God is not ignorant of human limitations, and God would not ask of us something beyond our capacity. Niebuhr trumps this argument, however, by appealing to *reason* (an empirical account of human history) and *experience* (the struggle of "every soul" with moral failure). These sources yield a better "analysis of human nature" and thus place us closer to the truth. In this case, to be sure, reason and experience do not contradict Scripture; rather, they show how Scripture should be read. The Bible's anthropology tallies with the evidence rationally discerned. Nonetheless, it is the empirical evidence that is decisive for Niebuhr. Significantly, he does not locate his dispute with Pelagius on exegetical ground; it is the rational and experiential judgments that finally matter most. Elsewhere, Niebuhr proposes that "lack of conformity to the facts of experience" is a certain "criterion of heresy."[40] As one reads through Niebuhr's essays, one sees again and again that political and moral questions are decided on the basis of rational assessments of efficacy. Scripture stands in the background as the ultimate source of the ideals that inform moral judgment, but its relation to specific political choices is distant and indirect.

(D) **PRAGMATIC** Finally, we must ask what sort of fruits Niebuhr's Christian realism has borne and might bear. If the Christian community shaped its life by applying a Niebuhrian hermeneutic to the New Testament, what would the result look like? Since Niebuhr was such an influential figure, the question need not be merely hypothetical. The mainstream U.S. Protestant denominations of the Cold War era—especially the boards and agencies headquartered at 475 Riverside Drive in New York City—were the institutional embodiments of Niebuhr's moral vision. These bodies have concerned themselves with articulating realistic social policies in the interest of social justice, seeking to influence the course of power politics. (Unfortunately, the bearers of Niebuhr's legacy have proven far less effective than Niebuhr himself in wielding influence within the political world.)

Niebuhr had little concern with the church as a distinctive institution; in fact, it would not be inaccurate to say that his theology lacks an ecclesiology. His writings address the individual Christian not as a member of the church but as a citizen of the democratic social order. Thus, the fruits of Niebuhr's ethic would be manifested in the guiding influence of Christians in positions of secular political responsibility. The corporate identity and life of the Christian community are not major themes in his work. Correspondingly, a community shaped by Niebuhr's vision would be far more concerned with pursuing political efficacy than with defining and maintaining its own confessional identity. Such a position might have made sense in the America of Niebuhr's time, in which the cultural vestiges of Christendom still persisted. As the culture of Christendom crumbles, however, the supposition that Christians can or should take responsibility for guiding the social struggle appears increasingly quaint and presumptuous.

One danger of such a strategy is that the Christian community might become so drawn into realistic and pragmatic discourse that it would lose its own peculiar voice, adopting instead the lowest-common-denominator values of popular politics. To some extent this has in fact happened to the mainstream denominations, which are now suffering precipitous membership losses. *Christianity and Crisis*, the journal that Niebuhr founded for the discussion of ethical issues, ceased publication in 1993. The demise of this once-important journal marks the massive cultural shift that has occurred since Niebuhr's heyday. A chastened Christian realism at the end of the century might require more attention to nurturing the life of the church community and fewer grand pretensions to shape the political order.

In any case, Niebuhr's "realistic," consequentialist approach to the use of the Bible in Christian ethics continues to command wide-ranging assent among Protestants in the United States. His hermeneutic is highly selective in its use of the New Testament, but it is methodologically clear and consistent. By adopting Niebuhr's hermeneutical perspective, the church can continue to claim Scripture as an authoritative source for general moral principles and for a soberly nuanced account of human nature, while at the same time allowing great latitude in the choice of particular courses of action.

2. Karl Barth: Obedience to the Command of God

The Swiss theologian Karl Barth (1886–1968) was among the most prodigious theological minds of the twentieth century.[41] His early commentary on Paul's letter to the Romans (the crucial second edition of which appeared in 1922), addressing the faith crisis of European Christianity in the aftermath of World War I, challenged both the standard paradigms of biblical criticism and the anthropocentric character of prewar European liberal theology. Later, Barth was the principal author of the Barmen Declaration (1934), the Confessing Church's theological manifesto against Nazism. As a vigorous critic of Rudolf Bultmann's hermeneutical program of "demythologizing" the New Testament, he became the most powerful voice for the neoorthodox project of reasserting the primacy of biblical categories for interpreting human experience; his multivolume *Church Dogmatics* stands as a monumental systematic attempt to rethink and present Christian doctrine on an explicitly biblical foundation.

Barth tirelessly resisted liberal Protestantism's tendency, exemplified classically in Schleiermacher, to reduce theological affirmations to expressions of the believer's religious consciousness; he insisted, instead, on proclaiming the givenness and potency of the Word of God apart from us, over against us, and for us. According to Barth's theology, God has claimed human beings as his covenant partners by his powerful act of self-revelation; indeed, God is to be known only in his action, for God is the One whose being is in his act.[42] Consequently, the truth is never to be found in universal abstractions but always in the particular, in God's concrete self-disclosure in Jesus Christ. Barth's theological vision accorded great importance to the biblical narratives, because he understood them as the form in which God's self-disclosure is made known specifically. Furthermore, unlike Niebuhr, Barth was acutely concerned to confront the methodological problems of biblical hermeneutics. Thus, Barth offers an interesting case for our investigation of the use of Scripture in Christian ethics.

Barth's Approach to Theological Ethics

A long methodological introduction in *Church Dogmatics* II/2 (hereafter generally referred to as *CD*) presents "Ethics as a Task of the Doctrine of God." Barth contends that "ethics belongs not only to dogmatics in general but to the doctrine of God,"[43] because it deals with the *command* of God to human beings.[44] Consequently, the discussion of ethics must reflect the trinitarian structure of God's self-revelation. "The concept of the command of God includes the concepts: the command of God the Creator, the command of God the Reconciler and the command of God the Redeemer."[45] Accordingly, Barth planned to treat ethics not in a single systematic location but in a concluding chapter to each of the different parts of *Church Dogmatics.* Unfortunately, since he did not live to complete his massive opus, we have only the programmatic introduction to ethics in *CD* II/2 and the treatment of "The Command of God the Creator" in III/4. As we shall see, the unfinished character of Barth's presentation of theological ethics will prove important for assessing his teaching on the issue of war, which appears in *CD* III/4.

Barth identifies three temptations that beset Christian ethics: (1) *apologetics:* the temptation to justify theological ethics on nontheological grounds; (2) *differentiation:* the temptation to isolate theological ethics as a special sphere of inquiry sharply distinguished from philosophical ethics; (3) *coordination:* the temptation to correlate theological ethics and philosophical ethics as mutually complementary.[46] The first two temptations Barth emphatically rejects. The third, historically exemplified by the Thomist tradition in Roman Catholicism, "merits the closest attention," but in the end it too must be decisively set aside:

> For . . . everything is compromised by the fact that revelation is not really accepted as revelation, but is constantly set against the light of reason with its independent, if limited, illumination. . . . The complaint which we have to make against the Roman construction of the relationship between theological ethics and general human ethics is that it . . . thinks it can combine the Christian and the human far too easily. To achieve this combination and co-ordination it has emptied out what is Christian. Therefore in spite of its inherent advantages we cannot accept it.[47]

As this quotation indicates, Barth seeks to articulate an account of theological ethics that is based entirely on revelation. In a striking metaphor, he compares the task of theological ethics to the mandate given to Israel to occupy the land of the Canaanites:

> We have to realize how far-reaching is this change in the conception of ethics. From the point of view of the general history of ethics, it means an annexation of the kind that took place on the entry of the children of Israel into Palestine. Other peoples had for a long time maintained that they had a very old, if not the oldest, right of domicile in this country. But, according to Josh. 9:27, they could now at best exist only as hewers of wood and drawers of water. On no account had the Israelites to adopt or take part in their culture. Their liveliest resistance, therefore, could be expected, and their existence would necessarily be for the Israelites an almost invincible temptation. . . . It may easily be forgotten . . . that the Word of God, and in its faithful proclamation the preaching of the Church, and with preaching dogmatics, and at the head of dogmatics the Christian doctrine of God, are always the aggressor in relation to everything else, to general human thinking and language. When they enter the field of ethical reflection and interpretation they must not be surprised at the contradiction of the so-called (but only so-called) original inhabitants of this land. They cannot regard them as an authority before which they have to exculpate themselves, and to whose arrangements they must in some way conform.[48]

The Word of God has invaded the world, and human reason can only bow before it. The task of Christian theological ethics must be to proclaim and explicate the Word, "[taking] every thought captive to obey Christ" (2 Cor. 10:5) and serving notice to all humanity of the truth disclosed in the biblical revelation.

For such ethics, there can be no concern about human processes of moral reasoning or about correlating Scripture with other sources of authority. "For the question of good and evil has been settled once and for all in the decree of God, by the cross and resurrection of Jesus Christ."[49] Thus, there can be no question of original thought in Christian ethics. "'[W]hat is good' has been 'said' to man (Mic. 6:8), so that man has been forbidden to try to say it to himself, and bidden simply and faithfully to repeat what has been said to him."[50] The only question that matters, then, is the question of obedience to the Word of God, for there is "no human action which does not stand under God's command." No human action is "exempted from decision in relation to God's command, or neutral in regard to it."[51] Because the obedience demanded by God has been fully disclosed in Jesus Christ, "we, for our part, have actually nothing to add, but have only to endorse this event by our action. The ethical problem of Church dogmatics can consist only in the question whether and to what extent human action is a glorification of the grace of Jesus Christ."[52]

The next major section of Barth's exposition of his method concentrates on "The Command as the Claim of God," developing the affirmation that Jesus Christ is himself the basis of the divine claim on humanity, as well as the content and form of that claim. Jesus "accomplished the great work of faith, so that it no longer requires to be accomplished for us, but we with our faith have only to look up to His, to approve and follow it, to endorse it with our own faith."[53] Barth's conception of faith emphatically includes obedience in action; his position is deeply rooted in the Pauline understanding of participation in the faith of Jesus Christ.[54] This theological position is crucial for Barth because it grounds the command of God in a determinate action of God played out in concrete human history: "What we find in the case of the man Jesus is a valid model for the general relationship of man to the will of God."[55] Thus, "[T]he command of God . . . does not confront us as an *ideal*, whether that of an obligation, that of a permission, or that of a combination of the two, but as the *reality* fulfilled in the person of Jesus Christ. This person as such is not only the ground and content but also the form of the divine claim."[56] The contrast to Niebuhr's treatment of Jesus could hardly be more striking.

But if Barth's way of connecting Christology and ethics differs sharply from Niebuhr's, his insistence on "the definiteness of the divine decision"[57] sets him apart still more dramatically, not only from Niebuhr but from almost all other theological ethicists as well. According to Barth's sweeping development of the Reformed conception of the sovereignty of God, the Word of God is always definite, the will of God always addressed specifically to individual situations. Barth's extraordinary articulation of this claim deserves to be quoted *in extenso*, for it is crucial to the comprehension of his normative ethics:

> Here we cannot try to secure for ourselves an advantage as against the command of God by understanding and asserting it as a general rule but regarding its application . . . as a matter for our judgment and action, so that the particular individual expression of what is laid down and prescribed in the command as a universal rule is only actualised in and with our own decisions—like the verdicts of a human judge, which are particular applications in each case, according to his own discretion, of what the law prescribes in general. The Law of God cannot be compared with any human law. *For it is not merely a general rule but also a specific prescription and norm for each individual case.* At one and the same time it is both the law and the judge who applies it. For as God is not only the God of the general but also of the particular, of the most particular, and the glory of the latter is His, so is it with His command. . . . The command of God is an integral whole. For in it form and content, general prescription and concrete application are not two things but one. The divine decision, in which the sovereign judgment of God is expressed on our decisions, is a very definite decision. This means that in the demand and judgment of His command God always confronts us with a specific meaning and intention, with a will which has foreseen everything and each thing in particular, which has not left the smallest thing to chance or our caprice. . . . [I]n every visible or invisible detail He wills of us precisely the one thing and nothing else, and measures and judges us precisely by whether we do or do not do with the same precision the one thing He so precisely wills.[58]

Barth's prevailing concern is that if we conceive of ethics as the application of general principles to specific situations, we will in the end indulge our own wishes and whims, all the while claiming religious—or even biblical—sanction. If so, "we have poured the dictates and pronouncements of our own self-will into the empty container of a formal moral concept, thus giving them the aspect and dignity of an ethical claim (although, in fact, it is we ourselves who will them)."[59] This is a weighty objection; examples of the abuse Barth fears could be multiplied endlessly. (Some would point, for example, to Niebuhr's appropriation of the ideal of love as a warrant for killing as an instance of this ethical fallacy.)

The difficulty for Barth, however, is that his account of the definiteness of the divine command requires him to adopt a hermeneutical position that strains credulity. The divine command, he insists, "does not need any interpretation, *for even to the smallest details it is self-interpreting.*"[60] Such an implausible claim—apparently refuted by the simple fact of serious interpretive disagreements in the church—is logically inescapable for Barth, for if the necessity of interpretation is admitted, then a loophole is provided for the assertion of sinful self-will. If and only if the Word of God is utterly self-interpreting can it be affirmed that "the command is unconditional, leaving us no other choice than that between obedience and disobedience."[61] A stronger and more explicit doctrine of the role of the Holy Spirit in guiding the interpretation of Scripture might provide a different route out of this dilemma, but Barth, for whatever reason, takes the "stonewall" option, affirming not just that Scripture is perspicuous but that it imposes its own interpretation on the reader.[62]

This line of thought leads inexorably to an account of how the divine command comes to us through Scripture. Barth's argument proceeds in two stages: "(1) that the divine law in the Bible is always a concrete command; and (2) that this concrete commanding to be found in the Bible must be understood as a divine command relevant to ourselves who are not directly addressed by it."[63]

The demonstration of the first point is a long exercise of descriptive exegesis, covering almost thirty pages of the *Dogmatics*, much of it in fine print.[64] The narrative character of the Bible, presenting the Word of God as encountering specific human beings in contingent historical situations, is the decisive indicator of the concrete particularity of the command of God. If the Bible presented the will of God as "the establishment and proclamation of general precepts and rules, . . . it would not be the Bible, but the code of a Hammurabi or the law of a Solon or Mohammed." As it is, however, the Bible presents itself as "the story [*Geschichte*] of God's covenant of grace." For this reason, "we may as little think of abstracting from this story as from the person of the God who commands. On the contrary, we must continually keep before us and therefore understand the person in the story and the story in the person."[65] This hermeneutical rule applies even to portions of Scripture that appear to offer general codes of conduct (e.g., the Ten Commandments or the Sermon on the Mount). To lift these passages out of their narrative context would be capricious, for "the theme of the Bible is something other than the proclamation of ethical principles." Those who merely extract principles "must realise that they are taking a disastrous freedom with the Bible, and if they appeal to the Bible they must be reminded that they are appealing to a Bible which they have first adjusted to their own convenience."[66]

All of this is both important and clear, but the second part of Barth's argument is more difficult to understand.[67] While recognizing that the command of God in the biblical stories was originally addressed to others long ago, he nonetheless insists that we too must understand ourselves to be *directly* addressed by it. We are not simply to find in these stories illuminating analogies to our experience; rather, we are to hear the Word spoken then as the Word spoken also now to us:

> The Bible speaks of God's command in order to call our attention not merely to what the will and work and self-revelation were there and then, but to what they are here and now for us ourselves. In its capacity as witness it claims not only our recognition of facts but also our faith, not merely our appreciation of the past events which it attests but also our realisation that matters are still the same here and now, and that as and what God commanded and forebade others, He now commands and forbids us. *The Bible wills that we should be contemporaneous with and of the same mind as these other men in regard to the divine command, our hearing and understanding of it, and our situation as affected by it.*[68]

What could it mean to assert that we should be "contemporaneous" with the prophetic and apostolic witnesses? On first encountering this suggestion, one is inclined to suppose it an instance of homiletical hyperbole, but as one reads and re-reads this section of the *Dogmatics*, it becomes evident that Barth makes this claim with full theological gravity. The claim is intelligible only in light of the very strong sense in which Barth conceives of the Bible as "the living speech of God":[69]

> . . . [I]f the meaning and substance of the biblical testimony is the revelation of the reality of God in His works, then we cannot avoid the conclusion that the Bible itself is this Word of command. . . . In practice, therefore, this God and the Bible, His commanding and its commanding, are not to be separated.[70]

In Scripture, we literally encounter the Word of God. Thus, we find ourselves not just in an analogous position to the original witnesses:

> We are not only exhorted to hear the command of God *as* they heard it. But at once the God who has spoken and acted in relation to them also becomes our God in virtue of their witness. And so the command given to them and heard by them becomes *directly* the command given to us and to be heard by us.[71]

In this way, Barth seeks to construct a hermeneutic that eliminates the necessity—indeed, the possibility—of independent human reckoning and moral calculation. God acts through Scripture to encounter and claim us, regardless of our intentions or interpretive abilities. Our place is to hear and obey.

> We stand under the arbitrament of God's precise and definite command and prohibition not as and because we realise it and think of it, but as and because he has issued His command once and for all, and therefore for us and our times and all the situations of our lives, in and with the history . . . of His covenant of grace. For by this covenant we are not only embraced by the fact of the death and resurrection of Jesus Christ. . . . We are also embraced (and closely so, without any empty or neutral zones) by His living command through which he wills to sanctify us, attract us to Himself, and therefore awaken us to obedience, as partners in his covenant.[72]

It remains for us to consider how this hermeneutical approach is worked out in Barth's handling of the ethical issues of war and violence.

Barth's Teaching on War

Barth's treatment of war as a topic for theological ethics appears in *CD* III/4 under the rubric of "The Protection of Life," in a section of the *Dogmatics* that offers an extended exposition of the commandment "Thou shalt not kill." The command of God in this case must be understood not just as a prohibition but also as a positive teaching that instills respect for life. Life is the "loan and blessing" of God, who has "unequivocally and fully accepted it in Jesus Christ, in the incarnation of His Word."[73] Thus, the commandment against killing expresses the will of God for the protection and affirmation of life.

Precisely because human life belongs to God, however, we must take care not to absolutize or idolize it. Knowing that life is God's gift, we must recognize that "human life has no absolute greatness or supreme value, that it is not a kind of second god, but that its proper protection must also be guided, limited and defined by the One who commands it, i.e., by the Lord of life."[74] The *freedom* of the God who commands (a major emphasis in Barth's theology) must be honored; in some exceptional cases, God may command killing. In such instances, the protection of life may, paradoxically, require "its surrender and sacrifice."[75] To exclude this possibility a priori would be to compromise the freedom of God.

> . . . [W]e cannot deny the possibility that God as the Lord of life may further its protection even in the strange form of its conclusion and termination rather than its preservation and advancement. Yet this exceptional case can and should be envisaged and accepted only as such, only as *ultima ratio*, only as highly exceptional, and therefore only with the greatest reserve on the exhaustion of all other possibilities.[76]

Because the fundamental norm is given by the biblical injunction against killing, the major aim of Barth's discussion, he explains, is to address the difficult problem of the *Grenzfall*, the exceptional case. By framing the problem in these terms, however, Barth appears to have created an insurmountable methodological problem for himself. On the one hand, he eschews casuistry, the attempt to specify ahead of time how general moral principles apply to various specific situations; on the other hand, he thinks it necessary to reflect theologically on the problem of how "exceptions" to the prohibition of killing may sometimes be recognized as the command of God. How does he solve this problem?

He begins with a brief but wide-ranging survey of pertinent biblical texts, attempting to summarize "the whole witness of the Bible" on this issue.[77] The citations range from the story of Cain and Abel in Genesis 4 to the warning against taking up the sword in Revelation 13:10. Curiously, Barth does not at this point mention the Old Testament's holy war texts; presumably, he is thinking initially of killing as the act of an individual rather than as the organized activity of a government. His interpretation of some of the New Testament passages that he cites is questionable; he infers, for example, that Peter "physically killed Ananias and his wife Sapphira by his word" (Acts 5:1–11). As other exceptional New Testament passages that seem to countenance killing, Barth cites 1 Corinthians 5:3–5, Romans 13:4, and John 19:10–11. Alongside these apparently anomalous passages he finds a preponderance of texts that forbid killing. He then summarizes the results of his survey in the following way:

> . . . [T]he whole witness of the Bible, although it recognises and does not exclude homicide which is not murder, is in fact a supreme summons to vigilance at this point. . . . It is indeed a matter for surprise that in the New Testament, as we have seen, not all cases of homicide are simply and absolutely prohibited as murder. . . . In the final New Testament form in which we have to hear and understand it, the commandment: "Thou shalt not kill," reaches us in such a way that in all the detailed problems that may arise we cannot exclude the exceptional case and yet we cannot assert too sharply that it is genuinely exceptional.[78]

With this result in hand, Barth moves to the discussion of a series of special issues in which the exceptional case of justified killing might be thought to arise: suicide, abortion, euthanasia, self-defense, and capital punishment. To summarize Barth's treatment of each of these issues would be too lengthy a task for our present purposes. In each case he attempts, insofar as possible, to set the discussion against the background of biblical texts; for example, despite "the remarkable fact that in the Bible suicide is nowhere forbidden," Barth adduces the stories of Saul, Ahitophel, and Judas, remarking that these narratives are "far better" for the purpose of moral instruction than a direct prohibition of suicide would be.[79]

The general tenor of his use of the Bible throughout the discussion of these problems is exemplified by his remarks, in the discussion of self-defense, concerning the Sermon on the Mount. After presenting Jesus' teachings that his followers should turn the other cheek and not resist an assailant, Barth comments on their normative force.

> We must not overlook them. We must not wrest nor misinterpret them. We must understand and respect them quite literally. *We cannot dismiss them simply by admiring or ridiculing them as the product of a heaven-storming idealism and then placing them in a corner and observing very different rules of life.* . . . The sayings of the Gospel are among those of which it is said that "they shall not pass away." For they do not merely express the well-meant exaggeration of humanitarianism, nor do they simply constitute a special rule for good or particularly good Christians. *They declare the simple command of God which is valid for all men in its basic and primary sense, and which is thus to be kept until further notice.* They do not refer to a peak of enthusiasm to which the obedient must finally climb; they refer soberly and realistically to a basis from which they must continually start and to which they must continually return in obedience. They give us the rule, whereas the rest of our discussion can deal only with exceptions.[80]

(Barth makes no mention of Niebuhr here, but had he written these words as a critique of Niebuhr's essay "The Relevance of an Impossible Ethical Ideal," they could hardly have been more apposite.)

As already noted, Barth has created a difficult problem for himself: the more strongly he stresses the situational particularity of the command of God, the more inappropriate it seems to speak of general "rules." On the other hand, the more strongly Barth stresses the binding character of the teaching of Jesus, the stranger the notion of "exceptions" appears. How are we to understand that tantalizing proviso, "until further notice"? In what form might such further notice come, and how are we to recognize it?

We have come at this juncture to a notoriously puzzling feature of Barth's theology. What does he mean when he speaks of hearing the command of God? To be sure, one hears the command of God through reading the Bible with careful attention. If, however, God in some cases commands exceptions to the commandments written in Scripture, it is difficult to see how Barth could be referring to anything other than direct experiences of divine revelation.[81] Among the five representative theologians we are considering in this book, only Barth, in his account of moral decision making, requires—at least implicitly—a constant reliance on prayer and listening for the guidance of God, believing that God can and does address individuals specifically with particular instructions. Apart from such convictions, Barth's whole discussion of "exceptions" would be nonsense.

Thus, Barth's hermeneutical strategy demands that we read Scripture thoroughly with the intent of obeying exactly what is commanded there, while always listening prayerfully for the unlikely revelation that in a particular case we may be commanded to do something contrary to the rule given by Scripture. How, then, does this hermeneutical strategy work itself out in Barth's discussion of war?

Writing this section of *Church Dogmatics* in 1951, in the shadow of the horrors of World War II, Barth mounts a powerful indictment of war as fundamentally contrary to the will of God.[82] Contrary to past illusions, war is not fought to protect honor, justice, and freedom; rather, it is a struggle between nations for economic power: "[T]he real issue in war . . . is much less man himself and his vital needs than the economic power which in war is shown not so much to be possessed by man as to possess him."[83] The deadly reality of modern warfare, with its capacity to annihilate whole populations, has disclosed the evil of war more vividly than the weaponry of previous historical periods. Consequently, "we to-day, unlike previous generations, are not merely qualified but compelled and certainly summoned to face the reality of war without any optimistic illusions. How unequivocally ugly war is!"[84]

Can war nevertheless be advocated by Christians as a legitimate or necessary course of action?

> All affirmative answers to this question are wrong from the very outset, and in Christian ethics constitute a flat betrayal of the Gospel, if they ignore the whole risk and venture of this Nevertheless. . . . All affirmative answers to this question are wrong if they do not start with the assumption that the inflexible negative of pacifism has almost infinite arguments in its favour and is almost overpoweringly strong.[85]

The burden of proof rests strongly on any theological argument in favor of war. Furthermore, the distinctive responsibility of Christian ethics is not to justify war but to pronounce God's judgment upon it and to promote conditions that are conducive to peace:

> The primary and supreme task of Christian ethics in this matter is surely to recover and manifest a distinctive horror of war and aloofness from it. . . . Christian ethics cannot insist too loudly that such mass slaughter might well be mass murder, and therefore that this final possibility should not be seized like any other, but only at the very last hour in the darkest of days. The Church and theology have first and supremely to make this detached and delaying movement. . . . Hence, the first basic and decisive point which Christian ethics must make in this matter is that the state, the totality of responsible citizens, and each individual in his own conduct should so fashion peace while there is still time that it will not lead to this explosion but make war superfluous and unnecessary instead of inevitable.[86]

In placing such emphasis on peacemaking as the fundamental task of Christian ethics, Barth's theology stands in impressive contrast to much of the Christian theological tradition from the time of Constantine onward. John Howard Yoder describes Barth's critique of war as "unique in the history of mainstream European Protestant theology."[87] Barth's distinctive stance is a result not only of his historical setting; it is also a consequence of his methodological insistence on according priority to the Bible as the source of theological norms. For Barth, the Christian tradition's acceptance of war as a normal task of the state is subject to severe challenge by the Word of God in Scripture.

Nevertheless, as the qualifying phrases in the above quotations suggest ("*almost* infinite arguments," and so on), Barth believes that in some extreme circumstances God may command war as an option of last resort. This possibility is required in principle by the freedom of God. Surprisingly, however, Barth goes on to argue that there are certain *specifiable circumstances* in which recourse to war may be understood as the command of God:

> [T]he conduct of one state or nation can throw another into the wholly abnormal situation of emergency in which not merely its greater or lesser prosperity but its very existence and autonomy are menaced and attacked. . . . Nothing less than this final question must be at issue if a war is to be just and necessary. . . . Indeed, it is only in answer to this particular question that there is a legitimate reason for war, namely, when a people or state has serious grounds for not being able to assume responsibility for the surrender of its independence, or, to put it even more sharply, when it has to defend within its borders the independence which it has serious grounds for not surrendering. The sixth commandment is too urgent to permit of the justification of war by Christian ethics on any other grounds.[88]

This permission for war is, furthermore, extended to situations in which "a state which is not itself directly threatened or attacked considers itself summoned by the obligation of a treaty or in some other way to come to the aid of a weaker neighbor which does actually find itself in this situation."[89] The United States' attack on Iraq in defense of Kuwait in the Gulf War of 1991, for example, would presumably be justified by this criterion.

This circumstantial justification for wars of national self-defense is baffling in the context of Barth's theological ethics for at least two reasons: it appears to be a lapse into precisely the sort of casuistic reasoning that Barth emphatically rejects in principle, and Barth is unable to adduce any specific biblical warrant for this alleged exception.[90] Why is the autonomy of a nation-state a value that Christians ought to defend? Barth merely remarks, mysteriously, that "there may well be bound up with the independent life of a nation responsibility for the whole physical, intellectual and spiritual life of the people comprising it, and therefore their relationship to God."[91] In such cases, Christians must fight and kill to protect the state. In a telling aside, Barth gives an illustration of what he has in mind:

> I may remark in passing that I myself should see it as such a case if there were any attack on the independence, neutrality and territorial integrity of the Swiss Confederation, and I should speak and act accordingly.[92]

Two corollaries of Barth's approach to the problem of war should be noted. First, conscientious objection to war must always be selective. The pacifist who absolutely refuses all participation in war is disobediently foreclosing the possibility that God may command war.[93] (This position is precisely the reverse of the policy of the United States during past eras when it practiced military conscription; only unconditional opposition to all wars was recognized as a legitimate ground for conscientious objector status.) Second, the traditional just war criterion concerning the probability of success as an indicator of *ius ad bellum* does not apply at all. The command of God is unconditional: "[I]t is independent of the success or failure of the enterprise, and therefore of the strength of one's own forces in comparison with the enemy."[94] No prudential reckoning of the prospects for victory can play a role in the decision to go to war. If war is ventured in obedience to God, "it is also ventured in faith and therefore with joyous and reckless determination."[95]

Thus, Barth presents a complex theological case that abhors war and insists on the weighty biblical case against it while at the same time holding open the possibility that obedience to the command of God may in exceptional cases require Christians to fight. We now turn to an analysis of his hermeneutical position in light of the diagnostic questions developed at the end of chapter 11.

Posing the Diagnostic Questions

(A) DESCRIPTIVE Barth offers sustained exegetical treatments of many biblical texts. His interpretations are not consistently informed by historical criticism, but they are consistently perceptive and interesting. Indeed, some of Barth's most compelling work is to be found in the fine-print exegetical sections of *Church Dogmatics*. This is not to say that his exegetical work is unimpeachable; his reading of the Ananias and Sapphira story (Acts 5:1–11) is an instance of unpersuasive interpretation. Still, Barth plunges into the thick of his exegetical work with impressive passion and discernment. He reads the texts with exemplary attention to context and large narrative patterns. This exegetical virtue carries with it, however, a corresponding temptation to read diverse texts—perhaps somewhat too readily—as part of a single grand narrative.

Barth, like Niebuhr, did most of his writing before the development of redaction criticism; consequently, he gives little attention to the individual theological perspectives of the evangelists. His reading of Paul, however, is rich and illuminating, perhaps because Barth's own emphasis on the priority and sufficiency of God's grace in Jesus Christ accords so well with Paul's major themes.

In sum, Barth deserves high marks as an exegete. No other systematic theologian of his time devoted so much energy to the exegetical task.

(B) SYNTHETIC Barth makes a serious attempt to deal with the whole witness of the canon—not just the New Testament but the Old Testament also. He cannot be faulted for selective use of texts, for he casts the exegetical net widely. Indeed, the range of his use of Scripture is so wide that it is difficult to identify a functional canon within the canon. One senses that the deepest roots of his thought are in Pauline theology, especially Paul's letter to the Romans—the text that launched his scholarly career—but in *Church Dogmatics* he ranges freely across the entirety of the canon, using all of it constructively.

How does he handle texts in tension with his position? There are no such texts for Barth. Even passages that appear to represent ethical anomalies merely serve to illustrate the freedom of the God who commands. God's ways are not our ways, and God cannot be bound by our limiting categories. Barth almost never explains intracanonical tensions by pointing to historical factors or developmental hypotheses. All of the biblical texts, even in their diversity, are revelatory of God's action and God's claim on our lives. Apparent contradictions in the canon become the springboard for Barth's dialectical theological reflection.

No reader of Barth will have any difficulty identifying the focal image that serves to unify his reading of Scripture. The person of Jesus Christ, who is the ground and content and form of the divine claim, is the unifying center; all Scripture bears witness to him and his truth. Thus, the command of God is brought into focus solely through the biblical portrayal of this person. For a full account of Barth's understanding of that portrayal, one must read through the fourth volume of the *Dogmatics*, but the same focal image is operative throughout Barth's work. The remarkable christocentric affirmations of the Barmen Declaration declare unmistakably the results of reading Scripture through this focal lens: "Jesus Christ, as He is attested to us in Holy Scripture, is the one Word of God, whom we have to hear and we have to trust and obey in life and in death."[96] This christocentric reading of biblical ethics causes Barth, in his discussion of war, to place an unusually heavy emphasis on peacemaking as the calling of the church.

(C) HERMENEUTICAL Barth's approach to ethics as "the command of God" is conducive to an emphasis on the *rules* in the Bible as directly normative, always with the twin provisos that the rules must be understood in their narrative context as belonging to the story of God's covenant election of a people, and that God is always free to decree particular exceptions to the rules. Subject to these qualifications, the New Testament's rules, such as those given in the Sermon on the Mount, are to be taken literally and obeyed "until further notice."

On the other hand, Barth polemicizes ferociously against the strategy of extracting *principles* from the biblical texts. The definiteness of the divine decision means that there can never be any latitude allowed for the application of general principles, never any "neutral zones" in which human reckoning can operate in deciding what is right. To leave room for such human reckoning would be to deny the particularity of the divine will and to adopt an ethic that is de facto atheistic. The effect of such an approach to ethics would be to leave the door open for selfish and sinful human beings to justify their own wills while cloaking their action in religious language.

By virtue of his attentiveness to narrative patterns, Barth values the biblical stories as *paradigms* (for example, note his remark that the stories of Saul, Ahitophel, and Judas are more instructive than an explicit prohibition of suicide). In particular, the story of Jesus Christ functions in Barth's theology as the single definitive template for obedience and authentic humanity. The "identity of authority and freedom" that is accomplished in the person of Jesus Christ "becomes normative for what is demanded of us."[97]

Barth is not content, however, to speak of the biblical stories as sources of analogies that might illumine our moral experience; he wants to press beyond mere analogy to "contemporaneousness." To speak of an analogical hermeneutic would again leave too much slack for our capricious interpretations. Rather, the paradigmatic stories are to confront us directly as the Word of God, in such a way that no process of analogical reasoning is necessary or even possible. With all good will and respect for Barth's concerns, it is difficult to see how this hermeneutical strategy can be distinguished, except rhetorically, from the exercise of the analogical imagination in reading the texts. In fact, much of Barth's own interpretive practice illustrates beautifully how such imaginative reading might be done: as an example, consider his use of the story of Israel's invasion of Canaan as a metaphor for the task of theological ethics.

With regard to the role of the New Testament's *symbolic world*, one might describe Barth's whole theological project as a resolute effort to place himself and his readers in "the strange new world within the Bible."[98] His reading of that world places all the accents on the character and activity of God as the one who is disclosed in Scripture; he shows relatively little interest in analyzing the New Testament's anthropological themes, except insofar as Jesus Christ himself is the revelation of humanity's true character and vocation.

How does Scripture relate to other sources of authority in Barth's ethics? The question answers itself: the Word of God is communicated through the Bible, and its authority is sovereign over all human wisdom. Throughout the *Dogmatics*, Barth carries on a running dialogue with the Christian theological *tradition*, employing the church fathers and the reformers as dialogue partners, and more recent theologians as foils. In every case, however, the New Testament provides the standard against which all tradition is to be measured; the tradition does not have normative weight in its own right.

Still less do *reason* and *experience* have any claim as authoritative sources for ethics. These are the "inhabitants of the land" that now have a right to exist only as "hewers of wood and drawers of water," only as servants of revelation. When theologians treat human wisdom as a source of theological knowledge, they have strayed into the clutches of "natural theology," against which Barth pronounced an emphatic "Nein!"[99] Natural theology is, for Barth, a form of idolatry. His stern conviction on this point was hardened by his struggle against Nazism's "German Christianity," which proffered a syncretistic blend of Christianity with elements of naturalism and nationalism. Against this syncretism, the Barmen Declaration was, at its heart, a disavowal of any authority other than the Word of God attested in Scripture.

Curiously, however, in Barth's discussion of war and killing his christocentric hermeneutic recedes into the background, while nonscriptural factors, such as the independence and integrity of the nation-state, come surprisingly to the fore as warrants for exceptions to the rule prohibiting killing. Why? Perhaps this is to some extent a consequence of the fact that *CD* III/4 treats ethics under the aspect of "The Command of God the Creator." How would Barth have dealt with war under the heading of "The Command of God the Reconciler"? Such a discussion might have compelled Barth to some rather different conclusions, more consonant with his professed determination to find the form and content of ethics in the person of Jesus Christ.[100] The more basic difficulty, however, is that human reason and experience cannot be summarily dismissed as factors in theological and ethical discourse. When one seeks to banish them, they tend to sneak in through the back door, unacknowledged. Barth's treatment of the problem of war offers a classic illustration of this problem. Precisely because he has so rigorously sought to exclude human moral wisdom and calculation from his program of ethics, his advocacy of military self-defense for the Swiss Confederacy appears abrupt and illogical; his experientially based conviction that Switzerland's independence ought to be defended has no theological foothold in his system.

The juxtaposition of Niebuhr and Barth demonstrates that, with respect to their hermeneutical methods, these two theologians stand in a converse relationship to one another, like a photograph and its negative. Niebuhr finds in Scripture ideals and principles that must be approximated by human choices, informed by a sober estimate of the likely consequences. Barth emphatically rejects all appeal to principles and consequentialist reckoning, while finding God's command in Scripture's explicit rules and in its paradigmatic narratives—elements that play no direct role in Niebuhr's ethics. While both theologians see the symbolic world of the New Testament as determinative for Christian ethics, their readings of that world stand in dramatic counterpoint. Niebuhr reads the symbolic world of the New Testament as an illuminating account of the tragic and transcendent *human* condition (*The Nature and Destiny of Man*), while Barth reads the symbolic world of the New Testament as a powerful account of the identity and action of *God*, who claims us through Jesus Christ for covenant partnership. Niebuhr insists that human reason and experience must be determinative for our interpretation of the New Testament and that inattention to "the facts of experience" is a sign of heresy; Barth insists that human reason and experience must bow in obedience before the Word of God and that deference to human experience is a sign of idolatry. The lesson to be learned: their disagreements on issues of normative ethics (e.g., Barth's much greater resistance to the use of violence by Christians) are not so much matters of exegetical disagreement as of hermeneutical method.

(D) PRAGMATIC What sort of fruits might Barth's theological ethics nurture? We have already noted his impressive role as a leading figure in the Confessing Church's resistance to the Hitler regime; the Barmen Declaration stands as an emblem of the practical consequences of a community formed by a Barthian hermeneutic, witnessing prophetically in the name of Jesus Christ against all earthly pretensions to authority. The goal of such witnessing is not so much to achieve political results as it is to proclaim the Word of God in the world.

Although Barth did not live to complete the sections of *Church Dogmatics* that would have dealt more extensively with the church, he was deeply concerned about the community of faith and the integrity of its confessional identity: it is apt that the final published fragment of the *Dogmatics* deals with baptism. A community shaped by Barth's hermeneutic would seek uncompromisingly to speak its message of the lordship of Jesus Christ over the world, without necessarily being concerned with practical means of implementing God's will in the political sphere.

One danger of such a strategy is that the Christian community might become so concerned with articulating its own proclamation that it would lose touch with the world to which it is supposed to speak. Barth's own career as a public figure who spoke compellingly to the issues of his day, however, shows that his theology does not necessarily or appropriately lead to such a conclusion.

In a time when the church is enervated by lukewarm indifference and conformity to the surrounding culture, Barth's theology offers it a potent shot of courage. His hermeneutic is comprehensive and radical in its incorporation of the witness of Scripture, though it is not always clear how Barth reasons from Scripture to his particular ethical judgments. In any case, by adopting Barth's hermeneutical perspective, the church can affirm its identity as a people whose vocation is above all obedience to the Word of God.

3. John Howard Yoder: Following the Way of Jesus

John Howard Yoder is an American theological ethicist whose roots are in the Mennonite tradition. He studied under Karl Barth at Basel, where his doctoral research dealt with the history of the Anabaptist movement in the sixteenth century. Subsequently, his intellectual pilgrimage led him into wide-ranging ecumenical conversations, as a Mennonite representative to the World Council of Churches and as a faculty member at the University of Notre Dame. His 1972 book *The Politics of Jesus*,[101] a pathbreaking attempt to do Christian ethics in vigorous dialogue with biblical scholarship, argues for three fundamental theses: (1) that the New Testament consistently bears witness to Jesus' renunciation of violence and coercive power; (2) that the example of Jesus is directly relevant and normatively binding for the Christian community; (3) that faithfulness to the example of Jesus is a political choice, not a withdrawal from the realm of politics. Yoder's work presented a frontal challenge to the Niebuhrian Christian realism that dominated Protestant social ethics in America during the period between World War II and the Vietnam War. Predating the emergence of liberation theology in the universe of theological discourse, *The Politics of Jesus* placed a formidable new proposal on the table for discussion.

Yoder has not produced a major systematic treatment of theological ethics; most of his writing has taken the form of occasional essays. *The Politics of Jesus,* on which we shall concentrate our attention, stands as his most significant constructive monograph. Also of importance for understanding Yoder's hermeneutic, however, is *The Priestly Kingdom,* a collection of essays published in 1984, emphasizing the communal context for Christian moral reasoning.[102] Taken together, these works provide the basis for an assessment of the role of Scripture in Yoder's thought.

Yoder's Approach to Theological Ethics

The opening chapter of *The Politics of Jesus* throws down the gauntlet: against "mainstream ethics," which asserts the irrelevance of Jesus for social ethics, Yoder affirms that "Jesus is, according to the biblical witness, a model of radical political action."[103] After sketching briefly several ways in which Christian theological ethicists have spiritualized or set aside the significance of Jesus' teaching and example, Yoder describes the alternative sources that typically have been adduced for ethical norms:

> [Social ethics] will derive its guidance from common sense and the nature of things. We will measure what is "fitting" and what is "adequate"; what is "relevant" and what is "effective." We shall be "realistic" and "responsible." All these slogans point to an epistemology for which the classic label is the *theology of the natural:* . . . it is by studying the realities around us, not by hearing a proclamation from God, that we discern the right.[104]

These are the assumptions Yoder seeks to challenge. If the sources and content of Christian ethics are discernible through natural wisdom, he asks, "Is there such a thing as a *Christian* ethic at all?" The theological stakes are high: at issue is not only the distinctiveness of Christian ethics but also the coherence between christological confession and ethical norms. If Jesus is not a model for conduct, the theological significance of his humanity may be diminished: "[W]hat becomes of the meaning of incarnation if Jesus is not normative man?"[105]

In order to demonstrate the biblical basis for his alternative position, Yoder proposes to undertake a fresh reading of "the Gospel narrative," constantly posing the heuristic question, "Is there here a social ethic?"

> I shall, in other words, be testing the hypothesis that runs counter to the prevalent assumptions: the hypothesis that the ministry and the claims of Jesus are best understood

> as presenting . . . not the avoidance of political options, but one particular social-political-ethical option.[106]

Yoder's reading focuses, as a test case, on the Gospel of Luke. Any of the canonical Gospels would serve to demonstrate the same point, he contends, but the Gospel of Luke is useful precisely because it presents the tough case for Yoder's hypothesis: "[Luke's] editorial stance is often taken to have been a concern to deny that the Christian movement was any threat to Mediterranean society or Roman rule."[107] Thus, if Yoder can demonstrate that the Gospel of Luke does represent Jesus as advocating a countercultural social ethic, the canonical basis for an apolitical portrait of Jesus will have been undermined.

Yoder seeks in the subsequent chapter, "The Kingdom Coming," to offer a series of "soundings" in Luke's narrative, showing that the kingdom of God proclaimed by the Lukan Jesus has a clear political dimension. The annunciation and birth stories show that Jesus "comes to break the bondage of his people," a bondage that "was discerned in all its social and political reality."[108] The temptation of Jesus in the wilderness depicts Jesus as rejecting "the idolatrous character of political power hunger and nationalism."[109]

Jesus' programmatic announcement of his mission in the synagogue at Nazareth (Luke 4:16–30) is a proclamation that the jubilee year of Leviticus 25 is at hand, when all slaves are to be freed, all debts canceled, and all property redistributed.

> *He has anointed me to preach good news to the poor;*
> *He has sent me to proclaim release to the captives;*
> *And recovering of sight to the blind;*
> *To set at liberty those who are oppressed,*
> *To proclaim the acceptable year of the Lord.*[110]

When Jesus declares that this Scripture is now fulfilled in the hearing of his listeners at Nazareth, he is pointing not just to some spiritual reality but to "a social event": "[W]hat the event was supposed to be is clear: it is a visible socio-political, economic restructuring of relations among the people of God, achieved by his intervention in the person of Jesus as the one Anointed and endued with the Spirit."[111]

Within the community of his followers, new patterns of leadership prevail: not dominance but servanthood and sharing. Jesus' teaching on discipleship reinforces this message. A new social order is in the process of formation. That new order, however, is inevitably a threat to the existing order. Consequently, those who join Jesus' movement will find rejection and suffering to be their lot:

> Jesus is here calling into being a community of *voluntary* commitment, willing for the sake of its calling to take upon itself the hostility of the given society. . . . [T]o be a disciple is to share in that style of life of which the cross is the culmination.[112]

To "take up the cross" and follow Jesus means to follow him in accepting "the fate of a revolutionary."[113]

The nonviolent character of Jesus' revolution, however, is decisively reaffirmed in Luke 22:39–53, the story of Jesus' prayer on the Mount of Olives and his subsequent arrest. At this climactic point in the story, Jesus once again is tempted by "the Zealot option" to seize power by force. Yoder asks acutely,

> What would it have meant for the petition to be answered, "Let this cup pass from me"? What else could possibly have happened then? . . . What was the option with which he was struggling? Was it that he might silently slip away to Qumran until the storm was over? Or could he have reconciled himself to the authorities by retracting some of his more extreme statements? Should he have announced a deescalation, renounced his candidacy for the kingship, and gone into teaching?

No, insists Yoder,

> The only imaginable real option in terms of historical seriousness, and the only one with even a slim basis in the text, is the hypothesis that Jesus was drawn, at this very last moment of temptation, to think *once again* of the messianic violence with which he had been tempted since the beginning. . . . Once more, now clearly for the last time, the option of the crusade beckons. Once more Jesus sees this option as real temptation. Once more he rejects it.[114]

By praying, "Not my will but yours be done," Jesus accepts his destiny of suffering and death on the cross.

This refusal of messianic violence, however, is not a renunciation of hope for the coming kingdom. It is, rather, precisely the way in which Jesus' obedience reveals the kingdom. "The cross is not a detour or a hurdle on the way to the kingdom, nor is it even the way to the kingdom; it is the kingdom come."[115] Once we have read Luke's Gospel in this way, according to Yoder, there can be no avoiding "an ethic marked by the cross, a cross identified as the punishment of a man who threatens society by creating a new kind of community leading a radically new kind of life."[116]

Following this survey of the Lukan story, Yoder takes up in subsequent chapters a series of particular topics that provide pertinent historical background to his interpretation: the meaning of the jubilee year, the way in which Israel's holy war tradition would have been understood by Jesus and his contemporaries, and the possibility of nonviolent resistance as a political option in that historical era. This leads to the pivotal chapter in the book, "Trial Balance," in which Yoder reflects hermeneutically on the normative consequences of reading the Gospels in the manner that he has proposed.

Anticipating the results of the latter half of the book, Yoder contends that the New Testament as a whole consistently points to Jesus' death on the cross as exemplary: "Only at one point, only on one subject—but then consistently, universally—is Jesus our example: in his cross."[117] The meaning of the cross, however, must not be generalized or abstracted away from the meaning that is given it by the Gospel narrative.

> The believer's cross is no longer any and every kind of suffering, sickness, or tension, the bearing of which is demanded. The believer's cross must be, like his Lord's, the price of social nonconformity. It is not, like sickness or catastrophe, an inexplicable, unpredictable suffering; it is the end of a path freely chosen after counting the cost. It is not . . . an inward wrestling of the sensitive soul with self and sin; *it is the social reality of representing in an unwilling world the Order to Come.*[118]

To bear the cross as Jesus' follower is to join the community of those who share his refusal of violence as an instrument of the will of God. This is not a peripheral theme in the Gospel narratives; it is their central concern.

> The one temptation the man Jesus faced—and faced again and again—as a constitutive element of his public ministry, was the temptation to exercise social responsibility, in the interest of justified revolution, through the use of available violent methods.[119]

Thus, theological ethics cannot proceed as though Jesus had nothing pertinent to say to the immediate problems of human life. "The Gospel record refuses to let the modern social ethicist off the hook. It is quite possible to refuse to accept Jesus as normative; but it is not possible on the basis of the record to declare him irrelevant."[120]

This account of Jesus' ethic receives additional resonance when heard in concert with the church's classic doctrine of the incarnation. Incarnation does not mean, insists Yoder,

> that God took all of human nature as it was, put his seal of approval on it, and thereby ratified nature as revelation. The point is just the opposite; that God broke through the borders of our standard definition of what is human and gave a new, formative definition in Jesus.[121]

Like his teacher Barth, Yoder affirms that Jesus reveals the true nature and vocation of human beings. This affirmation calls for a sweeping reformulation of our approach to theological ethics, for a christocentric ethic must take its bearings from the historical particularity of Jesus, who disclosed definitively that "God's will for God's Man in this world is that he should renounce legitimate defense."[122]

In the remaining chapters of the book, Yoder seeks to demonstrate that the model of Jesus as a politically relevant ethical example is carried consistently through the rest of the New Testament. The themes of "participation in Christ" and "imitation of Christ" that appear repeatedly in Paul and in the deutero-Pauline Epistles; the exhortation to love as Jesus loved that appears distinctively in the Johannine literature; the repeated calls throughout the New Testament canon to forgiveness and humble service as the characteristic marks of the believing community—all of these elements find their common logic in Jesus as the model for a life given in faithfulness to God. Repeatedly, this christologically defined faithfulness is characterized by self-emptying, by the relinquishment of coercive power. "Servanthood replaces dominion, forgiveness absorbs hostility. Thus—and only thus—are we bound by New Testament thought to 'be like Jesus.'"[123]

This claim can be sustained only through careful attention to a number of particular exegetical problems. Thus, in a series of chapters, Yoder addresses selected interpretive cruxes: Christ's victory over "the powers," the epistolary household codes as exhortations to "revolutionary subordination," the teaching of Romans 13 on the authority of the state, the social implications of the Pauline doctrine of justification, and "the war of the Lamb" in Revelation. Yoder does not attempt a complete survey of New Testament ethics; instead, these chapters seek to show that even the New Testament passages that seem most difficult do in fact support his overall thesis. To examine his exegetical arguments in each case would take us beyond the scope of this brief overview. We should, however, take careful note of a new theme that emerges in the chapter on "Christ and Power," the theme of the Christian community as the instrument of God's action in the world. In order to understand how the church can play this role, we must retrace Yoder's appropriation of the New Testament's cosmology.

Drawing on the work of Hendrik Berkhof, G. B. Caird, and other scholars,[124] Yoder focuses attention on a number of New Testament texts that speak of *archai kai exousiai* ("principalities and powers") as superpersonal systemic structures over which Christ has gained authority. These powers, created by God but in rebellion against him, have usurped mastery over human life and stand as oppressors of human beings: "These structures which were supposed to be our servants have become our masters and our guardians."[125] Through his life of freedom, however, Jesus challenged the rebellious powers; his denial of their ultimacy brought him into fatal conflict with the governmental and religious institutions that are the outward manifestation of the powers. By remaining steadfastly obedient to God even unto death and refusing to be co-opted into the systemic power game, Jesus exposed the illusion through which the powers hold us in bondage. Yoder quotes Berkhof's exposition of Colossians 2:13–15:

> Christ has "triumphed over them." The unmasking is actually already their defeat . . . . The resurrection manifests what was already accomplished at the cross: that in Christ God has challenged the Powers, has penetrated into their territory, and has displayed that He is stronger than they. . . . The weapon from which they heretofore derived their strength is struck out of their hands. This weapon was the power of illusion, their ability to convince men that they were the divine regents of the world. . . .[126]

By his refusal to fight violence with violence, Jesus shattered the illusionary power of the world's death-system and created a new pattern for life in peaceful obedience to God: "His very obedience unto death is itself not only the sign but also the first-fruits of an authentic restored humanity."[127]

The calling of the church, then, is to live in a way that reflects the politics of Jesus, thus continuing the unmasking and disarming of the powers. This is what Ephesians 3:9–11 means when it declares that "the manifold wisdom of God should henceforth be made known *by means of the church* to the principalities and powers in heavenly places, according to the eternal purpose which he set in Jesus Christ our Lord." The implications of this for understanding the community's responsibility are weighty:

> . . . [T]he very existence of the church is its primary task. It is in itself a proclamation of the lordship of Christ to the powers from whose dominion the church has begun to be liberated. The church does not attack the powers; this Christ has done. The church concentrates upon not being seduced by them. By existing the church demonstrates that their rebellion has been vanquished.[128]

Yoder insists that his concentration on the church's task of maintaining the integrity of its own life and witness is not to be construed as a withdrawal from the world or a retreat from social issues to private piety. "What needs to be seen is rather that the primary social structure through which the gospel works to change other structures is that of the Christian community."[129] The calling of the church is to be "the conscience and the servant within human society,"[130] a role that is possible only when the community resists the world's seductive pressures to live on the basis of values other than those directly exemplified by Jesus.

Posing the Diagnostic Questions

(A) DESCRIPTIVE Although Yoder disclaims any intention of exegetical originality, he achieves, through "the focusing effect of a consistent, persistent question,"[131] a fresh and illuminating reading of the New Testament texts. Because he seeks to focus on the biblical portrayal of Jesus, rather than on general sources of human wisdom, as the primary source of ethical norms, he gives priority to the exegetical task. Indeed, as a book about method in Christian ethics, *The Politics of Jesus* is remarkable in that it consists almost entirely of commentary on New Testament texts.

Furthermore, Yoder's interpretation of these texts is informed by detailed and sophisticated interaction with historical-critical scholarship. (In this respect, his work stands out clearly from Niebuhr and Hauerwas, and even from Barth.) At numerous points, his readings reflect an astute—indeed, almost prescient—grasp of important developments in the field of New Testament studies. For instance, his attention to the social context and meaning of the texts, his placement of Jesus within the political matrix of first-century Palestine, his emphasis on the apocalyptic horizons of the "powers" language in the Pauline traditions, his interpretation of Galatians as an argument about the social form of the church (rather than about the problem of individual guilt), his sympathetic understanding of the Torah as a vehicle of grace within Jewish tradition—all these elements of his presentation reflect careful harvesting of the best available insights of biblical scholarship in the early 1970s.

Yoder's readings also exhibit careful attention to the context and shape of the texts he treats. For example, in his interpretation of Romans 13:1–7, a passage whose teaching about submission to the authority of the state might appear seriously damaging to Yoder's Christian pacifism, he gains interpretive leverage by insisting that Romans 12 and 13 must be read as a literary unit:

> Christians are told (12:19) never to exercise vengeance but to leave it to God and to wrath. Then the authorities are recognized (13:4) as executing the particular function which the Christian was to leave to God. It is inconceivable that these two verses, using such similar language, should be meant to be read independently of one another. This makes it clear that the function exercised by government is not the function to be exercised by Christians.[132]

Thus, the distinct vocation of the Christian community is preserved and clarified. The passage summons the church "to a nonresistant attitude toward a tyrannical government. . . . [H]ow strange then," Yoder remarks, "to make it the classic proof for the duty of Christians to kill."[133] His exegetical treatment of the passage, which cannot be adequately summarized here, is detailed, subtle, and persuasive.

Not all of his exegesis, of course, is equally compelling. He is perhaps rather too sanguine about the correspondence between the historical Jesus and the shape of the canonical Gospel accounts;[134] he places more weight than most critics would think appropriate on André Trocmé's theory that Jesus was calling for the jubilee ordinances to be put into practice in 26 C.E.;[135] and his proposal that the *Haustafeln* should be read as a call for "revolutionary subordination" leans toward apologetic wishful thinking.[136] Even where we might be inclined to second-guess Yoder's arguments, however, it must be acknowledged that he is working seriously and deeply at the exegetical task, presenting his findings for all to see and inviting challenges to his exegesis of particular texts. Thus, *The Politics of Jesus* is an impressive foray by a theological ethicist into exegetical territory.

(B) SYNTHETIC Yoder, like Barth, aims to take the entire New Testament canon into account and succeeds to an impressive degree. *The Politics of Jesus*, however, does not aim at comprehensive coverage of the New Testament witnesses. Among the Gospels, primary emphasis is placed on Luke. The Gospel and Epistles of John receive slight attention, and—surprisingly, in light of the choice of Luke as the key test case—the Acts of the Apostles plays little role in Yoder's construction. If Yoder were attempting to write a systematic book on New Testament ethics (rather than what he has written: a programmatic proposal about Jesus as paradigm for Christian ethics), some of these gaps would have to be filled in.[137] Nonetheless, the scope of Yoder's canonical survey is remarkable; he offers a sustained and provocative attempt to ground the unity of the New Testament in Jesus' exemplary rejection of violence. On the final page of the book, he is prepared to claim that "[a] social style characterized by the creation of a new community and the rejection of violence of any kind is the theme of New Testament proclamation from beginning to end."[138]

Does Yoder have a functional canon within the canon? Perhaps one could point to the Gospel temptation and passion narratives as the texts that most clearly express the identity of Jesus and his acceptance of his vocation. In Yoder's view, all interpretations of the Gospel story must do justice to the cross as the definitive disclosure of Jesus' mission. The special attention given to the Gospel of Luke in *The Politics of Jesus* is in one sense accidental. Yoder does not regard Luke as somehow more important or revelatory than the other Gospels; indeed, the Gospel of Mark more clearly emphasizes the paradigmatic character of Jesus' renunciation of power. Luke merely serves to illustrate Yoder's methodology.

With the wisdom of hindsight, we can see that the focus on Luke does not quite achieve what Yoder intended. Scholarly interpretation of Luke during the time in which Yoder originally wrote *The Politics of Jesus* was dominated by Hans Conzelmann's thesis that Luke sought to portray the early Christian movement as politically innocuous to the Roman Empire. Hence, it was virtually axiomatic that the Lukan Jesus must be a nonthreatening, apolitical Jesus. This redaction-critical analysis served Yoder well as a foil: if even Luke's version of the story can be shown to represent Jesus as teaching and enacting a nonconforming social ethic, then (a fortiori) the same must be true of the other Gospels. Just as important, the *historical* truth about Jesus must be consistent with Yoder's portrayal, because Jesus' revolutionary political stance shines through the narrative despite Luke's attempt to filter it out. Since 1972, however, literary and redactional studies of Luke-Acts have called Conzelmann's interpretation fundamentally into question.[139] According to these studies, Luke, of all the evangelists, is the most concerned to tell the story of the liberation of a people,[140] the most concerned to show how the bursting forth of the gospel in the Roman world unsettled and reordered social conventions and arrangements. But if that is so, Yoder's argument has lost its foil; rather than describing the politics of Jesus, he may in fact be describing the politics of Luke.

To be sure, this is not necessarily a major setback for Yoder's basic claims.[141] Sometimes he writes as though the canonical portrait is all that matters for his purposes; if that is so, the newer accounts of Luke's politics would merely strengthen Yoder's position. At other times, however, Yoder indicates that the question of the historical reality behind the canonical stories is a matter of fundamental concern. "It would," he concedes, "be a count against my reading of the Jesus story if the historical questers were to come up with solid demonstrations that the 'real Jesus' they find is quite incompatible with what we find in the canonical account."[142] Yoder doubts that such demonstrations are possible. Nonetheless, his theoretical concession reveals that the historical events behind the story must somehow be factored into a synthetic reading of the canon. If the most politically telling elements of the story belong to the level of Lukan theology rather than historical reminiscence, then the "real Jesus" behind Luke's narrative becomes increasingly elusive. In that case, Yoder's hermeneutical craft would be in danger of losing its moorings, for he continues to regard Scripture "as witness to the historical baseline of the communities' origins and thereby as link to the historicity of their Lord's past presence."[143]

How does Yoder handle texts that stand in tension with his synthetic construal of the canon? As we have seen, his characteristic strategy is to engage in probing exegesis, seeking to diminish or resolve the tension. The conclusion of his chapter on Romans 13 exemplifies this approach to the synthetic problem:

> [T]he logic of the post-Constantinian position holds only under the assumption that the imperatives of Matthew 5 and Romans 13 are actually contradictory . . . but the above

> exposition should have shown that the assumption itself does not hold. It is not the case that two imperatives are affirmed in the New Testament, obedience to government on one hand and loving the enemy on the other, between which we must choose when they contradict. Romans 12–13 and Matthew 5–7 are not in contradiction or in tension. They *both* instruct Christians to be nonresistant in all their relationships, including the social. They *both* call on the disciples of Jesus to renounce participation in the interplay of egoisms which this world calls "vengeance" or "justice."[144]

In this case, the strategy works: a more careful descriptive reading resolves much of the synthetic difficulty. Inevitably, however, cases arise in which the attempt to find harmony seems strained, as in Yoder's handling of the *Haustafeln*.

One other strategy for confronting intracanonical tensions is of great importance with regard to the issues of war and violence. Yoder posits theological development within the canon, so that New Testament texts become hermeneutically determinative in relation to the Old Testament:

> One of the marks of the "believers' church" heritage is that it sees movement within the canonical story, and therefore a difference between the testaments. Instead of a timeless collection of parabolic anecdotes for allegorical application, or of propositional communications ready for deductive exposition, the Bible is a story of promise and fulfillment which must be read directionally. The New Testament, by affirming the Hebrew Scriptures which Christians have come to call the Old Testament, also interprets them. Abraham and Moses are read through Jesus and Paul.[145]

To read the Bible *directionally* is to follow its narrative logic, to see where the story points rather than seeking a conceptual synthesis of different moments in the story. For Yoder, this reading strategy discloses that the cross, as the decisive revelation of God's way of being in the world, supersedes all sanctions for war that might be drawn from the Old Testament read in isolation.

As this last observation suggests, the *cross* is for Yoder the focal image through which the entire canonical story must be read. "For the radical Protestant there will always be a canon within the canon: namely, that recorded experience of practical moral reasoning in genuine human form that bears the name of Jesus."[146] Yoder's use of the phrase "canon within the canon" here corresponds closely to what I have called a "focal image"; he is referring not to a text but to an element within Scripture that serves as the lens through which everything else must be read. Jesus as exemplar of practical moral reason walked the path that led to the cross, thus confounding and shaming all human wisdom and strength and thereby teaching us how to see and live rightly. That is the central message of the biblical story.

(C) HERMENEUTICAL While Yoder never denies that the specific *rules* found in Scripture are binding on the Christian community, he places strikingly little emphasis on them. For instance, in *The Politics of Jesus,* a book whose central claim is that Jesus rejected violence, he never quotes Matthew 5:39 ("If anyone strikes you on the right cheek, turn the other also"), and he refers to that verse only once in a footnote.[147] Jesus' role as teacher of moral rules is minimized in Yoder's presentation; the arguments against violence are constructed along other, more hermeneutically sophisticated lines. The basic role of Scripture is not to provide rules for conduct but to serve as "the collective scribal memory, the store *par excellence* of treasures old and new."[148]

Like Barth, Yoder eschews the hermeneutical strategy of extracting moral *principles* from Scripture, for the same reason: the exercise of applying principles to situations leaves too much room for straying away from the truth revealed in Jesus. The confession that "the Word became flesh and dwelt among us" means that

> . . . the business of ethical thinking has been taken away from the speculation of independent minds each meditating on the meaning of things and has been pegged to a particular set of answers given in a particular time and place. . . . [The] will of God is affirmatively, concretely knowable in the person and ministry of Jesus.[149]

Thus, Yoder fundamentally appeals to the New Testament as the source of a definitive *paradigm* for ethics: "[T]he most appropriate example of the difficult choice between effectiveness and obedience, and the most illuminating example, is that of Jesus himself."[150]

Unlike Barth, however, Yoder is entirely willing to describe the paradigmatic use of the New Testament as an exercise of the analogical imagination. In order to proclaim Christ's lordship in our time, we are called

> to renew in the language world of pluralism/relativism an *analogue* to what those first transcultural reconceptualizers [i.e., the New Testament writers] did; not to translate their results but to emulate their exercise. . . . What we need to find is the *interworld transformational grammar* to help us discern what will need to happen if the collision of the message of Jesus with our pluralist/relativist world is to lead to a reconception of the shape of the world, instead of rendering Jesus optional or innocuous.[151]

One might surmise that analogical "transcultural reconceptualization" would leave at least as much latitude for unfaithful capriciousness as would the application of general principles, but Yoder holds out the hope that this need not be so, as long as the Jesus portrayed in the New Testament remains the focal point of the message. His essay "'But We Do See Jesus': The Particularity of Incarnation and the Universality of Truth" seeks to make the case for this position.[152]

Furthermore, an important aspect of Yoder's vision is his emphasis on "communal moral process" as the means of discerning the will of God. The individual is not left alone to make private analogical applications of Scripture; rather, the gathered community of believers deliberates, expecting to receive guidance from the Holy Spirit. Proposed courses of action are tested by the witness of all in the community (cf. 1 Cor. 14:26–33). Individuals who veer away from the example of Jesus are to be admonished and corrected by the others, in accordance with the teachings of Matthew 18:15–20 and Galatians 6:1–2. Where such disciplines are practiced in the Christian community, the potential for hermeneutical aberration is greatly diminished. The outlines of such a communal discernment process are set forth in Yoder's programmatic essay "The Hermeneutics of Peoplehood."[153]

Yoder's reading of the New Testament's *symbolic world* also plays a significant role in the construction of his normative ethic. Unlike Niebuhr, who derives from the biblical sources a dialectical view of fallen human nature, Yoder places little hermeneutical weight on the New Testament's portrayal of human sin and finitude. His ethical approach is, as he forthrightly states, "more hopeful than others about the possibility of knowing and doing the divine will."[154] Yoder finds in the New Testament's symbolic world an account not of human fallenness but of human vocation and the mysterious divine order that confounds human wisdom. When we see "the shape of the world" as it is rendered in Scripture, we are given a different perspective on our moral situation, one that enables us to break out of the no-win dichotomies that conventional wisdom presents:

> When it *seems* to me that my unjust deed is indispensable to prevent some much greater evil being done by another, I have narrowed my scope of time, or of space, or of global variety, or of history. I have ruled some people out of my Golden Rule, or have skewed the coefficients in my utility calculus. . . . [155]

When, on the other hand, we see reality in the terms taught by Jesus' example, our entire frame of reference is transformed. We learn that the apparent efficacy of violence is illusory, that "suffering and not brute power determines the meaning of history."[156] Because the world is to be ruled by "the lamb that was slain," Jesus becomes "the standard by which Christians must learn how they are to look at the moving of history."[157] Thus, Yoder acknowledges, his ethic of nonviolence makes sense only within the confessional framework of Christian faith, only within the christologically determined symbolic universe of the New Testament texts.

> This conception . . . has the peculiar disadvantage—or advantage, depending upon one's point of view—of being meaningful only if Christ be he who Christians claim him to be, the Master. Almost every other kind of ethical approach espoused by Christians, pacifist or otherwise, will continue to make sense to the non-Christian as well. Whether Jesus be the Christ or not, whether Jesus Christ be Lord or not . . . most types of ethical approach will keep on functioning just the same. For their true foundation is in some reading of the human situation or some ethical insight which is claimed to be generally accessible to all people of good will. The same is not true for this vision of "completing in our bodies that which was lacking in the suffering of Christ." If Jesus Christ was not who historic Christianity confesses he was, *the revelation in the life of a real man of the character of God himself*, then this one argument for pacifism collapses.[158]

As this quotation intimates, Yoder stands close to Barth in rejecting the normative claims of nonbiblical sources of authority for ethics. In several ways, however, Yoder's position is more nuanced than Barth's, both because of his recognition of the historically contingent character of the New Testament documents themselves and because of his appreciation for the necessity of a continuing process of communal moral discernment.

Through this continuing process over time, the Christian community develops a *tradition* that shapes its distinctive identity in contrast to the values and norms of the world:

> Worship is the communal cultivation of an alternative construction of society and of history. That alternative construction of history is celebrated by telling the stories of Abraham (and Sarah and Isaac and Ishmael), of Mary and Joseph and Jesus and Mary, of Cross and Resurrection and Peter and Paul, of Peter of Cheltchitz and his Brothers, of George Fox and his Friends.[159]

Noteworthy here is the way that Yoder moves from the biblical stories to the stories of the radical Reformation without marking a distinction. While he affirms the normative primacy of Scripture, Yoder wants to maintain the legitimacy and necessity of the church's flexible response to changing historical situations, as long as that response maintains linear continuity with the New Testament. In his essay "The Authority of Tradition," Yoder formulates the problem in these terms:

> The clash is not tradition versus Scripture but faithful tradition versus irresponsible tradition. Only if we can with Jesus and Paul (and Francis, Savonarola, Milton, and others) denounce *wrong* traditioning, can we validly affirm the rest. Scripture comes on the scene not as a receptacle of all possible inspired truths, but rather as a witness to the historical baseline of the communities' origins and thereby as a link to the historicity of their Lord's past presence.[160]

Tradition will inevitably play a role in our moral deliberations, but it must meet the test of consistency with the historical roots of the community as definitively preserved in the New Testament.

The importance accorded to historical roots in Yoder's thinking suggests also that *reason*, in the form of historical criticism, has at least some role to play in grasping the historical events that are ultimately normative for Christian faith. This valuing of historical inquiry is more implicit than explicit in Yoder's methodology, and it is articulated more clearly in *The Priestly Kingdom* than in the earlier *The Politics of Jesus*. As the following quotation demonstrates, Yoder advocates a critical approach that attends to the history behind the New Testament witnesses:

> What we then find at the heart of our tradition is not some proposition, scriptural or promulgated otherwise, which we hold to be authoritative and to be exempted from the relativity of hermeneutical debate by virtue of its inspiredness. What we find at the origin is already a process of reaching back again to the origins, to the earliest memories of the event itself. . . .[161]

Because "Jesus participates in localizable, datable history," the gospel reports "an event that occurred in our listeners' own world."[162] Thus, Yoder believes that the hermeneutical gulf between the New Testament world and the present can be bridged by taking the "low road" of a historically oriented Christology. Yoder finds in *history* the hermeneutical point of contact with human reason that Barth steadfastly refused to acknowledge. The real issue, according to Yoder, "is not whether Jesus can make sense in a world far from Galilee, but whether—when he meets us in our world, as he does in fact—we want to follow him."[163]

At the same time, however, Yoder's conceptions of reason and history stand within and subordinate to the symbolic world created by Scripture: "The church precedes the world epistemologically. . . . The meaning and validity of concepts like 'nature' and 'science' are best seen not when looked at alone but in light of the confession of the lordship of Christ."[164]

Finally, Yoder's treatment of moral decison making within Christian community grants to *experience* a major hermeneutical role:

> [T]he gathered community expects Spirit-given newness to suggest answers previously not perceived. The transcendant appeal to authority is moved away from the inspiredness of holy writ and from the centralization of an episcopal magisterium, as well as from any personal, unaccountable "fanaticism". . . . The community . . . is believingly, modestly ready to say of consensus reached today, "it seemed good to the Holy Spirit and to us," and to commend this insight by encyclical to other churches.[165]

It is important to emphasize that Yoder develops his account of Spirit-led discernment in the church from the New Testament itself and that he does not treat experience as a source of revelation independent of Scripture; rather, the community under the guidance of the Spirit is given guidance about the meaning of Scripture for new historical situations. The Spirit enables the community to perceive senses of the biblical text that had previously remained hidden, just as the New Testament writers did in their hermeneutically revolutionary reinterpretations of the Old Testament. To explain the relation between text, Spirit, and community, Yoder offers a modern scientific analogy:

> There have always been radio waves bringing messages to us from distant stars. Only the development of radio technology has empowered us to receive those signals. The Bible was always a liberation storybook: now we are ready to read it that way.[166]

Those who live within the symbolic world of the New Testament will find no surprise or offense in this openness to the hermeneutical role of the Spirit in community. "There is continuing revelation. Jesus promised that there would be (John 14:12–26; 16:7–15). The Lucan and Pauline pictures of prophecy assume that there will be. 1 John 4:1ff, and 1 Corinthians 12:1ff assume that there will be and provide criteria for it."[167]

Thus, Yoder develops a hermeneutic that carefully acknowledges the necessary places of tradition, reason, and experience in the interpretive process. At the same time, he insists that the New Testament's portrayal of Jesus must remain the fundamental norm for all Christian ethics.

(D) PRAGMATIC What sort of fruits does Yoder's hermeneutic produce? The historic "peace churches" rooted in the sixteenth-century Anabaptist movement stand as instantiations of the vision. Yoder maintains resolutely, however, that his approach to ethics is not applicable only to "sectarian" communities: "[T]he convictions argued here do not admit to being categorized as a sectarian oddity or a prophetic exception," he writes. "Their appeal is to classical catholic Christian convictions properly understood."[168] He holds out the hope that the church at large might be reformed and renewed through attentiveness to the example of Jesus.

Throughout *The Priestly Kingdom*, he points to various other historical exemplifications of a similar vision, ranging from the Franciscans to the Mukyokai of Japan and the Kimbanguists of Zaire.[169] One might also identify groups such as Clarence Jordan's Koinonia Farm, Reba Place Fellowship in Evanston, Illinois, and the Sojourners community in Washington, D.C., as instances of radical Christian communities that exercise influence disproportionate to their size or visible power.

A community shaped by Yoder's hermeneutic will be engaged in "a modeling mission," embodying an alternative order that anticipates God's will for the reconciliation of the world:[170]

> Although immersed in this world, the church by her way of being represents the promise of another world, which is not somewhere else but is to come here. That promissory quality of the church's present distinctiveness is the making of peace, as the refusal to make war is her indispensable negative transcendence. . . . The church cultivates an alternative consciousness. Another view of what the world is like is kept alive by narration and celebration which fly in the face of some of the "apparent" lessons of "realism."[171]

In communities where this promise takes present form, violence will be renounced and mutual correction will be practiced in love and candor. Such communities will testify to the wider political order,[172] but they will not be seduced by the illusion that they might serve God's purposes by compromising in order to gain power. That is the temptation that Jesus faced and rejected, and the church is called to follow his example unwaveringly.

One danger of such a strategy is that the church might become increasingly withdrawn and ingrown, as Yoder's own biting critique of Mennonite "defensiveness and authoritarianism" suggests. He would maintain, however, that such "moral failures" result precisely from "following Jesus too little, not too much"[173]—that is, from absolutizing ethnic traditions and relinquishing the New Testament's historic witness as the effective foundation of the community's practices.[174]

Yoder's hermeneutic represents an impressive challenge to the church to remain faithful to its calling of discipleship, modeling its life after the example of the Jesus whom it confesses as Lord. As Christian theologians increasingly are forced to come to grips with the demise of Christendom and to acknowledge their minority status in a pluralistic world, Yoder's vision offers a compelling account of how the New Testament might reshape the life of the church.

4. Stanley Hauerwas: Character Shaped by Tradition

Through a steady stream of provocative essays and books over the past twenty years, Stanley Hauerwas has thrust the themes of narrative, community, and character formation into the spotlight in the field of theological ethics. His impassioned advocacy of the church's vocation to maintain its distinctive identity without succumbing to the values and pressures of liberal democratic culture has made him an important and controversial voice in contemporary theological debate. His popular works, such as *Resident Aliens*, coauthored by William Willimon, have received far wider attention in the church than is customary for works by academic theologians.[175]

Hauerwas, a United Methodist who teaches theological ethics at Duke Divinity School, has forged his position through an eclectic synthesis of improbably diverse influences. During his years as a student at Yale, he appropriated from Hans Frei an emphasis—derived ultimately from Karl Barth—on narrative as the basic and proper mode of presenting the gospel; at the same time, Hauerwas began to focus on Aristotle and Aquinas as key figures for developing an ethic of character and the virtues.[176] Later, during his years of teaching at Notre Dame, he discovered the work of John Howard Yoder and began to concentrate on Jesus as paradigm for Christian ethics, on the church as an alternative community of discipleship, and on nonviolence as "the hallmark of the Christian life."[177] Finally, in recent years (since his move to Duke), he has shifted—partly under the influence of Stanley Fish—into an aggressively postmodern phase, denying that texts, including the Bible, have meaning save as they are construed within particular interpretive communities.[178]

It is not easy to see how Hauerwas can hold these different elements together in a coherent hermeneutical position; indeed, given his rather freewheeling approach to biblical interpretation, it is not at all clear that he has done so. The purpose of the present discussion, however, is neither to trace Hauerwas's theological pilgrimage nor to seek some underlying unity of his thought through its various phases of development.[179] Our aim, rather, is to ask how the New Testament functions in his ethics, particularly in his formulation of a normative position on the issues of war and violence. For that purpose, we may concentrate on three major sources: *A Community of Character* (especially two of its key methodological essays, entitled "Jesus: The Story of the Kingdom" and "The Moral Authority of Scripture: The Politics and Ethics of Remembering"),[180] *The Peaceable Kingdom*, and *Unleashing the Scripture* (which contains an introductory section entitled "The Politics of the Bible: *Sola Scriptura* as Heresy?"[181] followed by a series of sermons illustrating Hauerwas's hermeneutic in action).

Hauerwas's Approach to Theological Ethics

Because Hauerwas has been significantly influenced by Yoder, his stance on the problem of violence is materially identical to Yoder's: the church is called to be a people that practices nonviolence, following the example of Jesus. His account of how that normative position is reached, however, reveals some noteworthy methodological differences from Yoder. The following sketch of Hauerwas's position will highlight some of the distinctive features of his approach.

Whereas Yoder maintains that a right reading of the New Testament's portrayal of Jesus must provide the norms for the life of the church, Hauerwas characteristically puts the matter the other way around: the church must be a truthful and peaceable community in order to be able to read the New Testament's portrayal of Jesus rightly. This may appear to be a chicken-and-egg paradox, but Hauerwas insists that the epistemological issue is real and crucial. He prefaces a telling quotation from Athanasius to his essay "Jesus: The Story of the Kingdom":

> For the searching and right understanding of the Scriptures there is need of a good life and a pure soul, and for Christian virtue to guide the mind to grasp, so far as human nature can, the truth concerning God the Word. One cannot possibly understand the teaching of the saints unless one has a pure mind and is trying to imitate their life. . . . [A]nyone who wishes to understand the mind of the sacred writers must first cleanse his own life, and approach the saints by copying their deeds.[182]

Thus, obedience must precede understanding. Athanasius formulates this hermeneutical dictum in terms of the character of the individual interpreter, but Hauerwas extends Athanasius's logic to the character of the church as an interpretive community. The most important task of the church is "to be a community *capable of hearing* the story of God we find in the scripture and living in a manner that is faithful to that story."[183] If and only if we are such a community can we seek to derive moral guidance from the story of Jesus. Readings of Scripture that occur outside the context of the church as a character-forming community will merely underwrite "the ideology of a politics quite different from the politics of the church";[184] in other words, such readings will promote individualism, self-indulgence, and violence. The extent to which Hauerwas is willing to press this methodological point is revealed in the opening paragraph of *Unleashing the Scripture*:

> Most North American Christians assume they have a right, if not an obligation, to read the Bible. I challenge that assumption. No task is more important than for the church to take the Bible out of the hands of individual Christians in North America. Let us no longer give the Bible to every child when they enter the third grade or whenever their assumed rise to Christian maturity is marked. . . . Let us rather tell them and their parents that they are possessed by habits far too corrupt for them to be encouraged to read the Bible on their own.[185]

Only a community already formed by the story of the kingdom of God can begin to read Scripture rightly.

But how, then, are we to learn the true "politics of the church," if not through reading the Bible? Hauerwas has two characteristic answers to this crucial question. First of all, we learn the truth, and therefore learn how to read Scripture rightly, through the example of the lives of the saints.

> The authority of Scripture is mediated through the lives of the saints identified by our community as most nearly representing what we are about. Put more strongly, to know what Scripture means, finally, we must look to those who have most nearly learned to exemplify its demands through their lives.[186]

By "saints," Hauerwas does not mean just those saints officially canonized by the Roman Catholic Church; rather, he refers to all our fathers and mothers in the faith, the great cloud of witnesses who have contributed to the stream of tradition in which we stand. By their lives of faithfulness they have kept Scripture's witness alive and have passed it on to us; similarly, our calling is to extend the chain of tradition: "By attending closely to the example of those who have given us our scripture, we learn how to be a people morally capable of forgiveness and thus worthy of continuing to carry the story of God we find authorized by scripture."[187]

The second way that we learn the truth is through the church's liturgy, especially the Eucharist: "Because the Christian story is an enacted story, liturgy is probably a much more important resource than are doctrines or creeds for helping us hear, tell, and live the story of God."[188] This emphasis on the Eucharist as the church's community-forming action that creates the necessary conditions for the interpretation of Scripture is a theme that has emerged with greater prominence in Hauerwas's later work. For example, in *Unleashing the Scripture,* the sermon "The Insufficiency of Scripture" takes the Emmaus road story (Luke 24:13–35) as a narrative showing that Jesus' disciples recognize him truly not through his explication of Scripture (24:25–27) but through the breaking of bread at table (24:30–31).[189] For Hauerwas, the story that shapes the community is definitively narrated in eucharistic table fellowship with the risen Lord. Thus, right reading of Scripture occurs preeminently in the worship of the gathered community.

In light of these considerations, we can see why Hauerwas maintains that it is a methodological mistake to ask how Scripture should be "used" in Christian ethics.[190] The question assumes that the ethicist has some privileged epistemological vantage point external to the Bible that allows one first to determine the meaning of the text and then to draw out useful tidbits of that meaning for the construction of an ethical system. But according to Hauerwas's account, the meaning of the text is knowable only for those who participate in a community whose identity is shaped by the story of Jesus and whose practices therefore already embody an ethic specifically determined by that story. To say that there is a "problem" about how the text is to be used is to declare oneself de facto an outsider to the community within which the New Testament functions as Scripture.[191]

Even so, if we grant all this, it is appropriate to ask what we do learn when we read Scripture in the context of the community of faith. What is the particular shape of the story of Jesus, and what are the distinctive practices of the community that lives within the world rendered by that story? Hauerwas's account of this story and the community whose life is rooted in it is more suggestive than systematic, but some of its major features may be summarized briefly.

In "Jesus: The Story of the Kingdom," Hauerwas points to the story of Peter's confession at Caesarea Philippi, the pivotal episode in the Gospel of Mark (Mark 8:27–9:1), as a redefinition of the kingdom of God in terms of the cross. This teaching is a great threat to the powers of this world:

> For here is one who invites others to participate in a kingdom of God's love, a kingdom which releases the power of giving and service. The powers of this world cannot compre-

> hend such a kingdom. Here is a man who insists it is possible, if God's rule is acknowledged and trusted, to serve without power.[192]

If the church is shaped by the story of this man, we learn that "Christian social ethics can only be done from the perspective of those who do not seek to control national or world history but who are content to live 'out of control.'"[193] The implications of this approach for ethics are not just individual but fundamentally communal: "To be a disciple is to be part of a new community, a new polity, which is formed on Jesus' obedience to the cross."[194] Or, as Hauerwas puts it in a pithy formulation, "[T]he church is the organized form of Jesus' story."[195]

So far Hauerwas follows Yoder closely. He goes on, however, to draw certain distinctive emphases from the story: he emphasizes that the story trains the community to accept *forgiveness*, to know itself as a forgiven people and thereby to live with an honesty and humility that is impossible for those who have not learned to interpret themselves as forgiven sinners.[196] By living as "a community that has no fear of the truth," the church is set free from the "fevered search to gain security through deception, coercion, and violence."[197]

Closely linked with this emphasis on forgiveness is an emphasis on *diversity* within the community of faith. Through the gospel we learn to value the diverse "particularity of our brothers and sisters in Christ" as necessary to the complex story of God's kingdom. "[T]he struggle of each to be faithful to the Gospel is essential to our own lives. I understand my own story through seeing the different ways in which others are called to be disciples."[198] Hauerwas notes that

> in contrast to all societies built on shared resentments and fears, Christian community is formed by a story that enables its members to trust the otherness of the other as the very sign of the forgiving character of God's kingdom. . . . The contention and witness of the church is that the story of Jesus provides a flourishing of gifts which other politics cannot know.[199]

Finally, Hauerwas highlights the way in which the Gospel narratives inculcate *flexibility* as a communal virtue. Trained by the story of Jesus that God's grace is unpredictable, we learn to welcome "the unexpected, especially as it comes in the form of strangers," as God's gift.[200] The church, living trustfully as a pilgrim people that cannot control its own destiny, must be ready to receive the unforeseeable gifts that God may send: "[W]e must be a people who have learned not to fear surprises as a necessary means to sustain our lives."[201]

These themes are further elaborated in *The Peaceable Kingdom*, particularly in the chapter entitled "Jesus: The Presence of the Peaceable Kingdom."[202] Here, however, Hauerwas also highlights the eschatological dimension of the story.

> To begin to understand Jesus' announcement of the kingdom we must first rid ourselves of the notion that the world we experience will exist indefinitely. We must learn to see the world as Israel had learned to understand it—that is eschatologically. Though it sounds

> powerful and intimidating, in fact it is quite simple, for to view the world eschatologically is to see it in terms of a story, with a beginning, a continuing drama, and an end.[203]

Only when we see the story whole, including its promised ending as foreshadowed in the resurrection of Jesus, do "the rigorous demands of the Sermon on the Mount" make sense, not as an impossible ideal but as pointers to the truth about reality.

> To be sure, Jesus' demand that we forgive our enemies challenges our normal assumptions about what is possible, but that is exactly what it is meant to do. We are not to accept the world with its hate and resentments as a given, but to recognize that we live in a new age which makes possible a new way of life.[204]

At the same time, the life of discipleship is necessarily a life "on the road," an unfinished story in which we participate. What the gospel offers is the opportunity to join in a great "common adventure" that gives our lives dignity and meaning.[205] The metaphor of pilgrimage emerges again and again in Hauerwas's work as the most apt description of the church's experience. The story of Israel depicts a journeying people, still awaiting God's final fulfillment of his promises, and the church finds itself in the continuation of that journey.

> The Christian claim that life is a pilgrimage is a way of indicating the necessary and never-ending growth of the self in learning to live into the story of Christ. He is our master and from him we learn the skills to live faithful to the fact that this is God's world and we are God's creatures.[206]

This account of Christian existence as life within an unfolding narrative discourages any attempt to formulate a systematic ethic.[207] Our need is not for rules and principles; rather, we need *skills* that can be taught us only by those who are more expert in the demanding craft of discipleship.

Thus, in Hauerwas's vision, the church is to be formed by the story of Jesus and by the example of those who have narrated it to us—formed as a "community of character," a people whose life "stands as a political alternative to every nation, witnessing to the kind of social life possible for those that have been formed by the story of Christ."[208] This alternative is the way of peace, forgiveness, and love of enemies; war and violence must be foreign to the polity of God's people, for "[v]iolence derives from the self-deceptive story that we are in control—that we are our own creators—and that only we can bestow meaning on our lives, since there is no one else to do so."[209] Since we know, however, that we are in the care and control of a God who loves us, violence is unnecessary and inconsistent with the storied truth in which we find our identity. That is why "nonviolence is not just one implication among others that can be drawn from our Christian beliefs; it is at the very heart of our understanding of God."[210]

Posing the Diagnostic Questions

(A) DESCRIPTIVE Hauerwas's interpretations of biblical texts rarely depend upon detailed exegesis or sustained close reading. His references to "the story of

Jesus" function as broad allusions to the Gospel narratives seen as a whole. When he does refer to a specific text, he often quotes it in full,[211] but rarely does he seek to justify his reading of the passage against alternative possibilities or to develop theological insights from careful analysis of its language or structure. The blocks of quoted material serve as retellings of the story, and Hauerwas explicates the meaning of that story in brief, pithy summaries.[212]

Even in the "sermonic exhibits" in *Unleashing the Scripture*, Hauerwas is less inclined to exposit the text than to propose conditions that must be met in order for the text to be understood. For example, in "A Sermon on the Sermon on the Mount," Hauerwas writes:

> I maintain that the Sermon on the Mount presupposes the existence of a community constituted by the practice of nonviolence, and it is unintelligible divorced from such a community. Or, put as contentiously as I can, you cannot rightly read the Sermon on the Mount unless you are a pacifist. . . . The Sermon does not generate an ethic of nonviolence, but rather a community of nonviolence is necessary if the Sermon is to be read rightly.[213]

Nowhere does Hauerwas engage in exegetical discussion of the structure and logic of the six antitheses in Matthew 5:21–48; nowhere does he explore the first-century historical background of such practices as turning the other cheek and going the second mile (Matt. 5:39–41); nowhere does he ask what source in Scripture or elsewhere might be said to instruct Jesus' hearers to hate their enemies (Matt. 5:43); nowhere does he investigate the meaning of the word *teleios* ("perfect"; Matt. 5:48). In short, he does not undertake any of the exegetical practices necessary to demonstrate how the specific language of the text might or might not warrant an ethic of nonviolence.[214] Such onerous interpretive tasks are said to be rendered unnecessary by participation in a community that already "rightly" knows and practices what the text means, without asking any of these questions. The reader must be a pacifist first; then he or she will see that the text teaches nonviolence. But can a nonpacifist reader ever be changed by reading such a text? Seemingly, Hauerwas's account leaves no possibility for such an event to occur. Nor does he explain how the overwhelmingly nonpacifist Christian tradition can be challenged or corrected by a minority reading such as the one that he offers.

Unleashing the Scripture is notable for its overt hostility toward historical criticism, which Hauerwas somewhat quaintly designates—using terminology that has been passé for at least a couple of generations—as "the higher-critical method."[215] In his earlier books, Hauerwas did sometimes acknowledge the importance of careful exegesis,[216] and he explicitly cited the work of biblical scholars. In "Jesus: The Story of the Kingdom," for example, his account of the Jesus story draws heavily not only on Yoder's exegesis but also on the work of scholars such as E. J. Tinsley, A. E. Harvey, John Riches, and Nils Dahl. Thus, even in his rejection of historical criticism as a method, Hauerwas acknowledges that he has in the past benefited from its results: "I certainly have learned from historical critics, whose work I often think better than their theory."[217] In his more recent work, however, Hauerwas has increasingly moved away from critical exegesis as a tool for interpreting the New Testament. In *Unleashing the Scripture,* he advocates and practices a style of exposition that does not depend on academic biblical studies for its insights. The problem, he declares, is that "higher criticism" is captive to an ideology alien to the politics of the church. "For example," he asserts, "most scholars trained in biblical criticism . . . regard the exegetical tradition prior to the development of historical criticism as an obstacle to proper understanding of the true meaning of the text."[218] To anyone conversant with the complex discussion of hermeneutics in recent biblical studies—particularly the acute attention being devoted to the *Wirkungsgeschichte* of the texts—this sweeping caricature can only sound like dismissive ignorance.[219]

Where, then, does Hauerwas derive his perspective on the interpretation of the Bible? A disarming admission in the foreword of *Unleashing the Scripture* locates the roots of his knowledge in the work of the church's great theologians:

> I really do not know the "text" of the Bible well—all my theological formation took place in curricula shaped by Protestant liberalism. Yet such formation was more "biblical" than I suspected because I now think it an advantage to learn Scripture through the work of Aquinas, Luther, Calvin, Barth, and Yoder.[220]

Thus, Hauerwas's descriptions of the content of the New Testament are, by his own account, eclectic and derivative. Still, despite his lack of exegetical specificity and his self-confessed lack of deep knowledge of the New Testament texts, his comprehensive vision of the life of the church corresponds closely to the New Testament witness. Should we attribute that—as he would like us to do—to the salutary effect of reading the Bible as mediated by tradition, or should we surmise that in this respect his work, like that of the historical critics whom he castigates, is "better than his theory"? In either case, Hauerwas's descriptive account of the New Testament's ethical vision is profoundly dependent upon the writings of great predecessors who have pursued the exegetical task with a rigor that he himself declines to attempt.

(B) SYNTHETIC Hauerwas's citations of the New Testament are wide-ranging but scattered. He has made no systematic attempt to work the full range of the canon into his synthesis. In an analysis of Hauerwas's quotations, Jeffrey Siker points out that while he is fond of appealing to the synoptic Gospels (especially the Sermon on the Mount, the Markan passion predictions, and Luke's stories of God's mercy to the poor and the weak), he almost never cites the Gospel of John.[221] The major Pauline letters, especially Romans and 1 Corinthians, are cited occasionally, and Ephesians seems to be a particular favorite.[222] On the other hand, the pastoral Epistles, Hebrews, and Revelation seem not to be part of Hauerwas's functional canon. Perhaps the most surprising observation, given Hauerwas's emphasis on story and the example of the saints, is that he makes very little use of the Acts of the Apostles; one would expect this text to serve him as a gold mine of stories about the saints. In fact, however, it is the synoptic Gospels that engage most of his attention, for it is there that the story of Jesus is most fully narrated.

How does Hauerwas deal with texts that stand in tension with his synthetic construal of the canon's message? Here two different answers can be given. On the one hand, he often simply ignores them. Since he makes no pretense of comprehensively incorporating all the New Testament witnesses into his account of the moral life, he apparently does not feel the necessity of showing how the pastoral Epistles or Revelation (for example) can be incorporated into the story of the kingdom. On the other hand, Hauerwas actively celebrates the canon's messy complexity, arguing that the diversity of the Gospels illustrates that there is a variety of ways to live faithfully.[223] He quotes with approval Joseph Blenkinsopp's remark that the diversity of the canon "suggests that the community must be prepared to accept creative tension as a permanent feature of its life."[224] This is not merely making a virtue of necessity: given Hauerwas's emphasis on flexibility and resourcefulness as hallmarks of the pilgrim community, the diversity of the canon provides the church with a range of options that may be useful in different times and places. "The canon marks off as scripture those texts that are necessary for the life of the church, without trying to resolve their obvious diversity and/or even disagreements."[225] Never does Hauerwas attempt to resolve intracanonical tensions through intensive exegetical scrutiny, in the manner of Yoder, or through proposing historical explanations of the origin and development of the New Testament traditions. The canon is construed as a large bag of stories that together constitute the church's untidy but useful heritage.

Is it possible, then, to identify focal images that serve to unify Hauerwas's reading of the New Testament? In "The Moral Authority of Scripture" he writes, "I am convinced that the most appropriate image . . . for characterizing scripture, for the use of the church as well as morally, is that of a narrative or a story."[226] The category of story is, however, a formal genre description rather than a particular image. The particular story of Jesus as Hauerwas retells it is best encapsulated—as our above discussion has suggested—by the images of *journey* and *cross*. (Major themes such as forgiveness and peaceableness are not independent images; they constitute Hauerwas's interpretation of the cross.) Unlike Yoder, who concentrates primarily on the cross as the focal point of the Gospel narratives, Hauerwas attends more consistently to the narrative depictions of Jesus' interactions with his disciples along the way, thus finding a basis in the story for the church's continuing pilgrimage. The cross is, to be sure, the *telos* of that pilgrimage, but other relationships and activities along the way are given equal weight in Hauerwas's narration of the tale. These images of journey and cross are dramatized in the church's liturgical celebrations, which teach us how to form our community life in order to read the story rightly: "The sacraments enact the story of Jesus and, thus, form a community in his image."[227]

(C) **HERMENEUTICAL** What is the mode of Hauerwas's appeal to the New Testament texts for the formation of ethical norms? *Rules* and *principles* play little role in his constructive ethic. Indeed, his emphasis on story and the formation of character is intended precisely as an alternative to such approaches:

> The nature of Christian ethics is determined by the fact that Christian convictions take the form of a story, or perhaps better, a set of stories that constitutes a tradition, which in turn creates and forms a community. Christian ethics does not begin by emphasizing rules or principles, but by calling our attention to a narrative that tells of God's dealing with creation.[228]

The stories carried by the tradition do serve as *paradigms* for the church's action. The example of the saints, which is in turn patterned upon the story of Jesus, provides a model for the community's continuing life:

> To be a disciple is to be part of a new community, a new polity, which is formed on Jesus' obedience to the cross. The constitutions of this new polity are the Gospels. The Gospels are not just the depiction of a man, but they are manuals for the training necessary to be part of the new community. To be a disciple means to share Christ's story, to participate in the reality of God's rule.[229]

It must always be remembered, however, that Hauerwas is leery of any attempt to "use" the New Testament as a source of informative analogies for ethical behavior; he prefers to say that "God uses the Scripture to help keep the church faithful."[230] Indeed, one finds in his writings relatively few instances of specific appeals to particular actions of Jesus as models for Christian behavior; instead, he sees the story as an agent that forms the community. He quotes approvingly Rowan Williams's assertion that the story of Jesus is "not only a paradigm" of the saving process. Rather, "it is a story which is itself an indispensable agent in the completion of this process."[231] Thus, unlike Yoder, who emphasizes the community's task of analogical reflection in modeling its life after the paradigm of Jesus, Hauerwas places more emphasis on the formation of virtue in the community's character in such a way that it intuitively does the will of God.

The *symbolic world* of the New Testament also plays a major role in Hauerwas's constructive ethic, for the "first task" of Christian ethics is "to help us rightly envision the world."[232] By making the story of Jesus the touchstone for their understanding of reality, "Christians are enabled to see the world accurately and without illusion."[233]

> The task of Christian ethics is imaginatively to help us understand the implications of [God's] kingdom. . . . Christian ethics is the disciplined activity which analyzes and imaginatively tests the images most appropriate to orchestrate the Christian life in accordance with the central conviction that the world has been redeemed by the work of Jesus Christ.[234]

Of course, the story of the kingdom teaches us not only to see the world rightly but also to know the God whose character is revealed in the story:

> The narrative of scripture not only "renders a character" but renders a community capable of ordering its existence appropriate to such stories. Jews and Christians believe this narrative does nothing less than render the character of God and in so doing renders us to be the kind of people appropriate to that character.[235]

Thus, the reality-making function of the New Testament narrative is perhaps even more fundamental for Hauerwas's ethics than its strictly paradigmatic function. The primary function of Scripture is to shape our vision.

How does the authority of Scripture stand in relation to other authorities in Hauerwas's theological ethics? Of the theologians examined in this chapter, Hauerwas places the greatest weight on the hermeneutical role of *tradition*. "Scripture can be rightly interpreted," he asserts, "only within the practices of a body of people constituted by the Eucharist."[236] He quotes with enthusiastic approval from the Vatican II document titled "Dogmatic Constitution on Divine Revelation":

> Sacred tradition and sacred Scripture form one sacred deposit of the word of God, which is committed to the Church. . . . The task of authentically interpreting the word of God, whether written or handed on, has been entrusted exclusively to the living teaching office of the Church, whose authority is exercised in the name of Jesus Christ.[237]

There can be no proper interpretation of Scripture apart from the interpretations sanctioned by community tradition. It is important to understand that Hauerwas, like the Catholic tradition that he reflects here, never sets Scripture and tradition in opposition to one another or subordinates Scripture to tradition. Rather, tradition embodies the meaning of Scripture, or—perhaps more accurately—Scripture is carried to us through the medium of tradition in such a way that there can be no "Scripture" apart from that tradition. There is no access to the truth of the Bible through any other method or medium, for "the Church creates the meaning of Scripture."[238]

Consequently, the classic Protestant idea that Scripture can challenge and judge tradition is simply an illusion, because it assumes an unmediated access to the meaning of the Bible that Hauerwas denies in principle. "You do not have or need 'a meaning' of the text when you understand that Church is more determinative than text."[239] This declaration is of momentous significance for hermeneutics; the crucial question is whether Hauerwas can in fact live by it.[240]

Reason, in the sense of autonomous human reason, plays no role in Hauerwas's ethics, because objective rationality is impossible. "There is no point outside our history where we can secure a place to anchor our moral convictions. We must begin in the middle, that is, we must begin within a narrative."[241] The church's tradition teaches us a rationality proper to Christian convictions.

The hermeneutical role of *experience* for Hauerwas is, however, a more complex matter. Sometimes he writes as though experience is a crucial factor in validating and illuminating the biblical texts. When confronting the question of why the texts contained in the Bible should have normative significance for the church, he appeals strongly to experience:

> My answer is simply: these texts have been accepted as scripture because they and they alone *satisfy* what Reynolds Price has called *our craving* for a perfect story which we *feel* to be true. . . . The scripture functions as an authority for Christians precisely because

> by trying to live, think, and feel faithful to its witness they find they are more nearly able to live faithful to the truth.[242]

On the whole, however, it seems that Hauerwas accords to experience only the role of confirming the truth of Scripture. It is difficult to find passages in Hauerwas's work that treat experience as a significant factor in determining the interpretation of any particular text, and it is impossible to find cases in which the witness of experience trumps the teaching of a biblical text or requires a modification of its traditional interpretation. The experience of the individual Christian is in any case a matter of small importance; it is the experience of the church through time that carries hermeneutical weight. But when the matter is put in these terms, the distinction between tradition and experience becomes elusive or inconsequential.

The serious conceptual problem dogging Hauerwas's presentation of Scripture and ethics is how the community's experience of the truth attested by Scripture can precede its actual reading of Scripture. The concluding paragraph of "The Moral Authority of Scripture" illustrates the difficulty:

> Finally, there can be no ethical use of scripture *unless* we are a community capable of following the admonition to put "away falsehood, let every one speak the truth with his neighbor, for we are members of one another. . . . "[243]

Hauerwas continues the quotation of Ephesians 4:25–32, but this much is sufficient to target the difficulty. Hauerwas thinks that only a community answering to the description given by Ephesians 4 can determine the proper "ethical use" of Scripture. But how does the church become such a community? Hauerwas enters the hermeneutical circle on the side of tradition and experience, trusting that they will lead us to a fuller and more truthful reading of the New Testament.

(D) PRAGMATIC For Hauerwas, the pragmatic task is an integral part of Christian ethics: "[T]he intelligibility and truthfulness of Christian convictions reside in their practical force."[244] That is why his writings have boldly addressed a wide range of practical moral issues in specific terms, taking strong stances on issues such as pacifism, abortion, euthanasia, and the care of retarded children.

Hauerwas is never shy about drawing normative conclusions and pressing them upon others. He regularly tells his first-year divinity students at Duke that he intends to convert them to pacifism before they get out of his introductory ethics course. Passionate action for the truth is a much greater virtue than cautious circumspection in Hauerwas's scheme of things, and profession without practice is of no value. This insistence upon putting faith into practice is deeply consistent with his Methodist heritage.

At the same time, however, the conviction that truth must be enacted in a community has long been a point of troubling tension for Hauerwas. In the introduction to A *Community of Character*, Hauerwas confessed his "ambiguous ecclesial position" as a Methodist "of doubtful theological background" who teaches (as he did then) in a Catholic institution and feels deep affinity with the Anabaptist tradition. He jokingly characterized himself as a "high-church Mennonite" before turning to a more serious reflection on the theological implications of his lack of firm location in a particular ecclesial tradition:

> Perhaps the reason I stress so strongly the significance of the church for social ethics is that I am currently not disciplined by, nor do I feel the ambiguity of, any concrete church. Such a position could be deeply irresponsible, as it invites intellectual dishonesty. . . . I find I must think and write not only for the church that does exist but for the church that should exist if we were more courageous and faithful.[245]

In the years since those words were written, Hauerwas has moved more clearly toward identification with and accountability to the United Methodist Church. This movement, however, has hardly resolved the practical ambiguity of his position. The United Methodist Church in the United States at the end of the twentieth century stands in contradiction to much of what Hauerwas professes as the substance of Christian ethics. It is a large, pluralistic, bureaucratic organization that champions precisely the values of liberal individualism that Hauerwas decries. It is, for the most part, not formed significantly by regular eucharistic practice, it has no clear tradition of standing against war and violence,[246] and it is separated from the Roman Catholic Church whose tradition-bearing Hauerwas so prizes. Thus, it falls under the indictment pronounced in *Unleashing the Scripture*: "[A]ny churches divided from Rome, which means they are divided from themselves, lack the ability to use faithfully Scripture for the whole church."[247] All this would seem to mean, according to Hauerwas's own standards, that he himself should be incapable of interpreting Scripture rightly, since he does not participate in a community capable of manifesting and nurturing the necessary virtues.

To put the problem another way, the logic of Hauerwas's hermeneutical position should require him to become a Roman Catholic. The Roman Catholic Church, however, historically teaches positions on major ethical issues (such as just war and the role of women in the church) that Hauerwas cannot accept. Thus, he refuses to have his mind and character formed by that tradition and chooses instead to live, anomalously, as a Protestant with no clear theological rationale for his ecclesial practice and no empirical community to exemplify his vision of ecclesial politics. There is no tradition of high-church Mennonites; the idealized tradition to which Hauerwas appeals is an idiosyncratic fiction. When challenged by friends to explain by what authority he, as an unordained person, preaches, he can only say, "I wish I had a good response to that troubling question."[248] He cannot appeal to the authority of the New Testament, because his theoretical program insists that the authority of the New Testament is mediated only through a traditioned community to whose traditions he chooses not to submit. Indeed, his very act of preaching is, paradoxically, an act of defiance against the authority that his theology advocates.

Thus, in the end, Hauerwas's hermeneutical position comes unraveled in the midst of the pragmatic task that he deems essential for the intelligibility of Christian ethics. The New Testament falls mute, muzzled by the unfaithful church, and Hauerwas finds himself with no theoretical grounds for an appeal to Scripture against the church's practices. Nonetheless, in *Unleashing Scripture* he does it anyway, despite the absence of a theoretical basis for such an appeal. The "sermonic exhibits" in the book repeatedly seek to draw the reader into the symbolic world of the New Testament. One comes to the end of the book sensing that we need a Reformation that will enable the church again to hear the New Testament's word of judgment on its life. If indeed the Bible "provides the resources necessary for the church to be a community sufficiently truthful so that our conversation with one another and God can continue across generations,"[249] it will yield those resources only to readers who are willing to let it speak apart from and *against* the church's traditions.

Despite Hauerwas's difficulties at the pragmatic level, his work bears eloquent witness to the power of the New Testament stories for forming the church. His testimony that the church is a journeying people constantly dependent on God's surprising grace is a salutary reminder for a community always tempted to try to seize control of its own destiny. In the end, Hauerwas's proposal that the Bible should be taken away from North American Christians is part of his larger hermeneutical strategy to restore the rightful place of the Bible in the church and to make the church "a community capable of hearing the story of God we find in the scripture and living in a manner that is faithful to that story."[250]

5. Elisabeth Schüssler Fiorenza: A Feminist Critical Hermeneutic of Liberation

Elisabeth Schüssler Fiorenza, a German Roman Catholic New Testament scholar who has held major teaching positions in the United States at Notre Dame and Harvard, has become the leading voice of feminist biblical criticism in the English-speaking world. Her 1983 book *In Memory of Her* created a sensation by offering, as its subtitle indicates, a major new "feminist theological reconstruction of Christian origins."[251] Deploying the standard tools of historical criticism, Schüssler Fiorenza sought to recover within and behind the texts of the New Testament the long-suppressed memory of an early Christianity in which women played a significant role as leaders and participants. This provocative work of historical reconstruction was followed in 1984 by *Bread Not Stone*, a collection of essays elaborating the feminist hermeneutical strategies employed in *In Memory of Her.*[252] Taken together, these books revolutionized the critical discussion of women in the New Testament and the role of the New Testament in feminist theology.[253]

The impact of Schüssler Fiorenza's contribution may be assessed by noting the roles she has come to occupy within the academy. She was the first woman elected to the office of president of the Society of Biblical Literature (SBL, 1987), and she is the cofounder and coeditor of *The Journal of Feminist Studies in Religion.* She now occupies a chair at Harvard Divinity School as the Krister Stendahl Professor of Divinity. Amidst the lively current discussion of feminist biblical hermeneutics, her pioneering studies remain the major systematic works that have defined the terms of the conversation.

Schüssler Fiorenza, unlike the other scholars treated in this chapter, is a professional biblical scholar; she is neither a theologian nor an ethicist by trade and training. Furthermore, unlike Niebuhr, Barth, Yoder, and Hauerwas, she does not focus on violence as an explicit issue for Christian ethics. Thus, to compare her work to that of the theological ethicists considered above is potentially to compare incommensurate bodies of writing. Nonetheless, Schüssler Fiorenza's hermeneutical methods are distinctive and important enough to merit careful attention as we examine the various ways in which New Testament texts are employed in ethical discourse; she remains the standard-bearer for feminist hermeneutics.[254] Furthermore, she has sounded a clear call for normative reflection about the use of biblical texts within communities that claim these texts as Scripture. Her SBL presidential address, for example, advocated "an *ethics of accountability* that stands responsible not only for the choice of theoretical interpretive models but also for the ethical consequences of the biblical text and its meanings."[255] Biblical scholars, she insists, cannot remain objectively detached from the *Wirkungsgeschichte* of the Bible; rather, they must take an active concern in the ethical uses made of the texts that they study. Such an approach to biblical interpretation will consistently ask, "What does the language of a biblical text 'do' to a reader who submits to its world of vision?"[256] Thus, it is appropriate to examine her work as a representative venture in the use of Scripture in Christian ethics, since she herself has insisted that the work of all biblical scholars should be evaluated in these terms.

Schüssler Fiorenza's Approach to Theological Ethics

For Schüssler Fiorenza, the ethical use of the New Testament requires a difficult process of sifting through patriarchal texts in order to recover a lost history of women's experience that has been buried there. Emblematic of the tradition's forgetfulness is the story of the woman who anoints Jesus at Bethany (Mark 14:3–9):

> Although Jesus pronounces in Mark: "And truly I say to you, wherever the gospel is preached in the whole world, what she has done will be told in memory of her" (14:9), the woman's prophetic sign-action did not become a part of the gospel knowledge of Christians. Even her name is lost to us. Wherever the gospel is proclaimed and the eucharist celebrated another story is told: the story of the apostle who betrayed Jesus. The name of the betrayer is remembered, but the name of the faithful disciple is forgotten because she was a woman.[257]

Thus, "in memory of her," the feminist biblical critic must try to restore what has been lost through interrogating these ancient texts with fresh questions, searching out the hints and traces of a time at the beginning of the Christian movement when women participated in "the discipleship of equals," and retelling in a critical light the story of the church's suppression of women.

Because the existing texts are predominantly patriarchal in character, Schüssler Fiorenza must give painstaking attention to questions of critical method. Unwilling to join Mary Daly and other post-Christian feminists in a categorical rejection of Scripture and history as irretrievable, she must work out carefully the procedures of "a feminist critical hermeneutics of liberation" that will "assert that the source of our power [i.e., the Bible] is also the source of our oppression."[258] The task of her hermeneutic, then, is to reconstitute historical memory in such a way that it will empower the struggle of women for liberation. "Rather than *abandon* the memory of our foresisters' sufferings and hopes in our common patriarchal Christian past, Christian feminists *reclaim* their sufferings and struggles in and through the subversive power of the 'remembered past.'"[259] Thus, the task that Schüssler Fiorenza sets for herself in *In Memory of Her* is the rewriting of early Christian history. That is why Part I of *In Memory of Her*, a long methodological introduction, is entitled "Seeing-Naming-Reconstituting": Schüssler Fiorenza seeks to reconstitute a usable past by looking at the texts afresh and (re)naming the experience of women that she finds there.

A feminist approach to New Testament ethics, according to Schüssler Fiorenza, must not attempt to "rescue the Bible" by distinguishing its allegedly timeless revealed truth from its patriarchal trappings. She is highly critical of "neoorthodox" feminist theology (particularly the earlier thought of Letty Russell and Rosemary Radford Ruether) for its attempt to distinguish between the androcentric *form* and the egalitarian *content* of the Bible's message—that is, the attempt "to distill the feminist kerygmatic essence from its culturally conditioned androcentric traditions."[260] The danger of this approach, in Schüssler Fiorenza's view, is that it fails to pose a fundamental theological critique of the ways in which the Bible has in fact legitimized the oppression of women. The problem is not just that the Bible has been misinterpreted by patriarchal interpreters; rather, the Bible itself, rightly interpreted, is full of androcentric perspectives. Schüssler Fiorenza desires, therefore, to render an unblinking historical description of the Bible's representation of women and then to subject this representation to critical evaluation in light of an experience of women's liberation that also finds fragmentary expression in the Bible.

The New Testament texts cannot provide the hermeneutical norms for theological ethics in any simple way; rather, they must be systematically reassessed in light of a liberating vision whose original historical expression is—paradoxically—embedded in oppressive texts that now obscure that vision. Thus, Schüssler Fiorenza is willing to speak of revelation in Scripture only selectively, only as something to be recovered by critical scrutiny: it is to be found only in texts that bring to expression the hope of the liberation of women. "Biblical revelation and truth are given only in those texts and interpretative models that transcend critically their patriarchal frameworks and allow for a vision of Christian women as historical and theological subjects and actors."[261]

In order to see how Schüssler Fiorenza's hermeneutic operates, it is necessary first of all to understand her general construal of the history of earliest Christianity, as set forth in Part II of *In Memory of Her*, which bears the subtitle "Women's History as the History of the Discipleship of Equals." In keeping with the methods of form criticism, as exemplified classically in Rudolf Bultmann's *History of the Synoptic Tradition*, she speaks only cautiously about the historical Jesus, instead seeing the Gospels primarily as witnesses to the experiences of the earliest communities of

Christians. The canonical Gospels, literary products of the second or third generation of emergent Christianity, preserve traditions that can be probed to uncover older layers of information about the first-generation "Jesus movement" in Palestine.

That movement, according to Schüssler Fiorenza's reconstruction, was a reform movement within Judaism that proclaimed a new vision of God's *basileia* ("kingdom" or "reign") as a present reality, offering wholeness and dignity to all members of Israel. The poor, the sick, and the socially marginal were all invited into an egalitarian community that anticipated God's eschatological future "when death, suffering, and injustice finally will be overcome and patriarchal marriage will be no more." Thus, "Jesus' *praxis* and *vision* of the *basileia* is the mediation of God's future into the structures and experiences of his own time and people."[262] For women, who were often victims of oppression and socioeconomic deprivation, this vision of the *basileia* came as liberating good news. Consequently, women were active in leadership of the movement, in preserving its earliest traditions, and in extending its reach to the Gentile world.

Schüssler Fiorenza argues that the early Christian community was—at least indirectly—critical of patriarchal social structures. In support of this claim, she adduces texts of three sorts: "(1) the pre-Markan controversy stories in which Jesus challenges patriarchal marriage structures (Mark 10:2–9 and 12:18–27); (2) the texts on the a-familial ethos of the Jesus movement [e.g., Mark 3:31–35 and 10:29–30; Luke 11:27–28 and 12:51–53]; and (3) the saying about domination-free relationships in the community of disciples [Mark 10:42–45 and parallels]."[263] Of particular interest is Matthew 23:9, which indicates that the distinctive early Christian practice of addressing God as "Father" had radically egalitarian implications with regard to relationships within the community: "Call no one your father on earth, for you have one Father—the one in heaven." Schüssler Fiorenza comments, "The saying of Jesus uses the 'father' name of God not as a legitimization for existing patriarchal power structures in society or church but as a critical subversion of all structures of domination."[264]

Also integral to Schüssler Fiorenza's account is her hypothesis that "the earliest Jesus traditions perceive [Israel's] God of gracious goodness in a woman's *Gestalt* as divine Sophia (wisdom)."[265] This claim, however, hangs by the thread of a single text: "Wisdom [*sophia*] is vindicated by all her children" (Luke 7:35). Schüssler Fiorenza interprets this to mean that "[t]he Sophia-God of Jesus recognizes all Israelites as her children and she is proven 'right' by all of them" (that is, including tax collectors, prostitutes, and sinners).[266] The explicit identification of Jesus himself with the figure of divine wisdom in Matthew's Gospel is regarded by Schüssler Fiorenza as a later development of this tradition. Without adducing any further evidence, however, Schüssler Fiorenza goes on through the rest of the book to speak of "Sophia-God" as a central emphasis of the message of the Jesus movement:

> The earliest Christian theology is sophialogy. It was possible to understand Jesus' ministry and death in terms of God-Sophia, because Jesus probably understood himself as the prophet and child of Sophia.[267]

This proposal is the most exegetically implausible element of Schüssler Fiorenza's reconstruction. It is not, however—despite its rhetorical prominence in her presentation—logically foundational for the other aspects of her account of the role of women in the Jesus movement.

Next, Schüssler Fiorenza turns to a treatment of "The Early Christian Missionary Movement: Equality in the Power of the Spirit." Here she seeks to reconstruct the role of women in the Hellenistic mission churches that came into existence around the Mediterranean before and alongside the Pauline churches. As she acknowledges, actual historical information about these communities is scanty:

> . . . [W]omen's actual contribution to the early Christian missionary movement largely remains lost because of the scarcity and androcentric character of our sources. It must be rescued through historical imagination as well as in and through a reconstruction of this movement which fills out and contextualizes the fragmentary information still available to us.[268]

The result of this imaginative exercise is a portrait of a missionary movement in which "women were among the most prominent missionaries and leaders." They were founders and leaders of house churches, and they exercised their wealth and social position as patrons of other missionaries.[269] This movement, according to Schüssler Fiorenza, "was not structured after the Greco-Roman patriarchal household"; rather, their ecstatic Spirit-led worship signaled a community in which all the members were "'full' of Sophia and Spirit."[270] The traditional formula cited by Paul in Galatians 3:28 expresses the self-understanding of these groups: "There is neither Jew nor Greek, neither slave nor free, no male and female. For you are all one in Christ Jesus." These groups believe that they "already participate in the power and 'energy' of Christ-Sophia, that they are the new creation because they have received the power of the Spirit in baptism."[271]

The apostle Paul, who was a major figure in this Hellenistic mission movement, played a "double-edged" role in the historical development of women's place within emergent Christianity:

> On the one hand, he affirms Christian equality and freedom. He opens up a new independent lifestyle for women by encouraging them to remain free of the bondage of marriage. On the other hand, he subordinates women's behavior in marriage and in the worship assembly to the interests of Christian mission, and restricts their rights not only as "pneumatics" but also as "women," for we do not find such explicit restrictions on the behavior of men *qua* men in the worship assembly.[272]

Thus, despite his theoretical affirmation of the equality of women, Paul "opens the door for the reintroduction of patriarchal values and sexual dualities."[273]

Not long after Paul's time, the one brief shining moment of sexual equality in the church was snuffed out. Women in the church rapidly suffered a constriction of their roles in ministry. We see the forceful reassertion of patriarchy in Colossians, Ephesians, and the pastoral Epistles, which—for the sake of gaining social respectability and acceptance—sought to conform the structures of the church's life to the prevailing patriarchal customs of Greco-Roman society. The patriarchal household became the model for the church, and women were explicitly relegated to subordinate roles. Schüssler Fiorenza suggests that the dualistic ideological schemes characteristic of emergent Gnostic and patristic theology in the second century and later are the conceptual corollaries and expressions of "patriarchal reality and structures": "Just as gnosticism transposed its cosmic-spiritual dualism into ecclesial-spiritual dualism and praxis, so did the patristic church."[274] Thus, emergent early catholicism suppressed Christianity's original egalitarian impulses.[275]

By the latter part of the first century, only the Gospels of Mark and John can be heard as alternative voices that describe women as "paradigms of true discipleship" and call women and men alike to love and humble service. Mark and John "highlight the alternative character of the Christian community, and therefore accord women apostolic and ministerial leadership."[276] Even though their alternative vision lost out historically to the power of patriarchy, it stands as a faithful witness to "Jesus' alternative praxis of *agape* and service."[277] Thus, the New Testament canon preserves voices and memories that perpetually counteract the repressive power of patriarchy.

Against the backdrop of this historical reconstruction, Schüssler Fiorenza sketches a programmatic vision for "the *ekklēsia* of women, the gathering of women as a free and decision-making assembly of God's people."[278] Women are summoned to claim their own religious powers, to "decide their own spiritual welfare," to experience the presence of God in and through one another, and to participate fully in the work of ministry. Anticipating the objection that an "*ekklēsia* of women" merely institutionalizes "reverse sexism," Schüssler Fiorenza responds that it is not possible to move directly from a church characterized by male domination to one characterized by full mutuality between the sexes; to appeal for immediate egalitarianism is to dream of "easy grace," underestimating the degree to which women have internalized the structures of patriarchal oppression. "Because the spiritual colonialization of women by men has entailed our internalization of the male as divine, men have to relinquish their spiritual and religious control over women as well as over the church as the people of God, if mutuality should become a real possibility."[279]

Throughout Schüssler Fiorenza's discussion of this issue, it is apparent that her primary polemical target is the exclusively male hierarchy of her own Roman Catholic Church, who "exclude women from 'breaking the bread and sharing the cup' in eucharistic table community."[280] Although this critique does not apply, strictly speaking, to the major Protestant denominations, it would be wrong to think that they are exempt from blame. According to Schüssler Fiorenza, patriarchy has infected the whole history and tradition of Christianity to such a degree that women must—at least for a time—form their own communities in which they can reclaim their spiritual identity.

Schüssler Fiorenza is not very explicit about whether such communities are to be conceived as communities of support and resistance within existing churches or whether they are to be formed as alternative churches that replace existing structures. In her essay "Women-Church" in *Bread Not Stone,* she writes, "[T]o speak of the church of women does not mean to advocate a separatist strategy but to underline the visibility of women in biblical religion and to safeguard our freedom from spiritual male control." This would seem to suggest that the *ekklēsia* of women would exist within the structure of the church as historically constituted. Her further explication, however, casts some doubt on this matter:

> Just as we speak of the church of the poor, of an African or Asian church, of Presbyterian, Episcopalian, or Roman Catholic churches, without relinquishing our theological vision of the universal Church, so we may speak of the church of women as a manifestation of this universal church. . . . [T]he church of women as a feminist movement of self-identified women and women-identified men transcends all traditional man-made denominational lines.[281]

If women-church is analogous to the Presbyterian Church, then it could be an organized independent entity; on the other hand, if it is a movement that transcends denominational lines, then its adherents could continue to work within existing churches. Schüssler Fiorenza offers little direct practical guidance on this point. Perhaps she is willing to leave such decisions to the decision-making power of women within the particular local *ekklēsia.*

In any case, her vision for the ethical character of life within the *ekklēsia* of women is clear. The church is to be a "discipleship of equals," where all participate fully in decision making, deciding their own affairs in freedom. Although this description might sound reminiscent of the Enlightenment ideal for democratic society, Schüssler Fiorenza's vision should not be understood in individualistic terms. The church of women is to be characterized by strong bonds of community: "Commitment, accountability, and solidarity in the *ekklēsia* of women are the life-praxis of such a feminist Christian vocation."[282] Furthermore, the community has a clearly defined mission:

> Like Jesus' own ministry, the ministry of the community called forth by Jesus, the messenger of divine wisdom, is not an end in itself. In the power of the Spirit the disciples are sent to do what he did: to feed the hungry, heal the sick, liberate the oppressed, and to announce the inbreaking of God's new world and humanity here and now.[283]

Schüssler Fiorenza's ethic for women-church rejects passivity and meek acquiescence in suffering. Rather, women are to act "in the angry power of the Spirit . . . to feed, heal, and liberate our own people who are women." Feminist Christian spirituality "sets us free from the internalization of false altruism and self-sacrifice that is concerned with the welfare and work of men first to the detriment of our own and other women's welfare and calling."[284]

While sounding the call to commitment to "the liberation struggle of women and all peoples,"[285] Schüssler Fiorenza does not specify what particular activities might constitute "the liberation struggle." Presumably, she is referring at least to organized political protest and action; whether she also envisions the literal use of violence against oppressive powers is not made clear.

Indeed, one finds in Schüssler Fiorenza's work no explicit deliberation about when or whether the use of violence by Christians might be justifiable. Rather, she writes about violence from the perspective of its victims:

> How can we point to the eucharistic bread and say "this is my body" as long as women's bodies are battered, raped, sterilized, mutilated, prostituted, and used to male ends? . . . As in the past so still today men fight their wars on the battlefields of our bodies, making us the targets of their physical or spiritual violence. Therefore, the *ekklēsia* of women must reclaim women's bodies as the "image and body of Christ." It must denounce all violence against women as sacrilege and maintain women's moral power and accountability to decide our own spiritual welfare, one that encompasses body and soul, heart and womb.[286]

The question for her is not whether to exercise violence but how to survive it, how to denounce it in a way that will effectively set women free from its destructive effects. It is evident that she deplores violence, but she makes no argument against it on the basis of biblical warrants. Rather, the experience of those who have suffered violence is taken as a sufficient testimony of its evil.

Here we encounter a poignant illustration of the impact of feminist hermeneutics on theological ethics: the angle of vision causes the problem of violence to appear in a completely different light. Violence as a topic for Christian ethics is not a major concern of Schüssler Fiorenza's work, but violence is constantly *presupposed* as an aspect of the experience of women who take up the task of interpreting the Bible. It is perhaps not an accident that much of Schüssler Fiorenza's scholarly writing has concentrated on Revelation, the New Testament book that seems most clearly to express the perspective of a persecuted community.[287] Like the seer of Revelation, she offers a cry of protest against the violence inflicted on her people and at the same time declares a vision for a future in which the destructive power of violence is overthrown.

Unlike the seer of Revelation, however, Schüssler Fiorenza nowhere reflects explicitly about "the Lamb who was slain" as a normative pattern for the life of discipleship. Her gospel does not focus upon the word of the cross. Rather, her normative vision of the church's life is that of the early Christianity that she has reconstructed: a Spirit-filled egalitarian community living out a new experience of the *basileia* of God.

Posing the Diagnostic Questions

(A) DESCRIPTIVE Historically sophisticated exegesis is, as one would expect, one of the strong points of Schüssler Fiorenza's program. She has reconstructed the history of women's roles in the early church in a way that has commanded serious attention, even among scholars unsympathetic to her perspective. It now seems impossible to deny that women played a much larger role in the early promulgation of the gospel than Christian tradition has generally acknowledged. If from time to time Schüssler Fiorenza's reconstruction seems somewhat fanciful, this is a consequence of her explicitly stated intention to fill in the gaps in the scanty evidence with "historical imagination." All historians do the same thing, to some extent. At some points, her imagination strains the reader's credulity, as in her claim that "the earliest Christian theology is sophialogy." For the most part, however, her positions are argued on the basis of detailed exegetical work. Those who would challenge her reconstruction must engage her at the point where she has chosen to do battle: the arena of serious exegesis.

Of course, one can always argue about particular exegetical points. One of Schüssler Fiorenza's most puzzling exegetical missteps is her repeated insistence that "the Greek New Testament notion of *ekklēsia*" refers to "the public assembly of free citizens who gather in order to determine their own and their children's communal, political and spiritual well-being."[288] This is an accurate account of what the term *ekklēsia* meant in the context of the Greek polis, but it is a wildly misleading interpretation of the New Testament's use of the term to describe the Christian assembly.[289] No New Testament writer thinks of the *ekklēsia* as an assembly of people who meet to decide their own affairs. The *ekklēsia* is a community called into being by God's grace; as such, it belongs to God, and it is called to obey God's will as set forth through the apostolic teaching and example, not to decide its own self-interest based on democratic processes. Schüssler Fiorenza's appeal to the Greek political meaning of the term allows her to employ it as a warrant for the right of self-determination that she wants to claim for "the *ekklēsia* of women," but this usage can hardly be grounded, as she contends, on exegesis of the New Testament.

A second possible complaint about Schüssler Fiorenza's exegetical work is that she produces skewed readings of the texts, concentrating not on the message that the New Testament writers sought to communicate but on tangential features and minor motifs. For example, she teases out of a few Gospel texts an indirect critique of patriarchy and treats this critique as a major theme, while at the same time largely ignoring the Gospel writers' portrayal of the death of Jesus as the focus of Christian proclamation. It must be remembered, however, that Schüssler Fiorenza, unlike Barth, does not *intend* to offer a sympathetic exposition of the message of the New Testament writers; rather, she is undertaking a critical evaluation, cross-examining the texts to recover concealed memories about women. Her interest lies not so much in the meaning of the canonical texts as in the historical experiences behind them. Thus, if her discussion of the New Testament texts seems skewed, that is not a result of bad exegesis; it is, instead, a result of her coming to the texts with a particular set of questions and using exegesis as a tool to seek answers to those questions. Her use of exegetical methods toward her goals is rigorous and skillful. Of the critics surveyed in this chapter, she is the most sophisticated in her handling of the complex critical problems surrounding the background and composition of the New Testament.

(B) SYNTHETIC One might suppose that a feminist reconstruction of Christian origins would find itself confined to a narrow range of New Testament texts that deal explicitly with women and their roles. Schüssler Fiorenza, however, explicitly rejects this limitation. A feminist vision of Christian origins cannot be attained "by analyzing merely the biblical passages on women, because such a topical analysis would take the androcentric dynamics and reality constructions of patriarchal texts at face value."[290] Thus, she undertakes a wide-ranging survey of the New Testament as a whole, contending that feminist critical criteria "must be applied to *all* biblical texts in order to determine how much they contribute to the 'salvation' or oppression of women."[291] Accordingly, *In Memory of Her* is structured very much like a traditional history of early Christianity, with major chapters on early Palestinian Christianity, the early Hellenistic mission movement, the Pauline churches, and the later development toward early catholicism: almost the entirety of the canon is encompassed by her treatment.

As we have already seen, however, her actual treatment of the material within these texts is highly selective. Attention is given especially to traditions that give hints of an egalitarian social vision, and critical scrutiny is given to materials that reflect patriarchal norms. Other passages not pertinent to this set of concerns receive little or no discussion. The passion and resurrection narratives, for example, receive scant treatment except for their depiction of the role of the women disciples as first witnesses to the resurrection.[292]

Is there an operative canon within the canon for Schüssler Fiorenza, a core of texts that she takes to be theologically authoritative? Initially, she leads us to expect that she will identify such a de facto canon: "Biblical revelation and truth are given only in those texts and interpretative models that transcend critically their patriarchal frameworks and allow for a vision of Christian women as historical and theological subjects and actors."[293]

In fact, however, all the New Testament texts are to some extent "androcentric codifications of patriarchal power and ideology that cannot claim to be the revelatory Word of God."[294] Consequently, they must be "demythologized" by a feminist critical hermeneutic:

> I would therefore suggest that the revelatory canon for theological evaluation of biblical androcentric traditions and their subsequent interpretations cannot be derived from the Bible itself but can only be formulated in and through women's struggle for liberation from all patriarchal oppression. . . . The personally and politically reflected experience of oppression and liberation must become the criterion of appropriateness for biblical interpretation and evaluation of biblical authority claims.[295]

This means that no single New Testament author or book can function as a canon within the canon. Only occasionally through the "patriarchalizing texts of the New Testament" can we catch "a glimpse of the egalitarian-inclusive practice and theology of early Christians. These texts are like the tip of an iceberg, indicating a rich heritage now lost to us."[296]

Thus, revelatory authority is lodged in a few scattered fragments of tradition, such as the baptismal formula of Galatians 3:28 ("In Christ . . . no male and female") or the egalitarian admonition of Matthew 23:8–9 (reconstructed by Schüssler Fiorenza to read, "But you are not to be called rabbi, for you have one teacher, and you are all disciples; call no one father, for you have one father, [and you are all siblings]").[297] The real locus of authority, then, is not the canonical New Testament but the present-day struggle of women for liberation, through which the submerged "iceberg" of early Christian experience can be discerned. The de facto canon for Schüssler Fiorenza is to be found in her critical reconstruction of the "Jesus movement" and the pre-Pauline Hellenistic missionary movement.

How does Schüssler Fiorenza handle texts that stand in tension with her reconstruction? Her consistent strategy is to subject them simultaneously to historical exegesis and to ideological critique. For example, with regard to the New Testament's household code texts, she declares:

> [N]o biblical patriarchal text that perpetuates violence against women, children, or "slaves" should be accorded the status of divine revelation if we do not want to turn the God of the Bible into a God of violence. That does not mean that we cannot preach . . . on the household code texts of the New Testament. It only means that we must preach them critically in order to unmask them as texts promoting patriarchal violence.[298]

One might seriously question Schüssler Fiorenza's characterization of a passage such as Ephesians 5:21–6:9 as promoting violence. She characterizes it in this way because—as a result of her historical reconstruction—she perceives the passage's benevolent patriarchalism as a repressive squelching of first-generation Christianity's more egalitarian vision; furthermore, she contends, the subsequent history of interpretation shows that such texts, regardless of their original intention, have been used to oppress women.

The important thing to note here is that Schüssler Fiorenza neither ignores the *Haustafeln*, nor tries to explain away their patriarchal implications, nor tries to synthesize them somehow with Galatians 3:28. Instead, she emphatically draws attention to their patriarchal character "in order to unmask them," in order to recover a "'dangerous memory' that reclaims our foremothers' and foresisters' sufferings and struggles through the subversive power of the critically remembered past."[299] This is her consistent strategy for dealing with every New Testament text that stands in tension with her critical vision of liberation.

Does Schüssler Fiorenza have a particular focal image that draws the ethical witness of the New Testament into a unified whole? In one sense, this question must be answered in the negative. "It is misleading to speak about a uniform biblical or New Testament ethics," she suggests, "since the Bible is not a book but a collection of literary texts that span almost a millennium of history and culture." Therefore, any systematization of its teaching "depends on the selective activity of the biblical interpreter."[300] Her critical hermeneutic is designed precisely to show that the New Testament does not bear witness univocally to a liberating vision.

On the other hand, she returns again and again to the image of "women's struggle for liberation" as a lens through which all of Scripture must be read. Reading through this lens will not yield a unified vision of the canon itself, but it will produce a consistent image of the truth about human experience, insofar as that experience is expressed in the biblical texts. She goes so far as to claim that this struggle of women for liberation and survival is "the fullest experience of God's grace in our midst," and therefore "the *locus* of divine revelation and grace."[301] Thus, it would not be inaccurate to say that for Schüssler Fiorenza "women's struggle for liberation" does indeed serve as the focal image that lends coherence to the New Testament, insofar as the New Testament can be appropriated for use in normative Christian ethics.

(C) **HERMENEUTICAL** What can be said about the mode in which Schüssler Fiorenza employs the New Testament as a basis for ethics? It is evident that the texts do not serve for her as a source of normative *rules*; indeed, most of the explicit rules in the New Testament are to be seen as expressions of oppressive patriarchalism ("Wives, be subject to your husbands as you are to the Lord"). Even those rules that she approves ("Call no one father") are treated less as rules than as pointers to a comprehensive ideological critique of patriarchy.

Nor does Schüssler Fiorenza find it helpful to isolate ethical *principles* within the New Testament as a source for ethical guidance. Indeed, she is sharply critical of "feminist neoorthodox" thinkers who think that the Bible can be theologically salvaged in this manner:

> Russell, Ruether, and Trible in turn argue with Cady Stanton that the Bible is not totally androcentric but also contains some absolute ethical principles and feminist liberating traditions. In order to do so, they adopt a feminist neo-orthodox model that is in danger of reducing the ambiguity of historical struggle to theological essences and abstract, timeless principles.[302]

This approach is emphatically rejected: "A Christian feminist theology must cease its attempts to rescue the Bible from its feminist critics and assert that the source of our power is also the source of our oppression."[303] Even "those biblical traditions and interpretations that have transcended their oppressive cultural contexts," such as Galatians 3:28, "should not be understood as abstract theological ideas or norms, but as responses of faith to concrete historical situations of oppression."[304]

This emphasis on "concrete historical situations" is the key to understanding Schüssler Fiorenza's constructive approach to the use of the New Testament in Christian ethics. A feminist reconstructive reading of the New Testament uncovers specific historical instances of grace in those moments where the church resisted and transcended its patriarchal cultural context and "contributed to the liberation of people, especially of women."[305] The texts that provide glimpses of these historical moments should not be understood as articulations of timeless truth but as windows opening upon past moments of liberating experience. Such texts can serve to inspire and sustain the continuing struggle for liberation, but they can never be frozen as timelessly normative ideals:

> Feminist theology therefore challenges biblical theological scholarship to develop a paradigm for biblical revelation that does not understand the New Testament as an archetype but as a prototype. Both archetype and prototype denote original models. However, an archetype is an ideal form that establishes an unchanging timeless pattern, whereas a prototype is not a binding timeless pattern or principle. A prototype, therefore, is critically open to the possibility of its own transformation.[306]

The task of feminist theology, and of women-church, is to carry forward and develop the liberating possibilities adumbrated by the prototype. In this way, the church maintains a flexible capacity to "respond to new social needs and theological insights, as well as to allow and to extrapolate new social-ecclesial structures, while preserving the liberating biblical vision by engendering new structural formations that belong to that vision."[307]

Thus, in terms of the analytic categories proposed in this book, Schüssler Fiorenza does find in the New Testament *paradigms* for ethics, but in a much looser sense than Yoder, who sees Jesus as the perfect and definitive paradigm for obedience to God. (The term "obedience" has no place in Schüssler Fiorenza's account of Christian ethics.) Insofar as the New Testament texts "remember the struggles of our foremothers and forefathers against patriarchal oppression and their experience of God's sustaining presence," they can offer, as Schüssler Fiorenza puts it, "an open-ended paradigm that sets experience in motion and structures transformations."[308]

The historical and cultural distance between the world of the New Testament and our world looms large in Schüssler Fiorenza's work. Consequently, though her historical exegesis seeks to make the *symbolic world* of the New Testament intelligible, she does not seek to establish that symbolic world as the normative context for ethical reflection. In fact, it might be suggested that her hermeneutic works the other way around: she seeks to show how the historical data can be reinterpreted in terms of categories drawn from the symbolic world of modern social science and political ideology. Her theological anthropology is resolutely modern, conceiving of human beings as autonomous persons whose greatest fulfillment is to be found in freely choosing and deciding their own destinies. She does not even attempt to ground this view in the New Testament; it is simply assumed as a self-evident truth.

Her conception of the character of God does draw selectively on some elements of the New Testament's symbolic world, especially the motif of Sophia, but she inflates the significance of this motif far beyond its New Testament scope. At the same time, her discourse about God often appears in danger of losing the element of transcendence, allowing God-language to become a form of symbolic speech about immanent realities or human religious experience.[309] For example, she quotes with emphatic approval an essay by Carol Christ:

> A woman who echoes Ntosake Shange's dramatic statement, "I found God in myself and I loved her fiercely" is saying "Female power is strong and creative." She is saying that the divine principle, the saving and sustaining power, is in herself, that she will no longer look to men or male figures as saviors.[310]

Schüssler Fiorenza then comments:

> I concur with Carol Christ that at the heart of the spiritual feminist quest is the quest for women's power, freedom, and independence. Is it possible to read the Bible in such a way that it becomes a historical source and *theological symbol for* such power, independence, and freedom?[311]

Elsewhere, she observes that "the 'option for our women selves' . . . allows us 'to find God in ourselves.'"[312] This is not the place for an extended examination of Schüssler Fiorenza's concept of God. The point to be made here is that even when Schüssler Fiorenza employs the New Testament's theological vocabulary, the meaning of her language is shaped less by the symbolic narrative world of the New Testament than by the experience of women in the present time.

This observation brings us directly to the question of the relationship between the New Testament and other sources of theological authority in Schüssler Fiorenza's thought. Her reflections on hermeneutical method are illuminating, because she confronts this problem forthrightly and takes an unambiguous stand.

Tradition—perhaps even more than the Bible itself—is, in Schüssler Fiorenza's view, a source of oppression that must be critically scrutinized rather than taken as a reliable guide: "A feminist hermeneutics cannot trust or accept Bible and tradition simply as divine revelation. Rather it must evaluate them as patriarchal articulations."[313] She insists that "the central commitment and accountability for feminist theologians is . . . not to *the* tradition as such but to a feminist transformation of Christian traditions."[314] Thus, the church's traditional teachings play no authoritative role in her construction of normative ethics.

The role of *reason* in Schüssler Fiorenza's scheme is difficult to assess. The substance of her work bears witness to her strong commitment to the value of historical-critical inquiry, and she has stood resolutely against feminists who argue that historical criticism is irrelevant to their concerns.[315] Her systematically worked out historical and hermeneutical program affirms the importance of reasoned discourse as an instrument of theological reform: to appeal only to experience and intuition would be to surrender both the past and the academic institutions of the present to the oppressive forces of the status quo. Nonetheless, one never finds in Schüssler Fiorenza's work—as one does in Niebuhr's—a direct appeal to rational considerations to overrule the teaching of the New Testament. Instead, her reasoned historical arguments seek to place the teachings of the New Testament in a context that will expose their patriarchal assumptions. On the whole, Schüssler

Fiorenza does not argue for reason in itself as a sufficient basis for the formation of ethical judgments.

The role of *experience* in Schüssler Fiorenza's theological ethics, however, is fundamental and explicit. A feminist critical hermeneutic "engenders a paradigm shift in biblical ethics insofar as it does not appeal to the Bible as its primary source but begins with women's own experience and vision of liberation."[316] This methodological commitment is hammered home forcefully in the opening chapter of *In Memory of Her*. We have already noted Schüssler Fiorenza's dictum that "the personally and politically reflected *experience* of oppression and liberation must become the criterion of appropriateness for biblical interpretation and evaluation of biblical authority claims."[317] This means, unambiguously, that "the model proposed here locates revelation not in texts but in Christian experience and community."[318] It would be possible to produce dozens of quotations to underscore this point, but one more will suffice: the "canon" for discerning inspired truth is derived "*not* from the biblical writings, but from the contemporary struggle of women against racism, sexism, and poverty as oppressive systems of patriarchy and from its systematic explorations in feminist theory."[319] This quotation is remarkable in its inclusion of feminist *theory* within the body of authoritative norms against which Scripture must be measured, but Schüssler Fiorenza's appeal to "the contemporary struggle of women" is consistent with her programmatic emphasis on experience.

Schüssler Fiorenza unflinchingly articulates the consequence of this methodological decision: "[T]he Bible no longer functions as authoritative source but as a *resource* for women's struggle for liberation."[320] All her cards are on the table. Her massive project of historical-critical investigation of the New Testament stands in service of a hermeneutic that explicitly subordinates the authority of Scripture to the authority of contemporary experience. Wherever she can retrieve from the New Testament information useful for the liberation of women from oppression, the contribution of the text is gladly received; wherever the New Testament seems inimical to these concerns, as interpreted by contemporary feminist criticism, it to be dismissed as a patriarchal ideological construct lacking theological authority.

(D) PRAGMATIC Where can we find the fruits of Schüssler Fiorenza's feminist critical hermeneutic of liberation? The place to look would be in the few small but intensely committed women-church communities that have come into being, partly under the influence of her work, in the late twentieth century. Somewhat less directly, one might look at the impact of the feminist movement within the established churches, within the seminaries, and within scholarly guilds such as the American Academy of Religion, where feminist criticism now exercises powerful influence.

Schüssler Fiorenza herself dreams of the establishment of "centers of pastoral-theological interpretation" that would integrate rigorous historical-critical study of the Bible with an equally rigorous concern for sociopolitical analysis of the contemporary situation and for the needs of the community of faith. Such centers would differ from our present seminaries in their more inclusive range of participants. They would encompass not only professional scholars and ministers-in-training but also "persons from different churches and communities, from different races, classes, sexes, ages, and cultures, from different professions and educational backgrounds."[321] However laudable the intention of this vision, it is difficult to see it as anything other than a utopian daydream.

Perhaps it is far too early to assess the pragmatic effects of Schüssler Fiorenza's hermeneutical proposals. We may need to wait a generation or two to allow feminist theology time to mature and bear fruit in the life of the church. At the present time, it appears that Schüssler Fiorenza has found relatively few followers who are willing to imitate her example of rigorous engagement with scholarly critical exegesis; on the other hand, she has found many followers who are glad to adopt her recommendation that contemporary experience must control the interpretation of the Bible.[322] In the long run, it is hard to see how the latter development could lead to anything other than the dissolution—or at least serious schism—of the Christian church. The more the weight of theological authority is placed on present experience, the more difficult it becomes to see why anyone should bother to recover hypothetical memories of women's history from ancient texts. The more "God" becomes identified with a divine principle within the (feminine) self, the more uncertain is the need for a gospel about Jesus of Nazareth who strangely died on a cross a long time ago. (It is hard to imagine what Prisca and Phoebe and the other early Christian women whose contributions Schüssler Fiorenza has highlighted would make of these theological developments. Presumably, as Paul's colleagues and coworkers, they preached the gospel of human reconciliation to God through the death of Jesus, not a theology of "self-affirmation"[323] through "deciding their own spiritual-political affairs.")[324]

Despite these serious reservations about the theological and pragmatic viability of Schüssler Fiorenza's hermeneutic, any fair assessment must acknowledge the importance of her work. It is a grave indictment against the Christian tradition that a book such as *In Memory of Her* needed to be written at all. Women have in fact been oppressed and marginalized in the church, and their history has been obscured and lost. By courageously undertaking "a feminist theological reconstruction of Christian origins" with scholarly rigor and hermeneutical sophistication, Schüssler Fiorenza has forced both church and academy to take a fresh look at the past and to confess their complicity in an androcentric distortion of our history. As a result of her work, many women have taken heart and discovered a new vision of their dignity as children of God and ministers of the gospel; furthermore, women and men alike have been challenged to dream anew about the church as a "discipleship of equals."

Schüssler Fiorenza's passion for reading the Bible as a resource to sustain those who "feed the hungry, heal the sick, and liberate the oppressed" is to be celebrated.

Of course, the Bible has long functioned in just this way, before and apart from the development of a feminist critical hermeneutic. The danger is that her approach might ultimately undermine the authority of the New Testament so thoroughly that its liberating power would also be lost, as the church finds its identity increasingly shaped by the ideals of liberal democracy and the apparent dictates of contemporary experience. The potential contribution of Schüssler Fiorenza's hermeneutic, however, lies in its capacity to bring clearly into focus the New Testament's witness that the power of God can transform us and create communities in which women and men minister together, one in Christ.

NOTES

1. See, for example, Fox 1985; R. M. Brown 1986; Harries 1986; Kellerman 1987; Neuhaus 1989; Rasmussen 1989; Stone 1992; C. C. Brown 1992; Clark 1994; Fackre 1994; Lovin 1995; McCann 1995. The following analysis of Niebuhr's hermeneutics is indebted to the insights of Ping-Cheung Lo, my former teaching assistant at Yale, who called my attention to several pertinent themes and passages in Niebuhr's writings.
2. Niebuhr 1979 [1935], 22–38, 62–83.
3. Because the aim of this analysis is to provide *sample* instances of the use of the NT in ethics, we need not be concerned to give a full account of Niebuhr's use of the NT throughout all his writings. A comprehensive investigation of his work might discover various emphases or nuances not present in his important early essays. For the purposes of our present study, however, we can be content with a snapshot showing how he appeals to the NT in these particular writings. Our goal is not to give a synopsis of Niebuhr's thought but to clarify various possible hermeneutical strategies.
4. See, e.g., Niebuhr 1932, 263.
5. Niebuhr 1979 [1935], 22.
6. Niebuhr 1979 [1935], 22.
7. Niebuhr 1979 [1935], 23–24, 25.
8. Niebuhr 1979 [1935], 27.
9. Niebuhr 1979 [1935], 32.
10. Niebuhr 1940, 10.
11. Niebuhr 1940, 29–30.
12. Niebuhr 1940, 73.
13. Niebuhr 1940, 28.
14. Niebuhr 1932, 263.
15. Niebuhr 1979 [1935], 23–24.
16. Niebuhr 1979 [1935], 91. At this point, Niebuhr appears to be under the influence of a tradition in NT scholarship influenced by Dibelius. Cf. Chapter 1.1.
17. Niebuhr elsewhere clearly indicates that he views Jesus as entirely above historical and political contingencies. "Nothing is more futile and pathetic," he opines, "than the effort of some Christian theologians who find it necessary to become involved in the relativities of politics . . . to justify themselves by seeking to prove that Christ was also involved in some of these relativities, that he used whips to drive the money-changers out of the Temple, or that he came 'not to bring peace but a sword,' or that he asked the disciples to sell a cloak and buy a sword" (1940, 8–9). Why these efforts are futile Niebuhr does not explain.
18. Niebuhr 1940, 73. For a more extended treatment of Christology, see Niebuhr 1943 (vol. 2), 35–97. In my judgment, this lengthier discussion is subject to the same fundamental criticisms raised here.
19. See, e.g., Tillich 1957 (vol. 2), 19–180.
20. Niebuhr 1979 [1935], 65. Cf. p. 80: "[A] religion which holds love to be the final law of life stultifies itself if it does not support equal justice as a political and economic approximation of the ideal of love."
21. Niebuhr 1979 [1935], 91.
22. Niebuhr 1979 [1935], 85.
23. Niebuhr 1979 [1935], 73–74.
24. Niebuhr 1932, 179–180, emphasis mine.
25. Niebuhr 1979 [1935], 116, emphasis mine.
26. Niebuhr 1979 [1935]. See also the essay "Why the Christian Church Is Not Pacifist" in 1940, 1–32, esp. pp. 4–5, 30–32.

27. Niebuhr 1979 [1935], 38.
28. Niebuhr 1979 [1935], 62, quoting Rom. 7:18–19, 24.
29. Niebuhr 1979 [1935], 71, quoting Rom. 7:23.
30. This point is noted by Jeffrey Siker in the chapter on Niebuhr in his forthcoming book, parts of which he has kindly made available to me in manuscript.
31. Niebuhr 1979 [1935], 29. Throughout this chapter, Scripture citations will follow the usage of the author under discussion in each section rather than the NRSV.
32. Niebuhr 1979 [1935], 62.
33. For a summation of the evidence, see Siker (forthcoming).
34. Niebuhr 1943 (vol. 2), 51.
35. Niebuhr 1943 (vol. 2), 50.
36. Niebuhr 1943 (vol. 2), 49.
37. Niebuhr explicitly describes the imminent expectation of Jesus and the early church as an "error" that must be corrected through the symbolic interpretation summarized here. See, e.g., Niebuhr 1943 (vol. 2), 49–50.
38. M. L. King, Jr., 1958, 100. This passage is cited by Kellerman 1987, 20.
39. Niebuhr 1979 [1935], 72, emphasis mine.
40. Niebuhr 1940, 6.
41. For an account of Barth's career, see Busch 1976. For overviews of his thought, see Mueller 1972; Jüngel 1986; Torrance 1990; and especially Hunsinger 1991.
42. *Church Dogmatics* II/1, 1964 [1957a] (henceforth abbreviated *CD*). This massive work contains partial volumes that were published separately. Therefore, the conventional system of reference designates the volume and parts by using both roman and arabic numerals: II/1 refers to volume II, part 1.
43. *CD* II/2, 512.
44. In Barth's view, ethics is a corollary of the doctrine of election, because God's act of forming covenant partnership with human beings requires us to ask "what it is that God wants from man" (*CD* II/2, 510).
45. *CD* II/2, 549.
46. For discussion of these temptations, see *CD* II/2, 520–535.
47. *CD* II/2, 533–534.
48. *CD* II/2, 518–520.
49. *CD* II/2, 536.
50. *CD* II/2, 537.
51. *CD* II/2, 535.
52. *CD* II/2, 540.
53. *CD* II/2, 558.
54. See Chapter 1.
55. *CD* II/2, 562.
56. *CD* II/2, 606, emphasis mine.
57. *CD* II/2, 661–708.
58. *CD* II/2, 663–664, emphasis mine.
59. *CD* II/2, 664.
60. *CD* II/2, 665, emphasis mine.
61. *CD* II/2, 669.
62. For a more recent instance of a similar claim about Scripture—though from an utterly different theological perspective—see Sternberg 1985.
63. *CD* II/2, 672.
64. *CD* II/2, 672–700.
65. *CD* II/2, 678. The English translation of *Church Dogmatics* alternates, even within this single passage, between "story" and "history" as the translation of the German *Geschichte*. I have modified the translation here for the sake of consistency, because it makes Barth's point much clearer. On Barth's reading of Scripture as narrative, see, e.g., Kelsey 1975, 39–50, and Ford 1981.
66. *CD* II/2, 680–681.
67. It would be possible to interrogate Barth's exegesis of specific texts—and thereby to challenge his broader thesis—but the scope of our present concern does not permit this sort of detailed examination of the passages.
68. *CD* II/2, 701, emphasis mine.
69. *CD* II/2, 706.
70. *CD* II/2, 705–706.
71. *CD* II/2, 706, emphasis mine.
72. *CD* II/2, 708.

73. CD III/4, 397.
74. CD III/4, 398.
75. CD III/4, 398.
76. CD III/4, 398.
77. CD III/4, 398–400.
78. CD III/4, 400.
79. CD III/4, 408–409.
80. CD III/4, 430, emphasis mine.
81. John Howard Yoder, in an incisive analysis of Barth's ethic, remarks, "We may be tempted to ask whether Barth himself has an 'intuitionist' conception of the command of God—and it is surprising that he has gone to so little trouble to ward off such a misunderstanding" (Yoder 1970, 48). Yoder seeks to deny that Barth's ethic depends on mystical discernment of God's will: "When Barth speaks thus of the Word which God addresses to a specific situation, he in no way means some kind of new superhuman channel of inside information whereby the Christian would receive a new truth specifically for his time and place. . . . The language which portrays God as speaking in the situation must not be understood as in disjunction from sober pragmatic calculation" (p. 49). Interestingly, however, Yoder can produce very little evidence from Barth's own work to support this denial. Indeed, if the command of God can in specific cases overrule the explicit teaching of the Bible, as Barth proposes, it is hard to see how Barth could have anything in mind other than a direct spiritual discernment of "inside information." For further discussion of this problem, however, see Nigel Biggar, "Hearing God's Command and Thinking About What's Right: With and Beyond Barth," in Biggar 1988, 101–118; Biggar, 1993.
82. For important discussions of Barth on war, see Yoder 1970; Rowan Williams, "Barth, War, and the State," in Biggar 1988, 170–190.
83. CD III/4, 452.
84. CD III/4, 453.
85. CD III/4, 455.
86. CD III/4, 456.
87. Yoder 1970, 38.
88. CD III/4, 461.
89. CD III/4, 462.
90. For an extended sympathetic critique of this apparently anomalous aspect of Barth's teaching, see Yoder 1970.
91. CD III/4, 462.
92. CD III/4, 462.
93. CD III/4, 468.
94. CD III/4, 463.
95. CD III/4, 463.
96. In Cochrane 1976, 237–247.
97. CD II/2, 606.
98. Barth 1957c [1928], 28–50.
99. This was the title of his polemic against Emil Brunner's book *Nature and Grace*.
100. This is, of course, a speculation, but note Yoder's intriguing discussion of this matter: Yoder 1970, 111–118, 133–137.
101. Yoder 1994. The second edition undertakes only minimal revision of the text but appends to each chapter of the original (1972) an epilogue in which Yoder comments on scholarly developments in the interim. In the following citations, I shall refer to the page numbering of the second edition, with page references for the 1972 edition appended in brackets.
102. Yoder 1984.
103. Yoder 1994, 2 [1972, 12].
104. Yoder 1994, 8–9 [1972, 20].
105. Yoder 1994, 10 [1972, 22].
106. Yoder 1994, 11 [1972, 22–23].
107. Yoder 1994, 11 [1972, 23]. The interpretation of Luke to which Yoder refers here is the widely influential work of Hans Conzelmann 1961 [1953], which was the pioneering redaction-critical study of Luke's Gospel.
108. Yoder 1994, 22–23 [1972, 27–28].
109. Yoder 1994, 26 [1972, 32].
110. Luke 4:18–19, as cited by Yoder 1994, 29 [1972, 35].
111. Yoder 1994, 32 [1972, 39].
112. Yoder 1994, 37–38 [1972, 45]. Yoder is commenting here on Luke 14:25–33.
113. Yoder 1994, 38 n. 28 [1972, 46 n. 28].

114. Yoder 1994, 46–48 [1972, 55–57].
115. Yoder 1994, 51 [1972, 61].
116. Yoder 1994, 53 [1972, 63].
117. Yoder 1994, 95 [1972, 97].
118. Yoder 1994, 96 [1972, 97], emphasis mine.
119. Yoder 1994, 96 [1972, 98].
120. Yoder 1994, 97 [1972, 99].
121. Yoder 1994, 99 [1972, 101]; here, of course, the influence of Barth on Yoder's understanding of incarnation is evident.
122. Yoder 1994, 98 [1972, 100].
123. Yoder 1994, 131 [1972, 134].
124. Berkhof 1962; Caird 1956. For other literature, see Yoder 1994, 140 n. 5 [1972, 142 n. 4].
125. Yoder 1994, 142 [1972, 143], citing passages such as Rom. 8:28, Eph. 2:2, Col. 2:20, and Gal. 4:3.
126. Yoder 1994, 146–147 [1972, 149–150].
127. Yoder 1994, 145 [1972, 148].
128. Yoder 1994, 150 [1972, 153].
129. Yoder 1994, 154 [1972, 157].
130. Yoder 1994, 155 [1972, 158].
131. Yoder 1994, 13 [1972, 25].
132. Yoder 1994, 198 [1972, 199].
133. Yoder 1994, 202–203 [1972, 204–205].
134. E.g., 1994, 12 n. 17 [1972, 24 n. 14].
135. In the second edition of the book (1994, 72–75), Yoder notes and summarizes several more recent scholarly works that lend support to Trocmé's emphasis on the jubilee. Nonetheless, these works have not exercised widespread influence on either Lukan scholarship or studies of the Jesus of history.
136. Yoder writes as follows:

> The voluntary subjection of the church is understood as a witness to the world. . . . The subordinate person becomes a free ethical agent when he voluntarily accedes to his subordination in the power of Christ instead of bowing to it either fatalistically or resentfully. . . . [I]t is the ethic of Jesus himself that was transmitted and transmuted into the stance of the servant church within society, as indicated precisely in the *Haustafeln*. . . . [I]t is precisely this attitude toward the structures of this world, this freedom from needing to smash them since they are about to crumble anyway, which Jesus had been the first to teach and in his suffering to concretize [1994, 185–187 (1972, 190–192)].

Yoder's suggestion in the second edition (1994, 190 n. 60) that Elisabeth Schüssler Fiorenza's interpretation of the *Haustafeln* parallels his is extremely puzzling. Concerning the household code in Ephesians, for example, she writes:

> [T]his christological modification of the husband's patriarchal position and duties does not have the power, theologically, to transform the patriarchal pattern of the household code, even though this might have been the intention of the author. Instead, Ephesians christologically cements the inferior position of the wife in the marriage relationship. . . . [T]he author was not able to 'Christianize' the code. The 'gospel of peace' has transformed the relationship of gentiles and Jews, but not the social roles of wives and slaves within the household of God. *On the contrary, the cultural-social structures of domination are theologized and thereby reinforced* [Schüssler Fiorenza 1983, 270, emphasis mine].

137. It is not difficult to see that John and Acts would fit into Yoder's hermeneutical program very nicely: both texts envision the church as a witness-bearing community sharply distinct from its cultural environment.
138. Yoder 1994, 242 [1972, 250].
139. Cassidy 1978; Pokorny 1992. In his second edition, Yoder takes note of this development in NT scholarship (1994, 53–54).
140. See especially the important work of Garrett 1989.
141. In the second edition, after noting the recent shift in critical assessment of Luke's politics, Yoder minimizes its significance for his argument: "I do not grant that my original reading was *limited* to the vision of Luke, in such a way that it would not be a coherent witness common to all the Gospels. Since all of the Gospels say enough of the same things to make my point, I have no stake in preferring one school of Gospel criticism to another" (1994, 54). It is certainly correct that Yoder does not build his cases solely on the basis of a single Gospel narrative or on one critical theory about the *Tendenz* of Luke; on the other hand, Yoder may be giving up too much to say that he has "no stake" in preferring some critical approaches to the Gospels to others.

The politically detached Cynic Jesus imagined by the historical critics of the Jesus Seminar, for example, would stand in fundamental tension with Yoder's Jesus. In fact, though one can find statements in Yoder downplaying the significance of historical work, it seems to me that his program does depend—perhaps more than Yoder himself realizes—on a particular construal of the historical Jesus behind the canonical accounts.

142. Yoder 1994, 12 n. 17 [1972, 24 n. 14].
143. Yoder 1984, 69.
144. Yoder 1994, 210 [1972, 214].
145. Yoder 1984, 9.
146. Yoder 1984, 37.
147. Yoder 1994, 202 n. 14 [1972, 204 n. 13].
148. Yoder 1984, 31.
149. Yoder 1994, 233 [1972, 239].
150. Yoder 1994, 233–234 [1972, 240].
151. Yoder 1984, 56, emphasis mine.
152. Yoder 1984, 46–62. The title of this essay alludes to Heb. 2:9.
153. Yoder 1984, 15–45.
154. Yoder 1984, 3. In private correspondence (Apr. 13, 1995), Yoder contests my characterization of the difference between him and Niebuhr on this point: "I largely agree with Niebuhr on that matter, except that he is much more optimistic (i.e. less realistic, less niebuhrian) than I about the ability of democracies and state governments to make and implement honest estimates of the application of just war restraints to their own cases. What I disagree with in Niebuhr is not his anthropology but his christology." Despite Yoder's demurral, I would continue to affirm that there is a real difference in the theological anthropologies of these two theologians.
155. Yoder 1984, 38.
156. Yoder 1994, 232 [1972, 238].
157. Yoder 1994, 233 [1972, 239].
158. Yoder 1994, 237 [1972, 244], emphasis mine. Yoder's unidentified quotation is a paraphrase of Col. 1:24.
159. Yoder 1984, 43.
160. Yoder 1984, 69.
161. Yoder 1984, 70.
162. Yoder 1984, 57, 59.
163. Yoder 1984, 62.
164. Yoder 1984, 11.
165. Yoder 1984, 35, citing Acts 15:28.
166. Yoder 1984, 71.
167. Yoder 1984, 72.
168. Yoder 1984, 9.
169. For one listing of such communities, see Yoder 1984, 5.
170. Yoder 1984, 92.
171. Yoder 1984, 94.
172. See Yoder's discussion of this aspect of the church's calling in Yoder 1964.
173. Yoder, private correspondence, Apr. 13, 1995.
174. Yoder 1984, 4.
175. Hauerwas and Willimon 1989. See also Hauerwas and Willimon 1991.
176. See especially Hauerwas 1985. The first edition of the book was published in 1975.
177. Hauerwas 1983, xxiv.
178. See, e.g., "Stanley Fish, the Pope, and the Bible," in Hauerwas 1993, 19–28. In private correspondence (Aug. 15, 1994), Hauerwas disputes this last point: "I use Stanley [Fish], but I'm not really 'influenced' by him."
179. For Hauerwas's own account of the development of his thought, see Hauerwas 1983, xv–xxvi, and—for a more recent update—Hauerwas 1990. For the suggestion that Hauerwas has failed to achieve integration of the various influences on his thought, see Jones 1990, 15–19.
180. Hauerwas 1981a, 36–52 and 53–71.
181. Hauerwas 1993, 15–44.
182. Hauerwas 1981a, 36. The quotation is taken from Athanasius, *The Incarnation of the Word of God*. The importance of this passage for Hauerwas is suggested by the fact that he cites it again in full in 1993, 37–38.
183. Hauerwas 1981a, 1, emphasis mine.
184. Hauerwas 1993, 15.
185. Hauerwas 1993, 15.
186. Hauerwas 1983, 70.

187. Hauerwas 1981a, 69. I take it that the phrase "those who have given us our scripture" refers not only to the writers of the biblical texts but also to those who have handed these texts down to us through many generations. See also the sermon "On the Production and Reproduction of the Saints" in Hauerwas 1993, 99–104.
188. Hauerwas 1983, 26.
189. Hauerwas 1993, 47–62.
190. Hauerwas 1981a, 55.
191. Hauerwas's formulation of the matter stands, of course, in significant tension with the way in which I have approached the relation between the NT and ethics in this book.
192. Hauerwas 1981a, 48. Note that Hauerwas introduces the motif of love, which is not present in Mark 8:27–9:1.
193. Hauerwas 1981a, 11. This is one of the "ten theses toward the reform of Christian social ethics" stated in the opening chapter of the book.
194. Hauerwas 1981a, 49.
195. Hauerwas 1981a, 50.
196. Cf. the section "On Learning to Be a Sinner" in Hauerwas 1983, 30–34.
197. Hauerwas 1981a, 51, 50.
198. Hauerwas 1981a, 52.
199. Hauerwas 1981a, 50–51.
200. Hauerwas 1981a, 10. This is another of Hauerwas's ten theses.
201. Hauerwas 1983, 89.
202. Hauerwas 1983, 72–95.
203. Hauerwas 1983, 82.
204. Hauerwas 1983, 85.
205. Hauerwas 1981a, 13.
206. Hauerwas 1983, 95.
207. For discussion of this methodological issue, see Stanley Hauerwas and David Burrell, "From System to Story: An Alternative Pattern for Rationality in Ethics," in Hauerwas and Burrell 1977, 15–39.
208. Hauerwas 1981a, 12. This is the last of Hauerwas's ten theses.
209. Hauerwas 1983, 94.
210. Hauerwas 1983, xvii.
211. This point is noted by Siker (forthcoming).
212. See, for example, Hauerwas 1981a, 46–49.
213. Hauerwas 1993, 64, 72.
214. It might be said in Hauerwas's defense that a sermon is not the place for such exegetical discussion. I would challenge that assumption; good preaching not only presupposes exegesis but also leads the congregation to a deeper reading of the text. In the case of Hauerwas's work, however, I am making two points: he rarely pursues exegetical inquiry in *any* of his writings, and he claims that such inquiry is *in principle* unnecessary.
215. Hauerwas 1993, 7.
216. E.g., Hauerwas 1981, 70: "Of course, before we decide that certain aspects of scripture are no longer relevant—e.g., the *Haustafeln*—we must make sure we understand them through an exegesis as accurate as we can muster." The following sentences, however, show where Hauerwas's basic hermeneutical commitments lie: "And we must remember that a set of historical-critical skills will not guarantee an accurate reading. Our analysis will also depend on the questions we learn to put to the text from participating in a community which acknowledges their formative role."
217. Hauerwas 1993, 7.
218. Hauerwas 1993, 34.
219. One example will suffice to make my point. In the preface to the first volume of his commentary on Matthew in the *Evangelisch-Katholischer Kommentar zum Neuen Testament*, Ulrich Luz writes, "[A] commentary which not only explains biblical texts but aids in their understanding must not remain simply in the past but must draw lines into the present. . . . I am convinced that the history of interpretation of a book can contribute greatly to this understanding. . . . I probably owe the most to the church fathers and the Protestant and Catholic exegesis of the 16th to 18th centuries. Their exegesis is in a magnificent way an occupation not only with the words but with the subject matter of the texts" (Luz 1989, 9).
220. Hauerwas 1993, 9. In passing, one might wish that theological students in the 1990s were still receiving such formation. Now in seminary curricula "shaped by Protestant liberalism," few students are reading Aquinas, Luther, Calvin, Barth, and Yoder in quantities sufficient to "learn Scripture" through them.
221. Siker (forthcoming).
222. See, e.g., Hauerwas 1981a, 70–71.

223. Hauerwas 1981a, 52.
224. Hauerwas 1981a, 63, citing Blenkinsopp 1977, 94.
225. Hauerwas 1981a, 66.
226. Hauerwas 1981a, 66.
227. As this quotation suggests, *community* is not itself a focal image in Hauerwas's reading of the NT, despite the important hermeneutical role given to the community in the process of interpretation.
228. Hauerwas 1983, 24–25.
229. Hauerwas 1981a, 49.
230. Hauerwas 1993, 16.
231. Hauerwas 1983, 90, quoting R. Williams 1982, 49.
232. Hauerwas 1983, 29.
233. Hauerwas 1981a, 50.
234. Hauerwas 1983, 69.
235. Hauerwas 1981a, 67.
236. Hauerwas 1993, 23.
237. Hauerwas 1993, 22, quoting *Documents of Vatican II* (New York: Guild Press, 1966), 117–118.
238. Hauerwas 1993, 36.
239. Hauerwas 1993, 23.
240. See the discussion of this problem in section 12.4.d (under the heading "Pragmatic").
241. Hauerwas 1983, 62. This section of the book is entitled "On Beginning in the Middle."
242. Hauerwas 1981a, 66, emphasis mine.
243. Hauerwas 1981a, 71, emphasis mine.
244. Hauerwas 1981a, 1.
245. Hauerwas 1981a, 6.
246. For critical reflection on this problem in the United Methodist Church, see Long 1992.
247. Hauerwas 1993, 23. In context, this statement is intended to summarize the Roman Catholic understanding of the relation between church and scriptural interpretation. It is clear, however, that Hauerwas is describing the Roman Catholic position with approval.
248. Hauerwas 1993, 10.
249. Hauerwas 1981a, 64.
250. Hauerwas 1981a, 1.
251. Schüssler Fiorenza 1983.
252. Schüssler Fiorenza 1984.
253. Schüssler Fiorenza's development of a feminist hermeneutic is carried forward in Schüssler Fiorenza 1992. While this work broadens Schüssler Fiorenza's repertoire of feminist interpretive strategies, her fundamental methodological commitments remain constant. For the purposes of our present concerns, we may focus our attention on her position as it was articulated in her work of the 1980s.
254. Regrettably, no one has yet undertaken the project of writing a major study of NT ethics from a feminist perspective.
255. Schüssler Fiorenza 1988, 3–17. The quotation is from p. 15.
256. Schüssler Fiorenza 1988, 15.
257. Schüssler Fiorenza 1983, xiii. The claim that "even her name is lost to us" is a little odd in light of the fact, duly noted by Schüssler Fiorenza in the next paragraph, that the Fourth Gospel identifies her as Mary of Bethany. Presumably Schüssler Fiorenza's point is that the Markan tradition has already obscured her identity, perhaps "to make the story more palatable to a patriarchal Greco-Roman audience" (Schüssler Fiorenza 1983, xiii).
258. Schüssler Fiorenza 1983, 35.
259. Schüssler Fiorenza 1983, 31.
260. Schüssler Fiorenza 1983, 21.
261. Schüssler Fiorenza 1983, 30.
262. Schüssler Fiorenza 1983, 121.
263. Schüssler Fiorenza 1983, 143.
264. Schüssler Fiorenza 1983, 151. It is not entirely clear why this passage ought to be read as evidence for the perspective of the early Jesus movement. Since the material is distinctive to Matthew, it could just as easily be read as reflecting the perspective of the late-first-century Matthean community. The latter hypothesis finds support in the close parallelism of Matt. 23:8: "You are not to be called 'rabbi,' for there is one teacher, and you are all brothers." This formulation looks very much as though it might have had its origin in the Matthean community's emergent rivalry with the synagogue.
265. Schüssler Fiorenza 1983, 132.

266. Schüssler Fiorenza 1983, 132.
267. Schüssler Fiorenza 1983, 134.
268. Schüssler Fiorenza 1983, 167.
269. Schüssler Fiorenza 1983, 183.
270. Schüssler Fiorenza 1983, 198. The evidence for this sketch comes primarily from Paul's letters to the Corinthians. Curiously, Schüssler Fiorenza seems not to acknowledge that the pneumatic wisdom enthusiasts at Corinth were elitists rather than egalitarians.
271. Schüssler Fiorenza 1983, 190.
272. Schüssler Fiorenza 1983, 236.
273. Schüssler Fiorenza 1983, 236.
274. Schüssler Fiorenza 1983, 278.
275. In significant respects, Schüssler Fiorenza's construction of the early church's descent into patriarchy parallels the construal of early Christian history that provides the organizational backbone of Bultmann's *Theology of the New Testament*, whose final section recounts the church's development toward early catholicism (Bultmann 1955 [vol. 2], 93–236).
276. Schüssler Fiorenza 1983, 334.
277. Schüssler Fiorenza 1983, 334.
278. Schüssler Fiorenza 1983, 349. This vision is set forth in an epilogue to the book (pp. 343–351), as well as in Schüssler Fiorenza 1984, 1–22.
279. Schüssler Fiorenza 1983, 347.
280. Schüssler Fiorenza 1983, 347.
281. Schüssler Fiorenza 1984, 7–8.
282. Schüssler Fiorenza 1983, 344.
283. Schüssler Fiorenza 1983, 345.
284. Schüssler Fiorenza 1983, 346.
285. Schüssler Fiorenza 1983, 346.
286. Schüssler Fiorenza 1983, 350–351.
287. See, e.g., Schüssler Fiorenza 1985 and 1991.
288. Schüssler Fiorenza 1984, xiv. See also 1983, 344.
289. Its connotations in the NT derive principally from the Septuagint's use of the term to translate the Hebrew *qahal*, the "congregation" of the covenant people Israel.
290. Schüssler Fiorenza 1983, 30.
291. Schüssler Fiorenza 1984, 41, emphasis hers.
292. Schüssler Fiorenza 1983, 319–323.
293. Schüssler Fiorenza 1983, 30.
294. Schüssler Fiorenza 1983, 32.
295. Schüssler Fiorenza 1983, 32.
296. Schüssler Fiorenza 1984, 111.
297. See Schüssler Fiorenza 1983, 149–150.
298. Schüssler Fiorenza 1984, 145.
299. Schüssler Fiorenza 1984, 86.
300. Schüssler Fiorenza 1984, 66.
301. Schüssler Fiorenza 1984, xv.
302. Schüssler Fiorenza 1983, 27. For Schüssler Fiorenza's more extended critique of feminist neoorthodoxy, see pp. 14–21.
303. Schüssler Fiorenza 1983, 35.
304. Schüssler Fiorenza 1984, 61.
305. Schüssler Fiorenza 1983, 33.
306. Schüssler Fiorenza 1983, 33.
307. Schüssler Fiorenza 1983, 34.
308. Schüssler Fiorenza 1984, xvi–xvii.
309. See, for example, Schüssler Fiorenza's thoroughly anthropocentric description of feminist worship in 1984, 21.
310. Carol P. Christ, "Why Women Need the Goddess: Phenomenological, Psychological, and Political Reflections," in Christ and Plaskow 1979, 277. Cited in Schüssler Fiorenza 1983, 18.
311. Schüssler Fiorenza 1983, 18–19, emphasis mine.
312. Schüssler Fiorenza 1984, xv–xvi.
313. Schüssler Fiorenza 1984, x.

314. Schüssler Fiorenza 1984, 3, emphasis hers.
315. See especially the essay "Remembering the Past in Creating the Future: Historical-Critical Scholarship and Feminist-Critical Interpretation," in Schüssler Fiorenza 1984, 93–115.
316. Schüssler Fiorenza 1984, 88. One wonders whether Schüssler Fiorenza intends a pun in her choice of the word "engenders."
317. Schüssler Fiorenza 1983, 32, emphasis mine.
318. Schüssler Fiorenza 1983, 34.
319. Schüssler Fiorenza 1984, 14, emphasis in original.
320. Schüssler Fiorenza 1984, 14.
321. Schüssler Fiorenza 1984, 42.
322. For Schüssler Fiorenza's account of an unsettling encounter with one such follower, see 1984, 92–93.
323. Schüssler Fiorenza 1984, xv.
324. Schüssler Fiorenza 1983, 344.

Chapter 13

How Shall We Use the Texts?

Normative Proposals

1. Summary and Normative Reflections

Having surveyed the use of the New Testament in the ethics of Reinhold Niebuhr, Karl Barth, John Howard Yoder, Stanley Hauerwas, and Elisabeth Schüssler Fiorenza, we may now draw some summary conclusions and offer normative proposals about the most faithful and fruitful approaches to shaping a Christian ethic in response to the New Testament's witness.

(A) THE DESCRIPTIVE AND SYNTHETIC TASKS: COMPARISON AND PROPOSALS First of all, it will be apparent that a theologian who wrestles with sustained close reading of the New Testament texts is likely to produce more compelling and sophisticated results than one who reads the texts casually or superficially. Serious exegesis is a sine qua non for New Testament ethics. In this respect, Barth, Yoder, and Schüssler Fiorenza, whose normative positions are argued on the basis of deep exegetical engagement with the New Testament documents, certainly command more attention than do Niebuhr and Hauerwas.

Likewise, those theologians who seek to attend to the entire range of canonical witnesses are on firmer theological ground than are those who base their normative positions on a limited sample of canonical evidence. In this regard, Barth and Yoder are once again exemplary for their thoroughgoing effort to listen obediently to the full witness of the canon. The canon as such carries less weight for Hauerwas, but his actual use of Scripture is more comprehensive in its range than that of Niebuhr, who needs only a few favorite loci as warrants for his normative principles. Schüssler Fiorenza stands in a different place on this issue: she reckons with the whole canon as evidence for her *historical* account of early Christianity, but at the same time she subjects the canon to critical scrutiny in light of extrinsic norms derived from the struggle of women for liberation. Consequently, her actual use of the New Testament as normative for theological ethics is highly selective, focusing on fragmentary or peripheral material more than on the themes and norms that are central in the texts themselves. (For example, Christology—the primary focus for the Gospel writers—recedes into the background.) As we have seen, this revisionary hermeneutical strategy is deliberately chosen, but it is of doubtful value for a community—that is, the church—that seeks to define its identity on the basis of the New Testament.

The question of how the interpreter handles New Testament texts that stand in tension with his or her normative vision has emerged as a crucial issue in our survey of these five theologians. We have seen that all five of them employ sophisticated hermeneutical strategies for dealing with this problem. All five are aware of the problems posed by the diversity of the canonical texts, and none of them tries to evade these difficulties through facile harmonization. Of the five, Yoder is the most inclined to argue for a comprehensive, unified vision within the canon, while Schüssler Fiorenza is the most insistent that the ideological diversity within the canon is irreducible. Despite standing at different ends of the spectrum on this issue, however, these two theologians are closely in agreement—over against Hauerwas—that historical investigation and explanation may inform our hermeneutical response to intracanonical diversity.

I have suggested that the unity-within-diversity of the New Testament witnesses can best be grasped with the aid of three focal images: *community*, *cross*, and *new creation*. We can encapsulate the theological implications of these images for the church in a single complex narrative summary: the New Testament calls the covenant *community* of God's people into participation in the *cross* of Christ in such a way that the death and resurrection of Jesus becomes a paradigm for their common life as harbingers of God's *new creation*. Of our five theologians, Barth, Yoder, and Hauerwas most adequately capture the full story adumbrated by these images. (The image of community receives less emphasis in Barth's treatment of the problem of war, however, than it does elsewhere in *Church Dogmatics*).[1]

Niebuhr notoriously neglects the covenant *community* as a theme in New Testament ethics and gives the *cross* the curiously indirect role of exemplifying a historically impossible self-abnegation that stands in judgment over all approximations of the ideal of love. In his handling of the New Testament's eschatology—which is central to his theological program—Niebuhr places far more emphasis on the "not yet" side of the dialectic than on the "already," with the result that the message of *new creation* is in danger of being swallowed up by the mundane "realism" of politics as usual.

Schüssler Fiorenza's vision of "the *ekklēsia* of women," on the other hand, results from reading the New Testament intently through the focal images of *community* and *new creation.* Indeed, the experience of the Christian feminist movement in the late years of the twentieth century offers a powerful analogue to the early Christians' consciousness of being a community "on whom the ends of the ages have come," living in the dawn of redemption while still beset by the vexing vestiges of an old order that is passing away. Reading the New Testament texts through the hermeneutical lens of such an experience, Schüssler Fiorenza brings several important aspects of New Testament ethics sharply into focus. Regrettably, however, the focal image of the *cross* virtually disappears from sight in her theology. One suspects that this omission is not so much an oversight as a reaction against perversions of Christian theology that appeal to the cross in order to inculcate women's passive acquiescence in their oppression. Still, her omission of the cross as a focal image for New Testament ethics produces a hermeneutical distortion at least as serious as Niebuhr's omission of community. *An ethic of the New Testament must be kept in balance through a reading that gives sustained and serious attention to all three of these images.*

(B) THE HERMENEUTICAL TASK: COMPARISON AND PROPOSALS In surveying the use of the New Testament by these five theologians, we have seen that each one appeals to the biblical text in certain characteristic *modes.* Niebuhr discovers in the New Testament *principles* of love, justice, and equity, along with a sober depiction of the human condition; Barth, on the other hand, eschews appeal to principle, preferring to find in the text specific *rules* and commandments that address the reader directly, along with a depiction of the character and action of God. Yoder and Hauerwas see in the story of Jesus a *paradigm* for the faithful life, and Hauerwas emphasizes the dialectical shaping of text and community that occurs when the text is read within the church. Schüssler Fiorenza joins Barth in refusing to factor abstract ethical principles out of the New Testament; however, rather than hearing in the Bible God's direct commanding word, she sees in the historical specificity of early Christianity an open-ended *paradigm,* a prototype that encourages imaginative elaboration and transformation. In this latter point, her perspective is not dissimilar to that of Hauerwas, though she does not share his interest in the New Testament as an instrument of character formation.

As I have noted previously, all of these different modes of ethical discourse may be found within the New Testament itself.[2] The logical corollary of this observation is that an ethic seeking to be responsive to the contours and emphases of the New Testament would seek to incorporate all of these modes appropriately within the church's ethical teaching.[3] The first step toward doing that is to attend carefully to the mode in which the individual New Testament texts themselves speak.

We may articulate this point as a normative guideline: *New Testament texts must be granted authority (or not) in the mode in which they speak.*[4] Claims about the authority of the text must respect not only its content but also its form. The interpreter should not turn narratives into law (for instance, by arguing that Acts 2:44–45 requires Christians to own all things in common) or rules into principles (for instance, by suggesting that the commandment to sell possessions and give alms [Luke 12:33] is not meant literally but that it points to the principle of inner detachment from wealth). Legalists and antinomians are equally guilty of hermeneutical gerrymandering to annex New Testament texts to foreign modes of ethical discourse. Christian preachers, at least since the time of Clement of Alexandria, have preached hundreds of thousands of disastrous sermons that say, in effect, "Now the text *says* x, but of course it couldn't really mean that, so we must see the underlying principle to which it points, which is y." Let there be a moratorium on such preaching! The New Testament's ethical imperatives are either normative at the level of their own claim, or they are invalid.

This hermeneutical guideline has a couple of corollaries. First, *we should guard against falling into a habit of reading New Testament ethical texts in one mode only.* If we read the New Testament and find only laws, we are obviously enmeshed in grave hermeneutical distortion. Likewise, if we read the New Testament and find only timeless moral principles, we are probably guilty, as Barth warned, of evading Scripture's specific claims upon our lives. Second, *we must be wary of attempts to use one mode of appeal to Scripture to override the witness of the New Testament in another mode.* Niebuhr, as we have seen, engages in this sort of hermeneutical trumping of the text in "The Relevance of an Impossible Ethical Ideal," when he argues that fidelity to the ideal of love exemplified in Jesus sometimes requires us to use violence to seek justice; thus, adherence to Jesus' love ideal requires rejection (in practice) of Jesus' explicit but unrealistic teaching against violence in the Sermon on the Mount. A community that has been taught to see the world through Matthew's eyes, however, will sense that something has gone awry here. In fact, Niebuhr's argument is finally a sophisticated dodge of Jesus' call to costly discipleship, allowing us to call Jesus "Lord, Lord," without doing what he commands.

Thus, to reiterate, a Christian ethic that seeks to be faithfully responsive to the New Testament texts will not move abstractly away from the form in which the texts present themselves to us. We must respect the particularity of the forms through which the whole witness of the whole canon lays claim upon us. The Christian tradition witnesses to the importance of the New Testament's claim in all four of the modes that we have delineated: rule, principle, paradigm, and symbolic world. The Scripture-shaped community will learn the skills necessary to respond to the voice of Scripture in each of these modes.

Having said that, however, we may also ask whether it is necessary to ascribe hermeneutical primacy to one of these modes. The shape of the New Testament canon suggests an answer: as Barth, Yoder, and Hauerwas have seen, the New Testament presents itself to us first of all in the form of story. The four Gospels present the figure of Jesus through the medium of narrative, the Acts of the Apostles relates the story of the earliest expansion of the gospel message in the Mediterranean world, and the Apocalypse offers a grand symbolic narrative of the consummation of God's dealings with the whole creation. Even the New Testament Epistles ought to be understood less as propositional theology than as reflection upon the story of Jesus Christ, as told in the early church's passion/resurrection kerygma.[5] Consequently, a Christian community that is responsive to the specific form of the New Testament texts will find itself drawn repeatedly to the *paradigmatic* mode of using the New Testament in ethics, seeking to shape analogies between the story told there and the life of the community. (This point is elaborated in the section that follows.) Thus, *narrative texts in the New Testament are fundamental resources for normative ethics.* The stories told in the Gospels and Acts subliminally form the Christian community's notions of what a life lived faithfully might look like. Those stories become the framework in which we understand and measure our lives; the narratives are more fundamental than any secondary process of abstraction that seeks to distill their ethical import.

What happens to normative theological ethics when the narrative particularity of the New Testament is deemphasized? We see a clear illustration in Niebuhr's treatment of the ethic of Jesus. As we have noted, he isolates the teachings of the Sermon on the Mount from their narrative context and ignores the story of the passion. Thus, he is able to characterize the ethic of Jesus as an "impossible ideal." Anyone who reads Matthew's Gospel all the way to the end, however, will see that nonresistant love of enemies is not an "impossible ideal." It is, rather, a horrifyingly costly human possibility. A hermeneutic that attends to the narrative form of the gospel message will insist that Jesus' disciples are called to follow him in the suffering love of enemies. Thus, the meaning of love as an ideal or principle is specified for us in and through the story. For Christian theology, rules and principles must find their place within the story of God's redemption of the world through Jesus Christ, and the symbolic world of the New Testament finds its coherence only in that story.

In addition to deciding how to employ the New Testament texts constructively, the interpreter must also reckon with the problem of how to coordinate the witness of the New Testament with the moral wisdom that comes from other sources: *tradition, reason,* and *experience.* No matter how earnestly we affirm the authority of Scripture, some role for these other sources is unavoidable, since our reading of Scripture is influenced by the church's tradition, by the recognized norms of rationality of the culture in which we live and move, and by the life experience that we bring to the text. Thus, it is well to acknowledge the impact of these other factors in shaping our construal of New Testament ethics and to identify their proper role as carefully as possible.

As we have seen, our five representative theologians take dramatically different stances on this issue, ranging from Barth's passionate anathema upon all merely "natural" sources for theology to Schüssler Fiorenza's equally passionate embrace of women's contemporary *experience* as the "revelatory canon" against which the teachings of the New Testament must be measured. Niebuhr also weighs human *experience* as a crucial normative factor for theology and adds a sturdy confidence in the capacity of human *reason* to make ethical decisions by predicting and assessing the consequences of our choices. Hauerwas champions the role of ecclesial *tradition* in shaping our reading of Scripture, and Yoder, while sharing Barth's conviction that the Bible is the fundamental source of revelation, gives a greater explicit role to the church's experience of receiving guidance through the Holy Spirit. In view of this survey of options, what shall we conclude? What role should sources of authority other than the Bible play in the formation of a constructive ethic?

I would propose the following minimal guideline: *extrabiblical sources stand in a hermeneutical relation to the New Testament; they are not independent, counterbalancing sources of authority.* In other words, the *Bible's* perspective is privileged, not ours. However tricky it may be in practice to apply this guideline, it is in fact a meaningful rule of thumb that discriminates significantly between different approaches to New Testament ethics. This guideline by no means excludes exceedingly serious consideration of other sources of wisdom, but it assigns those sources an explicitly subordinate role in normative judgments. They function instrumentally to help us interpret and apply Scripture. They must not, however, be allowed to stand as competing sources for theological norms.

Why should Scripture be accorded such hermeneutical primacy? A full answer to this question might require another book-length treatment engaging the history of canon formation, the history of the reception and use of Scripture in the church, and the complex debates in recent theology about authority and hermeneutics. The aim of the present book, however, is not to provide an apologetic justification for biblical authority but to reflect critically about how Scripture might form and inform moral judgment within the Christian church—that is, within a community whose identity is already fundamentally shaped by the gospel to which the New Testament texts are the original and uniquely authoritative witnesses. For that community, Scripture is not just one among several "classics," not just one source of moral wisdom competing in a marketplace of ideas, experiences, and feelings. Scripture is the wellspring of life, the fundamental source for the identity of the church. Thus, the hermeneutical primacy of the New Testament is an axiom for the life of the Christian community: tradition, reason, and experience must find their places within the world narrated by the New Testament witnesses.

Tradition must be heard and weighed; it carries indispensable insights both about the meaning of Scripture and about matters that Scripture does not address explicitly. Nonetheless, the tradition must be constantly resubmitted to critical scrutiny in light of the New Testament texts. (Indeed, Christian tradition itself witnesses to the authoritative primacy of Scripture.) Otherwise, tradition can smother the text or co-opt its radical challenges. Within the church, there is always the danger that we will fall under the same judgment that Jesus (quoting Isaiah) pronounced on the Pharisees and scribes:

> *Isaiah prophesied rightly about you hypocrites, as it is written,*
>
> > *"This people honors me with their lips,*
> > *but their hearts are far from me;*
> > *in vain do they worship me,*
> > *teaching human precepts as doctrines."*
>
> *You abandon the commandment of God and hold to human tradition.* (MARK 7:6–8)

When tradition comes into conflict with the New Testament's portrayal of the life and vocation of the Christian community, the time is at hand for judgment, repentance, and reformation. With regard to the issue of violence, for example, I would assert that Christendom's long-held and clearly formulated just war tradition is finally incompatible with the New Testament vision of the church as a people called to take up the cross and follow Jesus. If so, the tradition must be abandoned.

Reason plays an important role in clarifying and ordering our reading of Scripture and placing the biblical texts in the context of other sources of knowledge. But the gospel of the cross will frequently confound reason, "for God's foolishness is wiser than human wisdom" (1 Cor. 1:25a; see vv. 18–31). Reason—which is always specific to a particular human culture—must be healed and taught by God's wisdom, to which we have access primarily through the Scriptures. Reason can never operate in a vacuum. When reason seems to come into conflict with Scripture, the time is at hand for careful reassessment of our "knowledge" of the world. It may be that we are seeing things askew.

Experience, as we have already noted, can claim theological authority only when it is an experience shared broadly by the community of faith.[6] Its primary role is to confirm the truth of the teaching of Scripture, as it is confessed and lived out by the community. We know that our hope is not futile, because we have the experience of "God's love . . . poured into our hearts through the Holy Spirit that has been given to us" (Rom. 5:5). Of course, experience is a notoriously tricky guide: human beings are susceptible to all kinds of illusion and self-deception. That is why claims about experience as a theological authority must always be tested in light of Scripture and through the corporate discernment of the community of faith. Certainly, the private experience of an individual cannot overturn the theological authority of the New Testament. Are there cases, however, where the church as a whole might acknowledge some new experience as revelatory even against the apparent witness of Scripture? The paradigm case for such a possibility is found in the story of Peter's preaching to the household of the Gentile Cornelius in Acts 10 and 11, and the church's subsequent acknowledgment that God had given the Holy Spirit even to those who were "unclean" according to biblical norms. In Part IV of this book, we shall consider some issues concerning which this sort of authority is claimed for experience. Such possibilities cannot be excluded a priori; God is, as Barth would insist, free to act in surprising ways. It must be stated as a theological guideline, however, that claims about divinely inspired experience that contradicts the witness of Scripture should be admitted to normative status in the church only after sustained and agonizing scrutiny by a consensus of the faithful. Far more often, our experience, ambiguous and sin-riddled, will need to be judged and corrected in light of Scripture, which teaches us again and again not to be conformed to this age but to be transformed by the renewing of our minds so that we may rightly discern the will of God (Rom. 12:2).

We have not yet considered normative proposals for this *pragmatic* task of New Testament ethics. We shall begin to do so in section 3, below, and in Part IV. Before such proposals can be entertained, however, we must reflect briefly on the relationship between metaphor and the moral imagination.

2. Moral Judgment As Metaphor-Making

I suggested above that in order to practice New Testament ethics as a normative theological discipline, we will have to formulate imaginative *analogies* between the stories told in the texts and the story lived out by our community in a very different historical setting.[7] This is a point that requires further reflection.

To "understand" any text is to discover analogies between its words and our experience, between the world that it renders and the world that we know; thus, the mere act of reading is already a rudimentary exercise of the analogical imagination, even when the world of the text is very close to our own. It follows that the hermeneutical problem of reading an ancient text is only a special case of the hermeneutical problem that attends all acts of reading. To read the New Testament with understanding at the end of the second millennium, whether in New York or Sarajevo or Johannesburg or Tokyo, is to engage in the ambitious imaginative project of discerning analogies between our world and the world of the New Testament writers.[8]

Beyond this, however, to declare a text to be "Scripture" is to impose a still more ambitious demand upon the reading imagination. When we say that a text is "Scripture" for our community, we are committing ourselves to a diligent effort to discern analogical relations between the text and our community's life—but that is not all. We are also committing ourselves to form—and reform—our communal life in such a way that the analogies will be made more clearly visible. But that is to anticipate my conclusion: I shall return to this point presently.

For now, the central point is this: the use of the New Testament in normative ethics requires *an integrative act of the imagination,* a discernment about how our lives, despite their historical dissimilarity to the lives narrated in the New Testament, might fitly answer to that narration and participate in the truth that it tells. I reiterate here a major thesis articulated in the Introduction: *whenever we appeal to the authority of the New Testament, we are necessarily engaged in metaphor-making, placing our community's life imaginatively within the world articulated by the texts.* An exercise of aesthetic judgment is unavoidable if the two worlds are to be brought into conjunction. Here we speak, however, not merely of human artistic wit: in such acts of imaginative integration, the church has historically recognized the work of the Holy Spirit. Where faithful interpreters listen patiently to the Word of God in Scripture and discern fresh imaginative links between the biblical story and our time, we confess—always with reverent caution—that the Spirit is inspiring such readings.

Such imaginative integration would not be necessary if it were possible to separate out "timeless truth" in the New Testament from "culturally conditioned" elements. The timeless truth would constitute a special form of revelation that would be immediately pertinent in exactly the same way in all times, places, and cultures. The culturally conditioned elements could then be dismissed as contingent features with no normative significance. This is a very common strategy for dealing with New Testament texts that we find uncongenial: one encounters it often, for example, in debates about roles of women and sexual ethics in the New Testament. Unfortunately, the strategy is conceptually incoherent, because every jot and tittle of the New Testament is culturally conditioned. *The effort to distinguish timeless truth in the New Testament from culturally conditioned elements is wrongheaded and impossible.* These are texts written by human beings in particular times and places, and they bear the marks—as do all human utterances—of their historical location.

Even the most fundamental theological affirmations of the New Testament writers are intelligible only within the framework of first-century Judaism. A single example will illustrate the point:

> *For I handed on to you as of first importance what I in turn had received: that Christ died for our sins in accordance with the scriptures, and that he was buried, and that he was raised on the third day in accordance with the scriptures, and that he appeared to Cephas, then to the twelve.* (1 Cor. 15:3–5)

Every element of this early Christian confessional statement derives its sense from its participation in the particular symbolic universe of Jewish apocalyptic thought: *Christ* (i.e., "Messiah"), *sins, scriptures, resurrection, the twelve* (corresponding symbolically to the twelve tribes of Israel). What is the timeless suprahistorical truth here? The point hardly need be belabored. The earliest kerygma narrates the gospel within a very specific cultural tradition and setting. If the New Testament's fundamental theological statements are so thoroughly culturally specific, how much more will its ethical norms be thoroughly enculturated? Surely their validity or continuing normativity cannot depend upon their ahistorical character? Their roots are in the earth, not the air.

The illusory project of boiling away culturally conditioned elements so as to leave a residuum of timeless truth is the intellectual legacy of Kantian metaphysics.

The fundamental project of Enlightenment-era biblical criticism was "to uncover beneath the various manifestations of the Biblical religion a rational 'natural religion' common to all people."[9] Ever since Johann Philipp Gabler's famous inaugural address in 1787 proposed that the task of the biblical theologian was to distinguish between "true" biblical theology (i.e., a descriptive account of the explicit theology of the texts) and "pure" biblical theology (i.e., an account of the universal systematic truth implicit within or behind the texts), biblical scholars and theologians have been chasing the chimera of timeless truth.[10]

One would think that the intellectual climate of the late twentieth century would have exposed the futility of such a project, but one still encounters the distinction, perhaps most often and most astoundingly among Christians who imagine that it will somehow enable them to hold on to the authority of Scripture: authority is tacitly transferred from the historically conditioned text to the suprahistorical truth that is somehow packaged in a historical wrapper. The difficulty with this way of conceptualizing Scripture is evident: once we have the truth, we no longer need the wrapper.

The Christian understanding of incarnation, however, is fundamentally inimical to such Enlightenment idealism. Truth is given to us in a particular person in a particular time and place: Jesus of Nazareth. God has acted in history by calling a particular people (Israel/church) for a particular mission. To be sure, for many thinkers since the Enlightenment, Scripture's historical particularity has posed a stumbling block. G. E. Lessing described the gap between historical events and rational truths as "the ugly broad ditch which I cannot get across, however often and however earnestly I have tried to make the leap."[11] But how could the church ever have been deterred by Lessing's dictum that "the accidental truths of history can never become the proof of necessary truths of reason"?[12] The gospel is not a summary of "the necessary truths of reason"; rather, it is a revelation that shatters and reshapes human reason in light of God's foolishness. The Word is known in contingent human form, and only there. That is the scandal of the gospel.

Consequently, our hermeneutic must value rather than denigrate the particularity of the New Testament texts: the storied, culturally specific forms of the apostolic testimony are to be received and heeded just as they present themselves to us. But this leads back to my proposal that New Testament ethics is necessarily an exercise in metaphor-making. If we seek to honor the particular form of texts that are predominantly narrative and occasional, without subjecting them to analytic procedures that abstract general principles from them, we will find that the most promising hermeneutical strategy is one of metaphorical juxtaposition between the world of the text and our world.

Metaphors are incongruous conjunctions of two images—or two semantic fields—that turn out, upon reflection, to be like one another in ways not ordinarily recognized. They shock us into thought by positing unexpected analogies—analogies that could not be discerned within conventional categories of knowledge. Thus, metaphors reshape perception. For example, when the Gospel of John presents Jesus as saying, "I am the living bread that came down from heaven" (John 6:51a), the message jolts his hearers, who are looking for him to play the role of Moses by providing them with miraculous bread to eat (6:30–31). Jesus' striking response refuses the identification with Moses and posits instead a metaphorical conjunction between himself and the manna that fed the Israelites in the wilderness. The metaphor quickly takes a gruesome turn when Jesus goes on to say, "[T]he bread that I will give for the life of the world is my flesh," and affirms that "those who eat my flesh and drink my blood have eternal life" (6:51b, 54a). At one level, the metaphorical shock induces the reader to confront the scandal of John's claim that "the Word became flesh." (Indeed, the statement that the Word became flesh strikingly illustrates the power of metaphor to "mutilate our world of meanings" and create a new framework for perception.)[13] On another level, the metaphor leads the reader to make the imaginative connection between the Exodus story and the church's Eucharist, with the flesh of Jesus as the startling common term. The hearer of such a metaphor is confronted by two options. We can take offense at this jarring conjunction of images, as did those disciples who went away murmuring, "This teaching is difficult; who can accept it?" (John 6:60). Or, alternatively, we can "understand" the metaphor. To "understand" it, however, is to stand under its authority, to allow our life and perception of reality to be changed in light of the "ontological flash"[14] created by the metaphorical conjunction, so that we confess with Peter, "Lord, to whom [else] can we go? You have the words of eternal life" (6:68).

The metaphorical process can occur not only at the level of the individual image or sentence but also at the higher level of the story, as we see in the parables of the synoptic Gospels.[15] Luke's parable of the dishonest manager (Luke 16:1–9), for instance, offers an unsettling narrative of a shrewd operator who, on the verge of being fired by his master, ingratiates himself with the master's debtors by settling their accounts at a dramatic discount. In the parable's surprise punchline, the master, rather than being still more furious at the manager, commends him for his savvy dealings! We readers, expecting that the parable will end with a tidy moral condemnation of the dishonest manager, are caught off guard and forced to reconsider our understanding of the moral order of things. Why does the master not condemn the servant? Perhaps it is because he recognized that the moment of judgment was at hand and acted decisively, just as the hearers of Jesus' message of the kingdom of God are called to respond decisively rather than continuing with business as usual. Our discomfort with this conclusion to the tale forces us to recognize our affinity with the priggish older brother in the parable of the prodigal son (Luke 15:11–32), which immediately precedes the parable of the dishonest manager in Luke's story. Like the older brother, we stand offended outside the celebration if we continue to insist that people ought to get what is coming to them. To "understand" these parables is to be changed by them, to have our vision of the world reshaped by them. To "understand" them is to enter the process of reflecting about how our lives ought to change in response to the gospel—a gospel that unsettles what we "know" about responsibility and ethics.

A similar reorientation of our perceptions occurs—on an even larger scale—when we read and come to "understand" the Gospels, with their story of a crucified Messiah. This story is "a stumbling block to Jews and foolishness to Gentiles, but to those who are the called, both Jews and Greeks, Christ the power of God and the wisdom of God" (1 Cor. 1:23–24). The fundamental task of New Testament ethics is to call us again and again to see our lives shattered and shaped anew by "reading" them in metaphorical juxtaposition with this story.[16]

As Steven J. Kraftchick has summarized the matter, "Metaphor is a mode of creating dissonance of thought in order to restructure meaning relationships."[17] That is what the New Testament, read metaphorically in conjunction with our experience of the world, does. The world we know—or thought we knew—is reconfigured when we "read" it in counterpoint with the New Testament. The hermeneutical task is to relocate our contemporary experience on the map of the New Testament's story of Jesus. By telling us a story that overturns our conventional ways of seeing the world, the New Testament provides the images and categories in light of which the life of our community (the metaphorical "target domain") is reinterpreted.[18]

The temporal gap between the first-century Christians and Christians at the end of the twentieth century can be bridged only by a spark of imagination. How does this work of imaginative correlation inform the formation of normative judgments in New Testament ethics? Let us consider a few examples.

When we read the parable of the rich man and Lazarus (Luke 16:19–31), we are moved to reimagine our lives in light of this story. The parable is told, according to Luke, to Pharisees scoffing at Jesus' teaching because they "were lovers of money" (Luke 16:14), but when we read the text metaphorically, we hear it as told to us. This imaginative reading does not depend upon a one-to-one allegorical interpretation of characters and elements in the story; rather, a metaphorical shock occurs when we see our own economic practices projected side by side with those of the rich man who ignored poor Lazarus at his door. His fate of being tormented in the flames of Hades becomes a stern warning to us. We come away haunted by Abraham's sad declaration about the brothers that the rich man left behind: "If they do not listen to Moses and the prophets, neither will they be convinced even if someone rises from the dead." Does that become a word of warning for us who stand on this side of Jesus' resurrection? The Word leaps the gap.

The account of the early Jerusalem community in Acts 2:42–47 and 4:32–37 provides a positive paradigm, rather than a negative warning, for the church. But the normative function of this narrative is still metaphorical in the sense that I am describing: in this text, we are given neither rules for community life nor economic principles; instead, we are given a story that calls us to consider how in our own communities we might live analogously, how our own economic practices might powerfully bear witness to the resurrection so that those who later write our story might say, "And great grace was upon them all." The Word leaps the gap.

Such metaphorical mappings of the biblical stories onto our lives do not require us to imitate the narrated practices point for point or to repristinate ancient economic conventions in detail.[19] (Indeed, one of the salient characteristics of metaphor is its power to sustain the tension of simultaneous likeness and unlikeness between the semantic fields that are joined metaphorically.)[20] Rather, the metaphorical conjunction between the narrated church of Acts 2 and 4 and the church that we experience unsettles our "commonsense" view of economic reality and calls us to rethink our practices in radical ways.

This sort of metaphorical hermeneutic pervades Scripture itself. Consider the use that Paul makes of the story of Israel in the wilderness in 1 Corinthians 10. Writing to Gentile believers in Corinth, Paul spins a startling metaphor that links the wilderness events with the situation of Corinthians who are wrestling with the issue of whether to eat meat that has been sacrificed to idols; presumably, some of them justify the practice on the grounds that their participation in baptism and the Lord's Supper makes them immune to baleful spiritual influence. But Paul adopts a metaphorical reading strategy to induce a more complex reflection about the problem:

> *Our ancestors were all under the cloud,*
> *and all passed through the sea,*
> *and all were baptized into Moses[!] in the cloud and in the sea,*
> *and all ate the same spiritual food,*
> *and all drank the same spiritual drink. . . .*
> *Nevertheless, God was not pleased with most of them,*
> *and they were struck down in the wilderness.* 10:1–5

The metaphorical interaction here of the Exodus story and the Corinthian situation is complex. First, Paul rereads Israel's story anachronistically in terms of Christian symbolism, reading the sacraments back into the narrative; however, the hermeneutical logic then reverses direction as Paul reads the church's dangerous situation in terms of the fate that befell Israel: "Are we [i.e., we *too*] provoking the Lord to jealousy?" (1 Cor. 10:22a; cf. Deut. 32:21). Thus, the metaphorical conjunction between Israel and the Corinthian situation provides the warrant for the moral judgment that Paul calls the Corinthians to make: "Therefore, my dear friends, flee from the worship of idols" (1 Cor. 10:14).[21]

A moment's reflection will suggest that Paul's advice to the Corinthians can in turn become a metaphor for our own struggle to resist the temptations of idolatry. (In our case, the idols may tempt us with "national security" or sexual fulfillment or tokens of social status rather than with meat.) If and when that metaphorical transfer occurs, the Word leaps the gap from Corinth to America, just as it leaped from Exodus to Corinth.

If this sort of metaphorical hermeneutic is fundamental to New Testament ethics, then our normative appeals to Scripture will most often be in the *paradigmatic* mode or in the mode of *symbolic world* construction. We will seek, under the inspiration and guidance of the Holy Spirit, to reread our own lives within the narrative framework of the New Testament, discerning analogies—perhaps startling ones—between the canonical stories and our community's situation.

The great difficulty, of course, lies in knowing how to judge the validity of proposed metaphorical appropriations of the New Testament. There are no foolproof procedures. Our metaphorical readings must be tested prayerfully within the community of faith by others who seek God's will along with us through close reading of the text. The community that seeks to be shaped by Scripture must in the end claim responsibility for adjudicating between good and bad readings. In this book I have proposed one way to do this: we must ask whether any given interpretation is consonant with the fundamental plot of the biblical story as identified by the focal images of community, cross, and new creation.

3. The Church As Embodied Metaphor

Finally, the task of discerning metaphorical relations between the New Testament and the present time shades imperceptibly into the task of shaping our communities into living embodiments of the meaning of the New Testament texts.

Writing to his unruly and immature little congregation in Corinth, Paul coins a startling metaphor: "You are a letter of Christ, . . . written not with ink but with the Spirit of the living God, not on tablets of stone but on the tablets of fleshy hearts" (2 Cor. 3:3, AA).[22] Despite their squabbles and peccadilloes, he does not say to them, "Shape up; don't you know you're supposed to be a letter from Christ?" Instead, with metaphorical audacity, he says, "You *are* a letter from Christ . . . to be known and read by all." The existence of this struggling community is a communication of the gospel to the world.[23]

This remarkable claim opens a crucial insight into the hermeneutical relation between text and community, between the New Testament and the church. If moral judgment entails—as I have argued above—the making of metaphors through which the New Testament reconfigures our understanding of our communal identity, the converse is also true: the transformed community reflects the glory of God and thus illuminates the meaning of the text. According to Paul, apart from Christ a veil lies over the minds of the hearers when Scripture is read:

> *But when one turns to the Lord, the veil is removed. . . . And all of us, with unveiled faces, seeing the glory of the Lord as though reflected in a mirror, are being transformed into the same image from one degree of glory to another.* (2 Cor. 3:16, 18)

Thus, the church itself, being transformed into the image of Christ, becomes a *living* metaphor for the power of God to which the text also bears witness.[24] The power of metaphor is dialectical: the text shapes the community, and the community embodies the meaning of the text. Thus, there is a hermeneutical feedback loop that generates fresh readings of the New Testament as the community grows in maturity and as it confronts changing situations.

To be sure, this transformation of the community cannot be understood merely in terms of human hermeneutical ingenuity; as Paul insists, "this comes from the Lord, the Spirit" (2 Cor. 3:18). The church dares to articulate fresh and audacious readings of Scripture only because it relies upon the work of the Holy Spirit in the community—as promised in the New Testament texts themselves (cf. also 1 Cor. 2:6–16; John 16:12–15). The Spirit reshapes the community into unexpected metaphorical reflections of the biblical stories and thereby casts new light back onto the texts. Such illuminative conjunctions are impossible to predict and difficult to discern, but the church that seeks to deny or preclude them will find itself locked into the stifling grip of "the letter" (*gramma*, 2 Cor. 3:6), unable to hear the Word of God. Another way to put this point is to say that it is finally God who writes the metaphors.

These observations lead us to state a final dimension of the interpretive task: *right reading of the New Testament occurs only where the Word is embodied.* We learn what the text means only if we submit ourselves to its power in such a way that we are changed by it.[25] That is why George Steiner, in his important book *Real Presences*, wants to define hermeneutics as "the enactment of answerable understanding, of active apprehension."[26] The hermeneutical enterprise is not completed by the work of analysis and commentary; to interpret a text rightly is to put it to work, to perform it in a way that is self-involving so that our interpretations become acts of "commitment at risk."[27] As Nicholas Lash argues in his essay "Performing the Scriptures," "the fundamental form of the *Christian* interpretation of scripture is the life, activity, and organization of the believing community."[28]

One consequence of this hermeneutical guideline is that interpretation of the New Testament cannot be performed by isolated individuals; the embodiment of the Word happens in the body of Christ, the church. Hermeneutics is necessarily a communal activity.[29] "The performance of scripture," contends Lash, "*is* the life of the church. It is no more possible for an isolated individual to perform *these* texts than it is for him to perform a Beethoven quartet or a Shakespeare tragedy."[30] Those interpreters who not only acknowledge the importance of community but actually experience the enactment of Scripture in community are likely to provide far more perceptive and illuminating readings of the text.

It is of course paradoxical to assert that we can understand Scripture only after we see it enacted. Is it not necessary to have some understanding before action is possible? Two approaches to grasping this paradox may be suggested.

First, we are not starting from nowhere, reading the New Testament as though it had just been found sealed in a cave; we are the heirs of a community that has been reading and performing these texts for nineteen hundred years already. Our interpretation will be our own, just as a new performance of *King Lear* (Lash's example) will be a fresh product of the skills and sensibilities of the actors, but our interpretation will also stand on the shoulders of those who have gone before. We can point to prior performances that illuminate the meaning of the text. As Stanley Hauerwas is fond of saying, "The lives of the saints are the hermeneutical key to Scripture."

Second, as anyone who has ever participated in a dramatic production or a group musical performance or even a team sport can attest, something happens in the act of performance that transcends the experience of private rehearsal. The curtain goes up, the audience reacts, the interaction with other performers takes on an unforeseeable chemistry, and by the end of the play we have learned something we had not known before. In the best case—the serious performance of the great text—we learn something not only about the text but about ourselves as well.[31]

The New Testament itself repeatedly insists on the necessity of embodiment of the Word. The sequence of the verbs in Romans 12:1–2 is significant: "*Present* your bodies as a living sacrifice [Hear the metaphor!]. . . . Be *transformed* . . . that you may *discern* what is the will of God, what is good and acceptable and perfect." Knowledge of the will of God *follows* the community's submission and transformation. Why? Because until we see the text lived, we cannot begin to conceive what it means. Until we see God's power at work among us, we do not know what we are reading. Thus, the most crucial hermeneutical task is the formation of communities seeking to live under the Word.[32]

4. The Role of the Old Testament in New Testament Ethics

Some readers may wonder whether this book's focus on *New Testament* ethics has either the intent or the effect of excluding the *Old Testament* functionally from the biblical canon. Does the methodology employed here sponsor a crypto-Marcionite devaluing of Israel and Israel's Scriptures? By no means! The question is, however, an important one, and it demands a careful answer.

The first justification for concentrating primarily on the New Testament is simply the complexity of the problem. It is difficult enough to work out a coherent normative ethic on the basis of the New Testament alone; adding the entire Old Testament to the mix would complicate matters enormously. If it should prove possible to formulate a cogent New Testament ethic, the next logical step would be to ask how that ethic might fit into the larger canonical framework. Such a systematic undertaking is, unfortunately, beyond the scope of the present project.[33]

Nonetheless, no proposal about the normative use of the Bible in Christian ethics can proceed without taking the Old Testament[34] into account. How is that to be done, and where might the Old Testament fit into the process of ethical reflection? I offer three general responses to this significant problem.

(A) THE VOICE OF THE OLD TESTAMENT IN THE NEW The New Testament writings are formed within the generative matrix of Israel's Scriptures. Consequently, intertextual conversation with those Scriptures remains a major concern for the New Testament authors. It is impossible to read the New Testament rightly without hearing the voice of Israel's Scriptures *within* these early Christian documents. The New Testament texts are intelligible only as hermeneutical exercises grappling with the witness of the Scriptures, carrying on a theological conversation with a revered precursor.[35]

Paul, for example, opens his grand argument in Romans by declaring that the gospel was "promised beforehand through [God's] prophets in the holy scriptures" (Rom. 1:2), and he proceeds to make his case in the body of the letter, quoting the

Scriptures more than fifty times. In 1 Corinthians 15:3, he affirms as a matter of "first importance" the confessional tradition that designates Christ's death and resurrection as having happened "in accordance with the scriptures." Both passages just cited may preserve pre-Pauline confessional formulae; if so, this is evidence of the early and widespread conviction in early Christianity that the gospel must be understood in relation to the scriptural tradition. We see a similar concern for grounding Christian proclamation in the Old Testament in Matthew, Luke-Acts, John, Hebrews, and 1 Peter.

How does this situation bear upon the role of the Old Testament in New Testament ethics? It means that the full canon is the necessary context of intelligibility for the New Testament's treatment of any ethical topic. This recognition of the voice of the Old Testament in the New Testament can be developed only in detailed exegetical work with particular texts. In lieu of a full survey of the use of the Old Testament in New Testament ethical texts, a few examples will have to suffice as illustrations of this point.

Sometimes the authority of the Old Testament is tacitly assumed, without citation or comment. The New Testament teachings on sexual morality, for instance, regularly presuppose the Old Testament's explicit condemnations of fornication and homosexual intercourse. In other cases, the Old Testament's norms are evoked through a general reference. For example, the imperative of caring for the poor and homeless is grounded in Israel's covenant obligations, as passages such as Luke 16:19–31 show: if the rich man and his brothers would only listen to "Moses and the prophets," they would recognize their responsibility to care for the poor, as symbolized by Lazarus. The allusion here is to passages such as Deuteronomy 15:7–11, which commands the people of the covenant to "open your hand to the poor and needy neighbor in your land" (v. 11).

In situations where the New Testament writer is promulgating norms that go beyond Old Testament teaching, there is often a clear effort to recognize the difference and to explicate it in terms of the Old Testament's own deeper theological warrants. The treatment of divorce in Mark 10:2–12 and Matthew 19:1–9 is a clear instance of this hermeneutical strategy. Also noteworthy are the six antitheses in Matthew's Sermon on the Mount (Matt. 5:21–48), where Jesus' heightening of moral demand is presented as fulfillment, rather than abolition, of the Law.

In all these instances, we see that interpretation of the New Testament's ethical teachings requires us to read them in canonical context[36] and in dialogue with the Old Testament passages that are their necessary presupposition. Thus, even without an explicit survey of Old Testament ethics, the voice of the Old Testament will make itself heard in a responsible treatment of New Testament ethics.

(B) THE OLD TESTAMENT AS GROUNDING FOR COMMUNITY, CROSS, AND NEW CREATION In terms of the synthetic procedure that I have proposed for discerning unity within the New Testament's ethical witness, the whole canon is crucial to defining the focal images of *community* and *new creation*. One reason for putting *community* first, before *cross*, is to underscore Gerhard Lohfink's point that

Jesus didn't have to found a church because there already was one: Israel.[37] The meaning of the New Testament's vision of community is decisively conditioned by the covenant community of Israel. Jesus' appointment of twelve disciples was probably a symbolic act signaling his aim of bringing a restored Israel into being.[38] Paul interprets the identity of his Gentile mission communities as "Abraham's seed, heirs according to the promise" (Gal. 3:29), and he regards them as the spiritual descendants of the Israel of the Exodus generation, whom he calls "our fathers" (1 Cor. 10:1–13). There can be no understanding of the church as community in New Testament terms apart from the prior reality of God's election of a covenant people, as narrated in the Old Testament.

Likewise, the New Testament's hope for *new creation* is grounded in Old Testament prophetic traditions, especially Isaiah:

> *For I am about to create new heavens and a new earth;*
> *the former things shall not be remembered or come to mind.*
> *But be glad and rejoice forever in what I am creating;*
> *for I am about to create Jerusalem as a joy,*
> *and its people as a delight.* (ISA. 65:17–18)

The content of the New Testament's vision of new creation is informed by the rich Old Testament imagery of God as creator and eschatological redeemer of Israel. It is no accident that the Apocalypse constructs its portrayal of the New Jerusalem, in which God will wipe away every tear, out of building material supplied by Old Testament imagery.

The question of the relation of the *cross* to the Old Testament witness is, of course, a classic and fascinating problem. The focal image of the cross is far less explicitly grounded in the Old Testament than are the other two focal images that I have proposed. We should not get caught up in the artificial apologetic enterprise of trying to demonstrate that Jesus and the cross are predicted in the Old Testament; instead, it would be more accurate to say that the gospel of the cross gives the Christian tradition a hermeneutical lens through which Israel's Scripture must be read anew, so that new meanings are discerned. The death of Jesus comes to be understood as the saving event only when it is construed "according to the Scriptures" (i.e., as typological fulfillment of Abraham's sacrifice of Isaac, or of the Passover, or of the sacrifice on the Day of Atonement, or of Isaiah's suffering servant, or of the suffering figure in the royal lament psalms), but only retrospectively can it be seen that those Scriptures in any way prefigure such an event. More to the point of our immediate concerns, the cross as a paradigm for *ethics* is a distinctively new contribution of the New Testament; this is one of the features that most sharply differentiates the New Testament from the Old Testament. This observation leads to my final point.

(C.) THE NEW TESTAMENT AS LENS FOR READING THE OLD The New Testament has a normative role in Christian theology and ethics that is different from the Old Testament's role. We do not have a simple, undifferentiated canon running from Genesis to Revelation. The claim that Jesus' death and resurrection is *the* central decisive act of God for the salvation of humankind means that the cross becomes the hermeneutical center for the canon as a whole. Thus, within the canon the New Testament has a privileged hermeneutical function. This becomes especially important with regard to issues of war and violence. The Old Testament taken by itself can obviously be used to authorize armed violence; however, the New Testament radically redefines obedience through the cross in such a way that disciples of Jesus can no longer wield the sword. (This argument will be developed more fully in Part IV of this book.) The book of Revelation, as we have seen, subverts the Old Testament's holy war imagery by proclaiming that God's cosmic victory is won by the Lamb who was slaughtered and that the vocation of the saints is to participate in that victory not through violence but through "the word of their testimony."

A similar judgment would apply concerning other issues as well: wealth and material possessions, for example. Christian theology reads the Old Testament through the lens of the New Testament. Given the confession of a new and definitive disclosure of God through Jesus Christ, it could hardly be otherwise.

In sum, a treatment of New Testament ethics cannot simply fit the Old Testament into a discrete slot in the process of ethical deliberation. Rather, the Old Testament suffuses the entire enterprise, because the theological categories and images of the New Testament are pervasively drawn from the Old Testament. The story that the New Testament tells makes sense only as the continuation and climax of the story of Israel. Thus, the Old Testament is taken up dialectically and dialogically by the New Testament writers, who struggle to affirm the fundamental continuity of the gospel with Scripture and, at the same time, the newness of the gospel that requires a hermeneutical reappropriation of Scripture.[39] The only way to do justice to this complex situation in New Testament ethics is to read the New Testament texts with careful attention to their Old Testament subtexts. The exegetical work in Parts I and IV of this book is undertaken with that concern in mind.

5. Summary: Proposed Guidelines for New Testament Ethics

In the foregoing pages, I have set forth a number of methodological proposals about how the New Testament should function in the construction of normative Christian ethics. The task that remains before us is to illustrate how these proposals work in practice: in the final part of this book, we will examine a sample of ethical problems, asking how the New Testament witnesses might shape our response. Before undertaking that task, however, it may be useful to offer a final summary, gathering into one place the normative recommendations that I have offered about the use of the New Testament in ethical reflection.

I have set forth ten fundamental proposals, a few of which have corollaries attached to them. They are as follows:

1. Serious exegesis is a basic requirement. Texts used in ethical arguments should be understood as fully as possible in their historical and literary context.
   a. New Testament texts must be read with careful attention to their Old Testament subtexts.
2. We must seek to listen to the full range of canonical witnesses.
3. Substantive tensions within the canon should be openly acknowledged.
4. Our synthetic reading of the New Testament canon must be kept in balance by the sustained use of three focal images: community, cross, and new creation.
5. New Testament texts must be granted authority (or not) in the mode in which they speak (i.e., rule, principle, paradigm, symbolic world).
   a. All four modes are valid and necessary.
   b. We should not override the witness of the New Testament in one mode by appealing to another mode.
6. The New Testament is fundamentally the *story* of God's redemptive action; thus, the paradigmatic mode has theological primacy, and narrative texts are fundamental resources for normative ethics.
7. Extrabiblical sources stand in a hermeneutical relation to the New Testament; they are not independent, counterbalancing sources of authority.
8. It is impossible to distinguish "timeless truth" from "culturally conditioned elements" in the New Testament.
9. The use of the New Testament in normative ethics requires an integrative act of the imagination; thus, whenever we appeal to the authority of the New Testament, we are necessarily engaged in metaphor-making.
10. Right reading of the New Testament occurs only where the Word is embodied.

These ten proposals, I would suggest, offer practicable guidelines for New Testament ethics as a normative theological discipline. Not every reader will find these guidelines congenial; the proposals numbered 4, 5, 7, and 9 may be particularly controversial. However, those who do not accept these guidelines should take up the challenge to articulate alternative guidelines that will promote equal methodological clarity. In Part IV of this book, I shall address selected issues, bringing the New Testament to bear on the questions in light of these guidelines. The aim of this exercise will be to offer one possible model of a coherent approach to New Testament ethics.

NOTES

1. Consider, by way of contrast, this programmatic statement in *CD* I/2, 588:

> A common hearing and receiving is necessarily involved either way where the Church is the Church. The life of the Church is the life of the members of a body. Where there is any attempt to break loose from the community of hearing and receiving necessarily involved, any attempt to hear and receive the Word of God in isolation—even the Word of God in the form of Holy Scripture—there is no Church, and no real hearing and receiving of the Word of God; for the Word of God is not spoken to individuals,

> but to the Church of God and to individuals only in the Church. The Word of God itself, therefore, demands this community of hearing and receiving. Those who really hear and receive it do so in this community. They would not hear and receive it if they tried to withdraw from this community.

Or again, in II/2, 718, Barth writes:

> Whatever the divine command as focused by the apostolic exhortation may mean for each individual, it is certain that it will signify his share in the sacrificial act (Rom. 12:1) to be accomplished by a single race of brethren, in the service of God which as such is not the private business of any one individual, and in which none can act in opposition to the others in the name of God, but which can only be rendered in common.

The discussion of war and violence in III/4 should, therefore, be read within this communal frame of reference. I am indebted to Scott Saye for calling my attention to these passages.

2. See Chapter 11.1.

3. But see Verhey 1984, 176–177, who would exclude appeals to the NT at the "moral-rule" level.

4. Here I concur with Bartlett 1983, 5–6.

5. I have argued for this interpretation of Paul at considerable length in Hays 1983 and in my essay in Bassler 1991, 227–246. My treatment of Paul in this book—showing how his ethic ought to be read as an unfolding of the community's conformity to the pattern of the cross in the context of the apocalyptic world-story—should also be understood as one more attempt to demonstrate the narrative substructure of Pauline theology.

6. See Chapter 11.2.

7. This suggestion bears some resemblance to the constructive proposals of William Spohn (1995, 94–126), whose work unfortunately came to my attention too late to be integrated into the following discussion of moral judgment as an act of analogical imagination.

8. The distinction between analogy and metaphor is often pressed much too strictly. In fact, both linguistic phenomena have to do with the mapping of one semantic field onto another. The major difference between them is that metaphor is usually held to entail a greater wrenching or distortion of conventional perception, resulting in a more radical restructuring of meaning. The difference, however, is one of degree, not of kind; both metaphor and analogy posit connections between disparate entities or fields. In the discussion that follows, I will not distinguish sharply between them. In general, however, I prefer to speak of the role of the NT in shaping Christian ethics as a process of metaphor-making, because the gospel proclaimed in the NT has an apocalyptic character: it shatters and defamiliarizes the business-as-usual world. Thus, linkages between the NT stories and our world will characteristically effect the radical reorientation associated with metaphor. The literature on metaphor is massive. For useful discussions, see the following: Wheelwright 1962; Wheelwright 1968; Ricoeur 1976, 45–69; Ricoeur 1977; M. Johnson 1981, 3–47; McFague 1982; Gerhart and Russell 1984; Lash 1986, 95–119; Kittay 1987; Soskice 1985; Ollenburger 1990; Kraftchick 1993.

9. Räisänen 1990, 3.

10. Gabler 1980 [1787]. In private correspondence (Aug. 15, 1994), Stanley Hauerwas suggested to me the intriguing thesis that the project of factoring out a "pure" biblical theology from the actual historical form of the Bible was implicitly anti-Semitic: what the Enlightenment sought was a theology purified of its disagreeable historical (Jewish) particularity.

11. Lessing 1956 [1777], 55.

12. Lessing 1956 [1777], 53.

13. Gerhart and Russell 1984, 112–114.

14. Gerhart and Russell 1984, 114.

15. Ricoeur 1975, 75–106.

16. For an extended discussion of the way in which Paul's citation of an early Christian hymn (Phil. 2:5–11) enacts this sort of "remapping" of existence, see Kraftchick 1993. I am indebted to Steve Kraftchick for several illuminating conversations on the topic of metaphor and for a number of important bibliographical references.

17. Kraftchick 1993, 15, summing up insights of Kittay 1987.

18. Of course, the metaphorical juxtaposition allows the transfer of meaning both ways. The community also reinterprets the text in light of the church's experience: see section 3.

19. Again Kraftchick (1993, 23): "Because metaphor is not an isomorphic mapping of all relationships within one field to another, but a highlighting of some and suppression of others, it is not necessary to make a one to one mapping of the Christ onto the believer. . . . In the present case [the Philippians hymn] the content domain of Christian existence between the exaltation and final resurrection is ordered and given structure by the semantic field provided by the hymn."

20. Such tension is built into "the very copula of metaphorical utterance," which requires the reader to discern both the "is" and the "is not" of poetic assertion (Ricoeur 1976, 68). As Thomas Greene has observed (1982, 26), such metaphorical linkages conceal "profundities of unreason." Consider the following examples: "I am

the true vine, and my Father is the vinegrower" (John 15:1); "Beware of the leaven of the Pharisees and the leaven of Herod" (Mark 8:15, AA); "He will baptize you with the Holy Spirit and fire" (Matt. 3:11).

21. For more extended discussion of the metaphorical strategy at work in this text, see Hays 1989, 91–104.

22. For discussion of the passage and explanation of this translation, see Hays 1989, 125–131.

23. Here is yet another illustration of the way in which metaphorical statements defy literalistic isomorphic interpretation.

24. For more extensive discussion of this point, see Hays 1989, 131–149.

25. "Is it ever unethical to submit ourselves to a Biblical text?" This provocative question is posed to me by A. Katherine Grieb in private correspondence (June 15, 1995). I would answer along these lines: when I speak of submission to "the text," I do not mean individual texts (e.g., 1 Tim. 2:11–15) construed as prooftexts; rather, I mean the text of Scripture as a whole, construed in light of the images of community, cross, and new creation. To submit to isolated teachings might indeed sometimes be "unethical" or unfaithful to the will of God as disclosed in the fuller canonical witness.

26. Steiner 1989, 7.

27. Steiner 1989, 8.

28. Lash 1986, 42. Cf. Steiner 1989, 8: "The true hermeneutic of drama is staging."

29. See Fowl and Jones 1991.

30. Lash 1986, 43.

31. Cf. Lash 1986, 41.

32. See Meeks 1986a; Hays 1989, 125–131, 149–153, 191–192.

33. For various approaches to OT ethics, see J. Barton 1982; Kaiser 1983; Wilson 1988; Birch, 1991.

34. Many scholars in recent years have preferred to speak of "the Hebrew Bible" rather than "the Old Testament." This terminology reflects a laudable concern to respect the integrity of the religion of Israel and to avoid the possibly supersessionist connotations of the distinction between "Old" and "New" Testaments. In the context of a purely historical study of the texts, the term "Hebrew Bible" is both descriptively accurate and sensible. In the context of Christian theology, however, this term is not quite appropriate, for several reasons. First, it suggests that these texts really belong to someone else, that they are in some sense not part of the Christian Bible. The church, however, has from the beginning emphatically confessed these texts as Scripture, as a word of revelation and promise (hence, "testament") from the one God who spoke to Abraham, Moses, and the prophets, and who was also the God and Father of Jesus Christ. Thus, an inquiry into the normative use of these texts for the church will do better to designate them not as a neutral object for historical study ("Hebrew Bible") but as an integral part of the community's confessional heritage ("Old Testament"). Second, the Old Testament has been received in the church more often than not through a linguistic medium other than Hebrew. In the early centuries, Christians—including the writers of the NT books—read Scripture in Greek versions; subsequently, these texts were known to the church through Latin and vernacular translations. The Hebrew text remains, of course, the authority against which all these translations must be checked, but the fact remains that functionally this material has not operated as an authority in the church as the Hebrew Bible. The oddity of the usage might be illustrated if we ask whether it would be theologically felicitous to refer to the New Testament as "the Greek Bible." Such reference would make sense only in contexts where we seek to draw attention specifically to the original linguistic medium. Thus, rather than speaking of the Hebrew Bible and the Greek Bible, it makes more sense to retain the traditional designations of Old and New Testaments, with the clear proviso that "Old" does not mean "bad" or "obsolete." The notion that there is something pejorative in the term "Old Testament" is partly a feature of the late twentieth century's obsession with novelty. In antiquity, everyone believed that the new was suspect and trivial; only traditions that were certifiably old could claim dignity and authority. As a concession to the modern aversion to "old" things, James A. Sanders has proposed that Christians should call the two testaments of the Bible "the First Testament" and "the Second Testament." This usage implicitly preserves the theological emphasis on promise and continuity of action of the one God, but it leaves the reader wondering whether to expect a Third Testament, or even a continuing series. The terms "Old Testament" and "New Testament" convey the Christian confession that the death and resurrection of Jesus Christ is the decisive pivot-point in God's history of dealing with humanity. Thus, in view of all these considerations, I shall continue, in my discussion of the theological authority of the whole biblical canon, to refer to "the Old Testament."

35. See Hays 1989 for discussion of this phenomenon in the letters of Paul.

36. See the programmatic suggestions of Brevard Childs 1970, 123–138.

37. Lohfink 1984 [1982], xi.

38. E. P. Sanders 1985, 98–106.

39. For recent literature on this, see Hübner 1990; Hübner 1993; Childs 1992.

PART FOUR

The Pragmatic Task

Living Under the Word: Test Cases

We turn now to the task of making specific judgments about ethical issues. After surveying the various moral visions of the New Testament writers, defining the ground of coherence underlying those visions, and grappling with the problem of hermeneutical method, we come at last to the practical question that drives all the others: How shall the Christian community shape its life in obedience to the witness of the New Testament?

No single, definitive answer can be given to such a question, because the community of faith continually confronts new circumstances that require us to work out our salvation with fear and trembling, forming fresh imaginative judgments—just as the New Testament writers themselves did—in response to the challenges of our time. We can, however, seek to illustrate the implications of the proposed approach to New Testament ethics by considering a series of particular problems that stand before the church at the end of the twentieth century. In the final part of this book, we will examine, in light of the New Testament, five issues: violence, divorce, homosexuality, anti-Judaism, and abortion. These are by no means the only challenges confronting the church. Rather, they represent a cross-section of important ethical issues, chosen here for purposes of demonstrating the outworking of New Testament ethics according to the proposals that I have articulated in the first three parts of this study.

These issues are not necessarily the most important problems of our day, nor are they singled out here as the ethical concerns that receive the greatest emphasis within the New Testament itself. Indeed, my own judgment would be that if we were seeking to identify the ethical matters at the heart of Christian discipleship as spotlighted by the New Testament, we would be compelled to turn our attention to the following four issues: (1) the renunciation of violence, (2) the sharing of possessions, (3) the overcoming of ethnic divisions (particularly the division between Jew and Gentile), and (4) the unity of men and women in Christ. The final portion of this book will undertake extended discussions of (1) and (3) and will offer some brief reflections about (2) in the concluding summary section. The fourth issue—

the relation of men and women in Christ—will be addressed tangentially in my discussion of divorce and remarriage, but a full treatment of this complex problem would render an already lengthy study entirely unmanageable.[1] Thus, I reluctantly set it aside for the present.

What, then, is the logic of the selection and arrangement of the five issues picked for discussion? They are chosen to illustrate *methodologically* how the proposals made in Parts II and III work out in practice when applied to different configurations of evidence within the New Testament itself. By way of preview of the argument, I would summarize the situation in the following way:

- With regard to the issue of *violence,* the New Testament bears a powerful witness that is both univocal and pervasive, for it is integrally related to the heart of the kerygma and to God's fundamental elective purpose.
- With regard to *divorce,* the various New Testament texts share a common underlying perspective, but the casuistic development of that perspective leads to diverse judgments and applications.
- With regard to *homosexuality,* the New Testament evidence is univocal, but there are only a few directly pertinent texts, and these few passages are not closely related to the fundamental plot of the gospel story—at least not obviously so; furthermore, other serious moral arguments seem to weigh against the univocal witness of the canonical texts.
- With regard to *anti-Judaism,* the New Testament contains texts in fundamental tension with one another, some of which appear to the morally sensitive reader at the end of the twentieth century to be profoundly objectionable; thus, the interpreter is forced to make a choice between irreconcilable options.
- With regard to *abortion,* there are no New Testament texts at all that address the question directly.

Thus, our normative judgments about these five problems must respond appropriately to the different kinds and weights of evidence with which the New Testament presents us. In the pages that follow, I will take a stand on each of these questions and seek to demonstrate not only how the New Testament speaks to the issues but also how the methodological recommendations of the foregoing sections of this book inform my ethical response. One of the purposes for treating a range of different issues is to show that the decisions reached are not based on ad hoc prooftexting; rather, they represent the coherent outworking of a considered set of judgments about the way in which the New Testament ought to form the life of the church. One reason that appeals to the authority of Scripture often seem unconvincing is that the church has been inconsistent in shaping its life according to Scripture. For example, some voices in the church have insisted stoutly on the normative authority of a few texts dealing with sexual morality while ignoring or finessing equally clear New Testament teachings on possessions and violence. In such circumstances, is it any wonder that the church's witness is ineffectual? If the church is to have any credibility, any integrity, we must seek to be a Scripture-shaped community in *all* respects, not merely on selected issues of our own preference.

As I take a stand on these five issues, some of which are bitterly controversial, it is important to emphasize that I do not presume to speak *ex cathedra*. Rather, I offer a series of discernments to the church in prayerful humility. I offer them as *readings* of the New Testament witness on questions of urgent concern. These readings are set forth in a spirit analogous to Paul's advice to the Corinthian church "concerning virgins": "I have no command of the Lord, but I give my opinion as one who by the Lord's mercy is trustworthy" (1 Cor. 7:25). That is to say, I set forth my positions with conviction, but in the recognition that serious Christians can and do hold differences of opinion about these matters. Thus, I am seeking not to "excommunicate" those who differ from me but rather to *persuade* them of the biblical grounds for my position. I will not weary the reader's patience by repeating these qualifiers at every turn in the following pages. Let it be said once in the beginning: all the normative proposals set forth here should be understood as invitations to dialogue and to a deeper immersion in the New Testament texts themselves.

It will become clear as the discussion proceeds that the nature of the New Testament evidence warrants greater and lesser degrees of certainty, along with greater and lesser degrees of emphasis, on these particular test issues. For example, I will argue that the normative witness of the New Testament against armed violence is powerful, virtually univocal, and integrally related to the central moral vision of the New Testament texts. On the other hand, the issue of abortion, which is not treated explicitly in the New Testament at all, requires a more qualified set of judgments. The other topics treated here fall somewhere along the spectrum between these two extremes.

In sum, the following discussion offers one attempt to demonstrate in practice a coherent approach to New Testament ethics. For each test issue the general procedure will be the same: a preliminary sketch of the problem, followed by (1) discussion of key texts addressing the issue; (2) placement of the key texts in canonical context with the aid of the three focal images of *community*, *cross*, and *new creation*; (3) hermeneutical reflection about the mode in which the texts speak and their relation to other sources of authority; and (4) normative conclusions, with some attention to practical implications for the embodiment of the New Testament's message.

Advice to the reader: do not read Part IV of this book without having first read Parts I through III. The normative judgments offered here are meant to be read only in light of the foregoing analysis of the content of the New Testament and the methods appropriate to using it as an authority for Christian ethics.

NOTE

1. A full examination of this issue would require us to consider the relation between men and women not only in marriage but also in ministry, in friendship, and in the workplace. A massive cultural shift has occurred in this century that has required the church to reexamine its traditional teachings and practices on this question. A major aspect of this reexamination involves scrutiny of the NT texts that have traditionally warranted the subordination of women, as well as those texts that have sponsored visions of their dignity and freedom. The method for doing NT ethics that I have outlined would enable us to address this problem in fruitful ways; nonetheless, the task is too large to undertake here. I must leave it to the reader or for some future occasion. I would reiterate, however, that my decision to forego discussion of the problem in no way entails a judgment that the relation between men and women is of lesser importance as an ethical issue. As I have noted, I regard it as a central issue of our time.

Chapter 14

Violence in Defense of Justice

A small Episcopal church in Washington, D.C., features a lovely stained-glass window portraying Jesus as the Good Shepherd, carrying a lamb in his arms. The inscription at the bottom of the window reads, "Testimonial to the boys of this parish who served in the Great War." This touching tribute—obviously predating the tragic necessity of tallying World Wars with Roman numerals—joins countless other memorials in churches all over Europe and North America in bearing silent witness that the church has accepted war as a practice that Christians may at times be required to pursue. It may be seen as a sad duty; the church may lament as well as celebrate its dead soldiers. Rarely, however, has the church fundamentally questioned whether military service is consistent with Christian service. The stained-glass window suggests the hope that the "boys" who fought—and who may have been lost—in the war might be protected in the loving arms of Jesus. Yet the iconography unintentionally poses an ironic question: Is it appropriate for those who profess to be followers of this gentle Shepherd to take up lethal weapons against enemies?

More broadly, is it ever God's will for Christians to employ violence in defense of justice? The New Testament contains important texts that seem to suggest that this question must be answered in the negative, but human experience presents us over and over again with situations that appear to require violent action to oppose evil. An often-cited example is Dietrich Bonhoeffer's agonized decision to participate in a plot to kill Hitler. Similarly, some versions of liberation theology have advocated revolutionary violence against oppressors. And Christian theology, at least since the time of Augustine's *City of God*, has usually countenanced the participation of believers in police forces and armies deemed necessary for the preservation of order and a relative approximation of justice.

Of course, alongside such accounts of theologically principled recourse to violence, one can cite countless grim instances in which Christians have mindlessly embraced the logic of violence. A favorite example in my files is a newspaper story from 1986:

> An Ozzy Osbourne concert has been cancelled after protests and threats against the singer's life . . . in Tyler, Texas, where the controversial British rock star was to appear Saturday. Several groups, including religious leaders and the City Council of PTAs, said Osbourne represented anti-Christian values. . . . County Sheriff J. B. Smith told Osbourne's security chief of anonymous threats against the singer, including the use of fire and dynamite.[1]

When we hear of threats to commit terrorist murder as a way of preventing a singer from representing "anti-Christian values," we cannot help but wonder what "Christian" values are being defended. Though this case seems absurd, the mentality at work here is not materially different from the knee-jerk impulse that has afflicted humanity since Cain—the impulse to impose our will through violence.

History bears haunting witness that this impulse is all too easily baptized and confirmed, so that divine sanction is claimed for killing. We have seen this tragic scenario played out most recently in the former Yugoslavia, where the "ethnic cleansing" of Bosnian Muslims by nominally Christian Bosnian Serbs has been sanctioned by the church. Metropolitan Nikolaj, the highest-ranking church official in Bosnia, has publicly endorsed the architects of the ethnic-cleansing policy as followers of "the hard road of Christ," for example, and "Serbian priests have blessed militias on their return from kill-and-plunder expeditions."[2] The consequences of such ecclesiastical blessing of violence are predictable and tragic: "Ethnonationalists celebrated the feast of St. Sava, founder of the Serbian church, by burning down the 300-year-old mosque at Trebinje and massacring the town's Muslims."[3]

At this cultural distance, it appears easy to condemn such violence as a perversion of Christian ethics, but what are we to say about the Catholic military chaplain who administered mass to the Catholic bomber pilot who dropped the atomic bomb on Nagasaki in 1945? Father George Zabelka, chaplain for the Hiroshima and Nagasaki bomb squadrons, later came to repent of his complicity in the bombing of civilians, but his account of that time is a stunning judgment on the church's acquiescence in violence.

> To fail to speak to the utter moral corruption of the mass destruction of civilians was to fail as a Christian and as a priest as I see it. . . . I was there, and I'll tell you that the operational moral atmosphere in the church in relation to mass bombing of enemy civilians

> was totally indifferent, silent, and corrupt at best—at worst it was religiously supportive of these activities by blessing those who did them. . . . Catholics dropped the A-bomb on top of the largest and first Catholic city in Japan. One would have thought that I, as a Catholic priest, would have spoken out against the atomic bombing of nuns. (Three orders of Catholic sisters were destroyed in Nagasaki that day.) One would have thought that I would have suggested that as a minimal standard of Catholic morality, Catholics shouldn't bomb Catholic children. I didn't. I, like the Catholic pilot of the Nagasaki plane, "The Great Artiste," was heir to a Christianity that had for seventeen hundred years engaged in revenge, murder, torture, the pursuit of power, and prerogative violence, all in the name of our Lord.
>
> I walked through the ruins of Nagasaki right after the war and visited the place where once stood the Urakami Cathedral. I picked up a piece of censer from the rubble. When I look at it today I pray God forgives us for how we have distorted Christ's teaching and destroyed his world by the distortion of that teaching. I was the Catholic chaplain who was there when this grotesque process that began with Constantine reached its lowest point—so far.[4]

It is difficult to read such accounts without recalling the story of Jesus' weeping over Jerusalem, because "the things that make for peace" were hidden from their eyes (Luke 19:41–42).

The just war tradition—the subject of much public debate by pundits during and after the United States' Desert Storm offensive against Iraq in the Gulf War of 1991—was developed in Christian theology precisely as a check against the indiscriminate use of violence and, at the same time, as a way of articulating norms that would justify the participation of Christians in armed conflict under the authority of the state.[5] As our foregoing survey of theological ethicists has shown, however, there are serious questions to be raised about whether this tradition can itself be justified on the basis of the New Testament's teaching. As Zabelka remarked, the just war theory is "something that Christ never taught or even hinted at."[6]

What norms concerning the use of violence might be derived from the New Testament? In order to focus our consideration of the issue of violence, let us begin by considering the passage in the Sermon on the Mount that is often seen as the clearest call for Jesus' disciples to forsake violence.

1. Key Text: Matthew 5:38–48

> *You have heard that it was said, "An eye for an eye and a tooth for a tooth." But I say to you, Do not resist an evildoer. But if anyone strikes you on the right cheek, turn the other also; and if anyone wants to sue you and take your coat, give your cloak as well; and if anyone forces you to go one mile, go also the second mile. Give to everyone who begs from you, and do not refuse anyone who wants to borrow from you. You have heard that it was said, "You shall love your neighbor and hate your enemy." But I say to you, Love your enemies and pray for those who persecute you, so that you may be children of your Father in heaven; for he makes his sun rise on the evil and on the good, and sends rain on the righteous and*

on the unrighteous. For if you love those who love you, what reward do you have? Do not even the tax collectors do the same? And if you greet only your brothers and sisters, what more are you doing than others? Do not even the Gentiles do the same? Be perfect, therefore, as your heavenly Father is perfect.

The church has often been baffled by this text, which poses clear but terribly difficult requirements for those who would heed Jesus' teaching. Interpreters have generally sought to find ways to explain away the apparent literal force of the mandates of Matthew 5. The seeming impossibility of Jesus' teaching has led Christians to propose various ingenious interpretations that mitigate the normative claim of this text.[7] We may briefly summarize several of the most influential of these interpretations as follows:

- These words offer a vision of life in the eschatological kingdom of God; thus, they are not literally to be put into practice under the conditions of present earthly existence. Reinhold Niebuhr's "impossible ideal" interpretation is one permutation of this option.
- These words prescribe an "interim ethic" for Jesus' disciples on the assumption that the end of history and the final judgment of God are to occur very soon—so soon that one need not consider the long-term results of attempting to live this perfectionistic ethic. This option is the converse of the first, seeing the teaching not as an ultimate ideal but as a temporary arrangement born in the fever of eschatological enthusiasm.
- These words literally forbid self-defense, but they do not preclude fighting in defense of an innocent third party. This was Augustine's reading of the text.
- These words are a "counsel of perfection" (see v. 48); they apply only to those who aspire to belong to a special class of holy Christians, such as monks or clergy, not to the general run of believers.
- These words serve to show how impossible it is to live up to God's standard of righteousness (see 5:20); thus, they convict our consciences and show that we are sinners in need of grace.
- These words are located within a specific social setting. Therefore, the scope of the injunctions is delimited: for example, "Do not resist an evildoer" means "Do not oppose an evil person in court."[8] Likewise, the "enemy" refers only to personal enemies within the Palestinian village setting, not to foreign or political enemies.[9]

A careful exegetical consideration of the passage in its broader Matthean context, however, will demonstrate that none of these proposals renders a satisfactory account of Matthew's theological vision. Let us consider first of all how the passage fits into its immediate literary frame, the Sermon on the Mount (Matthew 5–7).

These verses comprise the climactic fifth and sixth antitheses ("You have heard that it was said. . . . But I say to you . . .") in the first chapter of the Sermon on the

Mount, Jesus' basic training on the life of discipleship. The placement of this material in Matthew's Gospel showcases it front and center. The Sermon, which constitutes the first of the five great blocks of teaching material in Matthew (see Chapter 4), stands at the beginning of Jesus' ministry in Galilee, immediately after he first calls disciples (Matt. 4:18–22) and begins to attract a crowd (4:23–25). Thus, the Sermon stands in Matthew's narrative scheme as Jesus' programmatic disclosure of the kingdom of God and of the life to which the community of disciples is called. The delivery of the Sermon from a mountain probably echoes the Exodus story of Moses and suggests that Jesus' teaching is a new Torah, a definitive charter for the life of the new covenant community.

This teaching material is presented in Matthew 5:1–2 as instruction for the *disciples* of Jesus. At the end of the Sermon, however (7:28–29), we are told that "the *crowds* were astounded at his teaching, for he taught them as one having authority"; thus, the instruction for the disciples takes place openly before the crowd, emphasizing Matthew's conviction that the community of disciples is called to be a light for the world (5:14–16). The disciples are called to live in accordance with the stringent standards articulated in the six antitheses precisely because of a concern to exemplify the reality of the kingdom of God in a pluralistic and sinful world.

The character of that kingdom, however, is surprising. The Beatitudes (5:3–12) contravene common sense by declaring that God's blessing rests upon the mourners, the meek, the peacemakers, and (especially) those who are persecuted. (Note that vv. 11–12 reiterate and expand the blessing pronounced on the persecuted in v. 10.) Thus, the Beatitudes limn an upside-down reality, or—more precisely—they define reality in such a way that the usual order of things is seen to be upside down in the eyes of God. The community's vocation to be "salt" and "light" for the world (5:13–16) is to be fulfilled precisely as Jesus' followers embody God's alternative reality through the character qualities marked by the Beatitudes. The community of Jesus' followers is to be "a city built on a hill," a model *polis* that demonstrates the counterintuitive peaceful politics of God's new order.

Matthew is concerned to affirm that this countercultural *polis* must be understood as a fulfillment rather than a negation of the Torah (5:17–20). The righteousness to which Jesus' followers are called intensifies and exceeds the most rigorous standards of Israel's most scrupulous interpreters of the Law. Thus, the six antitheses (5:21–48) raise the ante by radicalizing the demands of the Law. They sketch the identity of the new community that Jesus is bringing into being. That sketch can hardly be mistaken for a comprehensive new legal code; rather, it suggests by way of a few examples the character of this new community in which anger is overcome through reconciliation (5:21–26), lust is kept under discipline (5:27–30), marriage is honored through lifelong fidelity (5:31–32), language is simple and honest (5:33–37), retaliation is renounced (5:38–42), and enemy-love replaces hate (5:43–48). Even though this portrayal of the community of disciples is new and revelatory, it is at the same time a fulfillment of the deepest truth of the Law and the prophets (cf. also Matt. 22:34–40).

In sum, the kingdom of God as figured forth in Matthew 5 is full of surprises. Matthew offers a vision of a radical countercultural community of discipleship characterized by a "higher righteousness"—a community free of anger, lust, falsehood, and violence. The transcendence of violence through loving the enemy is the most salient feature of this new model *polis;* it is noteworthy that the antitheses dealing with these themes stand at the climactic conclusion of the unit (5:38–48). Instead of wielding the power of violence, the community of Jesus' disciples is to be meek, merciful, pure, devoted to peacemaking, and willing to suffer persecution—and blessed precisely in its faithfulness to this paradoxical vision.

How does this portrayal of discipleship fit into the wider Matthean context? It has sometimes been suggested that the Sermon on the Mount is a block of traditional material that stands in tension with Matthew's own theological perspective.[10] Such a view, however, fails to recognize the homology between the Sermon's account of discipleship and Matthew's overall portrayal of Jesus. In the temptation narrative (4:1–11), Jesus renounces the option of wielding power over the kingdoms of the world, choosing instead to worship and serve God alone. In the three passion predictions (16:21–23, 17:22–23, 20:17–19), Jesus foretells his fate as one who will be "persecuted for righteousness' sake," and he intimates that those who follow him will suffer the same fate (16:24–26).[11] In Gethsemane, Jesus struggles with this vocation but aligns his will with the Father's will that he should drink the cup of suffering (26:36–47). As Yoder has persuasively suggested, the temptation to refuse the cup is precisely the temptation to resort to armed resistance.[12] Jesus, however, chooses the way of suffering obedience instead of the way of violence. This point is even clearer in Matthew's story than in the synoptic parallels, for at the moment of Jesus' arrest, he admonishes the disciple who attempts armed resistance: "Put your sword back into its place; for all who take the sword will perish by the sword" (26:51–54). As Ulrich Mauser observes, "Jesus does not yield to the temptation to preserve his life by resisting evil with evil's own armor. If anything in Matthew's Gospel, this scene at the arrest is the authentic interpretation of the sentence in the Sermon on the Mount, 'Do not resist an evildoer' (Matt. 5:39)."[13] Thereafter, the passion narrative plays out to its inevitable conclusion: Jesus dies powerless and mocked (27:39–44). Thus, the death of Jesus exemplifies the same character qualities that are taught as normative for Jesus' disciples in Matthew 5.

The ending of Matthew once again reinforces the teaching of the Sermon on the Mount. The resurrection serves as God's decisive vindication of Jesus' authority to teach and guide the community. In the Gospel's final scene, Jesus appears to the eleven disciples, once again on a mountain, and declares, "All authority in heaven and on earth has been given to me. Go therefore and *make disciples of all nations,* baptizing them in the name of the Father and of the Son and of the Holy Spirit, *and teaching them to obey everything that I have commanded you*" (28:18a–20b, emphasis mine). The task of Jesus' disciples is to make more disciples; they are charged not merely to win converts but to train all who are baptized in the same disciplines that they have themselves learned from Jesus' teaching. And what disciplines are these? When we read Matthew as a whole, we see that what Jesus has commanded includes preeminently the teaching of the Sermon on the Mount.

This conclusion to the story makes it abundantly clear that Matthew does not regard the discipleship of the Sermon on the Mount as an impossible ideal. It is, rather, the way of life directly commanded by Jesus, who possesses "all authority in heaven and on earth." The calling of discipleship is not impossible, for the powerful risen Lord is present in and with the community: "Remember, I am with you always, to the end of the age" (28:20b). (This assurance indicates clearly that Matthew sees the age of the church's life not as a fleeting interim but as an extended historical period in which Jesus remains present to guide the church.) The only question is whether the disciples will heed what they have been taught. To be sure, there will be doubts and failures within the community of the faithful; as we have seen,[14] Matthew's apparently perfectionistic ethic acknowledges human sin and frailty and summons the community to practices of mutual correction and forgiveness. But this recognition of human fallibility by no means constitutes an abandonment of the directly normative claims of the Sermon; Matthew has only a word of judgment to pronounce on those who say, "Lord, Lord," but do not obey the will of God, as disclosed in Jesus' teaching. On the day of judgment, Jesus will say to them, "I never knew you; go away from me, you evildoers" (7:21–23). The commandments of the Sermon are not only divinely ordained, they are also finally eminently practical: the person who hears Jesus' words *and acts on them* will be like the wise man who built his house on rock, whereas the person who hears Jesus' words *and does not act on them* has built a house on sand (7:24–27). To live under the authority of Jesus' counterintuitive wisdom is to live securely in accord with God's ultimate order. That is the persistent message of Matthew the evangelist.

The foregoing discussion has laid to rest five of the six strategies listed above for mitigating the normative force of Matthew 5:38–48 within the church:

➢ The teaching of nonviolent enemy-love is not merely an eschatological vision or an ideal. Jesus practiced it to his own death, and the Gospel of Matthew presents this teaching as a commandment that is to be obeyed by Jesus' disciples.

➢ Matthew, writing at least fifty years after the death of Jesus, is well aware that history is continuing and that the church must reckon with an extended period of time "until the end of the age." During that time, he envisions the church's mission as one of discipling all nations to obey Jesus' commandments, including the commandment of nonviolent enemy-love.

➢ There is no basis in Matthew's Gospel for restricting the prohibition of violence merely to a prohibition of self-defense. The example given in Matthew 5:39 ("Turn the other cheek") certainly refers to self-defense—we might say *even* to self-defense. But the larger paradigm of Jesus' own conduct in Matthew's Gospel indicates a deliberate renunciation of violence as an instrument of God's will.

That is part of the temptation that Jesus rejects in the wilderness and again at Gethsemane. He does not seek to defend the interests of the poor and oppressed in Palestine by organizing armed resistance against the Romans or against the privileged Jewish collaborators with Roman authority. Rather, his activity consists of healing and proclamation. He preaches love and submits to being persecuted and killed. Perhaps most tellingly, he does not commend the disciple who takes up the sword to defend him against unjust arrest; rather, uttering a prophetic word of judgment against all who "take the sword," he commands that the sword be put away. Armed defense is not the way of Jesus. There is no foundation whatever in the Gospel of Matthew for the notion that violence in defense of a third party is justifiable. In fact, Matthew 26:51–52 serves as an explicit refutation of this idea.

- The suggestion that the teaching of the Sermon is intended only for a special class of supersanctified Christians is discredited by the Great Commission at the conclusion of the Gospel. *All* baptized believers are to be taught to observe *all* that Jesus commanded.
- The idea that the perfectionistic teachings of the Sermon are intended merely to compel us to recognize our need of grace is decisively refuted by the conclusion of the Sermon itself (Matt. 7:21–27). These words are meant to be put into practice.

All the arguments I have presented here get leverage on the interpretation of Matthew 5:38–48 by placing it within the narrative context of Matthew's Gospel, read as a literary and theological unity. Some proposals for reinterpreting the passage seek to get behind Matthew's construal of the tradition to what the historical Jesus "really" said or meant. Whatever the interest of such an attempt, we must insist that the canonical narrative context governs the normative theological use of the text; the historical reconstruction remains speculative.[15]

The above arguments leave untouched only that class of exegetical proposals that attempt to restrict the normative application of Matthew 5:38–48 by placing the original sense of the words in a limited social sphere. These proposals can be assessed only through closer exegetical attention to the passage itself. We turn now to that task.

In most of the six antitheses, the teaching of Jesus constitutes an intensification—rather than an abrogation—of the requirements of the Law. The Law prohibits murder, but Jesus forbids even anger; the Law prohibits adultery, but Jesus forbids even lust. In the fifth antithesis (5:38–42), however, Jesus actually overrules the Torah (despite 5:17–18). The *lex talionis* ("An eye for an eye and a tooth for a tooth") may have originated, as most commentators note, as a rule limiting the vengeance that might be exacted by an aggrieved party: that is, *no more than* an eye for an eye. That is how the rule apparently functions in Exodus 21:24. If the saying is understood in these terms, then Matthew 5:39 can be understood as conforming to the pattern of heightening the Torah's demand: where the Torah restricts retaliation, Jesus forbids it altogether.

In Deuteronomy 19:15–21, however, the *lex talionis* has a prescriptive function. False witnesses are to be punished with exactly the same punishment that would have been inflicted on the one whom they have falsely accused. Deuteronomy insists that the punishment must be exacted as a deterrent to future offenses:

> *If the witness is a false witness, having testified falsely against another, then you shall do to the false witness just as the false witness had meant to do to the other. So you shall purge the evil from your midst. The rest shall hear and be afraid, and a crime such as this shall never again be committed among you. Show no pity: life for life, eye for eye, tooth for tooth, hand for hand, foot for foot.* (Deut. 19:18b–21)

No bleeding-heart sympathy here! Just punishment must be meted out rigorously to ensure social order. But where Deuteronomy insists, "Show no pity," Jesus says, "Do not resist an evildoer." The Law's concern for maintaining stability and justice is supplanted by Jesus' concern to encourage nonviolent, long-suffering generosity on the part of those who are wronged.[16] This extraordinary change of emphasis constitutes a paradigm shift that effectually undermines the Torah's teaching about just punishment for offenders.

One important aspect of that shift is the identity of the implicit addressees of the teaching. In Deuteronomy 19:15–21, the implied addressees are the persons who wield judicial authority in society. In Matthew 5:43–48, however, the implied addressees are powerless persons, the victims of hostile actions by those who wield power; the responsibility for punishing offenders is left in the hands of God. This shift speaks volumes about the composition and social location of the community for which Matthew's Gospel was written. The community of Jesus' disciples, as envisioned in the Sermon on the Mount, stands outside the circle of power. This is a point to which we must return when we reflect on the hermeneutical appropriation of the passage.

Robert Guelich seeks to limit the scope of Matthew 5:39a to the courtroom setting by connecting the passage very closely with the legal scenario of Deuteronomy 19:15–21. He proposes that 5:39a "forbids the opposing of an evil person in court" and that the verb *antistēnai* ("resist") refers to seeking "legal vindication" against a false accuser.[17] This is a possible meaning for the word, although *antistēnai* is certainly not a technical term for legal opposition (and it does not normally have this special sense elsewhere in the New Testament). Guelich's suggestion does make Matthew 5:39a an apt response to the saying quoted in 5:38, and it establishes a plausible connection with 5:40, which also speaks of a legal proceeding. Guelich's proposal has difficulty, however, in accounting for the other specific illustrations in verses 39–42, including 5:39b: "But if anyone strikes you on the right cheek, turn the other also." Guelich follows David Daube's suggestion that the reference to the *right* cheek implies not a punch but a slap with the back of the hand, "an action that was particularly degrading to a Jew." Thus, "In Matthew's case of insult more than injury, one would need to take legal action to gain recompense and vindication."[18] It is this recourse to legal action, according to Guelich, that Jesus forbids here.

In response to this proposal, three observations must be made: (1) The scenario of declining to pursue legal remedies for an *insult* has nothing to do with the matter of resistance to *false accusation;* thus, the alleged logical connection to verses 38–39a and to Deuteronomy 19:15–21 is tenuous. (2) The notion of an insult that would require legal action to redress is imported into the text here on the basis of the arbitrary assumption that a blow on the right cheek could be delivered only with the back of the adversary's right hand.[19] Despite the widespread acceptance of this interpretation by commentators, however, nothing in the Matthean context explicitly indicates that such a scenario is envisioned. The text does *not* say, "If anyone insults you by slapping you with the back of the hand. . . ." Nor does it say, "If anyone strikes you on the right cheek, do not take him to court"; rather, it says, ". . . turn the other cheek," an action that emphasizes *physical* nonretaliation. (3) The larger argument falls apart if verses 41–42 cannot be integrated into the theory about forgoing legal defense. Guelich is forced to acknowledge that these illustrations (going the second mile and giving to all who ask) have nothing to do with his construal of 5:39. He can only say of these illustrations that "their presence here is . . . indicative of Matthew's faithful use of tradition even when only tangentially related to his primary redactional intention."[20] If that can be said of verses 41–42, however, why not of verse 39 also? A reading of Matthew's redactional intention, in order to be persuasive, must account for all the material that is present in the text.[21]

In fact, the loosely connected sayings of verses 39–42 all serve as illustrations of the peaceloving and generous character that the teaching of Jesus seeks to inculcate. Jesus' disciples are to relinquish the tit-for-tat ethic of the *lex talionis* and live in a way that eschews retaliation and defense of self-interest. The actions commanded here are fully consistent with the attributes singled out for blessing in the Beatitudes: humility, meekness, and a readiness to make peace and to suffer for the sake of righteousness.

The posture of the community is not to be one of supine passivity, however.[22] The actions positively prescribed here are parabolic gestures of renunciation and service. By doing more than what the oppressor requires, the disciples bear witness to another reality (the kingdom of God), a reality in which peacefulness, service, and generosity are valued above self-defense and personal rights. Thus, the prophetic nonresistance of the community may not only confound the enemy but also pose an opportunity for the enemy to be converted to the truth of God's kingdom.[23]

The teaching of Matthew 5:39, then, *is* about nonviolence, even though the passage as a whole has a larger vision of the kingdom of God in view. The admonition not to strike back is one of several "focal instances" that figuratively depict the Matthean vision for the community of discipleship.[24] It is not simply a rule prohibiting a certain action; rather, it is a symbolic pointer to the character of the peaceful city set on a hill.

The material in the sixth and final antithesis (Matt. 5:43–48) is less complex. The positive command to "love your enemies and pray for those who persecute you" is formulated unambiguously. By loving enemies, the disciples of Jesus, as the light of the world, reflect the character of God, who also offers mercy to the righteous and unrighteous alike.

There are, however, three problems in the unit that are immediately pertinent to our concern about the text's normative import: What is the source of the saying quoted in verse 43? What "enemies" are in view in verse 44? And what is the meaning of the exhortation to "be perfect" in verse 48? Let us examine each of these in turn.

(A) THE SOURCE OF THE SAYING In each of the first five antitheses, the foil to Jesus' pronouncement is a quotation from Scripture. In the final antithesis, the command to love the neighbor is taken from Leviticus 19:18, but there is no Old Testament command to "hate your enemy." Thus, it is not clear precisely what tradition Matthew is setting in opposition to the teaching of Jesus. The Psalms are full of bitter imprecations against the enemies of the righteous, and it is possible that a specific passage such as Psalm 139:21–22 might stand behind Matthew 5:43:

> *Do I not hate those who hate you, O Lord?*
> *And do I not loathe those who rise up against you?*
> *I hate them with perfect hatred;*
> *I count them my enemies.*

Perhaps more apt, however, is William Klassen's judgment that it is not necessary to look for a specific scriptural text.

> The formula "Be good to [or love] your friends and hate your enemies" was widespread in the ancient world and occurs in many layers of documentation. Rather than look in vain throughout Jewish sources, including Qumran, for these exact words, we should simply treat them as part of the general folk wisdom that Jesus' listeners had heard—words that were well known to Matthew's audience as well.[25]

On this view, the final antithesis would pose a new standard for obedience to God, not in opposition to the Torah but over against conventional attitudes and interpretations of the Torah. The limitation of love to the "neighbor"—that is, the fellow member of Israel's covenant community—is replaced by an expansive love that encompasses even the enemy. This dramatic extension of the imperative to love may be related to Matthew's general thematic interest in showing how the gospel reaches beyond Israel's ethnic boundaries to the Gentiles.

(B) THE NATURE OF THE "ENEMIES" Richard Horsley has argued that the term *echthroi* ("enemies," v. 44) referred in Jesus' original historical setting not to foreign or military enemies but only to "personal enemies," other residents of small Palestinian villages who found themselves pitted against one another for scarce economic resources. Since they are unable to express resentment against "the dominant system . . . , subject peoples tend to vent their frustration in attacks against one another."[26] The primary burden of Jesus' teaching, therefore, was to get the poor peasants to stop squabbling with one another and to cooperate for their mutual economic benefit. Thus, the exhortation to "love your enemies" cannot be construed as a general ethical principle, nor can it be applied directly to issues of war and enmity between nations.[27]

Against this interesting proposal, we offer several objections:

- There is nothing in the Matthean context to suggest the precise social situation that Horsley describes: no accounts of village squabbles or conflicts.
- Indeed, the immediate context suggests that the *echthroi* are those who persecute the followers of Jesus because of their adherence to "righteousness"—that is, the way of Jesus. Compare 5:10–12 and the synonymous parallelism of 5:44:

  Love your enemies

  Pray for those who persecute you.
- Horsley's proposal cannot be supported by lexicographical evidence. The term *echthroi* is generic. It is often used in biblical Greek of national or military enemies. It appears, for instance, in Deuteronomy 20:1 (the very next sentence after the "eye for an eye" passage quoted in Matt. 5:38): "When you go out to war against your enemies [LXX: *echthroi*], and see horses and chariots, an army larger than your own, you shall not be afraid of them; for the Lord your God is with you, who brought you up from the land of Egypt." (Note also Luke 19:43, which refers to *echthroi* laying siege to the city of Jerusalem.) In the absence of any explicit qualifiers in Matthew 5:44, there is no reason to restrict the application of the saying. As Heinz-Wolfgang Kuhn has correctly perceived, "The directive is without boundaries. The religious, the political, and the personal enemy are all meant."[28]
- Finally, Horsley's proposal seeks to reconstruct the hypothetical meaning of the saying in the lifetime of the Jesus of history, as opposed to its meaning within the setting of Matthew's Gospel. But it is the latter, as we have insisted, that must be determinative for the use of the text in normative New Testament ethics. (Horsley's historical reconstruction is in any case subject to serious question, but to argue the historical case against him would carry us too far afield from our present concerns.) His proposal cannot be sustained as a reading of the Sermon on the Mount in its canonical form. Horsley himself acknowledges that the Matthean context not only supports but actually requires the more general interpretation of enemies as outsiders and persecutors.[29]

(C) THE MEANING OF "PERFECT" Finally, how are we to understand the daunting directive of Matthew 5:48: "Be perfect [*teleios*], therefore, as your heavenly Father is perfect"? Is it a conclusion only to the sixth antithesis or to the whole series of six? There are good reasons to prefer the latter option. The admonition sums up the whole unit by blending echoes of two important Old Testament texts: Leviticus 19:1–2 ("The Lord spoke to Moses, saying: Speak to all the congregation of the people of Israel and say to them: You shall be holy, for I the Lord your God am holy") and Deuteronomy 18:13 LXX ("[When you come into the land that the Lord your God is giving you . . .] You shall be *teleios* before the Lord your God").[30] The concluding exhortation of Matthew 5 catches up these ideas together: the community of Jesus' disciples is to reflect the holiness of God in scrupulous obedience to the will of God as disclosed through the teaching of Jesus, who has taken the place of Moses as the definitive interpreter of the Law.[31] The result will be that those who see the "good works" of the new covenant community, the *polis* set on a hill, will "give glory to your Father in heaven" (5:16). The term "mature," another possible translation of *teleios*, is too weak to capture the full force of Matthew's theological claim. The point is that the community of Jesus' disciples is summoned to the task of showing forth the character of God in the world. That character is nowhere more decisively manifest than in the practice of loving enemies (5:44–45), a practice incompatible with killing them.[32] Those who are peacemakers are to be called "sons of God" (5:9) because, like God, they love their enemies (5:45, cf. 5:48).[33] Thus, the church's embodiment of nonviolence is—according to the Sermon on the Mount—its indispensable witness to the gospel.

2. Synthesis: Violence in Canonical Context

Our exegetical investigation of Matthew 5:38–48 has led to the conclusion that the passage teaches a norm of nonviolent love of enemies. Within the context of Matthew's Gospel, the directive to "turn the other cheek" functions as more than a bare rule; instead, as a "focal instance" of discipleship, it functions metonymically, illuminating the life of a covenant community that is called to live in radical faithfulness to the vision of the kingdom of God disclosed in Jesus' teaching and example. Taken alone, this text would certainly preclude any justification for Jesus' disciples to resort to violence. The question that we must now consider is how Matthew's vision of the peaceful community fits into the larger witness of the canonical New Testament. Do the other texts in the canon reinforce the Sermon on the Mount's teaching on nonviolence, or do they provide other options that might allow or require Christians to take up the sword?

When the question is posed this way, the immediate result—as Barth observed[34]—is to underscore how impressively univocal is the testimony of the New Testament writers on this point. The evangelists are unanimous in portraying Jesus as a Messiah who subverts all prior expectations by assuming the vocation of suffering rather than conquering Israel's enemies. Despite his stinging criticism of those in positions of authority, he never attempts to exert force as a way of gaining social or political power. (On the one possible exception to this generalization—the demonstration against commercial activity in the Temple—see further below.) He imposes an order of silence to keep his disciples from proclaiming him as Messiah until he has redefined the title in terms of the cross, and he instructs the disciples that their vocation must be the same as his (Mark 8:27–9:1). He withdraws from the crowd that wants to "take him by force to make him king" (John 6:15). At every turn he renounces violence as a strategy for promoting God's kingdom (e.g., Luke 9:51–56, where he rebukes James and John for wanting to call down fire from heaven to consume unreceptive Samaritans), and he teaches his followers to assume the posture of servanthood (Mark 10:42–45; John 13:1–17) and to expect to suffer at the hands of the world's authorities (Mark 13:9–13; John 15:18–16:4a). The hope of vindication and justice lies not with worldly force—that is the satanic temptation rejected at the beginning of his ministry—but in God's eschatological power. Jesus' death is fully consistent with his teaching: he refuses to lift a finger in his own defense, scolds those who do try to defend him with the sword, and rejects calling down "legions of angels" to fight a holy war against his enemies (Matt. 26:53). In Luke's account, he intercedes for the enemies responsible for his execution (Luke 23:34a, if this belongs to the text).[35]

In the Acts of the Apostles, Luke tells a story of an emergent movement whose activity consists of preaching, healing, worship, and sharing. Those who carry the word to the various outposts of the Roman world do not claim territory through military operations; rather, they proclaim the gospel and often find themselves the targets of violence. The Christian response to this violence is modeled by the martyr Stephen, who in turn mirrors Jesus in his death by praying for the forgiveness of his enemies (Acts 7:60).

In the letters of Paul, the death of Christ is interpreted as God's peace initiative:[36]

> *God proves his love for us in that while we were still sinners Christ died for us. Much more surely then, now that we have been justified by his blood, will we be saved through him from the wrath of God. For if while we were enemies, we were reconciled to God through the death of his Son, much more surely, having been reconciled, will we be saved by his life.* (Rom. 5:8–10)

How does God treat enemies? Rather than killing them, Paul declares, he gives his Son to die for them. This has profound implications for the subsequent behavior of those who are reconciled to God through Jesus' death: to be "saved by his life" means to enter into a life that recapitulates the pattern of Christ's self-giving. As we have argued above,[37] the imitation of Christ in his self-emptying service for the sake of others is a central ethical motif in Paul (e.g., Phil. 2:1–13). It is evident, then, that those whose lives are reshaped in Christ must deal with enemies in the same way that God in Christ dealt with enemies.

The most important Pauline hortatory passage that deals directly with the issue of violence (Rom. 12:14–21) bears so many material similarities to the Sermon on the Mount that some critics have sought to demonstrate Paul's dependence here on Jesus-tradition, despite the sparsity of verbatim agreement.[38] For the purposes of synthetic reflection about the problem of violence in New Testament ethics, we need not settle the question of Paul's direct knowledge of Jesus' teachings; we need only mark the significant convergence in their accounts of the calling of the community of God's people:

Bless those who persecute you; bless and do not curse them. . . . Live in harmony with one another. . . . Do not repay anyone evil for evil, but take thought for what is noble in the sight of all. If it is possible, so far as it depends on you, live peaceably with all. Beloved, never avenge yourselves, but leave room for the wrath of God, for it is written, "Vengeance is mine, I will repay, says the Lord." No, "if your enemies are hungry, feed them; if they are thirsty, give them something to drink; for by doing this you will heap burning coals on their heads."[39] *Do not be overcome by evil, but overcome evil with good.*

(ROM. 12:14, 16a, 17–21)

Though the governing authority bears the sword to execute God's wrath (13:4), that is not the role of believers. Those who are members of the one body in Christ (12:5) are never to take vengeance (12:19); they are to bless their persecutors and minister to their enemies, returning good for evil. There is not a syllable in the Pauline letters that can be cited in support of Christians employing violence. Paul's occasional uses of military imagery (e.g., 2 Cor. 10:3–6, Phil. 1:27–30) actually have the opposite effect: the warfare imagery is drafted into the service of the gospel, rather than the reverse. He appropriates battle imagery as a way of describing the apocalyptic context in which the community lives, but the actual "fighting" is done through the proclamation of the gospel and through obedient yielding of one's members to God as *hopla* ("weapons") of righteousness (Rom. 6:13). The implications of this metaphorical logic are nicely summarized in 2 Corinthians 10:3–4: "For though we live in the flesh, we do not wage war according to the flesh, for the weapons of our warfare are not fleshly" (RH). This revisionary imagery is subsequently further elaborated by Ephesians 6:10–20: the community's struggle is not against human adversaries but against "spiritual forces of darkness," and its armor and weapons are truth, righteousness, peace, faith, salvation, and the word of God. Rightly understood, these metaphors witness powerfully *against* violence as an expression of obedience to God in Christ.

Likewise, in Hebrews and the catholic Epistles we encounter a consistent portrayal of the community as called to suffer without anger or retaliation. The author of Hebrews asks the readers to recall their earlier experience:

[Y]ou endured a hard struggle with sufferings, sometimes being publicly exposed to abuse and persecution, and sometimes being partners with those so treated. For you had compassion on those who were in prison, and you cheerfully accepted the plundering of your possessions, knowing that you yourselves possessed something better and more lasting.

(HEB. 10:32b–34)

Having been through such experiences in the past, the readers are exhorted to maintain their confidence and to remain faithful in the present. The plundering of possessions is to be accepted "with joy" (*meta charas*) rather than resisted by force. Here, without the slightest verbal echo, we find a substantive parallel to Matthew 5:40. Similarly, 1 Peter is pervasively concerned with the community's response to trials and suffering (1 Pet. 1:6–7, 3:13–18, 4:12–19, 5:8–10). Such afflictions are interpreted, in a manner reminiscent of Paul, as "sharing Christ's sufferings" (4:13). Even more explicitly than Paul, however, the author of 1 Peter holds up the suffering of Christ as a paradigm for Christian faithfulness:

> *For to this you have been called, because Christ also suffered for you, leaving you an example, so that you should follow in his steps. . . . When he was abused, he did not return abuse; when he suffered, he did not threaten; but he entrusted himself to the one who judges justly.*[40] (1 PET. 2:21, 23; cf. 3:17–18)

The appeal is to Jesus' conduct in his passion, not to any specific teaching of Jesus, but the familiar picture that emerges here is thoroughly consonant with the texts that we have been considering in the Sermon on the Mount. A final passage that should be noted is James 4:1–3, which attributes "wars and fightings"[41] to the "cravings" that are at war within the individual: "You want something and do not have it; so you commit murder." James never entertains the notion that there might be circumstances in which fighting and killing are necessary for some good purpose.

The Apocalypse, as we noted in our descriptive account in Part I, has often been misconstrued as a warrant for warlike attitudes among Christians. In fact, as our analysis there demonstrated, such a reading of the text is far wide of the mark. In fact, the book seeks to inculcate in its readers precisely the same character qualities that we have seen extolled through the rest of the New Testament canon: faithful endurance in suffering, trust in God's eschatological vindication of his people, and a response to adversity modeled on the paradigm of "the Lamb who was slaughtered." The saints conquer the power of evil through "the blood of the Lamb and by the word of their testimony" (Rev. 12:11), not through recourse to violence.

Thus, from Matthew to Revelation we find a consistent witness against violence and a calling to the community to follow the example of Jesus in *accepting* suffering rather than *inflicting* it. There are, however, a few New Testament texts that are sometimes cited as warrants for Christian participation in war, or at least as qualifiers to the radical nonviolence of the Sermon on the Mount. We must now turn our attention to these passages that seem to stand in tension with the central witness of the New Testament concerning violence.

Matthew 10:34: "Do not think that I have come to bring peace to the earth; I have not come to bring peace, but a sword." Read out of context as a prooftext, this verse certainly would appear to contradict everything I have said so far about the witness of the New Testament. In context, however, the difficulty disappears. The saying occurs within Matthew's mission discourse (10:5–42), instructing the disciples about how to conduct the mission of preaching and healing that he is sending them to perform. The discourse is full of warnings that the disciples will face opposition, arrest, floggings, and calumny. They should expect to be opposed even by their own families. In this context, the "sword" of verse 34 is a metaphor for the division that will occur between those who proclaim the good news of the kingdom and those who refuse to receive it. The meaning of the saying is explicated in verses

35–36: "For [*gar*] I have come to set a man against his father, and a daughter against her mother, and a daughter-in-law against her mother-in-law; and one's foes will be members of one's own household." The Lukan version of the same saying paraphrases the metaphor of the "sword" to avoid any possible misunderstanding: "Do you think that I have come to bring peace to the earth? No, I tell you, but rather *division!*" (Luke 12:51, emphasis mine). If we are to think at all of any literal sword in Matthew 10:34, we will immediately see that the disciples of Jesus are to be its *victims* (as in vv. 18, 21, 28) rather than its wielders. The disciples are not to "fear those who kill the body." Their mission is to go without even a staff (v. 10)—and certainly without a sword—and to preach the good news. By so doing, they will be following the example of Jesus, taking up the cross and losing their lives for his sake (10:38–39). To read this verse as a warrant for the use of violence by Christians is to commit an act of extraordinary hermeneutical violence against the text.

Luke 22:36b: "The one who has no sword must sell his cloak and buy one." Again in this passage the reference to a sword has a figurative purpose. On the night of his arrest, just after his last supper with the disciples, Jesus reminds his followers of an earlier phase in their mission when they could rely on the goodwill and hospitality of those to whom they preached; however, they must now be prepared for a time of rejection and persecution. They will need to take along their own provisions, and the sword serves as a vivid symbol of the fact that they must now expect to encounter opposition. As I. Howard Marshall observes, "The saying can be regarded only as grimly ironical, expressing the intensity of the opposition which Jesus and the disciples will experience, endangering their very lives."[42] The disciples, however, give continuing evidence of their incomprehension of Jesus' destiny by taking the figurative warning as a literal instruction: "Lord, look, here are two swords." Jesus' response is one of impatient dismissal, indicating that they have failed to grasp the point: "Enough, already!"[43] Joseph Fitzmyer explains that "the irony concerns not the number of the swords, but the whole mentality of the apostles. Jesus will have nothing to do with swords, even for defense."[44] The truth of this reading is confirmed by the subsequent scene at Jesus' arrest: The disciples ask, "Lord, should we strike with the sword?" and one of them, without waiting for an answer, cuts off the ear of the high priest's slave. Jesus, however, rebukes him ("No more of this!") and *heals* the injured slave (Luke 22:49–51). Here again, literal armed resistance is exposed as a foolish misunderstanding of Jesus' message.

Such a misunderstanding is particularly ironic in view of Luke 22:37: the purpose of the figurative remark about buying a sword was to warn the disciples that the Scripture was about to be fulfilled. The passage cited is Isaiah 53:12: "And he was counted among the lawless."[45] It should not escape the attention of Luke's readers that this citation comes from the concluding verse of Isaiah's prophetic description of the suffering servant,[46] whose life was "handed over to death" for the sake of the sins of many. This is the sort of dramatic irony that Luke, as an author, savors:[47] while Jesus is trying to instruct the disciples about his destiny as the righteous sufferer, they are brandishing swords about, as though such pathetic weapons could promote God's kingdom. No wonder Jesus impatiently puts an end to the conversation.

Mark 11:15–19 and Parallels: The Temple Incident. A third passage that is sometimes cited to counter pacifist readings of the New Testament is the story of Jesus' protest action against commercial activity in the Temple.[48] He drives out those who are engaged in selling and buying, and he overturns "the tables of the moneychangers and the seats of those who sold doves" (Mark 11:15b). In the Johannine version of the story, he even makes "a whip of cords" in order to drive out sheep and cattle (John 2:15a). What are we to make of this narrative? Does it show that Jesus sometimes countenanced violence? Certainly, there is a sense in which the actions described here are violent, particularly the overturning of the tables; Jesus does not politely ask the sellers and moneychangers to leave. But the exact character of this "violent" activity must be carefully delineated.

Jesus' actions must be understood as acts of prophetic symbolism. He enters the Temple, stages a dramatic demonstration, offers public teaching about the meaning of his action, and then departs at the end of the day (Mark 11:19). He makes no effort to assume permanent control over the operation of the Temple. The action is interpreted by the two prophetic texts cited in Jesus' teaching (Mark 11:17 and parallels): Isaiah 56:7 and Jeremiah 7:11. The first of these ("My house shall be called a house of prayer for all the nations") evokes the eschatological vision of Isaiah 55–66 in which God will restore and redeem Jerusalem, bringing all nations to worship God truly there.[49] An integral part of that vision is the abolition of violence, as symbolized by the peaceful coexistence of the wolf and the lamb and the promise that "they shall not hurt or destroy on all my holy mountain" (Isa. 65:25). The other phrase ("You have made it a den of robbers") is an allusion to Jeremiah's Temple Sermon (Jer. 7:1–15), a vehement call for repentance that condemns Israel for stealing, murder, adultery, false swearing, and idolatry. To continue the charade of Temple worship while committing these offenses is to "trust in deceptive words to no avail" (Jer. 7:8). Thus, Jesus' demonstration in the Temple must be understood, in light of the prophetic passages cited, as *a call for repentance* and *a sign that the promised eschatological restoration is at hand.* By framing the incident with the story of the withered fig tree, Mark may also interpret Jesus' action as a prophecy of the Temple's destruction.[50] John, citing Psalm 69:9 ("Zeal for your house will consume me," John 2:17), reads the story as prefiguring Jesus' death; additionally, his account of Jesus' words ("Stop making my father's house a marketplace," John 2:16) may allude to Zechariah's apocalyptic vision of the day of the Lord, in which "there shall no longer be traders in the house of the Lord of hosts" (Zech. 14:21). In any case, none of the evangelists presents this incident as a coup attempt to seize power over the religious or political establishment in Jerusalem. It is, rather, an act of symbolic "street theater,"[51] in line with precedents well established in Israel's prophetic tradition (e.g., Jer. 27:1–22). Thus, it is an act of violence in approximately the same way that antinuclear protesters commit an act of violence when they break into a navy base and pour blood on nuclear submarines. No one is hurt or killed in Jesus'

Temple demonstration. The incident is a forceful demonstration against a prevailing system in which violence and injustice prevail, a sign that Jesus intends to bring about a new order in accordance with Isaiah's vision of eschatological peace. It is difficult to see how such a story can serve as a warrant for Christians to wage war and kill.

Soldiers in the New Testament. Finally, there are a number of New Testament passages in which soldiers appear as characters. In Luke's Gospel a group of soldiers, in response to the preaching of John the Baptist, ask what they should do. John replies, "Do not extort money from anyone by threats or false accusation, and be satisfied with your wages" (Luke 3:14–15). John does not suggest that they abandon their profession; they are merely charged to pursue it honestly without exploiting the civilian population. Similarly, Matthew and Luke relate a story of Jesus' healing of the servant of a centurion; Jesus marvels at the faith of the centurion and does not raise any questions about his military connections (Matt. 8:5–13, Luke 7:1–10). Another centurion at the foot of the cross is the first human character in Mark's Gospel to recognize Jesus as the Son of God (Mark 15:39).[52] Finally, the centurion Cornelius and his household are the first Gentile converts in Acts (10:1–11:18). Cornelius is said to be "an upright and God-fearing man" (10:22, cf. 10:34–35), and the outpouring of the Holy Spirit on his household is presented as the decisive sign of God's acceptance of Gentiles. Unlike the later case of the Ephesian converts who publicly burn their magic books as a sign of renouncing their former practices (Acts 19:18–20), there is no indication that Cornelius is required to renounce his service in the Roman army.

This evidence, taken cumulatively, suggests that the New Testament writers did not see participation in the army as sinful a priori, nor was the question of military service a question being debated in their communities. The role of these soldiers in the New Testament narratives, however, must be seen in proper context: precisely as Roman soldiers, they serve to dramatize the power of the Word of God to reach even the unlikeliest people. They are set beside tax collectors (Luke 3:12–13) as examples of how John's preaching reached even the most unsavory characters. Similarly, Mark makes a theological point through the shock value of having the true confession enunciated by a complete outsider at the moment of Jesus' death. Even the righteous centurion whose servant is healed by Jesus serves as a foil, a surprising exception whose faith stands in paradoxical contrast to Israel's lack of faith (Matt. 8:10–13). The narrative and theological force of this story is analogous to that of the saying, "Truly I tell you, the tax collectors and the prostitutes are going into the kingdom of God ahead of you" (Matt. 21:31); just as that saying does not necessarily commend extortionate tax-farming and prostitution as continuing practices, so these stories about centurions cannot be read as endorsements of military careers for Christians. To be fair, however, there is nothing within the New Testament itself that explicitly excludes or forbids such careers.[53] Thus, of the texts we have examined that might seem to stand in tension with the New Testament's central message of peacemaking, these narratives about soldiers provide the one possible legitimate basis for arguing that Christian discipleship does not necessarily preclude the exercise of violence in defense of social order or justice.

Old Testament Holy War Texts. Of course, the greatest intracanonical challenge to the witness of the Sermon on the Mount concerning nonviolence and love of enemies comes not from any New Testament text but from the Old Testament, particularly the holy war texts. Here we find texts that explicitly command Israel to kill its enemies. Deuteronomic legislation decrees that when Israel's army conquers a town, they are to "put all its males to the sword" and to take the women, children, and livestock as booty (Deut. 20:10–15). This law applies to towns outside Israel's immediate territory. But within the land claimed by Israel, captured towns are to be annihilated: "You must not let anything that breathes remain alive" (Deut. 20:16–18). We find a narrative illustrating this commandment in 1 Samuel 15, where the Lord, speaking through the prophet Samuel, commands King Saul to slaughter the Amalekites: "Now go and attack Amalek, and utterly destroy all that they have; do not spare them, but kill both man and woman, child and infant, ox and sheep, camel and donkey" (1 Sam. 15:3). Saul's subsequent failure to carry out this command to the letter, by sparing King Agag of the Amalekites, is presented in the narrative as a grievous fault, the basis for God's rejection of Saul as king of Israel. It is left to Samuel to fulfill the will of the Lord by hewing Agag in pieces before the altar (1 Sam. 15:7–35).

The Christian tradition has dealt with such texts in a variety of ways. Sometimes they have been claimed as literal warrants for violent crusades. Barth took these passages as indicators that we cannot constrain God's freedom to command, even to command violent action. (Thinking along similar lines, I, as a young Christian during the Vietnam War era, found myself unable to justify claiming conscientious objector status because I could not claim that I would never fight; God might command me, as he had commanded Saul, to slay an enemy.) Alternatively, Christians have sometimes read such texts allegorically as indicators that we should utterly extirpate all sin from our lives. Whatever validity such an interpretation may have for purposes of private edification, it can hardly pass muster as exegesis. Taken on its own terms, the Old Testament obviously validates the legitimacy of armed violence by the people of God under some circumstances.

This is the point at which one of the methodological guidelines proposed in Part III must come into play: the New Testament's witness is finally normative. If irreconcilable tensions exist between the moral vision of the New Testament and that of particular Old Testament texts, the New Testament vision trumps the Old Testament. Just as the New Testament texts render judgments superseding the Old Testament requirements of circumcision and dietary laws, just as the New Testament's forbidding of divorce supersedes the Old Testament's permission of it, so also Jesus' explicit teaching and example of nonviolence reshapes our understanding of God and of the covenant community in such a way that killing enemies is no longer a justifiable option. The sixth antithesis of the Sermon on the Mount marks the hermeneutical watershed. As we have noted, the Old Testament distinguishes the obligation of loving the neighbor (that is, the fellow Israelite) from the response to enemies: "[B]ut I say to you, Love your enemies and pray for those who persecute you, so that you may be children of your Father in heaven." Once that word has been spoken to us and perfectly embodied in the story of Jesus' life and death, we cannot appeal back to Samuel as a counterexample to Jesus. Everything is changed by the cross and resurrection. We now live in a situation in which we confess that "in Christ God was reconciling the world to himself, not counting their trespasses against them, and entrusting the message of reconciliation to us" (2 Cor. 5:19). Those who have been entrusted with such a message will read the Old Testament in such a way that its portrayals of God's mercy and eschatological restoration of the world will take precedence over its stories of justified violence.

Having completed this overview of the New Testament's teaching on the question of violence, we must ask how our reading of this material is brought into focus by the three images of *community*, *cross*, and *new creation*.

Community. When we read the New Testament material on violence through the focal lens of *community*, we recognize that the church as a whole is called to live the way of discipleship and to exemplify the love of enemies.[54] Matthew's call to be the light of the world, Paul's call to embody the ministry of reconciliation, Revelation's call to the saints to overcome the dragon through the word of their testimony—all these calls are addressed to the church corporately and can be answered only by the church as a body. The vocation of nonviolence is not exclusively an option for exceptionally saintly individuals, nor is it a matter of individual conscience; it is fundamental to the church's identity and *raison d'être*. Mainline Protestantism has usually treated this matter as though it were a question of individual moral preference, supporting the "right" of individual conscientious objection but also generally sanctioning Christian participation in war. In light of the New Testament's call to the community as a whole to embody the teaching of Jesus, however, this position is untenable and theologically incoherent. The church is called to live as a city set on a hill, a city that lives in light of another wisdom, as a sign of God's coming kingdom. That is one reason that the examples of individual "good soldiers" in the New Testament weigh negligibly in a synthetic statement of the New Testament's witness. Clearly it is *possible* for a Christian to be a soldier, possible for a Christian to fight. But if we ask the larger question about the vocation of the community, the New Testament witness comes clearly into focus: the community is called to the work of reconciliation and—as a part of that vocation—suffering even in the face of great injustice. When the identity of the community is understood in these terms, the place of the soldier within the church can only be seen as anomalous.

Cross. The other wisdom in light of which the community lives is the paradoxical wisdom of the cross (see 1 Cor. 1:18–2:5). Not only the teaching but, more important, the example of Jesus is determinative for the community of the faithful. The passion narrative becomes the fundamental paradigm for the Christian life.

This means that the community is likely to pay a severe price for its witness: persecution, scorn, the charge of being ineffective and irrelevant. When the New Testament canon is read through the focal lens of the *cross*, Jesus' death moves to the center of attention in any reflection about ethics. The texts cannot simply be scoured for principles (the imperative of justice) or prooftexts ("I have not come to bring peace but a sword"); rather, all such principles and texts must be interpreted in light of the story of the cross. The meaning of *dikaiosynē* ("justice") is transfigured in light of the one Just One who exemplifies it: Christ has become our *dikaiosynē* (1 Cor. 1:30). When we hear Jesus' saying that he has come to bring not peace but a sword, we can hear it only within the story of a Messiah who refuses the defense of the sword and dies at the hands of a pagan state that bears the power of the sword. The whole New Testament comes rightly into focus only within this story. Whenever the New Testament is read in a way that denies the normativity of the cross for the Christian community, we can be sure that the text is out of focus.

New Creation. None of the New Testament's witness makes any sense unless the nonviolent, enemy-loving community is to be vindicated by the resurrection of the dead. Death does not have the final word; in the resurrection of Jesus the power of God has triumphed over the power of violence and prefigured the redemption of all creation. The church lives in the present time as a *sign* of the new order that God has promised. All of the New Testament texts dealing with violence must therefore be read in this eschatological perspective. For example, even though Matthew 5:38–48 contains no explicit reference to eschatology, its directives must be read through the lens of the image of *new creation.* Otherwise, "Turn the other cheek" becomes a mundane proverb for how to cope with conflict. But this is ridiculous: if the world is always to go on as it does now, if the logic that ultimately governs the world is the immanent logic of the rulers of this age, then the meek are the losers and their cheek-turning only invites more senseless abuse. As a mundane proverb, "Turn the other cheek" is simply bad advice. Such action makes sense only if the God and Father of Jesus Christ actually is the ultimate judge of the world *and* if his will for his people is definitively revealed in Jesus. To use Matthew's own language, turning the other cheek makes sense if and only if it really is true that the meek will inherit the earth, if and only if it really is true that those who act on Jesus' words have built their house on a rock so that it will stand in the day of judgment. Turning the other cheek makes sense if and only if all authority in heaven and on earth has been given to Jesus.

Or, to take another example, Paul's counsel that we should bless our persecutors, eschew vengeance, and give food and drink to our enemies makes sense if and only if it really is true that "the night is far gone, the day is near" (Rom. 13:12)—the day when all creation will be set free from bondage (Rom. 8:18–25). To put this in theological shorthand, the New Testament's ethical teaching must always be situated within the context of eschatological hope. If we fail to read the New Testament texts on violence through the lens of *new creation,* we will fall into one of two opposing errors: either we will fall into a foolish utopianism that expects an evil world to receive our nice gestures with friendly smiles, or we will despair of the possibility of living under the "unrealistic" standards exemplified by Jesus. But if we do read the texts through the lens of *new creation*, we will see that the church is called to stand as God's sign of promise in a dark world. Once we see that, our way, however difficult, will be clear.

3. Hermeneutics: Responding to the New Testament's Witness Against Violence

Having reflected upon the way in which the images of *community*, *cross*, and *new creation* focus the New Testament's cumulative witness concerning violence, we must next ask how that witness is to be received. Can or should we adhere to the New Testament's teaching? If so, in what way? In what sense does it speak to the church after the passage of so much time?

In light of the extensive analysis in Part III of this book of different hermeneutical responses to the problem of violence, it will be possible to present succinctly a series of normative judgments about this complex problem, with frequent reference back to the options presented by the five theologians previously discussed.

(A) THE MODE OF NORMATIVE APPROPRIATION In Part III, I promulgated the guideline that *New Testament texts must be granted authority in the mode in which they speak.* One of the striking results of our survey of the New Testament evidence is that we find the testimony against the use of violence articulated in all four modes.

In the *rule* mode, we have a series of clear directives: if someone hits you, turn the other cheek; bless those who persecute you; never avenge yourselves; if your enemy is hungry, feed him. As we have suggested, these maxims function as more than simple rules: they hint, by metonymy, at the peacemaking character of the elect people of God. That observation, however, does not diminish their obligatory character as rules; to be a participant in the faithful community is to find one's life directly addressed and governed by these imperatives.

In the *principle* mode, we find several more generally formulated norms for ethics: love your enemies; take up the cross; live in harmony with one another; "as shoes for your feet put on whatever will make you ready to proclaim the gospel of peace" (Eph. 6:15). Perhaps the Beatitudes should also be classified under this heading: "Blessed are the peacemakers, for they will be called children of God," and so forth.[55] Nowhere in the New Testament is there an instance of any writer appealing to a principle such as love or justice to justify actions of violence.

The *paradigm* mode is the preeminent mode of the New Testament canon's pervasive witness against violence. The Gospel passion narratives are at the center of that witness, along with Paul's kerygma that tells the story of how God has reconciled enemies through the death of his Son. The story of Jesus' exemplary renunciation of violence is in turn reflected in stories such as the death of Stephen and in the exhortation of 1 Peter that believers should follow "in his steps." Nowhere does the New Testament provide any positive model of Jesus or his followers employing violence in defense of justice. (In this respect the New Testament is quite remarkable within the world's literature.) Jesus' protest action in the Temple—often seized upon as such a model warranting the use of violence—does not really answer very well to this description.[56] The soldiers who respond in faith to the gospel provide the one fragile basis in New Testament narrative for a more positive assessment of Christians serving in occupations that require the use of force; however, it is noteworthy that none of the positive stories about soldiers who become believers actually depicts them fighting or using force in God's service. Their military background is no more commended by these stories than are the occupations of other converts, such as tax collectors and prostitutes.

Finally, the New Testament texts depict a *symbolic world* in which the real struggle is not against flesh and blood, in which the only weapons that the church wields are faith and the Word of God. The truth about reality is disclosed in the cross: God's power is disclosed in weakness. Thus, all who are granted to see the truth through Jesus Christ will perceive the world through the lenses of the Beatitudes and the strange narrative of the Apocalypse, in which the King of kings and Lord of lords is the slaughtered Lamb. The power of violence is the illusory power of the Beast, which is unmasked by the faithful testimony of the saints. In this symbolic world, wars and fightings are caused by divided and unholy desires within the individual (James), but those who are made whole in Christ become ambassadors of reconciliation and participate in the body of Christ, the community whose oneness signifies the ultimate reconciliation of the world to God. And the deepest truth about reality is rooted in the character of God, who loves enemies and seeks to reconcile them to himself through the death of Christ.

Thus, in all four modes, the evidence accumulates overwhelmingly against any justification for the use of violence. As we have already noted, Niebuhr's attempt to justify violence—as a necessity in order to approximate the ideal of love through a relative enforcement of justice—is hermeneutically inappropriate, because it ignores the way in which the New Testament narratives exemplify the application of the principles of love and justice; furthermore, it ignores the way in which those principles are given specification in the *rule* mode within the New Testament writings. In light of the foregoing observations, however, Yoder and Hauerwas are shown to be on firm ground in their normative arguments against violence, particularly in their emphasis on the paradigmatic significance of the death of Jesus. Schüssler Fiorenza likewise stands decisively within the New Testament's symbolic world in her hermeneutical decision to perceive violence from the point of view of its victims rather than its perpetrators; however, her vision of that world becomes blurred insofar as she deemphasizes the paradigmatic significance of the *cross* for New Testament ethics.

(B) OTHER AUTHORITIES This is the place where New Testament ethics confronts a profound methodological challenge on the question of violence, because the tension is so severe between the unambiguous witness of the New Testament canon and the apparently countervailing forces of *tradition*, *reason*, and *experience*. The decisions made by the interpretive community about the relative weight of these sources of authority will go a long way toward determining the outcome of normative deliberation concerning the use of violence. For instance, Niebuhr is able to justify violence because he consciously and emphatically gives *reason* and *experience* decisive roles in Christian ethics. In Part III, however, I set forth the guideline that *extrabiblical sources stand in a hermeneutical relation to the New Testament; they are not independent, counterbalancing sources of authority*. That is to say, tradition, reason and experience come into play in enabling us to interpret Scripture; they cannot be used simply to overrule or dismiss the witness of Scripture. How does that guideline work itself out in normative deliberation about the problem of violence?

Although the *tradition* of the first three centuries was decidedly pacifist in orientation, Christian *tradition* from the time of Constantine to the present has predominantly endorsed war, or at least justified it under certain conditions. Only a little reflection will show that the classic just war criteria (just cause, authorized by legitimate ruler, reasonable prospect of success, just means of conduct in war, and so forth) are—as Barth realized—neither derived nor derivable from the New Testament; they are formulated through a process of reasoning that draws upon natural-law traditions far more heavily than upon biblical warrants. It is not possible to use the just war tradition as a hermeneutical device for illuminating the New Testament, nor have the defenders of the tradition ordinarily even attempted to do so.[57] Thus, despite the antiquity of the just war tradition and its fair claim to represent the historic majority position within Christian theology, it cannot stand the normative test of New Testament ethics—unless it could somehow be shown that its norms are consistent with the New Testament witness. We cannot undertake a comprehensive examination of this problem here. I simply venture the summary judgment—based on the above survey of the evidence—that the New Testament offers no basis for ever declaring Christian participation in war "just." If that be true, then our methodological guideline insists that the church's majority *tradition*, however venerable, must be rejected or corrected in light of the New Testament's teaching. At the same time, the church's tradition also carries a significant and eloquent minority cloud of witnesses against violence, beginning with the New Testament writers themselves and extending through the writer of the Epistle to Diognetus, Tertullian, St. Francis of Assisi, the Anabaptists, the Quakers, Dorothy Day, Martin Luther King, Jr., and on into the present time. These witnesses—characteristically appealing primarily to the New Testament and the example of Jesus—have spoken out firmly against all war and killing and have declared such practices incompatible with following Jesus. Such witnesses have had a historic influence vastly disproportionate to their meager numbers, because their vision resonated so deeply with the New Testament and because their Christian witness therefore possessed such evident integrity. To approach the question of violence through the New Testament might allow us to reclaim and celebrate more fully this stream of tradition within the church, for the stories of such people help us to see more clearly how the New Testament's testimony is to be received.

It is more difficult to know what to say about *reason* and *experience* on the matter of violence. On the one hand, some interpreters—such as Augustine and Niebuhr—believe that Christians are sometimes forced by the ambiguities of human historical *experience* to employ violence to secure the contingent peace of the *civitas terrena.* To do otherwise, on this account, is to ignore the consequences of our choices and actions (or inactions) and thus to abdicate moral responsibility for the world in which God has placed us. (For further elaboration of this position, see my discussion of Niebuhr in chapter 12.1) This approach reckons very seriously with the historical fact that the social and political context for Christian moral decision has changed dramatically from the time of the New Testament writers. If the Sermon on the Mount was addressed to a marginal community outside the circle of power, its teachings cannot be directly applied in a context where Christians hold positions of power and influence, or where they constitute the majority in a democratic political order.

On the other hand, an equally serious case can be made that, on balance, history teaches that violence simply begets violence. (Inevitably, someone raises the question about World War II: What if Christians had refused to fight against Hitler? My answer is a counterquestion: What if the Christians in Germany had emphatically refused to fight *for* Hitler, refused to carry out the murders in concentration camps?) The long history of Christian "just wars" has wrought suffering past all telling, and there is no end in sight. As Yoder has suggested, Niebuhr's own insight about the "irony of history" ought to lead us to recognize the inadequacy of our reason to shape a world that tends toward justice through violence. Might it be that reason and sad experience could disabuse us of the hope that we can approximate God's justice through killing? According to the guideline I have proposed, reason must be healed and taught by Scripture, and our experience must be transformed by the renewing of our minds in conformity with the mind of Christ. Only thus can our warring madness be overcome.

This would mean, practically speaking, that Christians would have to relinquish positions of power and influence insofar as the exercise of such positions becomes incompatible with the teaching and example of Jesus. This might well mean, as Hauerwas has perceived, that the church would assume a peripheral status in our culture, which is deeply committed to the necessity and glory of violence. The task of the church then would be to tell an alternative story, to train disciples in the disciplines necessary to resist the seductions of violence, to offer an alternative home for those who will not worship the Beast. If the church is to be a Scripture-shaped community, it will find itself reshaped continually into a closer resemblance to the socially marginal status of Matthew's nonviolent countercultural community. To articulate such a theological vision for the church at the end of the twentieth century may be indeed to take most seriously what *experience* is telling us: the secular *polis* has no tolerance for explicitly Christian witness and norms. It is increasingly the case in Western culture that Christians can participate in public governance only insofar as they suppress their explicitly Christian motivations. Paradoxically, the Christian community might have more impact upon the world if it were less concerned about appearing reasonable in the eyes of the world and more concerned about faithfully embodying the New Testament's teaching against violence.

Let it be said clearly, however, that the reasons for choosing Jesus' way of peacemaking are not prudential. In calculable terms, this way is sheer folly. Why do we choose the way of nonviolent love of enemies? If our reasons for that choice are shaped by the New Testament, we are motivated not by the sheer horror of war, not by the desire for saving our own skins and the skins of our children (if we are trying to save our skins, pacifism is a very poor strategy), not by some general feeling of reverence for human life, not by the naive hope that all people are really nice and will be friendly if we are friendly first. No, if our reasons for choosing nonviolence are shaped by the New Testament witness, we act in simple obedience to the God who willed that his own Son should give himself up to death on a cross. We make this choice in the hope and anticipation that God's love will finally prevail through the way of the cross, despite our inability to see how this is possible. That is the life of discipleship to which the New Testament repeatedly calls us. When the church as a community is faithful to that calling, it prefigures the peaceable kingdom of God in a world wracked by violence.

4. Living the Text: The Church As Community of Peace

One reason that the world finds the New Testament's message of peacemaking and love of enemies incredible is that the church is so massively faithless. On the question of violence, the church is deeply compromised and committed to nationalism, violence, and idolatry. (By comparison, our problems with sexual sin are trivial.) This indictment applies alike to liberation theologies that justify violence against oppressors and to establishment Christianity that continues to play chaplain to the military-industrial complex, citing just war theory and advocating the defense of a particular nation as though that were somehow a Christian value.

Only when the church renounces the way of violence will people see what the Gospel means, because then they will see the way of Jesus reenacted in the church. Whenever God's people give up the predictable ways of violence and self-defense, they are forced to formulate imaginative new responses in particular historical settings, responses as startling as going the second mile to carry the burden of a soldier who had compelled the defenseless follower of Jesus to carry it one mile first. The exact character of these imaginative responses can be worked out only in the life of particular Christian communities;[58] however, their common denominator will be conformity to the example of Jesus, whose own imaginative performance of enemy-love led him to the cross. If we live in obedience to Jesus' command to renounce violence, the church will become the sphere where the future of God's righteousness intersects—and challenges—the present tense of human existence. The meaning of the New Testament's teaching on violence will become evident only in communities of Jesus' followers who embody the costly way of peace.

NOTES

1. *New Haven Register*, Oct. 9, 1986.
2. Sells 1994, 5.
3. Sells 1994, 5.
4. Zabelka 1980, 14.
5. Augustine is generally considered the first Christian thinker to articulate a theory of just war. While he focused on when and whether to resort to violence (to defend the common good and protect the innocent), the just war tradition has developed subsequently to include guidelines for the right conduct of war. Modern just war theorists generally accept the following criteria for the just "practice" of war: There must be just cause (e.g., to defend innocent parties) and right intent (e.g., to bring about peace). The war may be waged only by a legitimate authority as a move of last resort, and there must be probability of success. Further, the means of waging war must be proportional to the ends, and the war must distinguish combatants from noncombatants. The presence of shared criteria, however, does not imply shared definitions of the terms (Hauerwas in DeCosse 1992, 83–105). Consequently, contemporary thinkers place emphasis on varying aspects of the tradition. Paul Ramsey (1968) focuses on the protection of noncombatants, while James Turner Johnson (1981; 1984) offers reflections defining the limits on the use of force. For a useful collection of recent essays on just war tradition and political theory, see Elshtain 1992b. For an excellent historical and conceptual overview of the debate between Christian pacifism and just war theory, see Cahill 1994. For discussion of the use of just war criteria in relation to the Gulf War, see Hauerwas and Neuhaus 1991; Yoder 1991; Elshtain 1992a.
6. Zabelka 1980, 14.
7. On the history of interpretation, see Kissinger 1975. For a briefer summary, see Guelich 1987.
8. Guelich 1982, 219–220.
9. Horsley 1987, 272–273.
10. This perspective is advocated by Betz 1985, who thinks that the Sermon is a pre-Matthean compendium originating from Jewish-Christian circles.
11. This material is taken over from Mark, but Matthew adopts it without significant alteration.
12. Yoder 1994 [1972], 45–48.
13. Mauser 1992, 80.
14. See Chapter 4.2.a.
15. See my discussion of the role of the historical Jesus in NT ethics in Chapter 7.
16. It is of interest that later rabbinic Judaism found hermeneutical means to mitigate the stringency of the *lex talionis* by allowing for monetary compensation to the injured party rather than literal bodily disfigurement of the offender (*b. B. Qam.* 83b–84a). This interpretive move toward more humane jurisprudence is still, however, a quite different matter from the teaching of Matt. 5:38–42.
17. Guelich 1982, 220.
18. Guelich 1982, 222, following Daube 1956, 260–263.
19. The detail of "the *right* cheek" is lacking in the Lukan version of the saying (Luke 6:29); this does not necessarily disprove Daube's theory about the Matthean version, but it does show that Luke unambiguously understood the tradition as referring to nonretaliation against violence.
20. Guelich 1982, 223.
21. For a more satisfying account of the logic that governs 5:38–42, see Strecker 1988, 83: the examples are "anticlimactically arranged. They form a downward sloping line from the greater evil to the lesser one."
22. This point is well made by Walter Wink, "Neither Passivity Nor Violence: Jesus' Third Way (Matt. 5:38–42 par.)," in Swartley 1992, 102–125. Less persuasive, however, is Wink's attempt to portray these actions as gestures of protest and defiance of oppressive authority.
23. I owe this insight to an unpublished paper ("Seeking the Redemption of Our Enemies") by my student Angie Wright, who in turn was influenced by Wink (see note 22, above).

24. The term "focal instance" is suggested by Tannehill 1975 as a description of the way that Jesus' language in this passage functions.

25. William Klassen, "'Love Your Enemies': Some Reflections on the Current Status of Research," in Swartley 1992, 1–31; the quotation is taken from p. 12.

26. Horsley 1987, 255.

27. The argument was originally set forth in "Ethics and Exegesis: 'Love Your Enemies' and the Doctrine of Nonviolence," *Journal of the American Academy of Religion* 54 (1986): 3–31, now reprinted in Swartley 1992, 72–101. A revised but substantially similar account of his position appears in Horsley 1987, 255–273.

28. Heinz-Wolfgang Kuhn, "Das Liebesgebot Jesu als Tora und als Evangelium: Zur Feindesliebe und zur christlichen und jüdischen Auslegung der Bergpredigt," in Frankemölle and Kertelge (eds.) 1989. The English translation here is from Klassen, "Love Your Enemies," in Swartley 1992, 11.

29. "Our understanding of these sayings individually and collectively has been decisively influenced by their Matthean rearrangement and setting. . . . Thus both the apparent contrast between the *lex talionis* and the 'do not resist' and 'turn the other cheek' and the contrast between loving your neighbor . . . and love of enemies are Matthean and not integral to the early tradition and are surely not from Jesus. It is only the Matthean setting, not the sayings themselves, that makes us think that the 'enemies' were outsiders" (Horsley 1987, 262).

30. The NRSV translates *teleios* here as "completely loyal." The temporal clause that introduces the quotation here is supplied from Deut. 18:9.

31. W. D. Davies comments perceptively on the significance of the motif of "perfection" in Matthew, comparing Matthew's teaching to that of Qumran: in both, "the community as a whole is called to a perfection rooted in a particular interpretation of the Law; the difference between the perfection demanded by Matthew and that at Qumran, was rooted in Jesus' interpretation of Law in terms of *agapē*. Qumran demanded more obedience, Matthew deeper" (Davies 1964, 212).

32. Contrary to the opinion of Augustine and Niebuhr.

33. I am indebted to Bruce Fisk for calling my attention to the close relation between Matt. 5:9, 5:45, and 5:48.

34. See Chapter 12.2.

35. On the text-critical problem, see Fitzmyer 1985 (vol. 2), 1503–1504. In favor of the authenticity of the reading, see L. T. Johnson 1991, 376; Marshall 1978, 867–868.

36. On the characteristic Pauline verb *katallassein* ("reconcile," e.g., in 2 Cor. 5:18–20) as a term belonging to the semantic field of political and diplomatic affairs, see Breytenbach 1989.

37. See Chapter 1.2.b.

38. For a recent survey of the evidence on Rom. 12:14, see Dunn (1988 [vol. 2], 745), who concludes that "the probability that the Pauline parenesis does reflect the exhortation of Jesus must be judged to be very strong." More broadly on the whole passage, Dunn remarks that "the spirit of the Sermon on the Mount breathes through these verses with a consistent call to open-handed goodness and generous response unmotivated by malice" (750–751). See also his summarizing remarks on the significance of Jesus' teaching and example for Paul in this passage (755–756).

39. Paul quotes Prov. 25:21–22. Despite the apparently harsh image, the burning coals may be a traditional symbol for repentance. See, e.g., Klassen 1963, 337–350.

40. This instruction is set forth explicitly in the context of teaching for slaves (2:18–20); however, as 3:17–18 suggests, the norms that apply to the conduct of slaves are not materially different from the norms for all Christians.

41. The NRSV translates *polemoi* and *machai* as "conflicts and disputes," thus making two questionable interpretive decisions: (1) to treat the language as figurative rather than literal and (2) to paraphrase the figure, rather than letting the metaphor speak for itself.

42. Marshall 1978, 823.

43. Fitzmyer 1985, 1428, translates, "Enough of that!"

44. Fitzmyer 1981, 1434.

45. The NRSV of Isa. 53:12 says he "was numbered with the transgressors." This is simply a variant English translation of the same text; there is no question that Luke 22:37 represents Jesus as quoting Isaiah 53.

46. Luke cites the same chapter of Isaiah again in Acts 8:28–35, where the evangelist Philip explicitly identifies it as being "about" Jesus.

47. Cf. Luke 24:13–35.

48. The story is traditionally referred to as the "cleansing" of the Temple. This term, however, does not appear in the story, and it is of doubtful propriety for several reasons. See, e.g., E. P. Sanders 1985, 61–69.

49. Matthew and Luke omit the phrase "for all the nations" from the quotation, presumably because both of them, writing after the destruction of the Temple, want to avoid tying the Gentile mission to a particular vision of restored Temple worship.

50. What Jesus intended historically speaking—as distinct from the intentions of the evangelists—is a complicated problem that we cannot take up in detail here.

51. The term is aptly suggested by Myers 1988, 294, as a description of Jesus' triumphal entry into Jerusalem (Mark 11:1–11). I am proposing that Mark 11:15–19 continues the street theater performance.

52. Matthew repeats the story (Matt. 27:54), though it does not have the same climactic significance in his narrative, since the disciples have long since acclaimed Jesus as Son of God (e.g. 14:33, 16:16). In Luke's version of the passion story, the centurion merely pronounces Jesus *dikaios* ("righteous" or "innocent," Luke 23:47).

53. The early church did subsequently come to regard service in the Roman army as incompatible with the gospel. For a review of recent studies of early Christian attitudes toward war and military service, see Hunter 1992.

54. For essays that clearly develop the implications of this insight, see Lischer 1987; Hauerwas 1993, 63–72.

55. The Beatitudes might also be categorized as shaping the *symbolic world* of the text: they render an alternative account of reality.

56. See my discussion of this episode in section 2 of this chapter.

57. The one significant exception to this generalization is Paul Ramsey. For an analysis of his contribution to the discussion of just war, see Long 1993.

58. Where do we see concrete instances of communities that live this vision? Every reader will be able to think of different examples. Some that come to mind are Clarence Jordan's Koinonia Farm in Americus, Georgia; Reba Place Fellowship in Evanston, Illinois; and the Sojourners community in Washington, D.C. (along with the network of communities associated with it).

Chapter 15

Divorce and Remarriage

Marriage is hard. For a man and a woman to build a life together, bringing their often conflicting needs and desires into a harmonious whole, is a great challenge, possible only through grace. When a couple is able over the long haul to build a successful marriage, they will find deep joy and consolation. Such joy and consolation, however, are attainable only through patience, mutual sacrifice, and disciplined fidelity. Consequently, particular marriages are often fragile entities, and the question of divorce looms over the church's life.

For a long time in Western culture, up until the middle of the twentieth century, the church's prohibition of divorce was supported by a powerful set of social conventions that made divorce a nearly unthinkable option, a last resort in desperate circumstances. In U.S. culture at the end of the twentieth century, however, divorce has become so commonplace that it is in some communities virtually the norm. The statistic that there is about one divorce for every two marriages in the United States has been widely reported,[1] and everyone can cite anecdotal evidence of the way in which divorce has touched his or her life or the lives of family and friends. My children have been in classes at school where more than half of the students did not live in homes with both of their birth parents.

The collapse of cultural strictures against divorce has left the church in serious need of fresh theological and pastoral reflection about divorce and remarriage. The pain and complications of divorce cast their shadows across almost every congregation, yet the church often fails to address the issue forthrightly. In some churches divorce remains a taboo, and divorced persons are ostracized.[2] In other churches, however, divorce is treated almost casually, and members are not in any serious way held accountable to their marriage vows.

For example, my own denomination, the United Methodist Church, drifting with the mainstream of U.S. society, has been carried along into an easy de facto acceptance of divorce. Insofar as there has been any theological rationale at all for this historic shift, it lies in the conviction that we must avoid being judgmental: the operative canon within the canon for Methodism—as for much of mainstream Protestantism—has been, "Do not judge, so that you may not be judged" (Matt. 7:1). (In its original context, this saying of Jesus warns that those who judge others are liable to the judgment of *God.* As popularly understood, however, the saying is heard as enjoining a tacit social agreement that we should all look the other way: "If you don't judge me, I won't judge you.") If someone opts out of a marriage commitment, that is his or her own business, and no one else should presume to pass judgment. Furthermore, if the gospel is a word of grace, so the thinking goes, then we must at all costs avoid legalism. To require people to stay in difficult marriages against their inclination would be to impose a harsh law contrary to the spirit of love. I am persuaded that this line of thought has had disastrous consequences for the church.

The church's permissive attitude toward divorce has developed within a wider cultural context that regards marriage as a purely private affair, based on feelings of romantic love. One "falls in love" and gets married; when the feeling of being "in love" dissipates, so does the basis for the marriage. Or, worse yet, in the reigning therapeutic worldview, marriage is seen as a means to the individual's achievement of fulfillment and personal wholeness; if the partner comes to be a hindrance rather than an aid to the goal of fulfillment, there exists not only a license but even a duty to dissolve the relationship and look for a better one. Such attitudes are to be found not only on TV talk shows and on the self-help shelves of shopping mall bookstores but also in the counseling practices of many Protestant clergy and in the pages of the church's journals. For example, Bishop John Shelby Spong of the Episcopal Church advocates the church's adoption of liturgical ceremonies to bless the end of marriages:

> Without compromising its essential commitment to the *ideal* of faithful, monogamous marriage, the church needs to proclaim that divorce is sometimes the alternative which gives hope for life, and that remaining in a marriage is sometimes the alternative which delivers only death. The fullness of life for each of God's creatures is the Christian church's ultimate goal for human life. When a marriage serves that goal, it is the most beautiful and complete of human relationships. When a marriage does not or cannot serve that goal, it becomes *less than ultimate* and may well prove less than eternal. In such a case the church needs to accept the reality and the pain that separation and divorce bring to God's people, and to help redeem and transform that reality and that pain.[3]

Noteworthy here is the description of faithful monogamous marriage as an "ideal" (echoes of Niebuhr should be heard in the background) and the suggestion that a marriage that is "less than ultimate" in its promotion of "fullness of life" should probably be terminated. The couple used as an example by Spong in this essay had experienced "growing alienation" and "an increasing inability to communicate" because the partners were taking "radically different life paths." Thus, they realized that there was "no more life or potential for life in their relationship," and they decided to part as "friends who respect and care about each other."[4] So they went to the bishop of Newark for blessing of their decision.

Can the church bless divorce? If so, under what conditions? What guidance might the New Testament provide on the questions of divorce and remarriage? In the following pages, I will review the pertinent New Testament texts and explore how my proposed approach to New Testament ethics might address the issue.[5]

1. Reading the Texts

There are five significant passages in the New Testament that directly address the issue of divorce: Mark 10:2–12 and its parallel in Matthew 19:3–12; Matthew 5:31–32; Luke 16:18; and 1 Corinthians 7:10–16. We will give brief consideration to each of these in turn.

(A) MARK 10:2–12

Some Pharisees came, and to test him they asked, "Is it lawful for a man to divorce his wife?" He answered them, "What did Moses command you?" They said, "Moses allowed a man to write a certificate of dismissal and to divorce her." But Jesus said to them, "Because of your hardness of heart he wrote this commandment for you. But from the beginning of creation, 'God made them male and female.' 'For this reason a man shall leave his father and mother and be joined to his wife, and the two shall become one flesh.' So they are no longer two, but one flesh. Therefore what God has joined together, let no one separate." Then in the house the disciples asked him again about this matter. He said to them, "Whoever divorces his wife and marries another commits adultery against her; and if she divorces her husband and marries another, she commits adultery."

Within Mark's Gospel, this teaching on divorce occurs in the central section of teachings on discipleship (8:31–10:45), bracketed between Peter's confession at Caesarea Philippi and Jesus' entry to Jerusalem. As we have seen in our discussion of Mark,[6] this portion of the Gospel repeatedly stresses the costliness of discipleship and the necessity of servanthood and suffering for those who are Jesus' followers. Disciples are called to take up the cross (8:34), to be "servant of all" (9:35, 10:42–45), to make whatever radical sacrifices are necessary to enter life (9:43–48), to become like little children (10:15), and to give up family and possessions for the sake of the gospel (10:29–30). At first glance, the controversy discourse pericope on divorce (10:2–12) seems to sit oddly in this context, both form-critically and materially. Why has Mark placed this unit here rather than in one of his two major collections of controversy materials (2:1–3:6 and 11:27–12:37)? Upon reflection, the answer becomes clear: by placing this material in its present narrative location, Mark presents marriage as one aspect of discipleship. In contrast to the Mosaic permission of divorce, Jesus issues a declaration against it and then teaches his disciples that divorcing one spouse to marry another is nothing more than a devious form of adultery. Divorce is a sign of hardness of heart; those who follow Jesus are called to a higher standard of permanent faithfulness in marriage. (It is noteworthy that husbands and wives are not included in the list of family members who should be left behind for the sake of Jesus and the gospel [10:29].) This framing of the passage may also suggest that marriage, like the other aspects of discipleship treated in this section of Mark's Gospel, should be understood as a form of sacrificial service, though this point is not made explicitly in the text.

The Pharisees pose the question about divorce to Jesus, Mark tells us, as a way of "testing him" (10:2). Why should this question be understood as a test? The practice of divorce was universally accepted within Judaism; the only debated issue was the legitimate *grounds* for divorce.[7] The most probable inference—in terms of the Markan story[8]—is that the Pharisees already had heard that Jesus opposed divorce and saw here an opportunity to expose his inconsistency with the Law of Moses.[9] In the ensuing dialogue, Jesus and his interlocutors engage in nuanced verbal fencing. Jesus responds to their question with a deftly worded question of his own: "What did Moses *command* [*eneteilato*] you?" Their answer substitutes a different verb: "Moses *allowed* [*epetrepsen*] a man to write a certificate of dismissal and to divorce her." The distinction between permission and command, marked by the verbs employed in this exchange, provides the basis for Jesus to escape the charge of opposing Moses: the Torah certainly does not *mandate* divorce. Indeed, the passage in question, Deuteronomy 24:1–4, presupposes the practice of divorce and merely prohibits a man from remarrying his divorced wife after an intervening second marriage; that is the only commandment actually stated in the passage. The certificate of divorce was no doubt originally intended as a document of legal protection for the woman, proving that she was free to remarry; again, however, this is presupposed rather than legislated by Deuteronomy 24:1.

Having forced his interlocutors to concede that the single pertinent Torah text expresses a permission to divorce rather than a commandment, Jesus makes two bold hermeneutical moves. First, he declares that the permission—and its accompanying commandment prohibiting the husband from reasserting any claim over a woman whom he has divorced—is a concession to "your hardness of heart"; for the reader of Mark's Gospel, the inference is clear that "hardness of heart" is associated with lack of faith in Jesus and resistance to the power of God (cf. 3:5, 8:17). Those who trust God as revealed through Jesus will not seek such an escape clause from their marriages. For with God all things are possible (cf. 10:27), and for those who believe, hardness of heart can be overcome. The second hermeneutical move is the more fundamental: he appeals "behind" the Mosaic Law to God's original intention, as disclosed in the creation story. Thus he trumps Scripture with Scripture: "From the beginning of creation" God made man and woman for each other (Gen. 1:27) and declared that their union made them "one flesh" (Gen. 2:24). The importance of this last point is underscored by verse 8b, Jesus' exegetical comment on

Genesis 2:24, which reiterates the "one flesh" affirmation. Sexual intercourse in marriage is not merely the satisfaction of individual appetites, as eating is, but it links two persons together—literally and spiritually. It effects what it symbolizes and symbolizes what it effects. Thus, the sexual union of man and woman creates a indissoluble bond.

Jesus' two hermeneutical moves prepare the way for his apodictic pronouncement in 10:9: "Therefore what God has joined together, let no one separate." The inclusive-language translation of the NRSV, just cited, slightly blunts the force of the opposition between *theos* and *anthropos* in this pronouncement. "What *theos* has joined together, let not *anthropos* separate." God does the joining; it is the fallen human being who does the separating. Jesus' response—as so often in the controversy dialogues—refuses to answer the question in the terms it was posed. In one sense, the Law of Moses is left in place, acknowledged but categorized as a concession to human sin. The concluding pronouncement, however, suggests that those who enter the kingdom of God will live in light of another vision, a vision that sees marriage in light of God's original creative will. When the frame of reference is shifted in this way, the Pharisees' question about divorce is shown to be not only a disingenuous effort at entrapment but also an exercise in small-minded quibbling, an attempt to circumvent the ultimate intention of God.[10] The new wine of the gospel bursts the old wineskins of the Law's restrictions and permissions (cf. 2:21–22).

Another way of putting this observation would be to say that the Pharisees quiz Jesus about the *rule* governing divorce, but Jesus reframes the issue by appealing to the Genesis narrative as constituting the *symbolic world* within which marriage must be understood. Once marriage is construed within the story told by Scripture, divorce—even if it is permissible in some narrow sense—is seen to be antithetical to God's design for male and female.

Having thus escaped the Pharisees' trap by demonstrating that his teaching against divorce is deeply grounded in the Torah, Jesus later gives further private "in-house" instruction to the disciples: "Whoever divorces his wife and marries another commits adultery against her; and if she divorces her husband and marries another, she commits adultery" (10:11–12). There are two different ways of interpreting this saying.

According to one interpretation, Jesus, while conceding that there may be situations (owing to human hardheartedness) in which divorce is permitted in accordance with the Law, excludes the option of remarriage. On this reading, Jesus' teaching would stand in agreement with the position of the Qumran community, as articulated in the Damascus Document. The Qumran community's blistering critique of establishment Judaism included the charge of committing fornication by "taking a second wife while the first is alive, whereas the principle of creation is, *male and female created He them.*"[11] Although this passage could be read as forbidding polygamy, scholarly opinion has inclined toward understanding it in the sense of Mark 10:11 as including the prohibition of remarriage after divorce.[12] Particularly interesting is the Damascus Document's citation of Genesis 1:27 as the scriptural basis for condemning remarriage (cf. Mark 10:6); this demonstrates that the position ascribed to Jesus in Mark 10 has clear points of contact with one stream of rigoristic pre-Christian Judaism.

The other way of reading Mark 10:11–12 is to interpret it as a restatement of verse 9: whoever divorces in order to remarry (the normal procedure) commits adultery, so divorce should be renounced altogether in the first place. This interpretation has the advantage of providing greater internal continuity in Mark 10. It is likely that Mark has taken a traditional saying of Jesus (cf. Matt. 5:31–32, Luke 16:18) forbidding remarriage after divorce and radicalized its implications by placing it in conjunction with the controversy story of verses 2–9.

On any reading, the teaching of Mark 10:11–12 contains surprises. The greatest of these is the statement that the man who remarries after divorcing his wife commits adultery *against her*. This declaration posits a fundamental redefinition of adultery; in Jewish Law and tradition, adultery was a property offense, a form of stealing a man's property by "taking" his wife.[13] Thus, adultery could by definition be committed only against a man, for the husband was not in any reciprocal sense regarded as the sexual property of the wife. Jesus' teaching, however, changes the rules of the game with one bold stroke. William Countryman underscores the wide-ranging implications of Jesus' innovative teaching on this point:

> Under the provisions of the Torah . . . it was impossible for a man to commit adultery against his own married state. In a single phrase, Jesus created such a possibility and thus made the wife equal in this regard, too. He not only forbade the man to divorce his wife, but also gave her a permanent and indissoluble claim on him as her sexual property. Henceforth, his sexual freedom was to be no greater than hers.[14]

Thus, Mark 10:11 is not merely a standard halakic ruling: it is a stunning reversal of convention that demands a rethinking of the character of marriage and the power relations between husbands and wives. The other surprise is the reference to the wife's action of divorcing her husband in verse 12. Since this option was not normally granted to women under Jewish Law,[15] this part of the saying is usually regarded as a Markan adaptation of the tradition to the legal situation of the Greco-Roman world, where wives could initiate divorce (cf. also 1 Cor. 7:10–16).

In sum, Mark 10:2–12, starting from a question about the legal permissibility of divorce, opens out into a symbolic reframing of marriage as an aspect of Christian discipleship and as a reflection of God's primal purpose in creating humanity male and female. When the question of divorce is seen in this perspective, it becomes clear that divorce is a violation of God's intent; those who are Jesus' disciples will renounce it, just as they renounce many other prerogatives in order to follow Jesus on the way of the cross.

(B) MATTHEW 19:3–12 Matthew, who is consistently concerned to place the teaching of Jesus in counterpoint with emergent rabbinic Judaism, reformulates the Pharisees' question to Jesus so that it corresponds to an issue actively debated among the rabbis in the first century: "Is it lawful for a man to divorce his wife *for any cause?*" The question alludes to the dispute between different rabbinic schools reported in the Mishnah:

> The School of Shammai say: A man may not divorce his wife unless he has found unchastity in her, for it is written, *Because he hath found in her* ***indecency*** *in anything.* And the School of Hillel say: [He may divorce her] even if she spoiled a dish for him, for it is written, *Because he hath found in her indecency in* ***anything.*** R. Akiba says: Even if he found another fairer than she, for it is written, *And it shall be if she find no favour in his eyes....*[16]

Thus, in Matthew's account, the Pharisees ask Jesus to take a position on a well-known controversy. Does the husband have the right to divorce the wife for anything that displeases him, or only for unchastity?

Matthew has rearranged the material so that Jesus, rather than answering the question with a question, as in Mark, gives a forceful direct response, ending with the pronouncement that human beings should not separate the one-flesh union that God has joined (Matt. 19:4–6). Consequently, his answer, as initially formulated, is more strict than even the school of Shammai. The Pharisees then protest Jesus' statement by appealing to Deuteronomy 24:1 (saying, in interesting contrast to the Markan account, "Why then did Moses *command* [*eneteilato*] us . . . ?"). Jesus offers the accusatory response that the Mosaic permission was a concession to their hardness of heart and concludes with a dictum that effectually locates him in agreement with the school of Shammai: "And I say to you, whoever divorces his wife, except for *porneia,* and marries another commits adultery" (19:9).[17]

This last formulation differs from Mark 10:11–12 in three crucial particulars: Matthew omits Mark's startling prepositional phrase "against her" and drops the provision against a woman divorcing her husband (Mark 10:12). Both of these changes have the effect of bringing Jesus' teaching back into line with conventional Jewish understanding of divorce practices by preserving a patriarchal understanding of marriage.[18] The third Matthean alteration of Mark, however, has proven the most difficult to interpret: Matthew adds an exception clause, specifying *grounds* on which the husband may after all legitimately divorce the wife. Such a provision is entirely lacking in the Markan tradition, as well as in the tradition as transmitted by Luke and Paul. There is therefore good reason to think that this exception clause—found also in Matthew 5:32—represents Matthew's own casuistic adaptation of the tradition. (It is possible that the exception clause, rather than being the evangelist's own contribution, was already traditional in Matthew's community.[19] For our present purposes it makes little difference; the point is that some early Christians—whether Matthew or his predecessors—found it necessary to supplement the received tradition with a qualification. For the sake of simplicity, I will continue to speak of this qualification as Matthew's modification of the saying.) The radicality of Jesus' teaching is softened to make it more readily applicable as a rule for the community's practice.

But what exactly does *porneia* mean? What is the exception that makes divorce permissible? To ask this question is, of course, to reprise the rabbinic debate about the meaning of "indecency in anything."[20] Three general lines of explanation are exegetically defensible:

- *Porneia* means adultery, the wife's illicit sexual relations with another man. Or, since the term in Hellenistic Greek can cover a broad range of sexual improprieties, it could refer here to some sort of unspecified sexual immodesty or misconduct. This interpretation would place Jesus' teaching, as already noted, in basic agreement with the school of Shammai. Some interpreters find this reading problematical, since it diminishes the "distinctiveness" of Jesus' point of view and makes the ending of the controversy discourse (19:2–9) anticlimactic. It is also sometimes noted that the word "adultery" (*moicheia*) is not used here, and that the punishment for adultery under the Law was not divorce but death (Deut. 22:22). To these objections it may be replied that the wording of the exception is deliberately formulated so as to encompass a slightly wider range of sexual offenses and that there is considerable evidence that the death penalty prescribed in the Torah had in practice been replaced by compulsory divorce. As Raymond Collins observes, "It is probable that adultery was not punished by the imposition of a death penalty in Palestine during Roman times."[21]
- A slight variation on the first view is that *porneia* refers not to adultery but to premarital unchastity, so that the exception clause would refer to the situation described in Deuteronomy 22:13–21, in which the husband finds his new bride not to be a virgin.[22] Under such circumstances, Deuteronomy prescribes capital punishment, but actual practice may have been for the man simply to dismiss the woman, as in Matthew 1:19, where Joseph resolves to send the pregnant Mary away quietly. This interpretation, which would restrict the range of application of the exception clause, would perhaps explain why the term *moicheia* is not used. As we have seen, however, the desire to formulate the rule in more general terms serves equally well as an explanation for the choice of the word *porneia*. In any case, it would be odd for the Matthean community to formulate an exception that would allow dissolution of a marriage on the basis of premarital fornication but not on the basis of adultery committed after the marriage.
- A rather different explanation has found acceptance among a number of scholars. *Porneia* refers to marriage within degrees of kinship prohibited by Jewish Law, as outlined in Leviticus 18:6–18.[23] *Porneia* would thus be a translation of the Hebrew term *zenut*, used by the rabbis to categorize these illicit unions. Such marriages were legal in the Hellenistic world, but they were regarded by Jews as incestuous. Thus, a problem might arise concerning proselytes to Judaism or Gentile converts to Christianity who were already married within the prohibited degree of consanguinity. It is sometimes argued that the apostolic decree of Acts 15:28–29 is based on the laws of Leviticus 17–18 and that the decree's prohibition of *porneia* must therefore refer to the incestuous marriages forbidden in

> Leviticus 18. Matthew, by inserting the exception clause in the case of *porneia*, would then be following the precedent of the apostolic decree by allowing for the dissolution of incestuous unions. Such a provision, it is argued, would make good sense in a community engaged, as Matthew's community was, in mission to the Gentiles; the termination of such abominations would be necessary for the Gentile converts to have fellowship with the Jewish Christians in the community. One strength of this explanation is that it makes Jesus' teaching still far more restrictive than the position of the school of Shammai: even adultery is not sufficient grounds for breaking a marriage; only marriages that are prohibited by the Law a priori are to be annulled.

This third solution, which has found favor particularly among Roman Catholic interpreters, has much to commend it in terms of what it affirms (that *porneia* can refer to incestuous marriage), but it is problematical in what it denies (that is, that adultery might also constitute legitimate grounds for divorce under the Matthean exception clause). The objections to this interpretation are as follows. First, Leviticus 18 prohibits not only incest (vv. 6–18) but also intercourse during menstruation, adultery, homosexuality, and bestiality (vv. 19–23). Thus, even if it is correct that *porneia* in the apostolic decree alludes to Leviticus 18, there is no reason to restrict the meaning of the term to incestuous marriage; it is a summary term for all the sexual offenses proscribed in the holiness code of Leviticus 18–20. Second, in terms of Matthew's theological program of presenting Jesus as one who calls his disciples to a standard of righteousness more exacting than what the Law requires, it hardly makes sense to tolerate adultery. Robert Guelich puts the question rightly: "[H]ow could a community or an evangelist pursuing a more rigorous intensification of the Law than found among the rabbis require divorce in the case of the forbidden marriages of Leviticus 18:6–18 but exclude adultery that brought the death penalty in the Old Testament . . . and required divorce according to the rabbis?"[24] Finally, any interpretation of the exception clause must do justice to the very general meaning of *porneia* in contemporary Greek usage: it is a generic term for all sorts of sexual misconduct. Unless the immediate context provides some good reason for limiting its sphere of application, it ought to be construed as a catch-all term, not as a *terminus technicus* for one specific offense.

Thus, the best interpretation is that the Matthean exception clause leaves the door open for divorce on the grounds of a variety of offenses related to sexual immorality. No matter what interpretation is put upon the clause, it is undeniable that we see here a process of adaptation, in which Jesus' unconditional prohibition of divorce is applied and qualified in the interest of practicability. Here, as elsewhere, we see Matthew the ecclesiastical politician and reconciler of differences seeking to work out a balance between rigor and mercy, between the demands of discipleship and the realities of the community's situation. "In harmony with his community tradition, Matthew lays down a practical instruction, with whose help the current problems of order can be resolved."[25] Exactly what those problems were we do not know. Perhaps Matthew was indeed wrestling with the issue of Gentile converts who had previously married within their own families; perhaps, as Collins suggests, he was trying to "assuage the consciences" of Christian Jews who had previously divorced adulterous wives in obedience to their understanding of the Law;[26] perhaps he simply could not believe that Jesus' unconditional prohibition of divorce was intended to bind Christians to adulterous spouses. Whatever the case, Matthew's exception clause stands as a clear sign of a process of moral deliberation, in which Mark's radical vision of marriage as indissoluble one-flesh union is accommodated in the interest of creating a workable rule for the community's life.

(C) MATTHEW 5:31–32, LUKE 16:18 The fact that Matthew includes two major passages in his Gospel dealing with this issue may indicate that it was a matter of significant concern for his community. Luke, on the other hand, has only a single brief saying, oddly disconnected from its narrative context, and he does not incorporate the controversy story of Mark 10:2–12 into his Gospel at all.

The third of the antitheses in the Sermon on the Mount, Matthew 5:31–32, gives a compressed treatment of the problem of divorce. The passage first paraphrases Deuteronomy 24:1 as a foil to Jesus' new teaching:

> *It was also said, "Whoever divorces his wife, let him give her a certificate of divorce." But I say to you that anyone who divorces his wife, except on the ground of unchastity, causes her to commit adultery; and whoever marries a divorced woman commits adultery.*

The wording of the exception clause here (*parektos logou porneias*) is different from the wording in 19:9 (*mē epi porneia*); the unidiomatic Greek of 5:32 is a very literal rendering of the Hebrew of Deuteronomy 24:1 (*'erwat dabar,* "a thing of indecency"),[27] and it thus seems even more clearly than 19:9 to identify the teaching of Jesus with the tradition of the school of Shammai. The noun *porneia* presents all the same possibilities and problems that have already been discussed above in relation to Matthew 19:9.

The new element here, however, is the assertion that the man who divorces his wife makes *her* into an adulteress and that the person who marries a legally divorced woman also is committing adultery. Presumably, the logic is that a certificate of divorce has no real effect; the marriage remains in force. If the divorced woman remarries—as she might have to do for legal and economic protection—she will thereby de facto commit adultery against the original husband who dismissed her, and the man who marries her will also be committing adultery against the first husband. The effect of this teaching is to declare the Deuteronomic divorce law null and void except in cases of *porneia.* Matthew's formulation of the saying, here as in chapter 19, frames the question within traditional Jewish parameters: adultery can be committed only against the husband through the wife's unfaithfulness.

It is sometimes argued that this teaching prohibits all remarriage after divorce, even in situations where divorce is permitted because of *porneia.* Strictly speaking, however, there is nothing in the saying to prevent a man who has divorced his wife on the ground of *porneia* from remarrying, as long as he marries a woman who has not previously been married. A divorced woman, however, could never remarry under the terms of this teaching without committing adultery.

It should be remembered that this saying is not just part of a list of moral rules; rather, it belongs to Matthew's depiction of the higher righteousness to which Jesus' disciples are called. The teaching is one of several examples that illustrate how the disciples are to go beyond the formal requirements of the Law to fulfill its deeper intent. The Law requires husbands who divorce their wives to set them free with a certificate of divorce, but Jesus' followers are not to divorce their wives at all. (The androcentric formulation is intentional; for Matthew, only the husband has the possibility of initiating divorce.) To dismiss a wife is to consign her to sin, or to singleness without protection in a patriarchal society; thus, Matthew calls husbands in the Christian community to a broader vision of the life of righteousness. They are to take full moral responsibility for maintaining their marriages faithfully—with the sole proviso that *porneia* can bring the marriage to an end. Here, as in chapter 19, the exception clause is a casuistic adaptation of the tradition that brings it more closely into line with Jewish custom and responds to specific issues that the blanket prohibition of divorce had not dealt with.

The Lukan form of this saying is closely parallel to Matthew 5:32 with two significant differences: it lacks the exception clause, and it shares with Mark 10:11 the surprising declaration that a husband who divorces his wife and marries another thereby commits adultery.[28] Unlike Mark, however, Luke 16:18 does not make the reciprocal statement that the wife who divorces her husband and marries another commits adultery; instead, the latter half of Luke's formulation agrees with Matthew 5:32 that a man who marries a divorced woman commits adultery. Thus, the force of the Lukan logion is that a man should neither divorce his wife nor marry a divorced woman. The effect of this pithy formulation is to exclude any option of remarriage after a divorce, for either partner.

(D) 1 CORINTHIANS 7:10–16 This passage, chronologically the earliest of our New Testament sources dealing with divorce, is the most interesting instance we have of a consciously reflective pastoral adaptation of the tradition concerning Jesus' teaching on this topic. The entire chapter deals with questions that the Corinthians had posed in an earlier letter to Paul (1 Cor. 7:1). The first issue is whether married Christians ought to abstain from sexual relations; Paul emphatically rejects radical asceticism and urges married couples to continue having sexual intercourse with one another (1 Cor. 7:1–7).[29] In verses 8–9, Paul advises the unmarried and widows to remain unmarried but at the same time gives those whose desires are strong permission to marry. Then he turns to a series of directives concerning divorce (7:10–16), another topic about which the Corinthians apparently had inquired.[30] It is possible that the issue had arisen in the Corinthian church for reasons similar to their interest in pursuing sexual abstinence within marriage: a concern for holiness. Perhaps some of the women were especially interested in dissolving their marriages as a sign of their new freedom in Christ and single-minded devotion to the Lord.[31]

Paul begins by citing the direct authority of the teaching of Jesus. This is one of the very few places in his letters where he makes a direct appeal to the words of Jesus as authoritative.

> *To the married I give this command—not I but the Lord—that the wife should not be separated from her husband (but if she does become separated, let her remain unmarried or else be reconciled to her husband), and that the husband should not send his wife away.*
> (1 Cor. 7:10–11, RH)

The NRSV translation, by using the verbs "separate" and "divorce," implies more of a distinction between the two directives than is appropriate. Ancient Mediterranean culture did not have the modern institution of "separation" as distinct from divorce. The verbs (*chōristhēnai* and *aphienai*) both refer to divorce. Reflecting his Jewish background, Paul uses a passive verb of the woman ("be separated from her husband")[32] and an active one of the man ("send his wife away"), but his comments presuppose the Hellenistic customs of Corinth, where the wife had the right to initiate divorce, as verse 13 clearly demonstrates. In relation to the Gospel traditions, Paul's formulation is closest to Mark 10:11–12 in applying the prohibition of divorce equally to husband and wife; the verbs used here, however, appear in none of the divorce texts in the Gospels: Paul is summarizing rather than quoting the tradition. The parenthetical remark in 1 Corinthians 7:11a appears to be Paul's own gloss on the tradition ("but if she does . . ."). Without characterizing remarriage as adultery, as the Gospel traditions do, Paul nonetheless discourages remarriage. Here he seems to be drawing an inference that extends the implications of the command of the Lord. The moderation of Paul's counsel, however, is noteworthy. He does not say, "But if she does separate, throw her out of the church" or "If she does separate, she is committing adultery." He articulates the tradition about Jesus' commandment against divorce but simultaneously reckons with the possibility that some of his readers may not heed this commandment.

In verses 12–16, however, Paul addresses a new topic not envisioned in Jesus' teaching, one that could arise only in the mission setting where there was a clearly drawn contrast between believers and nonbelievers, between the community of faith and the world. How are Christians to deal with marriages to non-Christians? In most cases, one assumes, these marriages predate the believer's conversion. It is not hard to imagine that such circumstances could create severe tensions in a marriage; one partner would join this strange new Jewish sect, with its odd rituals and fervent gatherings, while the other stood aloof, bewildered or disapproving. Some of the Corinthians no doubt questioned the propriety of maintaining such marriages, perhaps in words not unlike those found in 2 Corinthians 6:14–7:1:

> *Do not be mismatched with unbelievers. For what partnership is there between righteousness and lawlessness? Or what fellowship is there between light and darkness? What agree-*

ment does Christ have with Beliar? Or what does a believer share with an unbeliever? . . . Therefore come out from them, and be separate from them, says the Lord, and touch nothing unclean; then I will welcome you, and I will be your father, and you shall be my sons and daughters, says the Lord Almighty.[33] (2 Cor. 6:14–15, 17–18)

If, as Paul has insisted emphatically in 1 Corinthians 6:12–20, sexual union with a prostitute (described in 6:18 as *porneia*) defiles the body of Christ, would not the same argument apply to marriages with unbelievers, who have not been washed and sanctified through baptism (6:11), who still live under the power of sin? To pose the question is to realize what a deeply serious issue this must have been in a first-generation mission community such as the Corinthian church.

Paul's answer, then, is the more surprising:

To the rest I say—I and not the Lord—that if any believer has a wife who is an unbeliever, and she consents to live with him, he should not divorce her. And if any woman has a husband who is an unbeliever, and he consents to live with her, she should not divorce[34] *him.* (1 Cor. 7:12–13)

Three features of this passage command attention:

- Paul explicitly identifies this counsel as his own pastoral improvisation. The teaching of Jesus to which he has just alluded does not cover this situation; consequently, Paul gives advice on his own authority. We shall return to this point presently.
- Paul assumes that within the church there will be persons, both men and women, with unbelieving spouses. He does not assume that Christian wives will automatically have to defer to the religious preferences of their husbands, nor—perhaps more strikingly—does he assume that Christian husbands will have the authority to command their unbelieving wives to join the church. The scenario envisioned here is one in which participation in the community of faith cannot be coerced.[35] This view of the religious independence of the marriage partners stands in sharp contrast to the conventional expectation, articulated by Plutarch in a frequently quoted passage, that "it is becoming for a wife to worship and to know only the gods that her husband believes in, and to shut the front door tight upon all queer rituals and outlandish superstitions. For with no god do stealthy and secret rites performed by a woman find any favor."[36]
- Despite the seeming dangers of having the Christian spouse defiled through marital relations with the unbeliever, Paul counsels believers to stick with their unbelieving partners. The reasons given for this counsel (in 7:14) are still more remarkable than the counsel itself:

  For the unbelieving husband is made holy through his wife, and the unbelieving wife is made holy through her husband. Otherwise, your children would be unclean, but as it is, they are holy.

> Rather than having the holy polluted by the unholy, the opposite effect occurs: the holy "contaminates" the unholy and sanctifies it. Holiness is more powerful than uncleanness. Or, to put it a bit more provocatively, holiness is—as it were—a venereal disease, passed from one spouse to the other. This extraordinary reversal of conventional Jewish conceptualities about ritual defilement is diametrically opposed to the call for separation expressed in 2 Corinthians 6:14–7:1. The supporting argument in verse 14b about the holiness of the children is a bit obscure. Paul assumes that the children are in fact holy, even though one parent is not a Christian. (How can he assume this so confidently? Have they been baptized? Paul does not say.) From this assumption he deduces that the unbelieving spouse is sanctified through the believing spouse. This line of thought leads naturally to the idea expressed in verse 16, that perhaps the unbelieving spouse will be saved through the believer: "Wife, for all you know, you might save your husband. Husband, for all you know, you might save your wife." It is usually assumed that Paul refers here to the hope that the unbeliever will be converted through the love and witness of the believer; however, given Paul's mysterious notion of quasi-physical vicarious sanctification (v. 14), it seems equally possible that he holds out the hope for God somehow to save even the unbeliever on the soteriological coattails of the believer.

The final aspect of Paul's advice that must be considered here is the flip side of his counsel that believers should remain in mixed marriages when possible:

> *But if the unbelieving partner separates, let it be so [literally "let him/her separate"]; in such a case the brother or sister is not bound. It is to peace that God has called us.*[37] (7:15)

This declaration implies a crucial claim: participation in the community of faith is the most fundamental commitment, more basic than marriage. The line that divides the new creation from the old can run right through a marriage. Because of the continuing claim of the old age, and because of the hope of saving the unbelieving spouse, the believer is obligated to stay in the marriage as long as possible. But if a choice finally must be made, if the unbelieving partner wants to terminate the marriage, there is no doubt on which side of that line the believer finally must stand: "Let him/her separate." God has called *us* (i.e., the church, the community of God's elect people) to peace. Participation in that eschatological peace is finally more compelling—more a matter of vocation—than the attempt to save a futile marriage with one who does not know that peace.

Here we see Paul spinning out his response as he writes. In the situation of the Gentile mission, he is confronted by a problem for which the Jesus-tradition does not provide specific guidance; he devises a response grounded in his theological understanding of election and community. The specific counsel that emerges from this process is a daring revision that both extends and modifies the content of Jesus' teaching. Yes, says Paul, the believer should not initiate divorce, just as Jesus commanded. On the other hand, in the situation of the mixed marriage, the believer is not bound (*dedoulōtai*, literally "enslaved") to the marriage. It belongs to the form of this world that is passing away (7:31); thus, it represents a penultimate, not an ultimate, commitment.

Does the declaration that the believer is "not bound" imply the freedom to remarry in this situation? Paul does not address the problem explicitly. The situation is *not* directly covered by the parenthetical prohibition of verse 11a. The general tenor of Paul's advice throughout the chapter is clear: the unmarried person should not seek a change of status (vv. 8, 17–24, 25–27, 39–40). It is better to remain single and to serve the Lord with undivided attention (cf. vv. 32–35). At the same time, the provisional character of this advice is equally clear—at least for widows and virgins. If they choose to marry, they do not sin; indeed, in some instances such a choice is preferable to being "aflame with passion" (vv. 9, 28, 36–38, 39b). Thus, Paul expresses his own opinion, "as one who by the Lord's mercy is trustworthy" (v. 25), but then leaves the discernment in the hands of his readers. Would a similar discretionary freedom be granted to the believing spouse abandoned by an unbeliever? It is difficult to see anything against this interpretation either within 1 Corinthians 7 or elsewhere in Paul's letters. Paul does not seem to share the conviction expressed in the Damascus Document and in Luke 16:18 that all remarriage is adulterous. As we have seen, he is startlingly unconcerned about traditional conceptions of purity and defilement (conceptions that provide the underlying Levitical warrants for the prohibition of remarriage). For him, what matters most is freedom to serve the Lord with "unhindered devotion" (v. 35) and to experience the eschatological peace of the people of God (v. 15). It is difficult to come away from this chapter thinking that Paul would place a categorical prohibition on remarriage for the believers described in verses 12–16; rather, he would invite them to engage with him in a process of discernment about how they could best serve God in the "present necessity" (v. 26), in the time that remains.

2. Synthesis: Divorce and Remarriage in Canonical Context

In sum, we have seen that these five texts on divorce manifest simultaneously a deep unity and a bewildering diversity. The fundamental concern in all of them is to affirm marriage as a permanently binding commitment in which man and woman become one. This point cannot be stressed too strongly. All discussion of divorce must be understood only as a matter of exceptional—and tragic—qualification to this normative vision.

At the same time, there are complex differences among these texts in their interpretation of specific points. Mark and Paul offer a vision of marriage in which man and woman bear similar freedoms and equal responsibilities for sustaining the relationship, but Matthew's redaction of the tradition systematically reaffirms the patriarchal assumptions of Jewish Law and tradition. Both Matthew and Luke assume the traditional Jewish legal framework in which only the husband can initiate divorce, but Mark and Paul address the world of Hellenistic custom, where the wife has this right also. Mark and Luke categorically prohibit divorce, but Matthew and Paul both entertain the necessity of exceptions to the rule, situations in which a pastoral discernment is required. Paul gets the necessary leverage on the tradition by forthrightly distinguishing between the command of the Lord and his own opinion, whereas Matthew simply reads the exception clause back into his account of what Jesus taught.

What about remarriage? Luke excludes it altogether; Matthew thinks that divorced women cannot remarry without committing adultery but leaves the door open for husbands to remarry if their first wives have been guilty of *porneia.* Paul advises against remarriage for anybody, including widows, but presents his position in a way that invites his readers to enter a process of discernment about how best to serve the Lord in the eschatological interval between resurrection and parousia; the option of remarriage for those who have been divorced by unbelievers remains at least an open possibility. Mark vehemently rejects divorce as an instrument of serial polygamy but does not entertain the problem of remarriage under special circumstances, such as those envisioned by Matthew and Paul.

Thus the diversity of these passages lays before us a range of options. How can we speak synthetically about the witness of the New Testament on this issue? Mark's controversy story provides an important clue: it is a terrible mistake to isolate any particular rule about divorce from the wider canonical narrative context. We cannot read Deuteronomy 24:1 rightly without setting it in the framework of Genesis 1 and 2. By implication, then, we cannot make valid normative judgments about divorce without a broader understanding of the canonical witness concerning *marriage.* Taking our cue from Mark, we should return to the canon and trace its depiction of God's will for the union of man and woman. This would be a massive task, but I will venture a very brief sketch.

We would have to begin, as Mark's story does, with the Genesis narrative of God's creation of man and woman as complementary partners (Gen. 1:27, 2:18). The story represents the one-flesh union of man and woman (2:24) as a fundamental and good aspect of the Creator's design for the world. These are the elements of the story that Mark and Matthew highlight for us. Moving beyond Genesis, we might consider also the symbolic plot enacted by the prophet Hosea, who married Gomer, "a wife of whoredom," in order to symbolize God's relationship to an unfaithful people: "The Lord said to me again, 'Go, love a woman who has a lover and is an adulteress, just as the Lord loves the people of Israel, though they turn to other gods and love raisin cakes'" (Hosea 3:1). The symbol gives vivid expression to the horror of Israel's disloyalty to the covenant, but in the end it also serves as a vehicle of a still more powerful message: the covenant love of God will ultimately overcome Israel's unfaithfulness. The conclusion of the book offers a moving vision of reconciliation:

I will heal their disloyalty;
I will love them freely,

for my anger has turned from them. . . .
They shall again live beneath my shadow,
they shall flourish as a garden,
they shall blossom like the vine,
their fragrance shall be like the wine of Lebanon. (Hos. 14:4, 7)

The prophecy's primary message is about the unbreakable covenant love of God, but what does such a story teach us secondarily about marriage and divorce? Surely it models for us a love that overcomes even adultery and affirms the covenant of marriage as unbreakable.

The prophetic book of Malachi contains an oracle that powerfully condemns divorce and describes marriage as a *covenant*. This understanding of marriage was suggested by Hosea's symbolic action, but here it is brought to explicit expression. God does not accept Israel's offering with favor, says the prophet, because

> *. . . the Lord was a witness between you and the wife of your youth, to whom you have been faithless, though she is your companion and your wife by covenant. Did not one God make her? Both flesh and spirit are his. And what does the one God desire? Godly offspring. So look to yourselves, and do not let anyone be faithless to the wife of his youth. For I hate divorce, says the Lord, the God of Israel.* (Mal. 2:14–16a)

It is no accident that faithlessness to the marriage covenant and faithlessness to the covenant with God (2:10–12) are bracketed together by Malachi. One reflects and symbolizes the other. That is why God *hates* divorce. (It is a surprising fact that this powerful text is never quoted in the New Testament debates on this issue.)

Turning to the New Testament also we find fleeting images that represent marriage as a mirror of the relationship of God to his people. Ephesians 5:21–33 develops the trope of marriage as a symbol for the relationship between Christ and the church. "Husbands, love your wives, just as Christ loved the church and gave himself up for her" (Eph. 5:25). This passage again quotes Genesis 2:24 to proclaim the one-flesh character of the marriage union. Here, however, this idea is given a new hortatory spin. Instead of stressing the indissolubility of marriage, the image is used to impress upon husbands their duty to love their wives as themselves:

> *[H]usbands should love their wives as they do their own bodies. . . . For no one ever hates his own body, but he nourishes and tenderly cares for it, just as Christ does for the church, because we are members of his body.* (Eph. 5:28–30)

Thus the author of Ephesians sets up a three-level typology, linking the Genesis story with the actual marriages in the Christian community and with the relationship of Christ to the church.[38] Each element in the typology mirrors and illuminates the other two. Of course, this typology explicitly carries with it a hierarchical model of marriage: "Just as the church is subject to Christ, so also wives ought to be, in everything, to their husbands" (5:24). As I suggested in Chapter 2.2, the high ecclesiology of Ephesians somewhat mitigates the authoritarian potential of this paradigm, for the church is to grow into "the full stature of Christ." At the same time, Christ "gave himself up for the church," thus modeling the way husbands should treat their wives. Thus, although the symbolic world of Ephesians remains patriarchal, we see the beginnings of a remarkable hermeneutical revision of patriarchy through the story of the cross. More pertinent to our present concern with divorce, the Christ/church typology presents an extraordinarily high standard for marriage; if marriage truly reflects the love between Christ and the church, it should be characterized by infinite loyalty and self-sacrificial love. Divorce would be normatively unthinkable, and actual divorce within the community would grievously rend the fabric of the symbolic unity envisioned by Ephesians.

A passing hortatory remark in Hebrews also extols marriage: "Let marriage be held in honor by all, and let the marriage bed be kept undefiled; for God will judge fornicators and adulterers" (Heb. 13:4). Although nothing is said here directly about divorce, the high view of marriage as honorable and sacrosanct is consistent with the pronouncement of Jesus in Mark 10:6–9.

Finally, the Apocalypse, using an image similar to the marriage imagery of Ephesians 5, depicts the eschatological consummation of all things as "the marriage supper of the Lamb" (Rev. 19:6–9). In contrast to the great whore with whom the kings of the earth have committed fornication (Rev. 17–18), the bride of the Lamb appears in "fine linen, bright and pure," which is said to symbolize the righteous deeds of the saints (19:8). The bride is also identified, in symbolic opposition to Babylon, as the new Jerusalem that comes down from heaven (21:2, 9). She joins the Spirit in invoking the final glorious coming of Christ (22:17). All this imagery serves as a symbolic reversal of the Old Testament metaphor of Israel as the unfaithful wife.[39] In the consummation promised by the seer of Revelation, the people of God will finally experience the restoration and oneness adumbrated by Hosea. Given the pervasive Old Testament correlation between God's covenant with Israel and the marriage covenant, it is no surprise that the New Testament canon seals its triumphant vision of the new covenant by evoking the image of true marriage. Thus, although the Apocalypse says nothing about divorce as an issue, its symbolic structure supports and completes the picture we have already drawn. In the world rendered by this text, divorce can only be a step in the wrong direction, away from the wholeness ultimately promised to the people of God, when God himself will dwell with them and wipe every tear from their eyes (21:3–4).

In light of this very brief sketch of the canonical narrative context, we see that permanent marriage between one man and one woman is the literal embodiment of God's will in creation and, at the same time, a figurative sign of the longed-for eschatological union of Christ and the church. In this context, marriage can never be seen as ephemeral; rather, it figures forth the ultimate redemptive intention of God. For those in Christ, therefore, divorce is to be avoided in every way possible, for it is incongruous with the gospel of God's reconciling love.

Having completed a sweeping overview of the canonical witness, let us now consider this material through the lenses of the focal images of *community, cross,* and *new creation.*

Community. When we read the texts through this lens, we see in the first instance that divorce is not merely a private issue for individuals and couples to consider.

Rather, it is an issue that concerns the health and witness of the whole community. One of the problems with the Pharisees' fixation on the rule implied by Deuteronomy 24:1 is that it obscures the public covenantal character of marriage and treats divorce as a matter of the husband's discretion. (At least, however, the Pharisees were engaged in public debate about legitimate grounds for divorce rather than merely shrugging and leaving everything to individual conscience and whim, as the church is wont to do today!) When we examine the evidence through the *community* lens, 1 Corinthians 7 comes into prominent focus, for there Paul's pastoral reflections are offered in the interest of upbuilding the community, and his advice aims at enabling the Corinthians to pursue the community's mission without distraction. Or again, when we read the texts through this lens, the teaching of Matthew 5:31–32 comes into focus within its communal context in the Sermon on the Mount: the purpose of Jesus' instruction is to shape a community that will be the light of the world (Matt. 5:14–16). Decisions about divorce can never be made apart from a concern for the community's vocation to make disciples of all nations by exemplifying the righteousness that Jesus teaches. Similarly, for Mark, marriage—as an aspect of discipleship—must be understood as a practice shaped by the vocation of service to others in community.

Cross. To read these divorce texts through the lens of the *cross* is to perceive something important about the New Testament's vision of marriage: it can be difficult and costly. Furthermore, marriage calls the followers of Jesus to a reversal of the world's structures of power: this will have wide-ranging and costly consequences, especially for husbands who are summoned to follow Jesus' example of servanthood (cf. Mark 10:42–45). It is no accident that Mark locates his teaching against divorce in the midst of the central block of his Gospel—a block that is structured upon Jesus' threefold passion prediction. For Mark, discipleship is necessarily cruciform, and marriage is to be understood within the vocation of discipleship. The law of Deuteronomy 24:1 offers—at least to men—an easy escape from the hard demands of marriage, but Jesus calls his followers to live instead in faithful response to the original will of God. The specific costs of this are not spelled out in Mark; as usual, he is content to offer a provocative hint. The disciples in Matthew, however, articulate the offense of Jesus' saying: "If such is the case of a man with his wife, it is better not to marry" (Matt. 19:10). For a man to surrender the option of divorce (a startling renunciation of rights within Matthew's patriarchal cultural context), to enter marriage with the expectation of living it as a binding covenant, is to commit his life without reservation to one other particular human being. (For an interesting narrative example, see the story of Joseph and Mary in Matt. 1:18–25.) Thus, Matthew places the renunciation of divorce alongside renunciation of anger, alongside turning the other cheek—even alongside love of enemy—as a sign of the character of God's kingdom. Like the other examples in this inventory of antitheses, the relinquishment of divorce may entail suffering. If so, marriage is properly to be understood through the passion narrative, as Ephesians so provocatively suggests: husbands in particular are to give themselves up, surrendering power and prerogatives for the sake of their wives, just as Christ did for the church.

Marriage calls, of course, for mutuality of sacrifice by both partners, but in the foregoing summary I have highlighted its costliness for husbands, precisely to counteract the way in which calls for sacrificial suffering have often been one-sidedly applied to women. This sketch should be filled in by the recognition that, within the vision of marriage as discipleship that Mark articulates, women and men alike are called to the way of the cross, the way of service.

New Creation. If marriage may lead us to the cross, the way of suffering service, it is also a sign of the eschatological redemption of all things. It figuratively foreshadows, even in the ambiguities of the present time, God's unbreakable covenant faithfulness which will finally bring healing to the world. Thus, the community's renunciation of divorce is a signal, an outward and visible sign of the eschatological salvation of God. Mark, by pointing back behind the Mosaic Law to God's original design, dares to suggest that through unwavering faithfulness to the one-flesh union of marriage, Jesus' disciples embody *new creation,* manifesting what was meant to be "from the beginning of creation." Likewise, Matthew's placement of the teaching against divorce in the Sermon on the Mount makes this point with unmistakable clarity: the *polis* on a hill is a sign of hope for the world. In a community with such a sign-bearing vocation, divorce has no place. Matthew's exception clause, however, is a clear concession to the "not yet": until the kingdom arrives in its fullness, human unfaithfulness will necessitate realistic measures to cope with pastoral problems. Paul emphasizes even more clearly the "not yet" side of the eschatological dialectic. This is partly in reaction against Corinthians who may have been prematurely claiming eschatological blessedness and mistakenly using this claim as a warrant to dissolve marriages or to renounce sex within marriage. Consequently, Paul must exhort them to "remain in the condition in which you were called" (1 Cor. 7:20). Even though marriage is a matter of minor importance in view of the urgency of God's coming kingdom, marriages remain valid—even marriages to unbelievers. Indeed, for Christians to stay in mixed marriages is precisely a sign of hope for the future that we do not yet see (7:16). Both marriage and divorce, then, are framed within Paul's peculiarly poignant eschatological vision: on the one hand, the time has grown short and those who have wives should be as though they had none (7:29); on the other hand, as long as the present age continues, married couples owe one another sexual satisfaction and divorce is to be rejected. Hope and common sense are kept in delicate balance. In this passage, Paul—unlike Matthew and Mark—does not assign positive significance to the renunciation of divorce as a sign of the new creation. Finally, the marriage feast of the Lamb in Revelation is the figure in which all earthly marriages find their *telos.* If marriage is the New Testament's final symbol of eschatological redemption, then divorce cannot be consonant with God's redemptive will.

3. Hermeneutics: Responding to the New Testament's Witness Against Divorce

We have seen, despite the complexities of the New Testament's various teachings on divorce and remarriage, that there is a fundamentally coherent witness within the New Testament canon. Permanent monogamous marriage is the norm; Christians are called upon to see their marriages as expressions of discipleship and to renounce divorce, which was normally available as an option—at least for husbands—in the cultural setting of these writings. How are we to receive and respond to this witness of the New Testament in an age when divorce is widespread not only in our culture but in the church as well?[40]

(A) **THE MODE OF HERMENEUTICAL APPROPRIATION** Once again, as with the issue of violence, we find the New Testament speaking in all four of the modes that we have identified, though the weight of emphasis differs somewhat from our previous example. In this case, the New Testament texts place much more weight on specific rules and considerably less weight on narrative paradigms exemplifying the norm.

All five of the texts that speak specifically of divorce address the reader in the *rule* mode, as we have seen, and all of them attribute the original formulation of the rule against divorce directly to Jesus. Matthew's addition of the exception clause is a particularly clear indication that he construes the teaching as a rule that is intended to govern the behavior of Christians directly. Likewise, the detached saying in Luke 16:18 certainly reads as a rule. Paul goes on to elaborate some more rules of his own (1 Cor. 7:12–16), covering a situation that is deemed to fall outside the intended range of application of the original rule. In Mark's controversy story (Mark 10:2–9), Jesus initially rejects the Pharisees' request for a rule pronouncement but then later articulates a rule for his disciples (10:10–12). As with the rules concerning violence, Matthew's rule against divorce (5:31–32) is more than just a rule, but not less; that is, it points to the formation of the character of the community, but it does so precisely as a specific norm that is to be obeyed.

Only two of the statements in these passages could be read more broadly as *principles*: "Therefore what God has joined together, let no one separate" (Mark 10:9, Matt. 19:6b) and "It is to peace that God has called us" (1 Cor. 7:15c). The meaning of the latter is unclear unless it is read as a warrant for the immediately preceding rule allowing the believer to be separated from the unbelieving spouse.[41] The former principle (". . . let no one separate") stands as the punchline at the end of the controversy discourse; thus, its immediate narrative context specifies that it should be read as a prohibition of divorce. It will be evident, however, that the principle apart from the controversy in which it appears is also of very uncertain application. Some Christian might say, "I don't believe that my marriage was one in which *God* really joined us together; therefore, we're free to divorce." In this case, to take the principle out of its narrative context could lead to its being used in a sense diametrically opposed to the meaning of Jesus and the Gospel writers. (This example nicely illustrates why hermeneutical primacy should be given to narratives rather than principles.)

It is particularly noteworthy that none of our texts appeals to *love* as a principle that ought to determine whether a marriage should be dissolved. Modern readers would certainly expect to find some reference to love in a discussion of this topic, but the evangelists and Paul seem to regard it as irrelevant. Only in Ephesians, where divorce is not under consideration, do we find love mentioned; however, even here "love" is not so much a principle governing marriage as a narrative description of how Christ has treated the church. This narrative in turn provides the basis for an exhortation to husbands to love their wives in a way that will admit of no sundering.

Nor do we find the New Testament writers reasoning about divorce on the basis of other formal principles such as justice or personal wholeness. Principles play a decidedly minor role in the New Testament with regard to this issue.

In the *paradigm* mode, the New Testament also gives us surprisingly little to go on. In one sense, the creation story is treated as paradigmatic for marriage: the one-flesh union of Adam and Eve provides the pattern for all subsequent marriages. Very little of the story, however, is actually recounted in the New Testament, and Adam and Eve are certainly not held up as positive role models. The appeal to the Genesis narrative actually works in the *symbolic world* mode (see below). More pertinent is the paradigm of Christ and the church, both in Ephesians and in Revelation. But in neither case does the New Testament actually develop this paradigm as the basis for an argument against divorce. Furthermore, the fact that Jesus himself was not married—or at least none of our traditions ever suggest that he was—leaves the teaching against divorce without the powerful central example that we delineated in our discussion of violence. Paul also is able to offer himself only as a paradigm of celibacy (1 Cor. 7:7), even in the midst of an argument that seeks to persuade his readers *against* abstinence from sex within marriage.[42] We might wish that the New Testament offered us some moving stories of couples who overcome difficulties to maintain their marriages in obedience to Jesus' teaching, but our wish, sadly, would not be granted. The best example of this kind that we can find is the sketchy story of Hosea and Gomer in the Old Testament. Nor do we have stories illustrating the legitimate application of Matthew's exception clause or Paul's counsel to believers in mixed marriages.

There are a few negative paradigms to be found in texts that we have not considered—notably, the story of Herod and Herodias (Mark 6:17–29, Matt. 14:1–12). This example, however, does little normative work for us on the question of divorce, for these characters are bad examples for a whole variety of reasons; their marriage not only follows a divorce but is also incestuous by Jewish standards.

In the mode of *symbolic world* construction, however, the New Testament is richly instructive about the context in which marriage and divorce ought to be interpreted, as the above discussion has shown. This is the primary mode in which Ephesians 5:21–33 and Revelation become pertinent to the discussion of divorce. Likewise, the controversy discourse that is foundational for the New Testament's teaching on this matter (Mark 10:2–9) reframes the debate about divorce by shifting attention to the symbolic world set in place by the creation story. The point of Jesus' citation of this text is not that Adam and Eve were good examples of how to live out a marriage commitment; rather, the point is that God constituted a normative reality by making them male and female and joining them together as one flesh. Given that interpretation of the human condition and God's purpose in creation, the pronouncement against divorce follows inexorably. In the case of Paul, his *symbolic world* is constituted by the eschatological expectation of the Lord's return and the powerful consciousness of the church as an elect community where God's sanctifying power is at work. His pastoral discernments about divorce are formulated with reference to these perceptions of reality, and his particular counsel to those who have unbelieving spouses is intelligible only within a reality so construed.

Thus, the New Testament presents its witness against divorce primarily in the *rule* and *symbolic world* modes. Indeed, the rule forbidding divorce makes sense only within the symbolic world portrayed by these writings. It should be duly noted that this world is in the first instance the world charted out by the Old Testament and subsequently elaborated through the New Testament's Christology. Those who try to justify divorce among Christians—for reasons beyond those allowed by the New Testament—tend to appeal to general principles (e.g., "fullness of life," as in the Spong example at the beginning of this discussion) and to disregard the New Testament's specific rules. But, as we have seen, these rules are deeply grounded in the New Testament's symbolic world. Thus, in order to justify the dismissal of the rules, interpreters must also construct (or simply adopt) a different symbolic world. That observation leads us to consider the weight that ought to be given to other authorities on this question.

(B) OTHER AUTHORITIES Not surprisingly, in view of the diversity within the New Testament canon, the church's *tradition* regarding divorce and remarriage has not been entirely uniform. The Roman Catholic Church has incorporated into canon law a stringent interpretation of the teaching of the New Testament. Divorce is not recognized and remarriage is excluded, except in the case of the "Pauline privilege," which permits a Christian divorced from a non-Christian spouse to remarry. This has led in practice to the refining of a casuistic distinction between divorce and "annulment," in which the church declares that some particular marriages were never really legitimate marriages in the first place, thus allowing the partners to remarry and remain in communion. One might understand this as an extension of the process begun in Matthew and Paul of adapting the teaching to various circumstances; however, there is something disingenuous in the broad use of the term "annulment" to circumvent the New Testament's normative constraints in situations where people have actually lived as husband and wife. In a situation, for example, where a marriage is annulled because one partner is unwilling to have children, it would seem more straightforward to acknowledge that the dissolution of the marriage is simply a divorce, granted for reasons that the church deems just as weighty as Matthew deemed *porneia* to be—even though the New Testament itself offers no hint that the bearing of children is a marital obligation.

Protestantism, on the other hand—with its robust appreciation of human depravity—has generally treated divorce as a sad necessity in some cases, and it has not forbidden remarriage. Indeed, the English Reformation owes its origins partly to King Henry VIII's insistence on the legitimacy of remarriage under conditions that did not meet with Rome's approval. No Protestant theologian has ever been enthusiastic about divorce, but mainstream Protestantism has hesitated to impose the Bible's teaching as a form of ecclesiastical law. With its emphasis on love as the center of the Christian message and on the conscience as a sacrosanct center of moral decision for the individual, liberal Protestantism has found itself with little normative leverage against divorce as the wider cultural taboo against it has dissipated. In some conservative Protestant traditions, however, the New Testament prohibition of divorce and remarriage is taught and practiced rigorously. Often, though, in such traditions, the term "believer" is defined so narrowly that many baptized members of Christian churches are regarded as unbelievers; this has the effect of permitting divorce and remarriage under the provisions of 1 Corinthians 7:12–16 in a somewhat wider range of cases.

As this quick sketch indicates, the general tendency of the tradition has been to uphold the New Testament's rule against divorce but to expand the range of situations treated as exceptions to the rule, thereby extending a hermeneutical trajectory that we see within the New Testament itself. The range of the extension and the theological justifications for it have differed in different traditions. In some cases, the church's practice of accepting divorce has become so lax that the New Testament witness must be read primarily as a word of judgment on and correction for the church. In other cases, the church's rigid legalism in applying the New Testament teaching must be challenged by the New Testament's own modeling of flexibility in adapting Jesus' word to new situations.

Reason can make a subsidiary contribution to the debate on this issue. Studies can be performed on the effects of divorce on spouses and children; if divorce proves harmful to the psychological and economic well-being of the persons touched by it, one can mount consequentialist arguments against it. On the other hand, it is always possible to argue that in some cases the psychic damage of staying in a bad marriage outweighs the negative consequences of divorce. Alternatively, it could be argued positively that stable marriages are good for society at large in promoting order and the development of children. This sort of argument for the common good underlay the ubiquitous appeal of politicians to "family values" during the 1992 elections in the United States.[43] Everyone would probably agree that stable marriages are a good thing, but such an argument does not address the situation of individuals, nor is it likely to provide much motivational power for persons who are unhappy in their marriages.

The appeal to *experience* has come to play a major role in justifying divorces within the church. In the example cited by Bishop Spong, the couple—both "committed Christians" for whom the church had been "a central focus of their marriage"—had decided to divorce because they were experiencing "an increasing inability to communicate" and because they did not find "potential for life" in their relationship. Spong represents these factors as incontrovertibly valid reasons for divorce; in such circumstances, he writes, the church can only "accept the reality" of the divorce and try to provide a liturgical structure that will allow the former marriage partners and their friends to feel better about it. In our cultural setting, where such thinking has become commonplace, it requires a disciplined effort of the historical imagination to realize how strange and un-Christian such an argument would have sounded to virtually all Christian thinkers before, say, 1950. Only in a culture that exalts the therapeutic ideal of individual fulfillment over the binding character of covenant promises—and over the authority of Jesus' word—would such a line of thought be conceivable.

In Spong's description of the "Service for the Recognition of the End of a Marriage," the divorcing couple, standing before the altar and the congregation, "asked each other for forgiveness, and pledged themselves to be friends, to stand united in caring for their children, and to be civil and responsible to one another."[44] Can it really be that Christians who can say these things before God are incapable of finding God's healing in their marriage? Can it really be that the church can do no more than to say to them,

> We affirm you in the new covenant[!] you have made, one that finds you separated but still caring for each other and wishing each other good will; one that enables you to support and love your children, one that helps to heal the pain you feel. Count on God's presence. Trust our support and begin anew.[45]

Perhaps such a strange parody of the marriage covenant is better than parting in anger and abandoning the fellowship of the church.[46] But why does the bishop, in his role as a minister of the gospel of Jesus Christ, not feel compelled to say to them, "I give this command—not I but the Lord—that the wife should not separate from her husband and that the husband should not divorce his wife"? By what authority does the bishop say, "We affirm you in the new covenant you have made"?

The answer is clear: it is by the authority of *experience*, overriding everything in Scripture and tradition. The couple feels alienated and lacks the capacity to keep trying; that is the end of the matter. There is no suggestion in Spong's essay that the marriage was ended because of adultery or wife-beating, or because one spouse was an unbeliever who wanted a divorce; rather, there was just "more offense than forgiveness in their marriage." But these are Christians, who have been taught by Jesus to forgive seventy times seven (Matt. 18:21–22). What does it mean to be a follower of Jesus if it does not mean to learn the discipline of forgiveness even where it proves most difficult and painful, closest to home? William H. Willimon puts the matter in proper perspective:

> The pastor leading a marriage ceremony does not ask, "John, do you love Susan?" The pastor asks, "John, *will* you love Susan? Love is defined here as something we promise to do, a future activity, the result of marriage rather than its cause.[47]

The tragic separating couple in Spong's essay are at the mercy of their own feelings, because the church has failed to teach them that love is an act of the will, that marriage mirrors the costly fidelity of Christ to the church, and that the power of God can transform us and redeem situations that look hopeless.

What, then, can we conclude about the hermeneutical appropriation of the New Testament's witness concerning divorce and remarriage? I would offer the following suggestions:

First of all, we must recover the New Testament's vision for marriage as an aspect of *discipleship* and as a reflection of God's unbreakable *faithfulness*.

Second, the church must reaffirm its historic teaching that, since marriage is a *covenant* before God, divorce is therefore flatly contrary to God's will, save in certain extraordinary circumstances. The New Testament specifies two of these: sexual infidelity (Matthew) and the desire of an unbelieving spouse to separate (Paul). Are these the only possible grounds for divorce? On the contrary, I would argue that the list of possible legitimate causes might be extended. For instance, I would suggest (I and not the Lord!) that the physical violence of spousal abuse constitutes another circumstance that would justify marital separation, even though the New Testament does not address this problem directly.[48] In other words, I would take the New Testament's hermeneutical process of discerning exceptions to the rule of Jesus' teaching to be instructive about the *process* of moral deliberation in the church on this matter. *The canonical witness itself exemplifies a process of reflection and adaptation of the fundamental normative prohibition against divorce.*

Third, the church must recognize and teach that marriage is grounded not in *feelings* of love but in the *practice* of love. Nor is the marriage bond contingent upon self-gratification or personal fulfillment. The church has swallowed a great quantity of pop psychology that has no foundation in the biblical depiction of marriage; consequently, critical discrimination is necessary in order to restore an understanding of marriage based on the New Testament. When the marital union is rightly understood as a *covenant*, the question of divorce assumes a very different aspect. Those who have made promises before God should trust in God for grace sufficient to keep those promises, and they should expect the community of faith to help them keep faith, by supporting them and holding them accountable.

Fourth, there are occasions—as Matthew recognizes—when one partner so deeply wrongs the other that a marriage cannot continue. The hardness of heart that afflicts us all may overwhelm even our most conscientious efforts to live as Jesus' disciples. In such situations, divorce may result. If and when this happens, the church should continue to love and support the separated partners. Just as Paul in 1 Corinthians 7 does not invoke sanctions of church discipline against a couple that separates, so also the church today ought to continue to receive divorced persons as full participants in Christian fellowship.

Fifth, remarriage after divorce cannot be excluded as a possibility. Although some New Testament texts discourage or prohibit this option (Luke 16:18), others seem to leave the door open to the possibility of remarriage under certain circumstances. The Gospel of Matthew clearly allows the husband whose wife is guilty of *porneia* the option of remarriage (Matt. 5:31–32, 19:9), though Matthew does not accord this same privilege to the wife. Even the prohibitions of remarriage in Mark 10:11–12 and 1 Corinthians 7:10–11 are applied specifically only to the partner—male or female—who *initiates* the divorce; a reasonable case can be made that the silence of these texts concerning any restrictions on the spouse who is wrongly divorced implies the freedom for this "innocent" party to remarry.[49] The divorced become *agamoi* ("unmarried"), and they are therefore—I would suggest—subject to the advice that Paul gives in 1 Corinthians 7:8–9: it is good for them to remain unmarried, but if their desires are strong, it is better for them to marry than to burn with passion. The permission for remarriage would be particularly clear in the two cases stipulated by the New Testament as legitimate grounds for divorce: sexual infidelity of the partner and separation from a non-Christian spouse. (Even the stringent Roman Catholic teaching has recognized this last option on the basis of 1 Corinthians 7:15.) As I have suggested above, however, these are not the only possible cases. If the church assumes the authority to discern other exceptions to the rule against divorce, it must also acknowledge the possibility of remarriage in such cases, for "God has called us to peace." Indeed, if one purpose of marriage is to serve as a sign of God's love in the world (by symbolizing the relation between Christ and the church), how can we reject the possibility that a second marriage after a divorce could serve as a sign of grace and redemption from the sin and brokenness of the past? No New Testament writer entertains such a suggestion, but I offer it here as a constructive theological proposal. One dares to make such a suggestion precisely because the New Testament itself—especially 1 Corinthians 7—invites its readers into a process of constructive reflection and discernment about the issues of divorce and remarriage.

Sixth, the community of the church must seek to find ways to provide deep and satisfying *koinōnia* and friendships for those divorced persons who choose not to remarry in order to devote their lives to the service of God outside the married state. Such persons should be honored rather than pitied within the church, and their ministries should be recognized and supported. (These comments apply also, of course, to those who choose never to marry in the first place.) In other words, within the church we need to shatter the power of the myth that only married people are normal and that only marriage offers the conditions necessary for human fulfillment. We must work with compassion at recovering a vision for singleness as an authentic vocation (cf. 1 Cor. 7:25–40).

In sum, the controlling hermeneutical questions that we should ask in this process of discernment are these: What must we say to bear witness against shallow and false understandings of marriage in our culture, just as Jesus and Paul bore witness against shallow and false understandings of marriage in theirs? What must we say and do to form our communities so that they bear witness to God's creative intent for the permanent one-flesh union of man and woman in Christ? When these become the framing questions for our normative discourse, we will find creative ways to make the New Testament's witness against divorce speak to our time, just as the New Testament writers found creative ways to make Jesus' teaching against divorce speak to theirs.

4. Living the Text: The Church As Community Making the Love of God Visible

Writing in *Commonweal,* John Garvey offers a perceptive assessment of the future prospect for Christian marriage in a post-Christian culture:

> It could be that in time marriage seen as a sacrament, and lived as if it were a mystery of grace, will become nearly as radical a choice as monasticism, a counter-cultural thing. Maybe it is already, understood properly.[50]

How can we in the church form our life together so that the marriages in our midst do become signs of the mystery of grace? How can we enable our marriages to resist the corrosive cultural influences that make divorce seem inevitable?

In this matter, as in many others, the first great need of the church is for clear teaching. We should not wait until we are counseling couples in crisis to set forth the New Testament's teaching on marriage and divorce; rather, we must proclaim the New Testament's word on this matter in the regular course of preaching and teaching. Ministers will frequently avoid these issues in preaching, even when a text such as Mark 10:2–12 comes up in the lectionary, because the topic of divorce is regarded as too sensitive an issue for public discourse or because the teaching of the New Testament seems too hard. But avoidance of the issue merely perpetuates the cycle of ignorance and unfaithfulness that is undermining marriage in the church. Not only in premarital counseling with couples but also in proclamation from the pulpit, we need to start telling the truth about the difficult challenges of faithful marriage and about marriage as a covenantal commitment.

I have suggested above that the task of New Testament ethics is to perform an integrative act of the imagination that will bring the world of the New Testament together with our world. I offer here one small sample of such integrative reflection—an excerpt from a sermon that I preached at the wedding of two friends named Tim and Sue. This sermon articulates some of the things that we ought to be saying to bring the New Testament witness into contact with the practice of marriage in our time. The text chosen by the couple was 1 John 4:7–21.

> . . . Even though John is not writing about marriage, this text tells us two important truths about love that can shape our understanding of marriage—of the marriage between this man and this woman. The two truths are simple:
>
>> Love is made known through the death of Jesus for us.
>> Love enacted in community makes God known to the world.
>
> Let us think about these truths in turn.

Love is made known through the death of Jesus for us. That is the keynote of John's message: love proceeds from God. God is the initiator. "In this is love, not that we loved God but that he loved us and sent his Son to be the atoning sacrifice for our sins" (1 John 4:10). There is the pattern, the paradigm that defines love for us. What does love look like? There are so many counterfeits abroad. How will we recognize it when we see it? Over and over again, the Scriptures answer by pointing to Jesus' death on the cross. The love that comes from God expresses itself in sacrificial self-surrender. Jesus surrendered power and divine prerogatives and gave himself for us. That is what love is: self-giving for the beloved, not self-seeking to possess the beloved. Love that seeks only its own gratification is finally a disappointing and destructive illusion. But when we know the overflowing love of God, we let it flow through us to others. That points to the second important truth.

Love enacted in community makes God known to the world. The love of God continues to be visible, not only through the telling of the story of how God sent his Son for us but also through the ongoing life of the community of faith that lives by that story. John puts it this way: "No one has ever seen God. But if we love one another, God dwells among us, and his love is perfected among us" (1 John 4:12, RH). Do you see it? Through our acts of love, the invisible God is made visible—palpable—among us.

What does all this have to do with marriage? Just this: the love that binds man and woman in Christian marriage is not just warm spring evenings and roses, not the dizzy fantasy of fairy-tale romance. The love that binds man and woman in Christian marriage is the love of the *cross.*

That means, Tim and Sue, that your marriage is not just an arrangement that will last only as long as the rush of mutual joy lasts. It is a *covenant,* which will endure "for better for worse, . . . in sickness and in health." Not long ago, I sat and prayed with a friend whose wife was unconscious in the intensive care unit. She had gone into seizures during childbirth, and the doctors feared possible brain damage. But amidst my friend's suffering and uncertainty about the future, I saw in his love and tireless care for her a parable of the love of God, a love that surmounts fear and suffering.

But do not suppose that all suffering comes from outside through tragic mishaps. Your marriage is a covenant that must stand firm even if your spouse becomes a threat to your tranquility and personal fulfillment, even if the time should come when you feel that that other who shares your bed has become—for the moment, at least—your enemy. Jesus has taught us to love our enemies. Perhaps such a time will never come for you. But such times have come for Judy and me, and I suspect that they have come also to your parents and married friends. Certainly, in marriage there is joy. Certainly, there is companionship and comfort. But marriage in Christ can never be a tentative coupling that lasts only as long as the good times roll. The joy of marriage in Christ endures all pain because the love that binds you in Christ is rooted deeply in the love of God.

Thus, in making the covenant of marriage, you make a covenant to love one another as God has loved you—that means to love one another unconditionally, freely, sacrificially. In making the covenant of marriage, you promise to become servants of one another in love. In making the covenant of marriage, you form a union that reflects the love of God and stands as a *sign* of God's love in the world. Marriage is a sacrament in the true sense: it is both sign and vehicle of grace.

So, Tim and Sue, as you come to join your lives, this is our prayer for you:

May your marriage bear witness against all shallow, self-seeking visions of love.

May the community of faith stand about you to support you in love and to receive from your love.

May your marriage bear witness to the truth of the love of God and make God's love present to others in the world.

In confidence that God will answer that prayer, I invite you now to come forward and make your covenant before God with one another.

When marriage is understood along these lines, the logic of the New Testament's rigorous teaching against divorce comes clearly into focus. Such a countercultural interpretation of marriage as discipleship can be sustained only in a community that understands itself as the bearer of a distinct and peculiar vocation within the world. Thus, even on a matter as personal as marriage and divorce, the New Testament compels the recognition that the church's most urgent pastoral task is the formation of communities that embody the surprising hope of the new creation.

NOTES

1. Snodgrass 1989, 1, reports that in 1988 in the United States there were 2,389,000 marriages and 1,183,000 divorces.

2. For a serious attempt to address this problem from the point of view of the NT, see Keener 1991. Keener explicitly writes to offer pastoral correction of the tendency of some conservative churches to condemn and penalize "the innocent party" in divorces. As will become evident in the following discussion, my primary concern is instead to address churches that fail to provide any meaningful scripturally based teaching and discipline with regard to these matters.

3. Spong 1984. The quotation is from p. 1127, and the emphasis is mine.

4. Spong, 1984, 1126.

5. Since our interpretive work is always conditioned to some extent by the history that we bring to the text, it may be useful for me to clarify the perspective from which I speak to this problem. (1) My parents were divorced when I was two years old; neither ever remarried. Thus, I grew up in a one-parent household. (2) I am married, and have been—as of this writing—for twenty-five years.

6. See Chapter 3.

7. Schrage 1988, 94; R. F. Collins 1992, 74.

8. The matter looks different in Matthew, because of the different form in which the question is posed. See discussion below.

9. Readers of Mark's Gospel will also know that John the Baptist fell afoul of Herod by condemning his marriage to a divorced woman (Mark 6:17–29). The issue in this case, however, was not divorce as such but Herod's marriage to the former wife of his own brother (cf. Lev. 18:16, 20:21). Still, Jesus' debate with the Pharisees over divorce law occurs within a politically charged atmosphere.

10. Thus, the Pharisees are depicted in this story in a way consistent with Jesus' earlier charge that they hide behind human traditions (such as the practice of declaring material resources as *corban*—a sacrifice or offering to God—and thereby avoiding responsibility for supporting elderly parents) in order to reject the commandment of God (Mark 7:1–13).

11. *Damascus Document (CD)* 4:21, cited according to the translation of Vermes 1987, 86.

12. For an account of the argument on this point, see R. F. Collins 1992, 81–85.

13. For a clear discussion and summary, see Countryman 1988, 147–167, esp. 157–159.

14. Countryman 1988, 175.

15. See, however, Brooten 1982.

16. *m. Git.* 9.10, as translated by Danby 1933, 321.

17. In the final verses of this passage (Matt. 19:10–12), we encounter a puzzling dialogue between Jesus and the disciples. Space precludes a full consideration of the problems of this text, but the following observations

are pertinent to our present concerns. The disciples, astonished at Jesus' prohibition of divorce—even with the exception clause—exclaim, "If such is the case of a man with his wife, it is better not to marry." As David Hill (1972, p. 281) remarks, "They are virtually making the attractiveness of marriage contingent upon the possibility of easy divorce!" This response underscores our earlier observation that the call to renounce the option of divorce would have been understood in the first century as an extraordinary call to costly discipleship. Jesus' answer to the disciples, with its striking imagery about eunuchs, has served as an important basis for the church's traditional teaching about celibacy, but in the Matthean context it must be understood as a response to the disciples' complaint about the difficulty of Jesus' teaching against divorce. The major point of the saying is articulated in its opening and closing sentences: "Not everyone can accept this teaching, but only those to whom it is given. . . . Let anyone accept this who can." The words "this teaching" (*ton logon touton*, literally "this word") refer back to the teaching against divorce (vv. 3–9). In Matthew's context, the saying cannot be understood to posit two sorts of disciples: those who can accept the divorce teaching and those who cannot. Rather, the phrase "those to whom it is given" recalls Jesus' statement to the disciples in 13:11: "To you it is given to know the secrets of the kingdom of heaven." Those to whom it is given are Jesus' disciples, all of whom are instructed to obey his teachings without exception (28:16–20). Those who cannot accept the divorce teaching are the outsiders, such as the Pharisees (who remain closed and resistant to Jesus' authority). However difficult the teaching may appear—even if it leads disciples to "make themselves eunuchs" by choosing to forego marriage, even if Christian husbands feel castrated by losing their usual manly prerogative to divorce their wives—it is to be obeyed, in the knowledge that the capacity for obedience is itself a gift of God. The saying is thus exactly parallel to the teaching that follows in Matt. 19:23–26 about the renunciation of possessions: "For mortals it is impossible, but for God all things are possible." For a helpful exposition of this parallelism and of Matt. 19:10–12 more broadly, see R. F. Collins 1992, 115–134.

18. The formulation of Matt. 19:9, despite arguments to the contrary, does not forbid the husband who divorces his wife for *porneia* to remarry. Only the one who divorces his wife for some other reason and then remarries is said to be guilty of adultery. In Matthew 19, the exception clause appears to be a genuine exception; the normal expectation under Jewish Law is that a person legally divorced is free to remarry, and nothing is said in this passage to counter that expectation. (As we shall see, prohibitions of remarriage are based on other NT texts.)

19. R. F. Collins 1992, 207–208, argues this position on the basis of the wording of Matt. 5:32.

20. Rightly noted by R. F. Collins 1992, 206.

21. R. F. Collins 1992, 191.

22. See, e.g., Dumais 1977.

23. See, e.g., Bonsirven 1948; Baltensweiler 1959; Baltensweiler 1967; Guelich 1982.

24. Guelich 1982, 205.

25. Strecker 1988, 75.

26. R. F. Collins 1992, 212.

27. The NRSV translates this phrase in Deut. 24:1 as "something objectionable," thereby tacitly endorsing Hillel's interpretation of the passage. (I am indebted to A. Katherine Grieb for this observation.)

28. Luke, however, does not explicitly speak of adultery "against her."

29. See the discussion of this passage in Chapter 1.4.a.

30. Some scholars have suggested that Paul is responding to a single particular case in which a Corinthian wife is wanting to leave her husband, perhaps for ascetic spiritual reasons. I see no evidence for this in the text. The formulation of the address in vv. 10–11 is general: "To those who are married I give this command. . . ."

31. Wire 1990, 72–97.

32. This nuance is lost in the NRSV, which translates this passive verb in the active voice.

33. This much-disputed passage is often regarded as a non-Pauline interpolation in 2 Corinthians. For discussion of the arguments, see Furnish 1984, 371–383.

34. Here Paul uses the same verb (*aphienai*) with the woman as the subject that he used of the man in vv. 11 and 12.

35. This point is emphasized by Furnish 1985, 43.

36. Plutarch, "Advice to Bride and Groom," 140.19. (*Moralia*, vol. 2; LCL).

37. Here I have modified the translation to follow the NRSV margin. The reading "us" rather than "you" is strongly supported by the external manuscript evidence. On this issue, see Fee 1987, 297 n. 6.

38. For a less complex typology, omitting the element of literal marriages in the community, see 2 Cor. 11:2.

39. Or husband, as in Malachi 2.

40. This formulation once again reveals that I speak from within the ecclesial context of mainline Protestantism.

41. Some exegetes argue that 7:15c should be read with v. 16—i.e., that it provides not a reason for allowing the unbeliever to separate but rather a reason for the believer to seek to remain peacefully in the marriage. See,

e.g., Fee 1987, 303–305. It has not been possible to discuss this exegetical problem here, but the weight of probability lies with the reading adopted above.

42. It is tempting to turn to the Song of Solomon to find a joyous, sensual celebration of sex; the only difficulty with that text for our present purposes is that it does not explicitly describe the passionate lovers in the poem as married.

43. See Whitehead 1993.

44. Spong 1984, 1127.

45. Spong 1984, 1127.

46. One reader of my manuscript comments: "I would agree that such a pathetic 'parody' of the marriage covenant *might* be better than abandoning the fellowship of the church, but I would not say that it is 'better than parting in anger.' It seems to me that anger at injustice and unfaithfulness is something Christians today need to foster rather than avoid. It may be the case that the only faithful way to part is in anger."

47. Willimon 1990, 925.

48. This is merely one illustration. My aim here is not to produce a list of exceptions but to illustrate the sort of hermeneutical procedures that we might apply to the texts.

49. For an extended argument in defense of this position, see Keener 1991.

50. Garvey 1987, 169.

Chapter 16

Homosexuality

Gary came to New Haven in the summer of 1989 to say a proper farewell. My best friend from undergraduate years at Yale, he was dying of AIDS. While he was still able to travel, my family and I invited him to come visit us one more time.[1]

During the week he stayed with us, we went to films together (*Field of Dreams* and *Dead Poets Society*), we drank wine and laughed, we had long sober talks about politics and literature and the gospel and sex and such. Above all, we listened to music. Some of it was nostalgic music: the record of our college singing group, which Gary had directed with passionate precision; music of the sixties, recalling the years when we marched together against the Vietnam War—Beatles, Byrds, Bob Dylan, Joni Mitchell. Some of it was music more recently discovered: I introduced him to R.E.M. and the Indigo Girls; he introduced me to Johannes Ockeghem's *Requiem* (*Missa pro defunctis*). As always, his aesthetic sense was fine and austere; as always, he was determined to face the truth, even in the shadow of death.

We prayed together often that week, and we talked theology. It became clear that Gary had come not only to say goodbye but also to think hard, before God, about the relation between his homosexuality and his Christian faith. He was angry at the self-affirming gay Christian groups, because he regarded his own condition as more complex and tragic than their apologetic stance could acknowledge. He also worried that the gay apologists encouraged homosexual believers to "draw their identity from their sexuality" and thus to shift the ground of their identity subtly and idolatrously away from God. For more than twenty years, Gary had grappled with his homosexuality, experiencing it as a compulsion and an affliction. Now, as he faced death, he wanted to talk it all through again from the beginning, because he knew my love for him and trusted me to speak without dissembling. For Gary, there was no time to dance around the hard questions. As Dylan had urged, "Let us not talk falsely now; the hour is getting late."

In particular, Gary wanted to discuss the biblical passages that deal with homosexual acts. Among Gary's many gifts was his skill as a reader of texts. After leaving Yale and helping to found a community-based Christian theater group in Toronto, he had eventually completed a master's degree in French literature. Though he was not trained as a biblical exegete, he was a careful and sensitive interpreter. He had read hopefully through the standard bibliography of the burgeoning movement advocating the acceptance of homosexuality in the church: John J. McNeill, *The Church and the Homosexual;* James B. Nelson, *Embodiment;* Letha Scanzoni and Virginia Ramey Mollenkott, *Is the Homosexual My Neighbor?;* John Boswell, *Christianity, Social Tolerance, and Homosexuality.*[2] In the end, he came away disappointed, believing that these authors, despite their good intentions, had imposed a wishful interpretation on the biblical passages. However much he wanted to believe that the Bible did not condemn homosexuality, he would not violate his own stubborn intellectual integrity by pretending to find their arguments persuasive.

The more we talked, the more we found our perspectives interlocking. Both of us had serious misgivings about the mounting pressure for the church to recognize homosexuality as a legitimate Christian lifestyle. As a New Testament scholar, I was concerned about certain questionable exegetical and theological strategies of the gay apologists. As a homosexual Christian, Gary believed that their writings did justice neither to the biblical texts nor to his own sobering experience of the gay community that he had moved in and out of for twenty years.

We concluded that our witnesses were complementary and that we had a word to speak to the churches. The public discussion of this matter has been dominated by insistently ideological voices: on one side, gay rights activists demanding the church's unqualified acceptance of homosexuality; on the other, unqualified condemnation of homosexual Christians. Consequently, the church has become increasingly polarized. Gary and I agreed that we should try to encourage a more nuanced discourse within the community of faith. He was going to write an article about his own experience, reflecting on his struggle to live as a faithful Christian wracked by a sexual orientation that he believed to be incommensurate with the teaching of Scripture, and I agreed to write a response to it.

Tragically, Gary soon became too sick to carry out his intention. His last letter to me was an effort to get some of his thoughts on paper while he was still able to write. By May of 1990 he was dead.

This section of the present book, then, is an act of keeping covenant with a beloved brother in Christ who will not speak again on this side of the resurrection. I commit it to print in the hope that it will foster compassionate and carefully reasoned theological reflection within the community of faith.[3] The need for such reflection is great; no issue divides the church more sharply in the 1990s than the normative status of homosexuality. How is Scripture rightly to be employed in our deliberations about this matter?

1. Reading the Texts

The Bible hardly ever discusses homosexual behavior. There are perhaps half a dozen brief references to it in all of Scripture. In terms of emphasis, it is a minor concern—in contrast, for example, to economic injustice. The paucity of texts addressing the issue is a significant fact for New Testament ethics. What the Bible does say should be heeded carefully, but any ethic that intends to be biblical will seek to get the accents in the right place, not overemphasizing peripheral issues. (Would that the passion presently being expended in the church over the question of homosexuality were devoted instead to urging the wealthy to share with the poor! Some of the most urgent champions of "biblical morality" on sexual matters become strangely equivocal when the discussion turns to the New Testament's teachings about possessions.)[4]

As we deal with this issue, it will be useful first to comment briefly on the Old Testament texts usually cited. This procedure will enable us to clear away some possible misconceptions and to delineate the basis for the traditional Jewish teaching that is presupposed by the New Testament writers.

(A) **GENESIS 19:1–29** The notorious story of Sodom and Gomorrah—often cited in connection with homosexuality—is actually irrelevant to the topic. The "men of Sodom" come pounding on Lot's door, apparently with the intention of gang-raping Lot's two visitors—who, as we readers know, are actually angels. The angels rescue Lot and his family and pronounce destruction on the city. The gang-rape scenario exemplifies the wickedness of the city, but there is nothing in the passage pertinent to a judgment about the morality of consensual homosexual intercourse. Indeed, there is nothing in the rest of the biblical tradition, save an obscure reference in Jude 7, to suggest that the sin of Sodom was particularly identified with sexual misconduct of any kind.[5] In fact, the clearest statement about the sin of Sodom is to be found in an oracle of the prophet Ezekiel: "This was the guilt of your sister Sodom: she and her daughters had pride, excess of food, and prosperous ease, but did not aid the poor and needy" (Ezek. 16:49).

(B) **LEVITICUS 18:22, 20:13** The few biblical texts that *do* address the topic of homosexual behavior, however, are unambiguously and unremittingly negative in their judgment. The holiness code in Leviticus explicitly prohibits male homosexual intercourse: "You shall not lie with a male as with a woman; it is an abomination" (Lev. 18:22). (Nothing is said here about female homosexual behavior.) In Leviticus 20:10–16, the same act is listed as one of a series of sexual offenses—along with adultery, incest, and bestiality—that are punishable by death. It is worth noting that the *act* of "lying with a male as with a woman" is categorically proscribed: motives for the act are not treated as a morally significant factor. This unambiguous legal prohibition stands as the foundation for the subsequent universal rejection of male same-sex intercourse within Judaism.[6]

Quoting a law from Leviticus, of course, does not necessarily settle the question for Christian ethics. The Old Testament contains many prohibitions and commandments that have, ever since the first century, generally been disregarded or deemed obsolete by the church—most notably, rules concerning circumcision and dietary practices. Some ethicists have argued that the prohibition of homosexuality is similarly superseded for Christians: it is merely part of the Old Testament's ritual "purity rules" and therefore morally irrelevant today.[7]

The Old Testament, however, makes no systematic distinction between ritual law and moral law. The same section of the holiness code also contains, for instance, the prohibition of incest (Lev. 18:6–18). Is that a purity law or a moral law? Leviticus makes no distinction in principle. In each case, the church is faced with the task of discerning whether Israel's traditional norms remain in force for the new community of Jesus' followers. In order to see what decisions the early church made about this matter, we must turn to the New Testament.

(C) 1 CORINTHIANS 6:9–11, 1 TIMOTHY 1:10, ACTS 15:28–29 The early church did, in fact, consistently adopt the Old Testament's teaching on matters of sexual morality, including homosexual acts. In 1 Corinthians 6:9 and 1 Timothy 1:10, for example, we find homosexuals included in lists of persons who do things unacceptable to God.

In 1 Corinthians 6, Paul, exasperated with the Corinthians, some of whom apparently believe themselves to have entered a spiritually exalted state in which the moral rules of their old existence no longer apply to them (cf. 1 Cor. 4:8, 5:1–2, 8:1–9), confronts them with a blunt rhetorical question: "Do you not know that wrongdoers will not inherit the kingdom of God?" He then gives an illustrative list of the sorts of persons he means: "fornicators, idolaters, adulterers, *malakoi, arsenokoitai,* thieves, the greedy, drunkards, revilers, robbers."

I have left the terms pertinent to the present issue untranslated, because their translation has been disputed recently by Boswell and others.[8] The word *malakoi* is not a technical term meaning "homosexuals" (no such term existed either in Greek or in Hebrew), but it appears often in Hellenistic Greek as pejorative slang to describe the "passive" partners—often young boys—in homosexual activity. The other word, *arsenokoitai,* is not found in any extant Greek text earlier than 1 Corinthians. Some scholars have suggested that its meaning is uncertain, but Robin Scroggs has shown that the word is a translation of the Hebrew *mishkav zakur* ("lying with a male"), derived directly from Leviticus 18:22 and 20:13 and used in rabbinic texts to refer to homosexual intercourse.[9] The Septuagint (Greek Old Testament) of Leviticus 20:13 reads, "Whoever lies with a man as with a woman [*meta arsenos koitēn gynaikos*], they have both done an abomination" (my translation). This is almost certainly the idiom from which the noun *arsenokoitai* was coined. Thus, Paul's use of the term presupposes and reaffirms the holiness code's condemnation of homosexual acts. This is not a controversial point in Paul's argument; the letter gives no evidence that anyone at Corinth was arguing for the acceptance of same-sex erotic activity. Paul simply assumes that his readers will share his conviction that those who indulge in homosexual activity are "wrongdoers" (*adikoi*, literally "unrighteous"), along with the other sorts of offenders in his list.

In 1 Corinthians 6:11, Paul asserts that the sinful behaviors catalogued in the vice list were formerly practiced by some of the Corinthians. Now, however, since Paul's correspondents have been transferred into the sphere of Christ's lordship, they ought to have left these practices behind: "This is what some of you used to be. But you were washed, you were sanctified, you were justified in the name of the Lord Jesus Christ and in the Spirit of our God." The remainder of the chapter, then (1 Cor. 6:12–20), counsels the Corinthians to glorify God in their bodies, because they belong now to God and no longer to themselves.

The 1 Timothy passage includes *arsenokoitai* in a list of "the lawless and disobedient," whose behavior is specified in a vice list that includes everything from lying to slave-trading to murdering one's parents, under the rubric of actions "contrary to the sound teaching that conforms to the glorious gospel." Here again, the Old Testament prohibition is presupposed, but the context offers little discussion of sexual morality as such.

One other possibly relevant passage is the apostolic decree of Acts 15:28–29, which rules that Gentile converts to the new Christian movement must observe a list of minimal purity prohibitions in order to have fellowship with the predominantly Jewish early church:

> For it has seemed good to the Holy Spirit and to us to impose on you no further burden than these essentials: that you abstain from what has been sacrificed to idols and from blood and from what is strangled and from fornication [**porneia**].[10]

If, as seems likely, these stipulations are based on the purity regulations of Leviticus 17:1–18:30—which apply not only to Israelites but also to "the aliens who reside among them" (Lev. 17:8–16, 18:26)—then the umbrella term *porneia* might well include all the sexual transgressions enumerated in Leviticus 18:6–30, including *inter alia* homosexual intercourse. This suggestion about the Old Testament background for Acts 15:28–29 is probable but not certain. In any case, the immediate narrative context in Acts reflects a primary concern with the issue of whether Gentile converts must be circumcised; sexual morality is not the major point at issue. Thus the precise scope of the prohibited *porneia* is not explained in the story.

(D) ROMANS 1:18–32 The most crucial text for Christian ethics concerning homosexuality remains Romans 1, because this is the only passage in the New Testament that explains the condemnation of homosexual behavior in an explicitly theological context.

> *Therefore God gave them up in the lusts of their hearts to impurity, to the dishonoring*[11] *of their bodies among themselves, because they exchanged the truth about God for a lie and worshiped and served the creature rather than the Creator. . . . For this reason God gave them up to dishonorable passions. Their women exchanged natural intercourse for*

> *unnatural, and in the same way also the men, giving up natural intercourse with women, were consumed with passion for one another. Men committed shameless acts with men and received in their own persons the due penalty for their own error.* (ROM. 1:24–27)

(This is, incidentally, the only passage in the Bible that refers to lesbian sexual relations.) Because the passage is often cited and frequently misunderstood, a careful examination of its place in Paul's argument is necessary.

After the greeting and introductory thanksgiving (Rom. 1:1–15), the substance of Paul's exposition begins with a programmatic declaration in 1:16–17: the gospel is "the power of God for salvation to everyone who has faith, to the Jew first and also to the Greek. For in it the righteousness of God is revealed through faith for faith; as it is written, 'The one who is righteous will live by faith.'" This theologically pregnant formulation emphasizes first of all the character of the gospel as an active manifestation of God's power. The gospel is not merely a moral or philosophical teaching that hearers may accept or reject as they choose; it is rather the eschatological instrument through which God is working his purpose out in the world.[12]

Like Habakkuk long before him and like Milton long after, Paul is undertaking in his own way to "justify the ways of God to men"[13] by proclaiming that the righteousness of God (*dikaiosynē theou*) is now definitively manifest in the gospel. As a demonstration of his righteousness, God has "put forward" Jesus Christ, precisely in order "to prove at the present time that he himself [i.e., God] is righteous" (Rom. 3:25–26). The gospel is, among other things, a vindication of God. Of course, this vindication of God's righteousness entails more than an abstract declaration of God's moral uprightness; for Paul, the gospel that proclaims God's justice is also a power, "the power of God for salvation" (1:16), reaching out graciously to deliver humanity from bondage to sin and death.[14]

Having sounded this keynote, Paul abruptly modulates into a contrasting key by turning to condemn the unrighteousness of fallen humanity: "For the wrath of God is revealed from heaven against all ungodliness and wickedness of those who by their wickedness suppress the truth" (1:18). The Greek word that the NRSV translates as "wickedness" (*adikia*), used twice in 1:18 for unmistakable emphasis, is the direct antithesis of "righteousness" (*dikaiosynē*). Unless we translate it as "unrighteousness," we are apt to miss the intended contrast; the righteousness of God is manifest in God's wrath against the unrighteousness of humankind. The ensuing discussion (1:19–32) explains, documents, and elaborates this human unrighteousness. Humanity's unrighteousness consists fundamentally in a refusal to honor God and render him thanks (1:21). God has clearly shown forth his "power and divine nature" in and through the created world (1:19–20), but the human race in general has disregarded this evidence and turned on a massive scale to idolatry (1:23). The genius of Paul's analysis, of course, lies in his refusal to posit a catalog of sins as the cause of human alienation from God. Instead, he delves to the root: all other depravities follow from the radical rebellion of the creature against the Creator (1:24–31).

As Ernst Käsemann comments, "Paul paradoxically reverses the cause and consequence: moral perversion is the result of God's wrath, not the reason for it."[15]

In order to make his accusation stick, Paul has to claim that these human beings are actually in rebellion against God, not merely ignorant of him. The way in which the argument is framed here is crucial: ignorance is the consequence of humanity's primal rebellion. Because human beings did not acknowledge God, "they became futile in their thinking, and their senseless minds were darkened" (1:21; cf. 2 Thess. 2:10b–12). Paul does not argue on a case-by-case basis that every single individual has first known and then rejected God; instead, thinking in mythico-historical categories, he casts forth a blanket condemnation of humankind. The whole passage is "Paul's real story of the universal fall."[16] As Käsemann puts it, "For the apostle, history is governed by the primal sin of rebellion against the Creator, which finds repeated and universal expression."[17] The passage is not merely a polemical denunciation of selected pagan vices; it is a diagnosis of the human condition. The diseased behavior detailed in verses 24–31 is symptomatic of the one sickness of humanity as a whole. Because they have turned away from God, "all, both Jews and Greeks, are under the power of sin" (3:9).

According to Paul's analysis, God's "wrath" against his fallen human creatures takes the ironic form of allowing them the freedom to have their own way, abandoning them to their own devices.

> *Claiming to be wise, they became fools; and they exchanged the glory of the immortal God for images resembling a mortal human being or birds or four-footed animals or reptiles. Therefore God gave them up in the lusts of their hearts to impurity, to the dishonoring of their bodies among themselves, because they exchanged the truth about God for a lie and worshiped and served the creature rather than the Creator.* (1:22–25)

These and the following sentences, in which the refrain "God gave them up" occurs three times (1:24, 26, 28), repeatedly drive home Paul's point: idolatry finally debases both the worshiper and the idol. God's judgment allows the irony of sin to play itself out: the creature's original impulse toward self-glorification ends in self-destruction. The refusal to acknowledge God as Creator ends in blind distortion of the creation.

Thus, the particular depravities catalogued in verses 24–31 serve two basic purposes in Paul's argument. (Notice that the failings listed in verses 29–31 have nothing to do with sexual behavior.) First, these various forms of "debased mind" and "things that should not be done" are seen to be manifestations (not provocations) of the wrath of God, punishments inflicted upon rebellious humanity rather as the plagues were visited upon the Egyptians in Exodus.[18] Paul is not warning his readers that they will incur the wrath of God if they do the things that he lists here; rather, speaking in Israel's prophetic tradition, he is presenting an empirical survey of rampant human lawlessness as evidence that God's wrath and judgment are *already* at work in the world. Second, the heaping up of depravities serves to demonstrate

Paul's evaluation of humanity as deeply implicated in "ungodliness and wickedness" (1:18b). John Calvin saw clearly that Paul uses homosexuality as an illustration of his point because

> [u]ngodliness is a hidden evil, and therefore Paul uses a more obvious proof [i.e., homosexual acts] to show that they cannot escape without just condemnation, since this ungodliness was followed by effects which prove manifest evidence of the wrath of the Lord. . . . Paul uses these signs to prove the apostasy and defection of men.[19]

It is certainly true that Paul's portrayal of homosexual behavior is of a secondary and illustrative character in relation to the main line of argument;[20] however, the illustration is one that both Paul and his readers would have regarded as particularly vivid. Rebellion against this Creator who may be "understood and seen in the things that he has made" is made palpable in the flouting of sexual distinctions that are fundamental to God's creative design. The reference to God as Creator would certainly evoke for Paul, as well as for his readers, immediate recollections of the creation story in Genesis 1–3, which proclaims that "God created humankind in his own image . . . male and female he created them," charging them to "be fruitful and multiply" (Gen. 1:27–28).[21] Similarly, as we have noted in our discussion of divorce, Genesis 2:18–24 describes woman and man as created for one another and concludes with a summary moral: "Therefore a man leaves his father and his mother and clings to his wife, and they become one flesh." Thus the complementarity of male and female is given a theological grounding in God's creative activity. By way of sharp contrast, in Romans 1 Paul portrays homosexual behavior as a "sacrament" (so to speak) of the antireligion of human beings who refuse to honor God as Creator. When human beings engage in homosexual activity, they enact an outward and visible sign of an inward and spiritual reality: the rejection of the Creator's design. Thus, Paul's choice of homosexuality as an illustration of human depravity is not merely random: it serves his rhetorical purposes by providing a vivid image of humanity's primal rejection of the sovereignty of God the Creator.

The language of "exchange" plays a central role in this passage, emphasizing the direct parallelism between the rejection of God and the rejection of created sexual roles. The "exchange" imagery first appears in 1:23, where Paul charges that rebellious humans have "exchanged [*ēllaxan*] the glory of the immortal God for images resembling a mortal human being or birds or four-footed animals or reptiles." The accusation is recapitulated in 1:25, where it is for the first time connected directly to sexual impurity: because "they exchanged [*metēllaxan*] the truth about God for a lie and worshiped and served the creature rather than the Creator," God handed them over to "the dishonoring of their bodies among themselves." Up to this point, Paul's condemnation could apply equally well to all sexual offenses, heterosexual as well as homosexual.

In 1:26–27, however, he introduces a further development in his account of humanity's tragic rebellious trade-off: "Their women exchanged [*metēllaxan*] natural relations for unnatural, and the men likewise gave up natural relations with women and were consumed with passion for one another." The deliberate repetition of the verb *metēllaxan* forges a powerful rhetorical link between the rebellion against God and the "shameless acts" (1:27) that are themselves both evidence and consequence of that rebellion.

In describing what it is that straying humans have "exchanged," Paul for the first time introduces the concept of "nature" (*physis*) into the argument (1:26): they have exchanged (translating literally) "the natural use for that which is contrary to nature" (*tēn physikēn chrēsin eis tēn para physin*). What did Paul mean by "nature," and where does this idea come from?

There are abundant instances, both in the work of Greco-Roman moral philosophers and in literary texts, of the opposition between "natural" (*kata physin*) and "unnatural" (*para physin*) behavior. These categories play a major role in Stoicism, where right moral action is closely identified with living *kata physin*. In particular, the opposition between "natural" and "unnatural" is very frequently used (in the absence of convenient Greek words for "heterosexual" and "homosexual") as a way of distinguishing between heterosexual and homosexual behavior.[22]

This categorization of homosexual behavior as "contrary to nature" was adopted with particular vehemence by Hellenistic Jewish writers, who tended to see a correspondence between the philosophical appeal to "nature" and the teachings of the Law of Moses. "The Law recognizes no sexual connections," writes Josephus, "except for the natural [*kata physin*] union of man and wife, and that only for the procreation of children. But it abhors the intercourse of males with males, and punishes any who undertake such a thing with death."[23] In Paul's time, the categorization of homosexual practices as *para physin* was a commonplace feature of polemical attacks against such behavior, particularly in the world of Hellenistic Judaism. When this idea turns up in Romans 1 (in a form relatively restrained by comparison to the statements of some of Paul's contemporaries, both pagan and Jewish), we must recognize that Paul is hardly making an original contribution to theological thought on the subject; he speaks out of a Hellenistic-Jewish cultural context in which homosexuality is regarded as an abomination, and he assumes that his readers will share his negative judgment of it. In fact, the whole design and logic of his argument demands such an assumption. Though he offers no explicit reflection on the concept of "nature," it appears that in this passage Paul identifies "nature" with the created order. The understanding of "nature" in this conventional language does not rest on empirical observation of what actually exists; instead, it appeals to a conception of what ought to be, of the world as designed by God and revealed through the stories and laws of Scripture. Those who indulge in sexual practices *para physin* are defying the Creator and demonstrating their own alienation from him.

Let us summarize briefly our reading of Paul on this issue. The aim of Romans 1 is not to teach a code of sexual ethics; nor is the passage a warning of God's judgment against those who are guilty of particular sins. Rather, Paul is offering a *diagnosis* of the disordered human condition: he adduces the fact of widespread homosexual behavior as evidence that human beings are indeed in rebellion against their Creator. The fundamental human sin is the refusal to honor God and give God thanks (1:21); consequently, God's wrath takes the form of letting human idolatry run its own self-destructive course. Homosexual activity, then, is not a *provocation* of "the wrath of God" (Rom. 1:18); rather, it is a *consequence* of God's decision to "give up" rebellious creatures to follow their own futile thinking and desires. The unrighteous behavior catalogued in Romans 1:26–31 is a list of *symptoms:* the underlying sickness of humanity as a whole, Jews and Greeks alike, is that they have turned away from God and fallen under the power of sin (cf. Rom. 3:9).

When this context is kept clearly in view, several important observations follow:

- Paul is not describing the individual life histories of pagan sinners; not every pagan has first known the true God of Israel and then chosen to turn away into idolatry. When Paul writes, "They exchanged the truth about God for a lie," he is giving a global account of the universal fall of humanity.[24] This fall is manifested continually in the various ungodly behaviors listed in verses 24–31.
- Paul singles out homosexual intercourse for special attention because he regards it as providing a particularly graphic image of the way in which human fallenness distorts God's created order. God the Creator made man and woman for each other, to cleave together, to be fruitful and multiply. When human beings "exchange" these created roles for homosexual intercourse, they *embody* the spiritual condition of those who have "exchanged the truth about God for a lie."
- Homosexual acts are not, however, specially reprehensible sins; they are no worse than any of the other manifestations of human unrighteousness listed in the passage (vv. 29–31)—no worse in principle than covetousness or gossip or disrespect for parents.
- Homosexual activity will not *incur* God's punishment: it is its own punishment, an "antireward." Paul here simply echoes a traditional Jewish idea. The Wisdom of Solomon, an intertestamental writing that has surely informed Paul's thinking in Romans 1, puts it like this: "Therefore those who lived unrighteously, in a life of folly, [God] tormented through their own abominations" (Wisdom of Solomon 12:23).

Repeated again and again in recent debate is the claim that Paul condemns only homosexual acts committed promiscuously by heterosexual persons—because they "*exchanged* natural intercourse for unnatural." Paul's negative judgment, so the argument goes, does *not* apply to persons who are "naturally" of homosexual orientation. This interpretation, however, is untenable. The "exchange" is not a matter of individual life decisions; rather, it is Paul's characterization of the fallen condition of the pagan world. In any case, neither Paul nor anyone else in antiquity had a concept of "sexual orientation." To introduce this concept into the passage (by suggesting that Paul disapproves only those who act contrary to their individual sexual orientations) is to lapse into anachronism. The fact is that Paul treats *all* homosexual activity as prima facie evidence of humanity's tragic confusion and alienation from God the Creator.

But one more thing must be said: Romans 1:18–32 sets up a homiletical sting operation. The passage builds a crescendo of condemnation, declaring God's wrath upon human unrighteousness, using rhetoric characteristic of Jewish polemic against Gentile immorality. It whips the reader into a frenzy of indignation against others: those unbelievers, those idol-worshipers, those immoral enemies of God. But then, in Romans 2:1, the sting strikes: "Therefore you have no excuse, whoever you are, when you judge others; for in passing judgment on another you condemn yourself, because you, the judge, are doing the very same things." The reader who gleefully joins in the condemnation of the unrighteous is "without excuse" (*anapologētos*) before God (2:1), just as those who refuse to acknowledge God are *anapologētos* (1:20). The radical move that Paul makes is to proclaim that all people, Jews and Gentiles alike, stand equally condemned under the just judgment of a righteous God.

Consequently, for Paul, self-righteous judgment of homosexuality is just as sinful as the homosexual behavior itself. That does not mean that Paul is disingenuous in his rejection of homosexual acts and all the other sinful activities mentioned in Romans 1:24–32; all the evils listed there remain evils (cf. also Rom. 6:1–23).[25] But no one should presume to be above God's judgment; all of us stand in radical need of God's mercy. Thus, Paul's warning should transform the terms of our contemporary debate about homosexuality: no one has a secure platform to stand upon in order to pronounce condemnation on others. Anyone who presumes to have such a vantage point is living in a dangerous fantasy, oblivious to the gospel that levels all of us before a holy God.

2. Synthesis: Homosexuality in Canonical Context

Though only a few biblical texts speak of homoerotic activity, all that do mention it express unqualified disapproval. Thus, on this issue, there is no synthetic problem for New Testament ethics. In this respect, the issue of homosexuality differs significantly from matters such as slavery or the subordination of women, concerning which the Bible contains internal tensions and counterposed witnesses. The biblical witness against homosexual practices is univocal.

No theological consideration of homosexuality can rest content, however, with a short list of passages that treat the matter explicitly. We must consider how Scripture frames the discussion more broadly: How is human sexuality portrayed in the canon as a whole, and how are the few explicit texts treating homosexuality to be read in relation to this larger canonical framework? To place the prohibition of homosexual activity in a canonical context, we should keep in mind at least the following factors in the biblical portrayal of human existence before God.

(A) GOD'S CREATIVE INTENTION FOR HUMAN SEXUALITY From Genesis 1 onward, Scripture affirms repeatedly that God has made man and woman for one another and that our sexual desires rightly find fulfillment within heterosexual marriage. (See, for instance, Mark 10:2–9, 1 Thess. 4:3–8, 1 Cor. 7:1–9, Eph. 5:21–33, Heb. 13:4. The Song of Solomon, however it is to be interpreted, also celebrates love and sexual desire between man and woman.) The general lines of this portrait were sketched in the foregoing discussion of divorce and need not be repeated here. This normative canonical picture of marriage provides the positive backdrop against which the Bible's few emphatic negations of homosexuality must be read.

(B) THE FALLEN HUMAN CONDITION The biblical analysis of the human predicament, most sharply expressed in Pauline theology, offers a subtle account of human bondage to sin. As great-grandchildren of the Enlightenment, we like to think of ourselves as free moral agents, choosing rationally among possible actions, but Scripture unmasks that cheerful illusion and teaches us that we are deeply infected by the tendency to self-deception. As Jeremiah lamented, "The heart is deceitful above all things, and desperately corrupt; who can understand it?" (Jer. 17:9, RSV). Romans 1 depicts humanity in a state of self-affirming confusion: "They became futile in their thinking, and their senseless minds were darkened. Claiming to be wise, they became fools. . . . They know God's decree, that those who practice such things deserve to die—yet they not only do them but applaud others who practice them" (Rom. 1:21–22, 32). Once in the fallen state, we are not free not to sin: we are "slaves of sin" (Rom. 6:17), which distorts our perceptions, overpowers our will, and renders us incapable of obedience (Rom. 7). Redemption (a word that means "being emancipated from slavery") is God's act of liberation, setting us free from the power of sin and placing us within the sphere of God's transforming power for righteousness (Rom. 6:20–22, 8:1–11, cf. 12:1–2).

Thus, the Bible's sober anthropology rejects the apparently commonsense assumption that only freely chosen acts are morally culpable. Quite the reverse: the very nature of sin is that it is *not* freely chosen. That is what it means to live "in the flesh" in a fallen creation. We are in bondage to sin but still accountable to God's righteous judgment of our actions. In light of this theological anthropology, it cannot be maintained that a homosexual orientation is morally neutral because it is involuntary.

(C) THE DEMYTHOLOGIZING OF SEX The Bible undercuts our cultural obsession with sexual fulfillment. Scripture (along with many subsequent generations of faithful Christians) bears witness that lives of freedom, joy, and service are possible without sexual relations. Indeed, however odd it may seem to contemporary sensibilities, some New Testament passages (Matt. 19:10–12, 1 Cor. 7) clearly commend the celibate life as a way of faithfulness. In the view of the world that emerges from the pages of Scripture, sex appears as a matter of secondary importance. To be sure, the power of sexual drives must be acknowledged and subjected to constraints, either through marriage or through disciplined abstinence. But never within the canonical perspective does sexuality become the basis for defining a person's identity or for finding meaning and fulfillment in life. The things that matter are justice, mercy, and faith (Matt. 23:23). The love of God is far more important than any human love. Sexual fulfillment finds its place, at best, as a subsidiary good within this larger picture.

How then—keeping these larger canonical perspectives in mind—do we employ the three images of *community*, *cross*, and *new creation* in our interpretation of the New Testament witness concerning homosexuality? The role of these images, it should be remembered, is not to serve as independent theological motifs but to bring our reading of the New Testament texts into clear perspective. Since there are only a few directly pertinent texts, the focal images have a limited amount of work to do on this issue. Still, a few observations are in order.

Community. The biblical strictures against homosexual behavior are concerned not just for the private morality of individuals but for the health, wholeness, and purity of the elect *community*. This perspective is certainly evident in the holiness code of Leviticus. Almost immediately following the prohibition of homosexual conduct (Lev. 18:22), we find the following general warning, which refers to all the foregoing rules about sexual practices (Lev. 18:6–23):

> *Do not defile yourselves in any of these ways, for by all these practices the nations I am casting out before you have defiled themselves. Thus the land became defiled; and I punished it for its iniquity, and the land vomited out its inhabitants. But you shall keep my statutes and my ordinances and commit none of these abominations, either the citizen or the alien who resides among you.* (Lev. 18:24–26)

Israel as a holy nation is called upon, for the sake of the whole people's welfare, to keep God's commandments. Those who transgress the commandments defile not merely themselves but the whole land, jeopardizing the community as a whole. That is why "whoever commits any of these abominations shall be cut off from their people" (Lev. 18:29).

Similarly, Paul's exhortation to the Corinthians to "glorify God in your body" (1 Cor. 6:20) grows out of his passionate concern, expressed repeatedly in 1 Corinthians, for the unity and sanctification of the community as a whole. Fornication with a prostitute is wrong, among other reasons, because "your bodies are members of Christ" (6:15). Thus, to engage in sexual immorality defiles the body of Christ. Through baptism, Christians have entered a corporate whole whose health is at stake in the conduct of all its members. Sin is like an infection in the body; thus, moral action is not merely a matter of individual freedom and preference. "If one member suffers, all suffer" (1 Cor. 12:26). This line of argument is not applied specifically to every offense in the vice list of 6:9–10, but it does not require a great leap of imagination to see that for Paul the church is analogous (though not identical) to Israel as portrayed in the holiness code. That is the logic behind his demand that the Corinthian church expel the man engaged in a sexual relationship with his stepmother (5:1–13).[26] A similar logic would certainly apply, within Paul's frame of reference, to the *malakoi* and *arsenokoitai* of 1 Corinthians 6:9. The community of those who have been washed, sanctified, and justified in the name of the Lord Jesus Christ ought to have put such behaviors behind it. The New Testament never considers sexual conduct a matter of purely private concern between consenting adults. According to Paul, everything that we do as Christians, including our sexual practices, affects the whole body of Christ.

We must hasten to add that Paul's corporate concern is for the *church,* not the wider civil society; that is one of the major differences between Leviticus and 1 Corinthians. The right to privacy may well be a useful principle for a secular political order. Such a political right, however, does not extend carte blanche to sexual conduct within the church, where the question of each member's responsibility for the spiritual well-being of the community as a whole imposes a particular and far more stringent set of normative criteria for evaluating our actions. At the same time, the church also provides *koinōnia,* within which living out the obedience of faith is supported and sustained.

Cross. No New Testament text brings the issue of homosexuality into direct relationship with the story of Jesus' death. The connection is, however, implicit and crucial in Romans. The human rebellion and unrighteousness summarized in Romans 1:18–32 create the condition of crisis that makes the death of Jesus necessary. "God proves his love for us in that while we were still sinners Christ died for us" (Rom. 5:8). The human unrighteousness detailed in Romans 1 is answered by the righteousness of God, who puts forward Jesus to die for the unrighteous (Rom. 3:23–25), enabling them to walk in newness of life:

> *For God has done what the law, weakened by the flesh, could not do: by sending his own Son in the likeness of sinful flesh, and as a sin offering, he condemned sin in the flesh, so that the just requirement of the law might be fulfilled in us, who walk not according to the flesh but according to the Spirit.* (Rom. 8:3–4)

What are the implications of this act of God for understanding what Romans 1 says about homosexual practices?

First of all, the wrath of God—manifested in God's "giving up" of rebellious humanity to follow their own devices and desires—is not the last word. The gospel of the cross declares that God loves us even while we are in rebellion and that the sacrificial death of his own Son is the measure of the depth of that love. That is the fundamental theological logic underlying Paul's "sting" exposé of self-righteousness in Romans 2:1: we should not leap to condemnation of others, for we—no less than those who are engaged in "the dishonoring of their bodies"—are under God's judgment, and they—no less than we—are the objects of God's deeply sacrificial love. This has profound implications for how the Christian community ought to respond to persons of homosexual inclination. Even if some of their actions are contrary to God's design, the *cross* models the way in which the community of faith ought to respond to them: not in condemnation, but in sacrificial service. This is a particularly urgent word for the church in a time when the AIDS plague has wrought great suffering among homosexuals. (It should also be noted that many members of the gay community have responded to this crisis with actions of radical self-sacrificial love that powerfully reflect the paradigm of the cross; the church at large would do well to learn from such examples.)

Second, the cross marks the end of the old life under the power of sin (Rom. 6:1–4). Therefore, no one in Christ is locked into the past or into a psychological or biological determinism. Only in light of the transforming power of the cross can Paul's word of exhortation be spoken to Christians who—like my friend Gary—struggle with homosexual desires:

> *Therefore, do not let sin exercise dominion in your mortal bodies, to make you obey their passions. No longer present your members to sin as instruments of unrighteousness, but present yourselves to God as those who have been brought from death to life, and present your members to God as instruments of righteousness. For sin will have no dominion over you, since you are not under law but under grace.* (Rom. 6:12–14)

Paul's references to homosexual conduct place it within the realm of sin and death to which the cross is God's definitive answer. All of this is simply to say that the judgment of Romans 1 against homosexual practices should never be read apart from the rest of the letter, with its message of grace and hope through the cross of Christ.

New Creation. A similar point can be made here: neither the word of judgment against homosexuality nor the hope of transformation to a new life should be read apart from the eschatological framework of Romans. The Christian community lives in a time of tension between "already" and "not yet." Already we have the joy of the Holy Spirit; already we experience the transforming grace of God. But at the same time, we do not yet experience the fullness of redemption: we walk by faith, not by sight. The creation groans in pain and bondage, "and not only the creation, but we ourselves, who have the first fruits of the Spirit, groan inwardly while we wait for adoption, the redemption of our bodies" (Rom. 8:23). This means, among other things, that Christians, set free from the power of sin through Christ's death, must continue to *struggle* to live faithfully in the present time. The "redemption of our bodies" remains a future hope; final transformation of our fallen physical state awaits the resurrection. Those who demand fulfillment now, as though it were a right or a guarantee, are living in a state of adolescent illusion. To be sure, the transforming power of the Spirit really is present in our midst; on the other hand, the "not yet" looms large; we live with the reality of temptation, the reality of the hard struggle to live faithfully. Consequently, in this time between the times, some may find disciplined abstinence the only viable alternative to disordered sexuality. "For in hope we were saved. Now hope that is seen is not hope. For who hopes for what is seen? But if we hope for what we do not see, we wait for it with endurance" (Rom. 8:24–25).[27] The art of eschatological moral discernment lies in working out how to live lives free from bondage to sin without presuming to be translated prematurely into a condition that is free from "the sufferings of this present time" (Rom. 8:18).

3. Hermeneutics: Responding to the New Testament's Witness Against Homosexuality

As the foregoing exegetical discussion has shown, the New Testament offers no loopholes or exception clauses that might allow for the acceptance of homosexual practices under some circumstances. Despite the efforts of some recent interpreters to explain away the evidence, the New Testament remains unambiguous and univocal in its condemnation of homosexual conduct. The difficult questions that the church must face are all *hermeneutical* questions. In what way are we to apply these texts to the issues that confront us at the end of the twentieth century, as the church faces new and forceful demands for the acceptance and ordination of homosexuals?

(A) THE MODE OF HERMENEUTICAL APPROPRIATION One striking finding of our survey of the handful of relevant texts is that the New Testament contains no passages that clearly articulate a *rule* against homosexual practices. The Leviticus texts, of course, bluntly and explicitly prohibit male homosexual acts in a rule form. Paul, as we have seen, presupposes this prohibition—indeed, there may be an allusion in Romans 1:32 to Leviticus 20:13, with its prescription of the death penalty for a man who "lies with a male as with a woman"—but he neither repeats it explicitly nor issues any new rules on the subject. Consequently, if New Testament texts are to function normatively in the mode in which they speak, *no direct appeal to Romans 1 as a source for rules about sexual conduct is possible.* Similarly, 1 Corinthians 6:9–11 states no rule to govern the conduct of Christians; rather, it declares that they have already been transferred from an old life of sin to a new life of belonging to Jesus Christ. In other words, it presents a descriptive account of the new symbolic world within which discernments about Christian conduct are to be made (see further on this below). Indeed, in view of Paul's wider discussion of the role of the Mosaic Law in the Christian life, it would be at least mildly ironic to read and venerate Paul as the promulgator of a *nova lex* concerning homosexuality. If the prohibition of *porneia* in the apostolic decree (Acts 15:28–29) does include homosexual acts, that would be the one instance in the New Testament of a direct rule dealing with the issue. As we have seen, this reading of the passage is probable but not certain.

The New Testament passages in question do express ideas that can be read as *principles* governing sexual conduct. From Romans 1, one could properly infer the principle that human actions ought to acknowledge and honor God as Creator. When read against the specific background of the Genesis creation story, this principle yields for Paul the conclusion that homosexuality is contrary to the will of God. This application of the principle, however, is dependent on a particular construal of the order of creation. Taken by itself—apart from the biblical narrative context—the same principle could be used to authorize quite different judgments. For example, if homosexuality should be judged on the basis of empirical factors to be a "natural" part of the created order, this principle could be used to argue strongly in favor of its acceptance within the church. This example illustrates once again how little normative work general principles do, or—to speak more precisely—how the normative application of principles is fundamentally dependent on a particular narrative framework.

Similarly, from the slightly wider context of 1 Corinthians 6, we could derive this *principle*: "Glorify God in your body" (1 Cor. 6:20b). Good advice, no doubt, but how does it apply to the issue of our immediate concern? In its original context, the sense of the principle is governed by the more particular specifications of 1 Corinthians 6:9–10 and 6:15–18. If the principle is removed from these moorings, it could mean almost anything up to and including, "Celebrate the divinity of your own body by expanding the horizons of your sexual experience as far as possible." Of course, this would be a complete distortion of Paul's meaning. Thus, we must insist that our interpretation of "biblical principles" must be constrained and instructed by the way in which the New Testament writers themselves applied these principles.

The only *paradigms* offered by the New Testament for homosexual behavior are the emphatically negative and stereotypic sketches in the three Pauline texts (Rom. 1:18–32, 1 Cor. 6:9, 1 Tim. 1:10). The New Testament offers no accounts of homosexual Christians, tells no stories of same-sex lovers, ventures no metaphors that place a positive construal on homosexual relations. Occasionally, one encounters speculative claims that Jesus was gay (because of his relationship with the "beloved disciple"; see John 13:23) or that Mary and Martha were not really sisters but lesbian lovers.[28] Such exegetical curiosities, which have found no acceptance among serious New Testament scholars, can only be judged pathetic efforts at constructing a New Testament warrant for homosexual practice where none exists. If Jesus or his followers had practiced or countenanced homosexuality, it would have been profoundly scandalous within first-century Jewish culture. Such a controversy would surely have left traces in the tradition, as did Jesus' practice of having table fellowship with prostitutes and tax collectors. But there are no traces of such controversy. In the paradigmatic mode, the slender evidence offered by the New Testament is entirely disapproving of homosexuality.

A more sophisticated type of paradigmatic argument in defense of homosexuality is offered by those who propose that acceptance of gay Christians in the twentieth-century church is analogous to the acceptance of Gentile Christians in the first-century church.[29] The stories in Acts 10 and 11 provide, so it is argued, a paradigm for the church to expand the boundaries of Christian fellowship by recognizing that God's Spirit has been poured out upon those previously considered unclean. The analogy is richly suggestive, and it deserves careful consideration. The question is whether the analogy is a fitting one and whether it can overrule all the other factors enumerated here that create a strong presumption against the church's acceptance of homosexuality. (See further comments about the role of *experience*, below.)

The mode in which the New Testament speaks explicitly about homosexuality is the mode of *symbolic world* construction. Romans 1 presents, as we have seen, a portrayal of humankind in rebellion against God and consequently plunged into depravity and confusion. In the course of that portrayal, homosexual activities are—explicitly and without qualification—identified as symptomatic of that tragically confused rebellion. To take the New Testament as authoritative in the mode in which it speaks is to accept this portrayal as "revealed reality," an authoritative disclosure of the truth about the human condition. Understood in this way, the text requires a normative evaluation of homosexual practice as a distortion of God's order for creation.

Likewise, Romans 1 holds abundant resources for informing our understanding of God: God is a righteous God who creates human beings for obedience to his purposes, grants them freedom to rebel, stands in righteous judgment of their rebellion, and manifests his "wrath" by allowing them to suffer the just consequences of their sin. This characterization of God must be held together dialectically with the portrayal, developed at length elsewhere in Romans, of God as a merciful God whose righteousness is revealed preeminently in his act of deliverance through Jesus Christ, whose righteousness transforms and empowers us. In contrast, however, to other New Testament texts that present the character of God as a pattern for human emulation (e.g., Matt. 5:43–48), the understanding of God in Romans 1 provides not primarily a source of concrete norms but rather a ground of motivation for ethical action.

Thus, the New Testament confronts us with an account of how the ordering of human life before God has gone awry. To use these texts appropriately in ethical reflection about homosexuality, we should not try to wring rules out of them, nor should we abstract principles from them. Instead, we should attend primarily to the way the texts function to shape the *symbolic world* within which human sexuality is understood. If Romans 1—the key text—is to inform normative judgments about homosexuality, it must function as a diagnostic tool, laying bare the truth about humankind's dishonorable "exchange" of the natural for the unnatural. According to Paul, homosexual relations, however they may be interpreted (or rationalized: see Rom. 1:32) by fallen and confused creatures, represent a tragic distortion of the created order. If we accept the authority of the New Testament on this subject, we will be taught to perceive homosexuality accordingly. (Obviously, such a judgment leaves open many questions about how best to deal with the problem pastorally.) Still before us, however, is the problem of how the witness of the New Testament relates to other moral perspectives on this issue. Do we grant the normative force of Paul's analysis?

(B) OTHER AUTHORITIES Having recognized the New Testament's diagnosis of homosexual activity as a sign of human alienation from God's design, we must still consider how this teaching is to be weighted in relation to other sources of moral wisdom. An adequate discussion of this problem would be very long indeed. For the present, I offer only some brief reflections as places to start the discussion.

Far more emphatically than Scripture itself, the moral teaching *tradition* of the Christian church has for more than nineteen hundred years declared homosexual behavior to be contrary to the will of God. As Boswell's study amply documents, the mainstream of Christian ethical teaching has been relentlessly hostile to homosexual practice.[30] Only within the past twenty years has any serious question been raised about the church's universal prohibition of such conduct. It is extremely difficult to find in the tradition any firm point of leverage against the New Testament on this issue. If anything, a passage such as Romans 1 might serve to moderate tradition's harsh judgment of homosexuals as specially despicable sinners. (John Chrysostom, for example, an influential fourth-century bishop and theologian, declared that homosexual intercourse was a sin worse than fornication, worse even than murder.[31] Surely the biblical passages give no support to such a claim.) In any case, it is impossible to construct an argument for acceptance of homosexuality by juxtaposing the authority of tradition and the authority of Scripture. The result of the juxtaposition is to strengthen the Bible's prohibitions.

With regard to *reason* and scientific evidence, the picture is cloudy. A large body of modern psychological and scientific studies demonstrate the widespread incidence of homosexual activity. Some studies have claimed that as much as 10 percent of the population is inclined to same-sex erotic preference, and some theorists hold that homosexual orientation is innate (or formed by a very early age) and unchangeable. This is the opinion espoused by most advocates of full acceptance of homosexuality in the church: if homosexual orientation is a genetically determined trait, so the argument goes, then any disapproval of it is a form of discrimination analogous to racism. Others, however, regard homosexual orientation as a form of developmental maladjustment or "symbolic confusion." Some therapists claim significant clinical success in helping homosexual persons develop a heterosexual orientation; others challenge such claims. The conventional view at present is that therapeutic intervention can only impose behavior modification; it cannot effect change in a person's underlying sexual orientation.

There are, however, reasons to question the essentialist view that individuals have an innate sexual orientation. A major cross-cultural study published by David Greenberg, professor of sociology at New York University, contends that homosexual identity is socially constructed.[32] According to Greenberg, different cultures have constructed different conventions for same-sex erotic behavior, and the notion of homosexual "orientation" as a lifelong innate characteristic of some individuals is a relatively modern innovation. Of course, even if Greenberg's point is granted, it proves nothing one way or the other about whether some individuals have a genetic predisposition toward homosexuality.

In one sense, however, the etiology of homosexual orientation is not a significant factor for the formation of normative Christian ethics. We need not take sides in the debate of nature versus culture. Even if it could be shown that same-sex preference is somehow genetically programmed, that would not necessarily make homosexual behavior morally appropriate.[33] Surely Christian ethics does not want to hold that all inborn traits are good and desirable. The analogy of alcoholism, while only an analogy, is perhaps helpful: a considerable body of evidence suggests that some people are born with a predisposition to alcoholism. Once exposed to alcohol, they experience an attraction so powerful that it can be counteracted only by careful counseling, community support, and total abstinence. We now conventionally speak of alcoholism as a "disease" and carefully distinguish our disapproval of the behavior associated with it from our loving support of the person afflicted by it. Perhaps homoerotic attraction should be treated similarly.[34]

The argument from statistical incidence of homosexual behavior is even less useful in normative ethical deliberation. Even if 10 percent of the people in the United States should declare themselves to be of homosexual orientation (and that figure is a doubtful one),[35] that would not settle the *normative* issue; it is impossible to argue simply from an "is" to an "ought." If Paul were shown the poll results, he would reply sadly, "Indeed, the power of sin is rampant in the world."

The advocates of homosexuality in the church have their most serious case when they appeal to the authority of *experience*. There are individuals who live in stable, loving homosexual relationships and claim to experience the grace—rather than the wrath—of God therein. How are such claims to be assessed? Was Paul wrong? Or are such experiential claims simply another manifestation of the self-deception that he describes? Or, beside these irreconcilable alternatives, should we entertain the possible emergence of new realities that Paul could not have anticipated? Does the practice that Paul condemns correspond exactly to the experience of homosexual relations that exists in the present time? Scroggs, for example, argues that the New Testament's condemnation of homosexuality applies only to a certain "model" of exploitative pederasty that was common in Hellenistic culture; hence, it is not applicable to the modern world's experience of mutual, loving homosexual relationships.[36] Scroggs's position, in my judgment, fails to reckon adequately with Romans 1, where the relations are not described as pederastic and where Paul's disapproval has nothing to do with exploitation.

But the fact remains that there are numerous homosexual Christians—like my friend Gary and some of my ablest theological students—whose lives show signs of the presence of God, whose work in ministry is genuine and effective. How is such experiential evidence to be assessed? Should we, like the earliest Jewish Christians who hesitated to accept "unclean" Gentiles into the community of faith, acknowledge the work of the Spirit and say, "Who are we to stand in the way of what God is doing?" (cf. Acts 10:1–11:18)? Or should we see this as one more instance of a truth that all of us in ministry know sadly about ourselves: "We have this treasure in earthen vessels"? God gives the Spirit to broken people and ministers grace even through us sinners, without thereby endorsing our sin.

In Part III, I articulated the hermeneutical guideline that *claims about divinely inspired experience that contradicts the witness of Scripture should be admitted to normative status in the church only after sustained and agonizing scrutiny by a consensus of the faithful.* It is by no means clear that the community of the church as a whole is prepared to credit the experientially based claims being made at present for normative acceptance of homosexuality. Furthermore, in its rush to be "inclusive," the church must not overlook the experience reported by those Christians who, like Gary, struggle with homosexual desires and find them a hindrance to living lives committed to the service of God. This is a complex matter, and we have not heard the end of it.

In any case, it is crucial to remember that experience must be treated as a hermeneutical lens for reading the New Testament rather than as an independent, counterbalancing authority. This is the point at which the analogy to the early church's acceptance of Gentiles fails decisively. The church did not simply observe the experience of Cornelius and his household and decide that Scripture must be wrong after all. On the contrary, the experience of uncircumcised Gentiles responding in faith to the gospel message led the church back to a new reading of Scripture. This new reading discovered in the texts a clear message of God's intent, from the covenant with Abraham forward, to bless all nations and to bring Gentiles (*qua* Gentiles) to worship Israel's God. That is, for example, what Paul seeks to establish in the complex exegetical arguments conducted in Galatians and Romans. We see the rudiments of such a reflective process in Acts 10:34–35, where Peter begins his speech to Cornelius by alluding to Deuteronomy 10:17–18 and Psalm 15:1–2 in order to confess that "God shows no partiality, but in every nation anyone who fears him and does what is right is acceptable to him." Only because the new experience of Gentile converts proved *hermeneutically illuminating* of Scripture was the church, over time, able to accept the decision to embrace Gentiles within the fellowship of God's people. This is precisely the step that has not—or at least not yet—been taken by the advocates of homosexuality in the church. Is it possible for them to reread the New Testament and show how this development can be understood as a fulfillment of God's design for human sexuality as previously revealed in Scripture? In view of the content of the biblical texts summarized above, it is difficult to imagine how such an argument could be made.

Thus, in view of the considerable uncertainty surrounding the scientific and experiential evidence, in view of our culture's present swirling confusion about gender roles, in view of our propensity for self-deception, I think it prudent and necessary to let the univocal testimony of Scripture and the Christian tradition order the life of the church on this painfully controversial matter. We must affirm that the New Testament tells us the truth about ourselves as sinners and as God's sexual creatures: marriage between man and woman is the normative form for human sexual fulfillment, and homosexuality is one among many tragic signs that we are a broken people, alienated from God's loving purpose.

4. Living the Text: The Church As Community Suffering with the Creation

How, then, shall we respond in the church to the pastoral and political realities of our time? Having said that the New Testament will not permit us to condone homosexual behavior, we still find ourselves confronted by complex problems that demand rigorous and compassionate solutions. What decisions should the church make about the practical questions surrounding its response to homosexuality? How should the witness of the New Testament on this matter be embodied in the life of the church? In what follows, I pose several key issues and venture some discernments, based on the exegesis and theological reflections set forth above. Before and above all else, those who uphold the biblical teaching against homosexuality must remember Paul's warning in Romans 2:1–3: we are all "without excuse"; we all stand or fall under God's judgment and mercy.

(a) *Should the church support civil rights for homosexuals?* Yes. Any judgment about the church's effort to influence Caesar's social policies requires complex reasoning. (The complexity of the problem is illustrated by the controversy over admitting gay persons to the military in the United States. I have argued in this book that *Christians* have no place in the military. On what basis, then, shall we presume to call for admission of gays to an institution of which we disapprove?)[37] Certainly, however, the church should not single out homosexual persons for malicious discriminatory treatment: insofar as Christians have done so in the past, we must repent and seek instead to live out the gospel of reconciliation.

(b) *Can homosexual persons be members of the Christian church?* This is rather like asking, "Can envious persons be members of the church?" (cf. Rom. 1:29) or "Can alcoholics be members of the church?" De facto, of course, they are. Unless we think that the church is a community of sinless perfection, we must acknowledge that persons of homosexual orientation are welcome along with other sinners in the company of those who trust in the God who justifies the ungodly (Rom. 4:5). If they are not welcome, I will have to walk out the door along with them, leaving in the sanctuary only those entitled to cast the first stone.

This means that for the foreseeable future we must find ways to live within the church in a situation of serious moral disagreement while still respecting one another as brothers and sisters in Christ. If the church is going to start practicing the discipline of exclusion from the community, there are other issues far more important than homosexuality where we should begin to draw a line in the dirt: violence and materialism, for example.

At the same time, I would argue that the pastoral task of the church is to challenge self-defined homosexual Christians to reshape their identity in conformity with the gospel. Those who hold the offices of teaching and preaching in the church should uphold the biblical standard and call all who hear to follow. This is a tricky line to walk, but we do it on many issues. Can a racist be a member of the church? Probably so, but we hope and pray that the church will become a community of moral formation that will enable him or her to change. Can a soldier be a Christian? Probably so, but my understanding of the gospel requires me to urge that person to renounce the way of violence and to follow Jesus in the way of costly refusal of violence as a means to justice (see Chapter 14). My theological position on violence is a minority position both in the U.S. church at present and with respect to the church's historic mainstream position. I cannot excommunicate my militarist brothers and sisters, and I do not expect them to excommunicate me. But I do expect that there will be vigorous moral debate in which we try to persuade each other whether Christians can ever rightly take up the sword. Just as there are serious Christians who in good conscience believe in just war theory, so there are serious Christians who in good conscience believe that same-sex erotic activity is consonant with God's will. For the reasons set forth in this book, I think that both groups are wrong, but in both cases the questions are so difficult that we should receive one another as brothers and sisters in Christ and work toward adjudicating our differences through reflecting together on the witness of Scripture.

(c) *Is it Christianly appropriate for Christians who experience themselves as having a homosexual orientation to continue to participate in same-sex erotic activity?* No. The only one who *was* entitled to cast a stone instead charged the recipient of his mercy to "go and sin no more." It is no more appropriate for homosexual Christians to persist in homosexual activity than it would be for heterosexual Christians to persist in fornication or adultery. (Insofar as the church fails to teach clearly about heterosexual chastity outside of marriage, its disapproval of homosexual coupling will appear arbitrary and biased.) Unless they are able to change their orientation and enter a heterosexual marriage relationship, homosexual Christians should seek to live lives of disciplined sexual abstinence.

Despite the smooth illusions perpetrated by mass culture in the United States, sexual gratification is not a sacred right, and celibacy is not a fate worse than death. The Catholic tradition has something to teach those of us raised in Protestant communities. While mandatory priestly celibacy is unbiblical, a life of sexual abstinence can promote "good order and unhindered devotion to the Lord" (1 Cor. 7:35). Surely it is a matter of some interest for Christian ethics that both Jesus and Paul lived without sexual relationships. It is also worth noting that 1 Corinthians 7:8–9, 25–40, commends celibacy as an option for everyone, not just for a special caste of ordained leaders. Within the church, we should work diligently to recover the dignity and value of the single life.

My friend Gary, in his final letter to me, wrote urgently of the imperatives of discipleship: "*Are homosexuals to be excluded from the community of faith? Certainly not. But anyone who joins such a community should know that it is a place of transformation, of discipline, of learning, and not merely a place to be comforted or indulged.*" The community demands that its members pursue holiness, while it also sustains the challenging process of character formation that is necessary for Jesus' disciples. The church must be a community whose life together provides true friendship, emotional support, and spiritual formation for everyone who comes within its circle of fellowship. The need for such support is perhaps particularly felt by unmarried people, regardless of their sexual orientation. In this respect, as in so many others, the church can fulfill its vocation only by living as a countercommunity in the world.

(d) *Should the church sanction and bless homosexual unions?* No. The church should continue to teach—as it always has—that there are two possible ways for God's human sexual creatures to live well-ordered lives of faithful discipleship: heterosexual marriage and sexual abstinence.

(e) *Does this mean that persons of homosexual orientation are subject to a blanket imposition of celibacy in a way qualitatively different from persons of heterosexual orientation?* Here a nuanced answer must be given. While Paul regarded celibacy as a charisma, he did not therefore suppose that those lacking the charisma were free to indulge their sexual desires outside marriage. Heterosexually oriented persons are also called to abstinence from sex unless they marry (1 Cor. 7:8–9). The only difference—admittedly a salient one—in the case of homosexually oriented persons is that they do not have the option of homosexual "marriage." So where does that leave them? It leaves them in precisely the same situation as the heterosexual who would like to marry but cannot find an appropriate partner (and there are many such): summoned to a difficult, costly obedience, while "groaning" for the "redemption of our bodies" (Rom. 8:23). Anyone who does not recognize this as a description of authentic Christian existence has never struggled seriously with the imperatives of the gospel, which challenge and frustrate our "natural" impulses in countless ways.

Much of the contemporary debate turns on this last point. Many of the advocates of unqualified acceptance of homosexuality seem to be operating with a simplistic anthropology that assumes whatever is must be good: they have a theology of creation but no theology of sin and redemption. Furthermore, they have a realized eschatology that equates personal fulfillment with sexual fulfillment and expects sexual "salvation" now. The Pauline portrayal of human beings as fallen creatures in bondage to sin and yet set free in Christ for the obedience of faith would suggest a rather different assessment of our sexuality, looking to the future resurrection as the locus of bodily fulfillment. Thus, eschatology looms as the crucial question that divides the traditional position from those who would revise it.

(f) *Should homosexual Christians expect to change their orientation?* This tough question must also be answered in the critical framework of New Testament eschatology. On the one hand, the transforming power of the Spirit really is present in our midst; the testimonies of those who claim to have been healed and transformed into a heterosexual orientation should be taken seriously. They confess, in the words of the Charles Wesley hymn, that God "breaks the power of cancelled sin; He sets the prisoner free."[38] If we do not continue to live with that hope, we may be hoping for too little from God. On the other hand, the "not yet" looms large; the testimonies of those like Gary who pray and struggle in Christian community and seek healing unsuccessfully for years must be taken with no less seriousness. Perhaps for many the best outcome that is attainable in this time between the times will be a life of disciplined abstinence, free from obsessive lust. (Exactly the same standard would apply for unmarried persons of heterosexual orientation.) That seems to be the spiritual condition Gary reached near the end of his life:

> Since All Saints Day I have felt myself being transformed. I no longer consider myself homosexual. Many would say, big deal, you're forty-two—and are dying of AIDS. Big sacrifice. No, I didn't do this of my will, of an effort to improve myself, to make myself acceptable to God. No, he did this for me. I feel a great weight has been lifted off me. I have not turned "straight." I guess I'm like St. Paul's phrase, a eunuch for Christ.[39]

(g) *Should persons of homosexual orientation be ordained?* I save this question deliberately for last, where it belongs. It is unfortunate that the battle line has been drawn in the denominations at the question of ordination of homosexuals. The ensuing struggle has had the unfortunate effect of reinforcing a double standard for clergy and lay morality; it would be far better to articulate a single set of moral norms that apply to all Jesus' followers. Strictures against homosexuality belong in the church's moral catechesis, not in its ordination requirements. It is arbitrary to single out homosexuality as a special sin that precludes ordination. (Certainly, the New Testament does not do this.) The church has no analogous special rules to exclude from ordination the greedy or the self-righteous. Such matters are left to the discernment of the bodies charged with examining candidates for ordination; these bodies must determine whether the individual candidate has the gifts and graces requisite for ministry. In any event, a person of homosexual orientation seeking to live a life of disciplined abstinence would clearly be an appropriate candidate for ordination.

We live, then, as a community that embraces sinners as Jesus did, without waiving God's righteousness. We live confessing that God's grace claims us out of confusion and alienation and sets about making us whole. We live knowing that wholeness remains a hope rather than an attainment in this life. The homosexual Christians in our midst may teach us something about our true condition as people living between the cross and the final redemption of our bodies.

In the midst of a culture that worships self-gratification, and in a church that often preaches a false Jesus who panders to our desires, those who seek the narrow way of obedience have a powerful word to speak. As Paul saw in pagan homosexuality a vivid symbol of human fallenness, so I saw conversely in Gary, as I have seen in other homosexual friends and colleagues, a symbol of God's power made perfect in weakness (2 Cor. 12:9). Gary knew through experience the bitter power of sin in a twisted world, and he trusted in God's love anyway. Thus he embodied the "sufferings of this present time" of which Paul speaks in Romans 8: living in the joyful freedom of the "first fruits of the Spirit," even while groaning along with a creation in bondage to decay.

NOTES

1. At that time I was teaching at Yale Divinity School. I moved to Duke in 1991.

2. McNeill 1993; Nelson 1978; Scanzoni and Mollenkott 1978; Boswell 1980.

3. This section of the book represents a revision and expansion of my essay "Awaiting the Redemption of Our Bodies: The Witness of Scripture Concerning Homosexuality" (Hays 1991a). A revised version of that essay has appeared in an anthology: Siker 1994a, 3–17. Portions of the exegetical work on Romans 1 are also adapted from Hays 1986.

4. On the issue of possessions, see L. T. Johnson 1981; Wheeler 1995.

5. According to Jude 7, "Sodom and Gomorrah and the surrounding cities, which, in the same manner as they, indulged in sexual immorality and went after other flesh, serve as an example by undergoing a punishment of eternal fire." The phrase "went after other flesh" (*apelthousai opisō sarkos heteras*) refers to their pursuit of nonhuman (i.e., angelic!) "flesh." The expression *sarkos heteras* means "flesh of another kind"; thus, it is impossible to construe this passage as a condemnation of homosexual desire, which entails precisely the pursuit of flesh of the *same* kind.

6. In a recent article, Daniel Boyarin (1995) argues convincingly that these Levitical prohibitions were understood in later rabbinic tradition to pertain only to male homosexual intercourse in which anal penetration occurs. Other forms of male same-sex erotic activity would have been understood in this interpretive tradition as forms of masturbation, which was still frowned upon but subject to much less severe sanctions. Boyarin, noting that the Leviticus passages prohibit a specific act but say nothing about sexual "orientation," goes on to contend that the rabbis had no category corresponding to the modern idea of "homosexuality."

7. Countryman 1988.

8. Boswell 1980, 186–187, 338–353.

9. Scroggs 1983, 106–108.

10. The formula repeats the substance of James's earlier speech (Acts 15:19–20).

11. The NRSV translates *atimazesthai* as "degrading." This translation seems a bit too strong; I have rendered it here and throughout this discussion as "dishonoring," which is closer to the literal sense.

12. Schütz 1975, 40–53.

13. *Paradise Lost*, I.26.

14. On the meaning of "the righteousness of God," see Hays 1992, 1129–1133.

15. Käsemann 1980, 47.

16. Scroggs 1983, 110.

17. Käsemann 1980, 47.

18. As noted by Furnish 1985, 75–76. The idea is a familiar one in Hellenistic Judaism; for an interpretation of the Egyptian plagues in these terms, see Wisdom 11:15–16, 12:23: "In return for their foolish and wicked thoughts, which led them astray to worship irrational serpents and worthless animals, you sent upon them a multitude of irrational creatures to punish them, so that they might learn that one is punished by the very things by which one sins. . . . Therefore those who lived unrighteously, in a life of folly, you tormented through their own abominations."

19. Calvin 1960 [1556], 34.

20. Scroggs 1983, 113–114.

21. My colleague Dale Martin has recently argued that Rom. 1:18–32 does not allude to the universal fall of humanity but to an ancient Jewish myth about the origins of Gentile idolatry, as narrated, e.g., in Jubilees 11 (D. B. Martin 1995b). Thus, he questions any reference or allusion in these verses to the Genesis story of creation and fall. This exegetical issue is crucial for the interpretation of the passage. It is impossible to offer here a full reply, but the following points may be noted. (1) Though Paul does not explicitly cite Gen. 1–3, there is an explicit reference in Rom. 1:20 to "the creation of the world" and to "the things [God] has made"; no Jewish reader could read this language without thinking of the Genesis creation story. (2) Furthermore, the language used in Rom. 1:23 explicitly echoes Gen. 1:26–28: "They exchanged the glory of the immortal God for the *likeness* [*homoiōma*] of the *image* [*eikōn*] of a mortal human being or of birds or four-footed animals or reptiles." In Genesis, humankind, made in the *image* and *likeness* of God, is given dominion over the creatures; however, in Romans 1 human beings forfeit the glory of the divine image and instead worship images of the creatures over which God had given them dominion. Thus, idolatrous worship is an ironic inversion of the creation account. (3) Martin contends that Rom. 1:18–32 cannot be read as an account of the universal fallen condition of humanity because it refers only to the spiritual condition of Gentiles, not of Jews. At the first and most superficial level, this interpretation is correct, but it fails to reckon with the larger scope of Paul's argument. In Romans 1, he employs conventional Jewish polemic against Gentile immorality, but as the argument unfolds, the reader—who may have enthusiastically applauded the anti-Gentile polemic—finds him- or herself addressed

by the same word of judgment: all, including Jews, are "without apology" (2:1); all, Jews and Gentiles alike, are "under the power of sin" (3:9). Thus, the conventional attack on Gentile idolatry turns out to be also a description of the universal human condition. This claim is fundamental to the whole logic of the letter's argument.

22. For the following examples and others, see Furnish 1985, 58–67; Scroggs 1983, 59–60. For example, the Stoic-Cynic preacher Dio Chrysostom, after charging that brothel-keeping dishonors the goddess Aphrodite, "whose name stands for the natural [*kata physin*] intercourse and union of the male and female," goes on to suggest that a society that permits such practices will soon find its uncontrolled lusts leading to the still more deplorable practice of pederasty:

> Is there any possibility that this lecherous class would refrain from dishonoring and corrupting the males, making their clear and sufficient limit that set by nature [*physis*]? Or will it not, while it satisfies its lust for women in every conceivable way, find itself grown weary of this pleasure, and then seek some other worse and more lawless form of wantonness? . . . The man whose appetite is insatiate in such things . . . will turn his assault against the male quarters, eager to befoul the youth who will very soon be magistrates and judges and generals, believing that in them he will find a kind of pleasure difficult and hard to procure [*Discourse* 7.135, 151–152].

Likewise, Plutarch has Daphnaeus, one of the speakers in his Dialogue on Love, disparage "union contrary to nature with males" (*hē para physin homilia pros arrēnas*), as contrasted to "the love between men and women," which is characterized as "natural" (*tē physei*). A few sentences later, Daphnaeus complains that those who "consort with males" willingly are guilty of "weakness and effeminacy," because, "contrary to nature" (*para physin*), they "allow themselves in Plato's words 'to be covered and mounted like cattle'" (*Dialogue on Love* 751C, E). Plutarch's reference to Plato demonstrates the point that Paul did not originate the application of the *kata physin/para physin* dichotomy to heterosexual and homosexual behavior. Its common appearance in the writings of the Hellenistic moral philosophers is testimony to a convention that can be traced back at least as far as Plato (*Laws* I.636C), almost invariably in contexts where a negative judgment is pronounced on the morality or propriety of the "unnatural" homosexual relations.

23. Josephus, *Ap.* 2.199, Loeb translation corrected; the allusion, of course, is to Lev. 20:13; cf. Lev. 18:22, 29. Elsewhere in the same work, Josephus deplores "intercourse with males" as *para physin* and accuses the Greeks of inventing stories about homosexual behavior among the gods as "an excuse for the monstrous and unnatural [*para physin*] pleasures in which they themselves indulged" (*Ap.* 2.273, 275). Paul's contemporary Philo uses similar language in a long passage branding pederasty as "an unnatural pleasure" (*tēn para physin hēdonēn*) (*De spec. leg.* 3.37–42). Philo's distaste for homosexuality receives its most elaborate expression in his retelling of the Sodom story (*De Abr.* 133–141); he charges that the inhabitants of Sodom "threw off from their necks the law of nature [*ton tēs physeōs nomon*] and applied themselves to deep drinking of strong liquor and dainty feeding and forbidden forms of intercourse. Not only in their mad lust for women did they violate the marriages of their neighbors, but also men mounted males. . . ." After a lurid description of the homosexual practices of the people of Sodom, he leads into the conclusion of the tale with an account of God's judgment of the matter:

> But God, moved by pity for mankind whose Savior and Lover He was, gave increase in the greatest possible degree to the unions which men and women naturally [*kata physin*] make for begetting children, but abominated and extinguished this unnatural and forbidden intercourse, and those who lusted for such He cast forth and chastised with punishments.

24. As correctly noted by Käsemann 1980, 47; Scroggs 1983, 110.

25. This point is overlooked by C. L. Porter 1994, who defends the remarkable thesis that "Paul opposes and argues against Rom. 1:18–32 throughout Romans" (p. 221).

26. See my comment on this passage in Hays 1989, 97.

27. I have altered the final word of this translation from the NRSV's "patience." In English, to say "we wait for it with patience" suggests a docile contentment that is foreign both to the sense of the Greek word *hypomonē* ("endurance") and to the whole sense of Rom. 8:18–25: those who wait are said to "groan inwardly," suffering along with an unredeemed creation.

28. McNeill 1995, 132–139. Cf. the argument of van Tilborg (1993) that the portrayal of Jesus' relationship to the Beloved Disciple in the Fourth Gospel is modeled on the pattern of same-sex love relationships in Hellenistic antiquity.

29. L. T. Johnson 1983, 95–97; Siker 1994b.

30. Boswell 1980. In 1994, Boswell published a study claiming to demonstrate that Christian churches in premodern Europe had established liturgical forms for the blessing of "same-sex unions." The book briefly created a minor sensation: its thesis was even reported by Garry Trudeau in his "Doonesbury" comic strip. Serious

academic reviewers, however, have been withering in their criticism of the book. See, e.g., Young 1994; Shaw 1994. The ceremony of *adelphopoiēsis* that Boswell has "discovered" is well known to liturgical scholars as a rite celebrating adoption or special bonds of friendship, but its purpose was certainly not to give ecclesiastical sanction to "gay marriages," as Boswell seeks to suggest.

31. Chrysostom, "Commentary on Romans, Homily 4," *In Epistolam ad Romanos*; cited in Boswell 1980, 360–361.

32. Greenberg 1989.

33. Here recall the argument above that actions do not necessarily have to be "voluntary" in order to be sinful before God. For a nuanced and helpful discussion of the scientific and social-scientific evidence and the relation of such evidence to normative issues, see Van Leeuwen (forthcoming).

34. For an argument rejecting this analogy, see Siker 1994b.

35. See the study by Laumann et al. 1994, indicating that only 1.4 percent of women and 2.8 percent of men are of homosexual or bisexual orientation.

36. Scroggs 1983.

37. One cannot help recalling Arlo Guthrie's song "Alice's Restaurant," in which the sergeant at the draft induction center expresses dismay at discovering that Arlo had previously been arrested for littering. "Kid, have you rehabilitated yourself?" he asks. "Are you moral enough to kill people?" See the provocative essay of Stanley Hauerwas, "Why Gays (as a Group) Are Morally Superior to Christians (as a Group)," in Hauerwas 1994, 153–156.

38. Charles Wesley, "O For a Thousand Tongues to Sing," *United Methodist Hymnal* (Nashville: United Methodist Publishing House, 1989), 57.

39. Actually, Gary's phrase rather elegantly conflates 1 Cor. 4:10 with Matt. 19:12.

Chapter 17

Anti-Judaism and Ethnic Conflict

The Christian stance toward Jews and Judaism is rarely dealt with in books on New Testament ethics. This unfortunate omission is symptomatic of a blind spot in Christian theology that has—as our century has taught us all too well—contributed to tragic results in history. The standard New Testament ethics texts,[1] insofar as they offer normative discussions of ethical issues, deal with sexual ethics, divorce, possessions, obedience to government, violence and nonviolence—important topics all, but none so central to the self-definition of early Christian communities as the question of the relation of the emergent church to Israel. Perhaps the oversight occurs because the New Testament appears to contain little directly hortatory material on the subject of anti-Judaism or other forms of ethnic bias. As I have contended throughout this book, however, the study of ethics can be restricted neither to passages that give explicit moral exhortation nor to matters of individual moral decision; rather, the study of New Testament ethics must consider the fundamental symbols of communal identity and the way in which those symbols shape the ethos of particular communities.[2] Thus, the question of how Christians should regard Israel and treat Jews should be a central issue for any account of the ethics of the New Testament. The church's relation to Israel is an ethical issue that will never go away—as long as church and synagogue endure—because the church's identity as the people of God is rooted in the witness of early Christian communities that struggled bitterly with this problem.

Furthermore, the issue will not go away because the tangled history of church and synagogue for nineteen centuries has bequeathed us a shameful legacy of polemic and violence. The urgency of this problem—horrifyingly highlighted by Nazism's reign of terror in the middle of this century—is constantly reinforced by flare-ups of anti-Jewish sentiment and activity in unexpected places. Acts of vandalism are repeatedly directed against synagogues and Holocaust memorials both in Europe and America. In 1992, a survey conducted by the Anti-Defamation League of B'nai B'rith found that 20 percent of Americans "harbor strong prejudice against Jews."[3] As I write these pages, an account has just appeared in the newspaper of an excerpt from the diaries of H. R. Haldemann, the chief of staff in Richard Nixon's White House. According to Haldemann's account, Nixon once spent an hour and a half with the evangelist Billy Graham after a White House prayer breakfast, discussing "the terrible problem arising from the total Jewish domination of the media" and agreeing that "this was something that would have to be dealt with."[4] Or, to cite another instance, on the fiftieth anniversary of *Kristallnacht*, the speaker of the West German *Bundestag* made a laudatory speech about Hitler's success in rallying German national pride; though the ensuing controversy forced him to resign his post, the event was a chilling reminder that ethnic prejudice is not confined to villains of the past or skinheads of the present.

Steven Spielberg's powerful 1994 film *Schindler's List* once again pressed the event of the Holocaust into popular consciousness and debate. How is it possible that masses of Christians in Germany acquiesced in the terrible slaughter of Jewish people? Is there some sense in which Christian theology or even the New Testament itself underwrote the destructive anti-Jewish agenda of Nazism? Such questions demand thoughtful answers. An extensive literature has grown up around these issues, and it is impossible to engage it fully here.[5] My immediate aim in this book is to explore the various New Testament perspectives on the Jewish people and to reflect upon their normative implications for Christian theological ethics.

This issue of the relation between church and Israel brings sharply into focus a crucial issue of *method* in New Testament ethics: How do we deal with the diversity of the New Testament witnesses in a case where different texts stand fundamentally in tension with one another? Our previous test cases have not forced us to wrestle with this problem in a radical way. On the issue of homosexuality, the canonical witnesses, though few, are univocal. On the issues of violence and divorce, there is a fundamental basis of unity, with certain minor tensions or adaptations in the tradition; even where there are differences on matters of casuistic application, the witnesses point generally in the same direction: Christians are called to renounce violence and divorce. Similarly, even on a question such as the use of possessions (which we have not examined in this study), though we find many texts with various normative applications, all of them advocate concern for the poor and just sharing of resources. We may find the New Testament's vision difficult to obey, but there is little doubt about the direction in which it calls us to move. As we shall see, however, this is not the case when we ask about the New Testament writers' attitudes toward Judaism. In the case of the church-Israel question, we find texts that take radically divergent paths, some of which appear (in the retrospective light of history) to be vicious and morally reprehensible. Simple harmonization is impossible. Therefore, this issue, perhaps more than any other, impresses upon us the difficulty of seeking to formulate normative ethics in a way faithful to Scripture.[6]

While the issue of Jewish-Christian relations is of great ethical importance in its own right, there is still more at stake in this discussion, because the New Testament's treatment of the relation between Jew and Greek unavoidably becomes a paradigm for the Christian response to ethnic and racial divisions of all sorts. In a time wracked by ethnic conflict, it is imperative that Christians think clearly about how to take their bearings from New Testament documents whose legacy on such questions is decidedly mixed. We can return to these methodological and normative issues, however, only after exploring the content of the New Testament texts themselves.

1. Reading the Texts

The most important advance of New Testament scholarship in the second half of the twentieth century has been its dramatic reframing of the relationship between early Christianity and formative Judaism. This hard-won new understanding of the relation between these movements is foundational to understanding the New Testament's theological comments on Jews and Judaism; therefore, we must set the scene by sketching the historical setting from which the New Testament writings emerged. While many details are debated, the following broad summary represents the present consensus view of critical scholars, Christian and Jewish alike. We may group our observations under four headings:

First-century Judaism was diverse, not monolithic. Especially during the period before the war against Rome (66–70 C.E.), numerous varieties of Judaism flourished. The Pharisaic movement, which was the progenitor of later normative rabbinic Judaism, stood alongside numerous competing interpretations of Israel's faith and history: the Sadducees, the Essenes, various forms of militant and/or apocalyptic Judaism, and philosophically oriented diaspora Judaism (represented, e.g., by Philo of Alexandria) all prospered side by side and bid, with varying degrees of success, for popular adherence.[7]

Earliest Christianity began as a Jewish sectarian movement. Jesus himself was a Jew who observed Torah, participated in Israel's festivals, and—in the tradition of Israel's prophets—called for reform and renewal within Judaism. In the pre–70 period, followers of Jesus proclaimed him as the Messiah of Israel and promulgated new interpretations of Israel's Scriptures in light of their experience of his life, death, and resurrection. The first Christians, all of whom were Jews, did not believe that they had converted to another religion, or that they were starting a new one. They understood themselves as Jews offering a new construal of God's dealing with Israel, and they were understood in the same way by other Jews—even those (like Saul of Tarsus) who regarded them as apostates and therefore sought to discipline them.

By the late first century, the success of the preaching mission to Gentiles and the simultaneous relative failure of the mission to Jews had begun to create a major crisis of communal identity. How was the community to interpret the events of the time? There were "too many Gentiles, too few Jews," in this new messianic community,[8] which therefore was increasingly in danger of losing its Jewish identity altogether, particularly in light of the community's fateful decision not to require Gentile converts to be circumcised and keep the Jewish dietary laws. After the destruction of the Jerusalem Temple in 70 C.E., the question of the Jesus-movement's continuing continuity with Judaism became increasingly urgent. It was a volatile period socially and theologically for the formative Christian communities, as well as for the Jewish community, which also had to undergo fundamental reassessment of its identity now that the Temple, the cultic center of Jewish religious life, no longer stood. The various stances toward Judaism that we find in the New Testament writings must be understood as responses to this situation. It is a fateful fact that most of the canonical New Testament writings, especially the Gospels, date from precisely this period of "identity crisis" in early Christianity.

As a consequence of the above factors, the hostility toward Jews and Judaism that appears in some New Testament texts is to be understood as an expression of "sibling rivalry." The early Christians were engaged with their Jewish brothers and sisters in a struggle for possession of Israel's heritage.[9] In the heat of the rivalry, the Jewish followers of Jesus were not content to claim defensively that they were still legitimate Jews; instead, they went on the offensive, making the polemical claim that their rivals were *not* legitimate Jews, not real bearers of the authentic tradition of Israel.

For example, in Philippians 3:2–3, Paul warns his Greek readers in Philippi sternly against Jewish-Christian missionaries who might come preaching circumcision:

> *Beware of the dogs, beware of the evil workers, beware of those who mutilate the flesh. For it is we who are the circumcision,*[10] *who worship in the Spirit of God and boast in Christ Jesus and have no confidence in the flesh.*

The reversal of categories is startling. The literally uncircumcised Gentile church of Paul's mission is given the honorific title of "the circumcision," while those who literally practice and preach circumcision in accordance with the Law are said to be "evil workers" who put their confidence in the flesh rather than the Spirit.

Similarly, in the Apocalypse, a word of prophecy in the name of the one "who has the key of David" consoles the church in Philadelphia with these words:

> *I will make those of the synagogue of Satan who say that they are Jews and are not, but are lying—I will make them come and bow down before your feet, and they will learn that I have loved you.* (Rev. 3:9)

The "synagogue of Satan" refers, of course, not literally to Satan-worshipers; rather, it is a bitterly polemical epithet for non-Christian Jews, who may in fact be responsible for subjecting the small and powerless Christian group to persecution (cf. Rev. 2:9–10). The interesting point here is that the author of Revelation contends that such people are not really Jews at all; the obvious implication, here as in Philippians 3:2–3, is that the "real Jews" are those who confess Jesus as Lord. The prophecy envisions an eschatological vindication in which the "false Jews" (i.e., those of the synagogue) acknowledge that it is really the Christians whom God has loved.

Texts such as these show that we will create perspectival distortion if we superimpose a clear distinction between "Judaism" and "Christianity" on the New Testament documents. We must always remember that these texts originate around the time when these two groups were first coalescing into separate religious communities.[11] This is the background against which we must assess the various New Testament perspectives on Judaism.

To evaluate each of the New Testament witnesses on this question would be too lengthy a task for our present purposes.[12] We can, however, illustrate the methodological problem by sampling the perspectives of four major New Testament writers: Paul, Luke, Matthew, and John. This cross-section of examples will define a spectrum of responses, each interpreting the relation of the church to Israel in ways that have distinctive implications for the *ethical* issue of how Christians and Jews might relate to one another.

(A) PAUL: "GOD HAS NOT REJECTED HIS PEOPLE" The *locus classicus* for understanding Paul's teaching about the relation of the church to Israel is Romans 9–11, a passage that climaxes in the dictum that "all Israel will be saved" (Rom. 11:26a). Taken by itself, this saying closely resembles a well-known passage in the Mishnah: "All Israelites have a share in the world to come, for it is written, *Thy people also shall be all righteous, they shall inherit the land for ever; the branch of my planting, the work of my hands that I may be glorified.*"[13]

Thus, in Romans 11 Paul illustrates his deep affinity with traditional Jewish thought that affirms God's comprehensive covenant love for Israel. At the same time, however, Paul's vision for Israel's eschatological salvation differs in crucial ways from that of the rabbis. In order to delineate his vision, a close reading of Romans 9–11 is necessary.

Romans 11:26a has become a favorite text for interpreters who ascribe to Paul a two-covenant theory, in which the Sinai covenant remains soteriologically valid for the Jewish people, while the new covenant in Christ is exclusively for Gentiles.[14] Such an interpretation hardly does justice, however, to Paul's complex dialectical wrestling in Romans 9–11. If Paul had simply meant that Moses was for Jews and Jesus for Gentiles, he could have said so far more straightforwardly. An adequate exegesis must seek to place Romans 11:26 within the larger context of the letter's argument.

The entire letter to the Romans circles around two basic issues:

- *Is the grace of God extended to Gentiles who do not observe the Torah?* Paul answers emphatically yes: the righteousness of God is now revealed in Jesus Christ, apart from the Law. The gospel of "the power of God for salvation" is for "the Jew first and also to the Greek" (1:16).
- *If God receives Gentiles by grace without requiring circumcision and adherence to the Law, does that mean that he has broken the covenant with Israel?* This question, which is the focus of Romans 9–11, Paul answers even more emphatically than the first: *mē genoito*, by no means! "Let God be true, even if everyone is a liar" (3:4, RH). A major purpose of Romans is to offer an impassioned defense of the faithfulness of God to Israel, despite that people's manifest unfaithfulness (3:3).

The status of the Jewish people in God's design may well have been a controversial matter among the various Christian groups in Rome.[15] We know from a report by the Roman historian Suetonius that there were such severe civil disturbances in the Jewish community in Rome that the Emperor Claudius expelled the Jews from the city in the year 49 C.E. Suetonius says that the riots occurred *impulsore Chresto*, "at the instigation of Chrestus."[16] It is likely, however, that this is a corruption of "Christus," and that the turmoil among the Jews was actually sparked by controversy over the introduction of Christian preaching in the synagogues (cf. analogous reports of disturbances in other cities in Acts 13:44–50, 17:1–9). After the death of Claudius in 54 C.E., Jews were allowed to return to the city. Perhaps this situation provoked various tensions between the Gentile Christians, who would have remained in Rome during this five-year interval, and the returning Jewish groups, both Christian and non-Christian.[17] If so, Paul does not address the situation specifically—it is important to remember that Paul himself had not visited Rome at the time of this letter—but this background of civil conflict should be kept in mind as we read this letter that proclaims that the gospel is "the power of God for salvation to *everyone* who believes, *to the Jew first and also to the Greek*.

We pick up the discussion at the beginning of Romans 9. Paul has just affirmed that, despite all the sufferings of the present age, nothing in all creation "will be able to separate us from the love of God in Christ Jesus our Lord" (8:39). But what of Israel, unbelieving Israel which refuses to trust in Jesus? Are they included or excluded by Paul's "us"? Does their unbelief place them outside the bounds of God's love? At first it seems that Paul fears such a result. That is why he says,

> *I have great sorrow and unceasing anguish in my heart. For I could wish that I myself were accursed and cut off from Christ for the sake of my own people, my kindred according to the flesh. They are Israelites, and to them belong the adoption, the glory, the covenants, the giving of the Law, the worship, and the promises; to them belong the patriarchs, and from them, according to the flesh, comes the Messiah, who is over all, God blessed forever. Amen.* (9:2–5)

Despite these past glories and advantages, Israel has turned away from the proclamation of the gospel, away from God's Messiah who is the fruit of their own heritage. This tragic state of affairs brings Paul "great sorrow," and he finds himself wishing that he could even surrender his own salvation by being cut off from Christ for the sake of his people. This wish, however presumptuous or impossible, is not merely an empty rhetorical gesture. It shows how deeply Paul has internalized the "imitation of Christ" as a basis for Christian ethics, and it suggests how Christians should relate to those outside the faith: rather than being targets of resentment or contempt, they should be seen as the objects of sacrificial love, just as the lost and sinful world was the object of Christ's sacrificial love. Nonetheless, despite Paul's anguish, many of his fellow Jews continue to reject his preaching of the gospel.

The first theological response that Paul offers to this state of affairs is a defense of the efficacy of God's Word, on the basis of a theory of election:

> *It is not as though the word of God had failed. For not all Israelites truly belong to Israel [literally "not all those who are of Israel are Israel"], and not all of Abraham's children are his true descendants [**sperma,** literally "seed"];*[18] *but "It is through Isaac that descendants [**sperma**] shall be named for you" [Gen. 21:12]. This means that it is not the children of the flesh who are the children of God, but the children of the promise are counted as descendants [**sperma**].* (9:6–8)

The unbelieving Israelites, on this theory, are "children of the flesh" only, but they are not really part of the elect "Israel" that God has designated as heirs of the promise to Abraham. In the remainder of chapter 9, then, Paul offers a defense of the claim that God's purposes in history have always been selective: "[H]e has mercy on whomever he chooses, and he hardens the heart of whomever he chooses" (9:18). Thus, according to this initial phase of the argument, there is nothing surprising about God's decision to choose some from among the Jewish people and reject others, just as he chose Jacob and rejected Esau. Indeed, the image of a faithful "remnant" of Israel is a characteristic theme of the prophetic tradition (9:27, quoting Isa. 10:22–23). Physical descent and ethnic heritage cannot guarantee God's favor; the unfaithful ones will be destroyed by God's judgment, even if they are by birth and custom members of the community of Israel. This situation is prefigured by Isaiah's prophecy:

> *If the Lord of hosts had not left survivors [**sperma**] to us,*
> *We would have fared like Sodom*
> *and been made like Gomorrah.* (9:29, quoting Isa. 1:9)

The NRSV's translation of *sperma* as "survivors" here obscures the thematic linkage with the same term in 9:7: the whole unit of 9:6–29 is an artfully constructed midrash on a series of Old Testament passages, allowing Paul to claim that the faithful remnant of Isaiah is to be identified as the same *sperma* promised to Abraham, whereas the majority of the people of Israel are simply destined for destruction.[19]

If Paul had simply stopped at the end of 9:29, he would have presented a neat and clear theological argument, based on one significant strain of thought in Israel's prophetic tradition. But he is not content to rest with this solution. Part of the problem for Paul is that God has not just selected a faithful remnant from among the Jewish people; rather, he has created a new community that embraces Gentiles along with the Jewish remnant. Indeed, Paul's actual missionary experience has increasingly led to the disturbing conclusion that the uncircumcised, lawless Gentiles are far more receptive to the news of God's salvation in Jesus Christ than are the circumcised, Law-observant Jews. Something is amiss, Paul thinks, in this picture. Thus, he opens a new section of the argument with a question that probes the anomaly:

> *What then are we to say? Gentiles, who did not pursue righteousness, have grasped righteousness—that is, righteousness through faith—but Israel, who did pursue a Law of righteousness, did not attain the Law. Why not?* (9:30–32A, RH)

This whole middle section of the discussion grapples inconclusively with this problem. Not content to shrug off the unbelief of the Jewish people as a simple result of God's elective will, Paul continues to agonize over them:

> *Brothers and sisters, my heart's desire and prayer to God for them is that they may be saved. I can testify that they have a zeal for God, but it is not enlightened. For, being ignorant of the righteousness that comes from God, and seeking to establish their own, they have not submitted to God's righteousness. For Christ is the* **telos** *of the Law, so that there may be righteousness to everyone who believes.* (10:1–4, AA)

Answers of one sort can be given, to be sure. The Jewish people have pursued righteousness as though it were based on works, as though they could establish their own righteousness rather than submitting to God's righteousness revealed in Christ (9:32, 10:3–4). But why? Why, when the word was near them all along (10:6–8), could they not understand it? Why, when the word of the gospel was proclaimed to them, did they not accept it (10:18–21)? The mystery posed at the beginning of this section is restated at the end, again prefigured in a prophecy of Isaiah, now reinterpreted in a startling new way by Paul:

> *I have been found by those who did not seek me;*
> *I have shown myself to those who did not ask for me.*

This is the Septuagint version of Isaiah 65:1, read by Paul's revisionary hermeneutic as a reference to Gentile Christians who have responded to the preaching of the gospel. But the following verse from Isaiah 65:2 is read in Romans 10:21 as referring instead to unbelieving Israel:

> *All day long I have held out my hands to a disobedient and contrary people.*

Thus, by the end of chapter 10, Paul is left with the same vexing problem that he began with: the mystery of Israel's unbelief.[20]

The whole argument has led up to the explicit question that at last tumbles out in 11:1: "I ask, then, has God rejected his people?" And Paul, at this climactic point, declares, "By no means! . . . God has not rejected his people whom he foreknew." The unbelief of Israel is not allowed to have the final word in the story. How can such a claim be sustained?

First, Paul restates the remnant theory. Just as God kept seven thousand in the time of Elijah who did not bow the knee to Baal, "so too at the present time there is a remnant, chosen by grace" (11:2b–5). This elect remnant has received God's righteousness, "but the rest were hardened" (11:7). This is a reprise of the themes of Chapter 9. But now a slightly different nuance appears: the remnant must be understood not just as the lucky ones who are saved for their own sake; rather, they remain as a sign and witness of God's abiding faithfulness to the people Israel, a proof that God has not abandoned his people.

With verse 11, however, Paul introduces a new theme and turns a crucial corner in the argument:

> *So I ask, have they stumbled so as to fall? By no means! But through their stumbling salvation has come to the Gentiles, so as to make Israel jealous. Now if their stumbling means riches for the world, and if their defeat means riches for Gentiles, how much more will their full inclusion mean!* (11:11–12)

Thus, the judgment pronounced on Israel remains penultimate; the final fruition of God's dealing with them remains to be seen. In order to explain this strange situation, Paul employs the allegory of the cultivated olive tree (Israel) whose branches are broken off so that wild olive branches (Gentiles) can be grafted on (11:17–24). Here Paul's discussion takes an explicitly hortatory turn, as he admonishes the Gentiles not to boast or be proud:

> *Do not boast over the branches. If you do boast, remember that it is not you that support the root, but the root that supports you. You will say, "Branches were broken off so that I might be grafted in." That is true. They were broken off because of their unbelief, but you stand only through faith. So do not become proud, but stand in awe. For if God did not spare the natural branches, perhaps he will not spare you.* (11:18–21)

It appears that Paul is addressing an actual pastoral problem in the church: Gentile converts to Christian faith are despising and derogating Jews who do not believe the gospel and thus are "cut off." (If the problem is not actually occurring, Paul at least fears that it will.) Paul rebukes such an attitude and encourages the Gentile believers to adopt an attitude of greater humility and respect for the Jews. The Jewish people belong naturally to the tree, even though they may have been cut off temporarily for the sake of the Gentiles. No Gentile Christian can read this passage without hearing in it a summons to respect the Jewish people and to hope that they might be grafted in again (11:23–24). Indeed, Paul expresses this idea not just as a wistful wish but as a confidently held affirmation: "And even those of Israel, if they do not persist in unbelief, will be grafted in, for God has the power to graft them in again."

At this point Paul introduces his declaration that "all Israel will be saved." In context, it is a word addressed to Gentiles, warning them against complacent contempt for the Jewish people:

> *So that you may not claim to be wiser than you are, brothers and sisters, I want you to understand this mystery: a hardening has come upon part of Israel, until the full number of the Gentiles has come in. And so [**kai houtōs**] all Israel will be saved; as it is written,*
>
> *Out of Zion will come the Deliverer;*
> *he will banish ungodliness from Jacob.*
> *And this is my covenant with them,*
> *when I take away their sins.*
>
> *As regards the gospel they are enemies of God for your sake; but as regards election they are beloved for the sake of their ancestors; for the gifts and the calling of God are irrevocable. Just as you were once disobedient to God but have now received mercy because of their disobedience, so they have now been disobedient in order that, by the mercy shown to you, they too may now receive mercy. For God has imprisoned all in disobedience so that he may be merciful to all.* (11:25–32)

"As regards election," the Jewish people remain beloved by God, despite all disobedience, despite their rejection of the good news of the gospel. The "mystery" (11:25) is not that Israel will be saved; that was always expected, and it is assured by the constancy of God. The mystery is that the salvation of Israel will occur, contrary to all previous expectation, in this particular way; the emphatic words in Paul's elucidation of the mystery are *kai houtōs*, "in *this* way."[21] The mystery is the reversal of the prophetic scenario; Isaiah envisioned the restoration of Israel, followed by the gathering of Gentiles to Mount Zion to worship the God who had wrought the astonishing salvation of his people (Isa. 2:2–4, 60:1–16, 66:18–19). But Paul now declares that God has "hardened" Israel so that the Gentiles will come first to worship the Lord, making Israel "jealous" and thereby bringing them also at last to the obedience of faith. Though the gospel is for the Jew first and also the Greek, the Greeks have responded first. Nonetheless, Paul continues to hope for the eschatological salvation of all Israel.

Thus, the judgment and destruction announced in Romans 9 is at last subsumed in Paul's larger vision of eschatological hope. In this respect, Romans 9–11 adheres closely to the pattern of God's judgment and ultimate mercy that we find repeatedly in Israel's lament psalms and prophetic oracles.

But who constitutes the "Israel" that will ultimately be saved by God? We should never forget that Paul introduced this train of reflection by saying that "not all those who are of Israel are Israel" (9:6). The meaning of Paul's statement cannot be that all Jews who have ever lived will be saved. (Indeed, even in the Mishnah passage cited above, the statement that "all Israelites have a share in the world to come" stands as the introduction to a long discussion of the *exceptions* to this generalization; see *m. Sanh.* 10.1–3.) Paul is thinking of the fate of the people corporately, not the soteriological destiny of each individual. Just as significantly, "all Israel" in Romans 11:26 should be understood to encompass Gentile believers along with the Jewish ones. Karl Barth's exegetical remarks on the passage are pertinent:

> "All Israel" is the community of those elected by God in and with Jesus Christ both from Jews and also from Gentiles, the whole Church which together with the holy root of Israel will consist in the totality of all the branches finally united with and drawing sustenance from it, in the totality constituted by the remnant continuing in and with the original stem Jesus Christ, by the wild shoots added later from the Gentiles, and by the branches which were cut off and are finally grafted in again.[22]

Certainly, Paul does not think that the eschatological salvation of Israel will occur somehow apart from Jesus Christ; the clear indication of this is his statement in verse 23 that they will be grafted back in "if they do not persist in unbelief." The "Israel" of Romans 11:26 is the same as the "Israel of God" in Galatians 6:16, a description of the elect eschatological people of God consisting of Jews and Gentiles together in Christ.[23] This entails, of course, a "typically Pauline polemical redefinition" of the term "Israel."[24] But the ambiguity of the term also allows Paul to forestall closure of judgment in the present, to hold open the possibility that God will yet act in unforeseeable ways to effect the salvation of "a disobedient and contrary people," the empirical Israel. Within the present eschatological interval, Christians must maintain toward the Jewish people the delicately balanced dialectical position that Paul describes, simultaneously acknowledging their peculiar status as God's beloved people and yet hoping for their ultimate salvation in Christ.

Did Paul succeed in impressing this dialectical view upon the church? In retrospect, we can see that his letter to the Romans was only halfway successful. Paul carried the day on his first point: that the grace of God is extended to Gentiles. But on his second major point—that God has not broken covenant with Israel—Paul lost in a very real sense. Within a couple of generations, his concerns were no longer even intelligible to a Gentile church whose attitudes toward the Jewish people came to be shaped increasingly by Matthew and John.[25]

(B) LUKE: "THE FALLING AND RISING OF MANY IN ISRAEL" We turn now to the witness of three of the Gospel writers on the church's relation to Israel. None of them offers a sustained theological treatment comparable to Romans 9–11, but each weaves the theme of what we might anachronistically call "Jewish-Christian relations" into the fabric of his narrative.

As we have seen, a central theme of Luke's narrative is the continuity of salvation history, and Jesus appears in this Gospel as the fulfillment of God's promises to Israel. This keynote of Luke's proclamation is sounded in the birth narratives. At the annunciation, the angel Gabriel tells Mary that the Lord God will give her child "the throne of his ancestor David" (Luke 1:32). Thus, Mary's celebration song can declare that God

> . . . *has helped his servant Israel,*
> *in remembrance of his mercy,*

according to the promise he made to our ancestors,
to Abraham and his descendants forever. (LUKE 1:54–55)

Similarly, Zechariah, the father of John the Baptist, declares prophetically, with tongue at last loosed by the Holy Spirit, that these portentous births signify God's long-promised rescue of his people:

Blessed be the Lord God of Israel,
for he has looked favorably on his people and redeemed them.
He has raised up a horn of salvation[26] *for us*
in the house of his servant David,
as he spoke through the mouth of his holy prophets from of old,
that we would be saved from our enemies and from the hand of all who hate us.
Thus he has shown the mercy promised to our ancestors,
and has remembered his holy covenant,
the oath that he swore to our ancestor Abraham,
to grant us that we, being rescued from the hands of our enemies,
might serve him without fear, in holiness and righteousness
before him all our days. (1:68–75)

Finally, lest we miss Luke's point in chapter 1, the devout aged Simeon appears in chapter 2 to reinforce the identification of Jesus as the fulfillment of Israel's hope. Having awaited "the consolation of Israel" all his life (2:25), Simeon perceives in the eight-day-old child Jesus the appearance of the salvation for which he had hoped. Echoing Isaiah 49:6, Simeon declares this child to be "a light for revelation to the Gentiles and for glory to your people Israel" (2:32). The whole structure of the songs and speeches in Luke's opening chapters leads us to see Jesus as God's appointed agent for the fulfillment of the ancient covenant with Israel.

Simeon's final words to Mary, however, foreshadow dark and painful events as well: "This child is destined for the falling and rising of many in Israel, and to be a sign that will be opposed so that the inner thoughts of many will be revealed—and a sword will pierce your own soul too" (2:34–35). This is our first hint that Jesus' way will not be entirely triumphant and that through him Israel will come to face not only blessing but also judgment. The meaning of this prophecy of "falling and rising" remains to be seen.

As the story unfolds, we see different characters beginning to exemplify this divergence of falling and rising. Some, like Zacchaeus (19:1–10) and the crippled woman (13:10–17), who respond to Jesus in faith, show themselves to be true sons and daughters of Abraham (19:9, 13:16). Others, like the synagogue leader who protests Jesus' healing of the woman (13:14), by refusing to acknowledge the power of God at work in Jesus, find themselves "put to shame" (13:17). The crucial point of decision is articulated by Jesus himself in his response to those disciples of John who ask whether he is "the one who is to come" or whether they should look for another: "[B]lessed is anyone who is not caused to stumble by me" (7:23, RH).

In the end, the city of Jerusalem joins in the rejection of Jesus. Foreseeing this prophetically, Jesus weeps over the city and foretells its violent destruction because of its failure to recognize its "time of visitation" (19:41–44). For Luke, writing in the last quarter of the first century, this prophecy is seen to be a true one: the destruction of Jerusalem and the Temple—which has already occurred—is a sign of God's judgment on the people for their failure to receive Jesus.

The full import of Luke's "falling and rising" motif is not explained, however, until the story moves forward into the Acts of the Apostles. In Acts 3:17–26, Peter makes a speech to the Jews who have gathered in the Temple precincts to marvel at the healing of a man lame from birth. After proclaiming that the healing was done in the name of Jesus, whom the people had rejected, he calls on them to repent and to turn to God while awaiting "the time of universal restoration that God announced long ago through his holy prophets" (3:21). Then Peter explains the significance of Jesus by interpreting him as the fulfillment of the Old Testament expectation of a "prophet like Moses":

> *Moses said, "The Lord your God will raise up for you from your own people a prophet like me. You must listen to whatever he tells you.* ***And it will be that everyone who does not listen to that prophet will be utterly rooted out of the people****" [cf. Deut. 18:15–20; Acts 7:37]. And all the prophets, as many as have spoken, from Samuel and those after him, also predicted these days. You are the descendants of the prophets and the covenant that God gave to your ancestors, saying to Abraham, "And in your descendants all the families of the earth shall be blessed" [Gen. 22:18, 26:4]. When God raised up his servant, he sent him first to you, to bless you by turning each of you from your wicked ways.*
>
> (Acts 3:22–26, *emphasis mine*)

As the divinely appointed prophet, Jesus is "raised up"—the double sense, hinting at resurrection, serves Luke's purpose well—for the people, whose fate depends on their response to him. If they act as "descendants of the prophets" by believing Jesus, they will receive blessing, but if they do not listen to Jesus, they will be "utterly rooted out of the people." Interestingly, Luke's citation of Deuteronomy 18:19 agrees neither with the Hebrew text nor with the Septuagint, both of which merely say, "Anyone who does not heed the words that the prophet shall speak in my name, I myself will hold accountable." Luke has *introduced* the motif of exclusion from the people in order to specify the dire consequences of unbelief and in order to make it clear that Jews who refuse to accept the preaching of the gospel are, in his theological perspective, *opting out of Israel*. As Luke's Paul will say to the unbelieving Jews in Pisidian Antioch later in the story, "It was necessary that the word of God should be spoken first to you. *Since you reject it and judge yourselves to be unworthy of eternal life*, we are now turning to the Gentiles" (Acts 13:46, emphasis added; cf. 18:5–6). The way of salvation history runs through Jesus, and those who will not follow are in effect no longer part of the elect people. Thus the church *becomes Israel*, or, to put it more precisely, Israel after the resurrection of Jesus is composed entirely of those who believe and follow the prophet whom God has raised up. This is the sense in which Jesus is a sign "for the falling and rising of many in Israel."

This does not mean that the Jewish people as a whole have come under final judgment. The possibility always remains open for individuals to respond to the preaching of the Word and to join the people of God. This last point has been a debated issue in the interpretation of Luke-Acts.[27] Some scholars have interpreted the conclusion of Acts to mean that Luke regards the time of the Jewish mission to be over: Paul cites the prophecy of Isaiah 6:9–10 about the people's lack of understanding and then declares, "Let it be known to you then that this salvation of God has been sent to the Gentiles; they will listen" (28:25b–28). For several reasons, however, this passage should not be construed as marking a definitive end to the opportunity for Jews to accept the gospel. For one thing, within this very passage we are told that some of Paul's Jewish hearers at Rome were convinced by his arguments from Scripture about Jesus (28:23–24). For another, this is the third time in Acts that Paul makes such a statement (cf. 13:46–48, 18:5–6), yet after the first two times he continues his practice of preaching to Jews; indeed, it is tempting to read Acts 28:28 as a perfect illustration of what Paul means in Romans 11:13–14 when he says that he glorifies his ministry to the Gentiles "in order to make my own people jealous, and thus save some of them." Finally, Acts 28:30–31 indicates that during his house arrest in Rome, Paul continued to welcome "all who came to him"; there is no indication that the Jews who had shown considerable interest in his teaching (28:17–25) were excluded.

In general, Luke thinks of ongoing history as a time of triumphant expansion of the Christian mission. In the story that he tells in Acts, many thousands of Jews have become believers in the gospel. This is evident not only from Luke's description of the early church immediately after Pentecost (Acts 2:41–47, 5:12–16) but also from the later statement when Paul arrives in Jerusalem that there are "many thousands of believers . . . among the Jews" (21:20). Though the apostles also encounter opposition from Jewish authorities in Jerusalem and Jewish crowds in the diaspora, Acts is by no means a story of univocal Jewish rejection of the gospel. It is, rather, a story of the "falling and rising of many in Israel" as they encounter the Word and the signs and wonders that attend its proclamation.

For Luke, the history of Israel that began with patriarchs and prophets finds its true continuation in the community that gathers in response to the apostolic preaching. The apologetic agenda of his whole presentation is to argue for the continuity of the church with Israel, its rootedness in Israel. In that respect, despite the narrative emphasis on the Gentile mission in Acts, Luke-Acts is a strongly pro-Jewish work, even to the implausible extent of representing *Paul* as a strict observer of the Law (Acts 21:17–26). The action of Luke's two-volume work focuses on Jerusalem as the great symbolic center from which the Christian mission emanates, and the Scripture of Israel provides the entire symbolic/typological background for everything that happens in the narrative.

Jewish characters in the story are by no means stereotyped, for good or ill. The story has Jewish villains, of course, but all of Luke's heroes are also Jewish, beginning with Jesus himself. The attitude of Christians toward Jews, as modeled by the apostles, is one of urgent but respectful dialogue, "testifying" and "trying to convince" them on the basis of Scripture to believe the gospel. Only when the Jewish hearers become scornful—even in some cases instigating violence against the Christian preachers—do the apostles pronounce the word of prophetic rejection upon them.

In many respects, Luke's position on the Jewish people is similar to Paul's;[28] indeed, he may stress the continuity of the church with Israel even more strongly, without reckoning as Paul does with significant points of tension and discontinuity. The one great difference between Luke and Paul lies in Luke's virtual absorption of the line of salvation history into the church. We find in Luke none of the dialectical tension of Romans 9–11, no sense that even the unbelieving Jews are still in some mysterious way "beloved for the sake of their ancestors." We find in Luke no speculative hope for the ultimate salvation of all Israel, no sense that the covenant faithfulness of God somehow requires an eschatological reconciliation of the Jewish people as a whole to the truth of the gospel, no sense—and here is perhaps the most crucial point—that the people of the synagogue retain their identity alongside the church as a people with a special claim on God's favor, a people whose unbelief in the gospel creates an agonizing problem of theodicy. For Luke, the story is told in a simpler and more linear fashion: God has acted in Jesus to confirm and fulfill the promises to Israel, giving the people a clear choice. They can repent and believe, or they can reject the Word. If they do the latter, they are "utterly rooted out of the people." It is a clean choice, in or out. Nowhere in Acts does Luke overtly express any regrets or anguish over those who turn away. Only in Luke's haunting image of Jesus weeping over Jerusalem (Luke 19:41–44) do we find an echo of Paul's agonized lament for his own people.

(C) MATTHEW: "HIS BLOOD BE ON US AND ON OUR CHILDREN" In Matthew we encounter a peculiar combination of ardent affirmation of the Law and vehement rejection of Judaism, particularly as it is represented by the religious leadership of the Jewish community. Although Matthew is sometimes described as the most Jewish of the Gospels,[29] his narrative shows signs of bitter conflict between church and synagogue. The bitterness explodes into vicious polemic against the "scribes and Pharisees" in Matthew 23, a large block of distinctively Matthean anti-Jewish material. Furthermore, a number of clues in the narrative suggest that Matthew believes the Jewish people to have fallen into utter reprobation: they have missed their opportunity to respond to the messianic invitation, and now the door has closed upon them (cf. Matt. 25:10).

How are we to account for the polemical edge of Matthew's treatment of Judaism? The best hypothesis is that Matthew's Gospel is a classic expression of the "sibling rivalry" described above; it is a foundational document that claims for the community of Jesus' followers the exclusive possession of Israel's Scripture and tradition, against the counterclaims of the pharisaic movement. The figure of Jesus in Matthew becomes the one authentic and definitive interpreter of the Torah. Those who oppose him (and his disciples) can only be hypocrites and "blind guides" (23:24).

The remarkable claim in Matthew 5:17–20 that Jesus has come not to abolish the Law and the prophets but to fulfill them must be read in the context of the late-first-century struggle for ownership of Israel's heritage. No doubt the early Jewish Christians were being accused by their Jewish contemporaries of being "soft" on Law observance. Matthew responds by formulating, in the opening of the Sermon on the Mount, a programmatic denial of the charge:

> *Do not think that I have come to abolish the law or the prophets. I have come not to abolish but to fulfill. For truly I tell you, until heaven and earth pass away, not one letter, not one stroke of a letter, will pass from the law until all is accomplished. Therefore, whoever breaks one of the least of these commandments,*[30] *and teaches others to do the same, will be called least in the kingdom of heaven; but whoever does them and teaches them will be called great in the kingdom of heaven. For I tell you, unless your righteousness exceeds that of the scribes and Pharisees, you will never enter the kingdom of heaven.*
> (5:17–20, *emphasis added*)

Not only is the charge false that Jesus sponsors antinomianism, but in fact he demands a standard of legal obedience more stringent than that of the scribes and Pharisees, who merely require a minimal outward adherence to the literal sense of the Law. The six antitheses that follow (5:21–48) seek to show that Jesus' disciples are called to a higher standard, a more radical interpretation of the Law that "fulfills" the Law by dealing with the orientation of the heart. The scribes and Pharisees dabble with superficial concerns, suggests Matthew, but Jesus exposes the deep intention of the Law.

Jesus also "fulfills" the Law and the prophets in the events of his own life, which correspond in detail to predictive prophecies in Scripture. Matthew tirelessly documents this aspect of Jesus' career through the use of formula quotations that explicitly assert that "all this took place to fulfill what had been spoken by the Lord through the prophet" (1:22 and elsewhere). One intended effect of these citations is to emphasize the blindness and culpability of the Jews who do not believe in Jesus: despite the fact that the messianic predictions are being fulfilled before their eyes, they continue to resist his authority. In this respect Matthew is the point of origin for a major trajectory of anti-Jewish polemic in the Christian tradition; one sees the next fully developed stage of the trajectory in Justin's *Dialogue with Trypho*. (The effect on the critical reader of Matthew's Gospel, however, is almost exactly the reverse: Matthew's use of prooftexts is so farfetched and insensitive to the original Old Testament contexts that even the sympathetic Christian reader is led to question the legitimacy of his christological claims.)

Matthew also emphasizes more than the other synoptic evangelists the theme of Jewish persecution of Christians.[31] In the "mission discourse" of Matthew 10, Jesus sends his disciples explicitly to "the lost sheep of the house of Israel" (10:6) to preach the gospel of the nearness of the kingdom of heaven. But even in sending them out he warns them to expect persecution:

> *See, I am sending you out like sheep into the midst of wolves; so be wise as serpents and innocent as doves. Beware of them, for they will hand you over to councils [**synedria**] and flog you in their synagogues; and you will be dragged before governors and kings because of me, as testimony to them and the Gentiles.* (10:16–18)

The disciples will be betrayed to death by members of their own families (10:21); they are to flee from one town to the next under the threat of persecution, until the Son of Man comes (10:23). This is their inevitable fate as followers of Jesus: "If they have called the master of the house Beelzebul [cf. 9:34, 12:24], how much more will they malign those of his household" (10:25b). God will ultimately judge those who reject the disciples, however: "Truly I tell you, it will be more tolerable for the land of Sodom and Gomorrah on the day of judgment than for that town [that does not welcome you]" (10:15). A comparison of this passage to the Lukan parallel (Luke 9:2–5) is illuminating. Luke makes no mention of persecution and floggings in synagogues; he merely tells the Twelve to shake off the dust from their feet against towns that do not receive them. The motif of the judgment of Sodom is transferred over into Luke's longer account of the mission of the Seventy (Luke 10:1–16), but still there is no mention of persecution or violence against the disciples. The theme of persecution in synagogues does appear later among the signs of the apocalyptic tribulation in Mark 13:9–13 and Luke 21:12–19 (notice that the parallel in Matt. 24:9–14 envisions persecution by Gentiles), but Matthew—by connecting the warning of persecution directly with the earlier mission to Israel—highlights the adversarial relationship between church and synagogue.

The most crucial evidence, however, appears in Matthew's redactional modifications of several of Jesus' parables, which he turns into allegories of God's rejection of the Jewish people. We cannot consider all the relevant material here, but two instances will illustrate the phenomenon. Matthew incorporates Mark's parable of the wicked tenants who kill the son of the owner of the vineyard (Mark 12:1–12, Matt. 21:33–46). Though he follows the Markan source closely, Matthew appends his own moral to the tale: "Therefore I tell you, the kingdom of God will be taken away from you and given to a people [*ethnei*] that produces the fruits of the kingdom." Whereas the parable in Mark is clearly a condemnation of the chief priests, scribes, and elders (Mark 11:27; 12:1, 12), Matthew generalizes the allegory into a theory about the rejection of the Jewish people by God in favor of another "people" (i.e., the church) who will "produce fruits."[32]

Similarly, the immediately following parable of the wedding banquet (Matt. 22:1–14) becomes in Matthew's hands a proclamation of God's categorical judgment upon Israel. Whereas in the Lukan version (Luke 14:15–24) the snubbed host merely orders his slave to bring in "the poor, the crippled, the blind, and the lame" to replace the original guests, Matthew's host (a "king" in this version of the story) reacts more vehemently—perhaps not surprisingly in view of the fact that the invited guests have not merely refused the invitation but have actually mistreated and killed the king's slaves. (The link back to the wicked vineyard tenants is unmistakable.) So what does the king do? With the wedding banquet still steaming on the table, "[h]e sent his troops, destroyed those murderers, and burned their city" (Matt. 22:7). Only then, having worked up a good appetite through this military activity, does he order his slaves to invite people in from the streets for the wedding banquet. Though it cannot be proven, it is highly likely that the simpler Lukan version of the parable is closer to the tradition; Matthew has reworked it to make it into an allegorical account of the destruction of Jerusalem as God's judgment on the "murderers" who have rejected the emissaries of the king.

This observation leads us to note one final text in which Matthew fatefully lays the responsibility for the death of Jesus at the feet of the Jewish people as a whole:

> *So when Pilate saw that he could do nothing, but rather that a riot was beginning, he took some water and washed his hands before the crowd, saying, "I am innocent of this man's blood; see to it yourselves." Then the people as a whole [**pas ho laos**] answered, "His blood be on us and on our children!"* (MATT. 27:24–25)

With this chilling narrative detail, not present in any of the other Gospels, Matthew clearly ascribes responsibility for the death of Jesus to the whole Jewish people *and to their descendants*. Thus the allegorical description of them as "murderers" (22:7) becomes, in the passion narrative, literal fact.

We must defer discussion of how to deal with this text hermeneutically. For the moment, we simply record the exegetical conclusion that Matthew appears to have developed a clear dispensationalist construct that governs the logic of his narrative. Jesus' original mission was to the Jewish people, but they rejected him and—like the vineyard tenants—were responsible for killing him. Consequently, though God had originally designed to give them the kingdom, it has now been taken away from them and given to another "people," the church, who will be more faithful and obedient. This church, to be sure, includes (former?) Jews, but "all nations" are now to be made disciples (28:16–20). The future of the church is clearly among the Gentiles, because Israel has been irrevocably rejected by God. In short, Matthew (alongside the letter to the Hebrews) is the preeminent canonical voice of supersessionist Christian theology: the church *replaces* Israel.

(D) JOHN: "YOU ARE FROM YOUR FATHER THE DEVIL" In the Gospel of John, the church's bitter polemic against the synagogue is raised to its highest pitch in the New Testament. The Johannine church was a community of Jewish origin that had suffered the painful experience of being excluded from fellowship with the synagogue because of its conviction that Jesus was not only the Messiah but also the Son of God who was one with God the Father.[33] The entire Gospel thus reflects the painfully ironic vision of a community that believes that the Word "came to his own home, and his own people did not accept him" (John 1:11). Consequently, in this Gospel "the Jews" become the villains; whereas the term "the Jews" appears no more than five or six times in each of the synoptics, John uses it more than seventy times, almost always in a pejorative sense. Scholars sometimes argue that the phrase "the Jews" in John refers not to the people as a whole but to their leaders.[34] Even if this is correct in some passages, it makes little difference for our reflection about the ethical implications of the text. The leaders symbolize the Jewish community as a whole, a community from which John and his readers have become estranged.

The contention between the Johannine community and the synagogue is played out in this Gospel's repeated dramatic encounters between Jesus and "the Jews," always followed by long monologues from Jesus. These scenes, as J. Louis Martyn has shown, should be read as "two-level drama": Jesus' words to the Jews in the narrative (level one) express at the same time the message of the Johannine community (living near the end of the first century) to its contemporary rivals and opponents (level two).[35] Thus, Jesus' "revelation discourses" should be read less as reports of what Jesus said once upon a time than as prophetic-theological commentary directed to readers of the evangelist's own time. This construal of the text allows us to see—albeit through a glass darkly—the conflict between John's community and the Jewish community near the end of the first century.

For instance, in John 5, after Jesus heals a paralytic on the Sabbath, the healed man tells "the Jews" what Jesus has done:

> *Therefore the Jews started persecuting Jesus, because he was doing such things on the sabbath. But Jesus answered them, "My Father is still working, and I also am working." For this reason the Jews were seeking all the more to kill him, because he was not only breaking the sabbath, but was also calling God his own Father, thereby making himself equal to God.* (John 5:16–18)

In response to this hostility, Jesus offers a long discourse in which, among many other points, he castigates the Jews for failing to see that the Law, to which they are so devoted, actually bears witness to himself:

> *You search the scriptures because you think that in them you have eternal life; and it is they that testify on my behalf. Yet you refuse to come to me to have life. . . . Do not think that I will accuse you before the Father; your accuser is Moses, on whom you have set your hope. If you believed Moses, you would believe me, for he wrote about me. But if you do not believe what he wrote, how will you believe what I say?* (5:39–40, 45–47)

Here we see again the struggle for ownership of the tradition: John asserts, against the synagogue's repudiation of the church's claims about Jesus, that the Law of Moses actually points to Jesus. Nonetheless, in a few places in the Gospel, Jesus makes distancing references to Israel's Scriptures as "your law" (8:17, 10:34) or "their law" (15:25). The latter passage is particularly telling for our present concerns: "But now they have seen and hated both me and my Father. It was to fulfill the word that is written in their law, 'They hated me without a cause'" (15:24b–25, loosely quoting Ps. 69:4). Such passages are telltale signs of the growing rift between formative Judaism and Johannine Christianity.

Just as in Matthew, we find in the Fourth Gospel indications that the church has suffered (or expects to suffer) persecution at the hands of the Jews. Not only are those who confess Jesus to be the Messiah "put out of the synagogue" (9:22, 12:42, 16:2)—a flagrant anachronism when read back into the period of Jesus' own lifetime—but the disciples are warned of more severe persecutions to come. In the farewell discourse, for example, Jesus prepares the disciples for rejection and affliction:

> *If the world hates you, be aware that it hated me before it hated you. If you belonged to the world, the world would love you as its own. Because you do not belong to the world, but I have chosen you out of the world—therefore the world hates you. Remember the word that I said to you, "Servants are not greater than their master." If they persecuted me, they will persecute you; if they kept my word, they will keep yours also.*[36] *But they will do all these things to you on account of my name, because they do not know him who sent me. . . . They will put you out of the synagogues. Indeed, an hour is coming when those who kill you will think that by doing so they are offering worship to God. And they will do this because they have not known the Father or me.* (15:18–21; 16:2–3)

Whether this prophecy describes what John actually saw happening, or whether it merely expresses a fear of what might happen, it bears witness to a relation of deadly hostility between the two communities. It is one of history's great tragedies that texts such as this one, written from the point of view of a powerless minority group of Christians, later became the pretext for a Christian majority to hate and oppress and kill Jews, when the relations of social power were reversed.

Nowhere in John's Gospel does the superheated animosity toward the Jews come to more vigorous expression than in chapter 8. Here Jesus "models" a provocative and vicious invective against Jews. His words are all the more startling because they are directed not toward Jews who are seeking to persecute him but precisely toward those who are said to have believed in him (8:30–31). In response to their faith, Jesus tells them that if they *continue* in his word, they will know the truth and become free.[37] When they are puzzled by this admonition, declaring themselves to be already free children of Abraham, Jesus turns on them, suggests that they are in fact slaves to sin, and abruptly accuses them of trying to kill him. (The oddity of this accusation may be a sign that the discourse has slipped from one mode into another, from the once-upon-a-time story of Jesus to the later conflict between Christians and Jews.) The ensuing dialogue is the most deeply disturbing outburst of anti-Jewish sentiment in the New Testament.

> *Jesus said to them, "If you were Abraham's children, you would be doing what Abraham did, but now you are trying to kill me, a man who has told you the truth that I heard from God. This is not what Abraham did. You are indeed doing what your father does." They*

> *said to him, "We are not illegitimate children; we have one father, God himself." Jesus said to them, "If God were your father, you would love me, for I came from God and now I am here. I did not come on my own, but he sent me. Why do you not understand what I say? It is because you* ***cannot*** *accept my word.* ***You are from your father the devil, and you choose to do your father's desires.*** *He was a murderer from the beginning and does not stand in the truth, because there is no truth in him. . . . If I tell the truth, why do you not believe me?* ***Whoever is from God hears the words of God. The reason you do not hear them is that you are not from God.*** (8:39b–44a, 46b–47, *emphasis mine*)

Not surprisingly, the hostility continues to escalate from this point, and the scene ends with the Jews attempting to stone Jesus (8:59); thus, he has provoked them into fulfilling his characterization of them.

The scene makes no sense as a realistic account of an event in the life of Jesus; it can be read only as the Johannine community's frustrated and angry response to Jewish interlocutors who have refused to "continue" in accepting the community's extraordinary claims about Jesus. Even if some of the Jews have "believed" in some provisional way, they have not accepted the Fourth Gospel's cosmic claims about Jesus' preexistent unity with God (note the climax of the controversy in 8:58: "Very truly, I tell you, before Abraham was, I am"). But the evangelist and his community find this unbelief inexplicable: "Why do you not understand what I say?" How can it be that the Jewish people have resisted the truth that has been revealed by Jesus, who declares what he has seen in the Father's presence? How is it possible that they fail to recognize the glory that became flesh and lived among them? In answer to this agonized question, "Why do you not understand what I say?" John makes a fateful theological step: *from the empirical fact of the unbelief of the Jews, he infers an ontological dualism.* The Jews who do not believe must be children of the devil. The reason that they do not believe is that they *cannot.* Otherwise, surely they would be convinced of the truth. The conclusion of verse 47 articulates the chilling logic of this position: the reason they do not hear the word of God is that they are not from God.

One shudders to contemplate the ethical outworking of such a theological perspective on the Jews. Yet this passage's dualistic anthropology, which is well down the road toward Gnosticism, is not an aberration in the Fourth Gospel. In 10:26, for example, Jesus, walking in the Temple, declares to "the Jews" who are asking him to tell them plainly whether he is the Messiah that they do not believe "because you do not belong to my sheep." The world for John is divided into those who belong to God and those who do not. When Jesus appears on the scene, a polarization occurs so that the truth can be exposed. Those who are of divine origin believe; those who are "from below" do not. That is why John can speak of the moment of *krisis*, the point of judgment, as having already occurred: "Very truly, I tell you, anyone who hears my word and believes him who sent me has eternal life, and does not come under judgment, but has passed from death to life" (5:24). On the other hand, "[T]hose who do not believe are condemned already, because they have not believed in the name of the only Son of God" (3:18).

Thus, John's eschatology moves into a radically different theological universe from Paul's depiction of a church groaning in travail along with a creation that still awaits final redemption. For John, the judgment on the unbelieving Jewish people has already been definitively pronounced; indeed, the judgment is so final that he is willing to declare that they have always from the beginning been children of the devil in some primal metaphysical sense. For Paul, the continuing expectation of judgment and salvation in the future allows him to hope that God will yet act in some unforeseeable way to redeem all Israel. Thus, Paul and John define the opposite poles on the New Testament's spectrum of attitudes toward Judaism.

2. Synthesis: Israel in Canonical Context

A full treatment of the issue of New Testament attitudes toward Judaism would have to extend the survey to other canonical texts; the Epistle to the Hebrews would be an especially important text to consider. At the same time, a more detailed reading even of the four authors we have treated here would complicate the picture still further. For example, in 1 Thessalonians 2:14–16, we find a statement in Paul that is much closer in tone and content to what I have described as the Matthean position than it is to Romans 9–11. Some scholars have proposed that this passage is an interpolation, but I think it more likely that it simply reflects another facet—or perhaps an earlier phase—of Paul's thought on this matter. In any case, while acknowledging that the foregoing sketch of four major New Testament perspectives on Judaism is incomplete, we have enough evidence on the table to hint at the gravity of the synthetic problem. Is it possible to speak of a unity within New Testament ethics on the church's treatment of the Jewish people?

We can begin with a summary of several points in which our texts are in agreement.

- All the New Testament writings show puzzlement and frustration over Israel's failure to acknowledge Jesus as Messiah and Lord.
- No New Testament writer—including Paul—ever envisions a "separate but equal" salvation for Gentiles and Jews. The notion of a two-covenant theory in which Jews are saved apart from Jesus Christ will not stand the test of careful exegesis. All the New Testament authors agree that no one is saved by birth into a particular ethnic community. Responsive hearing, faith, and obedience are required. God has no grandchildren.
- All four of the writers we have surveyed testify to the persecution of Christians by Jews. Paul himself tells us, for example, that he once violently persecuted the church and tried to destroy it (Gal. 1:13). The statements that we find in the New Testament texts must be read as contextualized responses to this situation of conflict and persecution. There is no evidence either in the New Testament or in other historical sources of any Christian persecution of Jews during the

first century. This is perhaps in part a measure of the early Christian commitment to following Jesus' example of love of enemies, but—in light of the sordid subsequent history of Christian treatment of Jews—it is probably wiser to observe that the major reason for the absence of Christian persecution of Jews is simply that the Christians were in the first century a small and powerless minority within the Jewish community, to say nothing of the wider society. (In light of later tragic developments, it should also be noted that the Jewish persecution of Christians seems to have entailed primarily expulsion from the synagogue; despite isolated instances of martyrdom, such as the story of Stephen in Acts 7, there is no evidence that Jews undertook systematic campaigns of violence and mass murder against the followers of Jesus.)[38]

- In no case do the New Testament texts show any evidence of racially motivated "anti-Semitism." To speak of "anti-Semitism" in the New Testament is an anachronistic misnomer. The issues are entirely religious and confessional, hinging upon the acceptance of Jesus as Messiah and upon questions of observance of the Law. It should never be forgotten that the New Testament writers themselves were Jews,[39] as were Jesus and his original circle of followers.
- The conflict between the early Christian movement and pharisaic-rabbinic Judaism must be understood in the first instance as an intra-Jewish phenomenon. Paul and Luke quite clearly see themselves and their churches as standing within Israel and seeking to reshape the belief and practice of the Jewish people in accordance with their understanding of Jesus as God's Messiah. The evidence of Matthew and John shows us a more ambiguous situation. On the one hand, Matthew and John are forced to recognize that a split really has occurred, and they feel compelled to offer theological explanations for this situation; on the other hand, they continue to claim continuity with Scripture and the authentic heritage of Israel. Even John, for whom the division of church and synagogue is most sharply defined, continues to insist that Abraham and Moses bear witness to Jesus and that he is the fulfillment of all that Israel had awaited. There is, in other words, no opening for Marcionism in the New Testament. Nor is there any sense in which New Testament Christology is inherently anti-Jewish, as some theologians have contended.[40] Indeed, the development of New Testament Christology is originally comprehensible only within a Jewish context. Thus, despite the serious tensions between early Christians and Jews, their debate was being conducted within a fundamentally Jewish symbolic universe.

These observations help us to place our reading of the texts in an appropriate historical context. But wide divergences remain. How are we to deal with this problem?

First of all, we must let the tensions stand. If my reading of the individual witnesses is correct, there is no way of compromising or harmonizing their differences. The Gospel of John really does adopt a stance toward Judaism that can only engender polemics and hostility. If it could be shown through careful exegesis that my reading is incorrect, perhaps the intracanonical tensions could be reduced. For example, Amy-Jill Levine has offered an extended exegetical argument that Matthew's theology is not characterized by the sort of judgmental supersessionism that I have characterized here. She reads the polemic as directed toward the Jewish leaders, not the people, and proposes that Matthew's criticism is directed toward stasis and social inequality rather than toward Judaism as such.[41] Though I do not find her interpretation entirely persuasive, this is an example of the sort of exegetical initiative that might help to overcome the apparently irreducible diversity of perspectives within the New Testament. (Her work addresses only Matthew, however, and does not help us with the problem posed by the Gospel of John.)

Given the variety of incompatible positions within the New Testament canon, I believe that we are forced in this case to make a clear choice among the possible options offered us. No thoroughgoing synthesis is possible. For reasons that I will attempt to explain in what follows, I propose that the theological position taken by Paul in Romans 9–11 ought to be judged determinative for Christian attitudes and actions toward the Jewish people, and that the other New Testament writings must be either interpreted or critiqued within this Pauline framework.

Why should Paul be treated as the benchmark? First, Paul most adequately gives attention to the radical implications of the biblical understanding of election. More than any of the other New Testament writers, Paul sees clearly that the integrity and trustworthiness of God are at stake in this problem. Once one embraces Paul's radical conviction that salvation must depend finally on God's grace rather than on human will or performance, one sees that God's covenant with Israel commits God necessarily to a course of redemptive action that will not abandon the covenant people.

To put the same point in a slightly different way, Paul's approach to the church-Israel question most adequately preserves continuity with the larger scriptural story. (Luke also is attentive to this issue; the question of whether the Lukan and Pauline perspectives on Israel can be read as complementary is an important one.) It is no accident that Romans 9–11 is replete with citations of and arguments from Scripture. Paul understands the urgent importance of retelling the story in such a way that Israel—even if they are "a disobedient and contrary people"—is finally embraced by grace. Otherwise, the gospel is no gospel.

Another reason for choosing the Pauline stance—and this anticipates the hermeneutical discussion—is the weight of experience. The church's historic option of following the roads marked by Matthew and John has led to unmitigated disaster. Given another option within the canon, we ought to explore it. Because Paul's letters predate the irrevocable split of Judaism and Christianity into different religions, they offer us a fresh starting place for rethinking these painful issues.

Once one has made such a choice, one has to decide how to account for the presence of contrary positions in the New Testament canon. In this instance, I have suggested that the polemics of Matthew and John are to be understood first of all in light of the *historical* circumstances that produced them. The polemics in these texts must be set within the original context of *intra-Jewish* debate and conflict.[42] (This suggests, again to anticipate a hermeneutical point, that the same texts become hermeneutically skewed when they are reappropriated by Gentile Christians as part of an *Adversos Judaeos* tradition.)

Finally, we must consider how these divergent New Testament texts appear when viewed through the lenses of *community, cross*, and *new creation*. While these focal images cannot resolve the differences between the New Testament witnesses, they can help us see how to read those witnesses rightly.

Community. The New Testament texts do not frame the problem of the Christian response to Jews and Judaism either in terms of the relation of Christians to individual "neighbors" or in terms of a liberal ideal of tolerance of individual religious choice. Rather, the issue is the destiny of and relationship between particular communities of people: church and Israel. The formation of a corporate entity, the people of God, is the basic theological concern throughout these texts. Paul does not advise his Gentile readers in Rome to be nice to the Jews because each person should have religious freedom; rather, he makes an argument that "God has not rejected his people" and that Gentile Christians should therefore adopt a stance of respectful humility in relation to Jews, who are beloved for the sake of their ancestors. When Matthew, on the other hand, thinks of the kingdom of God as taken away from the Jews and given to "*a nation* producing the fruits of it," he is also thinking in corporate terms about God's dealings with the people. Likewise, Matthew's depiction of "all the people" taking Jesus' blood on themselves and on their children implies a strong notion of corporate responsibility and corporate destiny. Thus, while Matthew asserts that Israel's election is revoked and Paul argues that it cannot be, both writers are in agreement that it is a question of the destiny of a people as a whole. The ethic that will follow from such a way of conceiving the problem will naturally be an ethic of corporate responsibility: the community as a whole must take to heart Paul's admonitions in Romans 11.

Cross. When we read the New Testament witnesses on this question through the focal lens of the *cross*, we see above all else that Jesus' death is the enactment and proof of God's faithfulness to Israel. Paul has this truth the most sharply in focus, but the same theme is present in the Gospels as well, including Matthew and John. This interpretation of the cross as the fulfillment of God's promises to Israel is near the heart of the message of all the New Testament writers; thus, it provides a center point from which more peripheral teachings—such as Matthew's supersessionism and John's ontological dualism—can and must be critiqued. These peripheral explanatory theories, which seek to account ex post facto for the minimal success of Christian preaching among the Jewish people, are actually internally inconsistent with the deepest christological logic of the writings in which they appear.

Two illustrations will perhaps clarify what I mean. If Jesus dies, as John's Gospel has it, as the Passover Lamb, then surely the result of his death is to lead Israel again and finally out of bondage. Even if some fail or refuse to claim the protection of his blood on their doorposts, the deepest purpose of his death must be to rescue Israel. Or again, if, as Matthew has it, the cup at the Last Supper is Jesus' "blood of the covenant, which is poured out for many for the forgiveness of sins" (Matt. 26:28), then what ironic soteriological resonance is triggered when all the Jewish people cry, "His blood be on us and our children"? Surely Jesus' death reaffirms rather than negates God's forgiveness and covenant love for Israel?

Whether John and Matthew intend such interpretations is neither ascertainable nor of crucial significance. My point is simply that the message of the crucified Messiah, which stands at the center of the New Testament proclamation, makes sense precisely and only as a confirmation of God's redemptive will for the people Israel. Anything within the New Testament that denies or deemphasizes this foundational truth will have the effect of moving the texts out of focus.

Beyond this fundamental theological point, we may note several other consequences of interpreting the difficult texts on Judaism in light of the image of the *cross*. For instance, the Jesus who tells the parable of the wicked vineyard tenants (Matt. 21:33–46) must be identified with the son who is *killed* in the parable, not with the king in the following parable who exacts vengeance; judgment and vengeance are to be left to God. Even the angry and evasive Jesus of John's Gospel takes upon himself the vocation of dying for the salvation of a world that opposes him: "God did not send the Son into the world to condemn the world, but in order that the world might be saved through him" (John 3:17).[43] Thus, the negative statements about Israel ascribed to Jesus in these Gospels must be interpreted by the larger narrative in which they appear, which insists that Jesus died for all, including the Jews.

Because the statements of Matthew and John about the Jewish people originate in powerless communities under persecution, they bear the marks of pain and bitterness. They come out sounding like the indignant complaints of the righteous sufferer in the lament psalms. Such texts should be understood as cries of anguish that can be read with integrity only by a Christian community in a similar position of weakness and suffering. This guideline still does not justify the vituperative content of a text such as John 8, but it at least serves as a safeguard against the later appropriation of such a text by a powerful Christian community as a weapon against a weaker Jewish community. Our earlier discussion of violence becomes again pertinent here; the *cross* serves as a critical norm that governs Christian responses even—or especially—in the situation of persecution. In light of this norm, better patterns for the attitudes of a suffering community are offered in the Lukan narrative, where Jesus and Stephen, facing death, pray for the forgiveness of their persecutors (Luke 23:34, Acts 7:60); or again, we find a better pattern in Paul's wish that he could be cut off from Christ for the sake of the Jewish people (Rom. 9:3). Here we see another reason why the positions of Luke and Paul on this issue are to be given greater normative weight than those of John and Matthew.

Paul's discussion of Israel introduces one more significant factor that comes clearly into focus only when we read Romans 11 through the focal image of the cross. Israel's temporary rejection has occurred for the sake of the Gentiles. It is *God* who has broken the Jewish branches off in order to allow the Gentile branches to be grafted on. "God did not spare [*ouk epheisato*] the natural branches" (Rom. 11:21) in just the same way that God "did not spare [*ouk epheisato*] his own Son but gave him up for us all" (Rom. 8:32, RSV). Thus, in Paul's mind there is a definite—if mysterious—analogy between the "hardening" of Israel and the death of Jesus: God has ordained both of these terrible events for the salvation of the world. Thus, the fate of Israel is interpreted christomorphically, including the hope of the Jews' ultimate "life from the dead" (11:15).[44] Any Christian community that reckoned seriously with this soteriological analogy between a rejected Israel and a Christ who became a curse for us (Gal. 3:13) would certainly find its treatment of the Jewish people transformed.

New Creation. The danger of the Johannine eschatology is that it effectually locates the question of salvation in the present time, depending on the individual's response to Jesus: thus, the appearance of the Word made flesh—the new creation "already" present—has virtually eclipsed any form of future hope. (To the extent that this is not true of John's theology—to the extent that he continues to await the hope of resurrection at the last day, as in 5:28–29 and 6:39–40—the following critique of his position does not apply.) Consequently, it is easy for John to conclude that Jews who do not believe when they first hear the gospel presumably never will; indeed, he feels compelled, as we have seen, to ascribe their unbelief to an ontological alienation from God. The result of this way of thinking is evident and tragic: the future "not yet" dimension of New Testament eschatology dwindles away, leaving little hope for an unbelieving Israel. Somewhat less drastically, but in a similar way, Matthew ventures the theory that the kingdom has simply been taken away from Israel. Matthew certainly retains and indeed emphasizes a future eschatology, but there seems to be no place for Israel *qua* Israel in his future expectation.

In contrast to these positions, Paul's dialectical eschatology permits him to keep alive hope for what is not yet seen: the turning of Israel to trust in Christ. Thus, he continues to hope and pray for the eschatological reconciliation of Israel, and it is precisely this hope that allows him to live with the paradoxical tension of a present age in which only a remnant stands as a sign of the future salvation of all Israel.

This discussion suggests one more way of reading Matthew's condemnation of Israel. If we place Matthew's pronouncements that the kingdom is taken away from Israel within the larger framework of biblical eschatology, we might read these texts as analogous to prophetic judgment oracles, such as those of Amos and Jeremiah, which declare God's irrevocable sentence of destruction upon Israel. (Two concise examples: "Fallen, no more to rise, is maiden Israel; forsaken on her land, with no one to raise her up" [Amos 5:2]; "Thus says the Lord of hosts: So will I break this people and this city, as one breaks a potter's vessel, so that it can never be mended" [Jer. 19:11].) Yet even though God's judgment is inexorable, these judgment oracles never mark the absolute end of the people, or of God's dealing with them. Always on the horizon is the word of promise and the hope of restoration, whether later in the same book, as in the surprising ending of Amos, or elsewhere in the canon, as in Isaiah 40–66. Is it possible to read Matthew's words about Israel's guilt and God's rejection of that people within this prophetic tradition, so that the pronouncement of judgment might be understood as penultimate rather than final? Or perhaps even as a hortatory call to repentance? I think that this is indeed an appropriate synthetic reading strategy, an excellent example of what it would mean to read the Matthean text through the lens of the image of *new creation*. This construal of the text does not depend on a claim about Matthew's intention; it depends instead upon locating Matthew within a wider canonical frame of reference. Another way to put this point would be to say that Matthew's view of Israel, taken by itself, corresponds roughly to Romans 9, taken by itself. But a synthetic reading of the New Testament witness must allow Romans 11 to provide a dialectical response to Matthew, placing the word of judgment within a larger frame of reference.

Regrettably, I do not believe that this synthetic strategy will help with regard to the Gospel of John. If the unbelieving Jews in John's Gospel are by nature children of the devil, they have no eschatological prospect of redemption. Thus, forced to make a choice among conflicting New Testament witnesses, we choose to see John's position on this issue as a historically understandable but theologically misconceived development. The church will do far better to enter dialogue with Judaism on the basis of the Pauline position.

3. Hermeneutics: Responding to the New Testament's Witness Concerning Israel

In this test case, although our consideration of the synthetic task has been long and complex, the relevant hermeneutical issues can be presented concisely.

(A) THE MODE OF HERMENEUTICAL APPROPRIATION One reason that the relation between church and synagogue has not ordinarily been identified as an issue for New Testament ethics is that the New Testament writers do not address it by stating *rules* or *principles* to govern conduct. We find in the New Testament no *rules* either mandating or forbidding particular ways of treating Jews. Indeed, the New Testament writers could hardly have formulated their thought in such categories, because the distinction between Judaism and Christianity was only in an incipient stage. It must be emphatically stressed, however, that the New Testament's more general teachings against violence apply without exception to this case (see Chapter 14). Having been given a general mandate to love enemies and eschew violence, we hardly need a set of rules specifying that the prohibition of violence applies also to violence against Jews.

Although several important New Testament passages call for the tolerance of differences within the Christian community, nowhere do the New Testament writers appeal to the *principle* of tolerance toward Judaism (or toward any other religion or philosophy). Nor do *principles* of freedom, autonomy, or equality play any role in their reflection about this question. It might be argued on the basis of other considerations that such principles should play a role in a normative Christian ethic, but the New Testament itself does not argue along these lines. When Paul is faced with the pastoral problem of Gentile converts who are tempted to despise the Jewish people, he does not articulate general principles that should govern their thought and conduct; instead, he narrates the very *particular* way that God has dealt and is dealing with this particular people, and he asks Gentile Christians to shape their attitudes in response to this narrative.

By addressing the problem in these terms, Paul establishes a *paradigm* for subsequent Christian thought and action. In the midst of the olive tree allegory, he addresses his Gentile Christian readers at Rome directly: "So do not become proud, but stand in awe" (11:20b). This is not a general rule but a specific directive to Roman congregations still processing the social and political fallout from the expulsion of the Jewish community from Rome in 49 C.E. and their subsequent return after the death of Claudius. Reading this text more than nineteen hundred years later, in a time when we are still processing the far more lethal fallout of the Holocaust, we can find in Paul's directives to the Roman Christians an illuminating model for our own reflection. Lest we become wise in our own conceits, we are encouraged by this paradigm to pause silently before the mystery of God's election and sustenance of Israel, acknowledging that they are beloved by God and that none of us has seen the end of the story of God's mercy toward them.

This does not mean that Christians are simply to withdraw into a stance of benevolent neglect. The Pauline paradigm includes Paul's deep sense of anguish that the Jewish people as a whole have not come to believe that the righteousness of God is revealed in Jesus Christ. While awaiting the eschatological salvation of Israel, he fervently hopes through his preaching to "save some of them" (Rom. 11:14), to bring other Jews like himself to join the remnant chosen by grace in confessing that Jesus is Lord. This paradigm is clearly reinforced by the Acts narratives in which Paul and his apostolic colleagues urgently seek to convince Jewish audiences that Jesus is the Messiah and that "what God promised to our ancestors he has fulfilled for us, their children, by raising Jesus" (Acts 13:32–33a). Luke places great emphasis on efforts at persuasion through scriptural exposition and subsequent dialogue (see, e.g., Acts 13:42–43, 17:1–4, 28:23–24). The characteristic mode of address to Jewish audiences in most of the Acts speeches is one of invitation to accept the good news of God's fulfilled promises.[45]

The Matthean texts reflect a different historical situation, in which the effort at persuasion through argument from scriptural texts has been linked with—one fears superseded by—prophetic denunciation of the Jewish people for their rejection of Jesus. One might read Matthew's allegorical judgment parables as implicit calls to repentance, but, in contrast to most of the Lukan speeches, their tone is more threatening than inviting. Far more than in Romans and in Acts, the Matthean paradigm sets the church and pharisaic Judaism as separate communities in opposition to one another. The attitude modeled toward Jews by the dramatic dialogues in John's Gospel is alternately riddling (as with Nicodemus in John 3:1–10), inviting (as in 7:37–39), and imperiously hostile (as in 8:31–59). While the figure of Jesus in these dialogues symbolically represents the Christian community of the evangelist's own time, this paradigm is not one that the church at the end of the twentieth century can or should emulate. Thus we see that the New Testament texts offer us both positive and negative *paradigms* for our attitude and conduct toward the Jewish people. Our choice of one set of paradigms over the others has already been determined by the fork in the road taken in the synthetic section, above.

Even more important than the behavioral paradigm set forth in Romans 11 (which is, after all, not very specific) is the *symbolic world* sketched by Paul. The Epistle to the Romans tells a world-story within which Christians are to locate themselves. We find ourselves placed within the unfinished, unfolding story of God's righteousness, which entails both God's judgment on Israel and God's redemptive faithfulness to Israel. Gentile Christians should not fall prey to the supersessionist illusion that we are the culmination of God's saving work. The last act of the drama has not been played, and the mystery—of which Paul offers a sneak preview—is that its climax will be the reconciliation of all Israel. Such an account of the world makes sense only if the eschatological hope is literally real, only if we still expect God to act in the future. Paul (and Luke and Matthew as well) teach us to live with such an expectation and therefore to read Scripture as a continuous story within which we stand.[46] The ending of that story remains open, but it stands under the promise of God's grace, God's assurance that he will not abandon his people.

It is important to acknowledge that we do not stand in exactly the same place within the story that Paul stood. Much has happened: the church and synagogue have gone their separate ways, and the church has done much evil to the Jewish people, often blasphemously invoking God's sanction for atrocities committed. Whatever resolution may come in the story's future will have to include repenting, binding up the wounds of history, and reconciling Jews and Christians to one another. Despite all good will on our part, despite all godly sorrow for what has been done in the past, it is beyond our power of imagining to see how such a deep reconciliation can occur.

But we are taught by Paul that God can be trusted; his love for Israel and for the church overcomes all human unfaithfulness, even when we cannot see how it is possible. And it is God's design finally to bring Jews and Gentiles together in Christ in the worship of the one God.

> *Welcome one another, therefore, just as Christ has welcomed you, for the glory of God. For I tell you that Christ has become a servant of the circumcised on behalf of the truth of God in order that he might confirm the promises given to the patriarchs, and in order that the Gentiles might glorify God for his mercy.* (Rom. 15:7–9)

That is the ethical imperative that flows from the symbolic world that Paul describes: "Welcome one another as Christ has welcomed you." Paul is writing here to Jewish and Gentile Christians within the church, but the larger logic of his argument in Romans teaches us to see the church as a sign of the final eschatological reconciliation, which will embrace all Israel.

(B) OTHER AUTHORITIES The church's *tradition* conveys a mixed legacy, much of it tragically filled with prejudice and hatred toward Jews. While there have been times and places in which Christians and Jews have enjoyed peaceful coexistence, there has been a strong and persistent strain of Christian anti-Judaism, particularly in European Christianity.[47] Christians cannot disown the church's past abuses of Jews.[48] The notoriously polemical writings of Martin Luther, especially some anti-Jewish tracts written late in his life, have often been cited as providing historical background and theological justification for subsequent pogroms, up to and including the Nazi effort to exterminate the Jews. For example, in the treatise "On the Jews and Their Lies," written in 1543, Luther declared that God had "surely rejected" Israel for fifteen hundred years and that the Jewish people had been "wholly delivered into the devil's hands."[49] In Luther's view, the Jews constantly give evidence of their hardness of heart by their refusal to accept the gospel, even when it is plainly presented before their eyes (as it was through the Reformation). Consequently, "[W]henever you see a genuine Jew, you may with good conscience cross yourself and bluntly say, 'There goes a devil incarnate.'"[50] In light of these convictions, Luther argued that the Jews should be expelled from Germany.[51]

While Luther's rhetorical gift for invective was distinctive, his opinions were not; he was reflecting a tradition that was widespread in medieval Western Europe.[52] Indeed, as our discussion has shown, he was merely carrying forward themes that already come clearly to expression in the New Testament itself, especially in Matthew and John. Although some Protestant theological traditions, such as the Calvinist and Wesleyan, tend to hold a more favorable view of the Law (and therefore are less hostile to Judaism than the Lutheran tradition has been), it is really only in the aftermath of World War II that the churches have begun seriously to reassess the conscious and unconscious anti-Jewish bias that has infected their teaching.

Thus, in the case of attitudes toward Judaism, *tradition* is of relatively little help in disentangling the difficulties that Scripture presents to us. At best, we can return to historical studies of the tradition seeking to recover and highlight the witness of churches and individuals that reflected the Pauline hope of reconciliation and resisted the tide of anti-Judaism.[53]

The role of *reason* in normative reflection about this problem is potentially complementary to the case that has been put forward here. Insofar as the Enlightenment promoted freedom of religion and the acceptance of diversity within society, it created the conditions necessary for Christians to enter respectful dialogue with Jews. The historical study of the Bible and of ancient Judaism, a development made possible through the exercise of critical reason, has broken down unfair stereotypes.

of Judaism, illuminated the historical circumstances behind New Testament passages that express hostility toward Jews, and facilitated the hermeneutical recovery of Romans 9–11 as a text integral to Paul's theology. The free and candid discussions that now take place between Christian and Jewish scholars within the Society of Biblical Literature, for example, offer real signs of hope and an indispensable basis for ecumenical understanding.

The limits of *reason*, however, must also be recognized. No appeal to reason will ever settle the question of whether Jesus is Israel's Messiah. This is an issue that will continue to divide the Jewish and Christian communities on this side of the eschaton. More fundamentally, *reason*—if by that term we designate the heuristic fiction of a neutral, objective process of inquiry—can never credit the fundamental claims of either the church or the synagogue. The common ground offered by "reason" so understood is a ground where neither community can stand while retaining its identity and reason for being. Thus, even though the "reason" usually approved in modern liberal democracy might agree with Paul that Christians should remain respectful of Jews, the basis for that norm is entirely different from, or even incompatible with, Paul's basis. Liberal "reason" thinks that all individuals have a right to their religious convictions, no matter what they are, and that Christians should therefore leave Jews alone to believe whatever they want to, and vice versa; Paul, on the other hand, thinks that Jews are the elect people of God, whose faithfulness to them persists despite their unbelief. The difference between the two positions comes clear when we ask whether Christians ought to continue trying to persuade Jews to believe the gospel. The New Testament emphatically says yes; liberal "reason" finds the idea distasteful.

The role of *experience*, as we have noted already, is crucial in causing the church after the Holocaust to reassess its theology and its use of Scripture. The theological trajectory that begins in John 8 ends—one fears—in Auschwitz. (This is not to say that the New Testament writers themselves advocated or would have approved of killing Jews; it is a question of the *Wirkungsgeschichte* of the various New Testament traditions—how those traditions have been played out over time.) Of the test cases treated in this book, this is the one in which *experience* plays the most pivotal hermeneutical role. Since the New Testament gives us in Romans 9–11 another option, one that is deeply consonant with the wider biblical witness concerning Israel, our grievous past experience ought to lead us to explore the implications of this "road not taken."

4. Living the Text: The Church As Community Overcoming Ethnic Division

The foregoing discussion has made it clear that the church should seek to inculcate among its members an attitude of respect for Judaism and the Jewish people. In order to do this, it is necessary to pursue every possible opportunity for dialogue; many Christians are unfortunately ignorant of Jewish history and liturgy. Ignorance of Judaism not only allows prejudice to persist but also skews the church's understanding of its own history and faith. Thus, the first task is one of education. Correlated with the church's learning about Judaism is the task of critical scrutiny of its own traditions to see where false and malicious caricatures have persisted in our teaching and preaching.

In an adult Sunday School class that I was teaching once in Atlanta, one man expressed the opinion that we should be grateful to Jesus for setting us free from the dreadful works-righteousness of Judaism. "The Jews had to keep all those commandments and live in fear of an angry God all the time," he declared, "but then Jesus came along and taught that all we have to do is to *love* God with all our heart and soul and strength." When I informed him that Jesus was simply quoting Deuteronomy 6:5, which was part of the Shema, an act of devotion recited twice daily by the Jewish people,[54] he literally did not believe me until we looked up the passage in the Old Testament. We may laugh at this sort of misunderstanding, but in fact it is symptomatic of a problem in the church that is not funny at all. On that day in that Sunday School class a number of adult Christians who had grown up in the church were confronted with a paradigm shift in their understanding of Judaism; ultimately, such a shift must lead also to a corresponding shift in our understanding of Christianity.

Whether in local churches and synagogues, high-level ecumenical conferences, or exchanges within scholarly forums, we should seek to encourage sustained dialogue between Jews and Christians and serious study of one another's traditions. By "dialogue" I do not mean the renunciation or neutralizing of all convictions, nor am I simply calling for a kind of cultural enrichment program. As dialogue proceeds, there will be occasions when participants on both sides can appropriately debate the truth and relative merits of their beliefs. The conversation becomes serious only when it is a conversation between partners who are passionately convinced that ultimate questions are at stake. Thus, any serious dialogue between Jews and Christians will remain tense and risky, especially in light of the painful history that lies behind us. We go forward only by the grace of God.

In the beginning of this section, I hinted that the New Testament's treatment of Christian attitudes toward Judaism might function as a paradigm for Christian ethics in regard to other instances of ethnic or racial conflict. Although it is not possible to develop this suggestion fully here, the argument would have to proceed in at least two stages.

First, the New Testament can be shown in quite a powerful way to present an argument for the transcending of ethnic divisions *within the church*. Paul at Antioch opposed Peter to his face because he and his party had withdrawn from table fellowship with Gentile Christians. Paul saw this not merely as a social affront to the Gentile converts but as a betrayal of the truth of the Gospel (Gal. 2:11–14). To divide the church over ethnic particularity or dietary practices, Paul argues, is to build up again a principle of division that Christ's death had destroyed and thus to "nullify the grace of God." If righteousness is available only through observing such practices, "then Christ died for nothing" (Gal. 2:15–21). The church is to be a sign of God's eschatological reconciliation of the world, and therefore a community in which "there is no longer Jew or Greek, there is no longer slave or free, there is no longer male and female; for all of you are one in Christ Jesus" (Gal. 3:28). Thus the church's unity at table across ethnic boundaries is an outward and visible sign of the breaking down of these barriers, a prefiguration of the eschatological banquet of the people of God. That is why Paul insisted that the truth of the gospel was at stake in this Antioch incident.

In the Acts of the Apostles, Luke tells the story of how Peter and the Jerusalem church were led to a similar conclusion that "God shows no partiality" (10:34) and that the Gentile Cornelius and his household should be received into the community through baptism, without the requirement of circumcision (Acts 10:1–11:18). The divine voice in Peter's vision tells him, "What God has made clean, you must not call profane" (10:15). Thereby Peter comes to understand that he is to preach the gospel to the unclean Gentile Cornelius. As the story unfolds, God confirms the truth of this vision by pouring out the Holy Spirit on Cornelius and his household. The amount of space that Luke devotes to this story and its sequel in the Jerusalem Council (15:1–35) shows how crucial the issue was for his understanding of the development of the church: the church is called into being as a community that breaks ethnic barriers, carrying the gospel "away to the ends of the earth" and uniting Jews and Gentiles together in fellowship. It is noteworthy that the problem the church had to overcome in this early stage of its existence was not anti-Judaism but anti-Gentilism. No matter which way the barriers are erected, the Spirit breaks them down to create the one people of God.

This understanding of the church is given further theological development in Ephesians 2:11–22. Gentiles, who were at one time "aliens from the commonwealth of Israel, and strangers to the covenants of promise, having no hope and without God in the world," have now been "brought near by the blood of Christ."

> *For he is our peace; in his flesh he has made both groups into one and has broken down the dividing wall, that is, the hostility between us. He has abolished the law with its commandments and ordinances, that he might create in himself one new humanity in place of the two, thus making peace, and might reconcile both groups to God in one body through the cross, thus putting to death that hostility through it. So he came and proclaimed peace to you who were far off and peace to those who were near; for through him both of us have access in one Spirit to the Father. So then you are no longer strangers and aliens, but you are citizens with the saints and also members of the household of God.* (Eph. 2:14–19)

Through the cross, the one new community is created. The visible unity of the church is in fact the outward proclamation of "the mystery hidden for ages in God who created all things" (3:9–10). Thus, the cogency of the gospel is tied inextricably to the existence of the new community in Christ, which must therefore "maintain the unity of the Spirit in the bond of peace" (4:3).

Thus, the New Testament makes a compelling case for the church to live as a community that transcends racial and ethnic differences. Insofar as the church lives the reality of this vision, it has a powerful effect in society; insofar as it fails to live this reality, it compromises the truth of the gospel. Vivid examples of both possibilities are offered us by the civil rights struggle in the United States in the 1950s and 1960s and by the more recent struggles in South Africa. The continuing racial separatism of America's churches in the 1990s is a disturbing sign of unfaithfulness that can only reinforce the racial tensions abroad in our culture.

But how does all this relate to ethnic tensions that are not internal to the church? That would be the second—and far more difficult—stage of the argument. Once the church has caught the vision of living as a sign of the new creation in which racial and ethnic differences are bridged at the table of the Lord, how is it possible for the community of Christ's people to participate in animosity toward "outsiders"? If God is the creator of the whole world who wills ultimately to redeem the whole creation—if the death of Christ was the means whereby "God was pleased to reconcile to himself all things, whether on earth or in heaven, by making peace through the blood of his cross" (Col. 1:20)—then how can the church that is called to bear God's message of reconciliation in an unredeemed world (2 Cor. 5:17–20) scorn or reject people of any race or tongue, whether they are Christians or not? This is not to say that there is no difference between the church and the world. Far from it; the church has the task of embodying "the ministry of reconciliation" in the world. In other words, the church is called to expand and extend the same vocation that was Israel's:

I will give you as a light to the nations,
that my salvation may reach to the end of the earth. (Isa. 49:6)

When the identity of the community is understood in these terms, participation in any form of ethnic division or hatred becomes unthinkable, and ethnic division within the church becomes nothing other than a denial of the truth of the gospel. That is why racism is a heresy. One of the church's most urgent pragmatic tasks in the 1990s is to form communities that seek reconciliation across ethnic and racial lines.

NOTES

1. See, e.g., Houlden 1973; Schrage 1988; Lohse 1991; Meeks 1993. Houlden does have a section on "Toleration" in which he devotes one page of discussion to the NT writers' attitudes toward Judaism (pp. 95–96). A significant exception to the generalization is Longenecker 1984, 29–47, who structures his discussion on the basis of Gal. 3:28 and therefore accounts "neither Jew nor Greek" as a "cultural mandate" that stands at the foundation of his approach to NT ethics.

2. This formulation of the matter owes much to Meeks 1986b and 1993.

3. Reported in the *New York Times* (Nov. 22, 1992), p. 34.

4. Cited in a syndicated column by Clark Morphew, *Herald-Sun*, Durham, N.C. (June 11, 1994), p. B5.

5. See, e.g., Klein 1978 [1975]; Beck 1994; Charlesworth 1990; A. T. Davies 1979; Dunn 1991b; Evans and Hagner 1993; Gager 1983; Richardson and Granskou 1986; Ruether 1974; Sandmel 1978; Segal 1986; Smiga 1992.

6. The problem of obedience to the authority of the state poses similar methodological challenges. How do we cope normatively with a canon that offers us both Romans 13 and Revelation 13? For that matter, how do we cope with a canon that offers us both Romans 13 and Ephesians 6:10–20?

7. For a summary account, see Cohen 1987.
8. Fredriksen 1991, 562.
9. See Segal 1986.
10. Here the NRSV corrects the RSV, which reads "*true* circumcision." The word *true* does not appear in the Greek text.
11. See Dunn 1991b.
12. For more extended treatment of various texts on this theme, see, e.g., Hare 1967; Richardson 1970; Sandmel 1978; Martyn 1979; Harrington 1980; Williamson 1982; Gager 1983; Siker 1991.
13. *m. Sanh.* 10.1, quoting Isa. 60:21, as translated by Danby 1933, 397.
14. For example, see Gaston 1987.
15. Romans is the only one of Paul's letters that is not explicitly addressed to a particular church or churches. The address is more generally formulated: "To all God's beloved in Rome, who are called to be saints." Commentators have sometimes suggested that this may reflect a situation in which there is no single unified "church"; rather, there are various house-church communities that may be in some tension with one another over the sorts of issues noted in Romans 14. It is also possible that these communities might have been divided along the lines of Jewish or Gentile ethnic background.
16. Suetonius, *Life of Claudius* 25.3.
17. See Wolfgang Wiefel, "The Jewish Community in Ancient Rome and the Origins of Roman Christianity," in Donfried 1991, 85–101.
18. Here the NRSV rectifies the egregious mistranslation of the RSV, which reads: "Not all are children of Abraham because they are his descendants."
19. For a more detailed discussion of the passage, see Hays 1989, 63–68.
20. See Hays 1989, 73–83. It should be noted, in emphatic contrast to Robert Hamerton-Kelly (1992, 120–139) that the Jewish "rejection" of the gospel with which Paul wrestles in Romans 9–11 is *not* a reference to their act of killing Jesus! Paul is referring, rather, to the fact that the Jewish people as a whole have failed to accept his own preaching of the crucified and resurrected Christ.
21. As maintained by Wright 1991, 249–250.
22. Barth *CD* II/2, 300.
23. In Gal. 6:16, "the Israel of God" refers to all those—Jews and Gentiles alike (cf. Gal. 3:28)—who are crucified with Christ and thus participate in the new creation.
24. Wright 1991, 250.
25. The foregoing reading of Paul's attitude toward the Jewish people stands antithetically opposed to an astonishing recent monograph of Robert Hamerton-Kelly (1992), who argues (using the theoretical framework of René Girard) that Paul radically rejected his ancestral religion and came to understand it as the apotheosis of "the primitive Sacred" in all religion, which necessarily manifests itself in mimetic violence. Hamerton-Kelly's theory-driven reading leads to fundamental distortions of Paul's thought. One example will suffice to convey the tone of the argument: Hamerton-Kelly quotes 2 Cor. 5:21 ("[God] made him who knew no sin to be sin for us, in order that in him we might become the righteousness of God") and glosses it as follows: "The 'sin' that God made him is Jewishness, elsewhere called 'the likeness of sinful flesh'" (p. 126). Perhaps most remarkably, Hamerton-Kelly declares that, from the Girardian theoretical point of view that he himself has embraced in his work, "Paul was right in this estimate of his ancestral religion"—i.e., that it serves primitive violence (p. 9). The surest sign that Hamerton-Kelly's ideological commitments have skewed his reading of Paul is that he is forced finally to insist that Paul's defense of the election of Israel in Romans 9–11 is "inconsistent" with the hermeneutic that Hamerton-Kelly seeks to attribute to him. Paul's defense of a special elect status for Israel is simply "a case of nostalgia overwhelming his judgment" (p. 12). If he had been consistent, "He would have abandoned the category of election altogether and viewed the Mosaic Jews as simply an instance of sacred violence like all other scapegoating groups" (p. 12, cf. pp. 138–139). This would require, of course, the complete abandonment of the argument that Paul actually makes in Romans 9–11!
26. Here I follow the Greek text (as noted in the NRSV margin).
27. Jervell 1972, 41–74; Tiede 1980; J. T. Sanders 1987; Merkel 1994.
28. This suggestion was argued persuasively by Craig C. Hill in "A Future for the Historical Israel: A Link Between Pauline and Lukan Eschatology," a paper presented in the Pauline Epistles Section at the annual meeting of the Society of Biblical Literature in Washington, D.C., Nov. 1993.
29. I do not think this observation is either accurate or illuminating. All four of the Gospels are profoundly Jewish; they simply represent different facets of first-century Judaism. The statement that Matthew is "the most Jewish" reflects the correct observation that Matthew is closest in tone and content to pharisaic-rabbinic Judaism. As I have already indicated, however, first-century Judaism should not be identified strictly with the traditions that were later codified in the Mishnah.
30. A good exegetical case can be made that the phrase "these commandments" refers not to the commandments of Moses but to the commandments promulgated by Jesus within the following discourse; note the end-

ing of the Sermon on the Mount in 7:21–27, where the crucial eschatological test is obedience to "these words of mine."

31. Hare 1967.

32. Thus Trilling 1964, 45, 95–97, 162, 213. For a sustained argument against this reading, see Levine 1988, especially 206–211.

33. See the important studies of Martyn 1979 and R. E. Brown 1979b.

34. See, for a clear and helpful summary of the discussion, Smith 1990.

35. See also Meeks 1972.

36. Notice the verb tenses here: the most illuminating way to read this passage is to hear it as a prophetic revelation from the risen Lord, here transposed into the narrative framework of the last evening before his death.

37. The verb used here (*menein*, "to remain, abide, continue") is the same one used in the figure of the vine and the branches in 15:4–7, where Jesus says to his disciples, "Whoever does not *abide* in me is thrown away like a branch and withers; such branches are gathered, thrown into the fire and burned." Apparently the issue raised in 8:31 is whether these new Jewish believers will have staying power and allow themselves to be rooted and formed in Jesus' word.

38. One important implication of this point is that Christians can hardly seek to justify their persecution of Jews by pointing the finger and blaming the Jews for initiating hostilities.

39. The one possible exception is Luke, if the author of Luke-Acts is the same colleague of Paul mentioned in Col. 4:14, Philem. 24, and 2 Tim. 4:11. For a thorough discussion of Luke's ethnic background, see Fitzmyer 1981 (vol. 1), 35–53.

40. Most notably Ruether 1974.

41. Levine 1988.

42. L. T. Johnson 1989.

43. Does "the world" include "the Jews"? Apparently, in a passage such as 15:18–16:4a, the terms are synonymous. Thus, there is an unresolved tension even within John's Gospel about unbelieving Israel. Are the Jews ontologically children of the devil, or are they God's sheep for whom Jesus, the Good Shepherd, lays down his life?

44. For a more extensive development of this idea, see Hays 1989, 61–62.

45. A noteworthy exception is the lengthy speech of Stephen in Acts 7:2–53, which is strongly accusatory of the Jewish people as "a stiff-necked people, uncircumcised in heart and ears," who have now become the "betrayers and murderers" of the Righteous One, Jesus.

46. See Hays 1989, 156–160.

47. For a brief summary, see Carlo Maria Martini, "Christianity and Judaism: A Historical and Theological Overview," in Charlesworth 1990, 19–26.

48. It is startling that one still finds the expression of a sentiment such as that expressed by Richard R. DeRidder, writing in 1989 in response to a statement issued by the World Council of Churches Consultation on the Church and the Jewish People: "[The report] lays a heavy burden of guilt upon the Christian community for the past sins of the church in the treatment of the Jews. Why the church today is accused of being guilty for what the fathers have done is a mystery to me" (DeRidder 1989, 160).

49. Luther, "On the Jews and Their Lies," in *Luther's Works* (vol. 47), 1971 [1543], 139, 164.

50. Luther 1971 [1543] (vol. 47), 214.

51. Luther 1971 [1543] (vol. 47), 272, 288.

52. For a balanced assessment of Luther's teaching and influence on this question, see Hans J. Hillerbrand, "Martin Luther and the Jews," in Charlesworth 1990, 128–150, with bibliography cited. For a summary of anti-Jewish bias in law, art, and folklore, see Williamson 1982, 106–122.

53. John Calvin, with his usual exegetical attentiveness, is one voice in the tradition who understands and defends the Pauline witness concerning Israel:

> Nevertheless, when Paul cast them down from vain confidence in their kindred, he still saw, on the other hand, that the covenant which God had made once for all with the descendants of Abraham could in no way be made void. Consequently, in the eleventh chapter he argues that Abraham's physical progeny must not be deprived of their dignity. By virtue of this, he teaches that the Jews are the first and natural heirs of the gospel, except to the extent that by their ungratefulness they were forsaken as unworthy—yet forsaken in such a way that the heavenly blessing had not departed utterly from their nation. . . . [W]e must not despise them, while we consider that, for the sake of the promise, God's blessing still rests among them. For the apostle indeed testifies that it will never be completely taken away: "For the gifts and the calling of God are without repentance" (Rom. 11:29, Vulgate) [Calvin, *Institutes* IV.xvi.14].

I am indebted to Scott Saye for this reference.

54. See *m. Ber.* 1:1–3:6.

Chapter 18

Abortion

Christians in the United States are sharply and bitterly divided over the issue of abortion. On one side of the debate, "pro-life" advocates regard abortion as murder and are committed to stopping it by whatever means necessary, up to and sometimes including violent action against clinics and doctors performing abortions; on the other side, "pro-choice" advocates regard abortion as a right essential for women if they are to have dignity, equality with men, and freedom from oppressive social conditions. Many Christians find themselves in a position of paralyzing ambivalence, seeing merit in the arguments on both sides but recoiling from the excesses of zeal in both camps. The issue must, however, be faced in the church. Even apart from questions of law and public policy, the question arises within the community of faith every time a pregnancy occurs under difficult circumstances.

Several years ago, I found myself talking with close friends who were wrestling with a decision about abortion. I shall call them Bill and Jennifer—not their real names—for purposes of discussion. They were a talented and highly educated married couple in their forties, active in the community, successful in their careers, and economically comfortable. They were also devout Christians who practiced regular disciplines of prayer and spiritual reflection. They had raised two fine children, by this time teenagers on the verge of going to college. But now their life had been unsettled: Jennifer had unexpectedly become pregnant. Their initial response to this news was a mixture of pleasure, dismay, and resignation. Despite the major reconfiguration of their lives that this turn of fortune would necessitate, they decided that they would indeed receive and raise this unplanned child. As the pregnancy proceeded, however, tests indicated that the baby would be born with Down's syndrome. Faced with this situation, Bill and Jennifer began to rethink their position. Could they really handle a child with such a disability? Would it be the right and compassionate thing to bring such a child into the world? Would the responsibility of caring for a Down's syndrome child drain all their resources and energies from their important work and from their other children? Counting up all the costs, they were inclined to think that Jennifer should have an abortion. But they wanted to know what I, both as their friend and as a biblical scholar, thought. Could the New Testament provide any guidance on this agonizing decision?

How shall we approach this issue? Abortion is an extraordinarily challenging test case, because it is a major ethical issue not addressed explicitly by any New Testament texts at all. (Thus, I was not able to offer Bill and Jennifer any obvious answers; more complex reflection is required.) Does the approach to New Testament ethics that I have outlined in this book help us to think through problems that the New Testament itself does not address? Or must we fall silent or look to other sources of moral wisdom on questions of this sort?

The absence of explicit New Testament evidence suggests first of all that a certain humility about our claims and convictions concerning abortion is appropriate. Those with whom we differ are not necessarily monsters; they might have serious grounds for their position. The church is a community of moral discourse in which we must think hard together about this matter. Sloganeering and name-calling are not edifying to the community.

To locate the discussion *within* the Christian community (in the first instance) is already an enormously significant move, methodologically speaking. The first task of normative reflection about New Testament ethics is to form the thought and practice of the Christian community. Regardless of what others may do or think, regardless of what the law allows, how shall we as people who belong to Jesus Christ live faithfully under the gospel with regard to our treatment of the issues of pregnancy, abortion, and childbearing? How shall a couple like Bill and Jennifer decide prayerfully before God what to do?

Our deliberation about these matters should not be constrained by the categories and norms of a secular pluralistic society. Stanley Hauerwas describes the reasons for the futility of the usual debates about abortion:

> . . . Christian opposition to abortion on demand has failed because, by attempting to meet the moral challenge within the limits of public polity, we have failed to exhibit our deepest convictions that make our rejection of abortion intelligible. We have failed then in our first political task because we accepted uncritically an account of "the moral question of abortion" determined by a politics foreign to the polity appropriate to Christian convictions.[1]

We must not get trapped by the way the world defines the issue, by the questions that pollsters are likely to ask. Instead, the church must seek to frame its moral reflection within the categories offered us by Scripture.

If it should prove possible to achieve clarity within the church about the issue of abortion, a subsequent task of the community would be to bear witness to the world by embodying an alternative vision, demonstrating as a city set on a hill an alternative possibility, a better way to respond to the problem. We can return to this question of the church's witness to the world, however, only after we have first explored the New Testament's witness to us.

1. Reading the Texts

The Bible contains no texts about abortion. This simple fact—often ignored by those who would make opposition to abortion into a virtual litmus test of true Christian faith—places the issue of abortion in a very different category from the other test cases that we have examined in this book. Here it is not a question of how to interpret a contested text (as in the case of Matt. 5:38–48), or how to negotiate between texts in tension (as in the issues of anti-Judaism or submission to the authority of the state), or how to resolve the competing authority claims of the New Testament and contemporary experience (as in the issue of homosexuality). Here the Bible offers us no direct word at all.

Opponents of abortion, many of whom belong to theological traditions that stress the authority of Scripture, occasionally attempt to identify some biblical basis for their convictions.[2] Advocates of abortion, on the other hand, sometimes appeal to Exodus 21:22–25 in support of their contention that the fetus is not a "person." The passages adduced on both sides, however, make only the most oblique contribution to our reflection on this issue. Let us consider briefly some of the passages suggested as pertinent.

Exodus 20:13, Deuteronomy 5:17: "You shall not murder." To cite this passage against abortion begs the question. No one in the debate is arguing in favor of murder. The issue is one of definition: Is abortion murder or not? There is nothing in the context of the Decalogue, or indeed anywhere in the Torah, that offers an answer to this question.

Exodus 21:22–25. This text belongs to a section of laws dealing with payment of damages for injuries inflicted through violence:

> *When people who are fighting injure a pregnant woman so that there is a miscarriage, and yet no further harm follows, the one responsible shall be fined what the woman's husband demands, paying as much as the judges determine. If any harm follows, then you shall give life for life, eye for eye, tooth for tooth, hand for hand, foot for foot, burn for burn, wound for wound, stripe for stripe.*

The passage does not in any way deal with intentional abortion; rather, it is a piece of property law, prescribing how to deal with an unintentionally inflicted injury that results in a miscarriage. If the injured woman dies or suffers permanent injury, then the crime is treated like any other case of murder or assault, requiring capital or physical punishment on the offender, depending on the degree of injury sustained (vv. 23–25, cf. v. 12). But if only the fetus is lost, only a monetary fine is imposed (v. 22), to be paid to the woman's husband in compensation for his loss of potential progeny. Although the passage does not directly deal with abortion, it seems to posit a qualitative distinction between the fetus and the mother; only the latter is legally a person with reference to whom the *lex talionis* applies.

The Septuagint's translation of the same passage, however, puts a very different spin on the text. According to its rendering, the determining factor for liability is not whether the woman suffers injury but whether the miscarried child (*paidion*) is "formed" (*exeikonismenon*)—that is, whether it is sufficiently developed to bear the appearance of human form.[3] If not, the monetary penalty applies; if so, the *lex talionis*. This gives the already "formed" unborn child the same legal protection as any other person. The deformed or not-yet-formed fetus, however, is not reckoned as possessing the legal status of personhood. The crucial factor, according to this interpretation, would be how far advanced the pregnancy was at the time of the miscarriage.[4] It should be noted that Protestant theological tradition has historically affirmed the canonical priority of the Hebrew text over the Septuagint; thus, the problem of how to interpret the Septuagint of Exodus 21:22–25 is primarily of historical interest. In any case, it must be emphasized that the Greek text, like the Hebrew, deals with accidental injury, not with deliberate abortion.

Psalm 139:13–16: Of the passages adduced in the abortion debate, this one perhaps has the most pertinence. It portrays a symbolic world in which God is active in the formation of unborn life in the womb, and God knows the individual even before birth.

For it was you who formed my inward parts;
you knit me together in my mother's womb.
I praise you, for I am fearfully and wonderfully made.
Wonderful are your works;
that I know very well.
My frame was not hidden from you
When I was being made in secret,
intricately woven in the depths of the earth.
Your eyes beheld my unformed substance.
In your book were written
all the days that were formed for me,
when none of them as yet existed.

Certainly, such affirmations can inform the discussion of abortion. One should be careful, however, not to read too much into this text. It must be interpreted within the poetic genre to which it belongs, not as a scientific or propositional statement.

The passage is, after all, primarily a poetic affirmation of God's loving omniscience and foreknowledge, similar to Jeremiah 1:5:

Before I formed you in the womb I knew you,
and before you were born I consecrated you;
I appointed you a prophet to the nations.

Such statements cannot be pressed as a way of making claims about the status of the fetus as a "person"; rather, they are confessions about God's divine foreknowledge and care. God knows and calls us not just from the time of conception but even *before* conception—even from before the foundation of the world. Once we see that this is the tenor of Psalm 139:13–16, we recognize that its bearing on the abortion issue is very indirect indeed. Certainly, the passage is in no way explicitly concerned with abortion.

Luke 1:44. In this text, Elizabeth tells Mary that at the sound of her greeting, "the child in my womb leaped for joy." That child, of course, is John the Baptist, who—in Luke's artful narrative—is already, even before his birth, bearing inarticulate witness to the more powerful one who will come after him to baptize with the Holy Spirit (cf. Luke 3:16). To extrapolate from this text—whose theological import is entirely christological—a general doctrine of the full personhood of the unborn is ridiculous and tendentious exegesis; indeed, it should not be dignified with the label "exegesis." Again, the text might indirectly shape a symbolic world: the phrase "the *child* in my womb" implies an attitude toward the unborn that is very different from speaking clinically of "the fetus." But the text cannot be used to prove any particular claim about prenatal personhood, nor does it have the issue of abortion in any way in view.

Galatians 5:20. Included in Paul's list of "the works of the flesh" is the term *pharmakeia,* which means "sorcery." Some pro-life advocates, clutching at straws to find some New Testament prooftext, have proposed that this word refers to the practice of taking drugs to induce miscarriages.[5] This proposal is hardly worthy of discussion. Such practices did exist in antiquity,[6] but there is nothing in the context to suggest such an interpretation. The word *pharmakeia* is *not* a specific technical term for the taking of abortifacient drugs; it is an entirely generic term for the practice of magic arts (cf. Rev. 9:21, 18:23).

Matthew 19:14: "Let the little children come to me, and do not stop them; for it is to such as these that the kingdom of heaven belongs." This passage is sometimes cited as an antiabortion slogan.[7] This can only be judged as an embarrassing instance of decontextualized prooftexting. Anyone who reads the passage in context will see that it deals with born, not unborn, children.

In sum, we have no passages dealing with abortion, though a few texts poetically declare God's providential care for all life, even before birth or conception. This gives us very little material for the construction of a normative judgment.

2. Synthesis: Abortion in Canonical Context

There is nothing to synthesize. Since no texts deal with abortion, we have no problem of canonical diversity. The canon is unified in silence.

Consequently, the three focal images of *community*, *cross*, and *new creation* do not come into play here. This helps to underscore the observation that these images are not principles that can be applied generally to moral issues apart from any particular New Testament texts. Rather, they are guides for our interpretation and placement of specific texts within a wider canonical perspective. Where we have no texts, we cannot bring the focal images into play.

We could, however, undertake a more general survey of the biblical perspective on pregnancy and childbearing, in order to provide an interpretive context for the abortion question. For the sake of brevity, we shall not pursue such a survey here, but its general results should be evident to anyone with even a passing acquaintance with the Bible: children are a great blessing from God, and childlessness a terrible affliction.[8] Children are seen as a guarantee of posterity and as a source of economic blessing and security. To cite a single example, consider Psalm 127:3–5:

> *Sons are indeed a heritage from the Lord,*
> *the fruit of the womb a reward.*
> *Like arrows in the hand of a warrior*
> *are the sons of one's youth.*
> *Happy is the man who has his quiver full of them.*

As this particular example suggests, the biblical texts predominantly express a male point of view; however, we also find numerous narratives in which women long and pray for children. In such stories, news of pregnancy is welcomed by women with prayers and songs of joy (e.g., Gen. 21:6–7, 1 Sam. 1–2, Luke 1). Never do we find narratives that represent pregnancy as a problem. Of course, all the biblical texts presuppose a set of economic realities very different from the present day, and they also presuppose that women will find their primary social role as wives and mothers. Thus, this general perspective toward pregnancy and childbearing cannot be adopted without hermeneutical reflection (see below). Nonetheless, it is significant that the canon—though it does not address abortion specifically—portrays a world in which abortion would be not so much immoral as unthinkable or unintelligible.

3. Hermeneutics: Responding to the New Testament's Silence on Abortion

(A) THE MODE OF HERMENEUTICAL APPROPRIATION Since the New Testament provides no texts that speak to abortion, we will obviously find no *rules* pertinent to the topic there. Nor will an appeal to biblical *principles* resolve the impasse in the current debate. All parties agree that Christians should act justly and with respect for human life; the difficulty comes in knowing how to apply these principles to this particular dispute.[9] Consequently, I would propose that we can usefully bring the New Testament's witness into conversation with this issue only by placing the problem in the broader framework of the New Testament's *symbolic world*[10] and then reflecting analogically about the way in which the New Testament might provide implicit *paradigms* for our response to the question. The hermeneutical moves are not obvious, but some significant suggestions can be offered. In what follows, I reverse the order of discussion that I have followed previously, taking up the category of *symbolic world* first, because my observations about this category are more theologically foundational and less speculative than my proposals about analogical reading strategies.

Within the *symbolic world* of the New Testament, God is the creator and author of life. The prologue of John's Gospel asserts that all life comes into being through the creative agency of the Logos:

> *All things came into being through him, and without him not one thing came into being. What has come into being in him was life, and the life was the light of all people. The light shines in darkness, and the darkness did not overcome it.* (John 1:3–5)

Wherever new life begins to develop in any pregnancy, the creative power of God is at work, and Jesus Christ, who was the original agent of creation, has already died for the redemption of the incipient life *in utero*. That is why Barth can say, "The true light of the world shines already in the darkness of the mother's womb."[11] We are privileged to participate in the creative work of God through begetting and bearing and birthing children,[12] but there can be no new life without the generative power of God. We scatter seed, and it sprouts and grows without our knowing how.

As God's creatures, we are stewards who bear life in trust. To terminate a pregnancy is not only to commit an act of violence but also to assume responsibility for destroying a work of God, "from whom are all things and for whom we exist" (1 Cor. 8:6). To put the matter in these terms does not presume any particular decision about when the fetus becomes a "person." Whether we accord "personhood" to the unborn child or not, he or she is a manifestation of new life that has come forth from God. There might be circumstances in which we would deem the termination of such life warranted, but the burden of proof lies heavily upon any decision to undertake such an extreme action.[13] The normal response to pregnancy, within the Bible's symbolic world, is one of rejoicing for God's gift—even when that gift comes unexpectedly.

Thus, to understand ourselves and God in terms of the Bible's story is to know that we are God's creatures. We neither create ourselves nor belong to ourselves. Within this worldview, abortion—whether it be "murder" or not—is wrong for the same reason that murder and suicide are wrong: it presumptuously assumes authority to dispose of life that does not belong to us.

Within the framework of this general account of Scripture's symbolic world, is it possible to find New Testament *paradigms* to shape our decisions regarding abortion? I argued in Chapter 13.2 that the task of ethical discernment is necessarily an act of metaphor-making, of placing the New Testament texts and our world side by side in such a way that new and illuminating correlations result. The necessity for this sort of imaginative act is especially clear when we find ourselves dealing, as in the case of abortion, with an issue that is not explicitly addressed by the New Testament. In the following pages, I would like to propose three lines of metaphorical reasoning, three unlikely conjunctions between the New Testament story and the issue of abortion. These three examples all involve appealing to the New Testament in the *paradigmatic* mode; even though the New Testament passages invoked do not directly confront the problem of abortion, they narrate behaviors that might indirectly inform our response to the question. In the nature of the case, these examples will not be probative; they will prove persuasive only so far as the metaphorical correlations open up new perspectives on the issue.

The Good Samaritan (Luke 10:25–37). Jesus' parable offers a category-shattering answer to the question, "Who is my neighbor?" The double love command, citing Deuteronomy 6:5 and Leviticus 19:18, enjoins love of God and of neighbor (10:27), but the lawyer presses for a more precise delineation of the term "neighbor"—which in the original context of Leviticus meant "fellow Israelite." Jesus' story about the compassionate Samaritan, however, rather than narrowing down the definition of "neighbor," reshapes the whole issue in two ways: the hated Samaritan becomes included in the category of "neighbor," and the "neighbor" is defined as one who *shows*, rather than *receives*, mercy (10:36–37).

How does this story illuminate the issue of abortion? The point is not that the unborn child is by definition a "neighbor." Rather, the point is that we are called upon to *become* neighbors to those who are helpless, going beyond conventional conceptions of duty to provide life-sustaining aid to those whom we might not have regarded as worthy of our compassion. Such a standard would apply both to the mother in a "crisis pregnancy" and to her unborn child. When we ask, "Is the fetus a person?" we are asking the same sort of limiting, self-justifying question that the lawyer asked Jesus: "Who is my neighbor?" *Jesus, by answering the lawyer's question with this parable, rejects casuistic attempts to circumscribe our moral concern by defining the other as belonging to a category outside the scope of our obligation.* To define the unborn child as a nonperson is to narrow the scope of moral concern, whereas Jesus calls upon us to widen it by showing mercy and actively intervening on behalf of the helpless. The Samaritan is a paradigm of love that goes beyond ordinary obligation and thus *creates* a neighbor relation where none existed before. The concluding word of the parable addresses us all: "Go and do likewise." What would it mean for our decisions about abortion if we did indeed take the Samaritan as a paradigm?[14]

The Jerusalem Community (Acts 4:32–35). As we have seen in our discussion of Luke-Acts in Chapter 5, Luke's depiction of the early Jerusalem community exemplifies his vision for the church: the apostolic testimony to the resurrection is made effective through the community's practices of economic sharing and caring for the needy:

> *Now the whole group of those who believed were of one heart and soul, and no one claimed private ownership of any possessions, but everything they owned was held in common. With great power the apostles gave their testimony to the resurrection of the Lord Jesus, and great grace was upon them all. There was not a needy person among them, for as many as owned lands or houses sold them and brought the proceeds of what was sold. They laid it at the apostles' feet, and it was distributed to each as any had need.*

How does this story illuminate the issue of abortion? It suggests that the community should assume responsibility for the care of the needy. Thus, within the church, there should be no justification for abortion on economic grounds or on the ground of the incapacity of the mother to care for the child. The community assumes responsibility and creates whatever structures are necessary to provide for mother and child alike. Sharing, not abortion, is the answer. That is what it means for the community to live out the power of the resurrection. Surely the liberal Protestant church's advocacy of abortions for poor women who cannot afford to raise children is a tragic symbol that the church has lost its vision for communal sharing and has consequently acquiesced to the power of death. The church's confusion on the issue of abortion is a *symptom* of its more fundamental unfaithfulness to the economic imperatives of the gospel.[15]

A closely related point is the matter of church discipline: we should take responsibility not only for sharing resources but also for calling men to accountability. The fact that abortion is usually treated as a "women's issue" shows how disastrously the general culture has allowed males to abdicate responsibility for children. As Hauerwas rightly observes, "[A]bortion often is the coercive method men use to free themselves from responsibility to women."[16] In the church, it should not be so. A man who has fathered an unborn child should be required and helped, within the fellowship of the church, to take responsibility for supporting the pregnant woman both emotionally and financially and to assume continuing responsibility for the child after its birth. (I speak here of Christian men; obviously, the church cannot exert disciplinary authority over non-Christian fathers.) The community of faith should provide whatever support is necessary for both man and woman to assume their roles as parents. This would entail not only financial support but also the support of friendship, counsel, and prayer. If the church seriously adopted the paradigm of Acts 4:32–35 as a model for its life, many of the usual arguments for abortion would fall away.

The Imitation of Christ (Rom. 15:1–7; 1 Cor. 11:1; Gal. 6:2; Phil. 2:1–13). As interpreted by Paul, the call to "imitate Christ" means that the community is to forswear seeking its own self-defined freedom in order to render service to others, especially to the "weak."[17] If it is necessary to give up what appear to be reasonable rights or privileges—for example, the freedom to eat certain foods—for the sake of others, then those who are in Christ should readily relinquish these rights, just as Christ surrendered his divine prerogatives and suffered death on the cross in order to save those who are weak and helpless under the power of sin.

How does this paradigm illuminate the issue of abortion? It suggests that we should act in service to welcome children, both born and unborn, even when to do so is obviously difficult and may cause serious hardship. Let it be noted well that Paul's call to imitate Christ is addressed to the community of faith, not just to individuals. Thus, this word about welcoming children cannot be addressed just to the individual pregnant woman, as though the church could simply say to her, "You must imitate Christ by suffering for the sake of this child." Instead, this call is a charge laid upon the church as a whole. The church cannot literally go through the pregnancy and labor, but it can assume the burden of caring for the child, if necessary, as soon as it is born. This is what it would mean to "welcome one another . . . just as Christ has welcomed you, for the glory of God" (Rom. 15:7). Such a sacrificial welcome must be extended not only to the child but also to the mother in a crisis pregnancy; she should not be left alone to deal with her decision and its consequences. The community must welcome her, bear her burden, and so fulfill the law of Christ (Gal. 6:1–2). If it were so, there would almost never be any need for a Christian woman to seek an abortion. If this proposal sounds impractical, that is merely a measure of how far the church has drifted from its foundation in the New Testament.

(B) OTHER AUTHORITIES Where there is no explicit scriptural teaching, considerations of *tradition*, *reason*, and *experience* will inevitably assume a greater role in forming our norms and in subsequently discerning circumstances where exceptions to the general norms may be warranted. Let us turn then to a consideration of these other factors.

Although the New Testament does not mention abortion, the Christian *tradition* from a very early date bears strong and consistent witness against it. Among the factors regularly claimed by early Christians as marking their distinction from the pagan world was their rejection of abortion and infanticide. The earliest reference is to be found in the Didache (a late-first-century or early-second-century manual of Christian teaching), whose opening section contrasts the "Two Ways" of life and death; among the commandments that mark the "way of life" for Christians are these: "You shall not murder a child by abortion, nor shall you kill one who has been born" (Didache 2:2; cf. Epistle of Barnabas 19:5). The evidence concerning the witness of tradition has been ably summarized elsewhere and need not be repeated here.[18] The result of any such survey is to show that the entire Christian tradition has rejected the practice of abortion—while always being open to considering special cases, such as tragic instances where abortion is necessary to save the life of the mother. The recent shift in some branches of liberal Protestantism to advocacy for abortion rights is a major departure from the church's historic teaching.

Since those who argue for "freedom of choice" on abortion cannot appeal to Scripture or tradition, their arguments characteristically hinge upon reason and/or experience; consequently, the antiabortion party has felt itself constrained to answer in similar terms, seeking to articulate nonreligious arguments that will be persuasive in a pluralistic culture.[19] The role of *reason* in this debate has therefore been particularly extensive, because many of the issues are alleged to turn upon scientific questions about fetal development, psychological questions about the effects of abortion on women, and philosophical questions about when life begins and about the natural rights of persons. All these matters—scientific, psychological, philosophical, and legal—fall under the rubric of *reason* as an authority in theology. I have neither the space here nor the competence to address all these questions and arguments. It is possible, however, to indicate how and where the New Testament comes into collision with certain lines of argument from *reason*. Christian theology must judge some ways of framing the issue to be fundamentally inappropriate because they stand in irreconcilable tension with the New Testament's understanding of the community's life under God. Thus, even though the New Testament does not treat abortion explicitly, it plays a crucial *negative* role in the church's reflection by excluding some of the characteristic ways that the issues are formulated—both by "pro-life" and by "pro-choice" groups. I hasten to add that this does not mean that *reason* itself is excluded from the debate; my point is merely that certain argumentative strategies cannot be accommodated within the symbolic world rendered by the New Testament, the world within which the believing community is taught to live and move. In the interest of concision, I shall briefly describe how the New Testament excludes six commonly heard lines of reasoning about abortion:

- It is inappropriate to set up the issue as a conflict of "rights": the rights of the woman versus the rights of the unborn child. In Scripture, there is no "right to life." Life is a gift from God, a sign of grace. No one has a presumptive claim on it. Nor, on the other hand, do any of us—male or female—have a "right" to control our own bodies autonomously. "Do you not know that your body is a temple of the Holy Spirit within you, which you have from God, and that *you are not your own? For you were bought with a price*; therefore, glorify God in your body" (1 Cor. 6:19–20). We are always accountable to God for our decisions and actions.
- Still less is it appropriate to treat the issue as a matter of the "right to privacy," as in the *Roe* v. *Wade* decision, or exclusively as a matter of individual choice. (Remember, I am speaking of decisions about abortion by Christians within the church.) All our actions occur within the community of faith and must be judged by the twin standards of whether they edify the community and whether they witness faithfully to God's will in the world. A New Testament ethics must seek first of all to ask how the community's norms reflect the truth of its relation to God. Within the church, just as within Israel, to call for everyone to do what is right in his or her own eyes is a formula for moral chaos and disobedience to God (Deut. 12:8; Judg. 17:6, 21:25).
- The "sacredness of life" is a sacred cow that has no basis in the New Testament. This is a point made eloquently by Hauerwas:

  > The Christian prohibition against taking life rests not on the assumption that human life has overriding value but on the conviction that it is not ours to take. The Christian prohibition of abortion derives not from any assumption of the inherent

> value of life, but rather from the understanding that as God's creatures we have no basis to claim sovereignty over life. . . . The Christian respect for life is first of all a statement, not about life, but about God.[20]

- ➢ It is inappropriate to approach the issue of abortion by asking, "When does human life begin?" or "Is the fetus a 'person'?" Such questions are unanswerable, both from a scientific point of view and from the biblical evidence. There is no basis in Scripture for answering—or indeed even asking—such questions. They are also exceedingly dangerous questions if they seek to justify abortion by defining marginal cases out of the human race. This is, for obvious reasons, a bad precedent to set. Jesus' persistent strategy was, on the contrary, to define the marginal cases in.
- ➢ Even worse is the "quality of life" argument that advocates abortion by declaring that "no unwanted child ought ever to be born." Unwanted by whom? The mother? The argument proves too much and readily slides into an argument for infanticide among the poor. The whole historic witness of Jesus and the community he founded has been to receive and love the unwanted, not to recommend that they be terminated, "put out of their misery" through death. The community of faith should commit itself to seeking "quality of life" for all who are born into the world, whether their parents "want" them or not.
- ➢ The hypothetical consequentialist argument sometimes used against abortion is feeble: "What if Mary had decided to abort Jesus?" Counterquestion: "What if Hitler's mother had decided to abort him?" This juxtaposition of silly questions merely serves to show how strikingly indifferent is the New Testament—in contrast to much of the recent abortion debate—to consequentialist ethical reasoning. The New Testament teaches us to approach ethical issues not by asking "What will happen if I do x?" but rather by asking "What is the will of God?"

Experience has played a relatively lesser role in the abortion debate, because the various claims and counterclaims prove so inconclusive. There is a rapidly proliferating literature on the subject. Some accounts stress the sense of relief and liberation, even of empowerment, that women experience after abortion.[21] Others stress the struggle or psychic damage that women who choose abortion must work through.[22] The construal of the "experience" of abortion is of course heavily dependent on the cultural network surrounding the persons who go through it.

In contrast to the debate about homosexuality, there seems to be little inclination among Christians to provide positive religious-experiential accounts in justification of abortion. Abortion is usually treated simply as a "right" and as an unpleasant inconvenience that women must endure for the sake of the greater good of gaining autonomy and control over their own bodies.

Where does this discussion leave us with regard to forming normative judgments about abortion? Though the New Testament gives no explicit prohibition, its portrayal of God as the author and giver of life creates a general presumption against any human decision to terminate life. This presumption is reinforced by the paradigmatic arguments I have proposed: the church should follow the example of the compassionate Samaritan, of the early Jerusalem church, and of Jesus himself, all of whom acted sacrificially for the sake of others, particularly those who were weak, poor, or helpless. To act in imaginative response to these paradigms would bring the church into new practices of community and new relations to neighbors not previously acknowledged as neighbors. If the New Testament witness were put into practice, abortion would almost never be seen as necessary within the Christian community. Furthermore, the New Testament emphatically excludes some of the patterns of reasoning commonly used in support of abortion, particularly the appeal to the "right" of individuals to make autonomous moral decisions, the "right to privacy," and the "quality of life" argument. Such patterns of reasoning cannot be credited as valid arguments within normative Christian theology. When one adds to these considerations the historic Christian tradition's strong disapproval of abortion, the cumulative case becomes weighted heavily against abortion.

The debate, then, can only concern possible exceptions to the norm. Are there circumstances that might justify abortion as a tragic necessity for Christians? Surely if the New Testament writers could dare to formulate exceptions to Jesus' explicit teaching against divorce, the church can also act—in fear and trembling under the guidance of the Spirit—to identify exceptions to the traditional prohibition of abortion, a matter where we have no command of the Lord. There are two commonly cited situations that might plausibly be deemed exceptional cases: abortions performed to save the life of the mother and abortions performed where the pregnancy is a result of rape or incest. Particularly in the latter case (rape or incest), the argument to justify abortion rests heavily upon experiential warrants: we recoil instinctively from requiring a young woman to bear the burden of a child conceived through an act of violence against her. As I have already indicated, such an appeal to experience carries considerably more weight in theological argument in a case—such as this one—where there are no direct New Testament teachings on the subject. My own view would be that such exceptions are certainly justifiable options for Christians.[23]

Are there other possible exceptions? What about the case confronted by my friends Bill and Jennifer, the case of a pregnancy likely to yield a deformed or handicapped child? Here we confront a painfully difficult problem in which the strong general presumption of Scripture and tradition against abortion must be weighed against the heavy personal costs of bringing such a child to birth. (This is an instance in which modern medical technology has imposed upon us a burden of moral decision not borne by previous generations, who had no means of prenatal diagnosis of birth defects.) According to the proposals set forth in this book, such a decision ought to be addressed corporately by the local church community of which Bill and Jennifer are members, so that the burden of the decision and its consequences would not fall upon them alone. If the community finds itself compellingly summoned by metaphorical paradigms such as the three that I have proposed in relation to this issue (Samaritan, Jerusalem church, Jesus), it will de-cide to take upon itself whatever responsibilities are necessary to support Bill and Jennifer in the choice to bring their unplanned Down's syndrome child into the world. If, however, the community does not find these metaphorical readings illuminating, or if the cost of assuming responsibility for such a child is reckoned to be too great, then the church will assent to their decision to proceed with an abortion, all the while praying for God's mercy on all concerned: mother, father, child, doctor, and church.

My own judgment in this case is that the New Testament summons the community to eschew abortion and thus to undertake the burden of assisting the parents to raise the handicapped child. In the actual situation, however, Bill and Jennifer never brought the decision before the church, believing—perhaps rightly—that their local church was not in fact the sort of community that could meaningfully take responsibility for such a matter. Left alone with the decision, they decided to have the abortion. While I believe that the witness of the New Testament should have tipped the balance the other way on this decision, I respect the difficulty of their situation and the moral gravity of their action. In a case where the New Testament offers us no clear instruction, it is perhaps inevitable that Christians will in good conscience reach different conclusions. Bill and Jennifer did what they believed was right, seeing abortion as a tragic but necessary choice. If such a choice *is* necessary, the tragedy is primarily the tragedy of a church that has abdicated its calling to "bear one another's burdens, and so fulfill the law of Christ" (Gal. 6:2, AA). The New Testament envisions a more excellent way.

4. Living the Text: The Church As Community of Life

Throughout the foregoing discussion, I have steadfastly avoided addressing abortion as a political issue in U.S. culture. This strategy of avoidance was necessary in order to focus clearly upon the way in which the New Testament might be heard within the Christian church in relation to this wrenching problem. In light of this discussion, however, we may now ask what the church should do in relation to this matter. In what way shall we embody within our time God's Word on the question of abortion?

We must begin by recognizing that we cannot coerce moral consensus in a post-Christian culture. The United States is deeply divided on the question of abortion because there is no consensus about the cultural logic that ought to govern our decisions about this matter. We should recognize the futility of seeking to compel the state to enforce Christian teaching against abortion. This is neither because we advocate a dualistic separation of sacred and secular spheres of life nor because we acknowledge an alleged sacred right of individual conscience; rather, it is because we recognize that the convictions that cause us to reject abortion within the church are intelligible only within the symbolic world of Scripture. The church's rejection of abortion is persuasive only in light of the gospel of Jesus Christ; in this respect we stand in relation to our culture just as the early church stood in relation to the culture of the Roman Empire. Thus, the primary task of the Christian community on this issue is to form a countercommunity of *witness,* summoning the world to see the gospel in action.

That is why angry protests against abortion that employ invective and intimidation are both un-Christian and ineffective: rather than demonstrating the gospel in action, they manifest another spirit altogether. The occasional cases in which antiabortion activists have resorted to violence—such as the bombing of clinics or the murder of abortion clinic doctors—are incompatible with the gospel. (See my arguments against violence in defense of justice in Chapter 14.) Even peaceful efforts to legislate against abortion are simply doomed to failure in the present cultural climate. The world needs to be shown another way, not forced by law to abandon something it perceives as a "right."[24]

In such a situation, how should the church respond? The first and most basic task is for the community to act in ways that embody its commitment to receiving life as a gift from God. William Durland writes:

> We should not look to the state to compel women to complete, nor allow them to terminate, a pregnancy. Rather, God calls us to be our own people and our own community—to witness to the world's scandal, to love and bind up those harmed by its values. If the energy now being poured into attempts to affect Supreme Court decisions were dedicated to establishing viable alternatives to abortion and substantive support and long-range care for victimized women, "unwanted" children, and families struggling with poverty, mental illness, and domestic violence, perhaps we would begin to see Christian community being born in our midst—a light to the nations and a sure refuge for these needy ones.[25]

A similar vision is articulated by Bill Tibert, a Presbyterian minister from Colorado, who draws an apt analogy between the rejection of war and the rejection of abortion:

> During the 1960s and 70s there was an antiwar slogan that asked, "What if they gave a war and nobody came?" The point was what if there was a declaration of war and all the people just refused to participate? What if there were abortion clinics but nobody went in? What if abortion was a legal choice, but it was a choice nobody took? Changes in the law, blocking abortion clinics, demeaning name-calling will not stop abortions. The history of the church through the ages has been the history of changes brought about in society through the church demonstrating and living an alternative vision of life. We need to stop telling our nonbelieving neighbors how wrong their way of life is, and we need to start showing the power of the gospel in the way we live. . . . Let me ask you: Which has greater power? Ten thousand people who fill the streets in front of abortion clinics and shame those seeking abortions, or ten thousand people in California who take to the state capital a petition they have signed stating they will take any unwanted child of any age, any color, any physical condition so that they can love that child in the name of Jesus Christ?[26]

Notice how both of these statements point to the church's role of *witnessing* to an unbelieving world through its active assumption of responsibility for the needy and its willingness to receive women and children who otherwise would become the victims of the regnant cultural systems.

A similar theological—and particularly ecclesiological—logic shapes the Durham Declaration, a manifesto against abortion addressed specifically to the United Methodist Church by a group of United Methodist pastors and theologians. The declaration is addressed not to legislators or the public media but to the community of the faithful. It concludes with a series of pledges, including the following:

> We pledge, with God's help, to become a church that hospitably provides safe refuge for the so-called "unwanted child" and mother. We will joyfully welcome and generously support—with prayer, friendship, and material resources—both child and mother. This support includes strong encouragement for the biological father to be a father, in deed, to his child.[27]

No one can make such a pledge lightly. A church that seriously attempted to live out such a commitment would quickly find itself extended to the limits of its resources, and its members would be called upon to make serious personal sacrifices. In other words, it would find itself living as the church envisioned by the New Testament.

William H. Willimon tells the story of a group of ministers debating the morality of abortion. One of the ministers argues that abortion is justified in some cases because young teenage girls cannot possibly be expected to raise children by themselves. But a black minister, the pastor of a large African American congregation, takes the other side of the question.

> "We have young girls who have this happen to them. I have a fourteen year old in my congregation who had a baby last month. We're going to baptize the child next Sunday," he added.
>
> "Do you really think that she is capable of raising a little baby?" another minister asked.
>
> "Of course not," he replied. No fourteen year old is capable of raising a baby. For that matter, not many thirty year olds are qualified. A baby's too difficult for any one person to raise by herself."
>
> "So what do you do with babies?" they asked.
>
> "Well, we baptize them so that we all raise them together. In the case of that fourteen year old, we have given her baby to a retired couple who have enough time and enough wisdom to raise children. They can then raise the mama along with her baby. That's the way we do it."[28]

Only a church living such a life of disciplined service has the possibility of witnessing credibly to the state against abortion. Here we see the gospel fully embodied in a community that has been so formed by Scripture that the three focal images employed throughout this study can be brought to bear also on our "reading" of the church's action. *Community:* the congregation's assumption of responsibility for a pregnant teenager. *Cross:* the young girl's endurance of shame and the physical difficulty of pregnancy, along with the retired couple's sacrifice of their peace and freedom for the sake of a helpless child. *New creation:* the promise of baptism, a sign that the destructive power of the world is broken and that this child receives the grace of God and hope for the future.[29] There, in microcosm, is the ethic of the New Testament. When the community of God's people is living in responsive obedience to God's Word, we will find, again and again, such grace-filled homologies between the story of Scripture and its performance in our midst.

NOTES

1. Hauerwas 1981a, 212–213.
2. See, e.g., Davis 1985, 129–157.
3. According to later rabbinic tradition, the fetus was deemed "fully formed" on the forty-first day after conception (*m. Nid.* 3:7). Whether the Septuagint translators had in mind this specific tradition is doubtful. Philo of Alexandria—closer than the Mishnah to the Septuagint translators, both in date and in cultural milieu—interprets the passage as follows:

> If a man comes to blows with a pregnant woman and strikes her on the belly and she miscarries, then, if the result of the miscarriage is unshapen and undeveloped [*aplaston kai adiatypōton*], he must be fined both for the outrage and for obstructing the artist Nature in her creative work of bringing into life the fairest of living creatures, man [*anthrōpon*]. But, if the offspring is already shaped and all the limbs have their proper qualities and places in the system, he must die, for that which answers to this description is a human being [*anthrōpos*], which he has destroyed in the laboratory of Nature who judges that the hour has not yet come for bringing it out into the light [*De spec. leg.* 3.108–109].

4. On the historical and exegetical problems surrounding this passage, see Feldman 1975, 254–262; Feldman 1986, 82–83; Isser 1990.
5. Noonan 1970, 9; Davis 1985, 150.
6. See, e.g., Minucius Felix, *Octavius* 30:2: ". . . and there are women who swallow drugs to stifle in their womb the beginnings of a [person] on the way—committing infanticide even before they give birth to their infant."
7. The text is cited this way, for example, in the Durham Declaration, a statement issued by a group of United Methodist theologians and pastors (Stallsworth 1993, 11–16).
8. The exceptions to this norm (Luke 23:28–29; Isa. 54:1, quoted in Gal. 4:27) derive their force precisely as provocative reversals of convention. These texts do not actually challenge the norm; rather, they serve as poetic/prophetic statements that the hour of eschatological crisis is at hand (Luke 23) or that God is about to reverse the fortunes of barren, suffering Zion (Isa. 54).
9. Rightly observed by Hauerwas 1981a, 198. A helpful analysis of the way in which different ethicists employ the principle of love—with differing results—in dealing with this issue is offered by Gene Outka in his essay "The Ethics of Love and the Problem of Abortion" in his forthcoming book *God and the Moral Life: Explorations in the Protestant Tradition.*
10. For a discussion that follows this approach, see Hinlicky 1993.
11. *CD* III/4, 416.
12. As Hinlicky puts it, "Children are born of our love because the Creator wills so concretely to involve us in the continuation of creation" (1993, 192).
13. Here I follow Barth, *CD* III/4, 416.
14. I first encountered this line of argument in a paper by my student Michael A. Paulsen at Yale in 1984. A similar argument appears in O'Donovan 1994, 239–240.
15. See my remarks about this issue in the Conclusion of this book.
16. Hauerwas 1981a, 201, following Francke 1978, 81.
17. For discussion of this motif in Paul's ethics, see Chapter 1.2.b.
18. See, e.g., Connery 1977; Gorman 1982. For a brief summary, see Gorman, "Ahead to Our Past: Abortion and Christian Texts" (Stallsworth 1993, 25–43).
19. Hauerwas, of course, judges this strategy to be disastrous (1981a, 212–229).
20. Hauerwas 1981a, 225–226.

21. Hoshiko 1993; Zimmerman 1977.

22. Francke 1978; C. S. Williams 1991.

23. It is not my aim here to adjudicate all possible exceptional cases. My point is simply that good arguments can be made from an experiential point of view for these two exceptions (and that other similar exceptions cannot be precluded).

24. For a dramatically contrasting argument, see Kaveny 1991, who argues for "a pro-life jurisprudence" on the basis of Thomas Aquinas's understanding of the law as "a teacher of virtue."

25. Durland 1989.

26. Bill Tibert, unpublished sermon preached at Covenant Presbyterian Church, Colorado Springs, CO, May 23, 1993.

27. Stallsworth 1993, 14.

28. Willimon 1985, 65.

29. This example illustrates in a particularly interesting way how these focal images might assist us in "reading" (whether the text is the Bible or the church's life) and how a reading focused through these lenses might lead us to rethink our lives. My own inclination is to think that the church's normal practice should be to baptize believers upon profession of faith. Thus, I ordinarily regard infant baptism as a practice closely tied to Constantinian-era assumptions about the relation between the church and the social order; it is not exactly wrong, just misleading in a post-Christian culture. In this case, however, reading Willimon's story through the lens of new creation allows me to understand this action of infant baptism sympathetically, as a radical proclamation of the gospel's eschatological promise. The considerable power of such a reading gives me pause and forces me to return in a fresh way to reconsider infant baptism as one possible expression of the gospel.

Conclusion

We come to the conclusion of this book, though hardly to the end of the debate over the issues it addresses. In the foregoing pages, I have sought to present a coherent model for approaching New Testament ethics as a theological discipline and, consequently, for appropriating the ethical witness of the New Testament in the life of the church. I have proposed that such appropriation necessarily entails a complex fourfold task: reading the individual witnesses closely, reflecting synthetically about the common elements in their moral visions, considering the hermeneutical procedures that we employ in bringing the texts to bear upon our own situation, and performing the texts in Christian community. In order to illustrate how this procedure might work in practice, I have offered a series of discernments about five test cases: violence, divorce, homosexuality, anti-Judaism, and abortion.

The model I have proposed is not an exact method that can yield foolproof scientific results. It is nothing more nor less than a framework for *discernment*, a set of proposed guidelines for the church's ongoing task of seeking to understand and obey the will of God. Such discernment can take place only under the guidance of the Holy Spirit; thus, integral to the model itself is the insistence that all particular moral discernments—all readings of the Word—must be subject to the testing and confirming witness of the community. This book is certainly no exception to that proviso: the conclusions reached here are offered as one *performance* of the imaginative task of New Testament ethics—offered to the church at large for discussion and reflection. They constitute, therefore, an invitation to the community for renewed encounter with the witness of the New Testament itself. If I am correct in arguing that moral discernment requires the church to engage in the art of metaphor-making, bringing the New Testament into conjunction with our community's life in fresh and illuminating ways, it follows inevitably that other readers will produce performances of the Word that not only differ from my own but that will teach us aspects of the truth that we would never have seen apart from such enactments. Similarly, my own performance in the foregoing pages ought to be understood not as a collection of definitive pronouncements but as one person's effort to articulate a disciplined reading of the New Testament witness concerning issues of urgent concern for our time. This book is offered in the hope of opening, not terminating, conversation about the problems I have treated here.

I reiterate also a point made at the beginning of Part IV: the five test cases addressed here are not alleged to represent the central moral concerns of the New Testament, nor do they fully reflect my own judgment about the most pressing ethical issues facing the church at the end of the twentieth century. Rather, the range of problems posed in Part IV serves to illustrate how my proposed categories work with different patterns of evidence within the New Testament. The rationale for the selection is *methodological* rather than substantive.

One consequence of this selection procedure is that the conclusions drawn in Part IV represent very different levels of conviction. My proposals on the question of abortion, which is not treated directly by the New Testament, should be read as suggestions that attempt to develop indirect implications of the New Testament narratives. On the other hand, I understand my proposals concerning renunciation of violence to be integrally related to the center of the gospel story, and I would urge that this is the sort of issue over which Christians should lay down their lives; I would seek passionately to persuade those who think otherwise—the historic majority of Christians—that they are living as "enemies of the cross of Christ" (Phil. 3:18, where the reference is not to unbelievers but to believers who do not seek to live according to the apostolic *typos*, the paradigm of the cross). Even in this case, however, my argument does not constitute a claim that just war theorists should be excommunicated from the church. (None of us participates in the community of God's people save by God's mercy.) Rather, my argument seeks to draw a firm line that will facilitate authentic moral disagreement within the church and challenge the community to be confronted more urgently by the New Testament witness on this matter.

The goal of this entire project is to encourage the church in its efforts to become a Scripture-shaped community, to allow its life to be more fitly conformed to the stories narrated in the New Testament. I proposed at the beginning of Part IV that, if our moral concerns were shaped in accordance with the New Testament vision of Christian discipleship, we should direct our energy and attention to four fundamental issues: (1) the renunciation of violence, (2) the sharing of possessions, (3) the overcoming of ethnic divisions, particularly the division between Jew and Gentile, and (4) the unity of men and women in Christ. I have dealt in some detail with the first and third of these issues and have offered several passing observations about the fourth.[1] I want to conclude this book, then, by offering some brief reflections about the sharing of possessions, which has not received an emphasis in this study commensurate with its importance in the New Testament. These reflections will lead on to some final remarks about the task—and limitations—of New Testament ethics.

Sharing Possesions: A Challenge to the Church

There is always the danger that, in our complex hermeneutical deliberations about New Testament ethics, we might construct an elaborate system of rationalizations that simply justify the way we already live our lives. On no other topic is this danger so acute as on the issue of sharing possessions. Therefore, we cannot bring our treatment of New Testament ethics to a conclusion without attending—if only briefly—to the New Testament's teaching on this issue.[2]

The challenge of the New Testament is clear: from Matthew to Revelation, the New Testament writers bear witness passionately about the economic imperatives of discipleship. Without undertaking a full-scale descriptive reading of the individual texts, we can see even on the most cursory survey that the New Testament writers manifest a pervasive concern for just use of money and for sharing with the needy. Let us recall a few representative highlights of the New Testament's teaching on this question.

In Matthew's Gospel, Jesus teaches his disciples to relinquish anxiety about their own economic security and to seek first God's justice (Matt. 6:25–34); they are taught to pray for the provision of their daily needs and to forgive those who may owe them debts (Matt. 6:11–12, cf. 18:23–35). When the twelve disciples are sent out on a mission to Israel, they are to take no money with them and to receive no payment for their ministry (Matt. 10:8–9). Most tellingly, in the great Matthean parable of the last judgment (25:31–46), the sheep are separated from the goats on the basis of their treatment of those who are hungry, naked, sick, and in prison. Clearly, for Matthew authentic discipleship entails using one's resources to help those in need.

Mark tells the story of Jesus' challenge to the rich man who wants to know how to inherit eternal life: "Go, sell what you own, and give the money to the poor, and you will have treasure in heaven; then come, follow me." The man, stunned by this radical demand, goes away grieving, "for he had many possessions" (Mark 10:17–22). This becomes the occasion for Jesus' more general declaration that it is "easier for a camel to go through the eye of a needle than for someone who is rich to enter the kingdom of God" (10:23–27).[3] By way of contrast, Jesus praises the poor widow who puts her last two coins into the temple treasury (10:41–44).

Luke, as noted in the descriptive sketch of his moral vision in Chapter 5, proclaims God's liberating power on behalf of the poor and hungry (Luke 1:52–53, 4:18–19) and highlights the vision for a new community of believers who share all possessions in common so that there are no poor among them, in fulfillment of the Deuteronomic command. This new community is portrayed as manifesting the power of the message of the resurrection (Acts 2:42–47, 4:32–35). Accordingly, the concrete economic cost of discipleship receives consistent emphasis in Luke's story: Jesus proclaims bluntly, "None of you can become my disciple if you do not give up all your possessions" (Luke 14:25–35). The person who stores up provisions for himself is a fool (Luke 12:16–21), whereas Jesus' followers are exhorted to sell their possessions and give alms (Luke 12:33). Zacchaeus exemplifies authentic response to the coming of the kingdom of God by declaring that he will give half his goods to the poor (Luke 19:1–10).

Paul exhorts his churches to contribute to a collection for the poor among the saints in Jerusalem. Pointing to the story of God's provision of manna in the wilderness, which could not be hoarded and stored up for the future (2 Cor. 8:13–15, quoting Exod. 16:18),[4] he urges that there should be "a fair balance" (*isotēs*) between those who have abundance and those who are in need. Such a practice of sharing is the minimal expression of conformity to Christ's example of self-emptying, which ought to lead the community to "look not to [their] own interests, but to the interests of others" (Phil. 2:4) and therefore to act sacrificially.

According to 1 Timothy, those who are not shaped by "the sound words of our Lord Jesus Christ" are likely to fall into the trap of self-destructive greed:

> *Those who want to be rich fall into temptation and are trapped by many senseless and harmful desires that plunge people into ruin and destruction. For the love of money is a root of all kinds of evil, and in their eagerness to be rich some have wandered away from the faith and pierced themselves with many pains.* (1 TIM. 6:9–10)

Members of the community of faith are called instead to be "rich in good works" (6:18).

In language reminiscent of Amos and Isaiah, the letter of James denounces the rich, whose gold and silver will rust (cf. Matt. 6:19–21) and bear witness against them on the day of judgment. Their oppression of poor laborers will not escape God's notice: "You have lived on the earth in luxury and in pleasure; you have fattened your hearts in a day of slaughter" (James 5:1–6). By contrast, God has "chosen the poor in the world to be rich in faith and to be heirs of the kingdom that he has promised to those who love him" (James 2:5).

Even the Johannine literature, notable for its lack of specific ethical teaching, exhorts the community of faith to practice economic sharing:

> *How does God's love abide in anyone who has the world's goods and sees a brother or sister in need and yet refuses help? Little children, let us love, not in word or speech, but in truth and action.* (1 JOHN 3:17–18)

To fulfill the new commandment of Jesus ("Love one another") necessarily entails the sharing of possessions with the poorer members of the community.

Finally, Revelation draws a striking contrast between the church at Smyrna, living in affliction and poverty (2:9), and the church at Laodicea, which prides itself on its wealth (3:17). To the former, the prophetic word of the risen Christ offers consolation; to the latter, threatening to spit them out of his mouth, he says, "You do not realize that you are wretched, pitiable, poor, blind, and naked." Economic power and prosperity are consistently associated in this prophetic book with the power of the Beast that tries to delude the saints. At the fall of Babylon, the great city, in Revelation 18, "the merchants of the earth" weep and mourn, because they have lost their market for luxury items and because "in one hour all this wealth has been laid waste" (18:11–17a).

Thus, while the particular mandates and forms of expression may vary, the New Testament witnesses speak loudly in chorus: the accumulation of wealth is antithetical to serving God's kingdom, and Jesus' disciples are called at least to share their goods generously with those in need, and perhaps even to give everything away in order to follow him more freely.[5]

The focal images of community, cross, and new creation bring this material together into a compelling unified picture.

Community. The imperative of sharing material goods is addressed to the community as a whole. The New Testament writers are not concerned merely with how individuals might seek eternal life; rather, they are concerned with how the church as a whole might embody the economics of the kingdom of God. This communal dimension is explicit in the Acts narratives about the earliest community, in Paul's directives for his churches to participate in the collection for the poor among the saints as an expression of their *koinōnia* in Christ, in 1 John's exhortation to sharing as the authentic expression of loving one another within the church, and in Revelation's prophetic address to the churches of Smyrna and Laodicea *corporately.* Even where the corporate dimension of the economic imperative is less explicit, as in Matthew, it is implicit in the larger conception of discipleship: Matthew sees the community of Jesus' followers as a city set on a hill, a *polis* that manifests the righteousness of God. Thus, the good works (Matt. 5:16, cf. 25:31–46) of the community are a sign to the world of God's glory.

Cross. Relinquishment of material goods is closely linked to the way of the cross. This is directly stated in Luke 14:25–33, which begins with Jesus' call to "carry the cross" and ends with his challenge to his disciples to give up all their possessions. Paul also grounds his economic appeal to the Corinthians in the self-sacrificial example of Jesus (2 Cor. 8:9). The passage in 1 John that commands helping the brother or sister in need (1 John 3:17–18) is immediately prefaced by a direct allusion to the cross: "We know love by this, that he laid down his life for us—and we ought to lay down our lives for one another" (1 John 3:16). The meaning of "laying down our lives" is then immediately specified in terms of economic sharing. In this matter, as in others, the imperative of self-sacrificial love is rooted in the paradigm of Jesus's death on the cross.[6]

New Creation. The practices of sharing that characterize the New Testament church are to be understood as eschatological signs, demonstrating that the transforming power of God's kingdom has broken in upon the old age. Those who seek first the kingdom of God (Matt. 6:33) will, as a necessary consequence, put the old order's economic concerns in a secondary place. In Luke's Gospel, the mandate for sharing is premised directly on the promise of the coming kingdom:

> *Do not be afraid, little flock, for it is your Father's good pleasure to give you the kingdom. Sell your possessions, and give alms. Make purses for yourselves that do not wear out, an unfailing treasure in heaven, where no thief comes near and no moth destroys.*
> (Luke 12:32–33)

The message of such texts is not only that heavenly rewards relativize present economic anxieties but also that the kingdom impinges upon the present in such a way that we are freed to act with a generosity that figures forth God's good future. That claim is most powerfully made manifest, of course, in Luke's description of the Jerusalem church, where the power of the apostles' testimony to the resurrection of Jesus is confirmed by church members' practice of selling their property and sharing the proceeds so that "there was not a needy person among them" (Acts 4:32–35). The link between the kerygma of the resurrection and the community's sharing of goods is direct and material. The author of 1 John makes a similar point when he writes, "We know that we have passed from death to life because we love one another" (1 John 3:14a)—a love that is necessarily to be expressed, as we have seen, through sharing the world's goods (3:17). Thus, the church that lives in the time between the times—while still subject to mundane obligations such as paying taxes to Caesar (Mark 12:13–17, Rom. 13:1–7)—will also embody in its economic practices the sharing that prefigures the joy and justice of the world to come.

How are we to respond to the New Testament's challenge? A full discussion of the hermeneutical and pragmatic issues would require a lengthy discussion indeed. For the present, then, we must be content with a few basic observations:

- The New Testament's direct commands and general rules about possessions are embedded in a canonical context that complicates simple literal application. As Luke Johnson has demonstrated, even within Luke-Acts the rule that disciples of Jesus must give up all their possessions (Luke 14:33) is set alongside other teachings and narratives that pose different models of faithful response to the gospel.[7] Zacchaeus, for example, is commended for his repentant response ("Today salvation has come to this house" [Luke 19:9a]), even though he gives up considerably less than everything. Even the church in Jerusalem (Acts 2 and 4) is characterized by generous *sharing* of possessions rather than radical renunciation. The point is that we cannot derive simple or univocal rules for economic practice from the New Testament.
- Very little direct appeal is made in the New Testament texts to principles of equality and justice, though such principles may be implicit in some passages, such as 2 Corinthians 8:13–15. For the most part, the texts call the church to acts of sacrificial service far beyond what simple justice would require.

- The New Testament texts address us on this issue primarily through the medium of narrative. The various stories and parables of the Gospels and the narrative of Acts provide us with the fundamental paradigms to which we must respond faithfully. The particular exhortations and warnings about money found in the New Testament epistolary literature make sense only within the symbolic world narrated in these stories. On this matter, then, our basic orientation must be provided by the narrative texts, and our hermeneutical application of the New Testament will involve retelling these stories in such a way that we find our place within them; in other words, we will bring our communities metaphorically into conjunction with Acts 4—to cite one particularly important example—and ask ourselves, "How can we order our economic practices in the church in such a way that we give testimony with power to the resurrection of Jesus?"
- To ask that question in a serious and sustained way will require of us not only imaginative reflection but also costly change. No matter how much hermeneutical squirming we may do, it is impossible to escape the implications of the New Testament's address to us: imaginative obedience to God will require of us a sharing of possessions far more radical than the church has ordinarily supposed. To be sure, there have been many communities of Christians throughout history that perform the texts in impressive ways, sacrificing their own interests and sharing their goods with the poor. But such embodiments of the text are typically seen—at least in mainstream Protestantism—as the exception rather than the authentic norm of Christian faith and practice. For the church to heed the New Testament's challenge on the question of possessions would require nothing less than a new Reformation.

To bring the matter close to home, perhaps a word about myself, the author of this book, would be in order. As a tenured professor in a major U.S. university, I live a life of comfortable affluence and relative economic security. I participate in a church and support it financially, contribute money to good causes, and do the occasional service stint in a homeless shelter. But—let there be no mistake—such modest forms of economic discipleship fall far short of the New Testament vision, and most of the churches I have known have been formed by the forces of market capitalism as least as much as by the teaching of Jesus. I remain among the wealthy of the world, and the churches in which I have participated for the last twenty years have made only fitful and tepid attempts to respond to the New Testament's imperatives concerning the sharing of possessions. I say "for the last twenty years" because from 1971 to 1976 my wife and I participated in Metanoia Fellowship, a small church community in Massachusetts that practiced radical economic sharing through a common purse, seeking to have "all things in common." The ultimate demise of that particular communal-discipleship initiative in no way vitiates the legitimacy of its vision or excuses our subsequent failure to seek other communal expressions of the New Testament vision for sharing possessions.

Pressing On Toward the Goal: The Vision of New Testament Ethics

The purpose of the foregoing autobiographical remarks is simply to provide the necessary backdrop for some final remarks about the task of New Testament ethics.

First, the ethic envisioned by the New Testament writers is not an impossible ideal. If we fail to live in obedient responsiveness to their moral vision, that is because of a failure of the imagination—or perhaps a lack of courage—on our part. I include myself fully in this indictment, and I throw no stones at those who do not live according to the norms articulated in the other parts of this book. The difficulty of living in conformity with the New Testament vision does not, however, let us off the hook: my experience of struggle and failure to respond to the New Testament's challenge concerning possessions does not authorize me to disregard the New Testament's summons, or to pretend that the New Testament does not mean what it says, or to devise less costly standards for myself and for the church.

Second, with regard to the question of possessions, as with most of the other issues considered in this book, there is no single set of rules that can be promulgated for the community of faith. The New Testament is not a rulebook, not a cookie cutter for forming identical people or identical communities. Instead, the New Testament texts call us to respond in imaginative freedom, under the guidance of the Holy Spirit, to form communities that will embody the truth of the Word, demonstrating metaphorically the power of God's grace in our midst.

Third, such imaginative performances of obedience to the Word will prove costly: indeed, they may cost us not less than everything. That is what following Jesus requires.

Fourth, the whole vision for New Testament ethics developed in this book calls for a fundamental transformation of the church. To do New Testament ethics as I have proposed requires far more than the reconceptualization of an academic discipline; it requires the recovery of the church's identity as the eschatological people of God, prefiguring God's healing transformation of the world.[8] The church must be a *community* living in conformity to the paradigm of the *cross* and thereby standing as a sign of the *new creation* promised by God. Insofar as the church seeks to enact an obedient response to this vision, its reading of the New Testament texts will come more sharply into focus. For example, if we really want to understand the New Testament's challenging mandate concerning possessions, we must begin by being obedient to the light we have been given. For me and for my community, this would entail some immediate practical and sacrificial changes in what we do with our money.

Fifth, lest all of this sound utopian, we must never forget that the eschatological reservation, the "not yet," is an integral part of the New Testament's understanding of new creation. To acknowledge that the kingdom is not fully realized in our midst is not to compromise the New Testament's moral vision; it is, rather, to respect it. We cannot suppose that all our lives can be lived in the first enthusiasm of Pentecost; our ethical decisions and our actions must be performed over the long haul in the midst of a creation that still groans awaiting redemption. To acknowledge this truth will enable us in the church to admit our own fallibility and sinfulness, to live patiently with the dissonance between the eschatological vision and the present reality of our lives. If I have not yet found or formed a community in which possessions are shared freely and generously, in which there is no needy person, I should not be surprised or despairing. And yet, we continue to hope, pray, and work for something better, for a community more closely conformed to the will of God as disclosed in Scripture. Paul strikes the balance just right:

> *I want to know Christ and the power of his resurrection and the* **koinōnia** *of his sufferings by becoming like him in his death, if somehow I may attain the resurrection of the dead. Not that I have already obtained this or have already reached the goal; but I press on to make it my own, because Christ Jesus has made me his own. Beloved, I do not consider that I have made it my own; but this one thing I do: forgetting what lies behind and straining forward to what lies ahead, I press on toward the goal.* (PHIL. 3:10–14a, AA)

No complacency, no despair, no nostalgia: we reach forward, press on, knowing that we can trust God's grace because Christ Jesus has already claimed us. With this knowledge, we present our bodies as a living sacrifice to God, hoping and expecting that he will continue to transform the community of the church so that our moral discernments may indeed be true:

> *Do not be conformed to this age, but be transformed by the renewing of your minds, so that you may discern what is the will of God—what is good and acceptable and perfect.* (ROM. 12:2, AA)

That is the task of New Testament ethics.

NOTES

1. See the endnote to Part IV's introductory text for an explanation of my decision not to pursue an extended discussion of the fourth issue in this book.
2. For a full treatment of this issue—a treatment with which I am in substantial agreement—see Wheeler 1995.
3. These stories are also told, with only minor modifications, by Matthew and Luke.
4. For discussion of this passage, see Hays 1989, 88–91.
5. The texts cited here are only a representative sample. I have not tried to mention all the pertinent passages, nor have I flagged the texts that seem to represent a divergent perspective (e.g., Mark 14:7). Of course, a full descriptive survey would have to take such passages into account.
6. An interesting additional note: if James 5:6 alludes—as I believe it does—to the death of Jesus, then it is *the rich* (not, e.g., "the Jews") who are blamed for the murder of Jesus. The shadow of the cross looms over the image of the wealthy who "have lived on the earth in luxury and pleasure."
7. L. T. Johnson 1981.
8. This is not to imply that the church has totally lost an awareness of this identity; I am simply calling for a more intentional reclaiming of the NT's identity description for God's people.

Works Cited

Achtemeier, Paul J. 1970. "Toward the Isolation of Pre-Markan Miracle Catenae." *Journal of Biblical Literature* 89: 265–291.

______. 1972. "The Origin and Function of the Pre-Markan Miracle Catenae." *Journal of Biblical Literature* 91: 198–221.

Aland, Kurt, ed. 1985. *Synopsis Quattuor Evangeliorum*. Stuttgart: Deutsche Bibelgesellschaft.

Allison, Dale C. 1982. "The Pauline Epistles and the Synoptic Gospels: The Pattern of the Parallels." *New Testament Studies* 28: 1–32.

______. 1993. *The New Moses: A Matthean Typology*. Minneapolis: Fortress.

Althaus, Paul. 1966. *The Theology of Martin Luther*, trans. Robert C. Schultz. Philadelphia: Fortress.

______. 1972. *The Ethics of Martin Luther*, trans. Robert C. Schultz. Philadelphia: Fortress.

Augustine. 1949 [398 C.E.]. *Confessions*, trans. Edward B. Pusey. New York: Modern Library.

Baltensweiler, Heinrich. 1959. "Die Ehebruchklauseln bei Matthäus." *Theologische Zeitschrift* 15: 340–356.

______. 1967. *Die Ehe im Neuen Testament: Exegetische Untersuchungen über Ehe, Ehelosigkeit, und Ehescheidung*. Abhandlungen zur Theologie des Alten und Neuen Testaments 52. Zürich: Zwingli.

Banks, Robert. 1994. *Paul's Idea of Community: The Early House Churches in Their Historical Setting*. 2nd ed. Peabody, MA: Hendrickson.

Barclay, John. 1988. *Obeying the Truth: A Study of Paul's Ethics in Galatians*. Edinburgh: T & T Clark.

Barr, David L. 1984. "The Apocalypse as a Symbolic Transformation of the World: A Literary Analysis." *Interpretation* 38: 39–50.

Barrett, C. K. 1988. "Luke-Acts." In *It Is Written: Scripture Citing Scripture: Essays in Honour of Barnabas Lindars*, ed. D. A. Carson and H. G. M. Williamson, 231–244. Cambridge: Cambridge University Press.

Bartchy, S. Scott. 1991. "Community of Goods in Acts: Idealization or Social Reality?" In *The Future of Early Christianity: Essays in Honor of Helmut Koester*, ed. Birger A. Pearson, 309–318. Minneapolis: Fortress.

Barth, Karl. 1946. *Nein! Antwort an Emil Brunner*. Munich: Kaiser.

______. 1957a [1946]. *Church Dogmatics* II/1, trans. T. H. L. Parker et al. Edinburgh: T & T Clark.

______. 1957b [1946]. *Church Dogmatics* II/2, trans. G. Bromiley et al. Edinburgh: T & T Clark; New York: Charles Scribner's Sons.

______. 1957c [1928]. *The Word of God and the Word of Man*, trans. Douglas Horton. New York: Harper & Brothers.

______. 1961 [1951]. *Church Dogmatics* III/4, trans. A. T. Mackay et al. Edinburgh: T & T Clark; New York: Charles Scribner's Sons.

Bartlett, David. 1983. *The Shape of Scriptural Authority*. Philadelphia: Fortress.

Barton, John. 1982. "Approaches to Ethics in the Old Testament." In *Beginning Old Testament Study*, ed. John Rogerson, 113–130. Philadelphia: Westminster.
Barton, Stephen C. 1994. "Is the Bible Good News for Human Sexuality? Reflections on Method in Biblical Interpretation." *Theology and Sexuality* 1: 42–54.
Bassler, Jouette M. 1984. "The Widow's Tale: A Fresh Look at 1 Tim. 5:3–16." *Journal of Biblical Literature* 103: 23–41.
______, ed. 1991. *Pauline Theology*, vol. 1: *Thessalonians, Philippians, Galatians, Philemon*. Minneapolis: Fortress.
Batstone, David B. 1992. "Jesus, Apocalyptic, and World Transformation." *Theology Today* 49: 383–397.
Bauckham, Richard. 1993. *The Theology of the Book of Revelation*. New Testament Theology. Cambridge: Cambridge University Press.
Beardslee, William A. 1970. *Literary Criticism of the New Testament*. Guides to Biblical Scholarship. Philadelphia: Fortress.
Beck, Norman A. 1994. *Mature Christianity in the Twenty-First Century: The Recognition and Repudiation of the Anti-Jewish Polemic of the New Testament*. Rev. ed. New York: Crossroad.
Beker, J. Christiaan. 1980. *Paul the Apostle: The Triumph of God in Life and Thought*. Philadelphia: Fortress.
______. 1991. *Heirs of Paul: Paul's Legacy in the New Testament and in the Church Today*. Minneapolis: Fortress.
Berger, Peter L., and Thomas Luckmann. 1966. *The Social Construction of Reality*. Garden City, NY: Doubleday.
Berkhof, Hendrik. 1962. *Christ and the Powers*, trans. John Howard Yoder. Scottdale, PA: Herald.
Best, Ernest. 1979 [1972]. *A Commentary on the First and Second Epistles to the Thessalonians*. Black's New Testament Commentaries. London: Adam & Charles Black.
Betz, Hans Dieter. 1967. *Nachfolge und Nachahmung Jesu Christi im Neuen Testament*. Beiträge zur historischen Theologie 37. Tübingen: Mohr.
______. 1979. *Galatians*. Hermeneia Commentary. Philadelphia: Fortress.
______. 1985. *Essays on the Sermon on the Mount*. Philadelphia: Fortress.
Biggar, Nigel, ed. 1988. *Reckoning with Barth: Essays in Commemoration of the Centenary of Karl Barth's Birth*. London and Oxford: Mowbray.
______. 1993. *The Hastening That Waits: Karl Barth's Ethics*. Oxford: Clarendon.
Birch, Bruce C. 1991. *Let Justice Roll Down: The Old Testament, Ethics, and Christian Life*. Philadelphia: Westminster/John Knox.
Birch, Bruce C., and Larry L. Rasmussen. 1989. *Bible and Ethics in the Christian Life*. Rev. ed. Minneapolis: Augsburg.
Black, C. Clifton II. 1989. *The Disciples According to Mark: Markan Redaction in Current Debate*. Journal for the Study of the New Testament Supplement Series 27. Sheffield, UK: JSOT.
Blenkinsopp, Joseph. 1977. *Prophecy and Canon*. Notre Dame, IN: University of Notre Dame Press.
Bock, Darrell L. 1987. *Proclamation from Prophecy and Pattern: Lucan Old Testament Christology*. Journal for the Study of the New Testament Supplement Series 12. Sheffield, UK: JSOT.
Boers, Hendrikus W. 1979. *What Is New Testament Theology?* Guides to Biblical Scholarship. Philadelphia: Fortress.
Boesak, Alan. 1987. *Comfort and Protest: Reflections on the Apocalypse of John of Patmos*. Philadelphia: Westminster.
Bonsirven, Joseph. 1948. *Le divorce dans le Nouveau Testament*. Paris: Desclée.
Boring, M. Eugene. 1979. "The Influence of Christian Prophecy on the Johannine Portrayal of the Paraclete and Jesus." *New Testament Studies* 25: 113–123.
______. 1984. *Truly Human, Truly Divine*. St. Louis: CPB.
______. 1989. *Revelation*. Interpretation. Louisville: John Knox.
Bornkamm, Günther. 1960 [1956]. *Jesus of Nazareth*, trans. Irene and Fraser McLuskey. New York: Harper & Row.
Boswell, John. 1980. *Christianity, Social Tolerance, and Homosexuality*. Chicago and London: University of Chicago Press.
______. 1994. *Same-Sex Unions in Premodern Europe*. New York: Villard.
Boyarin, Daniel. 1994. *A Radical Jew: Paul and the Politics of Cultural Identity*. Berkeley: University of California Press.
______. 1995. "Are There Any Jews in 'The History of Sexuality'?" *Journal of the History of Sexuality* 5:333–355.
Braaten, Carl E. 1983. *Lutheranism: Principles of Lutheran Theology*. Philadelphia: Fortress.
Breytenbach, Cilliers. 1989. *Versöhnung: Eine Studie der paulinischen Soteriologie*. Wissenschaftliche Monographien zum Alten und Neuen Testament 60. Neukirchen-Vluyn: Neukirchener Verlag.

Brock, Rita Nakashima. 1988. *Journeys by Heart: A Christology of Erotic Power.* New York: Crossroad.
Brooten, Bernadette. 1982. "Konnten Frauen im alten Judentum die Scheidung betreiben? Überlegungen zu Mk. 10:11–12 und 1 Kor. 7:10–11." *Evangelische Theologie* 42: 65–80.
Brown, Charles C. 1992. *Niebuhr and His Age: Reinhold Niebuhr's Prophetic Role in the Twentieth Century.* Philadelphia: Trinity Press International.
Brown, Raymond E. 1966. *The Gospel According to John.* 2 vols. Anchor Bible 29 and 29A. Garden City, NY: Doubleday.
______. 1979a. *The Birth of the Messiah: A Commentary on the Infancy Narratives of Matthew and Luke.* Garden City, NY: Image Books.
______. 1979b. *The Community of the Beloved Disciple.* New York: Paulist.
______. 1982. *The Epistles of John.* Anchor Bible 30. Garden City, NY: Doubleday.
______. 1984. *The Churches the Apostles Left Behind.* New York: Paulist.
______. 1987. "The Gospel of Peter and Canonical Gospel Priority." *New Testament Studies* 33: 321–343.
______. 1994. *The Death of the Messiah: From Gethsemane to the Grave.* 2 vols. New York: Doubleday.
Brown, Robert McAfee. 1986. *The Essential Reinhold Niebuhr.* New Haven and London: Yale University Press.
Brunner, Emil. 1935. *Natur und Gnade: Zum Gespräch mit Karl Barth.* Zürich: Zwingli. (English edition: 1946. *Natural Theology: Comprising "Nature and Grace,"* trans. Peter Fraenkel. London: Centenary.)
Bultmann, Rudolf. 1951–1955. *Theology of the New Testament,* trans. Kendrick Grobel. 2 vols. New York: Charles Scribner's Sons.
Busch, Eberhard. 1976. *Karl Barth: His Life from Letters and Autobiographical Texts.* Philadelphia: Fortress.
Cahill, Lisa Sowle. 1994. *Love Your Enemies: Discipleship, Pacifism, and Just War Theory.* Minneapolis: Fortress.
Caird, G. B. 1956. *Principalities and Powers.* Oxford: Clarendon.
______. 1966. *The Revelation of St. John the Divine.* Harper's New Testament Commentaries. New York: Harper & Row.
Calvin, John. 1960 [1556]. *The Epistles of Paul the Apostle to the Romans and to the Thessalonians,* trans. Ross Mackenzie. Calvin's Commentaries, vol. 8. Grand Rapids: Eerdmans.
Carroll, John T. 1988. *Response to the End of History: Eschatology and Situation in Luke-Acts.* SBL Dissertation Series 92. Atlanta: Scholars Press.
Cartwright, Michael G. 1988. *Practices, Politics, and Performance: Toward a Communal Hermeneutic for Christian Ethics.* Ph.D. dissertation, Duke University. Ann Arbor, MI: University Microfilms.
Cassidy, Richard J. 1978. *Jesus, Politics, and Society: A Study of Luke's Gospel.* Maryknoll, NY: Orbis.
______. 1992. *John's Gospel in New Perspective: Christology and the Realities of Roman Power.* Maryknoll, NY: Orbis.
Cassidy, Richard J., and Philip Scharper, eds. 1983. *Political Issues in Luke-Acts.* Maryknoll, NY: Orbis.
Charlesworth, James H., ed. 1983. *The Old Testament Pseudepigrapha.* 2 vols. Garden City, NY: Doubleday.
______, ed. 1990. *Jews and Christians: Exploring the Past, Present, and Future.* New York: Crossroad.
Charry, Ellen T. 1993. "Is Christianity Good for Us?" In *Reclaiming Faith: Essays on Orthodoxy in the Episcopal Church and the Baltimore Declaration,* ed. E. Radner and G. Sumner, 169–193. Grand Rapids, MI: Eerdmans.
Childs, Brevard S. 1970. *Biblical Theology in Crisis.* Philadelphia: Westminster.
______. 1992. *Biblical Theology of the Old and New Testaments: Theological Reflection on the Christian Bible.* Minneapolis: Fortress.
Christ, Carol P., and Judith Plaskow, eds. 1979. *Womanspirit Rising.* San Francisco: Harper & Row.
Clark, Henry B. 1994. *Serenity, Courage, and Wisdom: The Enduring Legacy of Reinhold Niebuhr.* Cleveland: Pilgrim.
Cochrane, Arthur C. 1976. *The Church's Confession Under Hitler.* 2nd ed. Pittsburgh: Pickwick.
Cohen, Shaye J. D. 1987. *From the Maccabees to the Mishnah.* Library of Early Christianity. Philadelphia: Westminster.
Collange, J. F. 1980. *De Jesus à Paul: L'éthique du Nouveau Testament.* Geneva: Labor et Fides.
Collins, Adela Yarbro. 1977. "The Political Perspective of the Revelation to John." *Journal of Biblical Literature* 96: 241–256.
______. 1980. "The Function of 'Excommunication' in Paul." *Harvard Theological Review* 73: 251–263.
______. 1981. "Dating the Apocalypse of John." *Biblical Research* 26: 33–45.
______. 1984. *Crisis and Catharsis: The Power of the Apocalypse.* Philadelphia: Westminster.
Collins, John J. 1984. *The Apocalyptic Imagination: An Introduction to the Jewish Matrix of Christianity.* New York: Crossroad.
______. 1993. *Daniel.* Hermeneia Commentary. Minneapolis: Fortress.
Collins, Raymond F. 1984. *Studies on the First Letter to the Thessalonians.* Bibliotheca Ephemeridum Theologicarum Lovaniensium 66. Leuven, Belgium: Leuven University.

______. 1992. *Divorce in the New Testament.* Good News Studies 38. Collegeville, MN: Glazier.
Connery, John. 1977. *Abortion: The Development of the Roman Catholic Perspective.* Chicago: Loyola University Press.
Conzelmann, Hans. 1961 [1953]. *The Theology of St. Luke,* trans. Geoffrey Buswell. New York: Harper & Row.
______. 1987. *Acts of the Apostles,* trans. James Limburg, A. Thomas Kraabel, and Donald H. Juel. Hermeneia Commentary. Philadelphia: Fortress.
Countryman, L. William. 1988. *Dirt, Greed, and Sex: Sexual Ethics in the New Testament and Their Implications for Today.* Philadelphia: Fortress.
Cousar, Charles. 1990. *A Theology of the Cross: The Death of Jesus in the Pauline Letters.* Overtures to Biblical Theology 24. Minneapolis: Fortress.
Craddock, Fred B. 1985. "The Sermon and the Uses of Scripture." *Theology Today* 42: 7–14.
Crossan, John Dominic. 1975. *The Dark Interval: Towards a Theology of Story.* Niles, IL: Argus Communications.
______. 1988. *The Cross That Spoke: The Origins of the Passion Narrative.* San Francisco: Harper & Row.
______. 1991. *The Historical Jesus: The Life of a Mediterranean Jewish Peasant.* San Francisco: HarperSanFrancisco.
Cullmann, Oscar. 1956. *The State in the New Testament.* New York: Charles Scribner's Sons.
______. 1964 [1946]. *Christ and Time: The Primitive Christian Conception of Time and History,* trans. Floyd V. Filson. Rev. ed. Philadelphia: Westminster.
Culpepper, R. Alan. 1983. *Anatomy of the Fourth Gospel: A Study in Literary Design.* Philadelphia: Fortress.
Dahl, Nils Alstrup. 1976. *Jesus in the Memory of the Early Church.* Minneapolis: Augsburg.
______. 1991. *Jesus the Christ: The Historical Origins of Christological Doctrine.* Minneapolis: Fortress.
Danby, Herbert, trans. 1933. *The Mishnah.* Oxford: Oxford University Press.
Daube, David. 1956. *The New Testament and Rabbinic Judaism.* London: Athlone.
Davies, Alan T. 1979. *Anti-Semitism and the Foundations of Christianity.* New York: Paulist.
Davies, Glenn N. 1990. *Faith and Obedience in Romans.* Journal for the Study of the New Testament Supplement Series 39. Sheffield, UK: JSOT.
Davies, W. D. 1964. *The Setting of the Sermon on the Mount.* Cambridge: Cambridge University Press.
______. 1980. *Paul and Rabbinic Judaism: Some Rabbinic Elements in Pauline Theology.* 4th ed. Philadelphia: Fortress.
Davies, W. D., and Dale C. Allison. 1988–1991. *A Critical and Exegetical Commentary on the Gospel According to St. Matthew.* 2 vols. International Critical Commentary. Edinburgh: T & T Clark.
Davis, John Jefferson. 1985. *Evangelical Ethics.* Phillipsburg, NJ: Presbyterian and Reformed Publishing Company.
DeCosse, David. 1992. *But Was It Just? Reflections on the Morality of the Persian Gulf War.* New York: Doubleday.
de Jonge, Marinus. 1966. "The Use of the Word 'Anointed' in the Time of Jesus." *Novum Testamentum* 8: 132–148.
DeRidder, Richard R. 1989. "Reply to WCC's Sigtuna Statement, 'The Churches and the Jewish People.'" *International Bulletin of Missionary Research* 13: 159–160.
Dibelius, Martin. 1930. "Das christliche Leben (Eph. 4:17–6:9)." *Theologische Blätter* 9: 341–342.
______. 1936. [1926]. *A Fresh Approach to the New Testament and Early Christian Literature.* The International Library of Christian Knowledge. London: Ivor Nicholson and Watson.
Dibelius, Martin, and Heinrich Greeven. 1976 [1964]. *James,* trans. Michael A. Williams. Hermeneia Commentary. Philadelphia: Fortress.
Dibelius, Martin, and Heinz Kraft. 1953, 1956. *Botschaft und Geschichte: Gesammelte Aufsätze.* 2 vols. Tübingen: Mohr.
Documents of Vatican II. 1966. New York: Guild.
Dodd, C. H. 1936. *The Apostolic Preaching and Its Developments.* London: Hodder & Stoughton.
Donelson, Lewis R. 1988. "The Structure of Ethical Argument in the Pastorals." *Biblical Theology Bulletin* 18: 108–113.
Donfried, Karl P. 1991. *The Romans Debate.* Rev. ed. Peabody, MA: Hendrickson.
Dowd, Sharyn Echols. 1988. *Prayer, Power, and the Problem of Suffering: Mark 11:22–25 in the Context of Markan Theology.* SBL Dissertation Series 105. Atlanta: Scholars Press.
Duff, Nancy. 1995. "Response to Community, Cross, New Creation." Unpublished paper presented at symposium on "New Testament Ethics: Problems and Prospects," Duke University, Apr. 1, 1995.
Duke, Paul D. 1985. *Irony in the Fourth Gospel.* Atlanta: John Knox.
Dumais, Marcel. 1977. "Couple et sexualité selon le Nouveau Testament." *Église et Théologie* 8: 47–72.
Dungan, David L. 1971. *The Sayings of Jesus in the Churches of Paul.* Philadelphia: Fortress.

Dunn, J. D. G. 1977. *Unity and Diversity in the New Testament*. Philadelphia: Westminster.

______. 1983a. "The New Perspective on Paul." *Bulletin of the John Rylands Library* 65: 95–122.

______. 1983b. "The Incident at Antioch (Gal. 2:11–18)." *Journal for the Study of the New Testament* 18: 3–57.

______. 1988. *Romans*. 2 vols. Word Biblical Commentary 38A and 38B. Dallas: Word.

______. 1991a. "Once More, *Pistis Christou*." In *Society of Biblical Literature Seminar Papers 1991*, ed. David J. Lull, 730–744. Atlanta: Scholars Press.

______. 1991b. *The Partings of the Ways Between Christianity and Judaism and Their Significance for the Character of Christianity*. Philadelphia: Trinity Press International.

Durland, William. 1989. "Another Realm." *Sojourners* 18/10: 17.

Ehler, Bernhard. 1986. *Die Herrschaft des Gekreuzigten: Ernst Käsemanns Frage nach die Mitte der Schrift*. Beihefte zur Zeitschrift für die neutestamentliche Wissenschaft 46. Berlin and New York: de Gruyter.

Eliot, T. S. 1952 [1930]. *The Complete Poems and Plays 1909–1950*. New York: Harcourt, Brace & World.

Elshtain, Jean Bethke. 1992a. "Just War and American Politics." *The Christian Century* 109/2: 41–44.

______, ed. 1992b. *Just War Theory*. New York: New York University.

Evans, C. F. 1955. "The Central Section of Luke's Gospel." In *Studies in the Gospels*, ed. Dennis E. Nineham, 37–53. Oxford: Blackwell.

Evans, Craig A., and Donald A. Hagner, eds. 1993. *Anti-Semitism and Early Christianity: Issues of Polemic and Faith*. Minneapolis: Fortress.

Evans, Craig A., and James A. Sanders. 1993. *Luke and Scripture: The Function of Sacred Tradition in Luke-Acts*. Minneapolis: Fortress.

Fackre, Gabriel. 1994. *The Promise of Reinhold Niebuhr*. Rev. ed. Landham, MD: University Press of America.

Farmer, William R. 1974. *The Last Twelve Verses of Mark*. Society for New Testament Studies Monograph Series 25. Cambridge: Cambridge University Press.

Fee, Gordon D. 1987. *The First Epistle to the Corinthians*. New International Commentary on the New Testament. Grand Rapids, MI: Eerdmans.

Feldman, David M. 1975. *Marital Relations, Birth Control, and Abortion in Jewish Law*. New York: Schocken.

______. 1986. *Health and Medicine in the Jewish Tradition*. New York: Crossroad.

Finger, Thomas N. 1989. *Christian Theology: An Eschatological Approach*. 2 vols. Scottdale, PA: Herald.

Fish, Stanley. 1980. *Is There a Text in This Class? The Authority of Interpretive Communities*. Cambridge, MA: Harvard University Press.

Fitzmyer, Joseph A. 1981–85. *The Gospel According to Luke*. 2 vols. Anchor Bible 28 and 28A. Garden City, NY: Doubleday.

Ford, David F. 1981. *Barth and God's Story: Biblical Narrative and the Theological Method of Karl Barth in Church Dogmatics*. Studien zur interkulturellen Geschichte des Christentums 27. Frankfurt am Main and Bern: Peter Lang.

Fowl, Stephen E. 1990. *The Story of Christ in the Ethics of Paul: An Analysis of the Function of the Hymnic Material in the Pauline Corpus*. Journal for the Study of the New Testament Supplement Series 36. Sheffield, UK: JSOT.

Fowl, Stephen E., and L. Gregory Jones. 1991. *Reading in Communion: Scripture and Ethics in Christian Life*. Grand Rapids, MI: Eerdmans.

Fowler, Robert. 1981. *Loaves and Fishes: The Function of the Feeding Stories in the Gospel of Mark*. SBL Dissertation Series 54. Chico, CA: Scholars Press.

Fox, Richard Wightman. 1985. *Reinhold Niebuhr: A Biography*. New York: Pantheon.

France, R. T. 1989. *The Gospel According to Matthew*. Tyndale New Testament Commentaries. Grand Rapids, MI: Eerdmans.

Francke, Linda Bird. 1978. *The Ambivalence of Abortion*. New York: Random House.

Frankemöle, Hubert and Karl Kertelge, eds. 1989. *Vom Urchristentum zu Jesus*. Freiburg: Herder.

Fredriksen, Paula. 1991. "Judaism, the Circumcision of the Gentiles, and Apocalyptic Hope: Another Look at Galatians 1 and 2." *Journal of Theological Studies* 42: 532–564.

Frei, Hans. 1975. *The Identity of Jesus Christ: The Hermeneutical Bases of Dogmatic Theology*. Philadelphia: Fortress.

Frye, Northrop. 1957. *Anatomy of Criticism*. Princeton: Princeton University Press.

______. 1982. *The Great Code: The Bible and Literature*. New York: Harcourt Brace Jovanovich.

Fulkerson, Mary McClintock. 1994. *Changing the Subject: Women's Discourses and Feminist Theology*. Minneapolis: Fortress.

Funk, Robert. 1967. "Apostolic Parousia: Form and Significance." In *Christian History and Interpretation*, ed. W. R. Farmer, C. F. D. Moule, and R. R. Niebuhr, 249–268. Cambridge: Cambridge University Press.

______. 1985. "The Issue of Jesus." *Forum* 1/1: 1–6.

Furnish, Victor P. 1964. "The Jesus-Paul Debate: From Baur to Bultmann." *Bulletin of the John Rylands University Library of Manchester* 47: 342–381.
______. 1968. *Theology and Ethics in Paul.* Nashville: Abingdon.
______. 1984. *II Corinthians.* Anchor Bible 32A. Garden City, NY: Doubleday.
______. 1985. *The Moral Teaching of Paul: Selected Issues.* Rev. ed. Nashville: Abingdon.
______. 1993. *Jesus According to Paul.* Cambridge: Cambridge University Press.
Gabler, Johann Philipp. 1980 [1787]. "On the Proper Distinction Between Biblical and Dogmatic Theology and the Specific Objectives of Each," trans. John Sandys-Wunsch and Laurence Eldredge. *Scottish Journal of Theology* 33: 133–158.
Gager, John G. 1983. *The Origins of Anti-Semitism: Attitudes Toward Judaism in Pagan and Christian Antiquity.* New York: Oxford University Press.
Garrett, Susan R. 1989. *The Demise of the Devil: Magic and the Demonic in Luke's Writings.* Minneapolis: Fortress.
______. 1990. "Exodus from Bondage: Luke 9:31 and Acts 12:1–24." *Catholic Biblical Quarterly* 52: 656–680.
Gärtner, Bertil. 1965. *The Temple and the Community in Qumran and the New Testament.* Society for New Testament Studies Monograph Series 1. Cambridge: Cambridge University Press.
Garvey, John. 1987. "Fidelity and Faultlines: Marriage in a Radical Context." *Commonweal* 114/6: 168–169.
Gaston, Lloyd. 1987. *Paul and the Torah.* Vancouver: University of British Columbia Press.
Gaventa, Beverly Roberts. 1986. "Galatians 1 and 2: Autobiography as Paradigm." *Novum Testamentum* 28/4: 309–326.
______. 1990. "The Maternity of Paul." In *The Conversation Continues: Studies in Paul and John in Honor of J. Louis Martyn*, ed. Robert T. Fortna and Beverly Roberts Gaventa, 189–201. Nashville: Abingdon.
Geertz, Clifford. 1973. *The Interpretation of Cultures: Selected Essays.* New York: Basic Books.
Georgi, Dieter. 1986. *The Opponents of Paul in 2 Corinthians.* Philadelphia: Fortress.
Gerhart, Mary, and Allan Melvin Russell. 1984. *Metaphoric Process: The Creation of Scientific and Religious Understanding.* Fort Worth: Texas Christian University Press.
Goldsmith, Dale. 1988. *New Testament Ethics.* Elgin, IL: Brethren.
Gorman, Michael J. 1982. *Abortion and the Early Church: Christian, Jewish, and Pagan Attitudes in the Greco-Roman World.* Downer's Grove, IL: InterVarsity; New York: Paulist.
Green, Joel B. 1995. *The Theology of the Gospel of Luke.* New Testament Theology. Cambridge: Cambridge University Press.
Greenberg, David F. 1989. *The Construction of Homosexuality.* Chicago: University of Chicago Press.
Greene, Thomas. 1982. *A Light in Troy: Imitation and Discovery in Renaissance Poetry.* New Haven: Yale University Press.
Greene-McCreight, Kathryn. 1994. *Ad Litteram: Understanding of the Plain Sense of Scripture in the Exegesis of Augustine, Calvin, and Barth of Genesis 1–3.* Ph.D. dissertation, Yale University. Ann Arbor, MI: University Microfilms.
Gritsch, Eric W., and Robert W. Jenson. 1976. *Lutheranism: The Theological Movement and Its Confessional Writings.* Philadelphia: Fortress.
Guelich, Robert A. 1982. *The Sermon on the Mount: A Foundation for Understanding.* Waco, TX: Word.
______. 1987. "Interpreting the Sermon on the Mount. *Interpretation* 41: 117–130.
Gustafson, James M. 1970. "The Place of Scripture in Christian Ethics." *Interpretation* 24: 430–455.
Hamerton-Kelly, Robert. 1992. *Sacred Violence: Paul's Hermeneutic of the Cross.* Minneapolis: Fortress.
Hare, Douglas R. A. 1967. *The Theme of Jewish Persecution of Christians in the Gospel According to Saint Matthew.* Society for New Testament Studies Monograph Series 6. Cambridge: Cambridge University Press.
Harries, Richard, ed. 1986. *Reinhold Niebuhr and the Issues of Our Time.* Grand Rapids, MI: Eerdmans.
Harrington, Daniel J. 1980. *God's People in Christ: New Testament Perspectives on the Church and Judaism.* Overtures to Biblical Theology 7. Philadelphia: Fortress.
Harvey, A. E. 1982. *Jesus and the Constraints of History.* Philadelphia: Westminster.
Hauerwas, Stanley. 1981a. *A Community of Character: Toward a Constructive Christian Social Ethic.* Notre Dame, IN: University of Notre Dame Press.
______. 1981b. *Vision and Virtue: Essays in Christian Ethical Reflection.* Notre Dame, IN: University of Notre Dame Press.
______. 1983. *The Peaceable Kingdom: A Primer in Christian Ethics.* Notre Dame, IN: University of Notre Dame Press.
______. 1985. *Character and the Christian Life: A Study in Theological Ethics.* 2nd ed. San Antonio: Trinity University Press.
______. 1990. "The Testament of Friends." *Christian Century* 107: 212–216.
______. 1993. *Unleashing the Scripture: Freeing the Bible from Captivity to America.* Nashville: Abingdon.

______. 1994. *Dispatches from the Front: Theological Engagements with the Secular.* Durham, NC: Duke University Press.

Hauerwas, Stanley, and David B. Burrell. 1977. *Truthfulness and Tragedy: Further Investigations into Christian Ethics.* Notre Dame, IN: University of Notre Dame Press.

Hauerwas, Stanley, and L. Gregory Jones, eds. 1989. *Why Narrative? Readings in Narrative Theology.* Grand Rapids, MI: Eerdmans.

Hauerwas, Stanley, and Richard John Neuhaus. 1991. "Pacifism, Just War, and the Gulf." *First Things* 13: 39–45.

Hauerwas, Stanley, and William H. Willimon. 1989. *Resident Aliens.* Nashville: Abingdon.

______. 1991. "Why Resident Aliens Struck a Chord." *Missiology* 19: 419–429.

Hay, David M., ed. 1993. *Pauline Theology,* vol. 2: 1 and 2 *Corinthians.* Minneapolis: Fortress.

Hays, Richard B. 1983. *The Faith of Jesus Christ: An Investigation of the Narrative Substructure of Galatians* 3:1–4:11. SBL Dissertation Series 56. Chico, CA: Scholars Press.

______. 1986. "Relations Natural and Unnatural: A Response to John Boswell's Exegesis of Romans 1." *Journal of Religious Ethics* 14/1: 184–215.

______. 1987. "Christology and Ethics in Galatians: The Law of Christ." *Catholic Biblical Quarterly* 49: 268–290.

______. 1988. "'The Righteous One' as Eschatological Deliverer: Hermeneutics at the Turn of the Ages." In *The New Testament and Apocalyptic: Essays in Honor of J. Louis Martyn,* ed. Joel Marcus and Marion L. Soards. Journal for the Study of the New Testament Supplement Series 24. Sheffield, UK: JSOT.

______. 1989. *Echoes of Scripture in the Letters of Paul.* New Haven: Yale University Press.

______. 1990. "Scripture-Shaped Community: The Problem of Method in New Testament Ethics." *Interpretation* 44: 42–55.

______. 1991a. "Awaiting the Redemption of Our Bodies: The Witness of Scripture Concerning Homosexuality." *Sojourners* 20: 17–21.

______. 1991b. "*Pistis* and Pauline Christology: What Is at Stake?" In *Society of Biblical Literature Seminar Papers* 1991, ed. David J. Lull, 714–729. Atlanta: Scholars Press.

______. 1992. "Justification." *Anchor Bible Dictionary* 3: 1129–1133. New York: Doubleday.

______. 1993. "Christ Prays the Psalms: Paul's Use of an Early Christian Exegetical Convention." In *The Future of Christology: Essays in Honor of Leander E. Keck,* ed. Abraham J. Malherbe and Wayne A. Meeks, 122–136. Minneapolis: Fortress.

______. 1994. "The Corrected Jesus." *First Things* 43: 43–48.

Heyward, Carter. 1984. *Our Passion for Justice: Images of Power, Sexuality, and Liberation.* New York: Pilgrim.

Hill, David, 1972. *The Gospel of Matthew.* New Century Bible Commentary. London: Oliphants.

Hinlicky, Paul R. 1993. "War of Worlds: Re-Visioning the Abortion Dilemma." *Pro Ecclesia* 2: 187–207.

Holladay, Carl. 1977. *Theios Aner in Hellenistic Judaism.* SBL Dissertation Series 40. Missoula, MT: Scholars Press.

Holtz, Traugott. 1968. *Untersuchungen über die alttestamentlichen Zitate bei Lukas.* Berlin: Akademie-Verlag.

Hooker, Morna D. 1959. *Jesus and the Servant.* London: SPCK.

Horsley, Richard A. 1987. *Jesus and the Spiral of Violence: Jewish Resistance in Roman Palestine.* San Francisco: Harper & Row.

______. 1992. "Messianic Movements in Judaism." *Anchor Bible Dictionary* 4: 791–797. New York: Doubleday.

Hoshiko, Sumi. 1993. *Our Choices: Women's Personal Decisions About Abortion.* New York: Haworth.

Houlden, J. L. 1973. *Ethics and the New Testament.* New York: Oxford University Press.

Hübner, Hans. 1990–1993. *Biblische Theologie des Neuen Testaments.* 2 vols. Göttingen: Vandenhoeck & Ruprecht.

Hughes, Langston. 1992. *The Panther and the Lash: Poems of Our Times.* New York: Vintage.

Hunsinger, George. 1991. *How to Read Karl Barth.* New York: Oxford University Press.

Hunter, David G. 1992. "A Decade of Research on Early Christians and Military Service." *Religious Studies Review* 18/2: 87–94.

Hütter, Reinhard. 1994. "Ecclesial Ethics, the Church's Vocation, and Paraclesis." *Pro Ecclesia* 2/4: 433–450.

Isser, Stanley. 1990. "Two Traditions: The Law of Exodus 21:22–23 Revisited." *Catholic Biblical Quarterly* 52: 30–45.

Jervell, Jacob. 1972. *Luke and the People of God: A New Look at Luke-Acts.* Minneapolis: Augsburg.

Jewett, Robert. 1979. *A Chronology of Paul's Life.* Philadelphia: Fortress.

Johnson, James Turner. 1981. *Just War Tradition and the Restraint of War: A Moral and Historical Inquiry.* Princeton: Princeton University Press.

______. 1984. *Can Modern War Be Just?* New Haven: Yale University Press.

Johnson, Luke Timothy. 1977. *The Literary Function of Possessions in Luke-Acts.* Missoula, MT: Scholars Press.

______. 1981. *Sharing Possessions: Mandate and Symbol of Faith.* Overtures to Biblical Theology 9. Philadelphia: Fortress.

______. 1983. *Decision Making in the Church: A Biblical Model*. Philadelphia: Fortress.
______. 1986. *The Writings of the New Testament: An Interpretation*. Philadelphia: Fortress.
______. 1989. "The New Testament's Anti-Jewish Slander and the Conventions of Ancient Polemic." *Journal of Biblical Literature* 108: 419–441.
______. 1991. *The Gospel of Luke*. Sacra Pagina. Collegeville, MN: Liturgical Press.
______. 1992. "A Marginal Mediterranean Jewish Peasant." *Commonweal* 119: 24–26.
______. 1995. "The Use of the New Testament in Christian Ethics: A Response to Richard Hays' *New Testament Ethics: Community, Cross, New Creation*." Unpublished paper presented at symposium on "New Testament Ethics: Problems and Prospects," Duke University, Apr. 1, 1995.
______. 1996. *The Real Jesus: The Misguided Quest for the Historical Jesus and the Truth of the Traditional Gospels*. San Francisco: HarperSanFrancisco.
Johnson, Mark, ed. 1981. *Philosophical Perspectives on Metaphor*. Minneapolis: University of Minnesota Press.
Johnston, George. 1970. *The Spirit-Paraclete in the Gospel of John*. Society for New Testament Studies Monograph Series 12. Cambridge: Cambridge University Press.
Jones, L. Gregory. 1990. *Transformed Judgment*. Notre Dame, IN: University of Notre Dame Press.
Jüngel, Eberhard. 1986 [1982]. *Karl Barth: A Theological Legacy*, trans. Garrett E. Paul. Philadelphia: Westminster.
Kähler, Martin. 1964 [1896]. *The So-Called Historical Jesus and the Historic Biblical Christ*, trans. Carl E. Braaten. Philadelphia: Fortress.
Kaiser, Walter C., Jr. 1983. *Toward Old Testament Ethics*. Grand Rapids, MI: Zondervan.
Käsemann, Ernst. 1950. "Kritische Analyse von Phil. 2:5–11." *Zeitschrift für Theologie und Kirche* 47: 313–360.
______. 1964 [1960]. *Essays on New Testament Themes*, trans. W. J. Montague. Studies in Biblical Theology 41. London: SCM.
______. 1968. *The Testament of Jesus: A Study of the Gospel of John in the Light of Chapter 17*, trans. Gerhard Krodel. Philadelphia: Fortress.
______. 1969 [1965]. *New Testament Questions of Today*, trans. W. J. Montague and Wilfrid F. Bunge. Philadelphia: Fortress.
______. 1971 [1969]. *Perspectives on Paul*, trans. Margaret Kohl. Philadelphia: Fortress.
______. 1980. *Commentary on Romans*, trans. Geoffrey W. Bromiley. Grand Rapids, MI: Eerdmans.
Katz, Steven T. 1984. "Issues in the Separation of Judaism and Christianity after 70 C.E.: A Reconsideration." *Journal of Biblical Literature* 103: 43–76.
Kaveny, M. Kathleen. 1991. "Toward a Thomistic Perspective on Abortion and the Law in Contemporary America." *The Thomist* 55/3: 343–396.
Keck, Leander E. 1976. "Justification of the Ungodly and Ethics." In *Rechtfertigung*, ed. Johannes Friedrich, Wolfgang Pöhlmann, and Peter Stuhlmacher, 199–209. Tübingen: Mohr.
______. 1984. "Ethics in the Gospel of Matthew." *Iliff Review* 41: 39–56.
Kee, Howard Clark. 1977. *Community of the New Age: Studies in Mark's Gospel*. Philadelphia: Westminster.
Keener, Craig S. 1991. *And Marries Another: Divorce and Remarriage in the Teaching of the New Testament*. Peabody, MA: Hendrickson.
Kelber, Werner H. 1974. *The Kingdom in Mark: A New Place and a New Time*. Philadelphia: Fortress.
______. 1983. *The Oral and the Written Gospel: The Hermeneutics of Speaking and Writing in the Synoptic Tradition, Mark, Paul, and Q*. Philadelphia: Fortress.
Kellerman, Bill. 1987. "Apologist of Power: The Long Shadow of Reinhold Niebuhr's Christian Realism." *Sojourners* 16: 14–20.
Kelsey, David H. 1975. *The Uses of Scripture in Recent Theology*. Philadelphia: Fortress.
Kermode, Frank. 1979. *The Genesis of Secrecy*. Cambridge, MA: Harvard University Press.
Kimball, Charles A. 1994. *Jesus' Exposition of the Old Testament in Luke's Gospel*. Journal for the Study of the New Testament Supplement Series 94. Sheffield, UK: JSOT.
Kimelman, Reuven. 1981. "*Birkat ha-minim* and the Lack of Evidence for an Anti-Christian Jewish Prayer in Late Antiquity." In *Jewish and Christian Self-Definition*, ed. E. P. Sanders, A. I. Baumgarten, and Alan Mendelson, vol. 2: *Aspects of Judaism in the Greco-Roman Period*, 226–244. Philadelphia: Fortress.
King, Martin Luther, Jr. 1958. *Stride Toward Freedom: The Montgomery Story*. New York: Harper & Brothers.
______. 1963. "Letter from Birmingham City Jail." Philadelphia: American Friends Service Committee.
Kingsbury, Jack Dean. 1975. *Matthew: Structure, Christology, Kingdom*. Philadelphia: Fortress.
______. 1978. "The Verb *Akolouthein* ('To Follow') As an Index of Matthew's View of His Community." *Journal of Biblical Literature* 97: 56–73.
Kissinger, Warren S. 1975. *The Sermon on the Mount: A History of Interpretation and Bibliography*. ATLA Bibliography Series 3. Metuchen, NJ: ATLA.
Kittay, Eva Feder. 1987. *Metaphor: Its Cognitive Force and Linguistic Structure*. Oxford: Clarendon.

Klassen, William. 1963. "Coals of Fire: Sign of Repentance or Revenge?" *New Testament Studies* 9: 337–350.
______. 1984. *Love of Enemies: The Way to Peace.* Philadelphia: Fortress.
Klein, Charlotte. 1978 [1975]. *Anti-Judaism in Christian Theology,* trans. Edward Quinn. London: SPCK.
Kraftchick, Steven J. 1993. "A Necessary Detour: Paul's Metaphorical Understanding of the Philippian Hymn." *Horizons in Biblical Theology* 15/1: 1–37.
Kugel, James L., and Rowan A. Greer. 1986. *Early Biblical Interpretation.* Library of Early Christianity. Philadelphia: Westminster.
Kümmel, Werner G. 1929. *Römer 7 und die Bekehrung des Paulus.* Leipzig: Henrichs. (Reprint edition: 1974. Munich: Kaiser.)
______. 1975 [1973]. *Introduction to the New Testament,* trans. Howard Clark Kee. Nashville: Abingdon.
Lane, William L. 1974. *The Gospel According to Mark.* New International Commentary on the New Testament. Grand Rapids, MI: Eerdmans.
Langford, Thomas A., ed. 1991. *Doctrine and Theology in the United Methodist Church.* Nashville: Abingdon.
Lash, Nicholas. 1986. *Theology on the Way to Emmaus.* London: SCM.
Laumann, Edward D., John H. Gagnon, et al. 1994. *Social Organization of Sexuality: Sexual Practices in the United States.* Chicago: University of Chicago Press.
Lessing, Gotthold Ephraim. 1956 [1777]. "On the Proof of the Spirit and of Power." In *Lessing's Theological Writings,* trans. Henry Chadwick, 51–56. Stanford, CA: Stanford University Press.
Levenson, Jon D. 1993. *The Hebrew Bible, the Old Testament, and Historical Criticism.* Louisville: Westminster/John Knox.
Levine, Amy-Jill. 1988. *The Social and Ethnic Dimensions of Matthean Salvation History: "Go Nowhere Among the Gentiles . . . " (Matthew 10:56).* Studies in the Bible and Early Christianity, vol. 14. Lewiston, NY: Mellen.
Lindbeck, George. 1995. "Beginning or Ending? Commentary on Richard B. Hays' *New Testament Ethics: Community, Cross, New Creation.*" Unpublished paper presented at symposium on "New Testament Ethics: Problems and Prospects," Duke University, Apr. 1, 1995.
Lindsey, Hal. 1970. *The Late Great Planet Earth.* Grand Rapids, MI: Zondervan.
Lischer, Richard. 1987. "The Sermon on the Mount as Radical Pastoral Care." *Interpretation* 41: 157–189.
Lohfink, Gerhard. 1984 [1982]. *Jesus and Community: The Social Dimension of Christian Faith,* trans. John P. Galvin. Philadelphia: Fortress.
Lohse, Eduard. 1991 [1988]. *Theological Ethics of the New Testament,* trans. M. Eugene Boring. Minneapolis: Fortress.
Long, D. Stephen. 1992. *Living the Discipline: United Methodist Theological Reflections on War, Civilization, and Holiness.* Grand Rapids, MI: Eerdmans.
______. 1993. *Tragedy, Tradition, Transformism: The Ethics of Paul Ramsey.* Boulder, CO: Westview.
Longenecker, Richard N. 1984. *New Testament Social Ethics for Today.* Grand Rapids: Eerdmans.
Lovin, Robin W. 1995. *Reinhold Niebuhr and Christian Realism.* Cambridge: Cambridge University Press.
Lüdemann, Gerd. 1984 [1980]. *Paul, Apostle to the Gentiles: Studies in Chronology,* trans. F. Stanley Jones. Philadelphia: Fortress.
Luther, Martin. c. 1529. "A Mighty Fortress Is Our God." Traditional hymnal version, 1978. *Lutheran Book of Worship.*
______. 1971 [1543]. "On the Jews and Their Lies." In *Luther's Works,* vol. 47: *The Christian in Society,* trans. Martin H. Bertram, 137–306. Philadelphia: Fortress.
Luz, Ulrich. 1989 [1985]. *Matthew 1–7: A Commentary,* trans. Wilhelm C. Linss. Edinburgh: T & T Clark.
MacIntyre, Alasdair. 1988. *Whose Justice? Which Rationality?* Notre Dame, IN: University of Notre Dame Press.
Mack, Burton. 1988. *A Myth of Innocence: Mark and Christian Origins.* Philadelphia: Fortress.
Mack, Maynard, Leonard Dean, and William Frost, eds. 1961. *Modern Poetry.* 2nd ed. Englewood Cliffs, NJ: Prentice-Hall.
Marcus, Joel. 1986. *The Mystery of the Kingdom of God.* SBL Dissertation Series 90. Atlanta: Scholars Press.
______. 1992. *The Way of the Lord: Christological Exegesis of the Old Testament in the Gospel of Mark.* Louisville: Westminster/John Knox.
Marshall, I. Howard. 1978. *Commentary on Luke.* The New International Greek Testament Commentary. Grand Rapids, MI: Eerdmans.
Martin, Dale B. 1990. *Slavery as Salvation: The Metaphor of Slavery in Pauline Christianity.* New Haven and London: Yale University Press.
______. 1995a. *The Corinthian Body.* New Haven and London: Yale University Press
______. 1995b. "Heterosexism and the Interpretation of Romans 1:18–32." *Biblical Interpretation* 3/3: 332–355.
Martin, Ralph P. 1983. *Carmen Christi: Philippians 2:5–11 in Recent Interpretation and in the Setting of Early Christian Worship.* 2nd ed. Grand Rapids: Eerdmans.

Martyn, J. Louis. 1967. "Epistemology at the Turn of the Ages: 2 Corinthians 5:16." In *Christian History and Interpretation: Studies Presented to John Knox*, ed. W. R. Farmer, C. F. D. Moule, and R. R. Niebuhr, 269–287. Cambridge: Cambridge University Press.

______. 1979. *History and Theology in the Fourth Gospel*. Nashville: Abingdon.

Marxsen, Willi. 1969 [1956]. *Mark the Evangelist*, trans. J. Boyce et al. Nashville: Abingdon.

______. 1993 [1989]. *New Testament Foundations for Christian Ethics*, trans. O. C. Dean, Jr. Minneapolis: Fortress.

Mauser, Ulrich. 1992. *The Gospel of Peace*. Louisville: Westminster/John Knox.

McCann, Dennis. 1995. "The Case for Christian Realism: Rethinking Reinhold Niebuhr." *Christian Century* 112/19: 604–607.

McDonald, J. I. H. 1993. *Biblical Interpretation and Christian Ethics*. New Studies in Christian Ethics. Cambridge: Cambridge University Press.

McFague, Sallie. 1982. *Metaphorical Theology: Models of God in Religious Language*. Philadelphia: Fortress.

McNeill, John J. 1993. *The Church and the Homosexual*. 4th ed. Boston: Beacon.

______. 1995. *Freedom, Glorious Freedom*. Boston: Beacon.

Meeks, Wayne A. 1972. "The Man from Heaven in Johannine Sectarianism." *Journal of Biblical Literature* 91: 44–72.

______. 1974. "The Image of the Androgyne: Some Uses of a Symbol in Earliest Christianity." *History of Religions* 13: 165–208.

______. 1983. *The First Urban Christians: The Social World of the Apostle Paul*. New Haven: Yale University Press.

______. 1986a. "Understanding Early Christian Ethics." *Journal of Biblical Literature* 105: 3–11.

______. 1986b. *The Moral World of the First Christians*. Library of Early Christianity. Philadelphia: Westminster.

______. 1986c. "A Hermeneutics of Social Embodiment." *Harvard Theological Review* 79: 176–186.

______. 1993. *The Origins of Christian Morality: The First Two Centuries*. New Haven: Yale University Press.

Meier, John P. 1980. *Matthew*. New Testament Message. Wilmington, DE: Glazier.

______. 1991. *A Marginal Jew: Rethinking the Historical Jesus*. New York: Doubleday.

Merkel, Helmut. 1994. "Israel im lukanischen Werk." *New Testament Studies* 40: 371–388.

Metzger, Bruce M. 1975. *A Textual Commentary on the Greek New Testament*. Stuttgart: United Bible Societies.

Mickelsen, Alvera, ed. 1986. *Women, Authority, and the Bible*. Downer's Grove, IL: InterVarsity.

Minear, Paul S. 1968. *I Saw a New Earth: An Introduction to the Visions of the Apocalypse*. Washington: Corpus Books.

______. 1976. *To Heal and to Reveal: The Prophetic Vocation According to Luke*. New York: Seabury.

______. 1981. *New Testament Apocalyptic*. Interpreting Biblical Texts. Nashville: Abingdon.

______. 1984. *John: The Martyr's Gospel*. New York: Pilgrim.

Mitchell, Margaret M. 1992. *Paul and the Rhetoric of Reconciliation: An Exegetical Investigation of the Language and Composition of First Corinthians*. Louisville: Westminster/John Knox.

Moessner, David P. 1989. *Lord of the Banquet: The Literary and Theological Significance of the Lukan Travel Narrative*. Minneapolis: Fortress.

Morgan, Robert, ed. 1973. *The Nature of New Testament Theology: The Contribution of William Wrede and Adolf Schlatter*. Studies in Biblical Theology, Second Series 25. London: SCM.

Mueller, David L. 1972. *Karl Barth*. Waco, TX: Word.

Myers, Ched. 1988. *Binding the Strong Man: A Political Reading of Mark's Story of Jesus*. Maryknoll, NY: Orbis.

Nelson, James B. 1978. *Embodiment: An Approach to Sexuality and Christian Theology*. Minneapolis: Augsburg.

Neuhaus, Richard John, ed. 1989. *Reinhold Niebuhr Today*. New York: Pantheon.

Neusner, Jacob, ed., with William Scott Green and Ernest S. Frerichs. 1987. *Judaisms and Their Messiahs at the Turn of the Christian Era*. Cambridge: Cambridge University Press.

Nicklesburg, George W. E. 1992. "Son of Man." *Anchor Bible Dictionary* 6: 137–150. New York: Doubleday.

Niebuhr, H. Richard. 1951. *Christ and Culture*. New York: Harper & Row.

Niebuhr, Reinhold. 1932. *Moral Man and Immoral Society*. New York: Charles Scribner's Sons.

______. 1940. *Christianity and Power Politics*. New York: Charles Scribner's Sons.

______. 1943. *The Nature and Destiny of Man*. 2 vols. New York: Charles Scribner's Sons.

______. 1979 [1935]. *An Interpretation of Christian Ethics*. New York: Seabury.

Nietzsche, Friedrich. 1956 [1887]. *The Birth of Tragedy and the Genealogy of Morals*, trans. Francis Golffing. Garden City, NY: Doubleday.

Noonan, John T., Jr., ed. 1970. *The Morality of Abortion*. Cambridge, MA: Harvard University Press.

O'Day, Gail R. 1986. *Revelation in the Fourth Gospel.* Philadelphia: Fortress.
Oden, Thomas. 1979. *Agenda for Theology.* San Francisco: Harper & Row.
O'Donovan, Oliver. 1986. "The Political Thought of the Book of Revolation." *Tyndale Bulletin* 37: 61–94.
______. 1994. *Resurrection and Moral Order: An Outline for Evangelical Ethics.* Rev. ed. Grand Rapids, MI: Eerdmans.
Ogletree, Thomas W. 1983. *The Use of the Bible in Christian Ethics.* Philadelphia: Fortress.
Ollenburger, Ben. 1990. "We Believe in God, Maker of Heaven and Earth: Metaphor, Scripture, and Theology." *Horizons in Biblical Theology* 12: 64–96.
Outka, Gene. *God and the Moral Life: Explorations in the Protestant Tradition.* Forthcoming.
Pannenberg, Wolfhart. 1977 [1964]. *Jesus: God and Man,* trans. Lewis L. Wilkins and Duane A. Priebe, 2nd ed. Philadelphia: Westminster.
Payne, Philip. 1995. "Fuldensis, Sigla for Variants in Vaticanus, and 1 Cor. 14:34–5." *New Testament Studies* 41: 240–262.
Pelikan, Jaroslav. 1985. *Jesus Through the Centuries: His Place in the History of Culture.* New Haven and London: Yale University Press.
Pervo, Richard. 1987. *Profit with Delight: The Literary Genre of the Acts of the Apostles.* Philadelphia: Fortress.
Peterson, Dwight N. 1995. *The Origins of Mark: The Marcan Community in Current Debate.* Ph.D. dissertation, Duke University. Ann Arbor, MI: University Microfilms.
Petersen, Norman. 1980. "When Is the End Not the End? Literary Reflections on the Ending of Mark's Narrative." *Interpretation* 34: 151–166.
______. 1985. *Rediscovering Paul: Philemon and the Sociology of Paul's Narrative World.* Philadelphia: Fortress.
Petersen, William L. 1992. "Diatessaron." *Anchor Bible Dictionary* 2: 189–190. New York: Doubleday.
Pokorny, Petr. 1992. "Die Soziale Strategie in den lukanischen Schriften." *Communio Viatorum* 34: 9–19.
Porter, Calvin L. 1994. "Romans 1:18–22: Its Role in the Developing Argument." *New Testament Studies* 40: 210–228.
Porter, Stanley E. 1993. "What Does It Mean to Be 'Saved by Childbirth' (1 Timothy 2:15)?" *Journal for the Study of the New Testament* 49: 87–102.
Räisänen, Heikki. 1983. *Paul and the Law.* Wissenschaftliche Untersuchungen zum Neuen Testament 29. Tübingen: Mohr.
______. 1990. *Beyond New Testament Theology: A Story and a Programme.* London: SCM; Philadelphia: Trinity Press International.
Ramsey, Paul. 1968. *The Just War: Force and Political Responsibility.* New York: Charles Scribner's Sons.
Rasmussen, Larry. 1989. *Reinhold Niebuhr: Theologian of Public Life.* London: Collins.
Rensberger, David. 1988. *Johannine Faith and Liberating Community.* Philadelphia: Westminster.
Rese, Martin. 1969. *Alttestamentliche Motive in der Christologie des Lukas.* Studien zum Neuen Testament 1. Gütersloh: Gütersloher Verlagshaus Gerd Mohn.
Richardson, Peter. 1970. "The Israel-idea in the Passion Narratives." In *The Trial of Jesus: Cambridge Studies in Honor of C.F.D. Moule,* ed. Ernst Bammel, 1–10. Studies in Biblical Theology, Second Series 13. London: SCM.
Richardson, Peter, and David Granskou. 1986. *Anti-Judaism in Early Christianity,* vol. 1: Paul and the Gospels. Studies in Christianity and Judaism 2. Waterloo, Canada: Wilfrid Laurier University.
Riches, John K. 1982. *Jesus and the Transformation of Judaism.* New York: Seabury.
Ricoeur, Paul. 1975. "Biblical Hermeneutics." *Semeia* 4: 29–148.
______. 1976. *Interpretation Theory: Discourse and the Surplus of Meaning.* Fort Worth: Texas Christian University Press.
______. 1977. *The Rule of Metaphor: Multi-Disciplinary Studies in the Meaning of Language,* trans. Robert Czerny. Toronto: University of Toronto Press.
Ruether, Rosemary Radford. 1974. *Faith and Fratricide: The Theological Roots of Anti-Semitism.* New York: Seabury.
Sampley, J. Paul. 1991. *Walking Between the Times: Paul's Moral Reasoning.* Minneapolis: Fortress.
Sanders, E. P. 1977. *Paul and Palestinian Judaism: A Comparison of Patterns of Religion.* Minneapolis: Fortress.
______. 1985. *Jesus and Judaism.* Philadelphia: Fortress.
______. 1990. "Jewish Association with Gentiles and Galatians 2:11–14." In *The Conversation Continues: Studies in Paul and John in Honor of J. Louis Martyn,* ed. Robert Fortna and Beverly Roberts Gaventa, 170–188. Nashville: Abingdon.
______. 1992. *Judaism: Practice and Belief 63 B.C.E–66 B.C.E.* London: SCM.
______. 1993. *The Historical Figure of Jesus.* London: Allen Lane (Penguin Press).
Sanders, E. P., A. I. Baumgarten, and Alan Mendelson, eds. 1981. *Jewish and Christian Self-Definition,* vol. 2: *Aspects of Judaism in the Graeco-Roman Period.* Philadelphia: Fortress.

Sanders, E. P., and Margaret Davies. 1989. *Studying the Synoptic Gospels*. London: SCM.
Sanders, Jack T. 1975. *Ethics in the New Testament: Change and Development*. Philadelphia: Fortress.
______. 1987. *The Jews in Luke-Acts*. Philadelphia: Fortress.
Sandmel, Samuel. 1978. *Anti-Semitism in the New Testament?* Philadelphia: Fortress.
Scanzoni, Letha, and Virginia Ramey Mollenkott. 1978. *Is the Homosexual My Neighbor? Another Christian View*. San Francisco: Harper & Row.
Schnackenburg, Rudolf. 1965. *The Moral Teaching of the New Testament*, trans. J. Holland-Smith and W. J. O'Hara. New York: Herder & Herder.
Schneider, Gerhard. 1977. "Zur Bedeutung von *kathexēs* im lukanischen Doppelwerk." *Zeitschrift für die neutestamentliche Wissenschaft* 68: 128–131.
Schneiders, Sandra. 1982. "Women in the Fourth Gospel and the Role of Women in the Contemporary Church." *Biblical Theology Bulletin* 12: 35–45.
______. 1991. *The Revelatory Text: Interpreting the New Testament as Sacred Scripture*. San Francisco: HarperSanFrancisco.
Scholer, David M. 1986. "1 Timothy 2:9–15 and the Place of Women in the Church's Ministry." In *Women, Authority, and the Bible*, ed. Alvera Mickelsen, 193–219. Downer's Grove, IL: InterVarsity.
Schrage, Wolfgang. 1988 [1982]. *The Ethics of the New Testament*, trans. David E. Green. Philadelphia: Fortress.
Schulz, Siegfried. 1987. *Neutestamentliche Ethik*. Zürich: TVZ.
Schüssler Fiorenza, Elisabeth. 1983. *In Memory of Her: A Feminist Theological Reconstruction of Christian Origins*. New York: Crossroad.
______. 1984. *Bread Not Stone: The Challenge of Feminist Biblical Interpretation*. Boston: Beacon.
______. 1985. *The Book of Revelation: Justice and Judgment*. Philadelphia: Fortress.
______. 1988. "The Ethics of Interpretation: De-Centering Biblical Scholarship." *Journal of Biblical Literature* 107: 3–17.
______. 1991. *Revelation: Vision of a Just World*. Minneapolis: Fortress.
______. 1992. *But She Said: Feminist Practices of Biblical Interpretation*. Boston: Beacon.
Schütz, John. 1975. *Paul and the Anatomy of Apostolic Authority*. Society for New Testament Studies Monograph Series 26. Cambridge: Cambridge University Press.
Schweitzer, Albert. 1968 [1906]. *The Quest of the Historical Jesus*, trans. W. Montgomery. New York: Macmillan.
Schweizer, Eduard. 1975. *The Good News According to Matthew*, trans. David E. Green. Atlanta: John Knox.
Scroggs, Robin. 1983. *The New Testament and Homosexuality*. Philadelphia: Fortress.
______. 1993. *The Text and the Times: New Testament Essays for Today*. Minneapolis: Fortress.
Segal, Alan. 1986. *Rebecca's Children: Judaism and Christianity in the Roman World*. Cambridge, MA: Harvard University Press.
Sells, Michael A. 1994. "Bosnia: Some Religious Dimensions of Genocide." *Religious Studies News* 9/2: 4–5.
Shaw, Brent D. 1994. "A Groom of One's Own: The Medieval Church and the Question of Gay Marriage." *The New Republic* 211/3–4: 33–41.
Siker, Jeffrey S. 1991. *Disinheriting the Jews: Abraham in Early Christian Controversy*. Louisville: Westminster/John Knox.
______, ed. 1994a. *Homosexuality and the Church: Both Sides of the Debate*. Louisville: Westminster/John Knox.
______. 1994b. "How to Decide? Homosexual Christians, the Bible, and Gentile Inclusion." *Theology Today* 51/2: 219–234.
______. Forthcoming. *Scripture and Ethics: Twentieth Century Portraits*. New York: Oxford University Press.
Sleeper, C. Freeman. 1992. *The Bible and the Moral Life*. Louisville: Westminster/John Knox.
Smiga, George M. 1992. *Pain and Polemic: Anti-Judaism in the Gospels*. New York: Paulist.
Smith, D. Moody. 1984. *Johannine Christianity: Essays on Its Setting, Sources, and Theology*. Columbia: University of South Carolina Press.
______. 1990. "Judaism and the Gospel of John." In *Jews and Christians: Exploring the Past, Present, and Future*, ed. James H. Charlesworth, 76–96. New York: Crossroad.
______. 1991. *First, Second, and Third John*. Interpretation. Louisville: John Knox.
Snodgrass, Klyne. 1989. *Divorce and Remarriage*. Covenant Publications 3. Chicago: Covenant Publications.
Soards, Marion L. 1987. *The Apostle Paul: An Introduction to His Writings and Teachings*. New York: Paulist.
Soskice, Janet Martin. 1985. *Metaphor and Religious Language*. Oxford: Clarendon.
Spohn, William C. 1995. *What Are They Saying About Scripture and Ethics?* Rev. ed. New York: Paulist.
Spong, John Shelby. 1984. "Can the Church Bless Divorce?" *Christian Century* 101: 1126–1127.
______. 1991. *Rescuing the Bible from Fundamentalism*. San Francisco: HarperSanFrancisco.

Squires, John T. 1993. *The Plan of God in Luke-Acts.* Society for New Testament Studies Monograph Series 76. Cambridge: Cambridge University Press.

Stallsworth, Paul T., ed. 1993. *The Church and Abortion: In Search of New Ground for Response.* Nashville: Abingdon.

Stanton, Graham N., ed. 1983. *The Interpretation of Matthew.* Issues in Religion and Theology 3. Philadelphia: Fortress.

______. 1992. *A Gospel for a New People: Studies in Matthew.* Louisville: Westminster/John Knox.

Steiner, George. 1989. *Real Presences.* Chicago: University of Chicago Press.

Stendahl, Krister. 1968 [1954]. *The School of St. Matthew and Its Use of the Old Testament,* 2nd ed. Philadelphia: Fortress.

______. 1976. *Paul Among Jews and Gentiles.* Philadelphia: Fortress.

Sternberg, Meier. 1985. *The Poetics of Biblical Narrative: Ideological Literature and the Drama of Reading.* Bloomington: University of Indiana Press.

Stone, Ronald H. 1992. *Professor Reinhold Niebuhr: A Mentor to the Twentieth Century.* Louisville: Westminster/John Knox.

Strecker, Georg. 1988 [1985]. *The Sermon on the Mount: An Exegetical Commentary,* trans. O. C. Dean, Jr. Nashville: Abingdon.

Streeter, B. H. 1924. *The Four Gospels: A Study of Origins.* London: Macmillan.

Stringfellow, William. 1973. *An Ethic for Christians and Other Aliens in a Strange Land.* Waco, TX: Word.

Stuhlmacher, Peter. 1986 [1981]. *Reconciliation, Law, and Righteousness: Essays in Biblical Theology,* trans. Everett R. Kalin. Philadelphia: Fortress.

Swartley, Willard M. 1983. *Slavery, Sabbath, War, and Women: Case Issues in Biblical Interpretation.* Scottdale, PA: Herald.

______, ed. 1992. *The Love of Enemy and Nonretaliation in the New Testament.* Louisville: Westminster/John Knox.

Tannehill, Robert C. 1975. *The Sword of His Mouth.* Society of Biblical Literature Semeia Supplements. Philadelphia: Fortress; Missoula, MT: Scholars Press.

______. 1977. "The Disciples in Mark: The Function of a Narrative Role." *Journal of Religion* 57: 386–405.

Theissen, Gerd. 1982. *The Social Setting of Pauline Christianity: Essays on Corinth,* trans. John H. Schütz. Philadelphia: Fortress.

______. 1978 [1977]. *The Sociology of Early Palestinian Christianity,* trans. John Bowden. Phildelphia: Fortress.

Thompson, Leonard L. 1990. *The Book of Revelation: Apocalypse and Empire.* New York and Oxford: Oxford University Press.

Throckmorton, Burton H. 1992. *Gospel Parallels: A Comparison of the Synoptic Gospels,* 5th ed. Nashville: Nelson.

Tiede, David. 1980. *Prophecy and History in Luke-Acts.* Philadelphia: Fortress.

Tillich, Paul. 1957. *Systematic Theology,* vol. 2. Chicago: University of Chicago Press.

Tolbert, Mary Ann. 1989. *Sowing the Gospel: Mark's World in Literary-Historical Perspective.* Minneapolis: Fortress.

Tomson, Peter J. 1990. *Paul and the Jewish Law: Halakha in the Letters of the Apostle to the Gentiles.* Compendia Rerum Iudaicarum ad Novum Testamentum, section 3, vol. 1. Assen/Maastricht: Van Gorcum; Minneapolis: Fortress.

Torrance, Thomas F. 1990. *Karl Barth, Biblical and Evangelical Theologian.* Edinburgh: T & T Clark.

Towner, Philip H. 1989. *The Goal of Our Instruction: The Structure of Theology and Ethics in the Pastoral Epistles.* Journal for the Study of the New Testament Supplement Series 34. Sheffield, UK: JSOT.

Trilling, Wolfgang. 1964. *Das Wahre Israel.* 3rd ed. Studien zum Alten und Neuen Testament 10. Munich: Kösel.

Tuckett, C. M, ed. 1983. *The Messianic Secret.* Issues in Religion and Theology 1. Philadelphia: Fortress.

______. 1988. "Thomas and the Synoptics." *Novum Testamentum* 30: 132–157.

Van Leeuwen, Mary Stewart. Forthcoming. "To Ask a Better Question: The Heterosexuality/Homosexuality Debate Revisited." *Interpretation.*

van Tilborg, Sjef. 1993. *Imaginative Love in John.* Biblical Interpretation Series 2. Leiden: Brill.

Verhey, Allen. 1984. *The Great Reversal: Ethics and the New Testament.* Grand Rapids, MI: Eerdmans.

Vermes, Geza. 1987. *The Dead Sea Scrolls in English.* 3rd ed. New York and London: Penguin Books.

Verner, David. 1983. *The Household of God: The Social World of the Pastoral Epistles.* SBL Dissertation Series 71. Chico, CA: Scholars Press.

Via, Dan O., Jr. 1978. "Narrative World and Ethical Response: The Marvelous and Righteousness in Matthew 1–2." *Semeia* 12: 123–144.

______. 1985. *The Ethics of Mark's Gospel: In the Middle of Time.* Philadelphia: Fortress.

______. 1990. *Self-Deception and Wholeness in Paul and Matthew*. Minneapolis: Fortress.

Wall, Robert W. 1983. "Introduction: New Testament Ethics." *Horizons in Biblical Theology* 5/2: 49–94.

Watson, Francis. 1986. *Paul, Judaism, and the Gentiles: A Sociological Approach*. Society for New Testament Studies Monograph Series 56. Cambridge: Cambridge University Press.

Weeden, Theodore J., Sr. 1971. *Mark: Traditions in Conflict*. Philadelphia: Fortress.

Wengst, Klaus. 1983. *Bedrängte Gemeinde und Verherrlichter Christus: Der historische Ort des Johannesevangeliums als Schlüssel zu seiner Interpretation*. 2nd ed. Biblisch-Theologische Studien 5. Neukirchen-Vluyn: Neukirchener Verlag.

Wenham, David. 1995. *Paul: Follower of Jesus or Founder of Christianity?* Grand Rapids, MI: Eerdmans.

Westerholm, Stephen. 1988. *Israel's Law and the Church's Faith: Paul and His Recent Interpreters*. Grand Rapids, MI: Eerdmans.

Wheeler, Sondra Ely. 1995. *Wealth as Peril and Obligation: The New Testament on Possessions*. Grand Rapids, MI: Eerdmans.

Wheelwright, Philip. 1962. *Metaphor and Reality*. Bloomington: Indiana University Press.

______. 1968. *The Burning Fountain: A Study in the Language of Symbolism*. Bloomington: Indiana University Press.

Whitehead, Barbara Dafoe. 1993. "Dan Quayle Was Right." *The Atlantic Monthly* 271/4: 47–84.

Wilder, Amos N. 1971. *Early Christian Rhetoric: The Language of the Gospel*. Rev. ed. Cambridge, MA: Harvard University Press.

______. 1976. *Theopoetic: Theology and the Religious Imagination*. Philadelphia: Fortress.

Williams, Camille S. 1991. "Abortion and the Actualized Self." *First Things* 17: 27–32.

Williams, Delores S. 1993. *Sisters in the Wilderness: The Challenge of Womanist God-Talk*. Maryknoll, NY: Orbis.

Williams, Rowan. 1982. *Resurrection*. London: Darton, Longman & Todd.

Williamson, Clark M. 1982. *Has God Rejected His People? Anti-Judaism in the Christian Church*. Nashville: Abingdon.

Willimon, William H. 1985. *What's Right with the Church?* New York: Harper & Row.

______. 1988. *Acts*. Interpretation. Atlanta: John Knox.

______. 1990. "The People We're Stuck With." *Christian Century* 107: 924–925.

Wilson, Robert R. 1988. "Approaches to Old Testament Ethics." In *Canon, Theology, and Old Testament Interpretation: Essays in Honor of Brevard S. Childs*, ed. Gene M. Tucker, David L. Petersen, and Robert R. Wilson, 62–74. Philadelphia: Fortress.

Wire, Antoinette. 1990. *The Corinthian Women Prophets*. Minneapolis: Fortress.

Witherington, Ben III. 1980. *Women in the Earliest Churches*. Society for New Testament Studies Monograph Series 59. Cambridge: Cambridge University Press.

______. 1990. *The Christology of Jesus*. Minneapolis: Fortress.

______. 1994. *Paul's Narrative Thought World: The Tapestry of Tragedy and Triumph*. Louisville: Westminster/John Knox.

______. 1995. *The Jesus Quest: The Third Search for the Jew of Nazareth*. Downer's Grove, IL: InterVaristy Press.

Wolterstorff, Nicholas. 1995. *Divine Disclosure: Philosophical Reflections on the Claim That God Speaks*. Cambridge: Cambridge University Press.

Wrede, William. 1971 [1901]. *The Messianic Secret*, trans. J.C.G. Greig. Cambridge: Clarke.

Wright, N. T. 1987. "Reflected Glory: 2 Corinthians 3:18." In *The New Testament: Studies in Christology*, ed. L. D. Hurst and N. T. Wright, 139–150. Oxford: Oxford University Press.

______. 1991. *The Climax of the Covenant: Christ and the Law in Pauline Theology*. Minneapolis: Fortress.

______. 1992. *The New Testament and the People of God*. Minneapolis: Fortress.

Yarbrough, O. Larry. 1985. *Not Like the Gentiles: Marriage Rules in the Letters of Paul*. SBL Dissertation Series 80. Atlanta: Scholars Press.

Yoder, John Howard. 1964. *The Christian Witness to the State*. Institute of Mennonite Studies Series 3. Newton, KS: Faith & Life.

______. 1970. *Karl Barth and the Problem of War*. Studies in Christian Ethics. Nashville: Abingdon.

______. 1984. *The Priestly Kingdom: Social Ethics as Gospel*. Notre Dame, IN: University of Notre Dame Press.

______. 1991. "Just War Tradition: Is it Credible?" *Christian Century* 108: 295–298.

______. 1994. *The Politics of Jesus*. 2nd ed. Grand Rapids, MI: Eerdmans.

Young, Robin Darling. 1994. "Gay Marriage: Reimagining Church History." *First Things* 47: 43–48.

Zabelka, George. 1980. "I Was Told It Was Necessary" [interview]. *Sojourners* 9/8: 12–15.

Zimmerman, Mary K. 1977. *Passage Through Abortion: The Personal and Social Reality of Women's Experience*. New York: Praeger.

Permissions

Grateful acknowledgment is made for permission to reprint previously published material:

Bible quotations, unless otherwise noted, are from the New Revised Standard Version of the Bible, copyright © 1989 by the Division of Christian Education of the National Council of Churches of Christ in the U.S.A. Used by permission. Biblical quotations marked "(RH)" are the author's own translations and his adaptations of the NRSV are marked "(AA)."

Excerpt from *W. H. Auden: Collected Poems* by W. H. Auden. Copyright © 1976 by Edward Mendelson, William Meredith, and Monroe K. Spears, Executors of the Estate of W. H. Auden. Reprinted by permission of Random House, Inc., and Faber & Faber Ltd.

Excerpt from "East Coker" in *Four Quartets* by T. S. Eliot. Copyright 1943 by T. S. Eliot and renewed 1971 by Esme Valerie Eliot. Reprinted by permission of Harcourt Brace & Company and Faber & Faber Ltd.

Excerpt from "The Hollow Men" in *Collected Poems 1909–1962* by T. S. Eliot. Copyright 1936 by Harcourt Brace & Company, copyright © 1964, 1963 by T. S. Eliot. Reprinted by permission of Harcourt Brace & Company and Faber & Faber Ltd.

"Awaiting the Redemption of Our Bodies" by Richard B. Hays, which appeared in the July 1991 issue of *Sojourners*, is reprinted with permission from *Sojourners*, 2401 15th Street NW, Washington, DC 20009; (202) 328–8842; fax (202) 328–8757.

Excerpt from *The Panther and the Lash* by Langston Hughes. Copyright © 1951 by Langston Hughes. Reprinted by permission of Alfred A. Knopf Inc. and Harold Ober Associates Inc.

Quotations from ancient Greek and Latin authors are taken from the translations of the Loeb Classical Library, except where otherwise indicated.

Index of Scripture and Other Ancient Writings

Old Testament

New Testament

Mark

Luke

1 Corinthians

2 Corinthians

Galatians

Apocrypha and Pseudepigrapha

Dead Sea Scrolls

Early Christian Literature

Rabbinic Literature

Other Ancient Writings

Author Index

Topic Index